Fourth Edition

Practical Argument

A Text and Anthology

Laurie G. Kirszner

University of the Sciences, Emeritus

Stephen R. Mandell

Drexel University

bedford/st.martin's
Macmillan Learning

Boston | New York

For Bedford/St. Martin's

Vice President, Editorial, Macmillan Learning Humanities: Edwin Hill
Executive Program Director for English: Leasa Burton
Senior Program Manager: John E. Sullivan III
Executive Marketing Manager: Joy Fisher Williams
Director of Content Development, Humanities: Jane Knetzger
Senior Developmental Editor: Jesse Hassenger
Associate Content Project Manager: Matt Glazer
Senior Workflow Project Manager: Jennifer Wetzel
Production Coordinator: Brianna Lester
Media Project Manager: D. Rand Thomas
Media Editor: Julia Domenicucci
Assistant Editor: Cari Goldfine
Editorial Services: Lumina Datamatics, Inc.
Composition: Lumina Datamatics, Inc.
Text Permissions Manager: Kalina Ingham
Rights Platform Permissions Project Manager: Mark Schaefer, Lumina Datamatics, Inc.
Photo Permissions Editor: Angela Boehler
Photo Researcher: Krystyna Borgen, Lumina Datamatics, Inc.
Director of Design, Content Management: Diana Blume
Text Design: Jerilyn Bockorick
Cover Design: William Boardman
Cover Image: ViewStock/Getty Images
Printing and Binding: LSC Communications

Manufactured in the United States of America.

1 2 3 4 5 6   24 23 22 21 20 19

For information, write: Bedford/St. Martin's, 75 Arlington Street, Boston, MA 02116

ISBN 978-1-319-19445-1

In recent years, many college composition programs have integrated argumentation into their first-year writing sequence, and there are good reasons for this. Argumentation is central to both academic and public discourse, so students who are skilled at argumentation are able to participate in the dynamic, ongoing discussions that take place in their classrooms and in their communities. Argumentation teaches the critical-thinking skills that are valuable in an often contentious, sometimes divided sociopolitical landscape—and particularly necessary for academic success.

What has surprised and troubled us as teachers, however, is that many college argument texts are simply too difficult, with excessively technical terminology and unnecessarily abstract discussions. We want students to feel that they are part of a discourse community within which they can use the principles of argumentation with confidence and skill. With this in mind, we drew on our years of classroom experience to create *Practical Argument: A Text and Anthology*. In this fourth edition, *Practical Argument* remains a straightforward and accessible introduction to argumentative writing that explains concepts in understandable language and illustrates them with examples that actually mean something to students, covering contemporary issues that affect their lives as well as the kinds of visual arguments they see every day. *Practical Argument* is an ideal alternative for instructors who see currently available argument texts as too big, too complicated, and too intimidating for their students.

In short, our goal in this text is to demystify the study of argument. To this end, we focus on the things that students actually need to know. *Practical Argument* works because its approach is *practical*: It helps students make connections between what they learn in the classroom and what they experience outside of it. As they do so, they become comfortable with the rhetorical skills that are central to effective argumentation. We (and our many users) believe that there's no other book like it.

Organization

Practical Argument, both a text and a reader, includes everything students and instructors need for an argument course in a single book.

- **Part 1, Understanding Argument,** discusses the role of argument in everyday life and the value of studying argument, offers definitions of what argument is and is not, explains the means of persuasion (appeals to *logos*, *pathos*, and *ethos*), and defines and illustrates the basic elements of argument (thesis, evidence, refutation, and concluding statement).

- **Part 2, Reading and Responding to Arguments,** explains and illustrates critical thinking and reading; visual argument; writing a rhetorical analysis; logic and logical fallacies; and Rogerian argument, Toulmin logic, and oral arguments.

- **Part 3, Writing an Argumentative Essay,** traces and illustrates the process of planning, drafting, and revising an argumentative essay.

- **Part 4, Using Sources to Support Your Argument,** covers locating and evaluating print and online sources; summarizing, paraphrasing, quoting, and synthesizing sources; documenting sources in MLA style; and using sources responsibly.

- **Part 5, Strategies for Argument,** explains and illustrates the most common kinds of arguments—definition arguments, cause-and-effect arguments, evaluation arguments, ethical arguments, and proposal arguments, along with additional material covering stasis theory. Part 5 Review shows how these argumentative strategies can be combined in a single essay.

- **Part 6, Debates, Casebooks, and Classic Arguments,** includes both contemporary and classic arguments. The contemporary arguments are arranged in four pro-con debates and four in-depth casebooks on issues such as how to solve the opioid problem and whether the United States should have open borders. The classic arguments include well-known pieces by writers such as Jonathan Swift, George Orwell, Betty Friedan, and Rachel Carson.

- **Appendixes.** Appendix A provides instruction on writing literary arguments, and Appendix B covers APA documentation style.

Key Features

Accessible in a Thoughtful Way

Practical Argument covers everything students need to know about argument but doesn't overwhelm them. It limits technical vocabulary to what students and instructors actually need to understand and discuss key concepts in argument and argumentative writing. In short, *Practical Argument* is argument made accessible.

Argument Step by Step, Supported by Helpful Apparatus

Practical Argument takes students through a step-by-step process of reading and responding to others' arguments and writing, revising, and editing their own arguments. The book uses a classroom-tested, exercise-driven approach that encourages students to participate actively in their own learning process. Chapters progress in a clear, easy-to-understand sequence: students are asked to read arguments, identify their key elements, and develop a response to an issue in the form of a complete, documented argumentative essay based on in-book focused research.

Exercises and writing assignments for each selection provide guidance for students as they work toward creating a finished piece of writing. Throughout the text, checklists, grammar-in-context and summary boxes, and source and gloss notes provide support. In addition, more than a dozen unique templates for paragraph-length arguments—located with the end-of-chapter exercises—provide structures that students can use for guidance as they write definition arguments, cause-and-effect arguments, evaluation arguments, ethical arguments, and proposal arguments. Sentence templates also frequently appear in the questions that follow the readings, providing an opportunity for students to work up to arguments at the paragraph level.

A Thematically Focused Approach with Compelling Chapter Topics

Students learn best when they care about and are engaged in an issue. For this reason, *Practical Argument* uses readings and assignments to help students learn argumentation in the context of one high-interest contemporary issue per chapter. Chapter topics include environmental solutions, free speech, technology and privacy, student debt, student safety, and distinguishing between real news and misinformation—issues that have real meaning in students' lives.

Readings on Relevant and Interesting Issues

Practical Argument, Fourth Edition, includes over 110 accessible and thought-provoking professional readings on issues that students will want to read about and debate including selections from journals and blogs. The book also uses a variety of new visual argument selections, and seventeen sample student essays, more than in any other argument book, provide realistic models. Each student essay, including complete MLA and APA research papers, is annotated to further assist students through their own writing process. The mixture of professional and student essays, visual pieces, debates, and casebooks cover high-interest issues like campus speech, privacy in technology, immigration, women in science, technology, engineering, and mathematics (STEM), paying college athletes, student debt, self-driving cars, and more. A collection of ten classic arguments offers more challenging approaches to enduring issues.

To help students better understand the context of the sources included in *Practical Argument*, each is marked with an icon that shows how it was originally presented.

Magazine or journal

National newspaper

Poem

Professional essay

Report

Speech

Student essay

Student newspaper

Visual Argument

Website

An Open and Inviting Full-Color Design

The fresh, contemporary look of *Practical Argument* will engage students. This open, colorful design eliminates the sea of dense type that is typical of many other argument books. Over a hundred photographs and other visuals—such as advertisements, cartoons, charts and graphs, and web pages—provide appealing and instructive real-world examples. The use of open space and numerous images reinforces the currency of the book's themes and also creates an inviting and visually stimulating format.

New to This Edition

Essays, Topics, and Images

The fourth edition includes over seventy engaging new essays—a majority of the readings—covering such timely topics as campus environmental programs, the effects of social media, gun safety initiatives, and health care. These essays have been carefully selected for their high-interest subject matter as well as for their effectiveness as sources and as teaching models for student writing.

Debates and Casebooks

In addition to retaining some of the most popular debate and casebook topics and readings, we have added three new debates and two new casebooks to provide students with a variety of viewpoints on some of today's most compelling issues.

New debates:

- Should We Embrace Self-Driving Cars?
- Should College Athletes Be Paid?
- Should the United States Establish a Universal Basic Income?

New casebooks:

- How Should We Solve the Opioid Problem?
- Should the United States Have Open Borders?

Visual Arguments

Coverage of visual arguments has been expanded in this edition. Every chapter in Part 5, as well as each casebook, now includes a visual argument, accompanied by questions designed to focus students' attention on how to "read" a visual and understand its persuasive elements. Additional images throughout the book, including photos, advertisements, public-service announcements, cartoons, and more, add an extra dimension and additional perspective to the process of analyzing arguments.

New Coverage

Practical Argument continues to cover essential topics in argumentation, and the fourth edition has new coverage of stasis theory, refutation, and reading visual arguments.

Bedford/St. Martin's puts you first

From day one, our goal has been simple: to provide inspiring resources that are grounded in best practices for teaching reading and writing. For more than 35 years, Bedford/St. Martin's has partnered with the field, listening to teachers, scholars, and students about the support writers need. We are committed to helping every writing instructor make the most of our resources.

How can we help you?

- Our editors can align our resources to your outcomes through correlation and transition guides for your syllabus. Just ask us.

- Our sales representatives specialize in helping you find the right materials to support your course goals.

- Our *Bits* blog on the Bedford/St. Martin's English Community (**community.macmillan.com**) publishes fresh teaching ideas weekly. You'll also find easily downloadable professional resources and links to author webinars on our community site.

Contact your Bedford/St. Martin's sales representative or visit **macmillanlearning.com** to learn more.

Print and Digital Options for Practical Argument

Choose the format that works best for your course, and ask about our packaging options that offer savings for students.

Print

- *Short edition.* For instructors who only want to use Parts 1–4 of the book, we offer *Practical Argument, Short Fourth Edition*, featuring Chapters 1–11 to cover the basics of reading, writing, and researching arguments, for instructors who are looking to do more with less. To order the short edition, use ISBN 978-1-319-20721-2.

- *Loose-leaf edition.* This format does not have a traditional binding; its pages are loose and hole punched to provide flexibility and a lower price to students. It can be packaged with our digital space for additional savings.

Digital

- *Innovative digital learning space.* Bedford/St. Martin's suite of digital tools makes it easy to get everyone on the same page by putting student writers at the center. For details, visit **macmillanlearning .com/englishdigital**.

- *Popular e-book formats.* For details about our e-book partners, visit **macmillanlearning.com/ebooks**.

- *Inclusive Access.* Enable every student to receive their course materials through your LMS on the first day of class. Macmillan Learning's Inclusive Access program is the easiest, most affordable way to ensure all students have access to quality educational resources. Find out more at **macmillanlearning.com/inclusiveaccess**.

Your Course, Your Way

No two writing programs or classrooms are exactly alike. Our Curriculum Solutions team works with you to design custom options that provide the resources your students need. (Options below require enrollment minimums.)

- *ForeWords for English.* Customize any print resource to fit the focus of your course or program by choosing from a range of prepared topics, such as Sentence Guides for Academic Writers.

- *Macmillan Author Program (MAP).* Add excerpts or package acclaimed works from Macmillan's trade imprints to connect students with prominent authors and public conversations. A list of popular examples or academic themes is available upon request.

- *Bedford Select.* Build your own print handbook or anthology from a database of more than 900 selections, and add your own materials to create your ideal text. Package with any Bedford/St. Martin's text for additional savings. Visit **macmillanlearning.com/bedfordselect**.

Instructor Resources

You have a lot to do in your course. We want to make it easy for you to find the support you need—and to get it quickly.

Resources for Teaching Practical Argument is available as a PDF that can be downloaded from **macmillanlearning.com**. In addition to chapter overviews and teaching tips, the instructor's manual includes sample syllabi, sample answers to questions from the book, and suggested classroom activities.

Acknowledgments

The following reviewers gave us valuable feedback as we prepared the fourth edition of *Practical Argument*: Yaw Adu-Gyamfi, Liberty University; Emily Andrews, Volunteer State Community College; Kathryn Baker, Santa Fe College; Carol Bledsoe, Florida Gulf Coast University; Molly Brown, Clinton Community College; Jennifer Coenen, University of Florida; Emily Cosper, Delgado Community College; Joseph Couch, Montgomery College; Jason DePolo, North Carolina A&T State University; Andrea D. Green, Motlow State Community College; Lindsey Jungman, University of Minnesota Duluth; Jill Kronstadt, Montgomery College; Leslie LaChance, Volunteer State Community College; Felicia M. Maisey, LaSalle University; Danizete Martinez, University of New Mexico-Valencia; Carola Mattord, Kennesaw State University; James Mense, St. Louis Community College at Florissant Valley; Amanda Palleschi, University of the District of Columbia Community College; Barbara B. Parsons, Tacoma Community College; Christina Rothenbeck, Louisiana State University; David Seelow, Maria College; Wayne Sneath, Davenport University; Roger Swafford, Des Moines Area Community College—Ankeny Campus; David M. Taylor, St. Louis Community College—Meramec; Marlea Trevino, Grayson College; Ashley Whitmore, University of Michigan-Dearborn; Alex Wulff, Maryville University.

We thank Jeff Ousborne, Deja Ruddick, Elizabeth Rice, and Michelle McSweeney for their valuable contributions to this text.

At Bedford/St. Martin's, Joan Feinberg, Denise Wydra, Karen Henry, Steve Scipione, Leasa Burton, and John Sullivan were involved and supportive from the start of the project. John, in particular, helped us to shape this book and continues to provide valuable advice and support. In this fourth edition, we have had the pleasure of working with Jesse Hassenger, our knowledgeable, professional, and creative editor. His addition to our team has helped to make *Practical Argument* a better book. Coeditor Lexi DeConti and assistant editor Cari Goldfine devoted many hours to locating images and helping with manuscript prep where needed. Once again, Matt Glazer patiently and efficiently shepherded the book through the production process. Others on our team included project manager Nagalakshmi Karunanithi; Joy Fisher Williams who was instrumental in marketing the book; Krystyna Borgen and Angela Boehler, who obtained image permissions; Kalina Ingham and Mark Schaefer, who handled text permissions; and Diana Blume, who developed our design. We are grateful to everyone on our team for their help.

Finally, we would like to thank each other for lunches past—and lunches to come.

Laurie G. Kirszner

Stephen R. Mandell

How *Practical Argument* Supports WPA Outcomes for First-Year Composition

The following chart provides information on how *Practical Argument* helps students build proficiency and achieve the learning outcomes set by the Council of Writing Program Administrators, which writing programs across the country use to assess their students' work.

Rhetorical Knowledge	
Learn and use key rhetorical concepts through analyzing and composing a variety of texts.	**An Introduction to Argument** features a detailed section on determining the rhetorical situation, considering the writer, purpose, audience, and context, and more. **Part 2: Reading and Responding to Arguments** takes students through a scaffolded process of reading, analyzing, and responding to texts. **Part 3: Writing an Argumentative Essay** goes into greater detail on the writing process.
Gain experience reading and composing in several genres to understand how genre conventions shape and are shaped by readers' and writers' practices and purposes.	*Practical Argument* features over 100 readings from a variety of genres, sources, and authors, including sample student work throughout the book. **Part 5: Strategies for Argument** covers various approaches to argument, including definitions (**Chapter 12**), cause and effect (**Chapter 13**), evaluation (**Chapter 14**), ethics (**Chapter 15**), proposal (**Chapter 16**), and combined strategies. The book also covers Rogerian and Toulmin arguments in **Chapter 6**.
Develop facility in responding to a variety of situations and contexts calling for purposeful shifts in voice, tone, level of formality, design, medium, and/or structure.	**Chapters 1–16** include multiple exercises, building students up to writing responses to various types of arguments, including all of the strategies covered in **Part 5**.
Understand and use a variety of technologies to address a range of audiences.	*Practical Argument* covers **both written and oral arguments**, and discusses **a variety of technologies** particularly in the location and evaluation of sources.

Match the capacities of different environments (e.g., print and electronic) to varying rhetorical situations.	In addition to coverage noted above that helps students understand rhetorical situations, specific guidance on different environments includes the use of images of arguments (**Chapter 3**) and composing/delivering oral arguments (**Chapter 6**).
Critical Thinking, Reading, and Composing	
Use composing and reading for inquiry, learning, critical thinking, and communicating in various rhetorical contexts.	**Chapter 2** guides students through active reading, critical thinking, and composing critical responses based on those skills, while **Part 5** gets more specific in how to communicate in different rhetorical modes.
Read a diverse range of texts, attending especially to relationships between assertion and evidence, to patterns of organization, to the interplay between verbal and nonverbal elements, and to how these features function for different audiences and situations.	Over 70 readings are new to this edition of *Practical Argument*, with an emphasis on **diverse authors and sources**, and more visuals for analysis than ever before. Many of these readings are organized by different argument strategies in **Part 5**.
Locate and evaluate (for credibility, sufficiency, accuracy, timeliness, bias, and so on) primary and secondary research materials, including journal articles and essays, books, scholarly and professionally established and maintained databases or archives, and informal electronic networks and Internet sources.	**Part 4: Using Sources to Support Your Argument** includes two full chapters of material on locating and evaluating research materials: **Chapter 8** and **Chapter 9**.
Use strategies—such as interpretation, synthesis, response, critique, and design/redesign—to compose texts that integrate the writer's ideas with those from appropriate sources.	As mentioned above, **Chapter 9** gives students a complete picture of how to quote, summarize, paraphrase, synthesize, and otherwise integrate sourced material.

Processes	
Develop a writing project through multiple drafts.	**Chapter 7** covers drafting, revising, and polishing essays.
Develop flexible strategies for reading, drafting, reviewing, collaborating, revising, rewriting, rereading, and editing.	**Chapter 2** covers reading strategies including previewing, close reading, and looking for comprehension clues, while the above-mentioned **Chapter 7** includes drafting, reviewing, collaborating, revising, rewriting, and editing.
Use composing processes and tools as a means to discover and reconsider ideas.	**Chapter 4** gives the framework of composing as a means of students considering and analyzing ideas about arguments.
Experience the collaborative and social aspects of writing processes.	**Chapter 7** includes guidelines for peer review.
Learn to give and to act on productive feedback to works in progress.	**Chapter 7** also includes a section about getting feedback.
Adapt composing processes for a variety of technologies and modalities.	**Chapter 6** covers oral arguments, while **Part 4** includes digital-based sources.
Reflect on the development of composing practices and how those practices influence their work.	Checklists throughout the book invite students to reflect on their reading and writing processes, and scaffolded exercises throughout **Parts 1–5** provide opportunities for active reflection.

Knowledge of Conventions	
Develop knowledge of linguistic structures, including grammar, punctuation, and spelling, through practice in composing and revising.	**Grammar in Context** boxes throughout the text offer practical tips that can be applied to the processes of composing, revising, and editing.
Understand why genre conventions for structure, paragraphing, tone, and mechanics vary.	In addition to the book's grammar coverage, the "Understanding Your Purpose and Audience" section in **Chapter 7** helps students examine how an author's methods differ in relation to their purpose and audience.

Gain experience negotiating variations in genre conventions.	The exercises and assignments throughout **Chapters 1–16** offer a variety of writing assignments in different formats, including Rogerian, Toulmin, definition, cause-and-effect, ethical, evaluation, and proposal arguments.
Learn common formats and/or design features for different kinds of texts.	**Chapter 3** includes examination of design elements and visually augmented texts.
Explore the concepts of intellectual property (such as fair use and copyright) that motivate documentation conventions.	**Chapter 11** goes into detail about the responsibilities of using intellectual property in an academic context.
Practice applying citation conventions systematically in their own work.	**Chapter 10** offers all the essentials of MLA documentation.

Argument Step by Step, Supported by Helpful Apparatus

Practical Argument takes students through a step-by-step process of reading and responding to others' arguments and writing, revising, and editing their own arguments. The book uses a classroom-tested, exercise-driven approach that encourages students to participate actively in their own learning process. Chapters progress in a clear, easy-to-understand sequence: students are asked to read arguments, identify their key elements, and develop a response to an issue in the form of a complete, documented argumentative essay based on in-book focused research.

Exercises and writing assignments for each selection provide guidance for students as they work toward creating a finished piece of writing. Throughout the text, checklists, grammar-in-context and summary boxes, and source and gloss notes provide support. In addition, more than a dozen unique templates for paragraph-length arguments—located with the end-of-chapter exercises—provide structures that students can use for guidance as they write definition arguments, cause-and-effect arguments, evaluation arguments, ethical arguments, and proposal arguments. Sentence templates also frequently appear in the questions that follow the readings, providing an opportunity for students to work up to arguments at the paragraph level.

A Thematically Focused Approach with Compelling Chapter Topics

Students learn best when they care about and are engaged in an issue. For this reason, *Practical Argument* uses readings and assignments to help students learn argumentation in the context of one high-interest contemporary issue per chapter. Chapter topics include environmental solutions, free speech, technology and privacy, student debt, student safety, and distinguishing between real news and misinformation—issues that have real meaning in students' lives.

Readings on Relevant and Interesting Issues

Practical Argument, Fourth Edition, includes over 110 accessible and thought-provoking professional readings on issues that students will want to read about and debate including selections from journals and blogs. The book also uses a variety of new visual argument selections, and seventeen sample student essays, more than in any other argument book, provide realistic models. Each student essay, including complete MLA and APA research papers, is annotated to further assist students through their own writing process. The mixture of professional and student essays, visual pieces, debates, and casebooks cover high-interest issues like campus speech, privacy in technology, immigration, women in science, technology, engineering, and mathematics (STEM), paying college athletes, student debt, self-driving cars, and more. A collection of ten classic arguments offers more challenging approaches to enduring issues.

To help students better understand the context of the sources included in *Practical Argument*, each is marked with an icon that shows how it was originally presented.

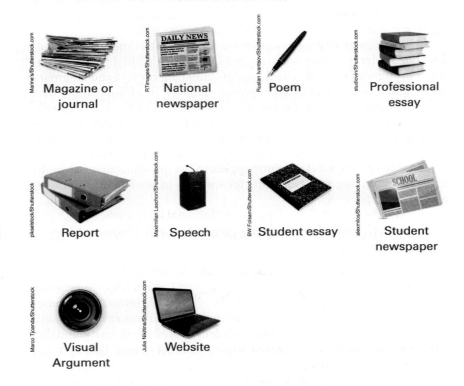

Magazine or journal

National newspaper

Poem

Professional essay

Report

Speech

Student essay

Student newspaper

Visual Argument

Website

An Open and Inviting Full-Color Design

The fresh, contemporary look of *Practical Argument* will engage students. This open, colorful design eliminates the sea of dense type that is typical of many other argument books. Over a hundred photographs and other visuals—such as advertisements, cartoons, charts and graphs, and web pages—provide appealing and instructive real-world examples. The use of open space and numerous images reinforces the currency of the book's themes and also creates an inviting and visually stimulating format.

BRIEF CONTENTS

CONTENTS

PART 2 Reading and Responding to Arguments 59

PART

3 Writing an Argumentative Essay   249

PART

4 Using Sources to Support Your Argument   283

CHAPTER 9   Summarizing, Paraphrasing, Quoting, and Synthesizing Sources   313

PART 5 Strategies for Argument   389

CHAPTER 12 Definition Arguments   393

CHAPTER 16   Proposal Arguments   563

PART
6 Debates, Casebooks, and Classic Arguments 605

DEBATES

DISCIPLINARY CONTENTS

Environmental Science

History

Law/Criminal Justice

Political Science

Psychology

Sociology

Practical
Argument
A Text and Anthology

PART

1

Understanding Argument

Ron Chapple/The Image Bank/Getty Images

An Introduction to Argument

Recognizing Arguments

Arguments are everywhere. Whenever you turn on the television, read a newspaper or magazine, talk to friends and family, enter an online discussion, or engage in a debate in one of your classes, you encounter arguments. In fact, it is fair to say that much of the interaction that takes place in society involves argument. Consider, for example, a lawyer who tries to persuade a jury that a defendant is innocent, a doctor who wants to convince a patient to undergo a specific form of treatment, a lawmaker who wants to propose a piece of legislation, an executive who wants to institute a particular policy, an activist who wants to pursue a particular social agenda, a parent who wants to convince a child to study harder, a worker who wants to propose a more efficient way of performing a task, an employee who thinks that he or she deserves a raise, or a spokesperson in an infomercial whose goal is to sell something: all these people are engaging in argument.

In college, you encounter arguments on a daily basis; in fact, both class discussions and academic writing often take the form of argument. Consider, for example, the following questions that might be debated (and written about) in a first-year writing class:

- Do the benefits of fossil fuels outweigh their risks?

- How free should free speech be?

- How far should schools go to keep students safe?

- Is organic food worth the cost?

- Do bystanders have an ethical responsibility to help in a crisis?

What these questions have in common is that they all call for argumentation. To answer these questions, students would be expected to state their opinions and support them.

Wake Up, America! (1917) James Montgomery Flagg. Published by the Hegeman Print, New York/ Library of Congress Prints and Photographs Division [LC-USZC4-3802].

World War I propaganda poster (1917)

Defining Argument

Now for the obvious question: exactly what is an argument? Perhaps the best way to begin is by explaining what argument is *not*. An argument (at least an academic argument) is not a **quarrel** or an angry exchange. The object of argument is not to attack someone who disagrees with you or to beat an opponent into submission. For this reason, the shouting matches that you routinely see on television or hear on talk radio are not really arguments. Argument is also not **spin**—the positive or biased slant that politicians routinely put on facts—or **propaganda**—information (or misinformation) that is spread to support a particular viewpoint. Finally, argument is not just a contradiction or denial of someone else's position. Even if you establish that an opponent's position is unwarranted or misguided, you still have to establish that your own position has merit by presenting evidence to support it.

There is a basic difference between **formal arguments**—those that you develop in academic discussion and writing—and **informal arguments**—those that occur in daily life, where people often get into arguments about politics, sports, social issues, and personal relationships. These everyday disputes are often just verbal fights in which one person tries to outshout another. Although they sometimes include facts, they tend to rely primarily on emotion and unsupported opinions.

Moreover, such everyday arguments do not have the formal structure of academic arguments: they do not establish a logical link between a particular viewpoint and reliable supporting evidence. There is also no real effort to address opposing arguments. In general, these arguments tend to be disorganized, emotional disputes that have more to do with criticizing an opponent than with advancing and supporting a position on an issue. Although such informal arguments can serve as starting points for helping you think about issues, they do not have the structure or the intellectual rigor of formal arguments.

So exactly what is an argument—or, more precisely, what is an academic argument? An **academic argument** is a type of formal argument that takes a stand, presents evidence, includes documentation, and uses logic to convince an audience to accept (or at least consider) the writer's position. Of course, academic arguments can get heated, but at their core they are civil exchanges. Writers of academic arguments strive to be fair and to show respect for others—especially for those who present opposing arguments.

Keep in mind that arguments take positions with which reasonable people may disagree. For this reason, an argument never actually proves anything. (If it did, there would be no argument.) The best that an argument can do is to convince other people to accept (or at least acknowledge) the validity of its position.

An angry exchange is not an academic argument.

Jim Watson/AFP/Getty Images

WHAT KINDS OF STATEMENTS ARE NOT DEBATABLE?

To be suitable for argument, a statement must be **debatable**: in other words, there must be conflicting opinions or conflicting facts that call the validity of the statement into question. For this reason, the following types of statements are generally *not* suitable for argument:

- **Statements of fact:** A statement of fact can be verified, so it is not debatable. For example, there is no point in arguing that your school makes instructors' lectures available as podcasts. This is a question of fact that can easily be checked. You can, however, argue that making instructors' lectures available as podcasts would (or would not) enhance education at your school. This is a debatable statement that can be supported by facts and examples.

- **Statements of personal preference or taste:** Expressions of personal preference or taste are not suitable for argument. For example, if you say that you don't like the taste of a particular soft drink, no one can legitimately argue that you are wrong. This statement is beyond dispute because it is a matter of personal taste. You could, however, argue that soft drinks should not be sold in school cafeterias because they contribute to obesity. To support this position, you would supply evidence—facts, statistics, and expert opinion.

> **NOTE**
>
> Although personal expressions of religious belief are difficult to debate, the interpretation of religious doctrine is a suitable subject for argument—and so are the political, social, philosophical, and theological effects of religion on society.

It is a mistake to think that all arguments have just two sides—one right side and one wrong side. In fact, many arguments that you encounter in college focus on issues that are quite complex. For example, if you were considering the question of whether the United States should ban torture of enemy combatants, you could answer this question with a yes or a no, but this would be an oversimplification. To examine the issue thoroughly, you would have to consider it from a number of angles:

- Should torture be banned in all situations?

- Should torture be used as a last resort to elicit information that could prevent an imminent attack?

- What actually constitutes torture? For example, is sleep deprivation torture? What about a slap on the face? Loud music? A cold cell? Are "enhanced interrogation techniques"—such as waterboarding—torture?

- Who should have the legal right to approve interrogation techniques?

If you were going to write an argument about this issue, you would have to take a position that adequately conveyed its complex nature—for example, "Although torture may be cruel and even inhuman, it is sometimes necessary." To do otherwise might be to commit the **either/or fallacy** (see p. 155)—to offer only two choices when there are actually many others.

Arguments in Real Life

In blogs, social media posts, work-related proposals, letters to the editor, emails to businesses, letters of complaint, and other types of communication, you formulate arguments that are calculated to influence readers. Many everyday situations call for argument:

- A proposal to the manager of the UPS store where you work to suggest a more efficient way of sorting packages

- A letter to your local newspaper in which you argue that creating a walking trail would be good use of your community's tax dollars

- An email to your child's principal asking her to extend after-school hours

- A letter to a credit card company in which you request an adjustment to your bill

- A blog post in which you argue that the federal government could do more to relieve the student loan burden

Because argument is so prevalent, the better your arguing skills, the better able you will be to function—not just in school but also in the wider world. When you have a clear thesis, convincing support, and effective refutation of opposing arguments, you establish your credibility and go a long way toward convincing readers that you are someone worth listening to.

Presenting a good argument does not guarantee that readers will accept your ideas. It does, however, help you to define an issue and to express your position clearly and logically. If you present yourself as a well-informed, reasonable person who is attuned to the needs of your readers—even those who disagree with you—you increase your chances of convincing your audience that your position is worth considering.

Arguments are also central to our democratic form of government. Whether the issue is taxation, health care, border control, the environment, abortion, gun ownership, energy prices, gay marriage, terrorism, or cyber-bullying, political candidates, media pundits, teachers, friends, and family members all try to influence the way we think. So in a real sense, argument is the way that all of us participate in the national (or even global) conversation about ideas that matter. The better you understand the methods of argumentation, the better able you will be to recognize, analyze, and respond to the arguments that you hear. By mastering the techniques of argument, you will become a clearer thinker, a more informed citizen, and a person who is better able to influence those around you.

Voting rights protest

Chip Somodevilla/Getty Images News/Getty Images

Winning and Losing Arguments

People often talk of "winning" and "losing" arguments, and of course, the aim of many arguments is to defeat an opponent. In televised political debates, candidates try to convince viewers that they should be elected. In a courtroom, a defense attorney tries to establish a client's innocence. In a job interview, a potential employee tries to convince an employer that he or she is the best-qualified applicant. However, the goal of an argument is not always to determine a winner and a loser. Sometimes the goal of an argument is to identify a problem and suggest solutions that could satisfy those who hold a number of different positions on an issue.

If, for example, you would like your college bookstore to lower the price of items (such as sweatshirts, coffee mugs, and backpacks) with a school logo, you could simply state your position and then support it with evidence. A more effective way of approaching this problem, however, might be to consider all points of view and find some middle ground. For example, how would lowering these prices affect the bookstore? A short conversation with the manager of the bookstore might reveal that the revenue generated by these products enables the bookstore to discount other items—such as art supplies and computers—as well as to hire student help. Therefore, decreasing the price of products with college logos would negatively affect some students. Even so, the high prices also make it difficult for some students to buy these items.

To address this problem, you could offer a compromise solution: the price of items with college logos could be lowered, but the price of other items—such as magazines and snacks—could be raised to make up the difference.

The Rhetorical Situation

In everyday use, the term *rhetoric* has distinctly negative connotations. When a speech is described as being nothing but *rhetoric*, the meaning is clear: the speech consists of empty words and phrases calculated to confuse and manipulate listeners. When writing instructors use the term *rhetoric*, however, it means something quite different: it refers to the choices someone makes to structure a message—written, oral, or visual.

The **rhetorical situation** refers to the factors that influence the creation of any type of communication—especially its words, images, and structure. Applied to argument, the rhetorical situation refers to five factors you should consider when planning an effective argument. Before you begin to write, you should analyze the rhetorical situation and consider the choices you will have to make to construct an effective argument.

Although every rhetorical situation is different, all rhetorical situations involve the following five elements: the *writer*, the *purpose*, the *audience*, the *question*, and the *context*. The following diagram shows the relationship of these elements to one another.

Considering the Writer

Every argument begins with a writer, the person who creates the text. For this reason, it is important to understand how your biases or preconceptions could affect what you produce. For example, if you were home schooled, you might have very definite ideas about education. Likewise, a former Navy Seal might have preconceptions concerning the war in Syria. Strongly held beliefs like these can,

Rhetorical situation

and often do, color arguments. The following factors can affect the tone and content of your argument:

age
education
gender
ethnicity
cultural experiences
political affiliation
religion
sexuality
social standing

Before you plan an argument, ask yourself what preconceived ideas you may have about a particular topic. Do your beliefs prevent you from considering all sides of an issue, reaching a logical and fair conclusion, or acknowledging the validity of opposing arguments? It is important that you present yourself as a fair and open-minded person, one whom readers can trust. For this reason, you should maintain a reasonable tone and avoid the use of words or phrases that indicate bias.

Considering the Purpose

A writer's **purpose** is his or her reason for writing. The purpose of an argument is to present a position and to change (or at least influence) people's ideas about an issue. In addition to this general purpose, a writer may have more specific goals. For example, you might want to criticize the actions of others or call into question a particular public policy. You may also want to take a stand on a controversial topic or convince readers that certain arguments are weak. Finally, you may want to propose a solution to a problem or convince readers to adopt a certain course of action.

When you write an argument, you may want to state your purpose directly—usually in your introduction. (Key words in your thesis statement can indicate the direction the argument will take as well as the points that you will discuss.) At other times, especially if you think readers will not readily accept your ideas, you may want to indicate your purpose later in your essay or simply imply it.

Considering the Audience

When you write argumentative essays, you don't write in a vacuum; you write for real people who may or may not agree with you. As you are writing, it is easy to forget this fact and address a general group of readers. However, this would be a mistake. Defining your audience and keeping this audience in mind as you write is important because it helps you decide what material to include and how to present it.

One way to define an audience is by its **traits**—the age, gender, interests, values, knowledge, preconceptions, and level of education of audience members. Each of these traits influences how audience members will react to your ideas, and understanding them helps you determine how to construct your argument. For instance, suppose you were going to write an essay with the following thesis:

Although college is expensive, its high cost is justified.

How you approach this subject would depend on the audience you were addressing. For example, college students, parents, and college administrators would have different ideas about the subject, different perspectives, different preconceptions, and different levels of knowledge. Therefore, the argument you write for each of these audiences would be different from the others in terms of content, organization, and type of appeal.

- **College students** have a local and personal perspective. They know the school and have definite ideas about the value of the education they are getting. Most likely, they come from different backgrounds and have varying financial needs. Depending on their majors, they have different expectations about employment (and salary) when they graduate. Even with these differences, however, these students share certain concerns. Many probably have jobs to help cover their expenses. Many also have student loans that they will need to start paying after graduation.

  An argumentative essay addressing this audience could focus on statistics and expert opinions that establish the worth of a college degree in terms of future employment, job satisfaction, and lifetime earnings.

- **Parents** probably have limited knowledge of the school and the specific classes their children are taking. They have expectations—both realistic and unrealistic—about the value of a college degree. Some parents may be able to help their children financially, and others may be unable to do so. Their own life experiences and backgrounds probably color their ideas about the value of a college education. For example, parents who have gone to college may have different ideas about the value of a degree from those who haven't.

  An argumentative essay addressing this audience could focus on the experience of other parents of college students. It could also include statistics that address students' future economic independence and economic security.

- **College administrators** have detailed knowledge about college and the economic value of a degree. They are responsible for attracting students, scheduling classes, maintaining educational standards, and providing support services. They are familiar with budget requirements, and they understand the financial pressures involved in running a school. They also know how tuition dollars are spent and how much state and federal aid the school needs to stay afloat. Although they are sympathetic to the plight of both students and parents, they have to work with limited resources.

An argumentative essay addressing this audience could focus on the need to make tuition more affordable by cutting costs and providing more student aid.

Another way to define an audience is to determine whether it is *friendly, hostile,* or *neutral.*

- A **friendly audience** is sympathetic to your argument. This audience might already agree with you or have an emotional or intellectual attachment to you or to your position. In this situation, you should emphasize points of agreement and reinforce the emotional bond that exists between you and the audience. Don't assume, however, that because this audience is receptive to your ideas, you do not have to address their concerns or provide support for your points. If readers suspect that you are avoiding important issues or that your evidence is weak, they will be less likely to take your argument seriously—even though they agree with you.

- A **hostile audience** disagrees with your position and does not accept the underlying assumptions of your argument. For this reason, you have to work hard to overcome their preconceived opinions, presenting your points clearly and logically and including a wide range of evidence. To show that you are a reasonable person, you should treat these readers with respect even though they happen to disagree with you. In addition, you should show that you have taken the time to consider their objections and that you value their concerns. Even with all these efforts, however, the best you may be able to do is get them to admit that you have made some good points in support of your position.

- A **neutral audience** has few or no preconceived opinions about the issue you are going to discuss. (When you are writing an argument for a college class, you should assume that you are writing for a neutral audience.) For this reason, you need to provide background information about the issue and about the controversy surrounding it. You should also summarize opposing points of view, present them logically, and refute them effectively. This type of audience may not know much about an issue, but it is not necessarily composed of unsophisticated or unintelligent people. Moreover, even though such readers are neutral, you should assume that they are **skeptical**—that is, that they will question your assumptions and require supporting evidence before they accept your conclusions.

> **NOTE**
>
> Some audiences are so diverse that they are difficult to categorize. In this case, it is best to define the audience yourself—for example, *concerned parents, prudent consumers*, or *serious students*—and then address them accordingly.

Keep in mind that identifying a specific audience is not something that you do at the last minute. Because your audience determines the kind of argument you present, you should take the time to make this determination before you begin to write.

Considering the Question

All arguments begin with a question that you are going to answer. To be suitable for argument, this question must have more than one possible answer. If it does not, there is no basis for the argument. For example, there is no point trying to write an argumentative essay on the question of whether head injuries represent a danger for football players. The answer to this question is so obvious that no thoughtful person would argue that they are not. The question of whether the National Football League (NFL) is doing enough to protect players from head injuries, however, is one on which reasonable people can (and do) disagree. Consider the following information:

- In recent years, the NFL has done much to reduce the number of serious head injuries.

- New protocols for the treatment of players who show signs of head trauma, stricter rules against helmet-to-helmet tackles, and the use of safer helmets have reduced the number of concussions.

- Even with these precautions, professional football players experience a high number of head injuries, with one in three players reporting negative effects—some quite serious—from repeated concussions.

Because there are solid arguments on both sides of this issue, you could write an effective argument in which you address this question.

Considering the Context

An argument takes place in a specific **context**—the set of circumstances that surrounds the issue. As you plan your argument, consider the social, political, historical, and cultural events that define the debate.

Assume that you were going to argue that the public school students in your hometown should be required to purchase iPads. Before you begin your argument, you should give readers the background—the context—they will need to understand the issue. For example, they should know that school officials have been debating the issue for over a year. School administrators say that given the advances in distance learning as well as the high quality of online resources, iPads will enhance the educational experience of students. They also say that it is time to bring the schools' instructional methods into the twenty-first century. Even so, some parents say that requiring the purchase of iPads will put an undue financial burden on them. In addition, teachers point out that a good deal of new material will have to be developed to take advantage of this method of instruction. Finally, not all students will have access at home to the high-speed internet capacity necessary for this type of instruction.

If it is not too complicated, you can discuss the context of your argument in your introduction; if it requires more explanation, you can discuss it in your first body paragraph. If you do not establish this context early in your essay, however, readers will have a difficult time understanding the issue you are going to discuss and the points you are going to make.

Logos, Pathos, and Ethos

To be effective, your argument has to be persuasive. **Persuasion** is a general term that refers to how a speaker or writer influences an audience to adopt a particular belief or to follow a specific course of action.

In the fifth century B.C.E., the philosopher Aristotle considered the issue of persuasion. Ancient Greece was primarily an oral culture (as opposed to a written or print culture), so persuasive techniques were most often used in speeches. Public officials had to speak before a citizens' assembly, and people had to make their cases in front of various judicial bodies. The more persuasive the presentation, the better the speaker's chance of success. In *The Art of Rhetoric*, Aristotle examines the three different means of persuasion that a speaker can use to persuade listeners (or writers):

- The appeal to reason (*logos*)
- The appeal to the emotions (*pathos*)
- The appeal to authority (*ethos*)

The Appeal to Reason (Logos)

According to Aristotle, argument is the appeal to reason or logic (***logos***). He assumed that, at their core, human beings are logical and therefore would respond to a well-constructed argument. For Aristotle, appeals to reason focus primarily on the way that an argument is organized, and this organization is determined by formal logic, which uses deductive and inductive reasoning to reach valid conclusions. Aristotle believed that appeals to reason convince an audience that a conclusion is both valid and true (see Chapter 5 for a discussion of deductive and inductive reasoning and logic). Although Aristotle believed that ideally, all arguments should appeal to reason, he knew that given the realities of human nature, reason alone was not always enough. Therefore, when he discusses persuasion, he also discusses the appeals to *ethos* and *pathos*.

Logos *in Action*

Notice how the ad below for the Tesla Model 3, an all-electric automobile, appeals primarily to reason. It uses facts as well as a logical explanation of the car's advantages to appeal to reason.

Andy Cross/Denver Post/Getty Images

You can assess the effectiveness of *logos* (the appeal to reason) in an argument by asking the following questions:

- Does the argument have a clear thesis? In other words, can you identify the main point the writer is trying to make?

- Does the argument include the facts, examples, and expert opinion needed to support the thesis?

- Is the argument well organized? Are the points the argument makes presented in logical order?

- Can you detect any errors in logic (**fallacies**) that undermine the argument's reasoning?

The Appeal to the Emotions (Pathos)

Aristotle knew that an appeal to the emotions (*pathos*) could be very persuasive because it adds a human dimension to an argument. By appealing to an audience's sympathies and by helping them to identify with the subject being discussed, emotional appeals can turn abstract concepts into concrete examples that can compel people to take action. After December 7, 1941, for example, explicit photographs of the Japanese attack on Pearl Harbor helped convince Americans that retaliation was both justified and desirable. Many Americans responded the same way when they saw pictures of planes crashing into the twin towers of the World Trade Center on September 11, 2001.

Although an appeal to the emotions can add to an already strong argument, it does not in itself constitute proof. Moreover, certain kinds of emotional appeals—appeals to fear, hatred, and prejudice, for example—are considered unfair and are not acceptable in college writing. In this sense, the pictures of the attacks on Pearl Harbor and the World Trade Center would be unfair arguments if they were not accompanied by evidence that established that retaliation was indeed necessary.

Pathos *in Action*

The following ad makes good use of the appeal to the emotions. Using a picture of children's shoes, the ad includes a tag that tells people that for every pair of children's shoes they buy, the manufacturer will donate a new pair of shoes to a needy child. The small shoes and their embroidered designs suggest the children who the shoes will be given to. Although the ad contains little supporting evidence, its emotional appeal is effective.

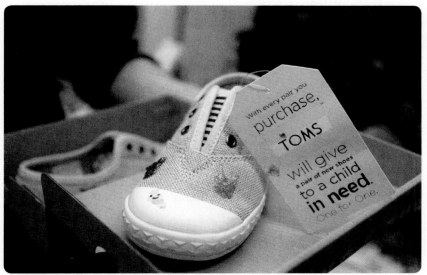

Rachel Murray/Getty Images Entertainment/Getty Images

You can assess the effectiveness of *pathos* (the appeal to the emotions) in an argument by asking the following questions:

- Does the argument include words or images designed to move readers?
- Does the argument use emotionally loaded language?
- Does the argument include vivid descriptions or striking examples calculated to appeal to readers' emotions?
- Are the values and beliefs of the writer apparent in the argument?
- Does the tone seem emotional?

The Appeal to Authority (Ethos)

Finally, Aristotle knew that the character and authority of a speaker or writer (*ethos*) could contribute to the persuasiveness of an argument. If the person making the argument is known to be honorable, truthful, knowledgeable, and trustworthy, audiences will likely accept what he or she is saying. If, on the other hand, the person is known to be deceitful, ignorant, dishonest, uninformed, or dishonorable, audiences will probably dismiss his or her argument—no matter how persuasive it might seem. Whenever you analyze an argument, you should try to determine whether the writer is worth listening to—in other words, whether the writer has **credibility**.

(For a discussion of how to establish credibility and demonstrate fairness in your own writing, see Chapter 7.)

Ethos *in Action*

The following ad uses an appeal to authority. It shows record producer and entrepreneur Dr. Dre and professional basketball player LeBron James wearing Beats headphones. The idea behind celebrity endorsements is simple. People like certain celebrities, so if they endorse a product, people will probably buy that product. (Recent studies seem to support this theory.)

You can assess the effectiveness of *ethos* (the appeal to authority) in an argument by asking the following questions:

- Does the person making the argument demonstrate knowledge of the subject?

- What steps does the person making the argument take to present its position as reasonable?

- Does the argument seem fair?

- If the argument includes sources, do they seem both reliable and credible? Does the argument include proper documentation?

- Does the person making the argument demonstrate respect for opposing viewpoints?

Dr. Dre and LeBron James in an ad promoting Beats headphones

Anthony J. Causi/Icon SMI 942/Newscom

The Rhetorical Triangle

The relationship among the three kinds of appeals in an argument is traditionally represented by a triangle.

LOGOS (reason)
Focuses on the text

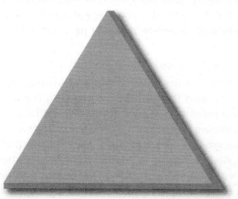

ETHOS (authority)   *PATHOS* (emotions)
Focuses on the writer   *Focuses on the audience*

In the diagram above—called the **rhetorical triangle**—all sides of the triangle are equal, implying that the three appeals occur in an argument in equal measure. In reality, however, this is seldom true. Depending on the audience, purpose, and situation, an argument may include all three appeals or just one or two. Moreover, one argument might emphasize reason, another might stress the writer's authority (or credibility), and still another might appeal mainly to the emotions. (In each of these cases, one side of the rhetorical triangle would be longer than the others.) In academic writing, for example, the appeal to reason is used most often, and the appeal to the emotions is less common. As Aristotle recognized, however, the three appeals often work together (to varying degrees) to create an effective argument.

Each of the following paragraphs makes an argument against smoking, illustrating how the appeals are used in an argument. Although each paragraph includes all three of the appeals, one appeal outweighs the others. (Keep in mind that each paragraph is aimed at a different audience.)

APPEAL TO REASON (*LOGOS*)

Among young people, the dangers of smoking are clear. According to the World Health Organization, smoking can cause a variety of problems in young people—for example, lung problems and shortness of breath. Smoking also contributes to heart attacks, strokes, and coronary artery disease (72). In addition, teenage smokers have an increased risk of developing lung cancer as they get older (CDC). According to one study, teenage smokers see doctors or other health professionals at higher rates than those who do not smoke (Ardly 112). Finally, teenagers who smoke tend to abuse alcohol and marijuana as well as engage in other risky behaviors (CDC). Clearly, tobacco is a dangerous drug that has serious health risks for teenage smokers. In fact, some studies suggest that smoking takes thirteen to fourteen years off a person's life (American Cancer Society).

APPEAL TO THE EMOTIONS (*PATHOS*)

Every day, almost four thousand young people begin smoking cigarettes, and this number is growing (Family First Aid). Sadly, most of you have no idea what you are getting into. For one thing, smoking yellows your teeth, stains your fingers, and gives you bad breath. The smoke also gets into your hair and clothes and makes you smell. Also, smoking is addictive; once you start, it's hard to stop. After you've been smoking for a few years, you are hooked, and as television commercials for the nicotine patch show, you can have a hard time breaking the habit. Finally, smoking is dangerous. In the United States, one out of every five deaths can be attributed to smoking (Teen Health). If you have ever seen anyone dying of lung cancer, you understand how bad long-term smoking can be. Just look at the pictures on the internet of diseased, blackened lungs, and it becomes clear that smoking does not make you look cool or sophisticated, no matter what cigarette advertising suggests.

APPEAL TO AUTHORITY (*ETHOS*)

My advice to those who are starting to smoke is to reconsider— before it's too late. I began using tobacco over ten years ago when I was in high school. At first, I started using snuff because I was on the baseball team and wanted to imitate the players in the major leagues. It wasn't long before I had graduated to cigarettes—first a few and then at least a pack a day. I heard the warnings from teachers and the counselors from the D.A.R.E. program, but they didn't do any good. I spent almost all my extra money on cigarettes. Occasionally, I would stop—sometimes for a few days, sometimes for a few weeks—but I always started again. Later, after I graduated, the health plan at my job covered smoking cessation treatment, so I tried everything—the patch, Chantix, therapy, and even hypnosis. Again, nothing worked. At last, after I had been married for four years, my wife sat me down and begged me to quit. Later that night, I threw away my cigarettes and haven't smoked since. Although I've gained some weight, I now breathe easier, and I am able to concentrate better than I could before. Had I known how difficult quitting was going to be, I never would have started in the first place.

When you write an argumentative essay, keep in mind that each type of appeal has its own particular strengths. Your purpose and audience as well as other elements of the rhetorical situation help you determine what strategy to use. Remember, however, that even though most effective arguments use a combination of appeals, one appeal predominates. For example, even though academic arguments may employ appeals to the emotions, they do so sparingly. Most often, they appeal primarily to reason by using facts and statistics—not emotions—to support their points.

AP Images/Butch Dill

CHAPTER

1

The Four Pillars of Argument

AT ISSUE

Is a College Education Worth the Money?

In recent years, more and more high school graduates have been heading to college, convinced that higher education will enhance their future earning power. At the same time, the cost of a college education has been rising, and so has the amount of student-loan debt carried by college graduates. (During 2017–18, average tuition and fees at nonprofit private four-year colleges rose 1.9 percent, to $34,740, while tuition for in-state students at four-year public schools went up 1.3 percent to $9,970. On average, 2017 graduates with student-loan debt owed nearly $40,000.) This situation has led some observers to wonder if the high cost of college actually pays off—not only in dollars

but also in future job satisfaction. Will a college degree protect workers who are threatened by high unemployment, the rise of technology, the declining power of labor unions, and the trend toward outsourcing? Given the high financial cost of college, do the rewards of a college education—emotional and intellectual as well as financial—balance the sacrifices that students make in time and money? These and other questions have no easy answers.

Later in this chapter, you will be introduced to readings that explore the pros and cons of investing in a college education, and you will be asked to write an argumentative essay in which you take a position on this controversial topic.

In a sense, you already know a lot more than you think you do about how to construct an argumentative essay. After all, an argumentative essay is a variation of the thesis-and-support essays that you have been writing in your college classes: you state a position on a topic, and then you support that position. However, with argumentative essays, some special concerns in terms of structure, style, and purpose come into play. Throughout this book, we introduce you to the unique features of argument. In this chapter, we focus on structure.

The Elements of Argument

An argumentative essay includes the same three sections—*introduction, body*, and *conclusion*—as any other essay. In an argumentative essay, however, the introduction includes an argumentative **thesis statement**, the body includes both the supporting **evidence** and the **refutation** of opposing arguments, and the conclusion includes a strong, convincing **concluding statement** that reinforces the position stated in the thesis.

The following diagram illustrates one way to organize an argumentative essay.

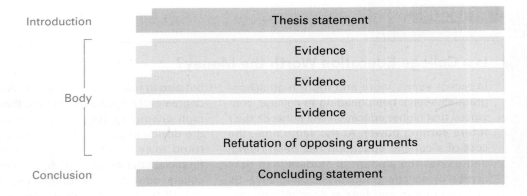

Introduction	Thesis statement
Body	Evidence
	Evidence
	Evidence
	Refutation of opposing arguments
Conclusion	Concluding statement

The elements of an argumentative essay are like the pillars of an ancient Greek temple. Together, the four elements—thesis statement, evidence, refutation of opposing arguments, and concluding statement—help you build a strong argument.

Ancient Greek temple

AP Images/Alessandro Fucarini

Thesis Statement

A **thesis statement** is a single sentence that states your position on an issue. An argumentative essay must have an **argumentative thesis**—one that takes a firm stand. For example, on the issue of whether colleges should require all students to study a language other than English, your thesis statement could be any of the following (and other positions are also possible):

- Colleges should require all students to study a foreign language.

- Colleges should require all liberal arts majors to study a foreign language.

- Colleges should require all students to study Spanish, Chinese, or Farsi.

- Colleges should not require any students to study a foreign language.

An argumentative thesis must be **debatable**—that is, it must have at least two sides, stating a position with which some reasonable people might disagree. To confirm that your thesis is debatable, you should see if you can formulate an **antithesis**, or opposing argument. For example, the statement, "Our school has a foreign-language requirement" has no antithesis because it is simply a statement of fact; you could not take the opposite position because the facts would not support it. However, the following thesis statement takes a position that *is* debatable (and therefore suitable for an argumentative thesis):

THESIS	Our school should institute a foreign-language requirement.
ANTITHESIS	Our school should not institute a foreign-language requirement.

(For more on thesis statements, see Chapter 7.)

Evidence

Evidence is the material—facts, observations, expert opinion, examples, statistics, and so on—that supports your thesis statement. For example, you could support your position that foreign-language study should be required for all college students by arguing that this requirement will make them more employable, and you could cite employment statistics to support this point. Alternatively, you could use the opinion of an expert on the topic—for example, an experienced college language instructor—to support the opposite position, arguing that students without an interest in language study are wasting their time in such courses.

You will use both *facts* and *opinions* to support the points you make in your arguments. A **fact** is a statement that can be verified (proven to be true). An **opinion** is always open to debate because it is simply a personal judgment. Of course, the more knowledgeable the writer is, the more credible his or her opinion is. Thus, the opinion of a respected expert on language study will carry more weight than the opinion of a student with no particular expertise on the issue. However, if the student's opinion is supported by facts, it will be much more convincing than an unsupported opinion.

FACTS

- Some community colleges have no foreign-language requirements.
- Some selective liberal arts colleges require all students to have two years or more of foreign-language study.
- At some universities, undergraduates must take as many as fourteen foreign-language credits.
- Some schools grant credit for high school language classes, allowing these courses to fulfill the college foreign-language requirement.

UNSUPPORTED OPINIONS

- Foreign-language courses are not as important as math and science courses.
- Foreign-language study should be a top priority on university campuses.
- Engineering majors should not have to take a foreign-language course.
- It is not fair to force all students to study a foreign language.

SUPPORTED OPINIONS

- The university requires all students to take a full year of foreign-language study, but it is not doing enough to support those who need help. For example, it does not provide enough student tutors, and the language labs have no evening hours.
- According to Ruth Fuentes, chair of the Spanish department, nursing and criminal justice majors who take at least two years of Spanish have an easier time finding employment after graduation than students in those majors who do not study Spanish.

Refutation

Because every argument has more than one side, you should not assume that your readers will agree with you. On the contrary, readers usually need to be convinced that your position on an issue has merit. This means that you need to do more than just provide sufficient evidence in support of your position; you also need to **refute** (disprove or call into question) arguments that challenge your position, possibly conceding the strengths of those opposing arguments and then pointing out their shortcomings.

For example, if you take a position in favor of requiring foreign-language study for all college students, some readers might argue that college students already have to take too many required courses. After acknowledging the validity of this argument, you could refute it by pointing out that a required foreign-language course would not necessarily be a burden for students because it could replace another, less important required course.

Other readers might point out that in today's competitive job market, which is increasingly dependent on technology, it makes more sense to study coding than to study a foreign language. In this case, you would concede the strength of the position, acknowledging the importance of proficiency in computer languages. You could then go on to refute the argument by explaining that foreign-language study expands students' ability to engage with people from other cultures, thereby becoming more competitive in a global economy. (You could also argue, of course, that students could benefit by studying *both* coding and foreign languages.) (For more on refutation, see Chapter 7.)

Concluding Statement

After you have provided convincing support for your position and refuted opposing arguments, you should end your essay with a strong **concluding statement** that reinforces your position. (The position that you want readers to remember is the one stated in your thesis, not the opposing arguments that you have refuted.) For example, you might conclude an essay in support of a foreign-language requirement by making a specific recommendation or by predicting the possible negative outcome of *not* implementing this requirement.

CHECKLIST

Does Your Argument Stand Up?

When you write an argumentative essay, check to make sure it includes all four of the elements you need to build a strong argument.

☐ Does your essay have an argumentative **thesis**?

☐ Does your essay include solid, convincing **evidence** to support your thesis?

☐ Does your essay include a **refutation** of the most compelling arguments against your position?

☐ Does your essay include a strong **concluding statement**?

🔽 The following student essay includes all four of the elements that are needed to build a convincing argument.

WHY FOREIGN-LANGUAGE STUDY SHOULD BE REQUIRED

NIA TUCKSON

Introduction

"What do you call someone who speaks three languages? Trilingual. 1 What do you call someone who speaks two languages? Bilingual. What do you call someone who speaks only one language? American." As this old joke illustrates, many Americans are unable to communicate in a language other than English. Given our global economy and American companies' need to conduct business with other countries, this problem

Thesis statement

needs to be addressed. A good first step is to require all college students to study a foreign language.

First body paragraph: Evidence

After graduation, many students will work in fields in which 2 speaking (or reading) another language will be useful or even necessary. For example, health-care professionals will often be called on to communicate with patients who do not speak English; in fact, a patient's life may depend on their ability to do so. Those who work in business and finance may need to speak Mandarin or Japanese; those who have positions in the military or in the foreign service may need to speak Persian or Arabic. A working knowledge of one of these languages can help students succeed in their future careers, and it can also make them more employable.

Second body paragraph: Evidence

In addition to strengthening a résumé, foreign-language study can 3 also give students an understanding of another culture's history, art, and literature. Although such knowledge may never be "useful" in a student's career, it can certainly enrich the student's life. Too narrow a focus on career can turn college into a place that trains students rather than educates them. In contrast, expanding students' horizons to include subjects beyond those needed for their careers can better equip them to be lifelong learners.

Third body paragraph: Evidence

When they travel abroad, Americans who can speak a language 4 other than English will find that they are better able to understand people from other countries. As informal ambassadors for the United States, tourists have a responsibility to try to understand other languages and cultures. Too many Americans assume that their own country's language and culture are superior to all others. This shortsighted attitude is not likely to strengthen relationships between the United States and other nations. Understanding a country's language can help students to build bridges between themselves and others.

Some students say that learning a language is not easy and that it takes a great deal of time. College students are already overloaded with coursework, jobs, and family responsibilities, and a new academic requirement is certain to create problems. In fact, students may find that adding just six credits of language study will limit their opportunities to take advanced courses in their majors or to enroll in electives that interest them. However, this burden can be eased if other, less important course requirements—such as physical education—are eliminated to make room for the new requirement.

5 Fourth body paragraph: Refutation of opposing argument

Some students may also argue that they, not their school, should be able to decide what courses are most important to them. After all, a student who struggled in high school French and plans to major in computer science might understandably resist a foreign-language requirement. However, challenging college language courses might actually be more rewarding than high school courses were, and the student who struggled in high school French might actually enjoy a college-level French course (or study a different language). Finally, a student who initially plans to major in computer science may actually wind up majoring in something completely different—or taking a job in a country in which English is not spoken.

6 Fifth body paragraph: Refutation of opposing argument

Entering college students sometimes find it hard to envision their personal or professional futures or to imagine where their lives may take them. Still, a well-rounded education, including foreign-language study, can prepare them for many of the challenges that they will face. Colleges can help students keep their options open by requiring at least a year (and preferably two years) of foreign-language study. Instead of focusing narrowly on what interests them today, American college students should take the extra step to become bilingual—or even trilingual—in the future.

7 Conclusion

Concluding statement

⊘ **EXERCISE 1.1 IDENTIFYING THE ELEMENTS OF ARGUMENT**

The following essay, "Learn a Language, but Not a Human One," by Andy Kessler, includes all four of the basic elements of argument discussed so far. Read the essay, and then answer the questions that follow it, consulting the diagram on page 24 if necessary.

This commentary appeared on July 17, 2017, in the *Wall Street Journal*.

LEARN A LANGUAGE, BUT NOT A HUMAN ONE

ANDY KESSLER

Donald Trump, whose wife speaks five languages, just wrapped up a pair 1 of trips to Europe during which he spoke only English. Good for him. If Mr. Trump studied a language in college or high school, as most of us were required to, it was a complete waste of his time. I took five years of French and can't even talk to a French poodle.

Maybe there's a better way for students to spend their time. Last month 2 Apple CEO Tim Cook urged the president: "Coding should be a requirement in every public school." I propose we do a swap.

Why do American schools still require foreign languages? Translating at 3 the United Nations is not a growth industry. In the 1960s and '70s everyone suggested studying German, as most scientific papers were in that language. Or at least that's what they told me. In the '80s it was Japanese, since they ruled manufacturing and would soon rule computers. In the '90s a fountain of wealth was supposed to spout from post-Communist Moscow, so we all needed to learn Russian. Now parents elbow each other getting their children into immersive Mandarin programs starting in kindergarten.

Don't they know that the Tower of Babel has been torn down? On your 4 average smartphone, apps like Google Translate can do real-time voice translation. No one ever has to say worthless phrases like *la plume de ma tante* anymore. The app Waygo lets you point your phone at signs in Chinese, Japanese, or Korean and get translations in English. Sometime in the next few years you'll be able to buy a Bluetooth-based universal translator for your ear.

Yet students still need to take at least two years of foreign-language classes 5 in high school to attend most four-year colleges. Three if they want to impress the admissions officer. Four if they're masochists. Then they need to show language competency to graduate most liberal-arts programs. We tried to get my son out of a college language requirement. He pointed to his computer skills and argued that the internet is in English. (It's true. As of March, 51.6 percent of websites were in English. Just 2 percent were Chinese.) We lost the argument. He took Japanese and has fun ordering sushi.

It's not as if learning another language comes with a big payday. In 2002 6 the Federal Reserve and Harvard put out a study showing those who speak a foreign language earn 2 percent more than those who don't.

High schools tend to follow colleges' lead, but maybe that's beginning to change. 7 I read through all 50 states' language requirements and only one requires either two years of a foreign language or two years of "computer technology approved for college admission requirements." Wow. Is that California? No. New York? No. Would you believe Oklahoma? South Dakota and Maryland also have flexible language skill laws. Foolishly, the Common Core State Standards are silent on coding.

The U.S. is falling behind. In 2014 England made computing a part of its national 8 primary curriculum. Estonia had already started coding in its schools as early as first grade. The Netherlands, Belgium, and Finland also have national programs.

Maybe the U.S. can start the ball rolling by requiring colleges and high 9 schools to allow computer languages to count as foreign languages. A handful of high schools already teach the Java computer language using a free tool called Blue J. Nonprofit Code.org exposes students to a visual programming language called Blockly. To compete in this dog-eat-dog world, America should offer Python and Ruby on Rails instead of French and Spanish.

Knowledge is good. Great literature reshuffles the mind. Tough trigonom- 10 etry problems provide puzzles for the brain. Yet there is no better challenge than writing code that teaches a machine to do exactly what you want. Some will respond, "So you want us to do vocational education?" As if computer programming is akin to auto shop and plumbing. Sorry, that's a *faux* argument. Even I remember the French word for bogus.

Let's face it, the world is headed toward one language anyway. The 11 American-based Germanic-named Uber was *originato* at the Le Web conference in Paris. In Shanghai, I've seen ads on trains and storefronts signs that read "Learn Wall Street English."

Mr. Cook is right to want more coders, though a tad self-serving as Apple 12 basically sells software wrapped in glass and metal. Same with Code.org, supported by Google and Microsoft. But every company requires coders. Even the formerly blue-collar job of operating machine tools now requires expertise in programming to control them. This will be increasingly true in workerless retail, doctorless medicine, and even teacherless education. Time to modernize the dated curriculum—*pronto*.

Identifying the Elements of Argument

1. What is this essay's thesis? Restate it in your own words.

2. List the arguments Kessler presents as evidence to support his thesis.

3. Summarize the main opposing argument the essay identifies. Then, summarize Kessler's refutation of this argument.

4. Restate the essay's concluding statement in your own words.

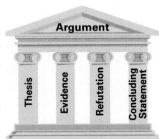

Is a College Education Worth the Money?

AP Images/Butch Dill

Reread the At Issue box on page 23, which summarizes questions raised on both sides of this issue. As the following sources illustrate, reasonable people may disagree about this controversial topic.

As you review the sources, you will be asked to answer some questions and to complete some simple activities. This work will help you understand both the content and the structure of the sources. When you have finished, you will be ready to write an essay in which you take a position on the topic "Is a College Education Worth the Money?"

SOURCES

This essay appeared in the *New York Times* on May 16, 2018.

COLLEGE MAY NOT BE WORTH IT ANYMORE

ELLEN RUPPEL SHELL

Last year, New York became the first state to offer all but its wealthiest residents tuition-free access to its public community colleges and four-year institutions. Though this Excelsior Scholarship didn't make college completely free, it highlights the power of the pro-college movement in the United States. 1

Recent decades have brought agreement that higher education is, if not a cure, then at least a protection against underemployment and the inequality it engenders. In 2012, President Barack Obama called a college degree an "economic imperative that every family in America has to be able to afford." 2

Americans strove to rise to that challenge: A third of them ages 25 to 29 now hold at least a bachelor's degree, and many paid heavily for the privilege. By last summer, Americans owed more than $1.3 trillion in student loans, more than two and a half times what they owed a decade earlier. 3

Young people and their families go into debt because they believe that college will help them in the job market. And on average it does. But this raises a question: Does higher education itself offer that benefit, or are the people who earn bachelor's degrees already positioned to get higher-paying jobs? 4

If future income was determined mainly by how much education people received, then you would assume that some higher education would be better than none. But this is often not the case. 5

People who have dropped out of college—about 40 percent of all who attend—earn only a bit more than do people with only a high school education: $38,376 a year versus $35,256. For many, that advantage is barely enough to cover their student loan debt. 6

And not all have even that advantage: African-American college dropouts on average earn less than do white Americans with only a high school degree. Meanwhile, low-income students of all races are far more likely to drop out of college than are wealthier students. Even with scholarships or free tuition, these students struggle with hefty fees and living costs, and they pay the opportunity cost of taking courses rather than getting a job. 7

The value of a college degree also varies depending on the institution bestowing it. The tiny minority of students who attend elite colleges do far better on average than those who attend nonselective ones. Disturbingly, black and Hispanic students are significantly less likely than are white and Asian students to attend elite colleges, even when family income is controlled for. That is, students from wealthy black and Hispanic families have a lower chance of attending an elite college than do students from middle-class white families. 8

It's a cruel irony that a college degree is worth less to people who most 9 need a boost: those born poor. This revelation was made by the economists Tim Bartik and Brad Hershbein. Using a body of data, the Panel Study of Income Dynamics, which includes 50 years of interviews with 18,000 Americans, they were able to follow the lives of children born into poor, middle-class, and wealthy families.

They found that for Americans born into middle-class families, a college 10 degree does appear to be a wise investment. Those in this group who received one earned 162 percent more over their careers than those who didn't.

But for those born into poverty, the results were far less impressive. College 11 graduates born poor earned on average only slightly more than did high school graduates born middle class. And over time, even this small "degree bonus" ebbed away, at least for men: By middle age, male college graduates raised in poverty were earning less than nondegree holders born into the middle class. The scholars conclude, "Individuals from poorer backgrounds may be encountering a glass ceiling that even a bachelor's degree does not break."

The authors don't speculate as to why this is the case, but it seems that 12 students from poor backgrounds have less access to very high-income jobs in technology, finance and other fields. Class and race surely play a role.

We appear to be approaching a time when, even for middle-class students, 13 the economic benefit of a college degree will begin to dim. Since 2000, the growth in the wage gap between high school and college graduates has slowed to a halt; 25 percent of college graduates now earn no more than does the average high school graduate.

Part of the reason is oversupply. Technology increased the demand for 14 educated workers, but that demand has been consistently outpaced by the number of people—urged on by everyone from teachers to presidents— prepared to meet it.

No other nation punishes the "uneducated" as harshly as the United 15 States. Nearly 30 percent of Americans without a high school diploma live in poverty, compared to 5 percent with a college degree, and we infer that this comes from a lack of education. But in 28 other wealthy developed countries, a lack of a high school diploma increases the probability of poverty by less than 5 percent. In these nations, a dearth of education does not predestine citizens for poverty.

It shouldn't here, either: According to the Bureau of Labor Statistics, fewer 16 than 20 percent of American jobs actually require a bachelor's degree. By 2026, the bureau estimates that this proportion will rise, but only to 25 percent.

Why do employers demand a degree for jobs that don't require them? 17 Because they can.

What all this suggests is that the college-degree premium may really be 18 a no-college-degree penalty. It's not necessarily college that gives people the leverage to build a better working life, it's that not having a degree decreases whatever leverage they might otherwise have.

This distinction is more than semantic. It is key to understanding the growing chasm between educational attainment and life prospects. For most of us, it's not our education that determines our employment trajectory but rather where that education positions us in relation to others.

> "No other nation punishes the 'uneducated' as harshly as the United States." [19]

None of this is to suggest that higher education is not desirable: I've [20] encouraged my own children to take that path. But while we celebrate the most recent crop of college graduates, we should also acknowledge the many more Americans who will never don a cap and gown. They, too, deserve the chance to prove themselves worthy of good work, and a good life.

◗ AT ISSUE: SOURCES FOR STRUCTURING AN ARGUMENT

1. Shell opens her essay by pointing to New York State's offer of free college tuition to most residents. Is this an appropriate introduction for the discussion that follows? Why or why not?

2. Paraphrase this essay's thesis statement by filling in the following template:

   Although college may be worth the cost for many students, _____
   _____.

3. Does Shell introduce arguments against her position? If so, where? If not, should she have done so, or is her essay convincing without mention of these counterarguments?

4. In paragraph 9, Shell refers to a study by two economists. How does this study support her position? What other kinds of supporting evidence does she include? Does she need to supply more?

5. In paragraph 18, Shell contrasts the "college-degree premium" with the "no-college-degree penalty." What is the difference? Why, according to Shell, is this distinction so important?

6. In her conclusion, Shell refers to her own children. Why? Do you think this is a good way for her to end her essay, or do you think she should have ended on a less personal note? Explain.

This undated essay is from MartyNemko.com.

WE SEND TOO MANY STUDENTS TO COLLEGE

MARTY NEMKO

Among my saddest moments as a career counselor is when I hear a story like 1 this: "I wasn't a good student in high school, but I wanted to prove to myself that I can get a college diploma—I'd be the first one in my family to do it. But it's been six years and I still have 45 units to go."

I have a hard time telling such people the killer statistic: According to the 2 U.S. Department of Education, if you graduated in the bottom 40 percent of your high school class and went to college, 76 of 100 won't earn a diploma, even if given 8½ years. Yet colleges admit and take the money from hundreds of thousands of such students each year!

Even worse, most of those college dropouts leave college having learned 3 little of practical value (see below) and with devastated self-esteem and a mountain of debt. Perhaps worst of all, those people rarely leave with a career path likely to lead to more than McWages. So it's not surprising that when you hop into a cab or walk into a restaurant, you're likely to meet workers who spent years and their family's life savings on college, only to end up with a job they could have done as a high school dropout.

Perhaps yet more surprising, even the high school students who are fully 4 qualified to attend college are increasingly unlikely to derive enough benefit to justify the often six-figure cost and four to eight years it takes to graduate— and only 40 percent of freshmen graduate in four years; 45 percent never graduate at all. Colleges love to trumpet the statistic that, over their lifetimes, college graduates earn more than nongraduates. But that's terribly misleading because you could lock the college-bound in a closet for four years and they'd earn more than the pool of non-college-bound—they're brighter, more motivated, and have better family connections. Too, the past advantage of college graduates in the job market is eroding: ever more students are going to college at the same time as ever more employers are offshoring ever more professional jobs. So college graduates are forced to take some very nonprofessional jobs. For example, Jill Plesnarski holds a bachelor's degree in biology from the private ($160,000 published total cost for four years) Moravian College. She had hoped to land a job as a medical research lab tech, but those positions paid so little that she opted for a job at a New Jersey sewage treatment plant. Today, although she's since been promoted, she must still occasionally wash down the tower that holds raw sewage.

Or take Brian Morris. After completing his bachelor's degree in lib- 5 eral arts from the University of California, Berkeley, he was unable to find a decent-paying job, so he went yet deeper into debt to get a master's degree from the private Mills College. Despite those degrees, the best job he could land was teaching a three-month-long course for $3,000. At that point, Brian was married and had a baby, so to support them, he reluctantly took a job as a truck driver. Now Brian says, "I just *have* to get out of trucking."

Colleges are quick to argue that a college education is more about enlight- 6 enment than employment. That may be the biggest deception of all. There is a Grand Canyon of difference between what the colleges tout in their brochures and websites and the reality.

Colleges are businesses, and stu-
dents are a cost item while research   **"Colleges are businesses, and**   7
is a profit center. So colleges tend to   **students are a cost item."**
educate students in the cheapest way
possible: large lecture classes, with small classes staffed by rock-bottom-cost graduate students and, in some cases, even by undergraduate students. Professors who bring in big research dollars are almost always rewarded, while even a fine teacher who doesn't bring in the research bucks is often fired or relegated to the lowest rung: lecturer.

So, no surprise, in the definitive *Your First College Year* nationwide survey 8 conducted by UCLA researchers (data collected in 2005, reported in 2007), only 16.4 percent of students were very satisfied with the overall quality of instruction they received and 28.2 percent were neutral, dissatisfied, or very dissatisfied. A follow-up survey of seniors found that 37 percent reported being "frequently bored in class," up from 27.5 percent as freshmen.

College students may be dissatisfied with instruction, but despite that, 9 do they learn? A 2006 study funded by the Pew Charitable Trusts found that 50 percent of college *seniors* failed a test that required them to do such basic tasks as interpret a table about exercise and blood pressure, understand the arguments of newspaper editorials, or compare credit card offers. Almost 20 percent of seniors had only basic quantitative skills. For example, the students could not estimate if their car had enough gas to get to the gas station.

What to do? Colleges, which receive billions of tax dollars with minimum 10 oversight, should be held at least as accountable as companies are. For example, when some Firestone tires were defective, the government nearly forced it out of business. Yet year after year, colleges turn out millions of defective products: students who drop out or graduate with far too little benefit for the time and money spent. Yet not only do the colleges escape punishment; they're rewarded with ever greater taxpayer-funded student grants and loans, which allow colleges to raise their tuitions yet higher.

What should parents and guardians do?   11

1. If your student's high school grades and SAT or ACT are in the bottom 12 half of his high school class, resist colleges' attempts to woo him. Their marketing to your child does *not* indicate that the colleges believe he will succeed there. Colleges make money whether or not a student learns, whether or not she graduates, and whether or not he finds good employ- ment. If a physician recommended a treatment that cost a fortune and

required years of effort without disclosing the poor chances of it working, she'd be sued and lose in any court in the land. But colleges—one of America's most sacred cows—somehow seem immune.

So let the buyer beware. Consider nondegree options: 13

- Apprenticeship programs (a great portal to apprenticeship websites: www.khake.com/page58.html)
- Short career-preparation programs at community colleges
- The military
- On-the-job training, especially at the elbow of a successful small business owner

2. Let's say your student *is* in the top half of his high school class and is moti- 14 vated to attend college by more than the parties, being able to say she went to college, and the piece of paper. Then have her apply to perhaps a dozen colleges. Colleges vary less than you might think, yet financial aid awards can vary wildly. It's often wise to choose the college that requires you to pay the least cash and take on the smallest loan. College is among the few products where you don't get what you pay for—price does not indicate quality.

3. If your child is one of the rare breed who, on graduating high school, 15 knows what he wants to do and isn't unduly attracted to college academics or the *Animal House* environment that college dorms often are, then take solace in the fact that in deciding to forgo college, he is preceded by scores of others who have successfully taken that noncollege road less traveled. Examples: the three most successful entrepreneurs in the computer industry, Bill Gates, Michael Dell, and Apple cofounder Steve Wozniak, all do not have a college degree. Here are some others: Malcolm X, Rush Limbaugh, Barbra Streisand, PBS *NewsHour*'s Nina Totenberg, Tom Hanks, Maya Angelou, Ted Turner, Ellen DeGeneres, former governor Jesse Ventura, IBM founder Thomas Watson, architect Frank Lloyd Wright, former Israeli president David Ben-Gurion, Woody Allen, Warren Beatty, Domino's pizza chain founder Tom Monaghan, folksinger Joan Baez, director Quentin Tarantino, ABC-TV's Peter Jennings, Wendy's founder Dave Thomas, Thomas Edison, Blockbuster Video founder and owner of the Miami Dolphins Wayne Huizenga, William Faulkner, Jane Austen, McDonald's founder Ray Kroc, Oracle founder Larry Ellison, Henry Ford, cosmetics magnate Helena Rubinstein, Benjamin Franklin, Alexander Graham Bell, Coco Chanel, Walter Cronkite, Walt Disney, Bob Dylan, Leonardo DiCaprio, cookie maker Debbi Fields, Sally Field, Jane Fonda, Buckminster Fuller, DreamWorks cofounder David Geffen, *Roots* author Alex Haley, Ernest Hemingway, Dustin Hoffman, famed anthropologist Richard Leakey, airplane inventors Wilbur and Orville Wright, Madonna, satirist H. L. Mencken, Martina Navratilova, Rosie O'Donnell, Nathan Pritikin (Pritikin diet), chef Wolfgang Puck, Robert Redford, oil billionaire John D. Rockefeller, Eleanor Roosevelt, NBC mogul David Sarnoff, and seven U.S. presidents from Washington to Truman.

4. College is like a chain saw. Only in certain situations is it the right tool. 16 Encourage your child to choose the right tool for her post–high school experience.

⊘ AT ISSUE: SOURCES FOR STRUCTURING AN ARGUMENT

1. Which of the following statements best summarizes Nemko's position? Why?

   ■ "We Send Too Many Students to College" (title)

   ■ "There is a Grand Canyon of difference between what the colleges tout in their brochures and websites and the reality" (para. 6).

   ■ "Colleges, which receive billions of tax dollars with minimum oversight, should be held at least as accountable as companies are" (10).

   ■ "College is like a chain saw. Only in certain situations is it the right tool" (16).

2. Where does Nemko support his thesis with appeals to logic? Where does he appeal to the emotions? Where does he use an appeal to authority? (Refer to the discussions of *logos*, *pathos*, and *ethos* on pages 14–18 if necessary.) Which of these three kinds of appeals do you find the most convincing? Why?

3. List the arguments Nemko uses to support his thesis in paragraphs 2–4.

4. In paragraph 4, Nemko says, "Colleges love to trumpet the statistic that, over their lifetimes, college graduates earn more than nongraduates." In paragraph 6, he says, "Colleges are quick to argue that a college education is more about enlightenment than employment." How does he refute these two opposing arguments?

5. Nemko draws an **analogy** between colleges and businesses, identifying students as a "cost item" (7). Does this analogy—including his characterization of weak students as "defective products" (10)—work for you? Why or why not?

6. What specific solutions does Nemko propose for the problem he identifies? To whom does he address these suggestions—and, in fact, his entire argument?

7. Reread paragraph 15. Do you think the list of successful people who do not hold college degrees is convincing support for Nemko's position? What kind of appeal does this paragraph make? How might you refute its argument?

This personal essay is from talk.onevietnam.org, where it appeared on May 9, 2011.

WHAT DOES IT MEAN TO BE A COLLEGE GRAD?

JENNIE LE

After May 14th, I will be a college graduate. By fall, there will be no more a cappella rehearsals, no more papers or exams, no more sleepless nights, no more weekday drinking, no more 1 a.m. milk tea runs, no more San Francisco Bay Area exploring. I won't be with the people I now see daily. I won't have the same job with the same awesome boss. I won't be singing under Sproul every Monday. I won't be booked with weekly gigs that take me all over California. I won't be lighting another VSA Culture Show.

I will also have new commitments: weekly dinner dates with my mom, brother/sister time with my other two brothers, job hunting and career building, car purchasing and maintenance. In essence, my life will be—or at least feel—completely different. From what college alumni have told me, I will soon miss my college days after they are gone.

But in the bigger picture, outside of the daily tasks, what does it mean to hold a college degree? My fellow graduating coworker and I discussed the importance (or lack thereof) of our college degrees: while I considered hanging up my two diplomas, she believed that having a bachelor's was so standard and insubstantial, only a professional degree is worth hanging up and showing off. Nowadays, holding a college degree (or two) seems like the norm; it's not a very outstanding feat.

> "Nowadays, holding a college degree (or two) seems like the norm."

However, I'd like to defend the power of earning a college degree. Although holding a degree isn't as powerful as it was in previous decades, stats still show that those who earn bachelor's degrees are likely to earn twice as much as those who don't. Also, only 27 percent of Americans can say they have a bachelor's degree or higher. Realistically, having a college degree will likely mean a comfortable living and the opportunity to move up at work and in life.

Personally, my degrees validate my mother's choice to leave Vietnam. She moved here for opportunity. She wasn't able to attend college here or in Vietnam or choose her occupation. But her hard work has allowed her children to become the first generation of Americans in the family to earn college degrees: she gave us the ability to make choices she wasn't privileged to make. Being the fourth and final kid to earn my degree in my family, my mom can now boast about having educated children who are making a name for themselves (a son who is a computer-superstar, a second son and future dentist studying at UCSF, another son who is earning his MBA and manages at Mattel, and a daughter who is thankful to have three brothers to mooch off of).

For me, this degree symbolizes my family being able to make and take the opportunities that we've been given in America, despite growing up with gang members down my street and a drug dealer across from my house. This degree will also mean that my children will have more opportunities because of my education, insight, knowledge, and support. 6

Even though a college degree isn't worth as much as it was in the past, it still shows that I—along with my fellow graduates and the 27 percent of Americans with a bachelor's or higher—will have opportunities unheard of a generation before us, showing everyone how important education is for our lives and our futures. 7

◯ AT ISSUE: SOURCES FOR STRUCTURING AN ARGUMENT

1. What purpose do the first two paragraphs of this essay serve? Do you think they are necessary? Do you think they are interesting? How else might Le have opened her essay?

2. Where does Le state her thesis? Do you think she should have stated it more forcefully? Can you suggest a more effectively worded thesis statement for this essay?

3. In paragraph 3, Le summarizes an opposing argument. What is this argument? How does she refute it? Can you think of other arguments against her position that she should have addressed?

4. In paragraphs 5–6, Le includes an appeal to the emotions. Does she offer any other kind of supporting evidence? If so, where? What other kinds of evidence do you think she should include? Why?

5. Echoing a point she made in paragraph 4, Le begins her conclusion with "Even though a college degree isn't worth as much as it was in the past, . . ." Does this concession undercut her argument, or is the information presented in paragraph 4 enough to address this potential problem?

This essay appeared in the January/February 2018 issue of *The Atlantic*.

THE WORLD MIGHT BE BETTER OFF WITHOUT COLLEGE FOR EVERYONE

BRYAN CAPLAN

I have been in school for more than 40 years. First preschool, kindergarten, 1 elementary school, junior high, and high school. Then a bachelor's degree at UC Berkeley, followed by a doctoral program at Princeton. The next step was what you could call my first "real" job—as an economics professor at George Mason University.

Thanks to tenure, I have a dream job for life. Personally, I have no reason 2 to lash out at our system of higher education. Yet a lifetime of experience, plus a quarter century of reading and reflection, has convinced me that it is a big waste of time and money. When politicians vow to send more Americans to college, I can't help gasping, "Why? You want us to waste even more?"

How, you may ask, can anyone call higher education wasteful in an age 3 when its financial payoff is greater than ever? The earnings premium for college graduates has rocketed to 73 percent—that is, those with a bachelor's degree earn, on average, 73 percent more than those who have only a high school diploma, up from about 50 percent in the late 1970s. The key issue, however, isn't whether college pays, but why. The simple, popular answer is that schools teach students useful job skills. But this dodges puzzling questions.

First and foremost: From kindergarten on, students spend thousands 4 of hours studying subjects irrelevant to the modern labor market. Why do English classes focus on literature and poetry instead of business and technical writing? Why do advanced-math classes bother with proofs almost no student can follow? When will the typical student use history? Trigonometry? Art? Music? Physics? Latin? The class clown who snarks "What does this have to do with real life?" is onto something.

The disconnect between college curricula and the job market has a banal 5 explanation: Educators teach what they know—and most have as little first-hand knowledge of the modern workplace as I do. Yet this merely complicates the puzzle. If schools aim to boost students' future income by teaching job skills, why do they entrust students' education to people so detached from the real world? Because, despite the chasm between what students learn and what workers do, academic success is a strong signal of worker productivity.

Suppose your law firm wants a summer associate. A law student with a 6 doctorate in philosophy from Stanford applies. What do you infer? The applicant is probably brilliant, diligent, and willing to tolerate serious boredom. If you're looking for that kind of worker—and what employer isn't?—you'll make an offer, knowing full well that nothing the philosopher learned at Stanford will be relevant to this job.

The labor market doesn't pay you for the useless subjects you master; it 7
pays you for the preexisting traits you signal by mastering them. This is not
a fringe idea. Michael Spence, Kenneth Arrow, and Joseph Stiglitz—all Nobel
laureates in economics—made seminal contributions to the theory of educational signaling. Every college student who does the least work required to get
good grades silently endorses the theory. But signaling plays almost no role in
public discourse or policy making. As a society, we continue to push ever larger
numbers of students into ever higher levels of education. The main effect is not
better jobs or greater skill levels, but a credentialist arms race.

Lest I be misinterpreted, I emphatically affirm that education confers some 8
marketable skills, namely literacy and numeracy. Nonetheless, I believe that signaling accounts for at least half of college's financial reward, and probably more.

Most of the salary payoff for college comes from crossing the graduation 9
finish line. Suppose you drop out after a year. You'll receive a salary bump compared with someone who's attended no college, but it won't be anywhere near
25 percent of the salary premium you'd get for a four-year degree. Similarly, the
premium for sophomore year is nowhere near 50 percent of the return on a bachelor's degree, and the premium for junior year is nowhere near 75 percent of that
return. Indeed, in the average study, senior year of college brings more than twice
the pay increase of freshman, sophomore, and junior years combined. Unless colleges delay job training until the very end, signaling is practically the only explanation. This in turn implies a mountain of wasted resources—time and money
that would be better spent preparing students for the jobs they're likely to do.

The conventional view—that education pays because students learn— 10
assumes that the typical student acquires, and retains, a lot of knowledge. She
doesn't. Teachers often lament summer learning loss: Students know less at
the end of summer than they did at the beginning. But summer learning loss
is only a special case of the problem of fade-out: Human beings have trouble retaining knowledge they rarely use. Of course, some college graduates use
what they've learned and thus hold on to it—engineers and other quantitative
types, for example, retain a lot of math. But when we measure what the average
college graduate recalls years later, the results are discouraging, to say the least.

In 2003, the United States Department of Education gave about 18,000 11
Americans the National Assessment of Adult Literacy. The ignorance it revealed
is mind-numbing. Fewer than a third of college graduates received a composite
score of "proficient"—and about a fifth were at the "basic" or "below basic" level.
You could blame the difficulty of the questions—until you read them. Plenty
of college graduates couldn't make sense of a table explaining how an employee's annual health-insurance costs varied with income and family size, or summarize the work-experience requirements in a job ad, or even use a newspaper
schedule to find when a television program ended. Tests of college graduates'
knowledge of history, civics, and science have had similarly dismal results.

Of course, college students aren't supposed to just download facts; they're 12
supposed to learn how to think in real life. How do they fare on this count?
The most focused study of education's effect on applied reasoning, conducted

by Harvard's David Perkins in the mid-1980s, assessed students' oral responses to questions designed to measure informal reasoning, such as "Would a proposed law in Massachusetts requiring a five-cent deposit on bottles and cans significantly reduce litter?" The benefit of college seemed to be zero: Fourth-year students did no better than first-year students.

Other evidence is equally discouraging. One researcher tested Arizona 13 State University students' ability to "apply statistical and methodological concepts to reasoning about everyday-life events." In the researcher's words:

> Of the several hundred students tested, many of whom had taken more than six years of laboratory science . . . and advanced mathematics through calculus, almost none demonstrated even a semblance of acceptable methodological reasoning.

Those who believe that college is about learning how to learn should 14 expect students who study science to absorb the scientific method, then habitually use it to analyze the world. This scarcely occurs.

College students do hone some kinds of reasoning that are specific to their 15 major. One ambitious study at the University of Michigan tested natural-science, humanities, and psychology and other social-science majors on verbal reasoning, statistical reasoning, and conditional reasoning during the first semester of their first year. When the same students were retested the second semester of their fourth year, each group had sharply improved in precisely one area. Psychology and other social-science majors had become much better at statistical reasoning. Natural-science and humanities majors had become much better at conditional reasoning—analyzing "if . . . then" and "if and only if" problems. In the remaining areas, however, gains after three and a half years of college were modest or nonexistent. The takeaway: Psychology students use statistics, so they improve in statistics; chemistry students rarely encounter statistics, so they don't improve in statistics. If all goes well, students learn what they study and practice.

Actually, that's optimistic. Educational psychologists have discovered that 16 much of our knowledge is "inert." Students who excel on exams frequently fail to apply their knowledge to the real world. Take physics. As the Harvard psychologist Howard Gardner writes,

> Students who receive honor grades in college-level physics courses are frequently unable to solve basic problems and questions encountered in a form slightly different from that on which they have been formally instructed and tested.

The same goes for students of biology, mathematics, statistics, and, I'm 17 embarrassed to say, economics. I try to teach my students to connect lectures to the real world and daily life. My exams are designed to measure comprehension, not memorization. Yet in a good class, four test-takers out of 40 demonstrate true economic understanding.

Economists educational bean counting can come off as annoyingly narrow. 18 Noneconomists—also known as normal human beings—lean holistic: We can't measure education's social benefits solely with test scores or salary premiums. Instead we must ask ourselves what kind of society we want to live in—an educated one or an ignorant one?

Normal human beings make a solid point: We can and should investigate 19 education's broad social implications. When humanists consider my calculations of education's returns, they assume I'm being a typical cynical economist, oblivious to the ideals so many educators hold dear. I am an economist and I am a cynic, but I'm not a typical cynical economist. I'm a cynical idealist. I embrace the ideal of transformative education. I believe wholeheartedly in the life of the mind. What I'm cynical about is people.

I'm cynical about students. The vast majority are philistines. I'm cyn- 20 ical about teachers. The vast majority are uninspiring. I'm cynical about "deciders"—the school officials who control what students study. The vast majority think they've done their job as long as students comply.

Those who search their memory will find noble exceptions to these sad 21 rules. I have known plenty of eager students and passionate educators, and a few wise deciders. Still, my 40 years in the education industry leave no doubt that they are hopelessly outnumbered. Meritorious education survives but does not thrive.

Indeed, today's college students are less willing than those of previous 22 generations to do the bare minimum of showing up for class and temporarily learning whatever's on the test. Fifty years ago, college was a full-time job. The typical student spent 40 hours a week in class or studying. Effort has since collapsed across the board. "Full time" college students now average 27 hours of academic work a week—including just 14 hours spent studying.

What are students doing with their extra free time? Having fun. As 23 Richard Arum and Josipa Roksa frostily remark in their 2011 book, *Academically Adrift,*

> If we presume that students are sleeping eight hours a night, which is a generous assumption given their tardiness and at times disheveled appearance in early morning classes, that leaves 85 hours a week for other activities.

Arum and Roksa cite a study finding that students at one typical college spent 24 13 hours a week studying, 12 hours "socializing with friends," 11 hours "using computers for fun," eight hours working for pay, six hours watching TV, six hours exercising, five hours on "hobbies," and three hours on "other forms of entertainment." Grade inflation completes the idyllic package by shielding students from negative feedback. The average GPA is now 3.2.

What does this mean for the individual student? Would I advise an aca- 25 demically well-prepared 18-year-old to skip college because she won't learn much of value? Absolutely not. Studying irrelevancies for the next four years will impress future employers and raise her income potential. If she tried to leap straight into her first white-collar job, insisting, "I have the right stuff to graduate, I just choose not to," employers wouldn't believe her. To unilaterally curtail your education is to relegate yourself to a lower-quality pool of workers. For the individual, college pays.

This does not mean, however, that higher education paves the way to 26 general prosperity or social justice. When we look at countries around the world, a year of education appears to raise an individual's income by 8 to 11 percent. By contrast, increasing education across a country's population by an average of one year per person raises the national income by only 1 to 3 percent. In other words, education enriches individuals much more than it enriches nations.

How is this possible? Credential inflation: As the average level of education 27 rises, you need more education to convince employers you're worthy of any specific job. One research team found that from the early 1970s through the mid-1990s, the average education level within 500 occupational categories rose by 1.2 years. But most of the jobs didn't change much over that span—there's no reason, except credential inflation, why people should have needed more education to do them in 1995 than in 1975. What's more, *all* American workers' education rose by 1.5 years in that same span—which is to say that a great majority of the extra education workers received was deployed not to get *better* jobs, but to get jobs that had recently been held by people with less education.

As credentials proliferate, so do failed efforts to acquire them. Students can 28 and do pay tuition, kill a year, and flunk their finals. Any respectable verdict on the value of education must account for these academic bankruptcies. Failure rates are high, particularly for students with low high school grades and test scores; all told, about 60 percent of full-time college students fail to finish in four years. Simply put, the push for broader college education has steered too many students who aren't cut out for academic success onto the college track.

The college-for-all mentality has fostered neglect of a realistic substitute: 29 vocational education. It takes many guises—classroom training, apprenticeships and other types of on-the-job training, and straight-up work experience—but they have much in common. All vocational education teaches specific job skills, and all vocational education revolves around learning by doing, not learning by listening. Research, though a bit sparse, suggests that vocational education raises pay, reduces unemployment, and increases the rate of high school completion.

> "Ignorance of the future is no reason to prepare students for occupations they almost surely won't have."

Defenders of traditional education often appeal to the obscurity of the 30 future. What's the point of prepping students for the economy of 2018, when they'll be employed in the economy of 2025 or 2050? But ignorance of the future is no reason to prepare students for occupations they almost surely won't have—and if we know anything about the future of work, we know that the demand for authors, historians, political scientists, physicists, and mathematicians will stay low. It's tempting to say that students on the college track can always turn to vocational education as a Plan B, but this ignores the disturbing possibility that after they crash, they'll be too embittered to go back and learn a trade. The vast American underclass shows that this disturbing possibility is already our reality.

Education is so integral to modern life that we take it for granted. Young 31 people have to leap through interminable academic hoops to secure their place in the adult world. My thesis, in a single sentence: Civilized societies revolve around education now, but there is a better—indeed, more civilized—way. If everyone had a college degree, the result would be not great jobs for all, but runaway credential inflation. Trying to spread success with education spreads education but not success.

⊙ AT ISSUE: SOURCES FOR STRUCTURING AN ARGUMENT

1. Why does Caplan begin his essay with a summary of his own educational and employment history? Is this introductory strategy an appeal to *logos*, *ethos*, or *pathos*? (See pages 19–21 for an explanation of these terms.)

2. Caplan identifies a number of shortcomings of today's college students—and of our higher education system in general. What problems does he identify? Where does he seem to place the blame for these problems? Does he offer solutions? If so, where?

3. Where does Caplan cite research studies? How does he use these studies to support his conclusions about the value of a college education?

4. Where does Caplan use personal experience as evidence in support of his points? Do you find this kind of evidence convincing here? Why or why not?

5. Do you think Caplan's use of the first-person pronoun *I* throughout strengthens or weakens his argument? Explain you conclusion.

6. In paragraph 7, Caplan says, "The labor market doesn't pay you for the useless subjects you master; it pays you for the preexisting traits you signal by mastering them." What does he mean? Do you think he is correct about the importance of what he calls "signaling" (para. 8)? Why or why not?

7. In paragraphs 4 and 10, Caplan summarizes arguments against his position. How does he refute these counterarguments? Does he include other arguments against his position? If so, where?

8. In paragraphs 23–24, Caplan says, "For the individual, college pays. This does not mean, however, that higher education paves the way to general prosperity or social justice." What point is he making here about the value of a college education?

9. What is "credential inflation" (29)? How is it related to what Caplan calls his "thesis, in a single sentence"? Do you think this "thesis" is actually the essay's main idea? Explain.

This economic letter was originally posted by the Federal Reserve Bank of San Francisco at www.frbsf.org, where it appeared on May 5, 2014.

IS IT STILL WORTH GOING TO COLLEGE?

MARY C. DALY AND LEILA BENGALI

Media accounts documenting the rising cost of a college education and rela- 1 tively bleak job prospects for new college graduates have raised questions about whether a four-year college degree is still the right path for the average American. In this *Economic Letter*, we examine whether going to college remains a worthwhile investment. Using U.S. survey data, we compare annual labor earnings of college graduates with those of individuals with only a high school diploma. The data show college graduates outearn their high school counterparts as much as in past decades. Comparing the earnings benefits of college with the costs of attending a four-year program, we find that college is still worth it. This means that, for the average student, tuition costs for the majority of college education opportunities in the United States can be recouped by age 40, after which college graduates continue to earn a return on their investment in the form of higher lifetime wages.

Earnings Outcomes by Educational Attainment

A common way to track the value of going to college is to estimate a col- 2 lege earnings premium, which is the amount college graduates earn relative to high school graduates. We measure earnings for each year as the annual labor income for the prior year, adjusted for inflation using the consumer price index (CPI-U), reported in 2011 dollars. The earnings premium refers to the difference between average annual labor income for high school and college graduates. We use data on household heads and partners from the Panel Study of Income Dynamics (PSID). The PSID is a longitudinal study that follows individuals living in the United States over a long time span. The survey began in 1968 and now has more than 40 years of data including educational attainment and labor market income. To focus on the value of a college degree relative to less education, we exclude people with more than a four-year degree.

Figure 1 shows the earnings premium relative to high school graduates 3 for individuals with a four-year college degree and for those with some college but no four-year degree. The payoff from a degree is apparent. Although the premium has fluctuated over time, at its lowest in 1980 it was about $15,750, meaning that individuals with a four-year college degree earned about 43 percent more on average than those with only a high school degree. In 2011, the latest data available in our sample, college graduates earned on average about $20,050 (61 percent) more per year than high school graduates. Over the entire sample period the college earnings premium has averaged about $20,300 (57 percent) per year. The premium is much smaller, although not zero, for workers with some college but no four-year degree.

Figure 1: Earnings Premium over High School Education

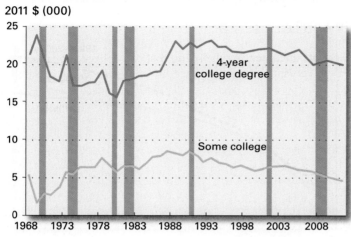

Data from: PSID and authors' calculations. Premium defined as difference in mean annual labor income. Blue bars denote National Bureau of Economic Research recession dates.

A potential shortcoming of the results in Figure 1 is that they combine the 4 earnings outcomes for all college graduates, regardless of when they earned a degree. This can be misleading if the value from a college education has varied across groups from different graduation decades, called "cohorts." To examine whether the college earnings premium has changed from one generation to the next, we take advantage of the fact that the PSID follows people over a long period of time, which allows us to track college graduation dates and subsequent earnings.

Using these data we compute the college earnings premium for three col- 5 lege graduate cohorts, namely those graduating in the 1950s–60s, the 1970s–80s, and the 1990s–2000s. The premium measures the difference between the average annual earnings of college graduates and high school graduates over their work lives. To account for the fact that high school graduates gain work experience during the four years they are not in college, we compare earnings of college graduates in each year since graduation to earnings of high school graduates in years since graduation plus four. We also adjust the estimates for any large annual fluctuations by using a three-year centered moving average, which plots a specific year as the average of earnings from that year, the year before, and the year after.

Figure 2 shows that the college earnings premium has risen consistently 6 across cohorts. Focusing on the most recent college graduates (1990s–2000s) there is little evidence that the value of a college degree has declined over time, and it has even risen somewhat for graduates five to ten years out of school.

Figure 2: College Earnings Premium by Graduation Decades

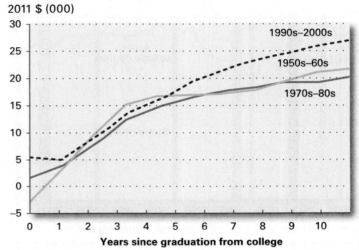

Data from: PSID and authors' calculations. Premium defined as difference in mean annual labor income of college graduates in each year since graduation and earnings of high school graduates in years since graduation plus four. Values are three-year centered moving averages of annual premiums.

The figure also shows that the gap in earnings between college and high 7 school graduates rises over the course of a worker's life. Comparing the earnings gap upon graduation with the earnings gap 10 years out of school illustrates this. For the 1990s–2000s cohort the initial gap was about $5,400, and in 10 years this gap had risen to about $26,800. Other analysis confirms that college graduates start with higher annual earnings, indicated by an initial earnings gap, and experience more rapid growth in earnings than members of their age cohort with only a high school degree. This evidence tells us that the value of a college education rises over a worker's life.

Of course, some of the variation in earnings between those with and 8 without a college degree could reflect other differences. Still, these simple estimates are consistent with a large and rigorous literature documenting the substantial premium earned by college graduates (Barrow and Rouse 2005, Card 2001, Goldin and Katz 2008, and Cunha, Karahan, and Soares 2011). The main message from these and similar calculations is that on average the value of college is high and not declining over time.

Finally, it is worth noting that the benefits of college over high school also 9 depend on employment, where college graduates also have an advantage. High school graduates consistently face unemployment rates about twice as high as those for college graduates, according to Bureau of Labor Statistics data. When the labor market takes a turn for the worse, as during recessions, workers with lower levels of education are especially hard-hit (Hoynes, Miller, and Schaller 2012). Thus, in good times and in bad, those with only a high school education face a lower probability of employment, on top of lower average earnings once employed.

The Cost of College

Although the value of college is apparent, deciding whether it is worthwhile means weighing the value against the costs of attending. Indeed, much of the debate about the value of college stems not from the lack of demonstrated benefit but from the overwhelming cost. A simple way to measure the costs against the benefits is to find the breakeven amount of annual tuition that would make the average student indifferent between going to college versus going directly to the workforce after high school.

> "Although the value of college is apparent, deciding whether it is worthwhile means weighing the value against the costs of attending." 10

To simplify the analysis, we assume that college lasts four years, students 11 enter college directly from high school, annual tuition is the same all four years, and attendees have no earnings while in school. To focus on more recent experiences yet still have enough data to measure earnings since graduation, we use the last two decades of graduates (1990s and 2000s) and again smooth our estimates by using three-year centered moving averages.

We calculate the cost of college as four years of tuition plus the earnings 12 missed from choosing not to enter the workforce. To estimate what students would have received had they worked, we use the average annual earnings of a high school graduate zero, one, two, and three years since graduation.

To determine the benefit of going to college, we use the difference 13 between the average annual earnings of a college graduate with zero, one, two, three, and so on, years of experience and the average annual earnings of a high school graduate with four, five, six, seven, and so on years of experience. Because the costs of college are paid today but the benefits accrue over many future years when a dollar earned will be worth less, we discount future earnings by 6.67 percent, which is the average rate on an AAA bond from 1990 to 2011.

With these pieces in place, we can calculate the breakeven amount of tui- 14 tion for the average college graduate for any number of years; allowing more time to regain the costs will increase our calculated tuition ceiling.

If we assume that accumulated earnings between college graduates 15 and nongraduates will equalize 20 years after graduating from high school (at age 38), the resulting estimate for breakeven annual tuition would be about $21,200. This amount may seem low compared to the astronomical costs for a year at some prestigious institutions; however, about 90 percent of students at public four-year colleges and about 20 percent of students at private nonprofit four-year colleges faced lower annual inflation-adjusted published tuition and fees in 2013–14 (College Board 2013). Although some colleges cost more, there is no definitive evidence that they produce far superior results for all students (Dale and Krueger 2011).

Table 1 shows more examples of maximum tuitions and the correspond- 16 ing percent of students who pay less for different combinations of breakeven years and discount rates. Note that the tuition estimates are those that make the costs and benefits of college equal. So, tuition amounts lower than our estimates make going to college strictly better in terms of earnings than not going to college.

Table 1: Maximum Tuitions by Breakeven Age and Discount Rates

	Breakeven age	
	33 (15 yrs after HS)	38 (20 yrs after HS)
Accumulated earnings with constant annual premium	$880,134	$830,816
Discount rate	Maximum tuition (% students paying less)	
5%	$14,385 (53–62%)	$29,111 (82–85%)
6.67%*	$9,869 (37–53%)	$21,217 (69–73%)
9%	$4,712 (0–6%)	$12,653 (53–62%)

*Average AAA bond rate 1990–2011 (rounded; Moody's).

Data from: PSID, College Board, and authors' calculations. Premia held constant 15 or 20 years after high school (HS) graduation. Percent range gives lower and upper bounds of the percent of full-time undergraduates at four-year institutions who faced lower annual inflation-adjusted published tuition and fees in 2013–14.

Although other individual factors might affect the net value of a col- 17 lege education, earning a degree clearly remains a good investment for most young people. Moreover, once that investment is paid off, the extra income from the college earnings premium continues as a net gain to workers with a college degree. If we conservatively assume that the annual premium stays around $28,650, which is the premium 20 years after high school gradua-tion for graduates in the 1990s–2000s, and accrues until the Social Security normal retirement age of 67, the college graduate would have made about

$830,800 more than the high school graduate. These extra earnings can be spent, saved, or reinvested to pay for the college tuition of the graduate's children.

Conclusion

Although there are stories of people who skipped college and achieved finan- 18 cial success, for most Americans the path to higher future earnings involves a four-year college degree. We show that the value of a college degree remains high, and the average college graduate can recover the costs of attending in less than 20 years. Once the investment is paid for, it continues to pay dividends through the rest of the worker's life, leaving college graduates with substantially higher lifetime earnings than their peers with a high school degree. These findings suggest that redoubling the efforts to make college more accessible would be time and money well spent.

References

Barrow, L., and Rouse, C. E. (2005). "Does college still pay?" *The Economist's Voice* 2(4), pp. 1–8.

Card, D. (2001). "Estimating the return to schooling: progress on some persistent econometric problems." *Econometrica* 69(5), pp. 1127–1160.

College Board. (2013). "Trends in College Pricing 2013."

Cunha, F., Karahan, F., and Soares, I. (2011). "Returns to Skills and the College Premium." *Journal of Money, Credit, and Banking* 43(5), pp. 39–86.

Dale, S., and Krueger, A. (2011). "Estimating the Return to College Selectivity over the Career Using Administrative Earnings Data." *NBER Working Paper* 17159.

Goldin, C., and Katz, L. (2008). *The Race between Education and Technology.* Cambridge and London: The Belknap Press of Harvard University Press.

Hoynes, H., Miller, D., and Schaller, J. (2012). "Who Suffers during Recessions?" *Journal of Economic Perspectives* 26(3), pp. 27–48.

⊘ AT ISSUE: SOURCES FOR STRUCTURING AN ARGUMENT

1. Why does the title of this essay include the word *still*? What does *still* imply in this context?

2. This essay is an "economic letter" from the Federal Reserve Bank of San Francisco, and its language is more technical, and more math- and business-oriented, than that of the other readings in this chapter. In addition, this reading selection *looks* somewhat different from the others. What specific format features set this reading apart from others in the chapter?

3. What kind of supporting evidence do the writers use? Do you think they should have included any other kinds of support—for example, expert opinion? Why or why not?

4. In paragraph 10, the writers make a distinction between the "value of college" and the question of whether a college education is "worthwhile." Explain the distinction they make here.

5. For the most part, this report appeals to *logos* by presenting factual information. Does it also include appeals to *pathos* or *ethos*? If so, where? If not, should it have included these appeals? (See pp. 14–21 for an explanation of these terms.)

TEMPLATE FOR STRUCTURING AN ARGUMENT

Write a one-paragraph argument in which you take a position on the topic of whether a college education is a good investment. Follow the template below, filling in the lines to create your argument.

> Whether or not a college education is worth the money is a controversial topic. Some people believe that _____
>
> _____
>
> _____. Others challenge this position, claiming that
>
> _____.
>
> However, _____. Although both
>
> sides of this issue have merit, it seems clear that a college education [is/is not] a worthwhile investment
>
> because _____
>
> _____.

⊙ EXERCISE 1.2 USING INTERVIEW NOTES

Interview two classmates on the topic of whether a college education is a worthwhile investment. Revise the one-paragraph argument that you drafted above so that it includes your classmates' views on the issue.

⊙ EXERCISE 1.3 WRITING AN ESSAY

Write an essay on the topic "Is a College Education Worth the Money?" Cite one or two of the readings on pages 33–48, and be sure to document your sources and to include a works-cited page. (See Chapter 10 for information on documenting sources.)

⊙ EXERCISE 1.4 REVISING YOUR ESSAY

Review the four-point checklist on page 27, and apply each question to your essay. Does your essay include all four elements of an argumentative essay? Add any missing elements. Then, label your essay's thesis statement, evidence, refutation of opposing arguments, and concluding statement.

⊙ EXERCISE 1.5 WRITING A RESPONSE

The following blog post promotes the University of the People, an accredited online university. To whom does this post seem to be addressed? Do you find it convincing? Does it include all four elements of an effective argument? Incorporating what you have learned about the structure and content of an effective argument, write a one-paragraph response to the blog post.

This essay appeared on Businessweek.com in March 2011.

DOES COLLEGE STILL MATTER IN 2018?

AYELET W., UNIVERSITY OF THE PEOPLE

The world seems to be changing faster than ever, doesn't it?   1

So understandably, people everywhere are questioning whether the edu- 2
cational trajectories of our parents' generation are still relevant for today's
fast-moving job market and global society.

We like this type of debate and encourage you to ask questions instead of 3
taking things for granted, so we thought we'd walk our talk and break down
one of the biggest questions facing today's young adults: Does college still matter in 2018?

1) The Financial Investment

College can be expensive. In some cases, crazy expensive. In 2016, Business 4
Insider reported that the University of Cambridge is developing a PhD business program, that's set to cost $332,000.

Yes, that's a PhD program, but bachelor's degrees aren't cheap either. Busi- 5
ness Insider reported that the bachelor's degree of music at Bard College might
be one of the most expensive BAs around, costing $253,520.

If these were the only options, college might be out of reach for many stu- 6
dents, but with degrees available in other top quality universities for as little as
$4,060 for the entire degree, it's something that can be in reach for all. Still, the
question remains—does it still matter in 2018?

2) Finding a Job and Remaining Employed

Let's face it, a college degree holds a higher prestige than a high school diploma, 7
and many people seem to appreciate those who've made the effort and graduated.

According to a 2016 study by Georgetown University, the majority of 8
the jobs still go to bachelor's degree graduates. Reporting on the study, CNN
Money noted that "of the 11.6 million jobs created after the Great Recession,
8.4 million went to those with at least a bachelor's degree." This is a substantial difference in proportional terms: Only 36 percent of Americans earned a
bachelor's degree or higher, compared to 30 percent of Americans holding an
associate degree and 34 percent holding a high school diploma or less.

If you still have doubts on whether a college degree is worth the invest- 9
ment, check out this 2016 report from the United States Bureau of Labor
Statistics about 2015's employment rates by educational attainment:

While the median unemployment rate in the country was 4.3 percent of 10
the population, those with a bachelor's degree were only 2.8 percent of the
unemployed population, and those with only a high school diploma were 5.4
percent of the unemployed population.

In other words, those who graduated from high school but did not go on 11
to college were twice as likely to become unemployed than those with a college
degree.

And according to Forbes, the demands for higher education is steadily 12
increasing in the job market.

"86 percent of companies planned to hire recent MBA graduates in 2017 13
compared with 79 percent in 2016, according to the GMAC report . . . 41 percent
of employers are now hiring college grads for jobs that high school grads formerly held. . . . Companies are increasingly hiring candidates with master's
degrees for jobs that previously required bachelor's degrees," reported Forbes.

3) Meeting People & Networking

Today's fellow students will become tomorrow's colleagues, so making friends 14
in college is an easy way to build your professional network early on. You'll
also be able to connect with professors, who might then be able to connect you
with their connections in the industry, which could make it easier to find a
great first professional job.

4) Developing Skills You Can Use in the Workplace

One of the main arguments of those who are not in favor of going to college is 15
that it doesn't train you to work in the "real world," but according to Entrepreneur, "academic assignments develop skills that are in high demand among top
employers," including general communication skills, writing skills, research
skills, and collaboration skills.

In the 2016 University of the People Students Satisfaction Survey, many of 16
our students shared that they already use the knowledge and skills they gained
in courses in their workplaces.

5) Starting Your Own Business

To be honest, there's more information
online now than ever before, not to mention a wealth of books on practically every
topic. If you're the kind of person who can
study for years on end without any exter-
nal motivation—then you can become an
entrepreneur with no extra costs.

> "These success stories 17
> happen to the minority
> of the population—and
> often seem a lot easier
> said than done."

However, this is more relevant if you're looking to start your own business 18
rather than getting a traditional job. We've all heard about successful entrepreneurs who never graduated from college—and about teenagers who built
successful businesses on YouTube or Instagram from their childhood bedroom
before they even graduated from high school.

But keep in mind that these success stories happen to the minority of the 19
population—and often seem a lot easier said than done.

Not to mention that according to Forbes, if you want to start your own busi- 20
ness, you need more than a first degree to become a successful entrepreneur—
which is why it might be beneficial to get a masters, too. "Graduate schools

actually have a rich tradition of entrepreneurship instruction. Indeed, MBAs have launched nearly a quarter of 'unicorn' startups, defined as those worth $1 billion or more," Forbes reported.

6) Your Potential Salary

If you look at the United States Bureau of Labor Statistics report we men- 21 tioned in the latter, you'll see that a degree significantly impacts your financial prosperity.

The median weekly salary in the general U.S. population is $860. How- 22 ever, those who hold a bachelor's degree can earn up to $1,137 and those with only a high school degree earn a smaller income at $678.

That's $54,576 a year if you have a bachelor's degree, versus $32,544 if you 23 only have a high school diploma.

7) The Return on Your Financial (and Time) Investment When You Get a University Degree

Once you graduate, and assuming you work in the U.S., you're expected to 24 earn $54,576 a year, versus $32,544 if you only have a high school diploma. That's $22,032 more a year, or $110,160 more in the next 5 years, and that's not counting promotions and salary increases, which will be more easily accessible as a university graduate.

As a side note, if you attend an online affordable university, like UoPeople, 25 you can choose your own class hours and study at your own pace, which makes it easier to combine a full-time job and earn more than the average student. Alternatively, because the cost of the degree is so low, you might be able to live off a part-time job and live a more balanced life than the average college student.

⊖ EXERCISE 1.6 CONSIDERING VISUAL ARGUMENTS

Study the image that opens this chapter. What argument about the value of a college education could it support? Could the image itself be considered an argument? Explain your conclusion.

Reading and Responding to Arguments

2

Thinking and Reading Critically

Does Recycling Really Accomplish Anything?

Recycling is woven into our lives; at home, in school, in public spaces, we're used to seeing those separate bins for waste disposal. Given that Americans produce about 254 million tons of trash each year, many probably take the advantages of this practice as a given. The United States now has a recycling rate of about 34 percent, which reduces both the garbage in overflowing landfills and the amount of carbon dioxide released into the atmosphere. There are less obvious benefits, too. In addition to helping the environment, recycling helps create jobs, even as it lowers the amount of energy required to create new products.

But what about the downsides? Critics point out that it is costly, as recycling programs are often prohibitively expensive for small, local communities. Moreover, recycling may be giving us a false sense of "sustainability." In fact, the process still uses a lot of energy, and its overall benefits to the environment are limited because many large industries still do not recycle. In addition, recycling some waste products (such as electronics) is inefficient or even dangerous, and some products made of recycled materials are low quality.

In this chapter and in the chapter that follows, you will be asked to read essays and study images that shed light on the advantages and limitations of recycling. In the process, you will learn critical-thinking and active reading strategies that will help you learn to examine and interpret texts and images.

Now that you understand the structure of an argumentative essay, you can turn your attention to reading arguments more closely. The arguments you encounter may be the subject of class discussion, or they may be source material for the essays you write. In any case, you will need to know how to get the most out of reading them.

Thinking Critically

When you **think critically**, you do not simply accept ideas at face value. Instead, you question the ideas you come across, analyzing them in order to understand them better. You also challenge their underlying assumptions and form your own judgments about them. Throughout this book, discussions and readings encourage you to think critically. The box below shows you where in this text to find material that will help you develop your critical-thinking skills.

USING CRITICAL-THINKING SKILLS

Reading (see Chapter 2): When you read a text, you use critical-thinking skills to help you understand what the text says and what it suggests. You ask questions and look for answers, challenging the ideas you read and probing for information. *Previewing*, *highlighting*, and *annotating* are active reading strategies that require you to use critical-thinking skills.

Analyzing Visual Texts (see Chapter 3): When you examine an image, you use critical-thinking skills to help you understand what you are seeing, using previewing, highlighting, and annotating to help you analyze the image and interpret its persuasive message.

Writing a Rhetorical Analysis (see Chapter 4): When you write a rhetorical analysis, you use critical-thinking skills to analyze the individual elements of a text and to help you understand how the writer uses various appeals and rhetorical strategies to influence readers. Critical-thinking skills can also help you to understand the argument's context. Finally, you use critical-thinking skills to evaluate the overall effectiveness of the argument.

Analyzing an Argument's Logic (see Chapter 5): When you analyze an argument's logic, you use critical-thinking skills to help you understand the relationships among ideas and the form the argument takes as well as to determine whether its conclusions are both valid and true. You also use critical-thinking skills to identify any **logical fallacies** that may undermine the argument.

Writing an Essay (see Chapter 7): When you plan an essay, you use critical-thinking skills to probe a topic, to consider what you already know and what you need to find out, to identify your essay's main idea, and to decide how to support it—that is, which ideas to include and how to arrange them. As you draft and revise, you use critical-thinking skills to evaluate your supporting evidence, to make sure your arguments are reasonable and fair, and to decide whether ideas are arranged effectively within paragraphs and in the essay as a whole. *Freewriting, brainstorming, clustering,* and *outlining* are activities that require you to use critical-thinking skills.

Refuting Opposing Arguments (see Chapter 7): When you refute opposing arguments, you use critical-thinking skills to identify and evaluate arguments against your position—and to challenge or possibly argue against them.

Evaluating Sources (see Chapter 8): When you evaluate sources, you use critical-thinking skills to assess your sources in terms of their *accuracy, credibility, objectivity,* and *comprehensiveness* and to determine whether a source is trustworthy and appropriate for your purpose and audience.

Summarizing (see Chapter 9): When you summarize a passage, you use critical-thinking skills to identify the writer's main idea.

Paraphrasing (see Chapter 9): When you paraphrase a passage, you use critical-thinking skills to identify the writer's main idea, the most important supporting details and examples, and the ways in which key ideas are related.

Synthesizing (see Chapter 9): When you synthesize material, you use critical-thinking skills to analyze sources and integrate them with your own ideas.

Reading Critically

When you read an argument, you should approach it with a critical eye. Contrary to what you may think, **reading critically** does not mean arguing with every idea you encounter. What it does mean is commenting on, questioning, and evaluating these ideas.

As a critical reader, you do not simply accept that what you are reading is true. Instead, you assess the accuracy of the facts in your sources, and you consider whether opinions are convincingly supported by evidence. You try to judge the appropriateness and reliability of a writer's sources, and you evaluate the scope and depth of the evidence and the relevance of that evidence to the topic. You also consider opposing arguments carefully, weighing them against the arguments developed in your sources. Finally, you watch out for possible **bias** in your sources—and you work hard to keep your own biases in check.

GUIDELINES FOR READING CRITICALLY

As a critical reader, you need to read carefully, keeping the following guidelines in mind:

- Assess the accuracy of a source's information, as well as the authors and publishers of the source itself.
- Be sure opinions are supported convincingly.
- Evaluate the supporting evidence.
- Consider opposing arguments.
- Be on the lookout for bias—in your sources and in yourself.

Becoming an Active Reader

Reading critically means being an active rather than a passive reader. Being an **active reader** means participating in the reading process by taking the time to preview a source and then to read it carefully, highlighting and annotating it. This process will prepare you to discuss the source with others and to respond in writing to what you have read.

Previewing

When you approach an argument for the first time, you **preview** it, skimming the text to help you form a general impression of the writer's position on the issue, the argument's key supporting points, and the context for the writer's remarks.

Begin by looking at the title, the first paragraph (which often contains a thesis statement or overview), and the last paragraph (which often includes a concluding statement or a summary of the writer's key points). Also look at the topic sentences of the essay's body paragraphs. In addition, note any headings, words set in boldface or italic type, and bulleted or numbered lists that appear in the body of the argument. If the argument includes visuals—charts, tables, graphs, photos, and so on—look at them as well. Finally, if an argument includes a headnote or background on the author or on the text, be sure to skim this material. It can help you to understand the context in which the author is writing.

When you have finished previewing the argument, you should have a good general sense of what the writer wants to communicate.

Close Reading

When you finish previewing the argument, you are ready to read through it more carefully. As you read, look for words and phrases that help to shape the structure of the argument and signal the arrangement of the writer's ideas. These words and phrases will help you to understand the flow of ideas as well as the content and emphasis of the argument.

COMPREHENSION CLUES

- Repeated words and phrases

- Phrases that signal emphasis (the *primary* reason, the *most important problem*)

- Words and phrases that signal addition (*also, in addition, furthermore*)

- Words and phrases that signal time sequence (*first, after that, next, then, finally*)

- Words and phrases that identify causes and effects (*because, as a result, for this reason*)

- Words and phrases that introduce examples (*for example, for instance*)

- Words and phrases that signal comparison (*likewise, similarly, in the same way*)

- Words and phrases that signal contrast (*although, in contrast, on the other hand*)

- Words and phrases that signal contradiction (*however, on the contrary*)

- Words and phrases that signal a move from general to specific (*in fact, specifically, in other words*)

- Words and phrases that introduce summaries or conclusions (*all things considered, to sum up, in conclusion*)

⊘ EXERCISE 2.1 PREVIEWING AN ESSAY

"The Reign of Recycling" is a *New York Times* opinion essay by John Tierney. In this essay, which begins on the following page, Tierney argues that although recycling remains popular, it may actually not be worth the time and trouble it requires.

In preparation for class discussion and other activities that will be assigned later in this chapter, preview the essay. Then, read it carefully, and answer the questions that follow it.

This article appeared in the *New York Times* on October 3, 2015.

THE REIGN OF RECYCLING

JOHN TIERNEY

If you live in the United States, you probably do some form of recycling. It's 1 likely that you separate paper from plastic and glass and metal. You rinse the bottles and cans, and you might put food scraps in a container destined for a composting facility. As you sort everything into the right bins, you probably assume that recycling is helping your community and protecting the environment. But is it? Are you in fact wasting your time?

In 1996, I wrote a long article for the *New York Times Magazine* argu- 2 ing that the recycling process as we carried it out was wasteful. I presented plenty of evidence that recycling was costly and ineffectual, but its defenders said that it was unfair to rush to judgment. Noting that the modern recycling movement had really just begun just a few years earlier, they predicted it would flourish as the industry matured and the public learned how to recycle properly.

So, what's happened since then? While it's true that the recycling message 3 has reached more people than ever, when it comes to the bottom line, both economically and environmentally, not much has changed at all.

Despite decades of exhortations and mandates, it's still typically more 4 expensive for municipalities to recycle household waste than to send it to a landfill. Prices for recyclable materials have plummeted because of lower oil prices and reduced demand for them overseas. The slump has forced some recycling companies to shut plants and cancel plans for new technologies. The mood is so gloomy that one industry veteran tried to cheer up her colleagues this summer with an article in a trade journal titled, "Recycling Is Not Dead!"

While politicians set higher and higher goals, the national rate of recy- 5 cling has stagnated in recent years. Yes, it's popular in affluent neighborhoods like Park Slope in Brooklyn and in cities like San Francisco, but residents of the Bronx and Houston don't have the same fervor for sorting garbage in their spare time.

The future for recycling looks even worse. As cities move beyond recycling 6 paper and metals, and into glass, food scraps, and assorted plastics, the costs rise sharply while the environmental benefits decline and sometimes vanish. "If you believe recycling is good for the planet and that we need to do more of it, then there's a crisis to confront," says David P. Steiner, the chief executive officer of Waste Management, the largest recycler of household trash in the

United States. "Trying to turn garbage into gold costs a lot more than expected. We need to ask ourselves: What is the goal here?"

Recycling has been relentlessly promoted as a goal in and of itself: an 7 unalloyed public good and private virtue that is indoctrinated in students from kindergarten through college. As a result, otherwise well-informed and educated people have no idea of the relative costs and benefits.

They probably don't know, for instance, that to reduce carbon emissions, 8 you'll accomplish a lot more by sorting paper and aluminum cans than by worrying about yogurt containers and half-eaten slices of pizza. Most people also assume that recycling plastic bottles must be doing lots for the planet. They've been encouraged by the Environmental Protection Agency, which assures the public that recycling plastic results in less carbon being released into the atmosphere.

But how much difference does it make? Here's some perspective: To offset 9 the greenhouse impact of one passenger's round-trip flight between New York and London, you'd have to recycle roughly 40,000 plastic bottles, assuming you fly coach. If you sit in business- or first-class, where each passenger takes up more space, it could be more like 100,000.

Even those statistics might be misleading. New York and other cities 10 instruct people to rinse the bottles before putting them in the recycling bin, but the E.P.A.'s life-cycle calculation doesn't take that water into account. That single omission can make a big difference, according to Chris Goodall, the author of "How to Live a Low-Carbon Life." Mr. Goodall calculates that if you wash plastic in water that was heated by coal-derived, electricity, then the net effect of your recycling could be *more* carbon in the atmosphere.

To many public officials, recycling is a question of morality, not cost- 11 benefit analysis. Mayor Bill de Blasio of New York declared that by 2030 the city would no longer send any garbage to landfills. "This is the way of the future if we're going to save our earth," he explained, while announcing that New York would join San Francisco, Seattle, and other cities in moving toward a "zero waste" policy, which would require an unprecedented level of recycling.

The national rate of recycling rose during the 1990s to 25 percent, meeting 12 the goal set by an E.P.A. official, J. Winston Porter. He advised state officials that no more than about 35 percent of the nation's trash was worth recycling, but some ignored him and set goals of 50 percent and higher. Most of those goals were never met and the national rate has been stuck around 34 percent in recent years.

"It makes sense to recycle commercial cardboard and some paper, as 13 well as selected metals and plastics," he says, "But other materials rarely make sense, including food, waste and other compostables. The zero-waste goal makes no sense at all—it's very expensive with almost no real environmental benefit."

One of the original goals of the recycling movement was to avert a sup- 14 posed crisis because there was no room left in the nation's landfills. But that media-inspired fear was never realistic in a country with so much open space. In reporting the 1996 article I found that all the trash generated by Americans for the next 1,000 years would fit on one-tenth of 1 percent of the land available for grazing. And that tiny amount of land wouldn't be lost forever, because landfills are typically covered with grass and converted to parkland, like the Freshkills Park being created on Staten Island. The United States Open tennis tournament is played on the site of an old landfill—and one that never had the linings and other environmental safeguards required today.

Though most cities shun landfills, they have been welcomed in rural com- 15 munities that reap large economic benefits (and have plenty of greenery to buffer residents from the sights and smells). Consequently, the great landfill shortage has not arrived, and neither have the shortages of raw materials that were supposed to make recycling profitable.

With the economic rationale gone, advocates for recycling have switched 16 to environmental arguments. Researchers have calculated that there are indeed such benefits to recycling, but not in the way that many people imagine.

Most of these benefits do not come from reducing the need for landfills 17 and incinerators. A modern well-lined landfill in a rural area can have relatively little environmental impact. Decomposing garbage releases methane, a potent greenhouse gas, but landfill operators have started capturing it and using it to generate electricity. Modern incinerators, while politically unpopular in the United States, release so few pollutants that they've been widely accepted in the eco-conscious countries of Northern Europe and Japan for generating clean energy.

Moreover, recycling operations have their own environmental costs, like 18 extra trucks on the road and pollution from recycling operations. Composting facilities around the country have inspired complaints about nauseating odors, swarming rats, and defecating seagulls. After New York City started sending food waste to be composted in Delaware, the unhappy neighbors of the composting plant successfully campaigned to shut it down last year.

The environmental benefits of recycling come chiefly from reducing the 19 need to manufacture new products—less mining, drilling, and logging. But that's not so appealing to the workers in those industries and to the communities that have accepted the environmental trade-offs that come with those jobs.

Nearly everyone, though, approves of one potential benefit of recycling: 20 reduced emissions of greenhouse gases. Its advocates often cite an estimate by the E.P.A. that recycling municipal solid waste in the United States saves the equivalent of 186 million metric tons of carbon dioxide, comparable to removing the emissions of 39 million cars.

According to the E.P.A.'s estimates, virtually all the greenhouse benefits— 21 more than 90 percent—come from just a few materials: paper, cardboard, and metals like the aluminum in soda cans. That's because recycling one ton of metal or paper saves about three tons of carbon dioxide, a much bigger payoff than the other materials analyzed by the E.P.A. Recycling one ton of plastic saves only slightly more than one ton of carbon dioxide. A ton of food saves a little less than a ton. For glass, you have to recycle three tons in order to get about one ton of greenhouse benefits. Worst of all is yard waste: it takes 20 tons of it to save a single ton of carbon dioxide.

Once you exclude paper products and metals, the total annual savings in 22 the United States from recycling everything else in municipal trash—plastics, glass, food, yard trimmings, textiles, rubber, leather—is only two-tenths of 1 percent of America's carbon footprint.

As a business, recycling is on the wrong side of two long-term global economic trends. For centuries, the real cost of labor has been increasing while the real cost of raw materials has been declining. That's why we can afford to buy so much more stuff than our ancestors could. As a labor-intensive activity, recycling is an increasingly expensive way to produce materials that are less and less valuable.

> "As a business, recycling is on the wrong side of two long-term global economic trends." 23

Recyclers have tried to improve the economics by automating the sorting 24 process, but they've been frustrated by politicians eager to increase recycling rates by adding new materials of little value. The more types of trash that are recycled, the more difficult it becomes to sort the valuable from the worthless.

In New York City, the net cost of recycling a ton of trash is now $300 more 25 than it would cost to bury the trash instead. That adds up to millions of extra dollars per year—about half the budget of the parks department—that New Yorkers are spending for the privilege of recycling. That money could buy far more valuable benefits, including more significant reductions in greenhouse emissions.

So what is a socially conscious, sensible person to do? 26

It would be much simpler and more effective to impose the equivalent of 27 a carbon tax on garbage, as Thomas C. Kinnaman has proposed after conducting what is probably the most thorough comparison of the social costs of recycling, landfilling and incineration. Dr. Kinnaman, an economist at Bucknell University, considered everything from environmental damage to the pleasure that some people take in recycling (the "warm glow" that makes them willing to pay extra to do it).

He concludes that the social good would be optimized by subsidizing the 28 recycling of some metals, and by imposing a $15 tax on each ton of trash that goes to the landfill. That tax would offset the environmental costs, chiefly the greenhouse impact, and allow each municipality to make a guilt-free choice based on local economics and its citizens' wishes. The result, Dr. Kinnaman predicts, would be a lot less recycling than there is today.

Then why do so many public officials keep vowing to do more of it? 29 Special-interest politics is one reason—pressure from green groups—but it's also because recycling intuitively appeals to many voters: It makes people feel virtuous, especially affluent people who feel guilty about their enormous environmental footprint. It is less an ethical activity than a religious ritual, like the ones performed by Catholics to obtain indulgences for their sins.

Religious rituals don't need any practical justification for the believers 30 who perform them voluntarily. But many recyclers want more than just the freedom to practice their religion. They want to make these rituals manda-tory for everyone else, too, with stiff fines for sinners who don't sort properly. Seattle has become so aggressive that the city is being sued by residents who maintain that the inspectors rooting through their trash are violating their constitutional right to privacy.

It would take legions of garbage police to enforce a zero-waste society, but 31 true believers insist that's the future. When Mayor de Blasio promised to elim-inate garbage in New York, he said it was "ludicrous" and "outdated" to keep sending garbage to landfills. Recycling, he declared, was the only way for New York to become "a truly sustainable city."

But cities have been burying garbage for thousands of years, and it's still the 32 easiest and cheapest solution for trash. The recycling movement is floundering, and its survival depends on continual subsidies, sermons and policing. How can you build a sustainable city with a strategy that can't even sustain itself?

Identifying the Elements of Argument

1. What is Tierney's thesis? Restate it in your own words.

2. What evidence does Tierney present to support his thesis?

3. What arguments against his position does Tierney identify? How does he refute them?

4. Paraphrase Tierney's concluding statement.

Highlighting

After you read an argument, the next step is to read through it again, this time highlighting as you read. When you **highlight**, you use underlining and symbols to identify the essay's most important points. (Note that the word *highlighting* does not necessarily refer to the underlining done with a yellow highlighter pen.) This active reading strategy will help you to understand the writer's ideas and to see connections among those ideas when you reread.

How do you know what to highlight? As a general rule, you look for the same signals that you looked for when you read the argument the first time—for example, the essay's thesis and topic sentences and the words and phrases that identify the writer's intent and emphasis. This time, how-ever, you physically mark these elements and use various symbols to indi-cate your reactions to them.

SUGGESTIONS FOR HIGHLIGHTING

- Underline key ideas—for example, ideas stated in topic sentences.

- Box or circle words or phrases you want to remember.

- Place a check mark or a star next to an important idea.

- Place a double check mark or double star next to an especially significant idea.

- Draw lines or arrows to connect related ideas.

- Insert a question mark near an unfamiliar reference or a word you need to look up.

- Number the writer's key supporting points or examples.

Here is how a student, Neena Thomason, highlighted the *Los Angeles Times* editorial "It's Time to Phase Out All Single-Use Plastic," which appears below. Thomason was preparing to write an essay about the advantages and disadvantages of recycling. She began her highlighting by underlining and starring the thesis statement (para. 4). After boxing the distinctive phrase "unholy tonnage" in the editorial's first line, she went on to underline key pieces of information, starring and placing check marks beside the points she considered the most important. She also circled a word ("pernicious," 4) and a term ("zero sum game," 9) with which she was unfamiliar and added question marks to remind her to look them up. Finally, she underlined and starred the editorial's strong concluding statement.

This essay first appeared in the *Los Angeles Times* on February 20, 2018.

IT'S TIME TO PHASE OUT SINGLE-USE PLASTIC

Faced with an unholy tonnage of chip bags, soda bottles, takeout containers, 1 and other disposable plastic items flowing into our landfills and our waters, winding up in wildlife, drinking water, and food, policymakers in California have tried reining in plastic waste bit by bit. For example, more than 100 cities have adopted restrictions on polystyrene takeout containers, and the state has banned single-use plastic grocery bags.

Considering the magnitude of the problem, however, this item-by-item, 2 ✓ city-by-city approach isn't going to cut it.

The state and local rules certainly have raised public awareness about the 3 problem. Denying free plastic bags at checkout or providing plastic straws only on request sends consumers an important message that there's a bigger cost to these everyday items than they may have considered. But the actual flow of trash has been disrupted only modestly.

✓ It's going to take more than a smattering of bans on single items to cure 4 society of its disposable-plastic habit. The sheer volume of plastic trash now littering Earth has become impossible to ignore. It's time for environmentalists, policymaker, and elected officials to start planning a broader response: ✳ phasing out *all* single-use plastic, not just the most pernicious.?

That's right, all of it. If that sounds like a pipe dream, consider what's happen- 5 ing across the pond. Last month, British Prime Minister Theresa May outlined a plan to eliminate plastic waste by 2042. Queen Elizabeth II kicked it off this month by banning plastic straws and bottles from royal estates, and the Church of England supported a nascent social media campaign, #plasticlesslent, to encourage its flock to give up plastic for Lent this year. Simultaneously, the European Union announced its own plan to significantly reduce plastic waste, including adopting a possible plastic tax, in a direct response to the news that China, the largest importer of plastic recyclable material, was no longer accepting "foreign garbage."

We don't expect President Trump or Congress to follow suit, even though 6 it's impossible to pretend that the trash filling up in the ocean is naturally ✓ occurring. That leaves it to states like California to step in.

One strategy is for lawmakers to adopt a reduction goal, as they did for 7 greenhouse-gas emissions and energy derived from fossil fuels, and then to adopt specific programs to meet that goal. It's a simple but effective approach to tackling such a formidable environmental threat. Also, it puts makers of disposable plastic on notice, so they can't complain they didn't have time to adapt or move into other, less harmful product lines.

But even forewarned, the plastic industry isn't likely to take an assault on 8 its bottom line well. Plastic makers spent millions of dollars trying to stop the state from banning single-use plastic bags. Imagine what they might unleash if all their disposable plastic products were threatened. As part of that, they will no doubt argue, as they did in the plastic bag fight, that the efforts to clean up plastic waste would mean lost jobs. 2

But it's not a zero-sum game. Cutting, jobs on a disposable plastic prod- 9 uct line doesn't automatically translate into fewer people employed. If the door ✓ closes on polystyrene takeout containers, for example, it will open for cardboard and other biodegradable alternatives.

No one expects consumers to give up convenience completely. In fact, the 10 market for bio-plastic alternatives, which are made from cornstarch and other biodegradable sources, is already growing thanks to public awareness and the sporadic efforts to curb plastic waste.

✓ Opponents will insist that the answer is just to encourage more recy- 11 cling. Not only is recycling not the answer (see China's diminished appetite for imported plastic trash), it has only enabled our addiction to convenient, disposable plastic packaging to deepen for some 60 years.

Yes, it's scary to think about a world where one has to carry around a reus- 12
able bag or worry about a paper drinking straw falling apart mid. . . . Oh, wait.
No, it's not. <u>Knowing that every piece of plastic manufactured on Earth is still
with us and that if we don't cut back now, there will eventually be more plastic
than fish in the ocean—that's the truly frightening thought.</u>

⊙ EXERCISE 2.2 EVALUATING A STUDENT'S HIGHLIGHTING

Look carefully at Neena Thomason's highlighting of the *Los Angeles Times*
editorial on pages 71–73. How would your own highlighting of this editorial be similar to or different from hers?

⊙ EXERCISE 2.3 HIGHLIGHTING AN ESSAY

Reread "The Reign of Recycling" (pp. 66–70). As you read, highlight the
essay by underlining and starring important points, boxing or circling key
words, writing question marks beside references that need further explanation, and drawing lines and arrows to connect related ideas.

Annotating

As you highlight, you should also annotate what you are reading. **Annotating** means making notes—of your questions, reactions, and ideas for discussion or writing—in the margins or between the lines. Keeping this kind
of informal record of ideas as they occur to you will prepare you for class
discussion and provide a useful source of material when you write.

As you read an argument and think critically about what you are reading, you can use the questions in the following checklist to help you make
useful annotations.

CHECKLIST

Questions for Annotating

- ☐ What issue is the writer focusing on?
- ☐ Does the writer take a clear stand on this issue?
- ☐ What is the writer's thesis?
- ☐ What is the writer's purpose (his or her reason for writing)?
- ☐ What kind of audience is the writer addressing?
- ☐ Does the argument appear in a popular periodical or in a scholarly journal?
- ☐ Does the writer seem to assume readers will agree with the essay's position?

- ☐ What evidence does the writer use to support the essay's thesis? Does the writer include enough evidence?
- ☐ Does the writer consider (and refute) opposing arguments?
- ☐ Do you understand the writer's vocabulary?
- ☐ Do you understand the writer's references?
- ☐ Do you agree with the points the writer makes?
- ☐ Do the views the writer expresses agree or disagree with the views presented in other essays you have read?

⬇ The following pages, which reproduce Neena Thomason's highlighting of the *Los Angeles Times* editorial on pages 71–73, also include her marginal annotations. In these annotations, Thomason put the editorial's thesis and some of its key points into her own words and recorded questions that she thought she might explore further. She also added definitions of the two items she questioned when she highlighted. Finally, she identified two arguments against the editorial's position and its refutation of those arguments.

This essay first appeared in the *Los Angeles Times* on February 20, 2018.

IT'S TIME TO PHASE OUT SINGLE-USE PLASTIC

THE TIMES EDITORIAL BOARD

Faced with an unholy tonnage of chip bags, soda bottles, takeout containers, 1 and other disposable plastic items flowing into our landfills and our waters, winding up in wildlife, drinking water, and food, policymakers in California have tried reining in plastic waste bit by bit. For example, more than 100 cities have adopted restrictions on polystyrene takeout containers, and the state has banned single-use plastic grocery bags.

Current restrictions

✓ Considering the magnitude of the problem, however, this item-by-item, 2 city-by-city approach isn't going to cut it.

The state and local rules certainly have raised public awareness about the 3 problem. Denying free plastic bags at checkout or providing plastic straws only on request sends consumers an important message that there's a bigger cost to these everyday items than they may have considered. But the actual flow of trash has been disrupted only modestly.

Limitations of current restrictions

It's going to take more than a smattering of bans on single items to cure 4 society of its disposable-plastic habit. The sheer volume of plastic trash now littering Earth has become impossible to ignore. It's time for environmentalists, policymaker, and elected officials to start planning a broader response: phasing out *all* single-use plastic, not just the most pernicious. ?

Harmful

Thesis: All single-use plastic should be eliminated ✳

Actions in England and EU

That's right, all of it. If that sounds like a pipe dream, consider what's happen- 5 ing across the pond. Last month, British Prime Minister Theresa May outlined a plan to eliminate plastic waste by 2042. Queen Elizabeth II kicked it off this month by banning plastic straws and bottles from royal estates, and the Church of England supported a nascent social media campaign, #plasticlesslent, to encourage its flock to give up plastic for Lent this year. Simultaneously, the European Union announced its own plan to significantly reduce plastic waste, including adopting a possible plastic tax, in a direct response to the news that China, the largest importer of plastic recyclable material, was no longer accepting "foreign garbage."

What has been done in other U.S. states?

We don't expect President Trump or Congress to follow suit, even though 6   *Why not?*
it's impossible to pretend that the trash filling up in the ocean is naturally
occurring. That leaves it to states like California to step in.   ✓

One strategy is for lawmakers to adopt a reduction goal, as they did for 7   *Possible action*
greenhouse-gas emissions and energy derived from fossil fuels, and then to
adopt specific programs to meet that goal. It's a simple but effective approach
to tackling such a formidable environmental threat. Also, it puts makers of disposable plastic on notice, so they can't complain they didn't have time to adapt
or move into other, less harmful product lines.

But even forewarned, the plastic industry isn't likely to take an assault on 8   *Problem: Likely industry*
its bottom line well. Plastic makers spent millions of dollars trying to stop the   *response*
state from banning single-use plastic bags. Imagine what they might unleash
if all their disposable plastic products were threatened. As part of that, they   *Opposing argument*
will no doubt argue, as they did in the plastic bag fight, that the efforts to clean
up plastic waste would mean lost jobs. ?

But it's not a zero-sum game. Cutting, jobs on a disposable plastic prod- 9   *Situation in which each side's*
uct line doesn't automatically translate into fewer people employed. If the door   *gain or loss is exactly balanced*
closes on polystyrene takeout containers, for example, it will open for card-   *by the other side's.*
board and other biodegradable alternatives.

No one expects consumers to give up convenience completely. In fact, the 10   *Refutation*
market for bio-plastic alternatives, which are made from cornstarch and other
biodegradable sources, is already growing thanks to public awareness and the
sporadic efforts to curb plastic waste.

Opponents will insist that the answer is just to encourage more recy- 11   *Opposing argument*
cling. Not only is recycling not the answer (see China's diminished appetite   ✓ ✓
for imported plastic trash), it has only enabled our addiction to convenient, *Refutation*
disposable plastic packaging to deepen for some 60 years.

Yes, it's scary to think about a world where one has to carry around a reus- 12
able bag or worry about a paper drinking straw falling apart mid. . . . Oh, wait.
No, it's not. Knowing that every piece of plastic manufactured on Earth is still
with us and that if we don't cut back now, there will eventually be more plastic   ✳   *Prediction for future w/o*
than fish in the ocean—that's the truly frightening thought.   *action*

⊙ EXERCISE 2.4 ANNOTATING AN ESSAY

Reread John Tierney's "The Reign of Recycling" (pp. 66–70). As you read,
refer to the "Questions for Annotating" checklist (p. 73), and use them as
a guide as you write your own reactions and questions in the margins of
Tierney's essay. In your annotations, note where you agree or disagree
with Tierney, and briefly explain why. Quickly summarize any points that
you think are particularly important. Look up any unfamiliar words or references you have identified, and write down brief definitions or explanations. Think about these annotations as you prepare to discuss "The Reign
of Recycling" in class (and, eventually, to write about it).

❂ EXERCISE 2.5 EVALUATING YOUR HIGHLIGHTING

Exchange books with another student, and read his or her highlighting and annotating. How are your written responses similar to the other student's? How are they different? Do your classmate's responses help you to see anything new about Tierney's essay?

❂ EXERCISE 2.6 THINKING CRITICALLY: ANALYZING AN ARGUMENT

The following essay, "Waste Not . . . ?" by Bob Holmes, focuses on how to recycle in an environmentally responsible manner. Read the letter, highlighting and annotating it.

Now, consider how this essay is similar to and different from John Tierney's essay (pp. 66–70). First, identify the writer's thesis, and restate it in your own words. Then, consider his views on recycling and his recommendations for supporting and encouraging the practice.

Where does Holmes identify limitations of recycling? Are the problems he identifies the same ones Tierney discusses? Finally, consider how Holmes's purpose for writing is different from Tierney's.

This essay was published on July 22, 2017, in the journal *New Scientist*.

WASTE NOT . . . ?

BOB HOLMES

Like altruism, The Beatles, and chocolate, recycling is universally acknowl- 1
edged as a good thing. For many of us, it is a way of life. Recycling rates have been rising since the 1970s, and in some places, including Germany, the Netherlands, and California, more than half of all domestic waste is recycled. But now some people are challenging the received wisdom with difficult questions. How do nonrecyclable styrofoam coffee cups compare with paper or ceramic ones, when all the costs of manufacturing are included? Is it worth recycling materials such as glass and plastic that yield only small environmental benefits? Might landfill be a greener option for plastic, much of which is trucked to seaports and shipped to China for recycling? If you've been left wondering whether it's worth it, here's what you need to know to make up your mind.

1. Which materials are worth recycling?

From the most basic environmental point of view, all materials are worth recy- 2
cling, because this reduces the need for energy-intensive mining and smelting of virgin materials. That makes a huge difference for some things—notably

aluminum—but even recycling glass leads to a small energy saving and consequent reduction in greenhouse-gas emissions. Recycling can also provide a reliable, nonimported source of scarce resources such as the rare earth metals that are crucial parts of touchscreens and other high-tech devices.

However, the answer gets muddier when we consider economics. The 3 price of recycled material fluctuates wildly, and some often aren't profitable to recycle, especially if the recovered material has to be shipped long distances to a reprocessing plant. Waste managers often have to pay recyclers to take glass off their hands, for example. That can make virgin glass look like a better deal—but only because we often fail to include the environmental costs of mining sand and the carbon emissions from glassmaking furnaces. Similarly, plastics are often reprocessed in China, so proximity to a seaport may dictate whether it is profitable to recycle them.

Other low-value materials such as wood and textiles need to be clean to be 4 recyclable. The extra effort and expense required to separate them from general waste means they often end up in landfill.

2. Can we make landfills greener?

Landfill sites emit methane, a potent greenhouse gas. A growing number cap- 5 ture this and convert it to energy but even in the most efficient systems up to 10 percent escapes. In the U.S. landfill accounts for 18 percent of methane emissions, making it the third-largest source of methane emissions after the fossil-fuel industry and livestock. What's more, most of the methane produced in landfill sites comes from organic waste, which can be disposed of in greener ways. The simplest is composting, but the carbon in organic waste can also be converted to carbon dioxide and carbon monoxide by high-temperature, high-pressure processes. This can then be reconstituted into liquid fuels such as ethanol or methanol, or used as feedstock in other industrial processes. In Edmonton, Canada, for example, one trash-to-methanol process is making headway. According to one calculation, the product has the smallest carbon footprint of any liquid fuel, when methane emissions avoided by not landfilling the waste are included.

3. Why do I have to separate my recyclables?

Keeping recyclables separate from the rest of your rubbish reduces contamina- 6 tion and makes recycling more effective. Recycling companies like it if we also segregate different types of recyclables because then they don't have to incur the extra expense of doing this.

Separate collections of organic waste, recycling, and other rubbish 7 can make waste-handling more efficient, Kitchen waste is dense and self-compacting, so organics can be collected frequently with simple vehicles. With the stinky organics gone, recycling and other rubbish can be collected less often—even once a month or two—which makes more efficient use of expensive compactor trucks.

But the more complex the household sorting task becomes, the more 8
likely householders are to give up and simply pitch something into the rubbish. As a result of this trade-off, local authorities often lump all recycling
into a single bin, or just separate paper and cardboard from plastic, metal,
and glass.

4. What if my carefully segregated load is contaminated?

Everyone makes mistakes, and recyclers accept a certain amount of contami- 9
nation. But too much of it can downgrade the quality of the batch and reduce
the price reprocessors will pay. In practical terms, that means you should take
reasonable steps to rinse and sort your recyclables according to your waste-
management system's protocol, but don't obsess over every last decision.

Pay particular attention, however, to instructions on how to handle plastic 10
wraps and plastic bags, because these can dog up the shredding and sorting
machinery in some systems. If your local authority asks you not to put them in
the recycling bin, don't.

5. Does recycling keep plastic from polluting the ocean?

Most of the plastic that ends up in the oceans is "leakage"—the stuff that gets 11
tossed out of car windows, dropped on the street, or otherwise escapes the
waste management system. That accounts for 32 percent of global plastic packaging. So, if plastic is recycled—or even sent to landfill or burned—it should
stay out of the ocean.

6. Is burning rubbish in incinerators better than dumping it?

Incinerators reduce the volume of waste that might otherwise be dumped into 12
landfill sites, and most also generate heat for electricity or heating homes.
Modern waste-to-energy incinerators are very clean, so toxic emissions aren't
generally an issue. But then modern landfill sites generally don't leach toxins
into their environment either. Incinerators do, however, release a lot of carbon dioxide for every kilowatt-hour of electricity produced—more than many
coal-fired power plants, in fact. And as the electricity grid shifts more towards
renewables, burning trash to generate electricity is likely to look increasingly
less attractive.

Another consideration is that burning waste may reduce levels of recy- 13
cling. Cities that rely too heavily on incineration can find themselves trapped
by the system's demands. "These things are hungry," says Thomas Kinnaman,
an environmental economist at Bucknell University in Pennsylvania. "They
need lots and lots of fuel to stay efficient, and they're increasingly looking at
that recycling pile."

7. Is there any point to composting?

Composting is one of the most useful things you can do. Compacted, airless 14
landfill sites are the perfect breeding ground for anaerobic bacteria called
methanogens that feed on organic waste. For every kilogram they digest, they

produce about 2 kilograms of the powerful greenhouse gas methane. That doesn't happen in a compost bin. Yet households in the UK binned 7.3 million tonnes of food waste in 2015, two-thirds of which could have been composted. Separating kitchen scraps, garden waste, and other organic waste from the rest of the rubbish stream means they can be used to generate high-quality compost to increase soil fertility for crops and gardens. Organic waste contaminated by household chemicals, glass, metal fragment, and the like may only produce compost fit for restoring industrial sites and roadsides.

8. Isn't "recycling" a misnomer?

Some materials, such as glass and aluminum, can be melted and recast into 15 new products that are just as good as those from virgin material. But others can only be "downcycled" into products of lower quality than the original. Each time paper is recycled, for example, its fibers break into shorter lengths so it can be used only for increasingly low-quality papers such as newspaper and toilet paper. Most plastics are downcycled into products that cannot themselves be recycled. In fact, only about 15 percent of recycled plastics end up in products of similar quality. Researchers are working on finding new ways to chemically break down plastics into their component molecules so that they can be rebuilt into high-quality material.

> "Can we create a world without rubbish?"

There is a move to redesign products and packaging to minimize waste. 16 In the meantime, environmentally aware consumers can reduce, reuse, avoid disposable items and repair broken ones instead of throwing them away.

Towards Zero Waste

Can we create a world without rubbish?   17

One of the big impediments to recycling is products made of mixed mate- 18 rials that can't easily be separated—but solutions are on the way. Sachets are a prime example. People living in poorer countries often purchase single-use sachets of things like ketchup and detergent because they cannot afford to buy in bulk. These sachets need to be durable as well as impermeable, so they are often made of layers of different materials. Hundreds of billions are produced annually. Unilever, a major manufacturer of sacheted products, pledged earlier this year to make all of its packaging recyclable by 2025, and is developing new ways to dissolve the polyethylene out of used sachets so that it can be reused. Others are developing ways to separate mixed plastics by shredding them and automatically sorting the millimeter-sized fragments.

Such efforts are part of the "new plastics economy," which recognizes that 19 plastics can have environmental benefits as well as costs, "We don't want to eliminate plastic, we want to eliminate plastic waste," says Joe Iles, a spokesperson for the Ellen MacArthur Foundation, which is leading the initiative. That will require coordination as well as innovation. For example, there's a new generation of biodegradable plastic made from cornstarch that can be used to make drinking bottles. But we need an easy way to distinguish them from bottles made from polyethylene terephthalate (PET), says Iles, because even a few can contaminate and ruin a batch of recycled PET.

Another way to encourage recycling is to require manufacturers to take 20 back and recycle the products they sell at the end of their useful life. This extended producer responsibility is increasingly being applied to products like electronics and batteries, It encourages manufacturers to think about the disposal of their products, possibly redesigning them to make that easier. Japan, one of the leaders in this approach, adds the price of recycling to new products and has seen an associated 27 percent increase in recycling rates for containers and packaging.

Initiatives like these are pushing society towards a "circular" econ- 21 omy, in contrast to today's "take, make, and dispose" economy. We have a long way to go and, even with the most advanced technologies and best intentions, zero waste is an impossible dream. But that shouldn't stop us dreaming. "I sometimes equate it to zero deaths in the emergency room of a hospital," says Jeffrey Morris, a waste consultant at the Sound Resources Management Group in Olympia, Washington. "Any other goal makes no sense."

⊖ EXERCISE 2.7 DRAFTING A THESIS STATEMENT

The following magazine article, "We Are So Forked" by Jenny Luna, focuses on the use of plastic utensils. What position does this essay take? Draft a thesis statement that summarizes this position. Then, consider how John Tierney (pp. 66–70) might respond to this thesis—and to Luna's specific recommendations.

This opinion piece appeared in the July/August 2017 issue of *Mother Jones*.

WE ARE SO FORKED

JENNY LUNA

Whether for stabbing salads at our desks or slurping up late-night Thai, plastic 1 cutlery has become a signature side to our growing takeout habit. It's hard to say exactly how many forks, spoons, and knives Americans throw away, but in 2015 we placed nearly 2 billion delivery orders. If at least half those meals involved single-use utensils, that would mean we're tossing out billions of utensils each year. They don't just disappear: A recent study in the San Francisco Bay Area found that food and beverage packaging made up 67 percent of all litter on the streets.

Apart from being an eyesore, disposable cutlery endangers wildlife. 2 A survey by four major environmental groups determined that plastic utensils ranked among the 10 most common trash items found in California—which contributes to a larger problem: The United Nations estimates that the oceans contain more than 8 million tons of plastic. As plastic breaks down, it can be mistaken for food by sea creatures, which can harm them and our seafood dinners.

A few options have surfaced in recent years. In 2010, a company in India 3 started selling edible spoons and forks made from grains. Closer to home, California-based SpudWare's forks are made from potato starch. But such alternatives, which cost about twice as much as plastic, still require a lot of energy and water to produce, according to Samantha Sommer, who runs a waste-prevention project for Clean Water Action. What's more, not all major cities compost. And even if biodegradable or compostable utensils make it to a facility, there's a chance they'll end up in a landfill, says Robert Reed, a spokesman for the West Coast recycling and compost plant Recology. Depending on what they're made of, he says, biodegradable utensils might not degrade completely; if they don't, they could be plucked out of the pile and thrown away.

Perhaps diners should take a page from China, where environmental protesters publicized how the roughly 80 billion pairs of disposable wooden chopsticks produced each year eat up 20 million trees in the process. Greenpeace China launched a BYOC (Bring Your Own Chopsticks) campaign and worked

> "Metal spoons have not yet graced American celebrity Instagram accounts, but maybe it's time." 4

with pop stars to promote reusable chopsticks as a trendy fashion accessory. As a result, disposable chopsticks were banned from use at many venues hosting events at Beijing's 2008 Olympics.

Metal spoons have not yet graced American celebrity Instagram 5 accounts, but maybe it's time: Encouraging customers to bring in their own utensils helps businesses cut down costs and waste. A few years ago, Clean Water Action ran a test case with restaurant owner Francisco Hernandez of El Metate in San Francisco. The restaurant staff used to include plastic utensils with every order. Now, sit-down diners get metal forks, and disposables are in a countertop container for to-go customers who need them. Hernandez saved money that year—now he buys just one case of disposable forks each week instead of three—and he decreased his restaurant's waste by more than 3,600 pounds. The change means El Metate has more to wash, but it's likely that the water used to run his dishwasher (one gallon for every one-minute cycle) is dwarfed by the amount needed to make those plastic forks.

Still, a sea change might require more research and toothier legislation— 6
something that worked in the fight against plastic bags. A 2013 study found
that after San Jose, California, enacted a bag ban, there was nearly 90 percent
less plastic in the city's storm drains and almost 60 percent less in its streets
than there had been before. Data like that helped California finalize a state-
wide ban—over the strenuous lobbying of plastics manufacturers—in 2016.
Such legislation appears to be catching on: Chicago, Seattle, and Austin, Texas,
have also enacted bag bans, and between 2015 and 2016, lawmakers proposed
at least 77 state-level plastic bag bills. Given that success, here's an idea: Charge
a small fee for disposable utensils to help nudge consumers to make a habit
out of carrying their own forks. Prettier streets, healthier oceans, and cheaper
takeout? Sold.

Writing a Critical Response

Sometimes you will be asked to write a **critical response**—a paragraph or
more in which you analyze ideas presented in an argument and express
your reactions to them.

Before you can respond in writing to an argument, you need to be sure
that you understand the writer's position and that you have a sense of how
supporting ideas are arranged—and why. You also need to consider how
convincingly the writer conveys his or her position.

If you have read the argument carefully, highlighting and annotating
it according to the guidelines outlined in this chapter, you should have a
good idea what the writer wants to communicate to readers as well as how
successfully the argument makes its point.

Before you begin to write a critical response to an argument, you
should consider the questions in the checklist on page 83.

Begin your critical response by identifying your source and its author;
then, write a clear, concise summary of the writer's position. Next, analyze the argument's supporting points one by one, considering the strength
of the evidence that is presented. Also consider whether the writer
addresses all significant opposing arguments and whether those arguments
are refuted convincingly. Quote, summarize, and paraphrase the writer's
key points as you go along, being careful to quote accurately and not to
misrepresent the writer's ideas or distort them by quoting out of context.
(For information on summarizing, paraphrasing, quoting, and synthesizing sources, see Chapter 9.) As you write, identify arguments you find
unconvincing, poorly supported, or irrelevant. At the end of your critical
response, sum up your assessment of the argument in a strong concluding
statement.

CHECKLIST

Questions for Critical Reading

☐ What is the writer's general subject?

☐ What purpose does the writer have for presenting this argument?

☐ What is the writer's position?

☐ Does the writer support ideas mainly with facts or with opinion?

☐ What evidence does the writer present to support this position?

☐ Is the evidence convincing? Is there enough evidence?

☐ Does the writer present opposing ideas and refute them effectively?

☐ What kind of audience does the writer seem to be addressing?

☐ Does the writer see the audience as hostile, friendly, or neutral?

☐ Does the writer establish himself or herself as well informed? As a fair and reasonable person?

☐ Does the writer seem to exhibit bias? If so, how does this bias affect the argument?

Neena Thomason, the student who highlighted and annotated the *Los Angeles Times* editorial on pages 74–75, used those notes to help her develop the following critical response to the editorial.

RESPONSE TO "IT'S TIME TO PHASE OUT ALL SINGLE-USE PLASTIC"

NEENA THOMASON

In "It's Time to Phase Out All Single-Use Plastic," the *Los Angeles Times* editorial board warns of a bleak future unless the "unholy tonnage" (para. 1) of disposable plastic items is controlled. The board's recommendation is a total ban of all single-use plastic items.

Although the editorial acknowledges steps that have been taken by state and local government to limit the use of various individual items, such as plastic bags and straws, the writers note that such efforts have not had much effect on the accumulation of trash. They are also not optimistic that the federal government will take significant steps to solve the problem. Therefore, they believe the time has come for the state of California to act.

One suggestion they make is the adoption of a "reduction goal" (7). The writers anticipate that industry will object to any such limitations, arguing that they will lead to a loss of jobs. They point out, however,

1 Article's source and author identified

2 Summary of writer's position

3 Analysis of supporting evidence

that any lost jobs would be replaced by jobs producing "biodegradable alternatives" (9) to plastic items.

Concluding statement

The editorial writers also expect industry to recommend recycling   4
as a better alternative than banning single-use plastic items. The writers believe, however, that recycling is not the answer—and may, in fact, be part of the problem because it has "enabled our addiction to convenient, disposable plastic packaging" (11).

In short, the writers of the editorial make a convincing case that the 5
only way to avoid a world with "more plastic than fish in the ocean" (12) is to take action now.

Work Cited

Los Angeles Times Editorial Board. "It's Time to Phase Out All Single-Use Plastic." *Practical Argument*, 4th ed., edited by Laurie G. Kirszner and Stephen R. Mandell. Macmillan, 2020, pp. 71–73.

TEMPLATE FOR WRITING A CRITICAL RESPONSE

Write a one-paragraph critical response to John Tierney's essay on pages 66–70. Use the following template to shape your paragraph.

According to John Tierney, recycling may not be worth the cost or effort required to achieve its goals. He points out, for example, that _____

_____

_____

_____. Tierney also observes that _____

_____

_____.

Tierney makes some convincing points. For example, he says that _____

_____

_____

_____. However, _____

_____

_____. All in

all, _____

_____.

❖ EXERCISE 2.8 WRITING A CRITICAL RESPONSE

Expand the one-paragraph critical response that you wrote above into a more fully developed critical response to John Tierney's essay on pages 66–70. Refer to the highlighting and annotations that you did for Exercises 2.3 and 2.4. (If you like, you can include references to other readings in this chapter.)

❖ EXERCISE 2.9 DEVELOPING VISUAL ARGUMENTS

What kind of images would you use to support the argument that recycling is necessary? What kinds of images might support the argument that recycling isn't worth the trouble? Develop two lists of possible visuals, one list for each side of the argument. Then, consider what these images might include and where they might appear.

When recyclable materials are mishandled, such as being dumped near recycling containers rather than placed inside them as in this photo, the process can break down. AP Images/Steve Parsons.

Reading and Responding to Visual Arguments

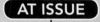

Does Recycling Really Accomplish Anything? (continued)

In Chapter 2, you read essays focusing on the advantages and limitations of recycling. Now, you will be introduced to a variety of visual texts that offer additional insights into this issue. At the same time, you will learn how to use the critical-reading strategies that you practiced in Chapter 2 to help you to interpret visual arguments and to use visuals as springboards for discussion and writing or as sources in your essays.

A **visual argument** can be an advertisement, a chart or graph or table, an infographic, a diagram, a web page, a photograph, a drawing, a cartoon, or a painting. Like an argumentative essay, a visual argument takes a position. Unlike an argumentative essay, however, a visual argument communicates its message (and offers evidence to support that message) largely through images rather than words.

When you approach a visual argument—particularly one that will be the subject of class discussion or writing—you should do so with a critical eye. Your primary goal is to understand the point that the creator of the visual is trying to make, but you also need to understand how the message is conveyed. In addition, you need to evaluate whether the methods used to persuade the audience are both logical and convincing.

VISUALS VERSUS VISUAL ARGUMENTS

Not every visual is an argument; many simply present information. For example, a diagram of a hunting rifle, with its principal parts labeled, tells viewers what the weapon looks like and how it works. However, a photo of two toddlers playing with a hunting rifle could make a powerful argument about the need for gun safety. Conversely, a photo of a family hunting trip featuring a teenager proudly holding up a rifle while his parents look on approvingly might serve as a positive argument for gun ownership.

Reading Visual Arguments

As you learned in Chapter 2, being a critical reader involves responding actively to the text of an argument. The active reading strategies that you practiced in Chapter 2—*previewing*, *close reading*, *highlighting*, and *annotating*—can also be applied to visual arguments.

When you approach a visual argument, you should look for clues to its main idea, or message. Some visuals, particularly advertising images, include words (sometimes called *body copy*) as well, and this written text often conveys the main points of the argument. (Such visuals are considered **multimodal** because they combine two methods of communication—in this case, words and images.) Apart from words, however, the images themselves can help you understand the visual's purpose, its intended audience, and the argument that it is making.

COMPREHENSION CLUES

Focusing on the following elements can help you to understand a visual argument:

- The individual images
- The relative distance between images (close together or far apart)
- The relative size of the images
- The relationship between images and background
- The use of empty space
- The use of color and shading (for example, contrast between light and dark)
- If people are pictured, their activities, gestures, facial expressions, positions, body language, dress, and so on

APPEALS: *LOGOS, PATHOS,* AND *ETHOS*

As you study a visual argument, you should consider the appeal (or appeals) that the visual uses to convince its audience:

- An ad produced by Mothers Against Drunk Drivers (MADD) that includes statistics about alcohol-related auto fatalities might appeal to logic (*logos*).

- Another MADD ad could appeal to the emotions (*pathos*) by showing photographs of an accident scene.

- Still another ad could appeal to authority (*ethos*) by featuring a well-known sports figure warning of the dangers of drunk driving.

(For more on these appeals, see pp. 14–21.)

The following photograph presents a strong visual argument, using a powerful image to make an emotional appeal to those concerned about the environment. This photograph appeared on the cover of the June 2018 issue of *National Geographic* magazine.

The visual below highlights one dramatic image: a floating plastic bag shaped like an iceberg. The placement of this image in the center of

the visual emphasizes its importance, and the contrast between the small portion of the image protruding from the water and the large submerged portion makes the visual's message clear: the environmental problems we see today are only "the tip of the iceberg." The clear demarcation of the gray sky and the blue ocean confirms the contrast between the placid surface and the unseen threat that lies beneath it.

The text that accompanies the image is brief and to the point. At the top right, the stark choice that confronts us—"planet or plastic?"—is expressed as a dilemma that seems to have only one reasonable solution. At the bottom left, in smaller type, two succinct sentences spell out the problem, reinforcing the conflict between the natural world (ocean) and the pollution (plastic) that threatens to destroy it.

Because it presents only one image, and because the subject matter is probably familiar to most people, this visual is easy to understand. Its powerful image and text are not difficult to interpret, and the visual's warning is straightforward: if we do not do something about the refuse that is polluting our oceans, we will risk losing them. The visual's accessibility (as well as its obvious emotional appeal) suggests that it is aimed at a wide general audience rather than, for example, environmentalists.

The visual might have been created for any of several purposes. Most obviously, it is intended to raise awareness and, perhaps, to inspire action—for example, to encourage readers to use fewer plastic bags and to dispose of them responsibly. In addition, because it is a magazine cover, it is also intended to encourage people to buy, and to read, this issue of *National Geographic.*

Now, turn your attention to the following bar graph, "U.S. Better at Recycling Some Things Than Others"; it appears in the article "Five Charts That Explain Why Recycling Efforts May Not Result in Zero Waste," published in the online newsletter *Waste Dive.* Unlike the *National Geographic* cover, which appeals to the emotions, this graph appeals to logic by providing evidence to support the article's position: that recycling is not a magic cure.

The graph uses a simple, open design and clearly labels each category it lists, presenting them in a logical order. It provides readily accessible information, in the form of percentages, to show which kinds of waste are most (and least) efficiently disposed of. The main idea, or message, this graph conveys is summarized in its boldfaced title: "U.S. better at recycling some things than others." This in turn supports the thesis of the article in which the graph appeared: that despite Americans' best efforts at recycling, achieving "zero waste" may not be an achievable goal.

This idea might surprise those readers who assume that recycling can lead to the elimination of the waste that pollutes our environment. In a sense, then, this graph can be seen as a **refutation** of a commonly held assumption. Because the graph (like the article in which it appeared) presents information intended to challenge the audience's probable assumptions, its purpose seems to be not just to inform readers but perhaps also to change the way they look at recycling.

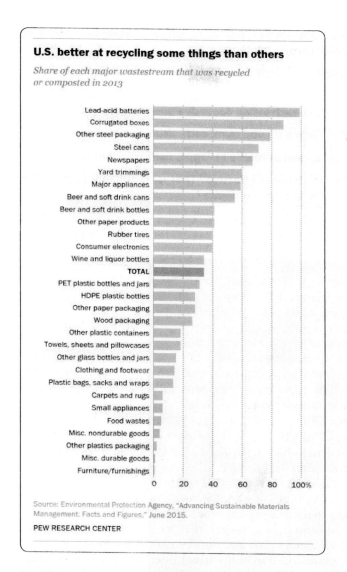

U.S. better at recycling some things than others

Share of each major wastestream that was recycled or composted in 2013

Source: Environmental Protection Agency, "Advancing Sustainable Materials Management: Facts and Figures," June 2015.

PEW RESEARCH CENTER

⊙ EXERCISE 3.1 READING VISUAL ARGUMENTS

Look carefully at each of the visuals on the pages that follow, and then answer the questions on page 99.

Reading Visual Arguments

1. Do you see all of the visuals on pages 92–98 as arguments, created to convey a message or make a point, or do you think any of them were created solely to present information?

2. What main idea does each visual communicate? State the main idea of each visual in a single sentence.

3. What elements (words and images) in each visual support this main idea?

4. What purpose does each visual seem designed to achieve?

5. What kind of audience do you think each visual is aimed at?

6. Does the visual appeal primarily to *logos*, *pathos*, or *ethos*?

7. Do you think the visual is effective? That is, is it likely to have the intended effect on its target audience?

Photo of a bird trapped in a plastic bag.

John Cancalosi/Photolibrary/Getty Images

David Sipress/Conde Nast/The Cartoon Bank

Cartoon commenting on public's lack of compliance with recycling guidelines.

"Waste pie chart" created from items found on a beach in Bali, Indonesia.

Making Oceans Plastic Free

TOWN OF NORTH ATTLEBOROUGH

WHAT TO RECYCLE	HOW TO PREPARE	DO NOT INCLUDE
GLASS Clear, green, brown, bottles and jars only	Rinse clean Place in recycling bin	No broken glass No other glass (light bulbs, window glass, mirrors, dishes, etc.)
PLASTIC CONTAINERS with necks (water bottles, mayonaise jars, detergent bottles, margarine tubs, etc.)	Rinse clean Labels, caps, lids, and neck rings are OK Place in recycling bin	No unmarked items No plastic wrap or film No plastic plant pots **No plastic bags** **No styrofoam**
ALUMINUM CANS Foil pie plates Aluminum trays	Rinse clean Place in recycling bin	**CLEAN foil ONLY** No other aluminum items
TIN cans ONLY	Rinse clean Cans can be flattened or nested to save space Place in recycling bin	No aerosol, paint, or motor oil cans No other metal items
PAPER Newspapers, Magazines, Junk Mail, Catalogs, Phone books Office paper	Place in recycling bin, brown paper grocery bags, or tie with string Do not put in plastic bags	**NO PIZZA BOXES WITH GREASE** No soiled newspapers, tissues, or napkins No wax paper No styrofoam packing or peanuts
CARDBOARD, PAPER Paperboard (cereal boxes, etc. with liners removed) Egg cartons (no styrofoam)	Cut or flatten cardboard Place in recycling bin **No Plastic Bags**	No food contaminated items No wax or foil coated items

SOLID WASTE DEPARTMENT, 43 SOUTH WASHINGTON STREET
P (508) 699-0105   F (508) 643-1268

Town of North Attleborough Massachusetts

Guidelines for town
recycling program.

Infographic encouraging consumers not to use nonbiodegradable straws.

Two Oceans Aquarium

Mckim Communications Group Ltd

Canadian public service
advertisement in sup-
port of recycling.

Highlighting and Annotating Visual Arguments

Now, it's time to look more closely at visual arguments and to learn how to *highlight* and *annotate* them. Unlike highlighting and annotating a written text, marking a visual text involves focusing your primary attention not on any words that appear but on the images.

After previewing the visual by looking at its overall appearance, begin highlighting to identify key images—perhaps by starring, boxing, or circling them—and then consider drawing lines or arrows to connect related images. Next, go on to make annotations on the visual, commenting on the effectiveness of its individual images in communicating the message of the whole. As in the case of a written text, your annotations can be in the form of comments or questions.

The visual on the following page shows how a student, Gabriel Dunn, highlighted and annotated a public-service advertisement prepared by the Surfrider Foundation.

When he first looked at this public-service ad, Gabriel Dunn was immediately struck by the way the large blue letters of the central message drew his eye to the blue plastic center of the sushi roll, thus emphasizing its importance. When he highlighted and annotated the ad, he made (and starred) a note about this effective use of color and drew arrows to connect the blue type with the roll's blue center. He then identified the largest (and most important) words and images and boxed the ad's central message, also noting the unexpected presence of plastic and commenting on the partial image of chopsticks. Finally, he underlined and starred a key piece of information in the written text.

Prominent image clearly reveals contamination

Plastic, not fish

Large capitalized words and central position emphasizes ad's message/warning

WHAT GOES IN THE OCEAN GOES IN YOU.

A RECENT STUDY FOUND THAT 35% OF FISH SAMPLED OFF THE WEST COAST HAD INGESTED PLASTIC. FIND OUT HOW YOU CAN HELP. VISIT WWW.SURFRIDER.ORG/RAP MAKE THE PLEDGE. BAN THE BAG.

Chopsticks suggest roll will be eaten

Blue type here highlights blue centers in rolls above

Use of capital letters makes information stand out

Surfrider

EXERCISE 3.2 HIGHLIGHTING AND ANNOTATING A VISUAL ARGUMENT

The visual that follows was created as a customizable template to illustrate the benefits of recycling and alternative energy sources. Rather than including text beneath its headings, the visual leaves blank space to be filled in with suitable text. (The images and headlines are designed to stay the same.) Look closely at the visual, and then highlight and annotate it to identify its most important images and their relationship to one another.

seamartini/iStock/Getty Images

Public service advertisement for recycling

Then, think about how the images work together to communicate a central message to the audience. What argument does this visual seem to make? How might that argument change based on the specific text that is supplied? How might it stay the same?

Responding Critically to Visual Arguments

As you learned in Chapter 2, a **critical response** analyzes the ideas in a text and expresses your reactions to them. When you respond in writing to a visual argument, you rely on your highlighting and annotations to help you understand the writer's ideas and see how the words and images work together to convey a particular message.

As you prepare to write a critical response to a visual argument, keep in mind the questions in the following checklist.

When you write a critical response, begin by identifying the source and purpose of the visual. Next, state your reaction to the visual, and then examine its elements one at a time, considering how effective each is and how well the various elements work together to create a convincing visual argument. End with a strong concluding statement that summarizes your reaction.

The critical response that follows was written by the student who highlighted and annotated the visual on page 97.

CHECKLIST

Questions for Responding to Visual Arguments

☐ In what source did the visual appear? What is the target audience for this source?

☐ For what kind of audience was the visual created? Hostile? Friendly? Neutral?

☐ For what purpose was the visual created?

☐ Who (or what organization) created the visual? What do you know (and what can you find out) about the background and goals of this person or group?

☐ What issue is the visual addressing? What position does the visual take on this issue? How does it support this position?

☐ Does the visual include words? If so, are they essential? What purpose do they serve? Does the visual need more—or different—written text?

☐ Does the visual seem to be a *refutation*—that is, an argument against a particular position?

☐ Is the visual interesting? Clear? Attractive? Convincing?

☐ Do you agree with the position the visual takes on the issue? Why or why not?

RESPONSE TO "WHAT GOES IN THE OCEAN GOES IN YOU"

GABRIEL DUNN

The public service advertisement produced by the Surfrider Foundation, an organization whose mission is to protect and enjoy "the world's oceans, waves, and beaches through a powerful activist network," clearly and effectively supports its stated goals.

Both words and images support the ad's message. In the center of the visual, large, capitalized blue letters spell out this message: "What goes in the ocean goes in you." At the top of the visual is a large cross section of a sushi roll. Although the rice remains, the roll is wrapped in plastic rather than seaweed, and it is filled with plastic rather than fish. The blue letters of the ad's central message make the blue of the roll's plastic center more prominent. Off to the side, chopsticks suggest that the roll is ready to be enjoyed. However, as the ad's visual elements show, this usually tasty delicacy is not fit to eat.

1   Identification of visual's source and purpose

Reaction to visual

2   Analysis of visual elements

Analysis, continued   Below the large letters of the central message, information from   3
recent research studies, set in smaller type, reinforces the accuracy and
seriousness of the message, and Surfrider's contact information offers
readers a way to "help turn the tide on plastic pollution."

Concluding statement   Because millennials are probably more likely than other groups to eat   4
sushi, the ad may be primarily directed at them. In any case, the message
the ad conveys to its audience is also a warning: When we pollute our
waters, we contaminate our food—and when we eat contaminated food,
we pollute our bodies.

TEMPLATE FOR RESPONDING TO VISUAL ARGUMENTS

Write a one-paragraph critical response to the visual you highlighted and annotated in
Exercise 3.2 on pages 97–98. Use the following template to shape your paragraph.

The visual created by Surfrider.org shows _____

_____.

The goal of this organization seems to be to _____

_____.

This visual makes a powerful statement about _____.

The central image shows _____

_____

Other visual elements enhance the central image by _____

_____. The visual includes words as well as images.

These words suggest _____

_____.

The visual [is/is not] effective because _____

_____.

⦿ EXERCISE 3.3 DEVELOP YOUR RESPONSE

Consulting the one-paragraph critical response that you wrote in the preceding template, write a more fully developed critical response to the visual on page 97. Refer to the highlighting and annotating that you did for Exercise 3.2.

⦿ EXERCISE 3.4 EVALUATING VISUAL ARGUMENTS

Look back at the images in this chapter. Which do you think is the strongest, most convincing visual argument? Why? Write a paragraph in which you explain and support your choice.

Fedor Selivanov/Alamy

4

Writing a Rhetorical Analysis

AT ISSUE

Is It Ethical to Buy Counterfeit Designer Merchandise?

The demand for counterfeit designer merchandise—handbags, shoes, and jewelry—has always been great. Wishing to avoid the high prices of genuine designer goods, American consumers spend hundreds of millions of dollars per year buying cheap imitations that are made primarily in factories in China (and in other countries as well). According to United States Customs and Border Protection statistics, the counterfeit goods seized in 2013 had a retail value of over $1.7 billion. In 2017, that figure went down to $1.2 billion, but much more counterfeit merchandise gets into the United States than is seized. However hard they try, law enforcement officials cannot seem to stem the tide of counterfeit merchandise that is sold in stores, in flea markets, and by street vendors as well as through the internet. As long as people want these illegal goods, there will be a market for them.

Purchasing counterfeit designer goods is not a victimless crime, however. Buyers are stealing the intellectual property of legitimate businesses that, unlike the manufacturers of fakes, pay their employees fair wages and provide good working conditions. In addition, because counterfeit goods are of low quality, they do not last as long as the genuine articles. This is not a serious problem when people are buying fake watches and handbags, but it can be life threatening when the counterfeit products include pharmaceuticals, tools, baby food, or automobile parts.

Later in this chapter, you will read a rhetorical analysis of an essay that takes a position on this issue, and you will be asked to write a rhetorical analysis of your own about another essay on this topic.

What Is a Rhetorical Analysis?

When you write a **rhetorical analysis**, you systematically examine the strategies a writer employs to achieve his or her purpose. In the process, you explain how these strategies work together to create an effective (or ineffective) argument. To carry out this task, you consider the argument's **rhetorical situation**, the writer's **means of persuasion**, and the **rhetorical strategies** that the writer uses.

OVERVIEW: "LETTER FROM BIRMINGHAM JAIL" BY MARTIN LUTHER KING JR.

Here and throughout the rest of this chapter, we will be analyzing "Letter from Birmingham Jail" by Martin Luther King Jr., which can be found online.

In 1963, civil rights leader Martin Luther King Jr. organized a series of nonviolent demonstrations to protest the climate of racial segregation that existed in Birmingham, Alabama. He and his followers met opposition not only from white moderates but also from some African-American clergymen who thought that King was a troublemaker. During the demonstrations, King was arrested and jailed for eight days. He wrote his "Letter from Birmingham Jail" on April 16, 1963, from the city jail in response to a public statement by eight white Alabama clergymen titled "A Call for Unity." This statement asked for an end to the demonstrations, which the clergymen called "untimely," "unwise," and "extreme." (Their letter was addressed to the "white and Negro" population of Birmingham, not to King, whom they considered an "outsider.")

King knew that the world was watching and that his response to the white clergymen would have both national and international significance. As a result, he used a variety of rhetorical strategies to convince readers that his demands were both valid and understandable and that contrary to the opinions of some, his actions were well within the mainstream of American social and political thought. Today, King's "Letter from Birmingham Jail" stands as a model of clear and highly effective argumentation.

Martin Luther King Jr. in Birmingham Jail (April 1963)

Bettmann/Getty Images

Considering the Rhetorical Situation

Arguments do not take place in isolation. They are written by real people in response to a particular set of circumstances called the **rhetorical situation** (see pp. 9–13). The rhetorical situation consists of the following five elements:

- The writer
- The writer's purpose
- The writer's audience
- The question
- The context

By analyzing the rhetorical situation, you are able to determine why the writer made the choices he or she did and how these choices affect the argument.

ANALYZING THE RHETORICAL SITUATION

To help you analyze the rhetorical situation of an argument, look for information about the essay and its author.

1. **Look at the essay's headnote.** If the essay you are reading has a headnote, it can contain useful information about the writer, the issue being discussed, and the structure of the essay. For this reason, it is a good idea to read headnotes carefully.

2. **Look for clues within the essay.** The writer's use of particular words and phrases can sometimes provide information about his or her preconceptions as well as about the cultural context of the argument. Historical or cultural references can indicate what ideas or information the writer expects readers to have.

3. **Search the web.** Often, just a few minutes online can give you a lot of useful information—such as the background of a particular debate or the biography of the writer. By looking at titles of the other books or essays the writer has written, you may also be able to get an idea of his or her biases or point of view.

The Writer

Begin your analysis of the rhetorical situation by trying to determine whether anything in the writer's background (for example, the writer's education, experience, race, gender, political beliefs, religion, age, and experiences) has influenced the content of the argument. Also consider whether the writer seems to have any preconceptions about the subject. (For a discussion of a writer's biases and preconceptions, see pp. 9–10.)

ANALYZING THE WRITER

- What is the writer's background?
- How does the writer's background affect the content of the argument?
- What preconceptions about the subject does the writer seem to have?

If you were analyzing "Letter from Birmingham Jail," it would help to know that Martin Luther King Jr. was pastor of the Dexter Avenue Baptist Church in Montgomery, Alabama. In 1956, he organized a bus boycott that led to a United States Supreme Court decision that outlawed segregation on Alabama's buses. In addition, King was a leader of the Southern Christian Leadership Conference and strongly believed in nonviolent protest. His books include *Stride towards Freedom* (1958) and *Why We Can't Wait* (1964). His "I Have a Dream" speech, which he delivered on the steps of the Lincoln Memorial on August 28, 1963, is considered by scholars to be one of the most influential speeches of the twentieth century. In 1964, King won the Nobel Prize for peace.

In "Letter from Birmingham Jail," King addresses the injustices that he sees in America—especially in the South—and makes a strong case for civil

"I Have a Dream" speech, Washington, D.C. (August 1963)

© Hulton-Deutsch Collection/CORBIS/Getty Images

rights for all races. Throughout his argument, King includes numerous references to the Bible, to philosophers, and to political and religious think-ers. By doing so, he makes it clear to readers that he is aware of the social, cultural, religious, and political implications of his actions. Because he is a clergyman, King suggests that by battling in-justice, he, like the apostle Paul, is doing God's work. This point is made clear in the following passage (para. 3):

> But more basically, I am in Birmingham because injustice is here. Just as the prophets of the eighth century B.C. left their villages and carried their "thus saith the Lord" far beyond the boundaries of their home towns, and just as the Apostle Paul left his village of Tarsus and carried the gospel of Jesus Christ to the far corners of the Greco-Roman world, so am I compelled to carry the gospel of freedom beyond my own home town. Like Paul, I must constantly respond to the Macedonian call for aid.

The Writer's Purpose

Next, consider what the writer hopes to achieve with his or her argument. In other words, ask yourself if the writer is trying to challenge people's ideas, persuade them to accept new points of view, or influence their behavior. (For a discussion of a writer's purpose, see p. 10.)

ANALYZING THE WRITER'S PURPOSE

- Does the writer state his or her purpose directly, or is the purpose implied?
- Is the writer's purpose simply to convince or to encourage action?
- Does the writer rely primarily on logic or on emotion?
- Does the writer have a hidden agenda?

It is clear that Martin Luther King Jr. wrote "Letter from Birmingham Jail" to convince readers that even though he had been arrested, his actions were both honorable and just. To get readers to understand that, like Henry David Thoreau, he is protesting laws that he considers wrong, he draws a distinction between just and unjust laws. For him, a law is just if it "squares with the moral law or the law of God" (16). A law is unjust if it "is out of harmony with the moral law" (16). As a clergyman and a civil rights leader, King believed that he had an obligation both to point out the immorality of unjust laws and to protest them—even if it meant going to jail.

The Writer's Audience

To analyze the writer's audience, begin by considering whether the writer seems to see readers as friendly, hostile, or neutral. (For a discussion of types of audiences, see pp. 10–13.) Also, determine how much knowledge the writer assumes that readers have. Then, consider how the writer takes into account factors like the audience's race, religion, gender, education, age, and ethnicity. Next, decide what preconceptions the writer thinks readers have about the subject. Finally, see if the writer shares any common ground with readers.

ANALYZING THE WRITER'S AUDIENCE

- Who is the writer's intended audience?

- Does the writer see the audience as informed or uninformed?

- Does the writer see the audience as hostile, friendly, or neutral?

- What values does the writer think the audience holds?

- What does the writer seem to assume about the audience's background?

- On what points do the writer and the audience agree? On what points do they disagree?

In "Letter from Birmingham Jail," King addresses more than one audience. First, he speaks directly to eight clergymen from Birmingham, who are at worst hostile and at best skeptical. They consider King an outsider whose actions are "unwise and untimely" (1). Before addressing their concerns, King tries to establish common ground, referring to his readers as "fellow clergymen" and "my Christian and Jewish brothers." He then goes on to say that he wishes that the clergymen had supported his actions instead of criticizing them. King ends his letter on a conciliatory note by asking his readers to forgive him if he has overstated his case or been unduly harsh.

King also speaks to white moderates, who he assumes are sympathetic to his cause but concerned about his methods. He understands that he has to influence this segment of his audience if he is to gain wide support for his cause. For this reason, King uses a restrained tone and emphasizes the universality of his message, ending his letter with a plea that is calculated to console and inspire those people who need reassurance (50):

> Let us all hope that the dark clouds of racial prejudice will soon pass away and the deep fog of misunderstanding will be lifted from our fear-drenched communities, and in some not too distant tomorrow the radiant stars of love and brotherhood will shine over our great nation with all their scintillating beauty.

Finally, King indirectly addresses the American people. He knows that because of his stature, his letter will be read by a broad, national audience, not just those who live in Birmingham, Alabama. King sees this audience as well meaning but confused about the racial situation in the United States. He realizes that to achieve his ends, he has to win over this audience and motivate them to take action. To do so, he appeals to their innate sense of justice and encourages them to do what's morally right, despite any misgivings.

The Question

Try to determine what question the writer is trying to answer. Is the question suitable for argument? Decide if there are good arguments on both sides of the issue. For example, what issue (or issues) is the writer confronting? Does he or she address them adequately? (For a discussion of the question, see p. 13.)

ANALYZING THE QUESTION

- What is the central question of the argument?
- Are there solid arguments on both sides of the issue?
- Has the writer answered the question fully enough?

The question King attempts to answer in "Letter from Birmingham Jail" is why he has decided to come to Birmingham to lead protests. Because the answer to this question is complicated, King addresses a number of issues. Although his main concern is with racial segregation in Alabama, he also is troubled by the indifference of white moderates who have urged him to call off his protests. In addition, he feels that he needs to explain his actions (for example, engaging in nonviolent protests) and address those who doubt his motives. King answers his critics (as well as his central question) by saying that because the people of the United States are interconnected, the injustices in one state will eventually affect the entire country.

The Context

The **context** is the set of circumstances that creates the need for the argument. As you analyze an argument, try to determine the social, historical, economic, political, and cultural events that set the stage for the argument and the part that these events play in the argument itself. (For a discussion of context, see p. 14.)

ANALYZING THE CONTEXT

- What situation (or situations) set the stage for the argument?
- What social, economic, political, and cultural events triggered the argument?
- What historical references situate this argument in a particular place or time?

The immediate context of "Letter to Birmingham Jail" is well known: Martin Luther King Jr. wrote an open letter to eight white clergymen in which he defended his protests against racial segregation. However, the wider social and political context of the letter is less well known.

In 1896, the U.S. Supreme Court ruled in *Plessy v. Ferguson* that "separate but equal" accommodations on railroad cars gave African Americans the equal protection guaranteed by the Fourteenth Amendment of the U.S. Constitution. Well into the twentieth century, this decision was used to justify separate public facilities—including restrooms, water fountains, and even schools and hospitals—for blacks and whites.

In the mid-1950s, state support for segregation of the races and discrimination against African Americans began to be challenged. For example, Supreme Court decisions in 1954 and 1955 found that segregation in the public schools and other publicly financed locations was unconstitutional. At the same time, whites and blacks alike were calling for an end

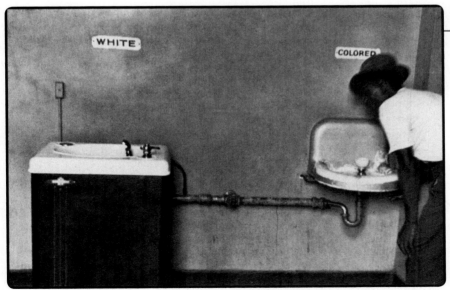

Segregated water fountains in North Carolina (1950)

© Elliott Erwitt/Magnum

to racial discrimination. Their actions took the form of marches, boycotts, and sit-ins (organized nonviolent protests whose participants refused to move from a public area). Many whites, however, particularly in the South, strongly resisted any sudden changes in race relations.

King's demonstrations in Birmingham, Alabama, took place within this larger social and political context. His campaign was a continuation of the push for equal rights that had been gaining momentum in the United States for decades. King, along with the Southern Christian Leadership Conference, had dispatched hundreds of people to Birmingham to engage in nonviolent demonstrations against those who were determined to keep African Americans from gaining their full rights as citizens.

Considering the Means of Persuasion: *Logos, Pathos, Ethos*

In the introduction to this book, you learned how writers of argument use three **means of persuasion**—*logos, pathos,* and *ethos*—to appeal to readers. You also saw how the **rhetorical triangle** represents the way these three appeals come into play within an argument. (See p. 19 for more information about the rhetorical triangle.) Of course, the degree to which a writer uses each of these appeals depends on the rhetorical situation. Moreover, a single argument can use more than one appeal—for example, an important research source would involve both the logic of the argument (*logos*) and the credibility of the writer (*ethos*). In "Letter from Birmingham Jail," King uses all three appeals.

The Appeal to Reason (Logos)

In "Letter from Birmingham Jail," King attempts to demonstrate the logic of his position. In paragraph 15, for example, he says that there are two types of laws—just and unjust. He then points out that he has both a legal and a moral responsibility to "disobey unjust laws." In paragraph 16, King supports his position with references to various philosophers and theologians—for example, St. Thomas Aquinas, Martin Buber, and Paul Tillich. He also develops the logical argument that even though all Americans should obey the law, they are responsible to a higher moral authority—God.

The Appeal to the Emotions (Pathos)

Throughout "Letter from Birmingham Jail," King attempts to create sympathy for his cause. In paragraph 14, for example, he catalogs the injustices of life in the United States for African Americans. He makes a particularly emotional appeal by quoting a hypothetical five-year-old boy who might ask, "Daddy, why do white people treat colored people so mean?" In addition, he includes vivid images of racial injustice to provoke anger against those who deny African Americans equal rights. In this way, King creates sympathy (and possibly empathy) in readers.

The Appeal to Authority (Ethos)

To be persuasive, King has to establish his credibility. In paragraph 2, for example, he reminds readers that he is the president of the Southern Christian Leadership Conference, "an organization operating in every southern state." In paragraph 3, he compares himself to the apostle Paul, who carried the gospel "to the far corners of the Greco-Roman world."

In addition, King attempts to show readers that what he is doing is well within the mainstream of American political and social thought. By alluding to Thomas Jefferson, Henry David Thoreau, and the 1954 U.S. Supreme Court decision that outlawed segregation in public schools, he tries to demonstrate that he is not the wild-eyed radical that some believe him to be. Thus, King establishes himself in both secular and religious terms as a leader who has the stature and the authority to present his case.

Finally, King repeatedly uses the words "we" and "us" to establish a connection to his readers. By doing so, he conveys the impression that like him, readers are part of the struggle to achieve social justice for African Americans.

Considering the Writer's Rhetorical Strategies

Writers use various **rhetorical strategies** to present their ideas and opinions. Here are a few of the elements that you should examine when analyzing and evaluating an argument.

Thesis

The **thesis**—the main idea or claim that the argument supports—is of primary importance in every argument. When you analyze an argument, you should always ask, "What is the essay's thesis, and why does the writer state it as he or she does?" You should also consider at what point in the argument the thesis is stated and what the effect of this placement is.

In "Letter from Birmingham Jail," Martin Luther King Jr. begins by telling readers that he is "confined here in the Birmingham city jail" and that he is writing his letter to answer clergymen who have called his demonstrations "unwise and untimely." King clearly (and unapologetically) states his thesis ("But more basically, I am in Birmingham because injustice is here") at the beginning of the third paragraph, right after he explains his purpose, so that readers will have no doubt what his position is as they read the rest of his argument.

Organization

The **organization** of an argument—how a writer arranges ideas—is also important. For example, after stating his thesis, King tells readers why he is in Birmingham and what he hopes to accomplish: he wants unjust laws to be abolished and the 1954 Supreme Court ruling to be enforced. King then **refutes**—disproves or calls into question—the specific charges that were leveled at him by the white clergymen who want him to stop his protests.

The structure of "Letter from Birmingham Jail" enables King to make his points clearly, logically, and convincingly:

- King begins his argument by addressing the charge that his actions are untimely. If anything, says King, his actions are not timely enough: after all, African Americans have waited more than 340 years for their "constitutional and God-given rights" (14).

- He then addresses the issue of his willingness to break laws and makes the distinction between just and unjust laws.

- After chiding white moderates for not supporting his cause, he addresses their claim that he is extreme. According to King, this charge is false: if he had not embraced a philosophy of nonviolent protest, the streets of the South would "be flowing with blood" (29).

- King then makes the point that the contemporary church must recapture the "sacrificial spirit of the early church" (42). He does this by linking his struggle for freedom with the "sacred heritage of our nation and the eternal will of God" (44).

- King ends his argument by asserting both his humility and his unity with the white clergy.

Evidence

To convince an audience, a writer must support the thesis with **evidence**—facts, observations, expert opinion, and so on. King presents a great deal of evidence to support his arguments. For instance, he uses numerous examples (both historical and personal) as well as many references to a wide range of philosophers, political thinkers, and theologians (such as Jesus, St. Paul, St. Augustine, Amos, Martin Luther, Martin Buber, and Abraham Lincoln). According to King, these individuals, who were once considered "extremists," were not afraid of "making waves" when the need arose. Now, however, they are well within the mainstream of social, political, and religious thought. King also presents reasons, facts, and quotations to support his points.

Stylistic Techniques

Writers also use stylistic techniques to make their arguments more memorable and more convincing. For example, in "Letter from Birmingham Jail," King uses figurative devices such as *similes*, *metaphors*, and *allusions* to enhance his argument.

Simile A **simile** is a figure of speech that compares two unlike things using the word *like* or *as*.

> Like a boil that can never be cured so long as it is covered up but must be opened with all its ugliness to the natural medicines of air and light, injustice must be exposed, . . . before it can be cured. (24)

> Isn't this like condemning a robbed man because his possession of money precipitated the evil act of robbery? (25)

Metaphor A **metaphor** is a comparison in which two dissimilar things are compared without the word *like* or *as*. A metaphor suggests that two things that are very different share a quality.

> Frankly, I have yet to engage in a direct-action campaign that was "well timed" in the view of those who have not suffered unduly from the disease of segregation. (13)

> [W]hen you see the vast majority of your twenty million Negro brothers smothering in an airtight cage of poverty . . . (14)

Allusion An **allusion** is a reference within a work to a person, literary or biblical text, or historical event in order to enlarge the context of the situation being written about. The writer expects readers to recognize the allusion and to make the connection to the text they are reading.

> I would agree with St. Augustine that "an unjust law is no law at all." (15)

> Of course, there is nothing new about this kind of civil disobedience. It was evidenced sublimely in the refusal of Shadrach, Meshach, and Abednego to obey the laws of Nebuchadnezzar, on the ground that a higher moral law was at stake. (21) [King expects his audience of clergymen to recognize this reference to the Book of Daniel in the Old Testament.]

In addition to those figurative devices, King uses stylistic techniques such as *parallelism*, *repetition*, and *rhetorical questions* to further his argument.

Parallelism **Parallelism**, the use of similar grammatical structures to emphasize related ideas, makes a passage easier to follow.

> In any nonviolent campaign there are four basic steps: collection of the facts to determine whether injustices exist; negotiation; self-purification; and direct action. (6)

> Shallow understanding from people of good will is more frustrating than absolute misunderstanding from people of ill will. Lukewarm acceptance is much more bewildering than outright rejection. (23)

> I wish you had commended the Negro sit-inners and demonstrators of Birmingham for their sublime courage, their willingness to suffer, and their amazing discipline in the midst of great provocation. (47)

Repetition Intentional **repetition** involves repeating a word or phrase for emphasis, clarity, or emotional impact.

> "Are you able to accept blows without retaliating?" "Are you able to endure the ordeal of jail?" (8)

> If I have said anything in this letter that overstates the truth and indicates an unreasonable impatience, I beg you to forgive me. If I have said anything that understates the truth and indicates my having patience that allows me to settle for anything less than brotherhood, I beg God to forgive me. (49)

Rhetorical questions A **rhetorical question** is a question that is asked to encourage readers to reflect on an issue, not to elicit a reply.

> One may well ask: "How can you advocate breaking some laws and obeying others?" (15)

> Will we be extremists for hate or for love? (31)

Assessing the Argument

No rhetorical analysis of an argument would be complete without an assessment of its **effectiveness**—whether the rhetorical strategies the writer uses create a clear and persuasive argument or whether they fall short. When you write a rhetorical analysis, you can begin with an assessment of the argument as a whole and go on to support it, or you can begin with a discussion of the various rhetorical strategies that the writer uses and then end with your assessment of the argument.

After analyzing "Letter from Birmingham Jail," you could reasonably conclude that King has written a highly effective argument that is likely to convince his readers that his presence in Birmingham is both justified and necessary. Using *logos*, *pathos*, and *ethos*, he constructs a multifaceted argument that is calculated to appeal to the various segments of his audience—Southern clergymen, white moderates, and a cross section of Americans. In addition, King uses similes, metaphors, and allusions to enrich his argument and to make it more memorable, and he uses parallelism, repetition, and rhetorical questions to emphasize ideas and to reinforce his points. Because it is so clear and powerful, King's argument—in particular, the distinction between just and unjust laws—addresses not only the injustices that were present in 1963 when it was written but also the injustices and inequalities that exist today. In this sense, King has written an argument that has broad significance beyond the audiences for which it was originally intended.

CHECKLIST

Preparing to Write a Rhetorical Analysis

As you read, ask the following questions:

- ☐ Who is the writer? Is there anything in the writer's background that might influence what is (or is not) included in the argument?

- ☐ What is the writer's purpose? What does the writer hope to achieve?

- ☐ What question has the writer decided to address? How broad is the question?

- ☐ What situation created the need for the argument?

- ☐ At what points in the argument does the writer appeal to logic? To the emotions? How does the writer try to establish his or her credibility?

- ☐ What is the argument's thesis? Where is it stated? Why?

- ☐ How does the writer organize the argument? How effective is this arrangement of ideas?

- ☐ What evidence does the writer use to support the argument? Does the writer use enough evidence?

- ☐ Does the writer use similes, metaphors, and allusions?

- ☐ Does the writer use parallelism, repetition, and rhetorical questions?

- ☐ Given your analysis, what is your overall assessment of the argument?

Sample Rhetorical Analysis

In preparation for a research paper, Deniz Bilgutay, a student in a writing class, read the following essay, "Terror's Purse Strings" by Dana Thomas, which makes an argument against buying counterfeit designer goods. Deniz then wrote the rhetorical analysis that appears on pages 119–121. (Deniz Bilgutay's research paper, "The High Cost of Cheap Counterfeit Goods," uses "Terror's Purse Strings" as a source. See Appendix B.)

This essay appeared in the *New York Times* on August 30, 2007.

TERROR'S PURSE STRINGS

DANA THOMAS

Luxury fashion designers are busily putting final touches on the handbags they 1
will present during the spring-summer women's wear shows, which begin next
week in New York City's Bryant Park. To understand the importance of the
handbag in fashion today consider this: According to consumer surveys conducted by Coach, the average American woman was buying two new handbags
a year in 2000; by 2004, it was more than four. And the average luxury bag
retails for 10 to 12 times its production cost.

"There is a kind of an obsession with bags," the designer Miuccia Prada 2
told me. "It's so easy to make money."

Counterfeiters agree. As soon as a handbag hits big, counterfeiters around 3
the globe churn out fake versions by the thousands. And they have no trouble
selling them. Shoppers descend on Canal Street in New York, Santee Alley in
Los Angeles, and flea markets and purse parties around the country to pick up
knockoffs for one-tenth the legitimate bag's retail cost, then pass them off as real.

"Judges, prosecutors, defense attorneys shop here," a private investigator 4
told me as we toured the counterfeit section of Santee Alley. "Affluent people
from Newport Beach." According to a study by the British law firm Davenport Lyons, two-thirds of British consumers are "proud to tell their family and
friends" that they bought fake luxury fashion items.

At least 11 percent of the world's clothing is fake, according to 2000 figures 5
from the Global Anti-Counterfeiting Group in Paris. Fashion is easy to copy:
counterfeiters buy the real items, take them apart, scan the pieces to make patterns, and produce almost-perfect fakes.

Most people think that buying an
imitation handbag or wallet is harmless,
a victimless crime. But the counterfeiting rackets are run by crime syndicates

> "At least 11 percent of the
> world's clothing is fake."   6

*An international criminal
police organization*

that also deal in narcotics, weapons, child prostitution, human trafficking, and
terrorism. Ronald K. Noble, the secretary general of Interpol,° told the House
of Representatives Committee on International Relations that profits from the
sale of counterfeit goods have gone to groups associated with Hezbollah, the
Shiite terrorist group, paramilitary organizations in Northern Ireland, and
FARC, the Revolutionary Armed Forces of Colombia.

Sales of counterfeit T-shirts may have helped finance the 1993 World 7
Trade Center bombing, according to the International AntiCounterfeiting
Coalition. "Profits from counterfeiting are one of the three main sources of
income supporting international terrorism," said Magnus Ranstorp, a terrorism expert at the University of St. Andrews, in Scotland.

Most fakes today are produced in China, a good many of them by chil- 8
dren. Children are sometimes sold or sent off by their families to work in

clandestine factories that produce counterfeit luxury goods. Many in the West consider this an urban myth. But I have seen it myself.

On a warm winter afternoon in Guangzhou, I accompanied Chinese 9 police officers on a factory raid in a decrepit tenement. Inside, we found two dozen children, ages 8 to 13, gluing and sewing together fake luxury-brand handbags. The police confiscated everything, arrested the owner, and sent the children out. Some punched their timecards, hoping to still get paid. (The average Chinese factory worker earns about $120 a month; the counterfeit factory worker earns half that or less.) As we made our way back to the police vans, the children threw bottles and cans at us. They were now jobless and, because the factory owner housed them, homeless. It was *Oliver Twist* in the 21st century.

What can we do to stop this? Much like the war on drugs, the effort to 10 protect luxury brands must go after the source: the counterfeit manufacturers. The company that took me on the Chinese raid is one of the only luxury-goods makers that works directly with Chinese authorities to shut down factories, and it has one of the lowest rates of counterfeiting.

Luxury brands also need to teach consumers that the traffic in fake goods 11 has many victims. But most companies refuse to speak publicly about counterfeiting—some won't even authenticate questionable items for concerned customers—believing, like Victorians,° that acknowledging despicable actions tarnishes their sterling reputations.

The people who lived during the reign of Victoria (1819–1901), queen of Great Britain and Ireland, who are often associated with prudish behavior

So it comes down to us. If we stop knowingly buying fakes, the supply 12 chain will dry up and counterfeiters will go out of business. The crime syndicates will have far less money to finance their illicit activities and their terrorist plots. And the children? They can go home.

A POWERFUL CALL TO ACTION

DENIZ BILGUTAY

In her *New York Times* essay, "Terror's Purse Strings," writer Dana   1   Context
Thomas uses the opening of New York's fashion shows as an opportunity
to expose a darker side of fashion—the impact of imitation designer   Topic
goods. Thomas explains to her readers why buying counterfeit luxury
items, like fake handbags, is a serious problem. Her first goal is to raise   Analysis of writer's
awareness of the dangerous ties between counterfeiters who sell fake   purpose
luxury merchandise and international criminal organizations that support
terrorism and child labor. Her second goal is to explain how people can
be a part of the solution by refusing to buy the counterfeit goods that   Thesis statement:
finance these criminal activities. By establishing her credibility, building   Assessment of essay

her case slowly, and appealing to both logic and emotions, Thomas succeeds in writing an interesting and informative argument.

Analysis of writer's audience

For Thomas's argument to work, she has to earn her readers' trust. 2 She does so first by anticipating a sympathetic, well-intentioned, educated audience and then by establishing her own credibility. To avoid sounding accusatory, Thomas assumes that her readers are unaware of the problem posed by counterfeit goods. She demonstrates this by presenting basic factual information and by acknowledging what "most people think" or what "many in the West consider": that buying counterfeit goods is harmless. She also acknowledges her readers' high level of education by drawing comparisons with history and literature—specifically, the Victorians and *Oliver Twist*. To further earn the audience's trust, she uses her knowledge and position to gain credibility. As the Paris correspondent for *Newsweek* and as the author of a book on luxury goods, Thomas has credibility. Showing her familiarity with the world of fashion by referring to a conversation with renowned designer Miuccia Prada, she further establishes this credibility. Later in the article, she shares her experience of witnessing the abuse that accompanies the production of fake designer handbags. This anecdote allows her to say, "I've seen it myself," confirming her knowledge not just of the fashion world but also of the world of counterfeiting. Despite her authority, she does not distance herself from readers. In fact, she goes out of her way to identify with them, using informal style and first person, noting "it comes down to us" and asking what "we" can do.

Writer's use of similes, metaphors, allusions

Writer's use of ethos

Analysis of the writer

Analysis of essay's organization

Writer's use of logos

In Thomas's argument, both the organization and the use of 3 evidence are effective. Thomas begins her article with statements that are easy to accept, and as she proceeds, she addresses more serious issues. In the first paragraph, she simply asks readers to "understand the importance of the handbag in fashion today." She demonstrates the wide-ranging influence and appeal of counterfeit designer goods, pointing out that "at least 11 percent of the world's clothing is fake." Thomas then makes the point that the act of purchasing these seemingly frivolous goods can actually have serious consequences. For example, crime syndicates and possibly even terrorist organizations actually run "the counterfeiting rackets" that produce these popular items. To support this point, she relies on two kinds of evidence—quotations from terrorism experts (specifically, the leader of a respected international police organization as well as a scholar in the field) and her own

Writer's use of evidence

personal experience at a Chinese factory. Both kinds of evidence appeal to our emotions. Discussions of terrorism, especially those that recall the terrorist attacks on the United States, create fear. Descriptions of child labor in China encourage readers to feel sympathy.

Writer's use of pathos

Thomas waits until the end of her argument to present her thesis 4 because she assumes that her readers know little about the problem she is discussing. The one flaw in her argument is her failure to provide the evidence needed to establish connections between some causes and their effects. For example in paragraph 7, Thomas says that the sale of counterfeit T-shirts "may have helped finance the 1993 World Trade Center bombing." By using the word *may*, she qualifies her claim and weakens her argument. The same is true when Thomas says that profits from the sale of counterfeit goods "have gone to groups associated with Hezbollah, the Shiite terrorist group." Readers are left to wonder what specific groups are "associated with Hezbollah" and whether these groups are in fact terrorist organizations. Without this information, her assertion remains unsupported. In spite of these shortcomings, Thomas's argument is clear and well organized. More definite links between causes and effects, however, would have made it more convincing than it is.

Analysis of the essay's weakness

⊙ EXERCISE 4.1 WRITING A RHETORICAL ANALYSIS

Read the following essay, "Sweatshop Oppression," by Rajeev Ravisankar. Then, write a one-paragraph rhetorical analysis of the essay. Follow the template on page 123, filling in the blanks to create your analysis.

This opinion essay was published in the *Lantern*, the student newspaper of the Ohio State University, on April 19, 2006.

SWEATSHOP OPPRESSION
RAJEEV RAVISANKAR

Being the "poor" college students that we all are, many of us undoubtedly place 1 an emphasis on finding the lowest prices. Some take this to the extreme and camp out in front of a massive retail store in the wee hours of the morning on Black Friday,° waiting for the opportunity to buy as much as we can for as little as possible.

The Friday after Thanksgiving, traditionally the biggest shopping day of the year

A work environment with long hours, low wages, and difficult or dangerous conditions

What often gets lost in this rampant, low-cost driven consumerism is the 2 high human cost it takes to achieve lower and lower prices. Specifically, this means the extensive use of sweatshop labor.

Many of us are familiar with the term sweatshop,° but have difficulty really 3 understanding how abhorrent the hours, wages, and conditions are. Many of these workers are forced to work 70–80 hours per week making pennies per hour. Workers are discouraged or intimidated from forming unions.

They must fulfill certain quotas for the day and stay extra hours (with no 4 pay) if these are not fulfilled. Some are forced to sit in front of a machine for hours as they are not permitted to take breaks unless the manager allows them to do so. Unsanitary bathrooms, poor ventilation, and extreme heat, upward of 90 degrees, are also prevalent. Child labor is utilized in some factories as well.

Facing mounting pressure from labor rights activists, trade unions, student 5 protests, and human-rights groups, companies claimed that they would make improvements. Many of the aforementioned conditions, however, persist. In many cases, even a few pennies more could make a substantial difference in the lives of these workers. Of course, multinational corporations are not interested in giving charity; they are interested in doing anything to increase profits. Also, many consumers in the West refuse to pay a little bit more even if it would improve the lives of sweatshop workers.

> "... Corporations are interested in doing anything to increase profits."

Free-market economic fundamentalists have argued that claims made by 6 those who oppose sweatshops actually have a negative impact on the plight of the poor in the developing world. They suggest that by criticizing labor and human-rights conditions, anti-sweatshop activists have forced companies to pull out of some locations, resulting in workers losing their jobs. To shift the blame in this manner is to neglect a simple fact: Companies, not the anti-sweatshop protestors, make the decision to shift to locations where they can find cheaper labor and weaker labor restrictions.

Simply put, the onus should always be on companies such as Nike, Reebok, 7 Adidas, Champion, Gap, Wal-Mart, etc. They are to blame for perpetuating a system of exploitation which seeks to get as much out of each worker for the least possible price.

By continuing to strive for lower wages and lower input costs, they are 8 taking part in a phenomenon which has been described as "the race to the bottom." The continual decline of wages and working conditions will be accompanied by a lower standard of living. This hardly seems like the best way to bring the developing world out of the pits of poverty.

So what can we do about it? Currently, the total disregard for human 9 well-being through sweatshop oppression is being addressed by a number of organizations, including University Students against Sweatshops. USAS seeks to make universities source their apparel in factories that respect workers' rights, especially the right to freely form unions.

According to an article in *The Nation*, universities purchase nearly 10 "$3 billion in T-shirts, sweatshirts, caps, sneakers and sports uniforms adorned with their institutions' names and logos." Because brands do not want to risk losing this money, it puts pressure on them to provide living wages and reasonable conditions for workers. Campaigns such as this are necessary if we are to stop the long race to the bottom.

TEMPLATE FOR WRITING A RHETORICAL ANALYSIS

Ravisankar begins his essay by _____
_____
_____. The problem he identifies is _____
_____
_____. Ravisankar assumes his readers are _____
_____
_____. His purpose in this essay is to _____
_____.

In order to accomplish this purpose, he appeals mainly to _____
_____
_____. He also appeals to _____
_____.

In his essay, Ravisankar addresses the main argument against his thesis, the idea that _____
_____
_____.

He refutes this argument by saying _____
_____
_____.

Finally, he concludes by making the point that _____
_____.

Overall, the argument Ravisankar makes [is/is not] effective because _____
_____
_____

⊘ EXERCISE 4.2 WRITING A RHETORICAL ANALYSIS

Read the following essay, "Sweatshops Are Good," by Jerome Sieger, a student at American University. Then, write a rhetorical analysis of Sieger's essay. Be sure to consider the rhetorical situation, the means of persuasion, and the writer's rhetorical strategies. End your rhetorical analysis with an assessment of the strengths and weaknesses of Sieger's argument.

This opinion column was published in *The Eagle*, American University's student newspaper, on February 15, 2017.

SWEATSHOPS ARE GOOD

JEROME SIEGER

If you can, take off one of your shoes. Go ahead; I'll wait. Check to see where it was made. Chances are your shoes, like most clothing we wear, were manufactured in a developing country in Asia or Latin America. Mine, for instance, were made in Vietnam. We all know that our clothes were made in factories commonly referred to as "sweatshops." If you're anything like most people, the thought of buying the products of such sweatshop labor makes you exceedingly guilty. Don't be. When put into their proper context, sweatshops are necessary and beneficial to workers. To quote the renowned Keynesian Jeffrey Sachs, "my concern is not that there are too many sweatshops, but that there are too few."

The ultimate problem for opponents of sweatshops is a failure of imagination. They simply lack empathy—the ability to imagine someone else's perspective. I would not want to work in a sweatshop, and if you have the privilege of attending a university in America, neither would you. But not everyone is a middle-class American. Our country is rich enough to afford such a high minimum wage and strict labor standards. But the truth is, for hundreds of millions of people, sweatshops offer the best hope to escape crippling poverty.

I will present data to back up this point, but just the story of how much effort people put in to work in sweatshops should suffice to prove it. Some 150 million people in China alone have left their homes and moved across the country to get factory jobs. One simply does not uproot their life and leave their home to get a job they don't really want. When factory jobs open up, thousands of people wait in line to apply. The fact that sweatshop workers choose their jobs, and that they put in so much effort to get them, must mean something. Simply put, as bad as sweatshops are, most alternatives are much worse.

And the numbers bear this out. This 2006 study in the *Journal of Labor Research* analyzed sweatshops across Asia and Latin America and found that in 90 percent of countries analyzed, working ten-hour days in sweatshops lifts the worker's income above the national average. In half of those countries, income rose to three times the national average. And this 2012 study from researchers at Duke University found that sweatshop workers in El Salvador believed that their factory jobs represented an improvement over their previous jobs in areas such as working conditions, job stability, location, benefits, and schedule.

The research is pretty clear that sweatshops are significantly better than alter- 5
natives, but something is lost when you reduce the difference to numbers alone.
It helps us empathize with sweatshop workers if we imagine the kinds of jobs they
go to when factory work is not an option. Before they work in sweatshops, most
factory workers in developing countries work in subsistence agriculture, which is
one of the three most dangerous industries in the world according to the International Labor Organization—rivaled only by construction and mining. And if
they're not in subsistence agriculture, they might be in commercial agriculture,
often as the slave of a chocolate company, for instance. Furthermore, in the past,
when sweatshops have shut down due to boycotts, many workers have "turned to
street hustling, stone crushing, and prostitution." When people bash sweatshops,
they are unknowingly advocating that poor workers take up these jobs instead.

And sweatshops not only reduce
poverty, but they also provide empow- 6
erment for women. Research has shown
that work in sweatshops delays marriage
and pregnancy for women and girls, and also increases their school enrollment. Poor women in developing countries are among the most vulnerable
people on the planet. Support of sweatshops is a feminist position.

> "Not everyone is a
> middle-class American."

So, what's the endgame here? Surely, even if sweatshop labor is better 7
than its wretched alternatives, we would ultimately want workers in developing countries to move to jobs even better than that. We would want to see an
eventual end to long hours and child labor. These wants are legitimate, and the
path to achieving them is through the arduous process of development. An
economy can't just jump from Bangladesh to Belgium over night, no matter
how much you protest GAP. The truth of the matter is that factory labor is
a necessary step in economic development. The notorious super liberal and
Nobel laureate economist Paul Krugman explains:

> "[T]he growth of manufacturing . . . has a ripple effect throughout the
> economy. The pressure on the land becomes less intense, so rural wages
> rise; the pool of unemployed urban dwellers always anxious for work
> shrinks, so factories start to compete with each other for workers, and
> urban wages also begin to rise."

The past success stories of sweatshops illustrate this principle and provide 8
a model for the rising economies of today. For instance, Hong Kong, South
Korea, Taiwan, and Singapore used sweatshop labor to raise incomes from 10
percent of American levels to 40 percent in just one generation.

Sweatshops are used as a stepping stone to open up new possibilities for 9
workers. Once these new jobs are made available, sweatshop work is no longer
preferable, and conditions inevitably improve. We cannot ascend a ladder by
knocking out the next few rungs.

For all these reasons, boycotting sweatshops is perhaps the worst thing 10
rich, American consumers can do to the world's poor. One more time, look at
your shoe. If you bought it, or anything else, from a sweatshop in a developing
country, pat yourself on the back. You made the world a better place.

5

Understanding Logic and Recognizing Logical Fallacies

How Free Should Free Speech Be?

Ask almost anyone what makes a society free and one of the answers will be free speech. The free expression of ideas is integral to freedom itself, and protecting that freedom is part of a democratic government's job.

But what happens when those ideas are offensive, or even dangerous? If free speech has limits, is it still free? When we consider the question abstractly, it's very easy to say no. After all, there is no shortage of historical evidence linking censorship with tyranny. When we think of limiting free speech, we think of totalitarian regimes, like Nazi Germany. On the other hand, what if the people arguing for the right to be heard are Nazis themselves? In places like Israel and France, where the legacy of Nazi Germany is still all too real, there are some things you simply cannot say. Anti-Semitic language is considered "hate speech," and those who perpetuate it face stiff fines, if not imprisonment. In the United States, speech—even speech that many would consider "hate speech"—is explicitly protected by the First Amendment of the Constitution. Nonetheless, many colleges and universities have sought to combat discrimination and harassment by instituting speech codes that prohibit speech that they deem inappropriate.

On American college campuses, freedom of speech has traditionally been considered fundamental to a liberal education. Indeed, encountering ideas that make you feel uncomfortable is a necessary part of a college education. But the question of free speech is easy to answer when it's theoretical: when the issue is made tangible by racist language or by a discussion of a traumatic experience, it becomes much more difficult to navigate. Should minorities be forced to listen to racists spew hate? Should a rape survivor have to sit through a discussion of rape in American literature? If you penalize a person for saying something hateful, will other subjects soon become off-limits for discussion?

Later in this chapter, you will be asked to think more about this issue. You will be given several sources to consider and asked to write a logical argument that takes a position on how free free speech should be.

The word *logic* comes from the Greek word *logos*, roughly translated as "word," "thought," "principle," or "reason." **Logic** is concerned with the principles of correct reasoning. By studying logic, you learn the rules that determine the validity of arguments. In other words, logic enables you to tell whether a conclusion correctly follows from a set of statements or assumptions.

Why should you study logic? One answer is that logic enables you to make valid points and draw sound conclusions. An understanding of logic also enables you to evaluate the arguments of others. When you understand the basic principles of logic, you know how to tell the difference between a strong argument and a weak argument—between one that is well reasoned and one that is not. This ability can help you cut through the tangle of jumbled thought that characterizes many of the arguments you encounter daily—on television, radio, and the internet; in the press; and from friends. Finally, logic enables you to communicate clearly and forcefully. Understanding the characteristics of good arguments helps you to present your own ideas in a coherent and even compelling way.

Specific rules determine the criteria you use to develop (and to evaluate) arguments logically. For this reason, you should become familiar with the basic principles of *deductive* and *inductive reasoning*—two important ways information is organized in argumentative essays. (Keep in mind that a single argumentative essay might contain both deductive reasoning and inductive reasoning. For the sake of clarity, however, we will discuss them separately.)

Student in a study group making a point

Johner Images/Getty Images

What Is Deductive Reasoning?

Most of us use deductive reasoning every day—at home, in school, on the job, and in our communities—usually without even realizing it.

Deductive reasoning begins with **premises**—statements or assumptions on which an argument is based or from which conclusions are drawn. Deductive reasoning moves from general statements, or premises, to specific conclusions. The process of deduction has traditionally been illustrated with a **syllogism**, which consists of a *major premise*, a *minor premise*, and a *conclusion*:

MAJOR PREMISE	All Americans are guaranteed freedom of speech by the Constitution.
MINOR PREMISE	Sarah is an American.
CONCLUSION	Therefore, Sarah is guaranteed freedom of speech.

Thomas Jefferson

A syllogism begins with a **major premise**—a general statement that relates two terms. It then moves to a **minor premise**—an example of the statement that was made in the major premise. If these two premises are linked correctly, a **conclusion** that is supported by the two premises logically follows. (Notice that the conclusion in the syllogism above contains no terms that do not appear in the major and minor premises.) The strength of deductive reasoning is that if readers accept the major and minor premises, the conclusion must necessarily follow.

Thomas Jefferson used deductive reasoning in the Declaration of Independence (see p. 732). When, in 1776, the Continental Congress asked him to draft this document, Jefferson knew that he had to write a powerful argument that would convince the world that the American colonies were justified in breaking away from England. He knew how compelling a deductive argument could be, and so he organized the Declaration of Independence to reflect the traditional structure of deductive logic. It contains a major premise, a minor premise (supported by evidence), and a conclusion. Expressed as a syllogism, here is the argument that Jefferson used:

MAJOR PREMISE	When a government oppresses people, the people have a right to rebel against that government.
MINOR PREMISE	The government of England oppresses the American people.
CONCLUSION	Therefore, the American people have the right to rebel against the government of England.

In practice, deductive arguments are more complicated than the simple three-part syllogism suggests. Still, it is important to understand the basic structure of a syllogism because a syllogism enables you to map out your argument, to test it, and to see if it makes sense.

Constructing Sound Syllogisms

A syllogism is **valid** when its conclusion follows logically from its premises. A syllogism is **true** when the premises are consistent with the facts. To be **sound**, a syllogism must be *both* valid and true.

Consider the following valid syllogism:

MAJOR PREMISE	All state universities must accommodate disabled students.
MINOR PREMISE	UCLA is a state university.
CONCLUSION	Therefore, UCLA must accommodate disabled students.

In the preceding valid syllogism, both the major premise and the minor premise are factual statements. If both these premises are true, then the conclusion must also be true. Because the syllogism is both valid and true, it is also sound.

However, a syllogism can be valid without being true. For example, look at the following syllogism:

MAJOR PREMISE	All recipients of support services are wealthy.
MINOR PREMISE	Dillon is a recipient of support services.
CONCLUSION	Therefore, Dillon is wealthy.

As illogical as it may seem, this syllogism is valid: its conclusion follows logically from its premises. The major premise states that *recipients of support services*—all such *recipients*—are wealthy. However, this premise is clearly false: some recipients of support services may be wealthy, but more are probably not. For this reason, even though the syllogism is valid, it is not true.

Keep in mind that validity is a test of an argument's structure, not of its soundness. Even if a syllogism's major and minor premises are true, its conclusion may not necessarily be valid.

Consider the following examples of invalid syllogisms.

Syllogism with an Illogical Middle Term

A syllogism with an illogical middle term cannot be valid. The **middle term** of a syllogism is the term that occurs in both the major and minor premises but not in the conclusion. (It links the major term and the minor term together in the syllogism.) A middle term of a valid syllogism must refer to *all* members of the designated class or group—for example, *all* dogs, *all* people, *all* men, or *all* women.

Consider the following invalid syllogism:

MAJOR PREMISE	All dogs are mammals.
MINOR PREMISE	Some mammals are porpoises.
CONCLUSION	Therefore, some porpoises are dogs.

Even though the statements in the major and minor premises are true, the syllogism is not valid. *Mammals* is the middle term because it appears in both the major and minor premises. However, because the middle term *mammal* does not refer to *all mammals*, it cannot logically lead to a valid conclusion.

In the syllogism that follows, the middle term *does* refer to all members of the designated group, so the syllogism is valid:

MAJOR PREMISE	All dogs are mammals.
MINOR PREMISE	Ralph is a dog.
CONCLUSION	Therefore, Ralph is a mammal.

Syllogism with a Key Term Whose Meaning Shifts

A syllogism that contains a key term whose meaning shifts cannot be valid. For this reason, the meaning of a key term must remain consistent throughout the syllogism.

Consider the following invalid syllogism:

MAJOR PREMISE	Only man is capable of analytical reasoning.
MINOR PREMISE	Anna is not a man.
CONCLUSION	Therefore, Anna is not capable of analytical reasoning.

In the major premise, *man* refers to mankind—that is, to all human beings. In the minor premise, however, *man* refers to males. In the following valid syllogism, the key terms remain consistent:

MAJOR PREMISE	All educated human beings are capable of analytical reasoning.
MINOR PREMISE	Anna is an educated human being.
CONCLUSION	Therefore, Anna is capable of analytical reasoning.

Syllogism with Negative Premise

If *either* premise in a syllogism is negative, then the conclusion must also be negative.

The following syllogism is not valid:

MAJOR PREMISE	Only senators can vote on legislation.
MINOR PREMISE	No students are senators.
CONCLUSION	Therefore, students can vote on legislation.

Because one of the premises of the syllogism above is negative ("No students are senators"), the only possible valid conclusion must also be negative ("Therefore, no students can vote on legislation").

If *both* premises are negative, however, the syllogism cannot have a valid conclusion:

MAJOR PREMISE	Disabled students may not be denied special help.
MINOR PREMISE	Jen is not a disabled student.
CONCLUSION	Therefore, Jen may not be denied special help.

In the preceding syllogism, both premises are negative. For this reason, the syllogism cannot have a valid conclusion. (How can Jen deserve special help if she is not a disabled student?) To have a valid conclusion, this syllogism must have only one negative premise:

MAJOR PREMISE	Disabled students may not be denied special help.
MINOR PREMISE	Jen is a disabled student.
CONCLUSION	Therefore, Jen may not be denied special help.

Recognizing Enthymemes

An **enthymeme** is a syllogism with one or two parts of its argument—usually, the major premise—missing. In everyday life, we often leave out parts of arguments—most of the time because we think they are so obvious (or clearly implied) that they don't need to be stated. We assume that the people hearing or reading the arguments will easily be able to fill in the missing parts.

Many enthymemes are presented as a reason plus a conclusion. Consider the following enthymeme:

Enrique has lied, so he cannot be trusted.

In the preceding statement, the minor premise (the reason) and the conclusion are stated, but the major premise is only implied. Once the missing term has been supplied, the logical structure of the enthymeme becomes clear:

MAJOR PREMISE	People who lie cannot be trusted.
MINOR PREMISE	Enrique has lied.
CONCLUSION	Therefore, Enrique cannot be trusted.

It is important to identify enthymemes in arguments you read because some writers, knowing that readers often accept enthymemes uncritically, use them intentionally to unfairly influence readers.

Consider this enthymeme:

Because Liz receives a tuition grant, she should work.

Although some readers might challenge this statement, others will accept it uncritically. When you supply the missing premise, however, the underlying assumptions of the enthymeme become clear—and open to question:

MAJOR PREMISE   All students who receive tuition grants should work.

MINOR PREMISE   Liz receives a tuition grant.

CONCLUSION   Therefore, Liz should work.

Perhaps some people who receive tuition grants should work, but should everyone? What about those who are ill or who have disabilities? What about those who participate in varsity sports or have unpaid internships? The enthymeme oversimplifies the issue and should not be accepted at face value.

At first glance, the following enthymeme might seem to make sense:

North Korea is ruled by a dictator, so it should be invaded.

However, consider the same enthymeme with the missing term supplied:

MAJOR PREMISE   All countries governed by dictators should be invaded.

MINOR PREMISE   North Korea is a country governed by a dictator.

CONCLUSION   Therefore, North Korea should be invaded.

Once the missing major premise has been supplied, the flaws in the argument become clear. Should *all* nations governed by dictators be invaded? Who should do the invading? Who would make this decision? What would be the consequences of such a policy? As this enthymeme illustrates, if the major premise of a deductive argument is questionable, then the rest of the argument will also be flawed.

BUMPER-STICKER THINKING

Bumper stickers often take the form of enthymemes:

- Self-control beats birth control.
- Peace is patriotic.
- A woman's place is in the House . . . and in the Senate.
- Ban cruel traps.
- Evolution is a theory—kind of like gravity.

- I work and pay taxes so wealthy people don't have to.

- The Bible says it, I believe it, that settles it.

- No one needs a mink coat except a mink.

- Celebrate diversity.

Most often, bumper stickers state just the conclusion of an argument and omit both the major and minor premises. Careful readers, however, will supply the missing premises and thus determine whether the argument is sound.

Bumper stickers on a car. B Christopher/Alamy Stock Photo.

⊖ EXERCISE 5.1 CONSTRUCTING A SYLLOGISM

Read the following paragraph. Then, restate its main argument as a syllogism.

Drunk Driving Should Be Legalized

In ordering states to enforce tougher drunk driving standards by making it a crime to drive with a blood-alcohol concentration of .08 percent or higher, government has been permitted to criminalize the content of drivers' blood instead of their actions. The assumption that a driver who has been drinking automatically presents a danger to society even when no harm has been caused is a blatant violation of civil liberties. Government should not be concerned with the probability and propensity of a drinking driver to cause an accident; rather, laws should deal only with actions that damage person or property. Until they actually commit a crime, drunk drivers should be liberated from the force of the law. (From "Legalize Drunk Driving," by Llewellyn H. Rockwell Jr., WorldNetDaily.com)

⊖ EXERCISE 5.2 ANALYZING DEDUCTIVE LOGIC

Read the following paragraphs. Then, answer the questions that follow.

Animals Are Equal to Humans

According to the United Nations, a person may not be killed, exploited, cruelly treated, intimidated, or imprisoned for no good reason. Put another way, people should be able to live in peace, according to their own needs and preferences.

Who should have these rights? Do they apply to people of all races? Children? People who are brain damaged or senile? The declaration makes it clear that basic rights apply to everyone. To make a slave of someone who is intellectually handicapped or of a different race is no more justifiable than to make a slave of anyone else.

The reason why these rights apply to everyone is simple: regardless of our differences, we all experience a life with its mosaic of thoughts and feelings. This applies equally to the princess and the hobo, the brain surgeon and the dunce. Our value as individuals arises from this capacity to experience life, not because of any intelligence or usefulness to others. Every person has an inherent value, and deserves to be treated with respect in order to make the most of their unique life experience. (Excerpted from "Human and Animal Rights," by AnimalLiberation.org)

1. What unstated assumptions about the subject does the writer make? Does the writer expect readers to accept these assumptions? How can you tell?

2. What kind of supporting evidence does the writer provide?

3. What is the major premise of this argument?

4. Express the argument that is presented in these paragraphs as a syllogism.

5. Evaluate the syllogism you constructed. Is it true? Is it valid? Is it sound?

⊖ EXERCISE 5.3 JUDGING THE SOUNDNESS OF A DEDUCTIVE ARGUMENT

Read the following five arguments, and determine whether each is sound. (To help you evaluate the arguments, you may want to try arranging them as syllogisms.)

1. All humans are mortal. Ahmed is human. Therefore, Ahmed is mortal.

2. Perry should order eggs or oatmeal for breakfast. She won't order eggs, so she should order oatmeal.

3. The cafeteria does not serve meat loaf on Friday. Today is not Friday. Therefore, the cafeteria will not serve meat loaf.

4. All reptiles are cold-blooded. Geckos are reptiles. Therefore, geckos are cold-blooded.

5. All triangles have three equal sides. The figure on the board is a triangle. Therefore, it must have three equal sides.

❯ EXERCISE 5.4 ANALYZING ENTHYMEMES

Read the following ten enthymemes, which come from bumper stickers. Supply the missing premises, and then evaluate the logic of each argument.

1. If you love your pet, don't eat meat.

2. War is terrorism.

3. Real men don't ask for directions.

4. Immigration is the sincerest form of flattery.

5. I eat local because I can.

6. Vote nobody for president 2020.

7. I read banned books.

8. Love is the only solution.

9. It's a child, not a choice.

10. Buy American.

Writing Deductive Arguments

Deductive arguments begin with a general principle and reach a specific conclusion. They develop that principle with logical arguments that are supported by evidence—facts, observations, the opinions of experts, and so on. Keep in mind that no single structure is suitable for all deductive (or inductive) arguments. Different issues and different audiences will determine how you arrange your ideas.

In general, deductive essays can be structured in the following way:

INTRODUCTION	Presents an overview of the issue
	States the thesis
BODY	Presents evidence: point 1 in support of the thesis
	Presents evidence: point 2 in support of the thesis
	Presents evidence: point 3 in support of the thesis
	Refutes the arguments against the thesis
CONCLUSION	Brings argument to a close
	Concluding statement reinforces the thesis

⊙ EXERCISE 5.5 IDENTIFYING THE ELEMENTS OF A DEDUCTIVE ARGUMENT

The following student essay, "College Should Be for Everyone," includes all the elements of a deductive argument. The student who wrote this essay was responding to the question, "Should everyone be encouraged to go to college?" After you read the essay, answer the questions on pages 138–141, consulting the outline above if necessary.

COLLEGE SHOULD BE FOR EVERYONE

CRYSTAL SANCHEZ

Overview of issue

Until the middle of the twentieth century, college was largely for the rich. The G.I. Bill, which paid for the education of veterans returning from World War II, helped to change this situation. By 1956, nearly half of those who had served in World War II, almost 7.8 million people, had taken advantage of this benefit (U.S. Department of Veterans Affairs). Even today, however, college graduates are still a minority of the population. According to the U.S. Census Bureau, only 30 percent of Americans age twenty-five or older have a bachelor's degree. Although this situation is gradually improving, it is not good for the country.

Thesis statement

Why should college be just for the privileged few? Because a college education provides important benefits, such as increased wages for our citizens and a stronger democracy for our nation, every U.S. citizen should have the opportunity to attend college.

1

One reason everyone should have the opportunity to go to college   2   Evidence: Point 1
is that a college education gives people a chance to discover what they
are good at. It is hard for people to know if they are interested in statistics or public policy or marketing unless they have the chance to explore
these subjects. College—and only college—can give them this opportunity. Where else can a person be exposed to a large number of courses
taught by experts in a variety of disciplines? Such exposure can open
new areas of interest and lead to a much wider set of career options—
and thus to a better life (Stout). Without college, most people have limited options and never realize their true potential. Although life and work
experiences can teach a person a lot of things, the best education is the
broad kind that college offers.

Another reason everyone should have the opportunity to go to   3   Evidence: Point 2
college is that more and more jobs are being phased out or moved
overseas. Americans should go to college to develop the skills that they
will need to get the best jobs that will remain in the United States. Over
the last few decades, midlevel jobs have been steadily disappearing. If
this trend continues, the American workforce will be divided in two. One
part will consist of low-wage, low-skill service jobs, such as those in food
preparation and retail sales, and the other part will be high-skill, high-wage
jobs, such as those in management and professional fields like business
and engineering. According to a recent report, to compete in the future job
market, Americans will need the skills that colleges teach. Future workers
will need to be problem solvers who can think both critically and creatively
and who can adapt to new situations. They will also need a global awareness, knowledge of many cultures and disciplines, and the ability to communicate in different forms of media. To master these skills, Americans
have to be college educated ("Ten Skills for the Future Workforce").

Perhaps the best reason everyone should have the opportunity to   4   Evidence: Point 3
go to college is that education is an essential component of a democratic society. Those without the ability to understand and analyze news
reports are not capable of contributing to the social, political, and economic growth of the country. Democracy requires informed citizens who
will be able to analyze complicated issues in areas such as finance, education, and public health; weigh competing claims of those running for
public office; and assess the job performance of elected officials.

By providing students with the opportunity to study subjects such as history, philosophy, English, and political science, colleges and universities help them to acquire the critical-thinking skills that they will need to participate fully in American democracy.

Refutation of opposing arguments

Some people oppose the idea that everyone should have the opportunity to attend college. One objection is that educational resources are limited. Some say that if students enter colleges in great numbers they will overwhelm the higher-education system (Stout). This argument exaggerates the problem. As with any other product, if demand rises, supply will rise to meet that demand. In addition, with today's extensive distance-learning options and the availability of open educational resources—free, high-quality, digital materials—it will be possible to educate large numbers of students at a reasonable cost ("Open Educational Resources"). Another objection to encouraging everyone to attend college is that underprepared students will require so much help that they will take time and attention away from better students. This argument is actually a red herring.° Most schools already provide resources, such as tutoring and writing centers, for students who need them. With some additional funding, these schools could expand the services they already provide. This course of action will be expensive, but it is a lot less expensive than leaving millions of young people unprepared for jobs of the future.

An irrelevant side issue used as a diversion

A college education gave the returning veterans of World War II many opportunities and increased their value to the nation. Today, a college education could do the same for many citizens. This country has an obligation to offer all students access to an affordable and useful education. Not only will the students benefit personally but the nation will also. If we do not adequately prepare students for the future, then we will all suffer the consequences.

Concluding statement

Works Cited

"Open Educational Resources." *Center for American Progress*, 7 Feb. 2012, www.americanprogress.org/issues/labor/news/2012/02/07/11114/open-educational-resources/.

Stout, Chris. "Top Five Reasons Why You Should Choose to Go to College." *Ezine Articles*, 2008, ezinearticles.com/?Top-Five-Reasons-Why-You-Should-Choose-To-Go-To-College&id=384395.

"Ten Skills for the Future Workforce." *The Atlantic,* 22 June 2011, www
.theatlantic.com/education/archive/2011/06/ten-skills-for-future-work
/473484/.

United States Census Bureau. "Highest Educational Levels Reached
by Adults in the U.S. Since 1940." *US Census Bureau Newsroom*,
23 Feb. 2017, www.census.gov/press-releases/2017/cb17-51.html.

---, Department of Veterans Affairs. "Born of Controversy: The GI Bill of
Rights." *GI Bill History*, 20 Oct. 2008, www.va.gov/opa/publications
/celebrate/gi-bill.pdf.

Identifying the Elements of a Deductive Argument

1. Paraphrase this essay's thesis.

2. What arguments does the writer present as evidence to support her thesis? Which do you think is the strongest argument? Which is the weakest?

3. What opposing arguments does the writer address? What other opposing arguments could she have addressed?

4. What points does the conclusion emphasize? Do you think that any other points should be emphasized?

5. Construct a syllogism that expresses the essay's argument. Then, check your syllogism to make sure it is sound.

What Is Inductive Reasoning?

Inductive reasoning begins with specific observations (or evidence) and goes on to draw a general conclusion. You can see how induction works by looking at the following list of observations:

- Nearly 80 percent of ocean pollution comes from runoff.

- Runoff pollution can make ocean water unsafe for fish and people.

- In some areas, runoff pollution has forced beaches to be closed.

- Drinking water can be contaminated by runoff.

- More than one-third of shellfish growing in waters in the United States are contaminated by runoff.

- Each year, millions of dollars are spent to restore polluted areas.

- There is a causal relationship between agricultural runoff and water-borne organisms that damage fish.

After studying these observations, you can use inductive reasoning to reach the conclusion that runoff pollution (rainwater that becomes polluted after it comes in contact with earth-bound pollutants such as fertilizer, pet waste, sewage, and pesticides) is a problem that must be addressed.

Children learn about the world by using inductive reasoning. For example, very young children see that if they push a light switch up, the lights in a room go on. If they repeat this action over and over, they reach the conclusion that every time they push a switch, the lights will go on. Of course, this conclusion does not always follow. For example, the light-bulb may be burned out or the switch may be damaged. Even so, their conclusion usually holds true. Children also use induction to generalize about what is safe and what is dangerous. If every time they meet a dog, the encounter is pleasant, they begin to think that all dogs are friendly. If at some point, however, a dog snaps at them, they question the strength of their conclusion and modify their behavior accordingly.

Scientists also use induction. In 1620, Sir Francis Bacon first proposed the **scientific method**—a way of using induction to find answers to questions. When using the scientific method, a researcher proposes a hypothesis and then makes a series of observations to test this hypothesis. Based on these observations, the researcher arrives at a conclusion that confirms, modifies, or disproves the hypothesis.

Runoff pollution —

Andrew Winning/Reuters

REACHING INDUCTIVE CONCLUSIONS

Here are some of the ways you can use inductive reasoning to reach conclusions:

- **Particular to general:** This form of induction occurs when you reach a general conclusion based on particular pieces of evidence. For example, suppose you walk into a bathroom and see that the mirrors are fogged. You also notice that the bathtub has drops of water on its sides and that the bathroom floor is wet. In addition, you see a damp towel draped over the sink. Putting all these observations together, you conclude that someone has recently taken a bath. (Detectives use induction when gathering clues to solve a crime.)

- **General to general:** This form of induction occurs when you draw a conclusion based on the consistency of your observations. For example, if you determine that Apple Inc. has made good products for a long time, you conclude it will continue to make good products.

- **General to particular:** This form of induction occurs when you draw a conclusion based on what you generally know to be true. For example, if you believe that cars made by the Ford Motor Company are reliable, then you conclude that a Ford Focus will be a reliable car.

- **Particular to particular:** This form of induction occurs when you assume that because something works in one situation, it will also work in another similar situation. For example, if Krazy Glue fixed the broken handle of one cup, then you conclude it will probably fix the broken handle of another cup.

Making Inferences

Unlike deduction, which reaches a conclusion based on information provided by the major and minor premises, induction uses what you know to make a statement about something that you don't know. While deductive arguments can be judged in absolute terms (they are either **valid** or **invalid**), inductive arguments are judged in relative terms (they are either **strong** or **weak**).

You reach an inductive conclusion by making an **inference**—a statement about what is unknown based on what is known. (In other words, you look at the evidence and try to figure out what is going on.) For this reason, there is always a gap between your observations and your conclusion. To bridge this gap, you have to make an **inductive leap**—a stretch of the imagination that enables you to draw an acceptable conclusion. Therefore, inductive conclusions are never certain (as deductive conclusions are) but only probable. The more evidence you provide, the stronger and more probable are your conclusions (and your argument).

Public-opinion polls illustrate how inferences are used to reach inductive conclusions. Politicians and news organizations routinely use public-opinion polls to assess support (or lack of support) for a particular policy, proposal, or political candidate. After surveying a sample population—registered voters, for example—pollsters reach conclusions based on their responses. In other words, by asking questions and studying the responses of a sample group of people, pollsters make inferences about the larger group—for example, which political candidate is ahead and by how much. How solid these inferences are depends to a great extent on the sample populations the pollsters survey. In an election, for example, a poll of randomly chosen individuals will be less accurate than a poll of registered voters or likely voters. In addition, other factors (such as the size of the sample and the way questions are worded) can determine the relative strength of an inductive conclusion.

As with all inferences, a gap exists between a poll's data—the responses to the questions—and the conclusion. The larger and more representative the sample, the smaller the inductive leap necessary to reach a conclusion and the more accurate the poll. If the gap between the data and the conclusion is too big, however, the pollsters will be accused of making a **hasty generalization** (see p. 154). Remember, no matter how much support you present, an inductive conclusion is only probable, never certain. The best you can do is present a convincing case and hope that your audience will accept it.

Constructing Strong Inductive Arguments

When you use inductive reasoning, your conclusion is only as strong as the **evidence**—the facts, details, or examples—that you use to support it. For this reason, you should be on the lookout for the following problems that can occur when you try to reach an inductive conclusion.

Generalization Too Broad

The conclusion you state cannot go beyond the scope of your evidence. Your evidence must support your generalization. For instance, you cannot survey just three international students in your school and conclude that the school does not go far enough to accommodate international students. To reach such a conclusion, you would have to consider a large number of international students.

Atypical Evidence

The evidence on which you base an inductive conclusion must be **representative**, not atypical or biased. For example, you cannot conclude that students are satisfied with the course offerings at your school by sampling just first-year students. To be valid, your conclusion should be based on responses from a cross section of students from all years.

Irrelevant Evidence

Your evidence has to support your conclusion. If it does not, it is **irrelevant**. For example, if you assert that many adjunct faculty members make substantial contributions to your school, your supporting examples must be adjunct faculty, not tenured or junior faculty.

Exceptions to the Rule

There is always a chance that you will overlook an exception that may affect the strength of your conclusion. For example, not everyone who has a disability needs special accommodations, and not everyone who requires special accommodations needs the same services. For this reason, you should avoid using words like *every*, *all*, and *always* and instead use words like *most*, *many*, and *usually*.

◉ EXERCISE 5.6 IDENTIFYING DEDUCTIVE AND INDUCTIVE ARGUMENTS

Read the following arguments, and decide whether each is a deductive argument or an inductive argument and write *D* or *I* on the lines.

1. Freedom of speech is a central principle of our form of government. For this reason, students should be allowed to wear T-shirts that call for the legalization of marijuana. _____

2. The Chevy Cruze Eco gets twenty-seven miles a gallon in the city and forty-six miles a gallon on the highway. The Honda Accord gets twenty-seven miles a gallon in the city and thirty-six miles a gallon on the highway. Therefore, it makes more sense for me to buy the Chevy Cruze Eco. _____

3. In Edgar Allan Poe's short story "The Cask of Amontillado," Montresor flatters Fortunato. He lures him to his vaults where he stores wine. Montresor then gets Fortunato drunk and chains him to the wall of a crypt. Finally, Montresor uncovers a pile of building material and walls up the entrance to the crypt. Clearly, Montresor has carefully planned to murder Fortunato for a very long time. _____

4. All people should have the right to die with dignity. Garrett is a terminally ill patient, so he should have access to doctor-assisted suicide. _____

5. Last week, we found unacceptably high levels of pollution in the ocean. On Monday, we also found high levels of pollution. Today, we found even higher levels of pollution. We should close the ocean beaches to swimmers until we can find the source of this problem. _____

⬣ EXERCISE 5.7 ANALYZING DEDUCTIVE AND INDUCTIVE ARGUMENTS

Read the following arguments. Then, decide whether they are deductive or inductive. If they are inductive arguments, evaluate their strength. If they are deductive arguments, evaluate their soundness.

1. *The Farmer's Almanac* says that this winter will be very cold. The National Weather Service also predicts that this winter will be very cold. So, this should be a cold winter.

2. Many walled towns in Europe do not let people drive cars into their centers. San Gimignano is a walled town in Europe. It is likely that we will not be able to drive our car into its center.

3. The window at the back of the house is broken. There is a baseball on the floor. A few minutes ago, I saw two boys playing catch in a neighbor's yard. They must have thrown the ball through the window.

4. Every time I go to the beach I get sunburned. I guess I should stop going to the beach.

5. All my instructors have advanced degrees. Richard Bell is one of my instructors. Therefore, Richard Bell has an advanced degree.

6. My last two boyfriends cheated on me. All men are terrible.

7. I read a study published by a pharmaceutical company that said that Accutane was safe. Maybe the government was too quick to pull this drug off the market.

8. Chase is not very good-looking, and he dresses badly. I don't know how he can be a good architect.

9. No fictional character has ever had a fan club. Harry Potter does, but he is the exception.

10. Two weeks ago, my instructor refused to accept a late paper. She did the same thing last week. Yesterday, she also told someone that because his paper was late, she wouldn't accept it. I'd better get my paper in on time.

⬣ EXERCISE 5.8 ANALYZING AN INDUCTIVE PARAGRAPH

Read the following inductive paragraph, written by student Pooja Vaidya, and answer the questions that follow it.

When my friend took me to a game between the Philadelphia Eagles and the Dallas Cowboys in Philadelphia, I learned a little bit about American football and a lot about the behavior of football fans. Many of the Philadelphia fans were dressed in green and white football jerseys, each with a player's name and number on the back. One fan had his face painted green and wore a green cape with a large white *E* on it. He ran up and down the aisles in his section and led cheers. When the team was ahead, everyone joined in. When the team fell behind, this fan literally fell on his knees, cried, and begged the people in the stands to support the Eagles. (After the game, several people asked him for his autograph.) A group of six fans sat without shirts. They wore green wigs, and each had one letter of the team's name painted on his bare chest. Even though the temperature was below freezing, none of these fans ever put on his shirt. Before the game, many fans had been drinking at tailgate parties in the parking lot, and as the game progressed, they continued to drink beer in the stadium. By the beginning of the second half, fights were breaking out all over the stadium. Guards grabbed the people who were fighting and escorted them out of the stadium. At one point, a fan wearing a Dallas jersey tried to sit down in the row behind me. Some of the Eagles fans were so threatening that the police had to escort the Dallas fan out of the stands for his own protection. When the game ended in an Eagles victory, the fans sang the team's fight song as they left the stadium. I concluded that for many Eagles fans, a day at the stadium is an opportunity to engage in behavior that in any other context would be unacceptable and even abnormal.

1. Which of the following statements could you *not* conclude from this paragraph?

   a. All Eagles fans act in outrageous ways at games.

   b. At football games, the fans in the stands can be as violent as the players on the field.

   c. The atmosphere at the stadium causes otherwise normal people to act abnormally.

   d. Spectator sports encourage fans to act in abnormal ways.

   e. Some people get so caught up in the excitement of a game that they act in uncharacteristic ways.

2. Paraphrase the writer's conclusion. What evidence is provided to support this conclusion?

3. What additional evidence could the writer have provided? Is this additional evidence necessary, or does the conclusion stand without it?

4. The writer makes an inductive leap to reach the paragraph's conclusion. Do you think this leap is too great?

5. Does this paragraph make a strong inductive argument? Why or why not?

Writing Inductive Arguments

Inductive arguments begin with evidence (specific facts, observations, expert opinion, and so on), draw inferences from the evidence, and reach a conclusion by making an inductive leap. Keep in mind that inductive arguments are only as strong as the link between the evidence and the conclusion, so the stronger this link is, the stronger the argument will be.

Inductive essays frequently have the following structure:

INTRODUCTION	Presents the issue
	States the thesis
BODY	Presents evidence: facts, observations, expert opinion, and so on
	Draws inferences from the evidence
	Refutes the arguments against the thesis
CONCLUSION	Brings argument to a close
	Concluding statement reinforces the thesis

⊘ EXERCISE 5.9 IDENTIFYING THE ELEMENTS OF AN INDUCTIVE ESSAY

The following essay includes all the elements of an inductive argument. After you read the essay, answer the questions on page 151, consulting the preceding outline if necessary.

This essay appeared in *Slate* on September 2, 2006.

PLEASE DO NOT FEED THE HUMANS

WILLIAM SALETAN

Dug

In 1894, Congress established Labor Day to honor those who "from rude 1 nature have delved° and carved all the grandeur we behold." In the century since, the grandeur of human achievement has multiplied. Over the past four decades, global population has doubled, but food output, driven by increases in productivity, has outpaced it. Poverty, infant mortality, and hunger are receding. For the first time in our planet's history, a species no longer lives at the mercy of scarcity. We have learned to feed ourselves.

We've learned so well, in fact, that we're getting fat. Not just the United 2
States or Europe, but the whole world. Egyptian, Mexican, and South African
women are now as fat as Americans. Far more Filipino adults are now overweight than underweight. In China, one in five adults is too heavy, and the
rate of overweight children is 28 times higher than it was two decades ago.
In Thailand, Kuwait, and Tunisia, obesity, diabetes, and heart disease are
soaring.

Hunger is far from conquered. But since 1990, the global rate of malnu- 3
trition has declined an average of 1.7 percent a year. Based on data from the
World Health Organization and the U.N. Food and Agriculture Organization, for every two people who are malnourished, three are now overweight
or obese. Among women, even in most African countries, overweight has
surpassed underweight. The balance of peril is shifting.

Fat is no longer a rich man's disease. For middle- and high-income 4
Americans, the obesity rate is 29 percent. For low-income Americans, it's
35 percent. Among middle- and high-income kids aged 15 to 17, the rate of
overweight is 14 percent. Among low-income kids in the same age bracket,
it's 23 percent. Globally, weight has tended to rise with income. But a study in
Vancouver, Canada, published three months ago, found that preschoolers in
"food-insecure" households were twice as likely as other kids to be overweight
or obese. In Brazilian cities, the poor have become fatter than the rich.

Technologically, this is a triumph. In the early days of our species, even 5
the rich starved. Barry Popkin, a nutritional epidemiologist at the University
of North Carolina, divides history into several epochs. In the hunter-gatherer
era, if we didn't find food, we died. In the agricultural era, if our crops per-
ished, we died. In the industrial era, famine receded, but infectious diseases
killed us. Now we've achieved such control over nature that we're dying not of
starvation or infection, but of abundance. Nature isn't killing us. We're killing
ourselves.

You don't have to go hungry anymore; we can fill you with fats and carbs 6
more cheaply than ever. You don't have to chase your food; we can bring it to
you. You don't have to cook it; we can deliver it ready-to-eat. You don't have
to eat it before it spoils; we can pump it full of preservatives so it lasts forever.
You don't even have to stop when you're full. We've got so much food to sell, we
want you to keep eating.

What happened in America is happening everywhere, only faster. Fewer 7
farmers' markets, more processed food. Fewer whole grains, more refined
ones. More sweeteners, salt, and trans fats. Cheaper meat, more animal fat.
Less cooking, more eating out. Bigger portions, more snacks.

Kentucky Fried Chicken and Pizza Hut are spreading across the planet. 8
Coca-Cola is in more than 200 countries. Half of McDonald's business is
overseas. In China, animal-fat intake has tripled in 20 years. By 2020, meat
consumption in developing countries will grow by 106 million metric tons,
outstripping growth in developed countries by a factor of more than five.
Forty years ago, to afford a high-fat diet, your country needed a gross national

product per capita of nearly $1,500. Now the price is half that. You no longer have to be rich to die a rich man's death.

Soon, it'll be a poor man's death. The rich have Whole Foods, gyms, and 9 personal trainers. The poor have 7-Eleven, Popeyes, and streets unsafe for walking. When money's tight, you feed your kids at Wendy's and stock up on macaroni and cheese. At a lunch buffet, you do what your ancestors did: store all the fat you can.

That's the punch line: Technology has changed everything but us. We 10 evolved to survive scarcity. We crave fat. We're quick to gain weight and slow to lose it. Double what you serve us, and we'll double what we eat. Thanks to technology, the deprivation that made these traits useful is gone. So is the link between flavors and nutrients. The modern food industry can sell you sweetness without fruit, salt without protein, creaminess without milk. We can fatten you and starve you at the same time.

And that's just the diet side of the equation. Before technology, adult men had to expend about 3,000 calories a day. Now they expend about 2,000. Look at the new Segway scooter. The original model relieved you of the need to walk, pedal, or balance. With the new one, you don't even have to turn the handlebars or start it manually. In theory, Segway is replacing the car. In practice, it's replacing the body.

> "We evolved to survive scarcity." 11

In country after country, service jobs are replacing hard labor. The folks 12 who field your customer service calls in Bangalore are sitting at desks. Nearly everyone in China has a television set. Remember when Chinese rode bikes? In the past six years, the number of cars there has grown from six million to 20 million. More than one in seven Chinese has a motorized vehicle, and households with such vehicles have an obesity rate 80 percent higher than their peers.

The answer to these trends is simple. We have to exercise more and change 13 the food we eat, donate, and subsidize. Next year, for example, the U.S. Women, Infants, and Children program, which subsidizes groceries for impoverished youngsters, will begin to pay for fruits and vegetables. For 32 years, the program has fed toddlers eggs and cheese but not one vegetable. And we wonder why poor kids are fat.

The hard part is changing our mentality. We have a distorted body image. 14 We're so used to not having enough, as a species, that we can't believe the problem is too much. From China to Africa to Latin America, people are trying to fatten their kids. I just got back from a vacation with my Jewish mother and Jewish mother-in-law. They told me I need to eat more.

The other thing blinding us is liberal guilt. We're so caught up in the idea 15 of giving that we can't see the importance of changing behavior rather than filling bellies. We know better than to feed buttered popcorn to zoo animals, yet we send it to a food bank and call ourselves humanitarians. Maybe we should ask what our fellow humans actually need.

Identifying the Elements of an Inductive Argument

1. What is this essay's thesis? Restate it in your own words.

2. Why do you think Saletan places the thesis where he does?

3. What evidence does Saletan use to support his conclusion?

4. What inductive leap does Saletan make to reach his conclusion? Do you think he should have included more evidence?

5. Overall, do you think Saletan's inductive argument is relatively strong or weak? Explain.

Recognizing Logical Fallacies

When you write arguments in college, you follow certain rules that ensure fairness. Not everyone who writes arguments is fair or thorough, however. Sometimes you will encounter arguments in which writers attack the opposition's intelligence or patriotism and base their arguments on questionable (or even false) assumptions. As convincing as these arguments can sometimes seem, they are not valid because they contain **fallacies**—errors in reasoning that undermine the logic of an argument. Familiarizing yourself with the most common logical fallacies can help you to evaluate the arguments of others and to construct better, more effective arguments of your own.

The following pages define and illustrate some logical fallacies that you should learn to recognize and avoid.

Begging the Question

The fallacy of **begging the question** assumes that a statement is self-evident (or obvious) when it actually requires proof. A conclusion based on such assumptions cannot be valid. For example, someone who is very religious could structure an argument the following way:

MAJOR PREMISE	Everything in the Bible is true.
MINOR PREMISE	The Bible says that Noah built an ark.
CONCLUSION	Therefore, Noah's ark really existed.

A person can accept the conclusion of this syllogism only if he or she accepts the major premise as self-evident. Some people might find this line of reasoning convincing, but others would not—even if they were religious.

Begging the question occurs any time someone presents a debatable statement as if it were true. For example, look at the following statement:

You have unfairly limited my right of free speech by refusing to print my editorial in the college newspaper.

This statement begs the question because it assumes what it should be proving—that refusing to print an editorial somehow violates a person's right to free speech.

Circular Reasoning

Closely related to begging the question, **circular reasoning** occurs when someone supports a statement by restating it in different terms. Consider the following statement:

Stealing is wrong because it is illegal.

The conclusion of the preceding statement is essentially the same as its beginning: stealing (which is illegal) is against the law. In other words, the argument goes in a circle.

Here are some other examples of circular reasoning:

- Lincoln was a great president because he is the best president we ever had.

- I am for equal rights for women because I am a feminist.

- Only someone who is deranged would carry out a school shooting, so he must be mentally ill.

All of the preceding statements have one thing in common: they attempt to support a statement by simply repeating the statement in different words.

Weak Analogy

An **analogy** is a comparison between two items (or concepts)—one familiar and one unfamiliar. When you make an analogy, you explain the unfamiliar item by comparing it to the familiar item.

Waterfall, by M. C. Escher. The artwork creates the illusion of water flowing uphill and in a circle. Circular reasoning occurs when the conclusion of an argument is the same as one of the premises.

Although analogies can be effective in arguments, they have limitations. For example, a senator who opposed a government bailout of the financial industry in 2008 made the following argument:

This bailout is doomed from the start. It's like pouring milk into a leaking bucket. As long as you keep pouring milk, the bucket stays full. But when you stop, the milk runs out the hole in the bottom of the bucket. What we're doing is throwing money into a big bucket and not fixing the hole. We have to find the underlying problems that have caused this part of our economy to get in trouble and pass legislation to solve them.

The problem with using analogies such as this one is that analogies are never perfect. There is always a difference between the two things being compared. The larger this difference, the weaker the analogy—and the weaker the argument that it supports. For example, someone could point out to the senator that the financial industry—and by extension, the whole economy—is much more complex and multifaceted than a leaking bucket.

This weakness highlights another limitation of an argument by analogy. Even though it can be very convincing, an analogy alone is no substitute for evidence. In other words, to analyze the economy, the senator would have to expand his discussion beyond a single analogy (which cannot carry the weight of the entire argument) and provide convincing evidence that the bailout was a mistake form the start.

The Granger Collection

Ad hominem attack against Charles Darwin, originator of the theory of evolution by natural selection.

Ad Hominem *Fallacy (Personal Attack)*

The ***ad hominem* fallacy** occurs when someone attacks the character or the motives of a person instead of focusing on the issues. This line of reasoning is illogical because it focuses attention on the person making the argument, sidestepping the argument itself.

Consider the following statement:

> Dr. Thomson, I'm not sure why we should believe anything you have to say about this community health center. Last year, you left your husband for another man.

The preceding attack on Dr. Thomson's character is irrelevant; it has nothing to do with her ideas about the community health center. Sometimes, however, a person's character may have a direct relation to the issue. For example, if Dr. Thomson had invested in a company that supplied medical equipment to the health center, this fact would have been relevant to the issue at hand.

The *ad hominem* fallacy also occurs when you attempt to undermine an argument by associating it with individuals who are easily attacked. For example, consider this statement:

> I think your plan to provide universal health care is interesting. I'm sure Marx and Lenin would agree with you.

Instead of focusing on the specific provisions of the health-care plan, the opposition unfairly associates it with the ideas of Karl Marx and Vladimir Lenin, two well-known Communists.

Creating a Straw Man

This fallacy most likely got its name from the use of straw dummies in military and boxing training. When writers create a **straw man**, they present a weak argument that can easily be refuted. Instead of attacking the real issue, they focus on a weaker issue and give the impression that they have effectively countered an opponent's argument. Frequently, the straw man is an extreme or oversimplified version of the opponent's actual position. For example, during a debate about raising the minimum wage, a senator made the following comment:

> If we raise the minimum wage for restaurant workers, the cost of a meal will increase. Soon, the average person won't be able to afford a cup of soup.

Instead of focusing on legitimate arguments against the minimum wage, the senator misrepresents an opposing argument and then refutes it. As this example shows, the straw man fallacy is dishonest because it intentionally distorts an opponent's position in order to mislead readers.

Hasty or Sweeping Generalization (Jumping to a Conclusion)

A **hasty or sweeping generalization** (also called **jumping to a conclusion**) occurs when someone reaches a conclusion that is based on too little evidence. Many people commit this fallacy without realizing it. For example, when Richard Nixon was elected president in 1972, film critic Pauline Kael

Soldiers practicing attacks against straw men

SOTK2011/Alamy Stock Photo

is supposed to have remarked, "How can that be? No one I know voted for Nixon!" The general idea behind this statement is that if Kael's acquaintances didn't vote for Nixon, then neither did most other people. This assumption is flawed because it is based on a small sample.

Sometimes people make hasty generalizations because they strongly favor one point of view over another. At other times, a hasty generalization is simply the result of sloppy thinking. For example, it is easier for a student to say that an instructor is an unusually hard grader than to survey the instructor's classes to see if this conclusion is warranted (or to consider other reasons for his or her poor performance in a course).

Either/Or Fallacy (False Dilemma)

The **either/or fallacy** (also called a **false dilemma**) occurs when a person says that there are just two choices when there are actually more. In many cases, the person committing this fallacy tries to force a conclusion by presenting just two choices, one of which is clearly more desirable than the other. (Parents do this with young children all the time: "Eat your carrots, or go to bed.")

Politicians frequently engage in this fallacy. For example, according to some politicians, you are either pro-life or pro-choice, pro–gun control or anti–gun control, pro-stem-cell research or anti-stem-cell research. Many people, however, are actually somewhere in the middle, taking a much more nuanced approach to complicated issues.

Consider the following statement:

> I can't believe you voted against the bill to build a wall along the southern border of the United States. Either you're for protecting our border, or you're against it.

This statement is an example of the either/or fallacy. The person who voted against the bill might be against building the border wall but not against all immigration restrictions. The person might favor loose restrictions for some people (for example, people fleeing political persecution and migrant workers) and strong restrictions for others (for example, drug smugglers and human traffickers). By limiting the options to just two, the speaker oversimplifies the situation and attempts to force the listener to accept a fallacious argument.

Equivocation

The fallacy of **equivocation** occurs when a key term has one meaning in one part of an argument and another meaning in another part. (When a term is used **unequivocally**, it has the same meaning throughout the argument.) Consider the following old joke:

> The sign said, "Fine for parking here," so because it was fine, I parked there.

Obviously, the word *fine* has two different meanings in this sentence. The first time it is used, it means "money paid as a penalty." The second time, it means "good" or "satisfactory."

Most words have more than one meaning, so it is important not to confuse the various meanings. For an argument to work, a key term has to have the same meaning every time it appears in the argument. If the meaning shifts during the course of the argument, then the argument cannot be sound.

Consider the following statement:

> This is supposed to be a free country, but nothing worth having is ever free.

In this statement, the meaning of a key term shifts. The first time the word *free* is used, it means "not under the control of another." The second time, it means "without charge."

Red Herring

This fallacy gets its name from the practice of dragging a smoked fish across the trail of a fox to mask its scent during a fox hunt. As a result, the hounds lose the scent and are thrown off the track. The **red herring fallacy** occurs when a person raises an irrelevant side issue to divert attention from the real issue. Used skillfully, this fallacy can distract an audience and change the focus of an argument.

Political campaigns are good sources of examples of the red herring fallacy. Consider this example from the 2016 presidential race:

> I know that Donald Trump says that he is for the "little guy," but he lives in a three-story penthouse in the middle of Manhattan. How can we believe that his policies will help the average American?

The focus of this argument should have been on Trump's policies, not on the fact that he lives in a penthouse.

Here is another red herring fallacy:

> **She:** I read that the Alexa virtual assistant records your conversations, even when it's off. This is an invasion of privacy.
>
> **He:** That certainly is a first-world problem. Think of all the poor people in Haiti. That should put things in perspective.

Again, the focus of the argument should be on a possible invasion of privacy, not on poverty in Haiti.

Person trying to follow the argument.

The actual issue being argued.

Red herring, a distraction not related to the argument.

Slippery Slope

The **slippery-slope fallacy** occurs when a person argues that one thing will inevitably result from another. (Other names for the slippery-slope fallacy are the **foot-in-the-door fallacy** and the **floodgates fallacy**.) Both these names suggest that once you permit certain acts, you inevitably permit additional acts that eventually lead to disastrous consequences. Typically, the slippery-slope fallacy presents a series of increasingly unacceptable events that lead to an inevitable, unpleasant conclusion. (Usually, there is no evidence that such a sequence will actually occur.)

We encounter examples of the slippery-slope fallacy almost daily. During a debate on same-sex marriage, for example, an opponent advanced this line of reasoning:

> If we allow gay marriage, then there is nothing to stop polygamy. And once we allow this, where will it stop? Will we have to legalize incest—or even bestiality?

Whether or not you support same-sex marriage, you should recognize the fallacy of this slippery-slope reasoning. By the last sentence of the preceding passage, the assertions have become so outrageous that they approach parody. People can certainly debate this issue, but not in such a dishonest and highly emotional way.

You Also (Tu Quoque)

The **you also fallacy** asserts that a statement is false because it is inconsistent with what the speaker has said or done. In other words, a person is attacked for doing what he or she is arguing against. Parents often encounter this fallacy when they argue with their teenage children. By introducing an irrelevant point—"You did it too"—the children attempt to distract parents and put them on the defensive:

- How can you tell me not to smoke when you used to smoke?

- Don't yell at me for drinking. I bet you had a few beers before you were twenty-one.

- Why do I have to be home by midnight? Didn't you stay out late when you were my age?

Arguments such as these are irrelevant. People fail to follow their own advice, but that does not mean that their points have no merit. (Of course, not following their own advice does undermine their credibility.)

Appeal to Doubtful Authority

Writers of research papers frequently use the ideas of recognized authorities to strengthen their arguments. However, the sources offered as evidence need to be both respected and credible. The **appeal to doubtful authority** occurs when people use the ideas of nonexperts to support their arguments.

Not everyone who speaks as an expert is actually an authority on a particular issue. For example, when movie stars or recording artists give their opinions about politics, climate change, or foreign affairs—things they may know little about—they are not speaking as experts; therefore, they have no authority. (They *are* experts, however, when they discuss the film or music industries.) A similar situation occurs with the pundits who appear on television news shows or whose ideas are posted on social media sites. Some of these individuals have solid credentials in the fields they discuss, but others offer opinions even though they know little about the subjects. Unfortunately, many people accept the pronouncements of these "experts" uncritically and think it is acceptable to cite them to support their own arguments.

How do you determine whether a person you read about or hear is really an authority? First, make sure that the person actually has expertise in the field he or she is discussing. You can do this by checking his or her credentials on the internet. Second, make sure that the person is not biased. No one is entirely free from bias, but the bias should not be so extreme that it undermines the person's authority. Finally, make sure that you can confirm what the so-called expert says or writes. Check one or two pieces of information in other sources, such as a basic reference text or encyclopedia. Determine if others—especially recognized experts in the field—confirm this information. If there are major points of discrepancy, dig further to make sure you are dealing with a legitimate authority. Be extremely wary of material that appears on social media sites, such as

Comedian/actor Amy Schumer boosts her credibility on the issue of gun control by appearing with her cousin, Senator Charles Schumer.

Andrew Burton/Getty Images News/Getty Images

Facebook and Twitter, even if it is attributed to experts. Don't use information until you have checked both its authenticity and accuracy.

Misuse of Statistics

The **misuse of statistics** occurs when data are misrepresented. Statistics can be used persuasively in an argument, but sometimes they are distorted—intentionally or unintentionally—to make a point. For example, a classic ad for toothpaste claims that four out of five dentists recommend Crest toothpaste. What the ad neglects to mention is the number of dentists who were questioned. If the company surveyed several thousand dentists, then this statistic would be meaningful. If the company surveyed only ten, however, it would not be.

Misleading statistics can be much subtler (and much more complicated) than the preceding example. For example, one year, there were 16,653 alcohol-related deaths in the United States. According to the National Highway Traffic Safety Administration (NHTSA), 12,892 of these 16,653 alcohol-related deaths involved at least one driver or passenger who was legally drunk. Of the 12,892 deaths, 7,326 were the drivers themselves, and 1,594 were legally drunk pedestrians. The remaining 3,972 fatalities were nonintoxicated drivers, passengers, or nonoccupants. These 3,972 fatalities call the total number into question because the NHTSA does not indicate which drivers were at fault. In other words, if a sober driver ran a red light and killed a legally drunk driver, the NHTSA classified this death as alcohol-related. For this reason, the original number of alcohol-related

"That's what I want to say. See if you can find some statistics to prove it."

deaths—16,653—is somewhat misleading. (The statistic becomes even more questionable when you consider that a person is automatically classified as intoxicated if he or she refuses to take a sobriety test.)

Post Hoc, Ergo Propter Hoc (After This, Therefore Because of This)

The *post hoc* **fallacy** asserts that because two events occur closely in time, one event must cause the other. Professional athletes commit the *post hoc* fallacy all the time. For example, one major league pitcher wears the same shirt every time he has an important game. Because he has won several big games while wearing this shirt, he believes it brings him luck.

Many events seem to follow a sequential pattern even though they actually do not. For example, some people refuse to get a flu shot because they say that the last time they got one, they came down with the flu. Even though there is no scientific basis for this link, many people insist that it is true. (The more probable explanation for this situation is that the flu vaccination takes at least two weeks to take effect, so it is possible for someone to be infected by the flu virus before the vaccine starts working. In addition, no flu vaccine is 100 percent effective, so even with the shot, it is possible to contract the disease.)

Another health-related issue also illustrates the *post hoc* fallacy. Recently, the U.S. Food and Drug Administration (FDA) studied several natural supplements that claim to cure the common cold. Because the study showed that these products were not effective, the FDA ordered the manufacturers to stop making false claims. Despite this fact, however, many people still buy these products. When questioned, they say the medications actually work. Again, the explanation for this phenomenon is simple. Most colds last just a few days. As the FDA pointed out in its report, people who took the medications would have begun feeling better with or without them.

Non Sequitur *(It Does Not Follow)*

The ***non sequitur* fallacy** occurs when a conclusion does not follow from the premises. Frequently, the conclusion is supported by weak or irrelevant evidence—or by no evidence at all. Consider the following statement:

> Megan drives an expensive car, so she must be earning a lot of money.

Megan might drive an expensive car, but this is not evidence that she has a high salary. She could, for example, be leasing the car or paying it off over a five-year period, or it could have been a gift.

Non sequiturs are common in political arguments. Consider this statement:

> Gangs, drugs, and extreme violence plague today's prisons. The only way to address this issue is to release all nonviolent offenders as soon as possible.

This assessment of the prison system may be accurate, but it doesn't follow that because of this situation, all nonviolent offenders should be released immediately.

Scientific arguments also contain *non sequiturs*. Consider the following statement that was made during a debate on climate change:

> Recently, the polar ice caps have thickened, and the temperature of the oceans has stabilized. Obviously, we don't need to do more to address climate change.

Even if you accept the facts of this argument, you need to see more evidence before you can conclude that no action against climate change is necessary. For example, the cooling trend could be temporary, or other areas of the earth could still be growing warmer.

Bandwagon Fallacy

The **bandwagon fallacy** occurs when you try to convince people that something is true because it is widely held to be true. It is easy to see the problem with this line of reasoning. Hundreds of years ago, most people believed that the sun revolved around the earth and that the earth was flat. As we know, the fact that many people held these beliefs did not make them true.

The underlying assumption of the bandwagon fallacy is that the more people who believe something, the more likely it is to be true. Without supporting evidence, however, this form of argument cannot be valid. For example, consider the following statement made by a driver who was stopped by the police for speeding:

> Officer, I didn't do anything wrong. Everyone around me was going the same speed.

As the police officer was quick to point out, the driver's argument missed the point: he was doing fifty-five miles an hour in a thirty-five-mile-an-hour zone, and the fact that other drivers were also speeding was irrelevant. If the driver had been able to demonstrate that the police officer was mistaken—that he was driving more slowly or that the speed limit was actually sixty miles an hour—then his argument would have had merit. In this case, the fact that other drivers were going the same speed would be relevant because it would support his contention.

Since most people want to go along with the crowd, the bandwagon fallacy can be very effective. For this reason, advertisers use it all the time. For example, a book publisher will say that a book has been on the *New York Times* best-seller list for ten weeks, and a pharmaceutical company will say that its brand of aspirin outsells other brands four to one. These appeals are irrelevant, however, because they don't address the central questions: Is the book actually worth reading? Is one brand of aspirin really better than other brands?

⊖ EXERCISE 5.10 IDENTIFYING LOGICAL FALLACIES

Determine which of the following statements are logical arguments and which are fallacies. If the statement is not logical, identify the fallacy that best applies.

1. Almost all the students I talked to said that they didn't like the senator. I'm sure he'll lose the election on Tuesday.

2. This car has a noisy engine; therefore, it must create a lot of pollution.

3. I don't know how Professor Resnick can be such a hard grader. He's always late for class.

4. A vote for the bill to limit gun sales in the city is a vote against the Second Amendment.

5. It's only fair to pay your fair share of taxes.

6. I had an internship at a government agency last summer, and no one there worked very hard. Government workers are lazy.

7. It's a clear principle of law that people are not allowed to yell "Fire!" in a crowded theater. By permitting protestors to hold a rally downtown, Judge Cohen is allowing them to do just that.

8. Of course this person is guilty. He wouldn't be in jail if he weren't a criminal.

9. Schools are like families; therefore, teachers (like parents) should be allowed to discipline their kids.

10. Everybody knows that staying out in the rain can make you sick.

11. When we had a draft in the 1960s, the crime rate was low. We should bring back the draft.

12. I'm not a doctor, but I play one on TV. I recommend Vicks Formula 44 cough syrup.

13. Some people are complaining about public schools, so there must be a problem.

14. If you aren't part of the solution, you're part of the problem.

15. All people are mortal. James is a person. Therefore, James is mortal.

16. I don't know why you gave me an *F* for handing in someone else's essay. Didn't you ever copy something from someone else?

17. First, the government stops us from buying assault-style rifles. Then, it tries to limit the number of handguns we can buy. What will come next? Soon, they'll try to take away all our guns.

18. Shakespeare was the world's greatest playwright; therefore, *Macbeth* must be a great play.

19. Last month, I bought a new computer. Yesterday, I installed some new software. This morning, my computer wouldn't start up. The new software must be causing the problem.

20. Ellen DeGeneres and Paul McCartney are against testing pharmaceutical and cosmetics products on animals, and that's good enough for me.

◯ EXERCISE 5.11 ANALYZING LOGICAL FALLACIES

Read the following essay, and identify as many logical fallacies in it as you can. Make sure you identify each fallacy by name and are able to explain the flaws in the writer's arguments.

This essay is from Buchanan.org, where it appeared on October 31, 1994.

IMMIGRATION TIME-OUT

PATRICK J. BUCHANAN

What do we want the America of the years 2000, 2020, and 2050 to be like? Do 1 we have the right to shape the character of the country our grandchildren will live in? Or is that to be decided by whoever, outside America, decides to come here?

By 2050, we are instructed by the chancellor of the University of California 2 at Berkeley, Chang Lin-Tin, "the majority of Americans will trace their roots to Latin America, Africa, Asia, the Middle East, and Pacific Islands."

Now, any man or woman, of any nation or ancestry can come here—and 3 become a good American.

We know that from our history. But by my arithmetic, the chancellor is 4 saying Hispanics, Asians, and Africans will increase their present number of 65 million by at least 100 million in 60 years, a population growth larger than all of Mexico today.

What will that mean for America? Well, South Texas and Southern 5 California will be almost exclusively Hispanic. Each will have tens of millions of people whose linguistic, historic, and cultural roots are in Mexico. Like Eastern Ukraine, where 10 million Russian-speaking "Ukrainians" now look impatiently to Moscow, not Kiev, as their cultural capital, America could see, in a decade, demands for Quebec-like status for Southern California. Already there is a rumbling among militants for outright secession. A sea of Mexican flags was prominent in that L.A. rally against Prop. 187, and Mexican officials are openly urging their kinsmen in California to vote it down.

If no cutoff is imposed on social benefits for those who breach our borders, 6 and break our laws, the message will go out to a desperate world: America is wide open. All you need do is get there, and get in.

Consequences will ensue. Crowding together immigrant and minority 7 populations in our major cities must bring greater conflict. We saw that in the 1992 L.A. riot. Blacks and Hispanics have lately collided in D.C.'s Adams-Morgan neighborhood, supposedly the most tolerant and progressive section of Washington. The issue: bilingual education. Unlike 20 years ago, ethnic conflict is today on almost every front page.

Before Mr. Chang's vision is realized, the United States will have at least two 8 official languages. Today's steady outmigration of "Anglos" or "Euro-Americans," as whites are now called, from Southern Florida and Southern California, will continue. The 50 states will need constant redrawing of political lines to ensure proportional representation. Already we have created the first "apartheid districts" in America's South.

Ethnic militancy and solidarity are on the rise in the United States; the old institutions of assimilation are not doing

> "Ethnic militancy and 9 solidarity are on the rise."

their work as they once did; the Melting Pot is in need of repair. On campuses we hear demands for separate dorms, eating rooms, clubs, etc., by black, white, Hispanic, and Asian students. If this is where the campus is headed, where are our cities going?

If America is to survive as "one nation, one people," we need to call a 10 "time-out" on immigration, to assimilate the tens of millions who have lately arrived. We need to get to know one another, to live together, to learn together America's language, history, culture, and traditions of tolerance, to become a new national family, before we add a hundred million more. And we need soon to bring down the curtain on this idea of hyphenated-Americanism.

If we lack the courage to make the decisions—as to what our country will 11 look like in 2050—others will make those decisions for us, not all of whom share our love of the America that seems to be fading away.

⊘ EXERCISE 5.12 CORRECTING LOGICAL FALLACIES

Choose three of the fallacies that you identified in "Immigration Time-Out" for Exercise 5.11. Rewrite each statement in the form of a logical argument.

How Free Should Free Speech Be?

CPL Archives/Everett Collection, Inc.

Go back to page 127, and reread the At Issue box that gives background on how free free speech should be. As the following sources illustrate, this question has a number of possible answers.

As you read this source material, you will be asked to answer questions and to complete some simple activities. This work will help you understand both the content and the structure of the sources. When you are finished, you will be ready to write an argument—either inductive or deductive—that takes a new position on how free free speech should actually be.

SOURCES

Sean McElwee, "The Case for Censoring Hate Speech," page 167

Sol Stern, "The Unfree Speech Movement," page 171

American Association of University Professors, "On Freedom of Expression and Campus Speech Codes," page 174

Jonathan Haidt, "Intimidation Is the New Normal," page 177

Laurie Essig, "Talking Past Each Other on Free Speech," page 182

Visual Argument: Football Players Kneeling, page 186

This essay originally appeared on the *Huffington Post* on July 24, 2013.

THE CASE FOR CENSORING HATE SPEECH

SEAN MCELWEE

For the past few years speech has moved online, leading to fierce debates 1 about its regulation. Most recently, feminists have led the charge to purge Facebook of misogyny that clearly violates its hate speech code. Facebook took a small step two weeks ago, creating a feature that will remove ads from pages deemed "controversial." But such a move is half-hearted; Facebook and other social networking websites should not tolerate hate speech and, in the absence of a government mandate, adopt a European model of expunging offensive material.

Stricter regulation of internet speech will not be popular with the 2 libertarian-minded citizens of the United States, but it's necessary. A typical view of such censorship comes from Jeffrey Rosen, who argues in *The New Republic* that,

> ". . . given their tremendous size and importance as platforms for free speech, companies like Facebook, Google, Yahoo, and Twitter shouldn't try to be guardians of what Waldron calls a 'well-ordered society'; instead, they should consider themselves the modern version of Oliver Wendell Holmes's fractious marketplace of ideas—democratic spaces where all values, including civility norms, are always open for debate."

This image is romantic and lovely (although misattributed to Oliver Wendell 3 Holmes, who famously toed both lines on the free speech debate, instead of John Stuart Mill) but it's worth asking what this actually looks like. Rosen forwards one example:

> "Last year, after the French government objected to the hash tag '#unbonjuif'— intended to inspire hateful riffs on the theme 'a good Jew . . .'—Twitter blocked a handful of the resulting tweets in France, but only because they violated French law. Within days, the bulk of the tweets carrying the hashtag had turned from anti-Semitic to denunciations of anti-Semitism, confirming that the Twittersphere is perfectly capable of dealing with hate speech on its own, without heavy-handed intervention."

It's interesting to note how closely this idea resembles free market funda- 4 mentalism: simply get rid of any coercive rules and the "marketplace of ideas" will naturally produce the best result. Humboldt State University compiled a visual map that charts 150,000 hateful insults aggregated over the course of 11 months in the U.S. by pairing Google's Maps API with a series of the most homophobic, racist, and otherwise prejudiced tweets. The map's existance draws into question the notion that the "Twittersphere" can organically combat hate speech; hate speech is not going to disappear from Twitter on its own.

The negative impacts of hate speech do not lie in the responses of third- 5 party observers, as hate speech aims at two goals. First, it is an attempt to tell bigots that they are not alone. Frank Collins—the neo-Nazi prosecuted in *National Socialist Party of America v. Skokie* (1977)—said, "We want to reach the good people, get the fierce anti-Semites who have to live among the Jews to come out of the woodwork and stand up for themselves."

The second purpose of hate speech is to intimidate the targeted minority, 6 leading them to question whether their dignity and social status is secure. In many cases, such intimidation is successful. Consider the number of rapes that go unreported. Could this trend possibly be impacted by Reddit threads like /r/rapingwomen or /r/mensrights? Could it be due to the harassment women face when they even suggest the possibility they were raped? The rape culture that permeates Facebook, Twitter, and the public dialogue must be held at least partially responsible for our larger rape culture.

Reddit, for instance, has become a veritable potpourri of hate speech; 7 consider Reddit threads like /r/nazi, /r/killawoman, /r/misogny, /r/killing-women. My argument is not that these should be taken down because they are offensive, but rather because they amount to the degradation of a class that has been historically oppressed. Imagine a Reddit thread for /r/lynchingblacks or /r/assassinatingthepresident. We would not argue that we should sit back and wait for this kind of speech to be "outspoken" by positive speech, but that it should be entirely banned.

American free speech jurisprudence relies upon the assumption that 8 speech is merely the extension of a thought, and not an action. If we consider it an action, then saying that we should combat hate speech with more positive speech is an absurd proposition; the speech has already done the harm, and no amount of support will defray the victim's impression that they are not truly secure in this society. We don't simply tell the victim of a robbery, "Hey, it's okay, there are lots of other people who aren't going to rob you." Similarly, it isn't incredibly useful to tell someone who has just had their race/gender/sexuality defamed, "There are a lot of other nice people out there."

Those who claim to "defend free speech" when they defend the right to 9 post hate speech online, are in truth backwards. Free speech isn't an absolute right; no right is weighed in a vacuum. The court has imposed numerous restrictions on speech. Fighting words, libel, and child pornography are all banned. Other countries merely go one step further by banning speech intended to intimidate vulnerable groups. The truth is that such speech does not democratize speech, it monopolizes speech. Women, LGBTQ individuals, and racial or religious minorities feel intimidated and are left out of the public sphere. On Reddit, for example, women have left or changed their usernames to be more male-sounding lest they face harassment and intimidation for speaking on Reddit about even the most gender-neutral topics.

Those who try to remove this hate speech have been criticized from left 10 and right. At *Slate*, Jillian York *writes*, "While the campaigners on this issue are to be commended for raising awareness of such awful speech on Facebook's platform, their proposed solution is ultimately futile and sets a dangerous precedent for special interest groups looking to bring their pet issue to the attention of Facebook's censors."

It hardly seems right to qualify a group fighting hate speech as an "interest 11 group" trying to bring their "pet issue" to the attention of Facebook censors. The "special interest" groups she fears might apply for protection must meet Facebook's strict community standards, which state:

> While we encourage you to challenge ideas, institutions, events, and practices, we do not permit individuals or groups to attack others based on their race, ethnicity, national origin, religion, sex, gender, sexual orientation, disability, or medical condition.

If anything, the groups to which York refers are nudging Facebook towards 12 actually enforcing its own rules.

People who argue against such rules generally portray their opponents as 13 standing on a slippery precipice, tugging at the question "what next?" We can answer that question: Canada, England, France, Germany, the Netherlands, South Africa, Australia, and India all ban hate speech. Yet, none of these countries have slipped into totalitarianism. In many ways, such countries are more free when you weigh the negative liberty to express harmful thoughts against the positive liberty that is suppressed when you allow for the intimidation of minorities.

As Arthur Schopenhauer said, "the 14 freedom of the press should be governed by a very strict prohibition of all and every anonymity." However, with the internet the public dialogue has moved online, where hate speech is easy and anonymous.

> "Free speech isn't an absolute right; no right is weighed in a vacuum."

Jeffrey Rosen argues that norms of civility should be open to discussion, 15 but, in today's reality, this issue has already been decided; impugning someone because of their race, gender, or orientation is not acceptable in a civil society. Banning hate speech is not a mechanism to further this debate because the debate is over.

As Jeremy Waldron argues, hate speech laws prevent bigots from, "trying 16 to create the impression that the equal position of members of vulnerable minorities in a rights-respecting society is less secure than implied by the society's actual foundational commitments."

Some people argue that the purpose of laws that ban hate speech is merely 17 to avoid offending prudes. No country, however, has mandated that anything be excised from the public square merely because it provokes offense, but rather because it attacks the dignity of a group—a practice the U.S. Supreme

Court called in *Beauharnais v. Illinois* (1952) "group libel." Such a standard could easily be applied to Twitter, Reddit, and other social media websites. While Facebook's policy as written should be a model, it's enforcement has been shoddy. Chaim Potok argues that if a company claims to have a policy, it should rigorously and fairly enforce it.

If this is the standard, the internet will surely remain controversial, but 18 it can also be free of hate and allow everyone to participate. A true marketplace of ideas must co-exist with a multi-racial, multi-gender, multi-sexually oriented society, and it can.

⊙ AT ISSUE: HOW FREE SHOULD FREE SPEECH BE?

1. McElwee states his thesis at the end of paragraph 1. Should he have given more background information about the issue before stating his thesis? Why or why not?

2. What evidence does McElwee provide to support his thesis? Should he have provided more evidence? If so, what kind?

3. In paragraph 8, McElwee compares a victim of robbery to a victim of hate speech. How strong is this **analogy**? At what points, if any, does this comparison break down?

4. What opposing arguments does McElwee address? What other opposing arguments could he have addressed?

5. In paragraph 12, McElwee says, "People who argue against such rules generally portray their opponents as standing on a slippery precipice. . . ." What is the "slippery precipice" to which McElwee refers? Is this characterization accurate? Fair?

6. What are the major strengths of McElwee's essay? What are its weaknesses? Overall, how effective is McElwee's argument?

This op-ed originally ran in the *Wall Street Journal* on September 24, 2014.

THE UNFREE SPEECH MOVEMENT

SOL STERN

This fall the University of California at Berkeley is celebrating the 50th anniver- 1
sary of the Free Speech Movement, a student-led protest against campus restrictions on political activities that made headlines and inspired imitators around the
country. I played a small part in the Free Speech Movement, and some of those
returning for the reunion were once my friends, but I won't be joining them.

Though the movement promised greater intellectual and political free- 2
dom on campus, the result has been the opposite. The great irony is that while
Berkeley now honors the memory of the Free Speech Movement, it exercises
more thought control over students than the hated institution that we rose up
against half a century ago.

We early-1960s radicals believed ourselves anointed as a new "tell it like it is" 3
generation. We promised to transcend the "smelly old orthodoxies" (in George
Orwell's phrase) of Cold War liberalism and class-based, authoritarian leftism.
Leading students into the university administration building for the first mass
protest, Mario Savio, the Free Speech Movement's brilliant leader from Queens,
New York, famously said: "There's a time when the operation of the machine
becomes so odious—makes you so sick at heart—that you can't take part. . . .
And you've got to indicate to the people who run it, to the people who own it
that unless you're free, the machine will be prevented from working at all."

The Berkeley "machine" now promotes Free Speech Movement kitsch. 4
The steps in front of Sproul Hall, the central administration building where
more than 700 students were arrested on December 2, 1964, have been
renamed the Mario Savio Steps. One of the campus dining halls is called the
Free Speech Movement Cafe, its walls covered with photographs and memen-
tos of the glorious semester of struggle. The university requires freshmen to
read an admiring biography of Savio, who died in 1996, written by New York
University professor and Berkeley graduate Robert Cohen.

Yet intellectual diversity is hardly embraced. Every undergraduate under- 5
goes a form of indoctrination with a required course on the "theoretical or analytical issues relevant to understanding race, culture, and ethnicity in American
society," administered by the university's Division of Equity and Inclusion.

How did this Orwellian inversion occur? It happened in part because 6
the Free Speech Movement's fight for free speech was always a charade. The
struggle was really about using the campus as a base for radical politics. I was
a 27-year-old New Left graduate student at the time. Savio was a 22-year-old
sophomore. He liked to compare the Free Speech Movement to the civil-rights
struggle—conflating the essentially liberal Berkeley administration with the
Bull Connors of the racist South.

During one demonstration Savio suggested that the campus cops who 7 had arrested a protesting student were "poor policemen" who only "have a job to do." Another student then shouted out: "Just like Eichmann." "Yeah. Very good. It's very, you know, like Adolf Eichmann," Savio replied. "He had a job to do. He fit into the machinery."

I realized years later that this moment may have been the beginning of 8 the 1960s radicals' perversion of ordinary political language, like the spelling "Amerika" or seeing hope and progress in Third World dictatorships.

Before that 1964–65 academic year, most of us radical students could not 9 have imagined a campus rebellion. Why revolt against an institution that until then offered such a pleasant sanctuary? But then Berkeley administrators made an incredibly stupid decision to establish new rules regarding political activities on campus. Student clubs were no longer allowed to set up tables in front of the Bancroft Avenue campus entrance to solicit funds and recruit new members.

The clubs had used this 40-foot strip of sidewalk for years on the assump- 10 tion that it was the property of the City of Berkeley and thus constitutionally protected against speech restrictions. But the university claimed ownership to justify the new rules. When some students refused to comply, the admin- istration compounded its blunder by resorting to the campus police. Not surprisingly, the students pushed back, using civil-disobedience tactics learned fighting for civil rights in the South.

The Free Speech Movement was born on October 1, 1964, when police 11 tried to arrest a recent Berkeley graduate, Jack Weinberg, who was back on campus after a summer as a civil-rights worker in Mississippi. He had set up a table on the Bancroft strip for the Berkeley chapter of the Congress of Racial Equality (CORE). Dozens of students spontaneously sat down around the police car, preventing it from leaving the campus. A 32-hour standoff ensued, with hundreds of students camped around the car.

Mario Savio, also back from Missis- sippi, took off his shoes, climbed onto the roof of the police car, and launched into an impromptu speech explaining why the students had to resist the immoral new rules. Thus began months of sporadic protests, the occupation of Sproul Hall on December 2 (ended by mass arrests), national media attention, and Berkeley's eventual capitulation.

"But others had mas- tered the new world of political theater, under- stood the weakness of American liberalism, and soon turned their ire on the Vietnam War." 12

That should have ended the matter. Savio soon left the political arena, say- 13 ing that he had no interest in becoming a permanent student leader. But others had mastered the new world of political theater, understood the weakness of American liberalism, and soon turned their ire on the Vietnam War.

The radical movement that the Free Speech Movement spawned eventually 14 descended into violence and mindless anti-Americanism. The movement waned in the 1970s as the war wound down—but by then protesters had begun their infiltration of university faculties and administrations they had once decried. "Tenured radicals," in *New Criterion* editor Roger Kimball's phrase, now dominate most professional organizations in the humanities and social studies. Unlike our old liberal professors, who dealt respectfully with the ideas advanced by my generation of New Left students, today's radical professors insist on ideological conformity and don't take kindly to dissent by conservative students. Visits by speakers who might not toe the liberal line—recently including former Secretary of State Condoleezza Rice and Islamism critic Ayaan Hirsi Ali—spark protests and letter-writing campaigns by students in tandem with their professors until the speaker withdraws or the invitation is canceled.

On October 1 at Berkeley, by contrast, one of the honored speakers at 15 the Free Speech Movement anniversary rally on Sproul Plaza will be Bettina Aptheker, who is now a feminist-studies professor at the University of California at Santa Cruz.

Writing in the Berkeley alumni magazine about the anniversary, 16 Ms. Aptheker noted that the First Amendment was "written by white, propertied men in the 18th century, who never likely imagined that it might apply to women, and/or people of color, and/or all those who were not propertied, and even, perhaps, not citizens, and/or undocumented immigrants. . . . In other words, freedom of speech is a Constitutional guarantee, but who gets to exercise it without the chilling restraints of censure depends very much on one's location in the political and social cartography. We [Free Speech Movement] veterans were too young and inexperienced in 1964 to know this, but we do now, and we speak with a new awareness, a new consciousness, and a new urgency that the wisdom of a true freedom is inexorably tied to who exercises power and for what ends." Read it and weep—for the Free Speech Movement anniversary, for the ideal of an intellectually open university, and for America.

⊘ AT ISSUE: HOW FREE SHOULD FREE SPEECH BE?

1. In your own words, summarize Stern's thesis. Where does he state it?

2. At what point (or points) in the essay does Stern appeal to *ethos*? How effective is this appeal?

3. In paragraph 4, Stern says, "The Berkeley 'machine' now promotes Free Speech Movement kitsch." First, look up the meaning of *kitsch*. Then, explain what Stern means by this statement.

4. Stern supports his points with examples drawn from his own experience. Is this enough? What other kinds of evidence could he have used?

5. In paragraph 5, Stern says that every undergraduate at Berkeley "undergoes a form of indoctrination." What does he mean? Does Stern make a valid point, or is he **begging the question**?

6. Why does Stern discuss Bettina Aptheker in paragraphs 15–16? Could he be accused of making an *ad hominem* attack? Why or why not?

This code came out of a June 1992 meeting of the American Association of University Professors.

ON FREEDOM OF EXPRESSION AND CAMPUS SPEECH CODES

AMERICAN ASSOCIATION OF UNIVERSITY PROFESSORS

Freedom of thought and expression is essential to any institution of higher 1 learning. Universities and colleges exist not only to transmit existing knowledge. Equally, they interpret, explore, and expand that knowledge by testing the old and proposing the new.

This mission guides learning outside the classroom quite as much as in 2 class, and often inspires vigorous debate on those social, economic, and political issues that arouse the strongest passions. In the process, views will be expressed that may seem to many wrong, distasteful, or offensive. Such is the nature of freedom to sift and winnow ideas.

> "On a campus that is free and open, no idea can be banned or forbidden."

On a campus that is free and open, 3 no idea can be banned or forbidden. No viewpoint or message may be deemed so hateful or disturbing that it may not be expressed.

Universities and colleges are also 4 communities, often of a residential character. Most campuses have recently sought to become more diverse, and more reflective of the larger community, by attracting students, faculty, and staff from groups that were historically excluded or underrepresented. Such gains as they have made are recent, modest, and tenuous. The campus climate can profoundly affect an institution's continued diversity. Hostility or intolerance to persons who differ from the majority (especially if seemingly condoned by the institution) may undermine the confidence of new members of the community. Civility is always fragile and can easily be destroyed.

In response to verbal assaults and use of hateful language some campuses 5 have felt it necessary to forbid the expression of racist, sexist, homophobic, or ethnically demeaning speech, along with conduct or behavior that harasses. Several reasons are offered in support of banning such expression. Individuals and groups that have been victims of such expression feel an understandable outrage. They claim that the academic progress of minority and majority alike may suffer if fears, tensions, and conflicts spawned by slurs and insults create an environment inimical to learning. These arguments, grounded in the need to foster an atmosphere respectful of and welcome to all persons, strike a deeply responsive chord in the academy. But, while we can acknowledge both the weight of these concerns and the thoughtfulness of those persuaded of the need for regulation, rules that ban or punish speech based upon its content cannot be justified. An institution of higher learning fails to fulfill its mission if it asserts the power to proscribe ideas—and racial or ethnic slurs, sexist epithets, or homophobic insults almost always express ideas, however repugnant. Indeed, by proscribing any ideas, a university sets an example that profoundly disserves its academic mission. Some may seek to defend a distinction between the regulation of the content of speech and the regulation of the manner (or style) of speech. We find this distinction untenable in practice because offensive style or opprobrious phrases may in fact have been chosen precisely for their expressive power. As the United States Supreme Court has said in the course of rejecting criminal sanctions for offensive words: Words are often chosen as much for their emotive as their cognitive force. We cannot sanction the view that the Constitution, while solicitous of the cognitive content of individual speech, has little or no regard for that emotive function which, practically speaking, may often be the more important element of the overall message sought to be communicated. The line between substance and style is thus too uncertain to sustain the pressure that will inevitably be brought to bear upon disciplinary rules that attempt to regulate speech. Proponents of speech codes sometimes reply that the value of emotive language of this type is of such a low order that, on balance, suppression is justified by the harm suffered by those who are directly affected, and by the general damage done to the learning environment. Yet a college or university sets a perilous course if it seeks to differentiate between high-value and low-value speech, or to choose which groups are to be protected by curbing the speech of others. A speech code unavoidably implies an institutional competence to distinguish permissible expression of hateful thought from what is proscribed as thoughtless hate. Institutions would also have to justify shielding some, but not other, targets of offensive language—not to political preference, to religious but not to philosophical creed, or perhaps even to some but not to other religious affiliations. Starting down this path creates an even greater risk that groups not originally protected may later demand similar solicitude—demands the institution that began the process of banning some speech is ill equipped to resist.

Distinctions of this type are neither practicable nor principled; their very 6 fragility underscores why institutions devoted to freedom of thought and expression ought not adopt an institutionalized coercion of silence.

Moreover, banning speech often avoids consideration of means more 7 compatible with the mission of an academic institution by which to deal with incivility, intolerance, offensive speech, and harassing behavior:

1. Institutions should adopt and invoke a range of measures that penalize conduct and behavior, rather than speech, such as rules against defacing property, physical intimidation or harassment, or disruption of campus activities. All members of the campus community should be made aware of such rules, and administrators should be ready to use them in preference to speech-directed sanctions.

2. Colleges and universities should stress the means they use best—to educate—including the development of courses and other curricular and

co-curricular experiences designed to increase student understanding and to deter offensive or intolerant speech or conduct. Such institutions should, of course, be free (indeed encouraged) to condemn manifestations of intolerance and discrimination, whether physical or verbal.

3. The governing board and the administration have a special duty not only to set an outstanding example of tolerance, but also to challenge boldly and condemn immediately serious breaches of civility.

4. Members of the faculty, too, have a major role; their voices may be critical in condemning intolerance, and their actions may set examples for understanding, making clear to their students that civility and tolerance are hallmarks of educated men and women.

5. Student personnel administrators have in some ways the most demanding role of all, for hate speech occurs most often in dormitories, locker-rooms, cafeterias, and student centers. Persons who guide this part of campus life should set high standards of their own for tolerance and should make unmistakably clear the harm that uncivil or intolerant speech inflicts.

To some persons who support speech codes, measures like these—relying 8 as they do on suasion rather than sanctions—may seem inadequate. But freedom of expression requires toleration of "ideas we hate," as Justice Holmes put it. The underlying principle does not change because the demand is to silence a hateful speaker, or because it comes from within the academy. Free speech is not simply an aspect of the educational enterprise to be weighed against other desirable ends. It is the very precondition of the academic enterprise itself.

⊘ AT ISSUE: HOW FREE SHOULD FREE SPEECH BE?

1. The writers of this statement rely primarily on deductive reasoning. Construct a syllogism that includes the selection's major premise, minor premise, and conclusion.

2. At what audience is this statement aimed—students, instructors, administrators, or the general public? How do you know?

3. What problem do the writers address? Where do they present their solution?

4. In paragraph 5, the writers discuss the major arguments against their position. Why do they address opposing arguments so early in the selection? How effectively do the writers refute these arguments?

5. Paragraph 7 is followed by a numbered list. What information is in this list? Why did the writers decide to set it off in this way?

6. What do the writers mean when they say that free speech "is the very precondition of the academic exercise itself" (para. 8)?

This essay first appeared in the *Washington Post* on February 20, 2015.

INTIMIDATION IS THE NEW NORMAL

JONATHAN HAIDT

Images of fires, fireworks, and metal barricades crashing through windows 1
made for great television, but the rioters who shut down Milo Yiannopoulos's talk at the University of California at Berkeley didn't just attack property.
Fewer cell phone cameras captured the moments when they punched and
pepper-sprayed members of the crowd, particularly those who seemed like
they might be supporters of Yiannopoulos or Donald Trump.

Although the violence on February 1 was clearly instigated by outside 2
agitators—"black bloc" anarchists who show up at events with their faces
masked—at least some of the people behind the masks were Berkeley students
who thought it was morally permissible to use violence to stop a lecture from
taking place. As one student wrote afterward, "Violence helped ensure the
safety of students." Another asked, "When the nonviolent tactics [for stopping
the talk] have been exhausted—what is left?"

Still, it was easy for the academic community to think of the riot as a spe- 3
cial case. After all, Yiannopoulos is a professional troll. He came to campus to
provoke, not to instruct. And he had exposed vulnerable individuals to danger
before, as when he posted the name and photo of a trans woman on-screen
while he mocked her.

A month later, on March 2, the violence was harder to justify. After stu- 4
dents shouted down Charles Murray's attempt to give a lecture at Middlebury
College, he was moved to a locked room in the student center from which
his talk was live-streamed. Angry students pounded on the walls and pulled
fire alarms to disrupt the broadcast. As Murray and his faculty host—Allison
Stanger, a political-science professor—left the building, they were blocked by
an "angry mob" (Stanger's words) including both students and nonstudents. As
Stanger and Murray tried to push their way through, with the help of two security guards, several people grabbed and pulled at them, sending her to the hospital with whiplash and a concussion. Stanger later wrote that she had feared
for her life.

Perhaps because it was a professor who was injured, Middlebury students 5
did not defend the use of violence in the way that some Berkeley students had.
But even the students' coordinated effort to silence Murray is harder to justify
than the effort to silence Yiannopoulos. Murray is mild-mannered, came with
co-sponsorship from the political-science department, and was there not to
provoke but to talk about an issue that is central to students' moral and political concerns: social and economic inequality. When two psychologists, Wendy
Williams and Stephen Ceci, asked 70 professors at various colleges to assess

the political leaning of Murray's speech—given to them as a transcript with no source attributed—they rated it as "middle of the road," leaning neither left nor right.

But for many students and professors, what Murray intended to say was not 6 relevant. The Southern Poverty Law Center had labeled him a "white supremacist" on the basis of his writings, and that was sufficient for many to believe that they had a moral duty to deny a platform to him. So perhaps Murray was a special case, too—some said his mere presence, like Yiannopoulos's at Berkeley, posed a direct danger to students. (I urge readers to see Murray's line-by-line corrections of the Southern Poverty Law Center's entry on him, then read some of his writings and decide for themselves.)

A month after the Middlebury fracas came the Heather Mac Donald 7 shout-down at Claremont McKenna College. But this was no special case. Mac Donald is a typical campus speaker—a journalist and political commentator who wrote a book challenging prevailing wisdom on a matter of current concern.

In her 2016 book, *The War on Cops*, she argued that overstated claims 8 about systemic racism among police officers have led police departments in some cities to adopt less assertive tactics, which has led to increased crime, including higher rates of murder, particularly of black men. Her thesis, popularly known as "the Ferguson effect," has been hotly debated, but as the left-leaning sociologist Neil Gross summarized the state of play last September, "there is now some evidence that when all eyes are on police misconduct, crime may edge up. Progressives should acknowledge that this idea isn't far-fetched."

Yet because Mac Donald challenged the dominant narrative and criticized 9 the Black Lives Matter movement, some students at Claremont McKenna decided that she, too, must be denied a platform. They mobilized a mass action via Facebook with a call to "show up wearing black" and "bring your comrades, because we're shutting this down." A mob outside the auditorium, estimated at around 300 people, prevented anyone from entering the building. The college decided to stream Mac Donald's talk live from the nearly empty hall as hundreds of protesters pounded on the windows. Immediately afterward, she was whisked away through a kitchen exit by the campus police in an unmarked car.

What are we to make of this? There were no reports of violence or prop- 10 erty damage. Yet this event is potentially more ominous than the Berkeley and Middlebury violence, for we are witnessing the emergence of a dangerous new norm for responding to speakers who challenge campus orthodoxy. Anyone offended by the speaker can put out a call on Facebook to bring together students and locals, including "antifa" (antifascist) and black-bloc activists who explicitly endorse the use of violence against racists and fascists. Because of flagrant "concept creep," however, almost anyone who is politically right of center can be labeled a racist or a fascist, and the promiscuous use of such labels is now part of the standard operating procedure. The call to shut down Mac Donald's talk asserted, without evidence, that her agenda is "racist, anti-Black, capitalist, imperialist, [and] fascist." As with accusations of witchcraft in earlier centuries, once such labels are attached to someone, few will dare to challenge their accuracy, lest they be accused of the same crimes.

It is crucial to note that at all three colleges—Berkeley, Middlebury, and 11 Claremont McKenna—the crowd included a mix of students and locals, some wearing masks. It is therefore no longer possible to assume that a crowd on a college campus will be nonviolent, as crowds of protesting students were in the fall of 2015. What would have happened to Mac Donald had she tried to enter or exit through the main entrance, without a police escort? From now on, any campus speaker who arouses a protest is at risk of a beating. Can this really be the future of American higher education?

I do not doubt that many students face indignities and insults because of 12 their race, gender, sexual orientation, or ability status. I respect students who take actions motivated by their concern for their fellow students. But these actions reflect choices that have far-reaching and potentially damaging consequences. First, there is the decision to appraise events in ways that amplify their harmfulness. A common feature of recent campus shout-downs is the argument that the speaker "dehumanizes" members of marginalized groups or "denies their right to exist." No quotations or citations are given for such strong assertions; these are rhetorical moves made to strengthen the case against the speaker. But if students come to believe that anyone who offends them has "dehumanized" them, they are setting themselves up for far greater vulnerability and isolation. Life, love, and work are full of small offenses and misunderstandings, many of which will now be experienced as monstrous and unforgivable.

Second, students in the past few years have increasingly opted for collective action to shut down talks by speakers they dislike, rather than taking the two traditional options available to all individuals: Don't go to the talk, or go and engage the speaker in the question-and-answer period. The decision to turn so many events into collective moral struggles has profound ramifications for the entire college. Everyone is pressured to take sides. Administrators are pressured to disinvite speakers, or at least to condemn their scholarship and morals while reluctantly noting their right to speak. Petitions are floated, and names of signers (and abstainers) are noted. 13

> "It is no longer possible to assume that a crowd on a college campus will be nonviolent."

The human mind evolved for violent intergroup conflict. It comes easily 14 to us, and it can be so emotionally rewarding that we have invented many ways of engaging in it ritually, such as in team sports. But the tribal mind is incompatible with scholarship, open-minded thinking, toleration of dissent, and the search for truth. When tribal sentiments are activated within an academic community, some members start to believe that their noble collective ends justify almost any means, including the demonization of inconvenient research and researchers, false accusations, character assassination, and sometimes even violence. Anyone not with the movement is against it, and its enemies—students, faculty members, administrators—are often intimidated into acquiescence. This is how professors and students are increasingly describing their campus climate, at least at elite four-year residential colleges.

What can be done to change course? College professors, more than anyone else in the country, have a professional duty to speak up for the freedom of scholars, authors, and journalists to present unpopular ideas, theories, and research findings, free from intimidation and harassment. The next time an unpopular speaker is invited to campus, professors should talk to their classes about the norms of the academy, the benefits of having one's cherished ideas challenged, and the impropriety of making slurs and *ad hominem* arguments. Then they should attend the event themselves—especially if they dislike the speaker. 15

But while professors are best placed to act as role models, it is only administrators who can set and enforce rules. At New York University, where I teach, the policy on protests is detailed and reasonable. It allows silent protests and brief outbursts within the lecture hall, but it states clearly that "chanting or making other sustained or repeated noise in a manner which substantially interferes with the speaker's communication is not permitted." Most colleges have such policies, but they are rarely enforced, even after the college president offers fine words about freedom of speech. From now on, administrators must ensure that any students who violate protest policies will be disciplined or expelled. There must be zero tolerance for mob rule, intimidation of speakers, and intimidation of political minorities among students as well as faculty members. Alumni can help by making it clear that they will give no further funds to colleges that permit students to shout down speakers with impunity. 16

And finally, when responsible campus leaders all fail to create a campus where diverse perspectives can be heard and discussed, students who desire such a campus must stand up and make their wishes known. There are encouraging signs on this front. In the wake of the unexpected outcome of the 2016 presidential election, the editors of Harvard's main student newspaper called on administrators and faculty members to "take active steps to ensure that students of all political stripes feel comfortable voicing their ideas, especially in the classroom." More recently, Northwestern University became the first in the country whose student government passed a resolution calling on the administration to promote viewpoint diversity and to enforce its policies against disruptive protests. 17

This year may become a turning point in the annals of higher education. It may be remembered as the year that political violence and police escorts became ordinary parts of campus life. Or it may be remembered as the year when professors, students, and administrators finally found the moral courage to stand up against intimidation, even when it is aimed at people whose ideas they dislike. 18

⊃ AT ISSUE: HOW FREE SHOULD FREE SPEECH BE?

1. Haidt begins his essay by devoting eight paragraphs to discussing three violent protests. How does this discussion set the stage for the rest of the essay?

2. At the end of paragraph 6, Haidt urges readers to do some research into Charles Murray's writings and then "decide for themselves" if his presence poses a danger to students. Why doesn't Haidt supply this information? What does he hope to gain by telling people to "decide for themselves"?

3. Is Haidt's argument primarily inductive or deductive? Why do you think he chose the strategy that he uses?

4. Does Haidt ever establish that the situation he describes is widespread enough to be a problem? Could he be accused of setting up a **straw man**? Explain.

5. Haidt begins paragraph 15 by asking a question. What is the function of this question?

6. What does Haidt want to accomplish with his essay? Is his purpose to convince readers of something? To move them to action? What is your reaction to his essay?

TALKING PAST EACH OTHER ON FREE SPEECH

LAURIE ESSIG

College free-speech controversies, I fear, will rage on because opposing sides 1 talk past each other.

On one side are those who insist that speech is simply free—no ifs, ands, 2 or buts. These are often the same people who insist that markets are free, disregarding, in both arenas, that society isn't made up only of individuals but also of structures and histories that give advantage to the elite while oppressing poor people and ethnic, racial, religious, and sexual minorities.

Those most disadvantaged by so-called free speech insist that we consider 3 its costs, and they see certain ideas as acts of symbolic violence. They consider blocking it a form of self-defense. When hate crimes are on the rise, when anti-immigrant and anti-minority sentiment is in the wind, to tolerate bigotry is to invite brutalization, the reasoning goes.

In fact, everyone—right, left, and center—can see the costs of speech 4 when it is directed at them and their sense of safety in the world.

After all, if the right really believes we should all be hearty enough to con- 5 sider views we find abhorrent, why did it cast off one of its media darlings? Free speech was the right's mantra with regard to its golden boy Milo Yiannopoulos, whose tweets were so racist and misogynist that he was kicked off Twitter. When he came to Berkeley on his "Dangerous Faggot" tour, students protested, black-bloc agitators rioted, and the right-wing Twittersphere went ballistic over those "precious snow-flake" students too fragile to bear his provocations.

But free speech, as it turns out, applies only when it doesn't touch on 6 matters one holds especially dear. The right became its own precious snow-flake when Yiannopoulos talked about teenaged boys as sexual subjects who could consent to sex with adult men. When his words undermined the idea that teenagers are children and that children are innocent, the "sticks and stones will break my bones but words will never hurt me" camp screamed "Shut him down," and shut him down it did: Yiannopoulos was forced to part ways with Breitbart News, disinvited to speak at the Conservative Political Action Conference, and lost his book deal with Simon & Schuster.

Targets of rhetoric like Yiannopoulos's reasonably insist that we acknowl- 7 edge symbolic violence not only in raucous provocations but in seemingly polite racist, sexist, or homophobic opining as well. Recently the very polite Charles Murray was invited by a student group to speak at Middlebury College, where I teach. His 1994 book with Richard J. Herrnstein, *The Bell Curve*, posited a racial basis of intelligence as measured through IQ tests.

The authors used spurious correlations, as well as a highly problematic measure of intelligence, to trot out old, eugenicist arguments that have oft been debunked.

When Murray came to Middlebury in 2007 to discuss his research, accord- 8 ing to some alumni of color, it felt pretty awful to sit in a room and have your intelligence and, by extension, your right to be at Middlebury, publicly debated. Many said they wished they had been more forceful in protesting Murray's presence then.

So this time, more than 450 alumni and over 70 faculty members (includ- 9 ing me) spoke up. We asked the political-science department to withdraw its cosponsorship of the event, or to at least make it a panel-type discussion so that Murray's views might be contested. We also asked President Laurie Patton not to introduce him.

We weren't trying to block Murray from speaking. We were seeking some 10 recognition that words can and do hurt, that they can be a form of symbolic violence, the sort pretty obvious to faculty, students, and staff of color, who are already told, in a million small ways, that they don't belong at Middlebury. They can be made fun of in Halloween costumes or "thug"-themed parties where white bros wear baggy jeans and carry malt liquor, casually using the N-word and laughing if anyone is offended. The white bros "belong" at Middlebury, you see. Many of them have relatives, parents, grandparents, even great-grandparents who went to Middlebury or places like it. No one ever debates *their* intelligence, no matter how little of it they display.

The Murray event's organizers encouraged us to debate his ideas and to 11 counter his eugenicist arguments with evidence and pointed questions. To be fair, many at Middlebury, including the president and the political-science faculty, were worried about censorship and committed to the idea that we must be able to hear ideas we find disagreeable. For people who feel threatened in the current political climate, however, polite debate about disagreeable ideas is a luxury they can no longer afford. We live in dangerous times, when immigrants fear expulsion and hate crimes are on the rise. Personal vulnerability drowns out the fear of censorship.

By the time Murray arrived on campus, the mood was explosive. Protest- 12 ers shut down his talk, and Allison Stanger, a political-science professor moderating Murray's appearance, was injured, although the circumstances around that are still murky.

Since then commentators in the *Atlantic*, the *New York Times*, and else- 13 where have attacked Middlebury for being against free speech. We receive emails and tweets calling us "brown-shirts" who seek to "muzzle" speakers. As I write this, my program, gender, sexuality, and feminist studies, is being trolled on Twitter by Murray's American Enterprise Institute colleague Christina Hoff Sommers. The right-wing website The Daily Wire suggests ludicrously that our curriculum is the reason "many leftist students felt compelled not only to disrupt Murray's speech, but also to rationalize the use of violence to combat ideas that they did not agree with." This is the sort of free speech the right loves: It targets feminist, critical race, postcolonial, and queer scholars in ways that are intimidating and designed to shut us up. It calls our courses "categorically insane."

The notion that our curriculum incited violence isn't just wrong, it's slan- 14 derous. But categorical insanity, differently read, is closer to the truth, for our curriculum does teach students to be critical thinkers, to question dominant ideologies and "common sense." The commonsensical notion that speech is free, for instance, and that we all enter fields of speech as equals is certainly a category of inquiry within our program. That must seem incomprehensible, or "insane," to those who do not want to question why things are the way they are. We expect our students to experience "category crisis" when looking from new vantage points at prevailing ways of seeing.

It is this sort of "categorical insanity," in fact, that might just extricate us all 15 from the speech quagmire. That kind of analysis shows that our ways of seeing the world are shaped by our circumstances: race, gender, sexual orientation, class, and so on. When people on the right say they feel their traditions and livelihoods are threatened, I don't question the strength of their feelings. When those on the left no longer want to bear the pain of having their human worth debated, I recognize their outrage. When those in the middle acknowledge that ostensibly free speech has costs, but that censorship is too high a price to ever pay, I trust their sincerity as well, and I agree with them.

> "If we can't untie these infinite knots, maybe we can at least remember how to live together."

Surely Christina Hoff Sommers, 16 a former philosophy professor, understands the nature and value of such category analysis. A free-speech advocate, as I am, she can no doubt find a critique of my department more articulate and empathetic than her tweeted "Oy vey."

I am a card-carrying member of the free-speech absolutist ACLU. I also 17 believe that when institutions support even polite racism and misogyny, they aggravate deep, ancient wounds, symbolically excluding those who have been historically excluded for many generations. I am truly concerned, too, about censorship, since when it is backed by the state it is usually targeted against the likes of me, not Charles Murray.

This queer inability, this refusal to be labeled, requires that I live with 18 unresolvable contradictions. So must we all. Neither Middlebury nor any other college can resolve them. Trite appeals to civility won't resolve them either, nor will columnists' scolds nor acts of violence.

But if we can't untie these infinite knots, maybe we can at least remem- 19 ber how to live together. Academe, and thoughtful people outside it, can begin to acknowledge not just intellectual but also circumstantial ways of perceiving speech.

Whether you're on the right or the left or in the topsy-turvy anxious mid- 20
dle, take a breath. Recognize the vastness of the gaps between us. Recognize
too the humanity and the life experiences of those you fear and scorn. Knowing that we understand speech, its costs and its freedoms, in radically different
ways isn't a tidy fix, but it is at least a first step toward actually hearing one
another.

⊘ AT ISSUE: HOW FREE SHOULD FREE SPEECH BE?

1. Throughout her essay, Essig accepts certain ideas as self-evident.
   What are they? Do you agree with her? Explain.

2. In paragraph 1, Essig says that the two sides to the free speech debate
   "talk past each other." What are two sides of the debate? Could Essig
   be accused of committing the **either/or fallacy**? Why or why not?

3. Does Essig appeal mainly to *logos, pathos,* or *ethos*? Explain.

4. Do Essig's sympathies lie with the protestors or those who wanted to
   give Charles Murray a platform for his ideas? How do you know? Why
   does Essig mention Christina Hoff Summers?

5. In her essay, Essig says that she is concerned about censorship
   because it is usually targeted against people like her. What does she
   mean? How do you know?

6. Essig concludes by saying the problem she has defined cannot be
   easily solved. Does this concession undercut her argument in any
   way? Explain.

VISUAL ARGUMENT: FOOTBALL PLAYERS KNEELING

AP Images/Marcio Jose Sanchez

⊙ AT ISSUE: HOW FREE SHOULD FREE SPEECH BE?

1. What point is this visual making? What course of action do you think it is advocating?

2. What visual elements are included in this picture? How does the arrangement of the people help the visual make its point?

3. How does this visual create an emotion appeal? Does it also appeal to *logos* and to *ethos*? Explain.

4. Write a caption for this visual that communicates its main point. Do you think that taking a knee at a football game is a legitimate form of protest? Do you think this type of protest reinforces or undermines our constitutional right to free speech? Explain.

TEMPLATE FOR WRITING A DEDUCTIVE ARGUMENT

Write a one-paragraph **deductive** argument in which you argue *against* your school imposing speech codes. Follow the template below, filling in the blanks to create your argument.

One of the basic principles of the United States government is the constitutional guarantee of freedom of speech. With few exceptions, all Americans _____ _____ _____. In college _____ _____. For example, _____ _____. By having the right to express themselves freely, _____ _____ _____. Therefore, _____ _____

Not everyone agrees with this view, however. Some people argue that _____ _____ _____ _____. This argument misses the point. When a university limits the speech of some students because others may be upset by their comments, _____ _____ _____

For this reason, colleges should _____ _____ _____ _____

TEMPLATE FOR WRITING AN INDUCTIVE ARGUMENT

Write a one-paragraph **inductive** argument in which you argue *in favor of* your school imposing speech codes. Follow the template below, filling in the blanks to create your argument.

The number of students demanding protection from distasteful ideas is growing yearly. Some students complain that _____

_____

_____. These students want _____

_____.

A number of studies have shown that so-called safe spaces and trigger warnings go a long way toward calming students' fears and creating a hospitable learning environment. For example, some

students _____

_____. As a result, _____

_____

_____. The best way for colleges to deal with this

problem is to _____

_____.

Free speech advocates, however, argue that _____

_____

_____

_____. Although this may be true, _____

_____

_____.

For this reason, it would make sense to _____

_____

_____.

⊘ EXERCISE 5.13 REVISING YOUR ARGUMENT PARAGRAPHS

Interview several of your classmates as well as one or two of your instructors about how free free speech should be. Then, revise the deductive and inductive arguments you wrote using the preceding templates so that they include some of these comments.

⊘ EXERCISE 5.14 WRITING DEDUCTIVE OR INDUCTIVE ARGUMENTS

Write an essay in which you take a position on the question, "Should Universities Be Able to Place Limits on Free Speech?" Make sure that your essay is organized primarily as either a deductive argument or an inductive argument. Use the readings on pages 166–185 as source material, and be sure to document all information that you get from these sources. (See Chapter 10 for information on documenting sources.)

⊘ EXERCISE 5.15 CHECKING FOR FALLACIES

Review the logical fallacies discussed on pages 162–163. Then, reread the essay you wrote for Exercise 5.14, and check to see if it contains any fallacies. Underline any fallacies you find, and identify them by name. Then, rewrite each statement so it expresses a logical argument. Finally, revise your draft to eliminate any fallacies you found.

⊘ EXERCISE 5.16 REVIEWING THE FOUR PILLARS OF ARGUMENT

Review the four pillars of argument discussed in Chapter 1. Does your essay include all four elements of an effective argument? Add anything that is missing. Then, label the key elements of your essay.

The 2016 film *Hidden Figures* adapted the stories of real-life black women who worked in STEM fields at NASA in the 1960s, including mathematician Dorothy Vaughan (played in the film by Octavia Spencer). Dorothy Vaughan: The Picture Art Collection/Alamy. *Hidden Figures:* LEVIATHAN FILMS/CHERNIN ENT/FOX 2000 PICTURES/Album/Alamy Stock Photo

6

Rogerian Argument, Toulmin Logic, and Oral Arguments

Why Are So Few Women in STEM Fields?

Until fairly recently, professions such as medicine, law, dentistry, and veterinary practices were overwhelmingly male. Beginning in the 1970s, however, this began to change, and today we can see a major shift within these professions. For example, in 2017, women outnumbered men in American medical schools for the first time in history. Similar shifts can be seen in other previously male-dominated professions—but not in the disciplines referred to as STEM (science, technology, engineering, and mathematics).

Despite the efforts of high schools and colleges, the percentage of women majoring in computer science and in engineering is below 20 percent. In the workplace, the numbers are even lower: only 10.7 percent of computer hardware engineers and 8 percent of mechanical engineers are women. Many people have tried to find an explanation for this disparity. In 2005, Larry Summers, the president of Harvard University, provoked a furor at a conference by suggesting that prejudice alone cannot explain the gender gap in science and math.

More recently, in 2017, James Damore, an engineer at Google, wrote an internal memo that criticized Google's diversity policy, referring to the company as an "ideological echo chamber." Although Damore asserted that he was opposed to workplace sexism and stereotyping, he went on to claim that the male/female imbalance in STEM fields is at least partly the result of biological differences and cannot be eliminated without resorting to discrimination against men. Damore's memo created an uproar at Google, and as a result, he was fired. Others take a more nuanced view of the situation and look for more complex explanations—for example, discrimination and lifestyle choices—to account for women's underrepresentation in STEM fields.

Later in this chapter, you will be asked to think more about this issue. You will be given several sources to consider and asked to write an argument—using one of the three approaches discussed in this chapter—that takes a position on why women are underrepresented in STEM fields.

Understanding Rogerian Argument

The traditional model of argument is **confrontational**—characterized by conflict and opposition. This has been the tradition since Aristotle wrote about argument in ancient Greece. The end result of this model of argument is that someone is a winner and someone is a loser or someone is right and someone is wrong.

Arguments do not always have to be confrontational, however. In fact, the twentieth-century psychologist Carl Rogers contended that in many situations, this method of arguing can actually be counterproductive, making it impossible for two people to reach agreement. According to Rogers, attacking opponents and telling them that they are wrong or misguided puts them on the defensive. The result of this tactic is frequently ill will, anger, hostility, and conflict. If you are trying to negotiate an agreement or convince someone to do something, these are exactly the responses that you do not want. To solve this problem, Rogers developed a new approach to argument—one that emphasizes cooperation and consensus over confrontation.

Rogerian argument begins with the assumption that people of good will can find solutions to problems that they have in common. Rogers recommends that you consider those with whom you disagree as colleagues, not opponents. Instead of entering into the adversarial relationship that is assumed in classical argument, Rogerian argument encourages you to enter into a cooperative relationship in which both you and your readers search for **common ground**—points of agreement about a problem. By taking this approach, you are more likely to find a solution that will satisfy everyone.

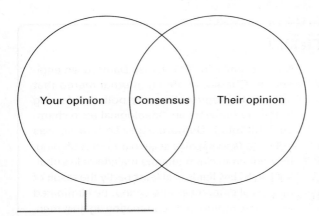

Rogerian argument as a Venn diagram

Structuring Rogerian Arguments

Consider the following situation. Assume that you bought a video game console that stopped working one week after the warranty expired. Also assume that the manager of the store where you purchased the game console has refused to exchange it for another console. His point is that because the warranty has expired, the store has no obligation to take the product back. As a last resort, you write a letter to the game console's manufacturer. If you were writing a traditional argument, you would state your thesis—"It is clear that I should receive a new game console"—and then present arguments to support your position. You would also refute opposing arguments, and you would end your letter with a strong concluding statement.

Because Rogerian arguments begin with different assumptions, however, they are structured differently from classical arguments. In a Rogerian argument, you would begin by establishing common ground—by pointing out the concerns you and the video game console's manufacturer share. For example, you could say that as a consumer, you want to buy merchandise that will work as advertised. If the company satisfies your needs, you will continue to buy its products. This goal is shared by the manufacturer. Therefore, instead of beginning with a thesis statement that demands a yes or no response, you would point out that you and the manufacturer share an interest in solving your problem.

Next, you would describe *in neutral terms*—using impartial, unbiased language—the manufacturer's view of the problem, defining the manufacturer's concerns and attempting to move toward a compromise position. For example, you would explain that you understand that the company wants to make a high-quality product that will satisfy customers. You would also say that you understand that despite the company's best efforts, mistakes sometimes happen.

In the next section of your letter, you would present your own view of the problem fairly and objectively. This section plays a major role in convincing the manufacturer that your position has merit. Here, you should also try to concede the strengths of the manufacturer's viewpoint. For example, you can say that although you understand that warranties have time limits, your case has some unique circumstances that justify your claim.

Then you would explain how the manufacturer would benefit from granting your request. Perhaps you could point out that you have been satisfied with other products made by this manufacturer and expect to purchase more in the future. You could also say that instead of requesting a new game console, you would be glad to send the console back to the factory to be repaired. This suggestion shows that you are fair and willing to compromise.

Finally, your Rogerian argument would reinforce your position and end with a concluding statement that emphasizes the idea that you are certain that the manufacturer wants to settle this matter fairly.

❍ EXERCISE 6.1 IDENTIFYING COMMON GROUND

Read through the At Issue topics listed in this book's table of contents. Choose one topic, and then do the following:

1. Summarize your own position on the issue.

2. In a few sentences, summarize the main concerns of someone who holds the opposite position.

3. Identify some common ground that you and someone who holds the opposite position might have.

4. Write a sentence that explains how your position on the issue might benefit individuals (including those who hold opposing views) or society in general.

Writing Rogerian Arguments

Rogerian arguments are typically used to address issues that are open to compromise. By making it clear that you understand and respect the opinions of others, you avoid an "I win/you lose" situation and demonstrate empathy and respect for all points of view. In this sense, Rogerian arguments are more like negotiations than classical arguments. Thus, in a Rogerian argument, you spend a good deal of time defining the common ground that exists between you and those with whom you disagree. Ideally, you demonstrate that it is possible to reach a consensus, one that represents the common ground that exists between opposing sides. The more successful you are in accomplishing this goal, the more persuasive your argument will be. Of course with some issues—usually the most polarizing—a consensus is difficult or even impossible to achieve. In these cases, the best you can hope for is to convince people to agree on just one or two points. With other issues, however, you will be able to demonstrate to readers how they would benefit by moving toward your position.

> **NOTE**
>
> Although the Rogerian approach to argument can be used to develop a whole essay, it can also be part of a more traditional argument. In this case, it frequently appears in the refutation section, where opposing arguments are addressed.

In general, a Rogerian argument can be structured in the following way:

INTRODUCTION   Introduces the problem, pointing out how both the writer and reader are affected (establishes common ground)

BODY   Presents the reader's view of the problem

Presents the writer's view of the problem (includes evidence to support the writer's viewpoint)

Shows how the reader would benefit from moving toward the writer's position (includes evidence to support the writer's viewpoint)

Lays out possible compromises that would benefit both reader and writer (includes evidence to support the writer's viewpoint)

CONCLUSION   Strong concluding statement reinforces the thesis and emphasizes compromise

➔ EXERCISE 6.2 ANALYZING A ROGERIAN ARGUMENT

The following student essay includes all the elements of a Rogerian argument. This essay was written in response to the question, "Is it fair for instructors to require students to turn off their cell phones in class?" After you read the essay, answer the questions on page 198, consulting the preceding outline if necessary.

WHY CELL PHONES DO NOT BELONG IN THE CLASSROOM

ZOYA KAHN

Some college students think it is unfair for instructors to require them to turn off their cell phones during class. Because they are accustomed to constant cell phone access, they don't understand how such a rule is justified. Granted, a strict, no-exceptions policy requiring that cell phones be turned off all over campus is not fair, but neither is a policy that prevents instructors from imposing restrictions. Both students and instructors know that cell phone use—including texting—during class can be disruptive. In addition, most would agree that the primary goal of a university is to create a respectful learning environment and that cell phone use during class undercuts this goal. For this reason, it is in everyone's interest for instructors to institute policies that require students to turn off cell phones during class.

1

Common ground

Thesis statement

Many students believe that requiring them to turn off their cell phones is unfair because it makes them feel less safe. Students are understandably concerned that, with their phones turned off, they will be unreachable during an emergency. For example, text message alerts are part of the emergency response system for most universities. Similarly, cell phones are a way for friends and family to contact students if there is an emergency. For these reasons, many students think that they should be free to make their own decisions concerning cell use. They believe that by turning their phones to vibrate or silent mode, they are showing respect for their classmates. Moreover, students need to learn how to regulate their own technology use, which will extend well beyond academia and graduation. As Dinesha Johnson, a student at

2

Reader's view of the problem

Henry Ford College notes in an opinion column, "Allowing students to have the freedom to practice self-discipline with their personal phone usage is necessary because when they are allowed such freedoms in the workplace they will handle it responsibly" (Johnson). Most students are honest, responsible, and courteous. However, those few students who cannot control themselves or are simply determined to misuse their phones will do so, regardless of the school's phone policy.

Writer's view of the situation

To protect the integrity of the school's learning environment, instructors are justified in requiring students to turn off their phones. Studies over the past several years have shown how distracting cell phones can be during a class. For example, a ringing cell phone significantly impairs students' performance, and a vibrating phone can be just as distracting (End et al. 56–57). In addition, texting in class decreases students' ability to focus, lowers test performance, and lessens students' retention of class material (Tindell and Bohlander 2). More recent research suggests that more daily use of cell phones correlate with lower grade point averages among high school students (Barnwell). Even more disturbing, cell phones enable some students to cheat. Students can use cell phones to text test questions and answers, to search the web, and to photograph exams. Although asking students to turn off their phones will not prevent all these problems, it will reduce the abuses, and this will benefit the majority of students.

Benefits for reader of writer's position

Even though students have good reasons for wanting to keep their phones on, there are even better reasons for accepting some reasonable restrictions. First, when students use cell phones during class, they distract themselves (as well as their classmates) and undermine everyone's ability to learn. Second, having their cell phones on gives students a false sense of security. A leading cell phone company has found that cell phones can actually "detract from school safety and crisis preparedness" in numerous ways. For example, the use of cell phones during a crisis can overload the cell phone system and make it useless. In addition, cell phones make it easy for students to spread rumors and, in some cases, cell phone use has created more panic than the incidents that actually caused the rumors ("Cell Phones").

Possible compromise

One possible compromise is for instructors to join with students to create cell phone policies that take into consideration various situations and settings. For example, instructors could require students to turn off their phones only during exams. Instructors could also try to find ways to engage students by using cell phone technology in the classroom. For example, in some schools teachers take advantage of the various functions available on most cell phones—calculators, cameras, dictionaries, and internet browsers ("Cell Phones"). In addition, schools should consider implementing alternative emergency alert systems. Such compromises would ensure safety, limit possible disruptions, reduce the potential for academic dishonesty, and enhance learning. They also would have a better chance of succeeding because students would have to buy-in to the policies. As Anita Charles, the director of Secondary Teacher Education at Bates College and a researcher who has studied this topic, states, "Negotiation, when [students] feel that they're being listened to, benefits everybody, because the teacher finds that students become more cooperative" (McConville).

It is understandable that students want instructors to permit the use of cell phones during class, but it is also fair for instructors to ask students to turn them off. Although instructors should be able to restrict cell phone use, they should also make sure that students understand the need for this policy. It is in everyone's best interest to protect the integrity of the classroom and to make sure that learning is not compromised by cell phone use. To ensure the success of their education, students should be willing to turn off their phones.

6

Concluding statement

Works Cited

Barnwell, Paul. "Should Smartphones Be Banned from Classrooms?" *The Atlantic*, Atlantic Media Company, 27 Apr. 2016, www.theatlantic.com/education/archive/2016/04/do-smartphones-have-a-place-in-the-classroom/480231/.

"Cell Phones and Text Messaging in Schools." *National School Safety and Security Services*, 2012, www.schoolsecurity.org/trends/cell-phones-and-text-messaging-in-schools/.

End, Christian M., Shaye Worthman, Mary Bridget Mathews, and Katharina Wetterau. "Costly Cell Phones: The Impact of Cell Phone Rings on Academic Performance." *Teaching of Psychology*, vol. 37, no. 1, 2010, pp. 55–57. *Academic Search Complete*, doi: 10.1080/00986280903425912.

Johnson, Dinesh A. Mirror News. "Why Students Should Be Using Their Phones in Class." *Mirror News.* Henry Ford College, 29 Jan. 2018, mirrornews.hfcc.edu/news/2018/01-29/why-students-should-be -using-their-phones-class.

McConville, Emily. "Why Banning Cellphones in Schools Misses the Point." Bates Wordmark, Bates College, 23 Mar. 2018, www.bates .edu/news/2018/03/23/why-banning-cellphones-in-schools -misses-the-point.

Tindell, Deborah R., and Robert W. Bohlander. "The Use and Abuse of Cell Phones and Text Messaging in the Classroom: A Survey of College Students." *College Teaching,* vol. 60, no. 1, 2012, pp. 1–9. *ERIC Institute of Education Services,* eric.ed.gov/?id=EJ951966.

Identifying the Elements of a Rogerian Argument

1. How does the writer attempt to establish common ground? Do you think she is successful?

2. What evidence does the writer supply to support her position?

3. Other than reinforcing the writer's position, what else is the conclusion trying to accomplish?

4. How does the concluding statement reinforce agreement and compromise?

5. How would this essay be different if it were written as a traditional argument (as opposed to a Rogerian argument)?

Understanding Toulmin Logic

Another way of describing the structure of argument was introduced by the philosopher Stephen Toulmin in his book *The Uses of Argument* (1958). Toulmin observed that although formal logic is effective for analyzing classical arguments, it is inadequate for describing the arguments that occur in everyday life. Although Toulmin was primarily concerned with the structures of arguments at the level of sentences or paragraphs, his model is also useful when dealing with longer arguments.

In its simplest terms, a **Toulmin argument** has three parts—the *claim*, the *grounds*, and the *warrant*. The **claim** is the main point of the essay—usually stated as the thesis. The **grounds** are the evidence that a writer uses to support the claim. The **warrant** is the **inference**—either stated or implied—that connects the claim to the grounds.

A basic argument using Toulmin logic would have the following structure.

CLAIM	Online education should be a part of all students' education.
GROUNDS	Students who take advantage of online education get better grades and report less stress than students who do not.
WARRANT	Online education is a valuable educational option.

Notice that the preceding three-part structure resembles the **syllogism** that is the backbone of classical argument. (See pp. 130–133 for a discussion of syllogisms.)

> **NOTE**
>
> When you use Toulmin logic to construct an argument, you still use deductive and inductive reasoning. You arrive at your claim inductively from facts, observations, and examples, and you connect the grounds and the warrant to your claim deductively.

Constructing Toulmin Arguments

Real arguments—those you encounter in print or online every day—are not as simple as the preceding three-part model implies. To be convincing, arguments often contain additional parts. To account for the demands of everyday debates, Toulmin expanded his model to include the following six interconnected elements.

CLAIM	The **claim** is the main point of your essay. It is a debatable statement that the rest of the essay will support.
	Online education should be a part of all students' education.
GROUNDS	The **grounds** are the concrete evidence that a writer uses to support the claim. These are the facts and observations that support the thesis. They can also be the opinions of experts that you locate when you do research.
	Studies show that students who take advantage of online education often get better grades than students who do not.
	Research indicates that students who take advantage of online education are under less stress than those who do not.

WARRANT
: The **warrant** is the inference that links the claim with the grounds. The warrant is often an unstated assumption. Ideally, the warrant should be an idea with which your readers will agree. (If they do not agree with it, you will need to supply **backing**.)

Online education is a valuable educational option.

BACKING
: The **backing** consists of statements that support the warrant.

My own experience with online education was positive. Not only did it enable me to schedule classes around my job but it also enabled me to work at my own pace in my courses.

QUALIFIERS
: The **qualifiers** are statements that limit the claim. For example, they can be the real-world conditions under which the claim is true. These qualifiers can include words such as *most, few, some, sometimes, occasionally, often,* and *usually*.

Online education should be a required part of most *students' education.*

REBUTTALS
: The **rebuttals** are exceptions to the claim. They are counterarguments that identify the situations where the claim does not hold true.

Some people argue that online education deprives students of an interactive classroom experience, but a course chat room can give students a similar opportunity to interact with their classmates.

● EXERCISE 6.3 PLANNING A TOULMIN ARGUMENT

Look through this book's table of contents, and select an At Issue topic that interests you (ideally, one that you know something about). Write a sentence that states your position on this issue. (In terms of Toulmin argument, this statement is the *claim*.)

Then, supply as many of the expanded Toulmin model elements as you can, consulting the preceding description of these elements.

Claim: _____

_____

Grounds: _____

_____

_____

_____

Warrant: _____

_____

_____

Backing: _____

_____

Qualifiers: _____

_____

_____

Rebuttals: _____

_____

Writing Toulmin Arguments

One of the strengths of the Toulmin model is that it recognizes that effective arguments often involve more than stating ideas in absolute terms. Unlike the classical model of argument, the Toulmin model encourages writers to make realistic and convincing points by including claims and qualifiers and by addressing opposing arguments in down-to-earth and constructive ways. In a sense, this method of constructing an argument reminds writers that arguments do not exist in a vacuum. They are often quite subtle and are aimed at real readers who may or may not agree with them.

In general, a Toulmin argument can be organized in the following way:

INTRODUCTION	Introduces the problem
	States the claim (and possibly the qualifier)
BODY	Possibly states the warrant
	Presents the backing that supports the warrant
	Presents the grounds that support the claim
	Presents the conditions of rebuttal
	States the qualifiers
CONCLUSION	Brings the argument to a close
	Strong concluding statement reinforces the claim

> ◯ **EXERCISE 6.4 ANALYZING A TOULMIN ARGUMENT**
> The following student essay, which includes all the elements of a Toulmin argument, was written in response to the question, "Are cheerleaders athletes?" After you read the essay, answer the questions on page 204, consulting the preceding outline if necessary.

COMPETITIVE CHEERLEADERS ARE ATHLETES

JEN DAVIS

Recently, the call to make competitive cheerleading an official college sport and to recognize cheerleaders as athletes has gotten stronger. Critics of this proposal maintain that cheerleading is simply entertainment that occurs on the sidelines of real sporting events. According to them, although cheerleading may show strength and skill, it is not a competitive activity. This view of cheerleading, however, misses the point. Because competitive cheerleading pits teams against each other in physically and technically demanding athletic contests, it should be recognized as a sport. For this reason, those who participate in the sport of competitive cheerleading should be considered athletes.

Acknowledging them as athletes gives them the respect and support they deserve. Many people associate cheerleading with pom-poms and short skirts and ignore the strength and skill that the competitive version requires. After all, cheerleaders are supposed to be cheering on boys and men who play "real" sports, right? Part of the problem is a stereotype from cheerleading in the National Football League, which "essentially comprises of dance routines performed by scantily clad women in glittery boots" (Pant). Not surprisingly then (and much like athletes in other female-dominated sports), cheerleaders have had to fight to be taken seriously. For example, Title IX, the law that mandates gender equity in college sports, does not recognize competitive cheerleading as a sport. This situation assumes a very narrow definition of sports, one that needs to be updated. For example, note how women's versions of long-accepted men's sports—such as basketball, soccer, and track—are easy for people to respect and to

Claim and qualifier

Warrant
Backing

Grounds

1

2

support. Competitive cheerleading, however, departs from this model and is not seen as a sport even though those who compete in it are skilled, accomplished athletes. Moreover, they do so at considerable physical risk: while overall injuries in the sport are low, college cheerleaders have the highest catastrophic injury rate (Lundy).

Recent proposals to rename competitive cheerleading "stunt" or "team acrobatics and tumbling" are an effort to reshape people's ideas about what cheerleaders actually do. Although some cheerleading squads have kept to their original purpose—to lead fans in cheering on their teams—competitive teams practice rigorously, maintain impressive levels of physical fitness, and risk serious injuries. Like other sports, competitive cheerleading involves extraordinary feats of strength and skill. Cheerleaders perform elaborate floor routines and ambitious stunts, including flips from multilevel human pyramids. Competitive cheerleaders also do what all athletes must do: they enter competitive contests, are judged, and emerge as winners or losers.

3 Backing

Grounds

Those in authority, however, are slow to realize that cheerleading is a sport. In 2010, a federal judge declared that competitive cheerleading was "too underdeveloped and disorganized" to qualify as a legitimate varsity sport under Title IX (Tigay). This ruling was shortsighted. Before competitive cheerleading can develop as a sport, it needs to be *acknowledged* as a sport. Without their schools' financial support, cheerleading teams cannot recruit, offer scholarships, or host competitions. To address this situation, several national groups are asking the National Collegiate Athletic Association (NCAA) to designate competitive cheerleading as an "emerging sport." By doing this, the NCAA would show its support and help competitive cheerleading to develop and eventually to flourish. This does not mean, however, that all cheerleaders are athletes or that all cheerleading is a sport. In addition, the NCAA does have reason to be cautious when it comes to redefining competitive cheerleading. Some schools have taken sideline cheerleading teams and recategorized them just so they could comply with Title IX. These efforts to sidestep the purpose of the law are, as one expert puts it, "obviously transparent and unethical" (Tigay). Even so, fear of possible abuse should not keep the NCAA from doing what is right and giving legitimate athletes the respect and support they deserve.

4 Rebuttal

Qualifiers

Competitive cheerleaders are athletes in every sense of the word. 5
They are aggressive, highly skilled, physically fit competitors. For this
reason, they deserve to be acknowledged as athletes under Title IX and
supported by their schools and by the NCAA. Biased and outdated ideas
about what is (and what is not) a sport should not keep competitive
cheerleading from being recognized as the sport it is. As one proponent
puts it, "If someone tries to tell you that cheerleading is not a sport,
send [him or her] to a college-level competition and ask if their favorite

Concluding statement professional athlete could do that" (Ruder). It is time to give competitive
cheerleaders the support and recognition they deserve.

Works Cited

Lundy, John. "'A Risk You Take': Cheerleaders Face Possibility of
Catastrophic Injuries." *West Central Tribune*, 8 Feb. 2018, www
.wctrib.com/sports/other/4399147-risk-you-take-cheerleaders-face
-possibility-catastrophic-injuries.

Pant, Bhavya. "To Cheer or Not to Cheer." *Massachusetts Daily
Collegian*, University of Massachusetts, 3 Apr. 2018, dailycollegian
.com/2018/04/to-cheer-or-not-to-cheer/.

Ruder, Rebecca. "Cheerleading Is a Sport." *Western Courier*, 15 Sept.
2017, westerncourier.com/38687/opinions/cheerleading-is-a-sport/.

Tigay, Chanan. "Is Cheerleading a Sport Protected by Title IX?" *CQ
Researcher*, 25 Mar. 2011, p. 276. library.cqpress.com/cqresearcher
/document.php?id=cqresrre2011032500.

Identifying the Elements of a Toulmin Argument

1. Summarize the position this essay takes as a three-part argument
   that includes the claim, the grounds, and the warrant.

2. Do you think the writer includes enough backing for her claim? What
   other supporting evidence could she have included?

3. Find the qualifier in the essay. How does it limit the argument? How
   else could the writer have qualified the argument?

4. Do you think the writer addresses enough objections to her claim?
   What other arguments could she have addressed?

5. Based on your reading of this essay, what advantages do you think
   Toulmin logic offers to writers? What disadvantages does it present?

Understanding Oral Arguments

Many everyday arguments—in school, on the job, or in your community—are presented orally. In many ways, an oral argument is similar to a written one: it has an introduction, a body, and a conclusion, and it addresses and refutes opposing points of view. In other, more subtle ways, however, an oral argument is different from a written one. Before you plan and deliver an oral argument, you should be aware of these differences.

The major difference between an oral argument and a written one is that an audience cannot reread an oral argument to clarify information. Listeners have to understand an oral argument the first time they hear it. To help your listeners, you need to design your presentation with this limitation in mind, considering the following guidelines:

- **An oral argument should contain verbal signals that help guide listeners.** Transitional phrases such as "My first point," "My second point," and "Let me sum up" are useful in oral arguments, where listeners do not have a written text in front of them. They alert listeners to information to come and signal shifts from one point to another.

- **An oral argument should use simple, direct language and avoid long sentences.** Complicated sentences that contain elevated language and numerous technical terms are difficult for listeners to follow. For this reason, your sentences should be straightforward and easy to understand.

- **An oral argument should repeat key information.** A traditional rule of thumb for oral arguments is, "Tell listeners what you're going to tell them; then tell it to them; finally, tell them what you've told them." In other words, in the introduction of an oral argument, tell your listeners what they are going to hear; in the body, discuss your points, one at a time; and finally, in your conclusion, restate your points. This intentional repetition ensures that your listeners follow (and remember) your points.

- **An oral argument should include visuals.** Visual aids can make your argument easier to follow. You can use visuals to identify your points as you discuss them. You can also use visuals—for example, charts, graphs, or tables—to clarify or reinforce key points as well as to add interest. Carefully selected visuals help increase the chances that what you are saying will be remembered.

Planning an Oral Argument

The work you do to plan your presentation is as important as the presentation itself. Here is some advice to consider as you plan your oral argument:

1. **Choose your topic wisely.** Select a topic that is somewhat controversial so listeners will want to hear your views. You can create interest in

a topic, but it is easier to appeal to listeners if they are already interested in what you have to say. In addition, try to choose a topic that you know something about. Even though you will probably have to do some research, the process will be much easier if you are already familiar with the basic issues.

2. **Know your audience.** Consider your audience and its needs before you begin to plan your presentation. For example, how much do listeners already know about your topic? Are they well informed, or do they know little about it? If listeners are unfamiliar with your topic, you will have to supply background information and definitions of key terms. If they already know a lot, you can dispense with this material and discuss your subject in more depth. Also, assess your audience members' likely response to your presentation. Will they be receptive? Hostile? Neutral? The answers to these questions will help you decide which arguments will most likely be effective (and which will not).

3. **Know your time limit.** Most oral presentations have a time limit. If you run over your allotted time, you risk boring or annoying your listeners. If you finish too soon, it will seem as if you don't know much about your subject. As you prepare your argument, include all the information that you can cover within your time limit. Keep in mind that you will not be able to go into as much detail in a short speech as you will in a long speech, so plan accordingly.

Visual aids can help listeners follow an oral presentation.

kasto80/iStock/Getty Images

4. **Identify your thesis statement.** Like a written argument, an oral argument should have a debatable thesis statement. Keep this statement simple, and make sure that it clearly conveys your position. Remember that in an oral argument, your listeners have to understand your thesis the first time they hear it. (See Chapter 7 for more on developing a thesis statement.)

5. **Gather support for your thesis.** Assume that your listeners are **skeptical**, that is, that they are not easily convinced. Even if you think that your audience is friendly, you still need to make a persuasive case. Don't make the mistake of thinking that listeners will automatically accept all your ideas just because they agree with your main point. For this reason, you need to support your thesis with compelling evidence if you expect listeners to conclude that your position is valid. Supporting evidence can be in the form of facts, observations, expert opinion, and statistics. Some of your support can come from your own experiences, but most will come from your research.

6. **Acknowledge your sources.** Remember that all of the information you get from your research needs to be acknowledged. As you deliver your presentation, let listeners know where the information you are using comes from—for example, "According to a 2020 editorial in the *New York Times . . .*" or "As Kenneth Davis says in his book *America's Hidden History. . . .*" This strategy enhances your credibility by showing that you are well informed about your topic. (Including source information also helps you protect yourself from unintentional **plagiarism**. See Chapter 11.)

7. **Prepare your speaking notes.** Effective speakers do not read their speeches. Instead, they prepare **speaking notes**—often on index cards—that list the points they want to make. (Microsoft's PowerPoint, as well as some other presentation software packages, has a section on each slide for speaking notes. Although the notes are displayed on the computer screen, they are not visible to the audience.) These notes guide you as you speak, so you should make sure that there are not too many of them and that they contain just key information. (If you use note cards, it is a good idea to number them so that you can be sure that they are in the correct order.)

8. **Prepare visual aids.** Visual aids help you to communicate your thesis and your supporting points more effectively. Visuals increase interest in your presentation, and they also strengthen your argument by reinforcing your points and making them easier for listeners to follow and to understand. In addition, visuals can help establish your credibility and thus improve the persuasiveness of your argument.

You can use the following types of visual aids in your presentations:

- Diagrams
- Photographs
- Slides
- Smartboards, flip charts
- Overhead transparencies
- Document cameras
- Handouts, objects

In order moving clockwise from top left: deomis/Shutterstock.com; Petr Vaclavek/ Shutterstock.com; Tarapong Siri/ Shutterstock.com; Brian A Jackson/ Shutterstock.com

In addition to these kinds of visual aids, you can also use **presentation software**, such as Microsoft's PowerPoint or the web-based application Prezi (Prezi.com). With presentation software, you can easily create visually appealing and persuasive slides. You can insert scanned photographs or drawings into slides, or you can cut and paste charts, graphs, and tables into them. You can even include YouTube videos and MP3 files. Keep in mind, however, that the images, videos, or sound files that you use must support your thesis; if they are irrelevant, they will distract or confuse your listeners. (See pp. 216–218 for examples of PowerPoint slides.)

9. **Practice your presentation.** As a general rule, you should spend as much time rehearsing your speech as you do preparing it. In other words, practice, practice, practice. Be sure you know the order in which you will present your points and when you will move from one visual to another. Rehearse your speech aloud with your speaking notes and your visuals until you are confident that you can get through your presentation effectively. Try to anticipate any problems that may arise with your visuals, and solve them at this stage of the process. If possible, practice your speech in the room in which you will actually deliver it. Bring along a friend, and ask for feedback. Finally, cut or add material as needed until you are certain that you can stay within your time limit.

CHECKLIST

Designing and Displaying Visuals

☐ Use images that are large enough for your audience to see and that will reproduce clearly.

☐ Make lettering large enough for your audience to see. Use 40- to 50-point type for titles, 25- to 30-point type for major points, and 20- to 25-point type for less important points.

☐ Use bulleted lists, not full sentences or paragraphs.

☐ Put no more than three or four points on a single visual.

☐ Make sure there is a clear contrast between your lettering and the background.

☐ Don't show your listeners the visual before you begin to speak about it. Display the visual only when you discuss it.

☐ Face your listeners when you discuss a visual. Even if you point to the screen, always look at your listeners. Never turn your back on your audience.

☐ Introduce and discuss each visual. Don't simply show or read the visual to your audience. Always tell listeners more than they can read or see for themselves.

☐ Don't use elaborate visuals or special effects that will distract your audience.

⮕ EXERCISE 6.5 PLANNING AN ORAL ARGUMENT

Look through the table of contents of this book, and select three At Issue topics that interest you. Imagine that you are planning to deliver an oral argument to a group of college students on each of these topics. For each topic, list three visual aids you could use to enhance your presentation.

Delivering Oral Arguments

Delivery is the most important part of a speech. The way you speak, your interaction with the audience, your posture, and your eye contact all affect your overall presentation. In short, a confident, controlled speaker will have a positive impact on an audience, while a speaker who fumbles with note cards, speaks in a shaky voice, or seems disorganized will lose credibility. To make sure that your listeners see you as a credible, reliable source of information, follow these guidelines:

1. **Accept nervousness.** For most people, nervousness is part of the speech process. The trick is to convert this nervousness into energy that you channel into your speech. The first step in dealing with nervousness is to make sure that you have rehearsed enough. If you have prepared adequately, you will probably be able to handle any problem you may encounter. If you make a mistake, you can correct it. If you forget something, you can fit it in later.

DEALING WITH NERVOUSNESS

If nervousness is a problem, the following strategies can help you to relax:

- **Breathe deeply.** Take a few deep breaths before you begin speaking. Research has shown that increased oxygen has a calming effect on the brain.

- **Use visualization.** Imagine yourself delivering a successful speech, and fix this image in your mind. It can help dispel anxiety.

- **Empty your mind.** Consciously try to eliminate all negative thoughts. Think of your mind as a room full of furniture. Imagine yourself removing each piece of furniture until the room is empty.

- **Drink water.** Before you begin to speak, take a few sips of water. Doing so will eliminate the dry mouth that is a result of nervousness. Don't, however, drink water during your speech.

- **Keep things in perspective.** Remember, your speech is a minor event in your life. Nothing that you do or say will affect you significantly.

2. **Look at your audience.** When you speak, look directly at the members of your audience. At the beginning of the speech, make eye contact with a few audience members who seem to be responding positively. As your speech progresses, look directly at as many audience members as you can. Try to sweep the entire room. Don't focus excessively on a single person or on a single section of your audience.

3. **Speak naturally.** Your presentation should sound like a conversation, not a performance. This is not to suggest that your presentation should include slang, ungrammatical constructions, or colloquialisms; it should conform to the rules of standard English. The trick is to maintain the appearance of a conversation while following the conventions of public speaking. Achieving this balance takes practice, but it is a goal worth pursuing.

4. **Speak slowly.** When you give a presentation, you should speak more slowly than you do in normal conversation. This strategy gives listeners time to process what they hear—and gives you time to think about what you are saying.

5. **Speak clearly and correctly.** As you deliver your presentation, speak clearly. Do not drop tense endings, and be careful to pronounce words correctly. Look up the pronunciation of unfamiliar words in a dictionary, or ask your instructor for help. If you go through an entire speech

pronouncing a key term or a name incorrectly, your listeners will question your competence.

6. **Move purposefully.** As you deliver your speech, don't pace, move your hands erratically, or play with your note cards. Try to stand in one spot, with both feet flat on the floor. Move only when necessary—for example, to point to a visual or to display an object. If you intend to distribute printed material to your listeners, do so only when you are going to discuss it. (Try to arrange in advance for someone else to give out your handouts.) If you are not going to refer to the material in your presentation, wait until you have finished your speech before you distribute it. Depending on the level of formality of your presentation and the size of your audience, you may want to stand directly in front of your audience or behind a podium.

7. **Be prepared for the unexpected.** Don't get flustered if things don't go exactly as you planned. If you forget material, work it in later. If you make a mistake, correct it without apologizing. Most of the time, listeners will not realize that something has gone wrong unless you call attention to it. If someone in the audience looks bored, don't worry. You might consider changing your pace or your volume, but keep in mind that the person's reaction might have nothing to do with your presentation. He or she might be tired, preoccupied, or just a poor listener.

8. **Leave time for questions.** End your presentation by asking if your listeners have any questions. As you answer questions, keep in mind the following advice:

   - *Be prepared.* Make sure you have anticipated the obvious counterarguments to your position, and be prepared to address them. In addition, prepare a list of websites or other resources that you can refer your audience to for more information.

   - *Repeat a question before you answer it.* This technique enables everyone in the audience to hear the question, and it also gives you time to think of an answer.

   - *Keep control of interchanges.* If a questioner repeatedly challenges your answer or monopolizes the conversation, say that you will be glad to discuss the matter with him or her after your presentation is finished.

   - *Be honest.* Answer questions honestly and forthrightly. If you don't know the answer to a question, say so. Tell the questioner you will locate the information that he or she wants and send it by email. Above all, do not volunteer information that you are not sure is correct.

   - *Use the last question to summarize.* When you get to the last question, end your answer by restating the main point of your argument.

Remember to project confidence and control as you speak.

Wavebreak Media/AGE Fotostock

Composing an Oral Argument

The written text of an oral argument is organized just as any other argument is: it has an introduction that gives the background of the issue and states the thesis, it has a body that presents evidence that supports the thesis, it identifies and refutes arguments against the thesis, and it ends with a concluding statement.

In general, an oral argument can be structured in the following way:

INTRODUCTION	Presents the background of the issue
	States the thesis
BODY	Presents evidence: Point 1 in support of the thesis
	Presents evidence: Point 2 in support of the thesis
	Presents evidence: Point 3 in support of the thesis
	Refutes opposing arguments
CONCLUSION	Brings the argument to a close
	Concluding statement restates thesis
	Speaker asks for questions

⊘ EXERCISE 6.6 ANALYZING AN ORAL ARGUMENT

The following oral argument was presented by a student in a speech course in response to the assignment, "Argue for or against the advantages of a 'gap year' between high school and college." (Her PowerPoint slides appear at the end of the speech.) After you read this argument, answer the questions on page 219, consulting the preceding outline if necessary.

AN ARGUMENT IN SUPPORT OF THE "GAP YEAR"

CHANTEE STEELE

College: even the word sounded wonderful when I was in high school. Everyone told me it would be the best time of my life. They told me that I would take courses in exciting new subjects and that I'd make lifelong friends. [Show slide 1.] What they didn't tell me was that I would be anxious, confused, and uncertain about my major and about my future. Although this is only my second year in college, I've already changed my major once, and to be honest, I'm still not sure I've made the right decision. But during the process of changing majors, my adviser gave me some reading material that included information about a "gap year." A gap year is a year off between high school and college when students focus on work or community service and learn about themselves—something that would have benefited me. Although gaining popularity in the United States, the gap year still suggests images of spoiled rich kids who want to play for a year before going to college. According to educator Christina Wood, however, in the United Kingdom a gap year is common; it is seen as a time for personal growth that helps students mature (Wood 36). [Show slide 2.] In fact, 230,000 British students take a gap year before going to college. As the rest of my speech will show, a well-planned gap year gives students time to mature, to explore potential careers, and to volunteer or travel.

[Show slide 3.] Apparently I'm not alone in my uncertainty about my major or about my future. The Educational Advisory Board estimates that between 75 percent and 85 percent of college students will switch majors at least once (Venit). As they go from high school to college, most students have little time to think about what to do with their lives. A gap year before college would give them time to learn more about themselves. According to Abigail Falik and Linda Frey, "The gap year has become increasingly popular with admissions leaders, who have witnessed firsthand its positive impact on students and campus culture" (Falik and Frey). A year off provides many students with the perspective they need to mature and to feel more confident about their decisions. It's also a choice that very few students regret, as those who take time

1

Thesis statement

2 Evidence: Point 1 in support of thesis

off overwhelmingly report that the experience increased their maturity and confidence (Hirsch).

Evidence: Point 2 in support of thesis

The gap year gives students many options to explore before going 3 to college. [Show slide 4.] This slide shows just some of the resources students can use as they prepare for their gap year. As you can see, they can explore opportunities for employment, education, and volunteer work. There are even resources for students who are undecided. The key is to make the year both "purposeful and practical" (Falik and Frey). Ideally, it should be challenging and allow students to build new skills; it should also include elements of service to others, as well as a balance between freedom and guidance from a mentor (Falik and Frey). That may include studying abroad in an exchange program or even working a full-time job to save money for tuition (Jones).

Evidence: Point 3 in support of thesis

Taking a gap year can also help students to get into better colleges. 4 According to an article by the dean of admissions at Harvard, "Occasionally students are admitted to Harvard or other colleges in part because they accomplished something unusual during a year off" (Fitzsimmons, McGrath, and Ducey). Depending on the scope of their service or work, a gap year could enable students to earn scholarships that they were not eligible for before. In fact, some colleges actually recommend that students take time off after high school. Harvard is one of several U.S. colleges that "encourages admitted students to defer enrollment for one year to travel, pursue a special project or activity, work, or spend time in another meaningful way" (Fitzsimmons, McGrath, and Ducey). Furthermore, evidence shows that a gap year can help students to be more successful after they begin in college. One Middlebury College admissions officer has calculated that "a single gap semester was the strongest predictor of academic success at his school" (Bull 7). Given this support for the gap year and given the resources that are now available to help students plan it, the negative attitudes about it in the United States are beginning to change.

Refutation of opposing arguments

In spite of these benefits, parental concerns about "slackerdom" and 5 money are common. Supporters of the gap year acknowledge that students have to be motivated to make the most of their experiences. Clearly, the gap year is not for everyone. For example, students who are not self-motivated may not benefit from a gap year. In addition, parents worry about how much money the gap year will cost them. This is a real concern when you add the year off to the expense of four years of college (Wood 37). However, if finances are a serious concern, students can spend their gap year working in their own communities or taking advantage of a paid experience like AmeriCorps—which, as the AmeriCorps website shows, covers students' room and board *and* offers an educational stipend after students complete the program. [Show slide 5.] Additionally, parents and students should consider the time and money that is wasted when a student who is not ready for college starts school and then drops out.

After considering the benefits of a gap year, I have concluded that more students should postpone college for a year. Many students (like me) are uncertain about their goals. We welcome new opportunities and are eager to learn from new experiences and may find a year of service both emotionally and intellectually rewarding. Given another year to mature, many of us would return to school with a greater sense of purpose, focus, and clarity. In some cases, the gap year could actually help us get into better schools and possibly get more financial aid. If we intend to take the college experience seriously, spending a gap year learning about our interests and abilities would help us to become better, more confident, and ultimately more focused students. [Show slide 6.]

6

Concluding statement

Are there any questions?

Works Cited

Bull, Holly. "Navigating a Gap Year." *TeenLife*, Feb. 2011, pp. 6–9.

Falik, Abigail, and Linda Frey. *The Chronicle of Higher Education*, 3 June 2018, www.chronicle.com/article/The-Best-Freshman-Year-Is-a/243563.

Fitzsimmons, William, et al. "Time Out or Burn Out for the Next Generation." *Harvard College Office of Admissions*, 2011, college.harvard.edu/admissions/preparing-college/should-i-take-time.

Hirsch, Leni M. G. "Ready, Set, Don't Go." *The Harvard Crimson*, 15 Apr. 2016, www.thecrimson.com/article/2016/4/15/take-a-gap-year/.

Venit, Ed. "How Late Is Too Late? Myths and Facts about the Consequences of Switching College Majors." *Student Success Collaborative*, *Education Advisory Board*, 29 Aug. 2018, www.eab.com/-/media/EAB/Technology/Student-Success-Collaborative/Success-Pages/EAB_Major%20Switching%20Myths%20and%20Facts.pd.

Wood, Christina. "Should You Take a 'Gap Year'?" *Careers and Colleges,* Fall 2007, pp. 36–37.

Slide 1

AnaBGD/iStock/Getty Images

Slide 2

230,000 students between 18 and 25 take a Gap
Year in the U.K.

—Tom Griffiths, founder and director
of GapYear.com

(qtd. in Christina Wood, "Should You Take a 'Gap Year'?,"
Careers and Colleges, Fall 2007)

Slide 3

50% of students change their major at least once.

—National Research Center for College
and University Admissions

Slide 4

A Few Links for the Potential "Gapster"

(links from Holly Bull, "The Possibilities of the Gap
Year," *Chronicle of Higher Education* 52.44 [2006])

Employment

Cool Works: CoolWorks.com (domestic jobs)

Working Abroad: WorkingAbroad.org (jobs overseas)

Education

Global Routes: GlobalRoutes.org (semester-long courses)

Sea-mester: Seamester.com (sea voyage programs)

Volunteer Work

AmeriCorps: AmeriCorps.gov

City Year: CityYear.org

Thoughtful Texts for Fence Sitters

Karl Haigler and Rae Nelson, *The Gap-Year
    Advantage* (Macmillan, 2005)

Colin Hall, *Taking Time Off* (Princeton Review, 2003)

Charlotte Hindle and Joe Bindloss, *The Gap Year
    Book* (Lonely Planet, 2005)

Slide 5

Corporation for National and Community Service.

Slide 6

In order moving clockwise from the top left: © Roger Cracknell 01/classic/Alamy Stock Photo; © Steve Stock/Alamy Stock Photo; David Cordner/Getty Images; Sportstock/E+/Getty Images

Identifying the Elements of an Oral Argument

1. Where does this oral argument include verbal signals to help guide readers?

2. Does this oral argument use simple, direct language? What sections of the speech, if any, could be made simpler?

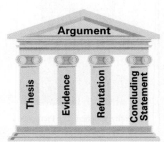

3. Where does this oral argument repeat key information for emphasis? Is there any other information that you think should have been repeated?

4. What opposing arguments does the speaker identify? Does she refute them convincingly?

5. How effective are the visuals that accompany the text of this oral argument? Are there enough visuals? Are they placed correctly? What other information do you think could have been displayed in a visual?

6. What questions would you ask this speaker at the end of her speech?

Why Are So Few Women in STEM Fields?

Dorothy Vaughan: The Picture Art Collection/Alamy. *Hidden Figures:* LEVIATHAN FILMS/CHERNIN ENT/FOX 2000 PICTURES/ Album/Alamy Stock Photo.

Go back to page 191, and reread the At Issue box, which gives background about whether online education is better than classroom instruction. As the following sources illustrate, this question has a number of possible answers.

After you review the sources listed below, you will be asked to answer some questions and to complete some simple activities. This work will help you to understand both the content and the structure of the sources. When you are finished, you will be ready to develop an argument—using one of the three alternative approaches to argument discussed in this chapter—that takes a position on whether online education is better than classroom learning.

SOURCES

 Olivia Nicholas, "What Are You Going to Do with That Major?," page 221

 Olga Khazan, "The More Gender Equality, the Fewer Women in STEM," page 224

 Stuart Reges, "Why Women Don't Code," page 227

 Rosalind C. Barnett and Caryl Rivers, "We've Studied Gender and STEM for 25 Years. The Science Doesn't Support the Google Memo," page 237

 Barbara Oakley, "Why Do Women Shun STEM? It's Complicated," page 242

 Visual Argument: STEM PSA, page 245

The following essay appeared in the *Whitman Wire*, the student newspaper of Whitman College, on February 8, 2018.

WHAT ARE YOU GOING TO DO WITH THAT MAJOR?

OLIVIA NICHOLAS

The problem is not that we have too few women in STEM; it is that we have too 1 few men in the humanities. Increasing women's access to STEM is an important and worthy cause, but in our efforts to improve access, we have devalued the humanities. Somehow, for once in our lives, we have forgotten to ask: what about the men?

We've known for a while that there is a gender divide in academic disci- 2 plines. The national response was to strive to increase the number of women in STEM. In 2011 First Lady Michelle Obama made a speech on the subject: "We need all hands on deck, and that means clearing hurdles for women and girls as they navigate careers in science, technology, engineering, and math." This call to action is warranted, since many women have certainly been dissuaded from studying STEM, but why is no one talking about increasing the number of men studying the humanities? Because, whether we acknowledge it or not, we have concluded that STEM is more important than the humanities.

At liberal arts colleges, majors are often segmented along gender lines. 3 Women make up a disproportionate share of the humanities majors at liberal arts colleges, while men make up the majority in the hard sciences and mathematics. According to the U.S. Department of Education's most recent statistics, in 2008, engineering ranked third on the list of most popular majors for men in the United States and 83.2 percent of engineering students were male. Men also make up 82.4 percent of computer and information science majors. Meanwhile, men only made up about 33.8 percent of all liberal arts and sciences, humanities and general studies majors.

Whitman follows this trend. Considering currently declared majors by per- 4 centage and eliminating majors with fewer than five people, those with the highest number of men at Whitman are computer science (90 percent male), physics (73 percent), economics (72 percent) and chemistry (71 percent). Meanwhile, the majors with the lowest number of men include race and ethnic studies (0 percent), environmental science-sociology (7 percent), French (11 percent) and English (21 percent). Nine out of the top ten woman-dominated majors at Whitman are in the humanities (with the exception being sociology, which is a social science). Meanwhile, only two of the top ten male-dominated majors at Whitman are in the humanities: philosophy and German.

Paula England and Li Su in an essay from the 2010 book *Gender &* 5 *Society*, find that women have contributed to the decrease in major segregation through their decisions to enter male-dominated fields of study, while very few men have chosen to enter woman-dominated fields. So, where are the men?

> "The arts and humanities are devalued precisely because women study them."

Evelyn Fox Keller offers one explanation in her 1985 book *Reflections on Gender and Science*, where she states that people often associate masculinity with objectivity and femininity with subjectivity. Those fields that are objective and therefore seen as masculine are viewed as more legitimate and worthy, while fields that are subjective and therefore seen as feminine are devalued. The arts and humanities, in other words, are devalued precisely because women study them. One might argue that perhaps men are simply more interested in more objective fields and the fact that society places greater importance on these fields is a mere coincidence. However, England and Li's findings suggest otherwise. They found that when women do enter previously male-dominated fields, men begin to leave those fields. Men do not want to study fields that women study, not because they are not rigorous or interesting, but because they believe that what interests women is decidedly unimportant.

Currently, women are the majority in American higher education. The U.S. Department of Education states that women make up 56 percent of college students enrolled this fall 2017. As women increase in numbers in higher education, their decisions about disciplinary focus have a greater and greater impact on the colleges and universities they attend. Women's steady decline in the humanities in favor of social sciences and STEM presents the humanities with the threat of extinction. Women's turn away from the humanities could very likely be their kiss of death. So, again, I ask: what about the men?

⊘ AT ISSUE: WHY ARE SO FEW WOMEN IN STEM FIELDS?

1. Nicholas begins her essay by saying, "The problem is not that we have too few women in STEM; it is that we have too few men in the humanities" (para. 1). Is this statement an example of the **either/or fallacy**? Explain.

2. According to Nicholas, men are not going into the humanities because they "have concluded that STEM is more important than the humanities" (2). What other explanations might there be for men not studying the humanities?

3. In this essay, where does the claim appear? How is the claim qualified? How does the qualifier set up the rest of the essay?

4. Is Nicholas's argument aimed primarily at an audience of women in STEM fields or a general audience? How do you know?

5. Throughout her essay, Nicholas supports her argument with statistics. How effective is this support?

6. Consider the following facts:

   - Computer science, biophysics, and physics tend to be male dominated.
   - Neurobiology, environmental biology, and biology of global health tend to be female dominated.
   - Social work, English, and psychology tend to be female dominated.
   - History, economics, and finance tend to be male dominated.

   How would Nicholas explain these disparities? How do you?

7. Where does Nicholas address opposing arguments? How effectively does she refute them?

This piece first appeared online at TheAtlantic.com on February 18, 2018.

THE MORE GENDER EQUALITY, THE FEWER WOMEN IN STEM

OLGA KHAZAN

Though their numbers are growing, only 27 percent of all students taking the 1 AP Computer Science exam in the United States are female. The gender gap only grows worse from there: Just 18 percent of American computer-science college degrees go to women. This is in the United States, where many college men proudly describe themselves as "male feminists" and girls are taught they can be anything they want to be.

Meanwhile, in Algeria, 41 percent of college graduates in the fields of 2 science, technology, engineering, and math—or "STEM," as it's known—are female. There, employment discrimination against women is rife and women are often pressured to make amends with their abusive husbands.

According to a report I covered a few years ago, Jordan, Qatar, and the 3 United Arab Emirates were the only three countries in which boys are significantly *less* likely to feel comfortable working on math problems than girls are. In all of the other nations surveyed, girls were more likely to say they feel "helpless while performing a math problem."

So what explains the tendency for nations that have traditionally *less* 4 gender equality to have *more* women in science and technology than their gender-progressive counterparts do?

According to a new paper published in *Psychological Science* by the 5 psychologists Gijsbert Stoet, at Leeds Beckett University, and David Geary, at the University of Missouri, it could have to do with the fact that women in countries with higher gender inequality are simply seeking the clearest possible path to financial freedom. And often, that path leads through STEM professions.

The issue doesn't appear to be girls' aptitude for STEM professions. In 6 looking at test scores across 67 countries and regions, Stoet and Geary found that girls performed about as well or better than boys did on science in most countries, and in almost all countries, girls would have been capable of college-level science and math classes if they had enrolled in them.

But when it comes to their *relative* strengths, in almost all the countries— 7 all except Romania and Lebanon—boys' best subject was science, and girls' was reading. (That is, even if an average girl was as good as an average boy at science, she was still likely to be even better at reading.) Across all countries, 24 percent of girls had science as their best subject, 25 percent of girls' strength was math, and 51 percent excelled in reading. For boys, the percentages were 38 for science, 42 for math, and 20 for reading. And the more gender-equal the country, as measured by the World Economic Forum's Global Gender Gap Index, the larger this gap between boys and girls in having science as their best subject. (The most gender-equal countries are the typical snowy utopias you hear about, like Sweden, Finland, and Iceland. Turkey and the United Arab Emirates rank among the least equal, according to the Global Gender Gap Index.)

The gap in reading "is related at least in part to girls' advantages in basic 8 language abilities and a generally greater interest in reading; they read more and thus practice more," Geary told me.

What's more, the countries that minted the most female college graduates 9 in fields like science, engineering, or math were also some of the least gender-equal countries. They posit that this is because the countries that empower women also empower them, indirectly, to pick whatever career they'd enjoy most and be best at.

"Countries with the highest gender equality tend to be welfare states," they 10 write, "with a high level of social security." Meanwhile, less gender-equal countries tend to also have less social support for people who, for example, find themselves unemployed. Thus, the authors suggest, girls in those countries might be more inclined to choose STEM professions, since they offer a more certain financial future than, say, painting or writing.

When the study authors looked at the "overall life satisfaction" rating of 11 each country—a measure of economic opportunity and hardship—they found that gender-equal countries had more life satisfaction. The life-satisfaction ranking explained 35 percent of the variation between gender equality and women's participation in STEM. That correlation echoes past research showing that the genders are actually more segregated by field of study in more economically developed places.

The upshot of this research is neither especially feminist nor especially sad: It's not that gender equality discourages girls from pursuing science. It's that it allows them not to if they're not interested. The findings will likely seem controversial, since the idea that men and women have different inherent abilities is often used as a reason, by some, to argue we should forget trying to recruit more women into the STEM fields. But, as the University of Wisconsin gender-studies professor Janet Shibley Hyde, who wasn't involved with the study, put it to me, that's not quite what's happening here.

> "There's something in even the most liberal societies that's nudging women away from math and science." 12

"Some would say that the gender STEM gap occurs not because girls can't 13 do science, but because they have other alternatives, based on their strengths in verbal skills," she said. "In wealthy nations, they believe that they have the freedom to pursue those alternatives and not worry so much that they pay less."

Instead, this line of research, if it's replicated, might hold useful takeaways 14 for people who do want to see more Western women entering STEM fields. In this study, the percentage of girls who did excel in science or math was still larger than the number of women who were graduating with STEM degrees.

That means there's something in even the most liberal societies that's nudging women away from math and science, even when those are their best subjects. The women-in-STEM advocates could, for starters, focus their efforts on those would-be STEM stars.

Then again, it could just be that, feeling financially secure and on equal 15 footing with men, some women will always choose to follow their passions, rather than whatever labor economists recommend. And those passions don't always lie within science.

◯ AT ISSUE: WHY ARE SO FEW WOMEN IN STEM FIELDS?

1. A *paradox* is an absurd or self-contradictory statement that could possibly be true. In what sense is Khazan's thesis a paradox?

2. In paragraph 4, Khazan asks a question. What function does this question have in her essay?

3. Speaking of the research done by Gijsbert Stoet and David Geary, Khazan says, "The upshot of this research is neither especially feminist nor especially sad" (para. 12). What does she mean? Why, according to Khazan, are their findings controversial?

4. Should Khazan have provided more details about Stoet and Geary's study? For example, how many children did they interview? Were the samples randomly chosen? How did they measure "overall life satisfaction" (11)? Explain.

5. In her concluding paragraphs, Kazan uses the following phrases:

   ■ "Some would say. . . ." (13)
   ■ "Instead, this line of research, if it's replicated. . . ." (14)
   ■ "Then again, it could just be that. . . ." (15)

   What do these phrases indicate about Khazan's assessment of Stoet and Geary's study?

6. Suppose Khazan wanted to present her ideas in a speech. What parts of the essay would you suggest she expand? What parts would you advise her to condense or delete? What visuals would you suggest she use?

7. Use Toulmin logic to analyze Khazan's essay, identifying the argument's claim, its grounds, and its warrant. Does Khazan appeal only to *logos*, or does she appeal to *pathos* and *ethos*? Explain.

This essay was posted to the online magazine *Quillette* on June 19, 2018.

WHY WOMEN DON'T CODE

STUART REGES

Ever since Google fired James Damore for "advancing harmful gender stereo- 1
types in our workplace," those of us working in tech have been trying to figure
out what we can and cannot say on the subject of diversity. You might imagine
that a university would be more open to discussing his ideas, but my experience suggests otherwise.

For the last ten months I have been discussing this issue at the Allen 2
School of Computer Science & Engineering where I work. I have tried to
understand why Damore's opinions generated such anger and have struggled to decide what I want to do in response. As a result of my attempts to
discuss this, our mailing list known as "diversity-allies" is now a moder-
ated list to prevent "nuanced, and potentially hurtful, discussion." Instead,
I have been encouraged to participate in face-to-face meetings that have
often been tense, but which have helped me to understand where others are
coming from.

I embarked on this journey because I worry that tech companies and uni- 3
versities are increasingly embracing an imposed silence, in which one is not
permitted to question the prevailing wisdom on how to achieve diversity goals.
I intend to fight this imposed silence and I encourage others to do the same.
We can't allow the Damore incident to establish a precedent. Damore's Twitter
handle briefly claimed that he had been "fired for truth," but really he was fired
for honesty. Those of us who disagree with current diversity efforts need to
speak up and share our honest opinions, even if doing so puts us at risk.

Saying controversial things that might get me fired is nothing new for me. 4
I've been doing it most of my adult life and usually my comments have generated a big yawn. I experienced a notable exception in a 1991 case that received
national attention, when I was fired from Stanford University for "violating
campus drug policy" as a means of challenging the assumptions of the war
on drugs. My attitude in all of these cases has been that I need to speak up
and give my honest opinion on controversial issues. Most often nothing comes
of it, but if I can be punished for expressing such ideas, then it is even more
important to speak up and try to make the injustice plain.

So let me go once more unto the breach by stating publicly that I believe 5
that women are less likely than men to want to major in computer science and
less likely to pursue a career as a software engineer and that this difference
between men and women accounts for most of the gender gap we see in computer science degree programs and in Silicon Valley companies.

My Diversity Work

My friends advise me that only someone who has fought for diversity can dis- 6
cuss the state of the movement, so let me describe some details of my 32-year
career teaching computer science. I worked for ten years at Stanford managing
introductory computer science courses, receiving the Dinkelspiel Award for
Outstanding Service to Undergraduate Education along the way. I spent eight
years at the University of Arizona doing similar work where I won the College
of Science Distinguished Teaching Award and the Honors College Outstanding
Advisor Award. For the last fourteen years I have worked at the University of
Washington where I manage introductory computer science courses, winning
the Distinguished Teaching Award in 2014.

I have been a champion of using undergraduate TAs in introductory 7
programming classes. I set up undergraduate TA programs at Stanford and
Arizona that continue to this day and we have a thriving program at UW. I was
co-author of an IEEE article entitled, "Broadening Participation: The Why and
the How." My work with introductory courses and undergraduate TAs factored
into the selection in 2015 of UW as the inaugural winner of the Excellence in
Promoting Women in Undergraduate Computing prize awarded by NCWIT
(the National Center for Women & Information Technology).

In my years of teaching nothing has brought me more joy and sense of 8
accomplishment than helping young people discover a love of computer
science. Many of them have been men but more often they have been women.
I have helped hundreds of women to learn to love computer science and for
most it has been life changing.

As a result, I am absolutely convinced that for many years there have 9
been—and even today still are—many women who have not yet discovered the
bright future they can have in the field of computer science. Half of the women
in our undergraduate major are "interest changers," which means they weren't
intending to apply to the major when they started our first course. For men the
figure is closer to 20 percent, so there is a big gender gap.

In short, I have always been and continue to be a strong advocate of many 10
aspects of the diversity agenda.

The Equality Agenda versus the Equity Agenda

Arguments over diversity have been going on for decades at universities with 11
bitter fights along the way over affirmative action, political correctness, and
speech codes. These arguments have acquired renewed urgency as major tech
companies have joined the fray in response to increased scrutiny from the
media about the lack of diversity in their workforce.

No company has done more than Google to create and share resources 12
in this space. They developed a popular workshop on unconscious bias that
has been copied by many other organizations, and they extended those ideas
to create a second workshop called "Bias Busters" that many universities have
also adopted.

Like most of us who work in tech, I heard mention of these things but 13 didn't take the time to investigate them. But when Damore was fired, I started looking more closely at the content of these workshops and I found much to criticize. In talking to professional staff who work in this area and students and faculty who are deeply committed to this issue, I have found that there are two visions of diversity and inclusion.

I favor what I call the "equality agenda" in computer science. Advocates of 14 the equality agenda want to see the most talented and passionate individuals joining us regardless of their life circumstances or unalterable characteristics. For us, diversity has its usual dictionary definition of having a variety of individuals, which implies racial, ethnic, and gender diversity but also political and religious diversity. Inclusion involves welcoming a broad range of individuals to consider pursuing computer science as a career. The equality agenda, then, is about encouragement and removal of artificial barriers.

Professionals and activists who work in this area tend to see it differ- 15 ently. For them, diversity involves a commitment to righting the wrongs of the past. Political and religious diversity are not on their list because they don't represent the immutable characteristics previously used to justify discrimination. They may concede that Damore's claim that Google has become an echo chamber might be an issue worth addressing, but they will deny that this is a diversity issue. By contrast, working with the LGBTQ community is important because of the historical oppression they have experienced even though there is no evidence that LGBTQ individuals are currently discriminated against in the field.

Their understanding of inclusion is also quite different. Inclusion is about 16 culture, and in a twist worthy of Orwell, inclusion often demands the exclusion of ideas and opinions. Google's Bias Busters workshop trains people to intervene when they hear examples of bias. Microaggression training fosters inclusion by preparing people to recognize and eliminate small slights that could make some people uncomfortable. Google CEO Sundar Pichai used the word in this sense when he justified Damore's firing with the observation that, "It's important for the women at Google, and all the people at Google, that we want to make an inclusive environment."

The word "equity" has the most variability in how it is understood. For 17 example, Steven Pinker uses the term "equity feminism" to refer to something similar to what I am calling the equality agenda. But among professionals and activists, "equity" has the specific meaning of working to dismantle existing power structures as a way to redress privilege.

I refer to this combination of ideas as the "equity agenda." While the equal- 18 ity agenda focuses on equality of opportunity, the equity agenda is concerned with outcomes. Its proponents don't demand equal outcomes but instead use unequal outcomes as evidence that there is more work to be done. So, unless or until we reach perfect gender parity, they will continue to argue for more diversity programs for women.

Why So Much Anger?

When I tried to discuss Damore at my school, I found it almost impossible. 19
As a thought experiment, I asked how we could make someone like Damore
feel welcome in our community. The pushback was intense. My question was
labeled an "inflammatory example" and my comments were described as
"hurtful" to women. When I mentioned that perhaps we could invite Damore
to speak at UW, a faculty member responded, "If he comes here, we'll hurt
him." She was joking, but the sentiment was clear.

One faculty member gave a particularly cogent response. She said, "Is 20
it our job to make someone with those opinions feel welcome? I'm not sure
whether academic freedom dictates that." She argued that because we know
that women have traditionally been discriminated against, perhaps it is more
important to support them because the environment will not be sufficiently
inclusive if they have to deal with someone like Damore. She said it "is up to
us" to decide, but that, "choosing to hold a viewpoint does not necessarily give
you the right to feel comfortable."

As Damore mentions in his essay, this issue has acquired a moral dimen- 21
sion, which is why the response is often anger. Jonathan Haidt, author of *The
Righteous Mind*, has described this as elevating certain ideas to a sacred status.
In this case, suggesting that men and women are different either in interests or
abilities is considered blasphemy. So let me commit some blasphemy.

Men and Women Are Different

As Sundar Pichai said in his memo to employees explaining why he fired 22
Damore, "To suggest a group of our colleagues have traits that make them
less biologically suited to that work is offensive and not OK." This is a fairly
egregious misrepresentation of what Damore actually wrote, but fortunately
we don't need to turn to biology or Damore for evidence that men and women
are different. The gender diversity movement itself has spent the better part of
30 years cataloguing differences between men and women. Indeed, the entire
goal of achieving gender diversity makes no sense unless you believe that men
and women work in fundamentally different ways.

One of the earliest ideas I encountered was that men believe in their suc- 23
cesses and discount their failures while women believe in their failures and discount their successes. If you attend almost any diversity event today you will
hear that "stereotype threat" and "imposter syndrome" should be discussed with
our students because women disproportionately suffer from these problems.
Lack of confidence, therefore, is held to be a particular problem for women.

The diversity literature also discusses how men and women have different 24
priorities, as in this passage from the seminal book *Unlocking the Clubhouse* by
Jane Margolis and Allan Fisher:

A critical part of attracting more girls and women to computer science is
providing multiple ways to "be in" computer science. Concern for people,
family, "balance in life," novels, and a good night's sleep should not come

at the cost of success in computer science. But the full acceptance of this proposition cuts across the dominant culture of the field.

They claim that men have created a culture that matches their values and inter- 25 ests. How is that possible if men and women don't differ in fundamental ways?

Diversity advocates have also started claiming that diverse teams perform 26 better. In a CNBC interview discussing her book *Own It: The Power of Women at Work*, Wall Street veteran Sallie Krawcheck said, "It's the qualities that women bring to the workforce—not better than the men, but somewhat different than the men—where our holistic decision making, our risk awareness, our relationship orientation skills that we tend to bring are becoming actually more valuable going forward, not less valuable."

The Oppression Narrative

A dangerous narrative has been taking hold in recent years that the gender gap is 27 mostly the fault of men and the patriarchal organizations they have built to serve their interests. Emily Chang's new book *Brotopia* asserts that, "the environment in the tech industry has become toxic for women," and that, "women have been systematically excluded from the greatest wealth creation in the history of the world and denied a voice in the rapid remolding of our global culture."

Chang and I clearly know different people because the women I talk to 28 who are working in Silicon Valley are enjoying their experiences as software engineers. Certainly there are bad actors and companies where the culture is broken, but the vast majority of women work at companies that make significant efforts to provide a supportive work experience.

Another example of this false narrative comes from NPR's *Planet Money*, 29 which produced a segment entitled "When Women Stopped Coding." They identify 1984 as the year that "something changed" and they highlight a theory that around that time the personal computer revolution was affecting college campuses. Young men were arriving who had used personal computers young women lacked because families disproportionately bought computers for boys. NPR claims that, "As personal computers became more common, computer science professors increasingly assumed that their students had grown up playing with computers at home," and includes an anecdote from a woman who had a bad experience in her introductory programming class. I don't doubt that this woman had a bad experience, but the claim that computer science faculty were gearing their courses towards men with prior experience is simply not true.

I ran the introductory programming courses at Stanford in the 1980s and 30 I met regularly with faculty who taught introductory programming at other schools. We were on a mission to make CS1 a universal course taken by a broad range of students. We loved Rich Pattis's 1981 book, *Karel the Robot*, because it was, as it's subtitle claimed, "A Gentle Introduction to the Art of Computer Programming." Many schools were experimenting with new courses, new textbooks, and new programming environments, all of which were intended to make it easier for novices to learn how to program.

The NPR piece also noted that we have experienced a slow but steady 31 decrease in women majoring in computer science since 1984. Even as women were taking a greater share of slots in medicine, law, and the physical sciences, they represented a decreasing percentage of computer science degrees. This is consistent with the idea that women simply chose to pursue other interests, but NPR chose to highlight the suggestion that professors teaching introductory courses were creating courses unfriendly to women.

It's Complicated

The more I study the gender gap in computer science the more I become con- 32 vinced that there are no simple answers. When I hear a claim or encounter a graph, I find that it takes a great deal of effort to drill down into the details and I almost always end up concluding, "It's complicated." This article would become a book if I were to drill down on everything, but the NPR graph provides a nice example of what you find when you dig into the data.

To better understand the level of interest by gender, I used data from the 33 same source, the Digest of Education Statistics put out annually by the National Center for Education Statistics. I computed separate statistics for the percentage of men and women obtaining computing degrees, comparing men against other men and women against other women.

Graphing the data this way allows us to see a phenomenon that those of us 34 who lived through these years understand all too well. Computer science has gone through two major boom and bust cycles in the last 40 years. The idea that men drove women from the field is not supported by the data. There has been no period of time when men have been increasing while women have been decreasing. In 48 of the last 50 years the trend was the same for men and women with the percentage of women going up at the same time that the percentage of men went up and the percentage of women going down when the percentage of men went down. But while the trend has been the same, the magnitude of the response has differed significantly.

In both cycles, men disproportionately reacted to the boom part of the 35 cycle and women disproportionately reacted to the bust. And as the graph illustrates, men are once again responding faster and more forcefully to the new boom we are experiencing today. The cumulative effect of these differences has been devastating for the goal of increasing the participation of women in computer science.

We don't yet understand why men rush in during the boom years and why 36 women turn away during the bust years, but it seems likely that multiple factors are at work. Men disproportionately respond to economic incentives, so they are more likely to respond favorably to reports of high salaries for tech workers. Women tend, on average, to be more risk averse, and are more likely to respond strongly to negative stories about dwindling job prospects in tech. Perhaps women also react differently to changes in messaging as departments desperate to meet demand during the boom part of the cycle shift from an attitude of welcoming prospective students to one of pushing them away.

The Free Choice Explanation

I suggest a variation of Hanlon's Razor that one should never attribute to oppres- 37
sion that which is adequately explained by free choice. If men and women are
different, then we should expect them to make different choices. In 2010, the
National Academy of Sciences published a paper entitled "Understanding
Current Causes of Women's Under-Representation in Science." As in the NPR
piece, the authors describe the great success women have had in other fields:

> Since 1970, women have made dramatic gains in science. Today, half of all
> MD degrees and 52 percent of PhDs in life sciences are awarded to women,
> as are 57 percent of PhDs in social sciences, 71 percent of PhDs to psychol-
> ogists, and 77 percent of DVMs to veterinarians. Forty years ago, women's
> presence in most of these fields was several orders of magnitude less; e.g., in
> 1970 only 13 percent of PhDs in life sciences went to women. In the most
> math-intensive fields, however, women's growth has been less pronounced.

But they reject discrimination as an explanation: 38

> We conclude that past initiatives to combat discrimination against women
> in science appear to have been highly successful. Women's current under-
> representation in math-intensive fields is not caused by discrimination
> in these domains, but rather to sex differences in resources, abilities, and
> choices (whether free or constrained).

In 2013, *Psychological Science* published a paper that explored this ques- 39
tion further entitled "Not Lack of Ability but More Choice: Individual and Gender Differences in Choice of Careers in Science, Technology, Engineering, and
Mathematics." The authors included Jacquelynne Eccles who is well known for
a career spanning decades studying student motivation and gender differences.

They concluded that women may choose non-STEM careers because they 40
have academic strengths that many men lack. They found that individuals
with high math ability but only moderate verbal ability were the most likely
to choose a career in STEM (49 percent) and that this group included more
men than women (70 percent men). By contrast, individuals with both high
math ability and high verbal ability were less likely to pursue a career in STEM
(34 percent) and this group had more women than men (63 percent women).
They write that, "Our study provides evidence that it is not lack of ability that
causes females to pursue non-STEM careers, but rather the greater likelihood
that females with high math ability also have high verbal ability and thus can
consider a wider range of occupations."

In 2018, another paper explored the same question from a different per- 41
spective using international data from the PISA survey (the Programme for
International Student Assessment). Olga Khazan summarized the paper well
in an article for the *Atlantic*:

> The issue doesn't appear to be girls' aptitude for STEM professions. In
> looking at test scores across 67 countries and regions, Stoet and Geary

found that girls performed about as well or better than boys did on science in most countries, and in almost all countries, girls would have been capable of college-level science and math classes if they had enrolled in them.

But when it comes to their *relative* strengths, in almost all the countries—all except Romania and Lebanon—boys' best subject was science, and girls' was reading. (That is, even if an average girl was as good as an average boy at science, she was still likely to be even better at reading.) Across all countries, 24 percent of girls had science as their best subject, 25 percent of girls' strength was math, and 51 percent excelled in reading. For boys, the percentages were 38 for science, 42 for math, and 20 for reading.

The study found that gender differences increased in countries that have 42 greater gender equality as measured by the World Economic Forum's annual *Global Gender Gap* Report. They noted that countries with the highest gender equality tend to be "welfare states . . . with a high level of social security for all its citizens," which they believe can (influence women's choices. They describe this as a paradox because it implies that the more progress we make towards achieving the equality agenda, the further we are likely to be from achieving the equity agenda. As Khazan says in the conclusion to her article, "it could just be that, feeling financially secure and on equal footing with men, some women will always choose to follow their passions, rather than whatever labor economists recommend. And those passions don't always lie within science."

I was curious to see how this relates to computing degrees, so I checked 43 out the data for the top ten countries in terms of gender equality. Of the eight countries that include statistics for undergraduate degrees, the average percentage of women majoring in computing was 1.9 percent versus 8.2 percent for men. Taking into account the higher number of undergraduate degrees received by women, the Nordic countries which have the highest scores for gender equality (Iceland, Norway, and Finland) are producing computing graduates who are 18.6 percent, 17 percent, and 15.9 percent female, respectively. These percentages are very close to what we see in the United States.

Where Do We Go from Here?

I believe we have reached a significant crossroads in the campaign to increase 44 the representation of women in tech. We have harvested the low-hanging fruit by eliminating overt discrimination and revamping policies and procedures that favored men. Now we more often focus on minutia such as replacing *Star Trek* posters with travel posters. And yet, the campaign has stalled.

At the University of Washington, we have managed over the last ten years to 45 increase the percentage of women taking our first course from 26 percent to 41 percent and to increase the percentage taking the second course from 18 percent to 31 percent. In the early years, we were able to go from 16 percent women in our major to 30 percent, but we have made no additional progress since. I have heard from friends at Stanford that they have been stalled for several years at 30 percent and a colleague at Princeton reports that they are stuck in the mid-30s for percentages of women. CMU and Harvey Mudd have reported percentages at or above 50 percent, but they have a highly selective student body and have put special emphasis on tweaking admissions criteria and creating special programs for women in computing.

The sad truth is that UW, Stanford, and Princeton are among the best 46 performing schools and part of that success is likely due to being a top-10 department. For most schools, the percentage of women is much lower. Over the last ten years the percentage of undergraduate computing degrees going to women nationwide has bounced around in a tight range, varying from 17.6 percent to 18.7 percent.

Computer science departments have never put more attention and resources into the diversity campaign than they have in the last few years, and we have

> "Women *can* code, but often they don't *want* to." 47

seen a small but steady increase in the percentage of women choosing a computing major, going from 0.9 percent in 2008 to 1.1 percent in 2017. But at the same time, and with no special encouragement from us, the percentage of men choosing a computing major has also increased, going from 5.3 percent in 2008 to 6.4 percent in 2017.

I worry that lack of progress will make us more likely to switch from pos- 48 itive messages about women succeeding in tech to negative stories about men behaving badly in tech, which I think will do more harm than good. Women will find themselves wondering if they should resent men and men will feel guilty for sins committed by other men. Women are not going to find this message appealing and men will find themselves feeling even more awkward around women than they would be otherwise.

Our community must face the difficult truth that we aren't likely to make 49 further progress in attracting women to computer science. Women *can* code, but often they don't *want* to. We will never reach gender parity. You can shame and fire all of the Damores you find, but that won't change the underlying reality.

It's time for everyone to be honest, and my honest view is that having 50 20 percent women in tech is probably the best we are likely to achieve. Accepting that idea doesn't mean that women should feel unwelcome. Recognizing that women will be in the minority makes me even more appreciative of the women who choose to join us.

Obviously many people will disagree with my assessment. I have already 51 been told that expressing such ideas is hurtful to women. But it is exactly because I care so much about diversity that I value honesty above politeness. To be effective, we have to commit ourselves to a search for the truth and that search can succeed only if everyone feels comfortable sharing their honest opinions.

In the last ten months I have taken the time to talk to those who dis- 52 agree with me. I welcome such conversations. I have strong opinions, but I also realize that I could be wrong. The big question is whether there is room in tech for a James Damore or for me when we question basic tenets of the equity agenda. I believe that the uproar over Damore's firing underscores how extreme his case was. This article will probably produce a big yawn like most of my other controversial stands over the years. If so, then I encourage all of the closet Damores out there to join the discussion and to let people know what you really think.

⊙ AT ISSUE: WHY ARE SO FEW WOMEN IN STEM FIELDS?

1. Reges begins his essay by asserting his need to address controversial ideas. He goes on to describe his "32-year career teaching computer science" (para. 6). Why do you think he includes this information before he begins to discuss the gender gap in computer science?

2. In paragraph 13, Reges says that there are "two visions of diversity and inclusion." What are they? Which one does he favor? Why?

3. In paragraph 21, Reges says that he is going to commit "blasphemy." To what idea is he referring? Why does he consider this idea blasphemy?

4. What is Reges's opinion of James Damore? What is his opinion of those who disagree with Damore? What does he think of Sundar Pichai's decision to fire him? How do you know?

5. Draw a **rhetorical triangle** (p. 19) that represents the relative importance of various appeals in this essay. Which appeal does the longest side of the triangle represent? What does the shortest side represent? Do you think this is a good balance?

6. What evidence does Reges present to support his thesis? How convincing is this evidence? Explain.

7. Suppose Reges wanted to present his ideas as a Rogerian argument. How would he have to change his essay?

This essay was posted to the technology news website *Recode* on August 11, 2017.

WE'VE STUDIED GENDER AND STEM FOR 25 YEARS. THE SCIENCE DOESN'T SUPPORT THE GOOGLE MEMO.

ROSALIND C. BARNETT AND CARYL RIVERS

A Google engineer who was fired for posting an online claim that women's 1 biology makes them less able than men to work in technology jobs has charged that he is being smeared and is a victim of political correctness.

James Damore, 28, questioned the company's diversity policies and 2 claimed that scientific data backed up his assertions. Google CEO Sundar Pichai wrote that Damore's 3,300-word manifesto crossed the line by "advancing harmful gender stereotypes" in the workplace. Pichai noted that "To suggest a group of our colleagues have traits that make them less biologically suited to that work is offensive and not OK."

Damore argued that many men in the company agreed with his senti- 3 ments. That's not surprising, since the idea that women just can't hack it in math and science has been around for a very long time. It has been argued that women's lack of a "math gene," their brain structures and their inherent psychological traits put most of them out of the game.

Some critics sided with Damore. For example, columnist Ross Douthat of 4 the *New York Times* found his scientific arguments intriguing.

But are they? What are the real facts? We have been researching issues 5 of gender and STEM (science, technology, engineering, and math) for more than 25 years. We can say flatly that there is no evidence that women's biology makes them incapable of performing at the highest levels in any STEM fields.

Many reputable scientific authorities have weighed in on this question, 6 including a major paper in the journal *Science* debunking the idea that the brains of males and females are so different that they should be educated in single-sex classrooms. The paper was written by eight prominent neuroscientists, headed by professor Diane Halpern of Claremont McKenna College, past president of the American Psychological Association. They argue that "There is no well-designed research showing that single-sex education improves students' academic performance, but there is evidence that sex segregation increases gender stereotyping and legitimizes institutional sexism."

They add, "Neuroscientists have found few sex differences in children's 7 brains beyond the larger volume of boys' brains and the earlier completion of girls' brain growth, neither of which is known to relate to learning."

Several major books have debunked the idea of important brain differ- 8 ences between the sexes. Lise Eliot, associate professor in the Department of Neuroscience at the Chicago Medical School, did an exhaustive review of the scientific literature on human brains from birth to adolescence. She concluded, in her book *Pink Brain, Blue Brain.* that there is "surprisingly little solid evidence of sex differences in children's brains."

Rebecca Jordan-Young, a sociomedical scientist and professor at Barnard 9 College, also rejects the notion that, there are pink and blue brains, and that the differing organization of female and male brains is the key to behavior. In her book *Brain Storm: The Flaws in the Science of Sex Differences*, she says that this narrative misunderstands the complexities of biology and the dynamic nature of brain development.

And happily, the widely held belief that boys are naturally better than girls at 10 math and science is unraveling among serious scientists. Evidence is mounting that girls are every bit as competent as boys in these areas. Psychology professor Janet Hyde of the University of Wisconsin–Madison has strong U.S. data showing no meaningful differences in math performance among more than seven million boys and girls in grades 2 through 12.

Also, several large-scale international testing programs find girls closing 11 the gender gap in math, and in some cases outscoring the boys. Clearly, this huge improvement over a fairly short time period argues against biological explanations.

Much of the data that Damore provides in his memo is suspect, outdated, 12 or has other problems.

In his July memo, titled "Google's Ideological Echo Chamber: How bias 13 clouds our thinking about diversity and inclusion," Damore wrote that women on average have more "openness directed towards feelings and aesthetics rather than ideas." And he stated that women are more inclined to have an interest in "people rather than things, relative to men."

Damore cites the work of Simon Baron-Cohen, who argues in his widely 14 reviewed book *The Essential Difference* that boys are biologically programmed to focus on objects, predisposing them to math and understanding systems, while girls are programmed to focus on people and feelings. The British psychologist claims that the male brain is the "systematizing brain" while the female brain is the "empathizing" brain.

This idea was based on a study of day-old babies, which found that the 15 boys looked at mobiles longer and the girls looked at faces longer. Male brains, Baron-Cohen says, are ideally suited for leadership and power. They are hardwired for mastery of hunting and tracking, trading, achieving and maintaining power, gaining expertise, tolerating solitude, using aggression, and taking on leadership roles.

The female brain, on the other hand, is specialized for making friends, 16 mothering, gossip, and "reading" a partner. Girls and women are so focused on others, he says, that they have little interest in figuring out how the world works.

But Baron-Cohen's study had major problems. It was an "outlier" study. 17 No one else has replicated these findings, including Baron-Cohen himself. It is so flawed as to be almost meaningless. Why?

The experiment lacked crucial controls against experimenter bias and was 18 badly designed. Female and male infants were propped up in a parent's lap and shown, side by side, an active person or an inanimate object. Since newborns can't hold their heads up independently, their visual preferences could well have been determined by the way their parents held them.

> "Media stories continue to promote the idea of very different brains on little evidence."

There is much literature that flat- 19 out contradicts Baron-Cohen's study, providing evidence that male and female infants tend to respond equally to people and objects, notes Elizabeth Spelke, co-director of Harvard's Mind Brain Behavior Interfaculty Initiative. But media stories continue to promote the idea of very different brains on little evidence.

Damore also claims that women experience more stress and anxiety 20 than men, and that "This may contribute to the higher levels of anxiety women report on Googlegeist and to the lower number of women in high-stress jobs."

He implies that stress and anxiety are personality traits inherent in 21 females, but more likely they are due to the pressures and discrimination women face on the job that men do not. For example, a 2008 report sponsored by major companies, "The Athena Factor," found that women in high positions in male-dominated fields, such as tech, suffer harsher penalties than men when they slip up. Women don't get second chances. Men do.

One of the report's authors, Sylvia Ann Hewlett, founding president of 22 the Center for Work-Life Policy in New York, notes in the *Harvard Business Review* that in tech firms, "the way to get promoted is to do a diving catch. Some system is crashing in Bulgaria, so you get on the plane in the middle of the night and dash off and spend the weekend wrestling with routers and come back a hero."

But what if you don't make the catch? "Women have a hard time taking 23 on those assignments because you can dive and fail to catch. If a man fails, his buddies dust him off and say, 'It's not your fault; try again next time.' A woman fails and is never seen again."

Add to that conundrum the fact that just getting in the door is harder for a 24 woman than it is for a man.

Her résumé may look exactly like his, but because her name is Mary and not 25 John, she may not get a second look. A review of studies of U.S. decision makers who have the power to hire candidates found that clearly competent men were rated higher than equally competent women. This bias is especially rampant in the high-tech industry. One study, conducted by professors at Columbia, Northwestern, and the University of Chicago, found that two-thirds of managers selected male job candidates, even when the men did not perform as well as the women on math problems that were part of the application process.

Throw in the facts that, according to research, competent men are seen 26 as likeable, while competent women are seen as bitchy, that women get less credit for their accomplishments than men do, that men are often promoted on promise while women get elevated only on the basis of performance, and that sexual harassment is a constant problem for women in tech.

All of these are issues that males simply do not have to face. The "anxiety 27 gap" exists for a reason, and it is not about biology.

Many of Damore's controversial conclusions rest heavily on one recent 28 study and much older, now-discredited research, ignoring reams of data that tell a very different story. The argument that men, especially affluent men, are more focused on their "male" breadwinner role than on their more "female" family roles, does not reflect either research data or observational data.

For example:

- Over the past two decades, men in the U.S. are spending more and more time on housework and childcare on both workdays and weekends. Indeed, their time spent on such tasks is close to that spent by their wives, according to the National Study of the Changing Workforce.

- The psychological well-being of employed married fathers is as closely linked to their family as to their employee roles, according to a study directed by Dr. Barnett.

- Today, companies are offering more and more paternity leave, because male employees are clamoring for it. Generous leave policies are seen as a recruitment tool, as companies are in an arms race with competitors to attract millennials and retain their best talent.

- In 2016, Mark Zuckerberg, CEO of Facebook, caused banner headlines when his daughter was born and he took a two-month paternity leave. He set an example for his employees and those of other companies.

And they seem to have noticed. According to SmartAsset.com, "in just the past 29 year . . . at least 17 big employers have either introduced or expanded paid-leave options for new dads." They include Hilton, Netflix, Spotify, Microsoft, and Fidelity.

"The rate of expansion is unprecedented," said Ellen Bravo, executive 30 director of Family Values @ Work.

But many men who would opt for paternity leave hesitate, not because of 31 innate biological dispositions, but because of fear of retribution. Cultural stereotypes exert a powerful effect, punishing men for the caring, family-oriented behavior that they desire. Damore's article may make it even harder for such men to take the paternity leave they so clearly crave.

The recent history of Sweden's legislation on paternity leave highlights 32 dramatically the overwhelming role of cultural stereotypes on male parental behavior. It's not biology at work here, but laws mandating at least two months of the nation's well-paid, 13-month parental leave exclusively for fathers that have created profound social change.

"In perhaps the most striking example of social engineering, a new defini- 33 tion of masculinity is emerging," notes the *New York Times*. Birgitta Ohlsson,

European affairs minister, put it this way: "Machos with dinosaur values don't make the top-10 lists of attractive men in women's magazines anymore. Now men can have it all—a successful career and being a responsible daddy. It's a new kind of manly. It's more wholesome."

Damore, on the other hand, argues for downplaying empathy in American 34 companies.

Creating more dinosaurs doesn't seem like a healthy way to go. 35

⊘ AT ISSUE: WHY ARE SO FEW WOMEN IN STEM FIELDS?

1. Why do Barnett and Rivers wait until paragraph 5 to state their thesis? What information do they provide before stating it? Why is this information necessary?

2. At what point in their essay do Barnett and Rivers appeal to *ethos*? What do they hope to establish with this appeal?

3. According to Barnett and Rivers, "the 'anxiety gap' exists for a reason" (para. 27). What do they mean?

4. In paragraph 5 Barnett and Rivers say, "there is no evidence that women's biology makes them incapable of performing at the highest levels in any STEM field." Do they include enough facts and examples to support this assertion? Could they be accused of making a **sweeping generalization**? Why or why not?

5. Much of this essay is devoted to refuting James Damore's Google memo. How do Barnett and Rivers characterize this memo? How effectively do they refute its assertions? (If you wish, go online and read Damore's memo.)

6. Barnett and Rivers end their essay by saying, "Creating more dinosaurs doesn't seem like a healthy way to go" (41). To what are they referring? How fair is this statement?

7. Is Barnett and Rivers's argument primarily inductive or deductive? Why do you think that they chose this structure?

This essay first appeared in the July 13, 2018, issue of the *Wall Street Journal*.

WHY DO WOMEN SHUN STEM? IT'S COMPLICATED

BARBARA OAKLEY

Why do relatively few women work in science, technology, engineering, and 1 mathematics? University of Washington lecturer Stuart Reges—in a provocative essay, "Why Women Don't Code"—suggests that women's verbal and analytical skills lead to career choices outside STEM. Mr. Reges's critics say he is making women feel inferior by implying they aren't interested in tech. I'm a female engineering professor with decades of experience as well as a background in the humanities and social sciences, so perhaps I can lend some perspective to the controversy.

I've observed that women tend to choose disciplines other than STEM, 2 often for the reasons Mr. Reges mentions. Yet his argument is incomplete. An important but often neglected factor is the attitudes of undergraduate professors. Not STEM professors, but professors in the humanities and social sciences.

Professors have profound influence over students' career choices. I'm 3 sometimes flabbergasted at the level of bias and antagonism toward STEM from professors outside scientific fields. I've heard it all: STEM is only for those who enjoy "rote" work. Engineering is not creative. There's only one right answer. You'll live your life in a cubicle. It's dehumanizing. You'll never talk to anyone. And, of course, it's sexist. All this from professors whose only substantive experience with STEM is a forced march through a single statistics course in college, if that.

My colleagues in the humanities unthinkingly malign STEM in front of 4 me. Their bias has become so deeply ingrained that they don't think twice. My students tell me it's worse when I'm not around. With joking asides during class or more-pointed conversations about careers, the STEM disciplines are caricatured as a gulag for creative types. Even a few untoward remarks like this to students can have profound effects. It's too bad, because science, technology, engineering, and math can be among the most creative and satisfying disciplines.

Many studies, including a critical review by Elizabeth Spelke in *American Psychologist*, have shown that on average men and women have the 5 same abilities in math and science. But as Mr. Reges notes, women tend to do better than men verbally—a consequence of early developmental advantages.

How does this alter career choice? A student named Bob might get 6 a C in physics 101 but a D in English composition. His English professor probably won't try to recruit him into the field. Bob's choice to become an engineer makes sense because he's less likely to be good at the social sciences or humanities.

Women who are average in physics classes, on the other hand, are often 7 better at other subjects. When Sara has a C in physics 101, she's more likely to have a B or even an A in English composition. Her English professor is more likely to recruit her. And, crucially, the "STEM is only for uncreative nerds" characterization can play well here. It can provide a mental boost for Sara to hear a powerful figure like her professor denigrate the subject she's struggling with.

Even when a professor isn't working to recruit Sara to the social sciences or human- ities, she might be recruiting herself. Grades mean something; if Sara's working hard to get a C in calculus, but she earns an A in English with less effort, she's going to experience a powerful pull toward the humanities.

> "Jerks exist in every workplace." 8

Consider a student who gets an A in every subject. Let's call her Nadine. 9 She's the type of student who could excel in whatever she chooses. Her engineering professors might be telling her that an electrical engineering degree is a great career choice that will open doors and pay well. But her non-STEM professors may be telling her something completely different: "You won't use your fantastic writing skills. And besides, you'll just sit in a cubicle crunching numbers." Nadine can begin to feel she's untrue to her full set of talents if she picks engineering. So Nadine jumps the STEM ship.

What about the women who go into STEM and discover bias in the work- 10 place? Jerks exist in every workplace. Bullying is so prevalent in nursing, for example, that it's the subject of dozens of studies. "Bullying behaviors fall on a continuum ranging from eye-rolling and exclusion to humiliation, withholding information, scapegoating, intimidation, and backstabbing," a 2016 article in *American Nurse Today* notes. "The bully sets out to destroy the victim's confidence and credibility as a way to gain power and control."

If I drew a Venn diagram to see the intersection between a jerk and a 11 sexist, it would show almost total overlap—in male-dominated disciplines, that is. It can be easy for a woman who has landed in a toxic software-development environment to say, "There's horrible bias here!" And she'd be right. But there are toxic pockets in every discipline or field. STEM is no different.

I have experienced bias in my career, but I also would not be where I am 12 today without the strong support of many wonderful men. Women are vitally important to STEM. Professors outside these disciplines should stop mischaracterizing to poach the best students, who are often women. And it's time for everyone to step back, take a breath, and acknowledge that good and bad bosses and co-workers exist everywhere.

⊘ AT ISSUE: WHY ARE SO FEW WOMEN IN STEM FIELDS?

1. Explain the essay's title.

2. Regarding STEM, how does Oakley characterize students? How does she characterize instructors? Based on your experience, are these characterizations fair? Accurate? Explain.

3. In paragraph 2, Oakley concedes an opposing argument. Why? What weakness does she go on to identify?

4. In her essay, Oakley discusses three hypothetical students. What point (or points) does she make about each one? How effective is this rhetorical strategy? Would her argument have been stronger had she used the experiences of actual students to support her argument? What other kinds of evidence could she have used?

5. Addressing the fact that women in STEM workplaces experience bias, Oakley says, "Jerks exist in every workplace" (para. 10). Should she have done more to address this issue? Explain.

6. Oakley begins her essay by saying that she is a female engineer "with decades of experience" (1). She ends her essay by saying, "I have experienced bias in my career" (12). What does she hope to accomplish by including this personal information?

7. What preconceptions about women in STEM fields does Oakley assume her readers have? How do you know?

VISUAL ARGUMENT: STEM PSA

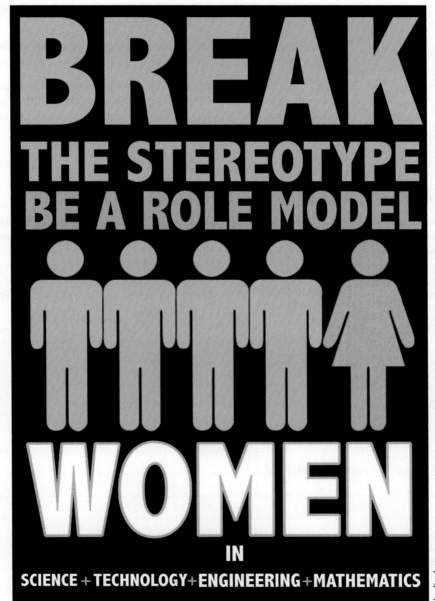

⊘ AT ISSUE: WHY ARE SO FEW WOMEN IN STEM FIELDS?

1. What is the purpose of this public-service ad? In general, do you think it is successful? Explain.

2. How do the variations in type size highlight the ad's main points? Is the use of this visual element effective? Explain.

3. How does the ad use color to emphasize its main point? Does this use of color reinforce gender stereotypes in any way? Explain.

4. Is this ad easy to read, or does it seem crowded? If you were going to edit this ad, which elements would you change? Which would you keep the same? Why?

TEMPLATE FOR WRITING A ROGERIAN ARGUMENT

Write a one-paragraph **Rogerian** argument in which you argue that the drawbacks of STEM education have to be addressed before it can appeal to the majority of women. Follow the template below, filling in the blanks to create your argument.

With more and more women taking STEM courses, both the students and the colleges benefit. For example, _____

_____. In addition, _____

_____.

However, STEM education does have some drawbacks for women. For instance, _____

_____

_____.

These problems could be easily solved. First, _____

_____. Second, _____

_____.

If these problems are addressed, both students and colleges would benefit because _____

_____.

TEMPLATE FOR WRITING A TOULMIN ARGUMENT

Write a one-paragraph **Toulmin** argument in which you argue in favor of changes to STEM education. Follow the template below, filling in the blanks to create your argument.

> Many colleges and universities have instituted programs to encourage women to consider STEM majors. These programs are the best way _____
>
> _____.
>
> If colleges are going to meet the rising demand for STEM graduates, they _____
>
> _____
>
> _____.
>
> The science and math courses I took _____
>
> _____
>
> _____.
>
> Recent studies show that _____
>
> _____. In addition, _____
>
> _____. However, some people argue that _____
>
> _____
>
> _____. They also say that _____
>
> _____
>
> These arguments _____
>
> _____.
>
> For this reason, STEM education is _____
>
> _____
>
> _____.

● EXERCISE 6.7 DISCUSSING AN ARGUMENT

Discuss your ideas about STEM education with one or two of your classmates. Consider both the strengths and the limitations of these courses. What classes do you think women avoid? Why do you think this is so? What changes could be made to make majoring in STEM more appealing? Then, edit the Rogerian and Toulmin arguments that you wrote on the previous templates so that they include some of these comments.

⊖ EXERCISE 6.8 WRITING AN ARGUMENTATIVE ESSAY

Write an argumentative essay on the topic, "Why are so few women in STEM fields?" Use the principles of either Rogerian argument or Toulmin logic to structure your essay. Cite sources in the Reading and Writing about the Issue section on pages 221–246, and be sure to document the sources you use and to include a works-cited page. (See Chapter 10 for information on documenting sources.)

⊖ EXERCISE 6.9 CONSIDERING THE FOUR PILLARS OF ARGUMENT

Review the four pillars of argument that are discussed in Chapter 1. Does your essay include all four elements of an effective argument? Add anything that is missing. Then, label the elements of your argument.

⊖ EXERCISE 6.10 CONSTRUCTING AN ORAL ARGUMENT

Assume that you have been asked to present the information in the essay you wrote for Exercise 6.8 as an oral argument. What information would you include? What information would you eliminate? Find two or three visuals that you would use when you deliver your speech. Then, make an outline of your speech and indicate at what points you would display these visuals.

3

Writing an Argumentative Essay

AP Images/The Herald-Palladium/Don Campbell

Planning, Drafting, and Revising an Argumentative Essay

Should All College Campuses Go Green?

In recent years, more and more American colleges and universities have become "green campuses," emphasizing **sustainability**—the use of systems and materials that will not deplete the earth's natural resources. Various schools have taken steps such as the following:

- Placing an emphasis on recycling and reducing nonbiodegradable waste
- Creating green buildings and using eco-friendly materials in construction projects
- Instituting new curricula in environmental science
- Monitoring their greenhouse gas emissions and evaluating their carbon footprint
- Growing crops on campus to feed students
- Hiring full-time "sustainability directors"
- Encouraging students to use bikes instead of cars
- Purchasing wind-generated electricity to supply the campus's energy
- Eliminating trays in college cafeterias

Although many schools continue to launch ambitious programs and projects to reduce their energy dependence, some have been more cautious, citing the high cost of such programs and the need to allocate resources elsewhere. Moreover, some critics of the green movement object to the notion that colleges should help to make students "sustainability literate." Such critics consider the green movement to be an expression of political correctness that at best does no more than pay lip service to the problem and at worst threatens academic freedom by furthering a political agenda.

The question remains whether the green movement that is spreading rapidly across college campuses is here to stay or just a fad—or something between these two extremes. This chapter takes you through the process of writing an argumentative essay on the topic of whether all college campuses should go green. (Exercises guide you through the process of writing your own argumentative essay on a topic of your choice.)

Before you can write a convincing argumentative essay, you need to understand the **writing process**. You are probably already familiar with the basic outline of this process, which includes *planning, drafting,* and *revising.* This chapter reviews this familiar process and explains how it applies to the specific demands of writing an argumentative essay.

Choosing a Topic

The first step in planning an argumentative essay is to choose a topic you can write about. Your goal is to select a topic that you have some emotional stake in—not simply one that interests you. If you are going to spend hours planning, writing, and revising an essay, you should care about your topic. At the same time, you should be able to keep an open mind about your topic and be willing to consider various viewpoints. Your topic also should be narrow enough to fit the boundaries of your assignment—the time you have to work on the essay and its length and scope.

Typically, your instructor will give you a general assignment, such as the following.

Assignment
Write a three- to five-page argumentative essay on a topic related to college services, programs, facilities, or curricula.

The first thing you need to do is narrow this general assignment to a topic, focusing on one particular campus service, program, facility, or curriculum. You could choose to write about any number of topics—financial aid, the writing center, athletics, the general education curriculum—taking a position, for example, on who should receive financial aid, whether to expand the mission of the writing center, whether college athletes should receive a salary, or why general education requirements are important for business majors.

If you are interested in environmental issues, however, you might decide to write about the green movement that has been spreading across college campuses, perhaps using your observations of your own campus's programs and policies to support your position.

Topic
The green movement on college campuses

Topics to Avoid

Certain kinds of topics are not appropriate for argumentative essays.

- **Topics that are statements of fact.** Some topics are just not arguable. For example, you could not write an argumentative essay on a statement of fact, such as the fact that many colleges saw their endowments decline after the financial crisis of 2008. (A fact is not debatable, so there can be no argument.)

- **Topics that have been overused.** Some familiar topics also present problems. These issues—the death penalty, abortion rights, and so on—are important (after all, that's why they are written about so often), but finding an original argument on either side of the debate can be a challenge. For example, you might have a hard time finding something new to say that would convince some readers that the death penalty is immoral or that abortion is a woman's right. In many people's minds, these issues are "settled." When you write on topics such as these, some readers' strong religious or cultural beliefs are likely to prevent them from considering your arguments, however well supported they might be.

- **Topics that rely on subjective judgments.** Some very narrow topics depend on subjective value judgment, often taking a stand on issues readers simply will not care much about, such as whether one particular video game or TV reality show is more entertaining than another. Such topics are unlikely to engage your audience (even if they seem compelling to you and your friends).

❷ EXERCISE 7.1 CHOOSING A TOPIC

In response to the boxed assignment on the previous page, list ten topics that you could write about. Then, cross out any that do not meet the following criteria:

- The topic interests you.
- You know something about the topic.
- You care about the topic.
- You are able to keep an open mind about the topic.
- The topic fits the boundaries of your assignment.

Now, decide on one topic to write an essay about.

Thinking about Your Topic

Before you can start to develop a thesis statement or plan the structure of your argument, you need to think a bit about the topic you have chosen. You can use *invention strategies*—such as **freewriting** (writing without stopping for a predetermined time), **brainstorming** (making quick notes on your topic), or **clustering** (creating a diagram to map out your thoughts)—to help you discover ideas you might write about. You can also explore ideas in a writing journal or in conversations with friends, classmates, family members, or instructors.

Freewriting

People say green is good, but I'm not sure why. Do we really need a separate, smelly container for composting? Won't the food decompose just as fast in a landfill? In middle school, we learned about the "three Rs" to save the environment—one was Recycle, but I forget the other two. Renew? Reuse? Remember? Whatever. OK, I know not to throw trash on the ground, and I know we're supposed to separate trash and recycling, etc. I get that. But does all this time and effort really do any good?

Brainstorming

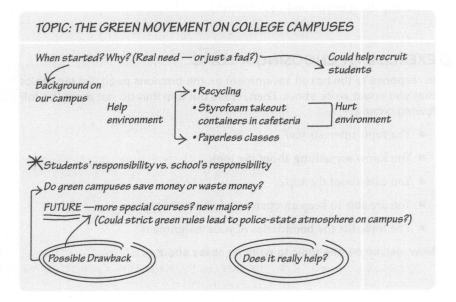

TOPIC: THE GREEN MOVEMENT ON COLLEGE CAMPUSES

When started? Why? (Real need — or just a fad?) ——→ Could help recruit students

Background on our campus

Help environment
• Recycling
• Styrofoam takeout containers in cafeteria
• Paperless classes
Hurt environment

✱ Students' responsibility vs. school's responsibility

Do green campuses save money or waste money?

FUTURE — more special courses? new majors?
(Could strict green rules lead to police-state atmosphere on campus?)

(Possible Drawback)   (Does it really help?)

Clustering

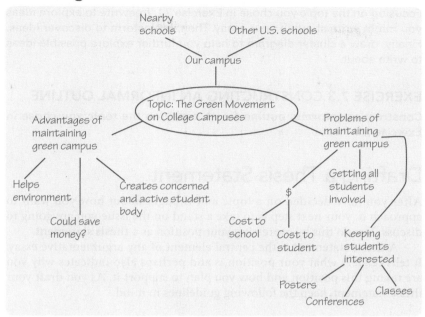

When you finish exploring ideas, you should be able to construct a quick **informal outline** that lists the ideas you plan to discuss.

Informal Outline

Topic: The Green Movement on College Campuses
    History/background
        National
        Our campus
    Positive aspects
        Helps environment
        Attracts new students
    Negative aspects
        Cost
        Enforcement
    Future

By grouping your ideas and arranging them in a logical order, an informal outline like the preceding one can help lead you to a thesis statement that expresses the position you will take on the issue.

⊘ EXERCISE 7.2 EXPLORING IDEAS

Focusing on the topic you chose in Exercise 7.1, freewrite to explore ideas you might write about in your essay. Then, brainstorm to discover ideas. Finally, draw a cluster diagram to help you further explore possible ideas to write about.

⊘ EXERCISE 7.3 CONSTRUCTING AN INFORMAL OUTLINE

Construct an informal outline for an essay on the topic you chose in Exercise 7.1.

Drafting a Thesis Statement

After you have decided on a topic and thought about how you want to approach it, your next step is to take a stand on the issue you are going to discuss. You do this by expressing your position as a **thesis statement**.

A thesis statement is the central element of any argumentative essay. It tells readers what your position is and perhaps also indicates why you are taking this position and how you plan to support it. As you draft your thesis statement, keep the following guidelines in mind:

- An argumentative thesis statement is not simply a statement of your topic; rather, it expresses the point you will make about your topic.

TOPIC	The green movement on college campuses
THESIS STATEMENT	College campuses should go green.

- An argumentative thesis statement should be specific, clearly indicating to readers exactly what position you will take in your essay.

TOO GENERAL	Colleges need to do more to get students involved in environmental issues.
REVISED	Colleges should institute programs and classes to show students the importance of using sustainable resources.

- An argumentative thesis statement should get right to the point, avoiding wordy, repetitive language.

WORDY	Because issues that revolve around the environment are so crucial and important, colleges should do more to increase student involvement in campus projects that are concerned with sustainability.

REVISED   Because environmental issues are so important, colleges should take steps to involve students in campus sustainability projects.

■ Many argumentative thesis statements include words such as *should* and *should not*.

- College campuses should _____.

- Because _____, colleges should _____.

- Even though _____, colleges should not _____.

> **NOTE**
>
> At this point, any thesis that you come up with is tentative. As you think about your topic and perhaps read about it, you will very likely modify your thesis statement, perhaps expanding or narrowing its scope, rewording it to make it more precise, or even changing your position. Still, the thesis statement that you decide on at this point can give you some focus as you explore your topic.

TENTATIVE THESIS STATEMENT

College campuses should go green.

⊘ EXERCISE 7.4 DEVELOPING A THESIS STATEMENT

List five possible thesis statements for the topic you chose in Exercise 7.1. (To help you see your topic in several different ways, you might experiment by drafting at least one thesis statement that evaluates, one that considers causes and/or effects, and one that proposes a solution to a problem.) Which thesis statement seems to suggest the most promising direction for your essay? Why?

Understanding Your Purpose and Audience

When you write an argument, your primary purpose is to convince your audience to accept your position. Sometimes you will have other goals as well. For example, you might want to change readers' ideas about an issue, perhaps by challenging a commonly held assumption. You might even want to move readers to take some action in support of your position.

To make the best possible case to your audience, you need to understand who your audience is—what knowledge, values, beliefs, and opinions your readers might have. You will also need to have some idea whether your audience is likely to be receptive, hostile, or neutral to the ideas you propose.

In most cases, it makes sense to assume that your readers are receptive but **skeptical**—that they have open minds but still need to be convinced. However, if you are writing about a topic that is very controversial, you will need to assume that at least some of your readers will not support your position and may, in fact, be hostile to it. If this is the case, they will be scrutinizing your arguments very carefully, looking for opportunities to argue against them. Your goal in this situation is not necessarily to win readers over but to make them more receptive to your position—or at least to get them to admit that you have made a good case even though they may disagree with you. At the same time, you also have to work to convince those who probably agree with you or those who are neutral (perhaps because the issue you are discussing is something they haven't thought much about).

An audience of first-year college students who are used to the idea that sound environmental practices make sense might find the idea of a green campus appealing—and, in fact, natural and obvious. An audience of faculty or older students might be more skeptical, realizing that the benefits of green practices might be offset by the time and expense they could involve. College administrators might find the long-term goal of a green campus attractive (and see it as a strong recruitment tool), but they might also be somewhat hostile to your position, anticipating the considerable expense that would be involved. If you wrote an argument on the topic of green campuses, you would need to consider these positions—and, if possible, address them.

⊝ EXERCISE 7.5 CONSIDERING YOUR AUDIENCE

Consider how different audiences might respond to the thesis statement you found the most promising in Exercise 7.3. Identify five possible groups of readers on your college campus—for example, athletes, history majors, or part-time faculty. Would you expect each group to be receptive, hostile, or neutral to your position? Why?

Gathering Evidence

After you have a sense of who your audience will be and how these readers might react to your thesis, you can begin to collect **evidence** to support your thesis. As you look for evidence, you need to evaluate the usefulness and relevance of each of your sources, and you need to be alert for possible bias.

Evaluating the Evidence in Your Sources

As you read each potential source, consider the quality of the supporting evidence that the writer marshals to support his or her position. The more compelling the evidence, the more willing you should be to accept the writer's ideas—and, perhaps, to integrate these ideas into your own essay.

> **NOTE**
>
> Don't forget that if you use any of your sources' ideas, you must document them. See Chapter 10 for information on MLA documentation format and Appendix B for information on APA documentation format.

To be convincing, the evidence that is presented in the sources you review should be *accurate, relevant, representative,* and *sufficient*:

- **Accurate** evidence comes from reliable sources that are quoted carefully—and not misrepresented by being quoted out of context.

- **Relevant** evidence applies specifically (not just tangentially) to the topic under discussion.

- **Representative** evidence is drawn from a fair range of sources, not just those that support the writer's position.

- **Sufficient** evidence is enough facts, statistics, expert opinion, and so on to support the essay's thesis.

(For more detailed information on evaluating sources, see Chapter 8.)

> **NOTE**
>
> Remember, the evidence you use to support your own arguments should also satisfy the four criteria listed above.

Detecting Bias in Your Sources

As you select sources, you should be alert for **bias**—a writer's use of preconceived ideas (rather than factual evidence) as support for his or her arguments. A writer who demonstrates bias may not be trustworthy, and you should approach such a writer's arguments with skepticism. To determine whether a writer is biased, follow these guidelines:

- *Consider what a writer explicitly tells you* about his or her beliefs or opinions. For example, if a writer mentions that he or she is a lifelong member of the Sierra Club, a vegan, and the owner of a house heated by solar energy, then you should consider the possibility that he or she might downplay (or even disregard) valid arguments against maintaining a green campus rather than presenting a balanced view.

- *Look for slanted language.* For example, a writer who mocks supporters of environmental issues as "politically correct" or uses pejorative terms such as *hippies* for environmentalists should not earn your trust.

- *Consider the supporting evidence* the writer chooses. Does the writer present only examples that support his or her position and ignore valid opposing arguments? Does the writer quote only those experts who agree with his or her position—for example, only pro- (or only anti-) environmental writers? A writer who does this is presenting an unbalanced (and therefore biased) case.

- *Consider the writer's tone.* A writer whose tone is angry, bitter, or sarcastic should be suspect.

- *Consider any overtly offensive statements or characterizations* that a writer makes. A writer who makes negative assumptions about college students (for example, characterizing them as selfish and self-involved and therefore dismissing their commitment to campus environmental projects) should be viewed with skepticism.

> **NOTE**
>
> As you develop your essay, be alert for any biases you hold that might affect the strength or logic of your own arguments. See "Being Fair," page 267.

⊘ EXERCISE 7.6 EXAMINING YOUR BIASES

In writing an essay that supports the thesis statement you have been working with in this chapter, you might find it difficult to remain objective. What biases do you have that you might have to watch for as you research and write about your topic?

⊘ EXERCISE 7.7 GATHERING EVIDENCE

Now, gather evidence to support the thesis statement you decided on in Exercise 7.3, evaluating each source carefully (and consulting Chapter 8 as necessary). Be on the lookout for bias in your sources.

USING VISUALS AS EVIDENCE

As you draft your essay, you might want to consider adding a **visual**—such as a chart, graph, table, photo, or diagram—to help you make a point more forcefully. For example, in a paper on the green campus movement, you could include anything from photos of students recycling to a chart comparing energy use at different schools. Sometimes a visual can be so specific, so attractive, or so dramatic that its impact will be greater than words would be; in such cases, the image itself can constitute a visual argument. At other times, a visual can expand and support a written argument.

You can create a visual yourself, or you can download one from the internet, beginning your search with Google Images. If you download a visual and paste it into your paper, be sure to include a reference to the visual in your discussion to explain the argument it makes—or to show readers how it supports your argument.

> **NOTE**
>
> Don't forget to label any visuals with a figure number, to use proper documentation, and to include a caption explaining what the visual shows, as the student essay that begins on page 278 does. (For information on documentation, see Chapter 10.)

Refuting Opposing Arguments

As you plan your essay and explore sources that might supply your supporting evidence, you will encounter evidence that contradicts your position. You may be tempted to ignore this evidence, but if you do, your argument will not be very convincing. Instead, as you review your sources, identify the most convincing arguments against your position and prepare yourself to **refute** them (that is, to disprove them or call them into question), showing them to be illogical, unfair, or untrue. Indicating to readers that you are willing to address these arguments—and that you can respond effectively to them—will help convince them to accept your position.

Of course, simply saying that your opponent's position is "wrong" or "stupid" is not convincing. You need to summarize opposing arguments accurately and clearly identify their weaknesses. In the case of a strong opposing argument, be sure to concede its strengths (that is, acknowledge that it is a valid position) before you refute it; if you do not, readers may see you as uninformed or unfair. For example, you could refute the argument that maintaining a green campus is too expensive by acknowledging that although expenditures are high at first, in the long run, a green campus is not all that costly considering its benefits.

In assessing the strength of an opposing argument, you should always try to identify its limitations. Even a strong opposing argument may be addressing only one part of the problem. For example, an argument might focus on students' reluctance to comply with campus environmental guidelines and ignore efforts by the school's administration to overcome that reluctance. Or, an argument might focus on the current lack of green buildings on campus and ignore the school's requirement that green materials be used in all campus construction projects.

Also be careful not to create a **straw man**—that is, do not distort an opposing argument by oversimplifying it so it can be easily refuted (for example, claiming that environmentalists believe that sustainability should always be a college's first priority in its decisions about allocating resources). This unfair tactic will discourage readers from trusting you and thus will undermine your credibility.

Strategies for Refuting Opposing Arguments

In order to do a convincing job of refuting an argument that challenges your position, you need to consider where such an argument might be weak and on what basis you could refute it.

WEAKNESS IN OPPOSING ARGUMENT	REFUTATION STRATEGY
Factual errors or contrary-to-fact statements	Identify and correct the errors, perhaps explaining how they call the writer's credibility into question.
Insufficient support	Point out that more facts and examples are needed; note the kind of support (for example, statistics) that is missing.
Illogical reasoning	Identify fallacies in the writer's argument, and explain why the logic is flawed. For example, is the writer setting up a straw man or employing the either/or fallacy? (See Chapter 5 for more on logic.)
Exaggerated or over-stated claims	Identify exaggerated statements, and explain why they overstate the case.
Biased statements	Identify biased statements, and show how they exhibit the writer's bias. (See page 259, "Detecting Bias in Your Sources.")
Irrelevant arguments	Identify irrelevant points and explain why they are not pertinent to the writer's argument.

⊘ EXERCISE 7.8 EVALUATING OPPOSING ARGUMENTS

Read paragraphs 7 and 8 of the student essay on page 278. Summarize the opposing argument presented in each of these paragraphs. Then, consulting the preceding list, identify the specific weakness of each opposing argument. Finally, explain the strategy the student writer uses to refute the argument.

Revising Your Thesis Statement

Before you can begin to draft your argumentative essay, and even before you can start to arrange your ideas, you need to revise your tentative thesis statement so it says exactly what you want it to say. After you have gathered and evaluated evidence to support your position and considered the merits of opposing ideas, you are ready to refocus your thesis and state it in more precise terms. Although a tentative thesis statement such as "College campuses should go green" is a good start, the thesis that guides your essay's structure should be more specific. In fact, it will be most useful as a guide if its phrasing actually acknowledges opposing arguments.

> ### REVISED THESIS STATEMENT
>
> Colleges should make every effort to create and sustain green campuses because by doing so they will not only improve their own educational environment but also ensure their institutions' survival and help solve the global climate crisis.

⊘ EXERCISE 7.9 REVISING YOUR THESIS STATEMENT

Consulting the sources you gathered in Exercise 7.7, list all the arguments against the position you express in your thesis statement. Then, list possible refutations of each of these arguments. When you have finished, revise your thesis statement so that it is more specific, acknowledging the most important argument against your position.

After you have revised your thesis statement, you will have a concise blueprint for the essay you are going to write. At this point, you will be ready to plan your essay's structure and write a first draft.

Structuring Your Essay

As you learned in Chapter 1, an argumentative essay, like other essays, includes an introduction, a body, and a conclusion. In the introduction of an argumentative essay, you state your thesis; in the body paragraphs, you present evidence to support your thesis and you acknowledge and refute opposing arguments; and in your conclusion, you bring your argument to a close and reinforce your thesis with a strong concluding statement. As you have seen, these four elements—thesis, evidence, refutation, and concluding statement—are like the four pillars of the ancient Greek temple, supporting your argument so that it will stand up to scrutiny.

SUPPLYING BACKGROUND INFORMATION

Depending on what you think your readers know—and what you think they need to know—you might decide to include a background paragraph that supplies information about the issue you are discussing. For example, in an essay about green campuses, you might briefly sum up the history of the U.S. environmental movement and trace its rise on college campuses. If you decide to include a background paragraph, it should be placed right after your introduction, where it can prepare readers for the discussion to follow.

Understanding basic essay structure can help you as you shape your essay. You should also know how to use induction and deduction, how to identify a strategy for your argument, and how to construct a formal outline.

Using Induction and Deduction

Many argumentative essays are structured either **inductively** or **deductively**. (See Chapter 5 for explanations of induction and deduction.) For example, the body of an essay with the thesis statement that is shown on page 263 could have either of the following two general structures:

INDUCTIVE STRUCTURE

- Colleges have been taking a number of steps to follow green practices.

- Through these efforts, campuses have become more environmentally responsible, and their programs and practices have had a positive impact on the environment.

- Because these efforts are helping to save the planet, they should be expanded.

DEDUCTIVE STRUCTURE

- Saving the planet is vital.

- Green campuses are helping to save the planet.

- Therefore, colleges should continue to develop green campuses.

These structures offer two options for arranging material in your essay. Many argumentative essays, however, combine induction and deduction or use other strategies to organize their ideas.

Identifying a Strategy for Your Argument

There are a variety of different ways to structure an argument, and the strategy you use depends on what you want your argument to accomplish. In this text, we discuss five options for presenting material: *definition arguments, cause-and-effect arguments, evaluation arguments, ethical arguments,* and *proposal arguments.* (See p. 390 for more on these options.)

Any of the five options listed above could guide you as you develop an essay on green campuses:

- You could structure your essay as a **definition argument**, explaining the concept of a green campus and giving examples to show its positive (or negative) impact.

- You could structure your essay as a **cause-and-effect argument**, showing how establishing a green campus can have positive results for students and for the campus—or how it might cause problems.

- You could structure your essay as an **evaluation argument**, assessing the strengths and weaknesses of various programs and policies designed to create and sustain a green campus.

- You could structure your essay as an **ethical argument**, explaining why maintaining a green campus is the right thing to do from a moral or ethical standpoint.

- You could structure your essay as a **proposal argument**, recommending a particular program, service, or course of action and showing how it can support a green campus.

Constructing a Formal Outline

If you like, you can construct a **formal outline** before you begin your draft. (Later on, you might also construct an outline of your finished paper to check the logic of its structure.) A formal outline, which is more detailed and more logically organized than the informal outline shown on page 255, presents your main points and supporting details in the order in which you will discuss them.

A formal outline of the first body paragraph (para. 2) of the student essay on page 278 would look like this:

I. Background of the term *green*
   A. 1960s environmental movement
      1. Political agenda
      2. Environmental agenda

B. Today's movements
   1. Eco-friendly practices
   2. Green values

Following a formal outline makes the drafting process flow smoothly, but many writers find it hard to predict exactly what details they will use for support or how they will develop their arguments. In fact, your first draft is likely to move away from your outline as you develop your ideas. Still, if you are the kind of writer who prefers to know where you are going before you start on your way, you will probably consider the time you devote to outlining to be time well spent.

◉ EXERCISE 7.10 CONSTRUCTING A FORMAL OUTLINE

Look back at the thesis you decided on earlier in this chapter, and review the evidence you collected to support it. Then, construct a formal outline for your argumentative essay.

Establishing Credibility

Before you begin drafting your essay, you need to think about how to approach your topic and your audience. The essay you write will use a combination of logical, emotional, and ethical appeals, and you will have to be careful to use these appeals reasonably. (See pp. 15–21 for information on these appeals.) As you write, you will concentrate on establishing yourself as well informed, reasonable, and fair.

Being Well Informed

If you expect your readers to accept your ideas, you will need to establish yourself as someone they should believe and trust. Achieving this goal depends upon showing your audience that you have a good command of your material—that is, that you know what you are talking about.

If you want readers to listen to what you are saying, you need to earn their respect by showing them that you have done your research, that you have collected evidence that supports your argument, and that you understand the most compelling arguments against your position. For example, discussing your own experiences as a member of a campus or community environmental group, your observations at a Greenpeace convention, and essays and editorials that you have read on both sides of the issue will encourage your audience to accept your ideas on the subject of green campuses.

Being Reasonable

Even if your evidence is strong, your argument will not be convincing if it does not seem reasonable. One way to present yourself as a reasonable person is to **establish common ground** with your readers, stressing possible points of agreement instead of attacking those who might disagree with your position. For example, saying, "We all want our planet to survive" is a more effective strategy than saying, "Those who do not support the concept of a green campus are out to destroy our planet." (For more on establishing common ground, see the discussion of Rogerian argument in Chapter 6.)

Another way to present yourself as a reasonable person is to **maintain a reasonable tone**. Try to avoid absolutes (words like *always* and *never*); instead, use more conciliatory language (*in many cases, much of the time*, and so on). Try not to use words and phrases like *obviously* or *as anyone can see* to introduce points whose strength may be obvious only to you. Do not brand opponents of your position as misguided, uninformed, or deluded; remember, some of your readers may hold opposing positions and will not appreciate your unfavorable portrayal of them.

Finally, be very careful to treat your readers with respect, addressing them as your intellectual equals. Avoid statements that might insult them or their beliefs ("Although some ignorant or misguided people may still think . . ."). And never assume that your readers know less about your topic than you do; they may actually know a good deal more.

Being Fair

If you want readers to respect your point of view, you need to demonstrate respect for them by being fair. It is not enough to support your ideas convincingly and maintain a reasonable tone. You also need to avoid unfair tactics in your argument and take care to avoid **bias**.

In particular, you should be careful not to *distort evidence, quote out of context, slant evidence, make unfair appeals,* or *use logical fallacies.* These unfair tactics may influence some readers in the short term, but in the long run such tactics will alienate your audience.

- **Do not distort evidence. Distorting** (or misrepresenting) **evidence** is an unfair tactic. It is not ethical or fair, for example, to present your opponent's views inaccurately or to exaggerate his or her position and then argue against it. If you want to argue that expanding green programs on college campuses are a good idea, it is not fair to attack someone who expresses reservations about their cost by writing, "Mr. McNamara's concerns about cost reveal that he has basic doubts about saving the planet." (His concerns reveal no such thing.) It is, however, fair to acknowledge your opponent's reasonable concerns about cost and then go on to argue that the long-term benefits of such programs justify their expense.

- **Do not quote out of context.** It is perfectly fair to challenge someone's stated position. It is not fair, however, to misrepresent that position by

quoting out of context—that is, by taking the words out of the original setting in which they appeared. For example, if a college dean says, "For schools with limited resources, it may be more important to allocate resources to academic programs than to environmental projects," you are quoting the dean's remarks out of context if you say, "According to Dean Levering, it is 'more important to allocate resources to academic programs than to environmental projects.'"

- **Do not slant evidence.** An argument based on slanted evidence is not fair. **Slanting** involves choosing only evidence that supports your position and ignoring evidence that challenges it. This tactic makes your position seem stronger than it actually is. Another kind of slanting involves using biased language to unfairly characterize your opponents or their positions—for example, using a dismissive term such as *tree hugger* to describe a concerned environmentalist.

- **Do not make unfair appeals.** If you want your readers to accept your ideas, you need to avoid **unfair appeals** to the emotions, such as appeals to your audience's fears or prejudices. For example, if you try to convince readers of the importance of using green building materials by saying, "Construction projects that do not use green materials doom future generations to a planet that cannot sustain itself," you are likely to push neutral (or even receptive) readers to skepticism or to outright hostility.

- **Do not use logical fallacies.** Using **logical fallacies** (flawed arguments) in your writing is likely to diminish your credibility and alienate your readers. (See Chapter 5 for information about logical fallacies.)

MAINTAINING YOUR CREDIBILITY

Be careful to avoid phrases that undercut your credibility ("Although this is not a subject I know much about") and to avoid apologies ("This is just my opinion"). Be as clear, direct, and forceful as you can, showing readers you are confident as well as knowledgeable. And, of course, be sure to proofread carefully: grammatical and mechanical errors and typos will weaken your credibility.

Drafting Your Essay

Once you understand how to approach your topic and your audience, you will be ready to draft your essay. At this point, you will have selected the sources you will use to support your position as well as identified the strongest arguments against your position (and decided how to refute them). You may also have prepared a formal outline (or perhaps just a list of points to follow).

As you draft your argumentative essay, keep the following guidelines in mind:

- **Follow the general structure of an argumentative essay.** State your thesis in your first paragraph, and discuss each major point in a separate paragraph, moving from least to most important point to emphasize your strongest argument. Introduce each body paragraph with a clearly worded topic sentence. Discuss each opposing argument in a separate paragraph, and be sure your refutation appears directly after your mention of each opposing argument. Finally, don't forget to include a strong concluding statement in your essay's last paragraph.

- **Decide how to arrange your material.** As you draft your essay, you may notice that it is turning out to be an ethical argument, an evaluation argument, or another kind of argument that you recognize. If this is the case, you might want to ask your instructor how you can arrange your material so it is consistent with this type of argument (or consult the relevant chapter in Part 5, "Strategies for Argument").

- **Use evidence effectively.** As you make your points, select the evidence that supports your argument most convincingly. As you write, **summarize** or **paraphrase** relevant information from your sources, and respond to this information in your own voice, supplementing material that you find in your sources with your own original ideas and conclusions. (For information on finding and evaluating sources, see Chapter 8; for information on integrating source material, see Chapter 9.)

- **Use coordination and subordination to make your meaning clear.** Readers shouldn't have to guess how two points are connected; you should use coordination and subordination to show them the relationship between ideas.

Choose **coordinating conjunctions**—*and, but, or, nor, for, so,* and *yet*—carefully, making sure you are using the right word for your purpose. (Use *and* to show addition; *but, for,* or *yet* to show contradiction; *or* to present alternatives; and *so* to indicate a causal relationship.)

Choose **subordinating conjunctions**—*although, because,* and so on—carefully, and place them so that your emphasis will be clear.

Consider the two ideas expressed in the following sentences.

> Achieving a green campus is vitally important. Creating a green campus is expensive.

If you want to stress the idea that green measures are called for, you would connect the sentences like this:

> Although creating a green campus is expensive, achieving a green campus is vitally important.

If, however, you want to place emphasis on the high cost, you would connect the sentences as follows:

> Although achieving a green campus is vitally important, creating a green campus is expensive.

■ **Include transitional words and phrases.** Be sure you have enough transitions to guide your readers through your discussion. Supply signals that move readers smoothly from sentence to sentence and paragraph to paragraph, and choose signals that make sense in the context of your discussion.

SUGGESTED TRANSITIONS FOR ARGUMENT

- To show causal relationships: *because, as a result, for this reason*
- To indicate sequence: *first, second, third; then; next; finally*
- To introduce additional points: *also, another, in addition, furthermore, moreover*
- To move from general to specific: *for example, for instance, in short, in other words*
- To identify an opposing argument: *however, although, even though, despite*
- To grant the validity of an opposing argument: *certainly, admittedly, granted, of course*
- To introduce a refutation: *however, nevertheless, nonetheless, still*

■ **Define your terms.** If the key terms of your argument have multiple meanings—as *green* does—be sure to indicate what the term means in the context of your argument. Terms like *environmentally friendly, climate change, environmentally responsible, sustainable,* and *sustainability literacy* may mean very different things to different readers.

■ **Use clear language.** An argument is no place for vague language or wordy phrasing. If you want readers to understand your points, your writing should be clear and direct. Avoid vague words like *good, bad, right,* and *wrong,* which are really just unsupported judgments that do nothing to help you make your case. Also avoid wordy phrases such as *revolves around* and *is concerned with,* particularly in your thesis statement and topic sentences.

GRAMMAR IN CONTEXT

Using Parallelism

As you draft your argumentative essay, you should express corresponding words, phrases, and clauses in **parallel** terms. The use of matching parts of speech to express corresponding ideas strengthens your argument's impact because it enables readers to follow your line of thought.

In particular, use parallelism in sentences that highlight *paired items* or *items in a series.*

- **Paired Items**

UNCLEAR	Maintaining a green campus is important because <u>it sets</u> an example for students and the <u>environment will be protected</u>.
PARALLEL	Maintaining a green campus is important because it <u>sets</u> an example for students and <u>protects</u> the environment.

- **Items in a Series**

UNCLEAR	Students can do their part to support green campus initiatives in four ways—by <u>avoiding</u> bottled water, use of electricity <u>should be limited</u>, and they <u>can recycle</u> packaging and also <u>educating</u> themselves about environmental issues is a good strategy.
PARALLEL	Students can do their part to support green campus initiatives in four ways—by <u>avoiding</u> bottled water, by <u>limiting</u> use of electricity, by <u>recycling</u> packaging, and by <u>educating</u> themselves about environmental issues.

- **Finally, show your confidence and your mastery of your material.** Avoid qualifying your statements with phrases such as *I think, I believe, it seems to me,* and *in my opinion.* These qualifiers weaken your argument by suggesting that you are unsure of your material or that the statements that follow may not be true.

⮞ EXERCISE 7.11 DRAFTING YOUR ARGUMENTATIVE ESSAY

Keeping the preceding guidelines in mind, write a draft of an argumentative essay that develops the thesis statement you have been working with. If you like, include a visual to support your argument.

Revising Your Essay

After you have written a draft of your essay, you will need to revise it. **Revision** is "re-seeing"—looking carefully and critically at the draft you have written. Revision is different from editing and proofreading, which focus on grammar, punctuation, mechanics, and the like. In fact, revision can involve substantial reworking of your essay's structure and content. The strategies discussed on the pages that follow can help you revise your arguments.

Asking Questions

Asking some basic questions, such as those in the three checklists that follow, can help you to focus on the individual elements of your essay as you revise.

CHECKLIST

Questions about Your Essay's Purpose and Audience

- ☐ What was your primary purpose in writing this essay? What other purposes did you have?
- ☐ What appeals, strategies, and evidence did you use to accomplish your goals?
- ☐ Who is the audience for your essay? Do you see your readers as receptive, hostile, or neutral to your position?
- ☐ What basic knowledge do you think your readers have about your topic? Have you provided enough background for them?
- ☐ What biases do you think your readers have? Have you addressed these biases in your essay?
- ☐ What do you think your readers believed about your topic before reading your essay?
- ☐ What do you want readers to believe now that they have read your essay?

CHECKLIST

Questions about Your Essay's Structure and Style

☐ Does your essay have a clearly stated thesis?

☐ Are your topic sentences clear and concise?

☐ Have you provided all necessary background and definitions?

☐ Have you refuted opposing arguments effectively?

☐ Have you included enough transitional words and phrases to guide readers smoothly through your discussion?

☐ Have you avoided vague language and wordy phrasing?

☐ Does your essay have a strong concluding statement?

CHECKLIST

Questions about Your Essay's Supporting Evidence

☐ Have you supported your opinions with *evidence*—facts, observations, examples, statistics, expert opinion, and so on?

☐ Have you included enough evidence to support your thesis?

☐ Do the sources you rely on present information accurately and without bias?

☐ Are your sources' discussions directly relevant to your topic?

☐ Have you consulted sources that represent a wide range of viewpoints, including sources that challenge your position?

☐ Have you included one or more visuals to support your argument?

The answers to the questions in the checklists may lead you to revise your essay's content, structure, and style. For example, you may want to look for additional sources that can provide the kind of supporting evidence you need, or you may want to add visuals or replace a visual with one that more effectively supports your argument. Then, you may notice you need to revise the structure of your essay, perhaps rearranging your points so that the most important point is placed last, for emphasis. You may also want to revise your essay's introduction and conclusion, sharpening your thesis statement or adding a stronger concluding statement. Finally, you may decide to add more background material to help your readers understand the issue you are writing about or to help them take a more favorable view of your position.

Using Outlines and Templates

To check the logic of your essay's structure, you can prepare a revision outline or consult a template.

- To make sure your essay's key points are arranged logically and supported convincingly, you can construct a **formal outline** of your draft. (See pp. 265–66 for information on formal outlines.) This outline will indicate whether you need to discuss any additional points, add supporting evidence, or refute an opposing argument more fully. It will also show you if paragraphs are arranged in a logical order.

- To make sure your argument flows smoothly from thesis statement to evidence to refutation of opposing arguments to concluding statement, you can refer to one of the paragraph **templates** that appear throughout this book. These templates can help you to construct a one-paragraph summary of your essay.

Getting Feedback

After you have done as much as you can on your own, it is time to get feedback from your instructor and (with your instructor's permission) from your school's writing center or from other students in your class.

Instructor Feedback You can get feedback from your instructor in a variety of different ways. For example, your instructor may ask you to email a draft of your paper to him or her with some specific questions ("Do I need paragraph 3, or do I have enough evidence without it?" "Does my thesis statement need to be more specific?"). The instructor will then reply with corrections and recommendations. If your instructor prefers a traditional face-to-face conference, you may still want to email your draft ahead of time to give him or her a chance to read it before your meeting.

Writing Center Feedback You can also get feedback from a writing center tutor, who can be either a student or a professional. The tutor can give you another point of view about your paper's content and organization and also help you focus on specific questions of style, grammar, punctuation, and mechanics. (Keep in mind, however, that a tutor will not edit or proofread your paper for you; that is your job.)

Peer Review Finally, you can get feedback from your classmates. **Peer review** can be an informal process in which you ask a classmate for advice, or it can be a more structured process, involving small groups working with copies of students' work. Peer review can also be conducted electronically. For example, students can exchange drafts by email or respond to one another's drafts that are posted on the course website. They can also use Word's comment tool, as illustrated in the following example.

DRAFT

Colleges and universities have no excuse for ignoring the threat of global climate change. Campus leaders need to push beyond efforts to recycle or compost and instead become models of sustainability. Already, many universities are hard at work demonstrating that reducing their institution's environmental impact is not only possible but worthwhile. They are overhauling their entire infrastructure, their buildings, systems, and even curriculum. While many students, faculty, staff, and administrators are excited by these new challenges, some still question this need to go green. Is it worth the money? Is it promoting "a moral and behavioral agenda rather than an educational one" (Butcher)? In fact, greening will ultimately save institutions money while providing their students with a good education. Colleges should make every effort to create green campuses because by doing so they will help solve the global climate crisis.

Comment [LB]: Your first two sentences are a little abrupt. Maybe you could ease into your argument more slowly?

Comment [KS]: I like these two questions. They really got me thinking.

Comment [PL]: Could you be more specific? I'm not sure what you mean.

Comment [PL]: You definitely talk about this in your paper, but you also talk about other reasons to go green. You might consider revising this thesis statement so it matches your argument.

FINAL VERSION

In recent years, the pressure to go green has led colleges and universities to make big changes. The threats posed by global climate change are inspiring campus leaders to push beyond efforts to recycle to become models of sustainability. Today, in the interest of reducing their environmental impact, many campuses are seeking to overhaul their entire infrastructure—their buildings, their systems, and even their curriculum. While many students, faculty, staff, and administrators are excited by these new challenges, some question this need to go green. Is it worth the money? Is it promoting "a moral and behavioral agenda rather than an educational one" (Butcher)? In fact, greening will ultimately save institutions money while providing their students with the educational opportunities necessary to help them solve the crisis of their generation. Despite the expense, colleges should make every effort to create and sustain green campuses because by doing so they will not only improve their own educational environment but also ensure their institutions' survival and help solve the global climate crisis.

GUIDELINES FOR PEER REVIEW

Remember that the peer-review process involves *giving* feedback as well as receiving it. When you respond to a classmate's work, follow these guidelines:

- Be very specific when making suggestions, clearly identifying errors, inconsistencies, redundancy, or areas that need further development.

- Be tactful and supportive when pointing out problems.

- Give praise and encouragement whenever possible.

- Be generous with your suggestions for improvement.

⊜ EXERCISE 7.12 REVISING YOUR ARGUMENTATIVE ESSAY

Following the guidelines for revision discussed earlier, get some feedback from others, and then revise your argumentative essay.

Polishing Your Essay

The final step in the writing process is putting the finishing touches on your essay. At this point, your goal is to make sure that your essay is well organized, convincing, and clearly written, with no distracting grammatical or mechanical errors.

Editing and Proofreading

When you **edit** your revised draft, you review your essay's overall structure, style, and sentence construction, but you focus on grammar, punctuation, and mechanics. Editing is an important step in the writing process because an interesting, logically organized argument will not be convincing if readers are distracted by run-ons and fragments, confusingly placed modifiers, or incorrect verb forms. (Remember, your grammar checker will spot some grammatical errors, but it will miss many others.)

When you **proofread** your revised and edited draft, you carefully read every word, trying to spot any remaining punctuation or mechanical errors, as well as any typographical errors (typos) or misspellings that your spellchecker may have missed. (Remember, a spellchecker will not flag a correctly spelled word that is used incorrectly.)

Choosing a Title

After you have edited and proofread your essay, you need to give it a title. Ideally, your title should create interest and give readers clear information about the subject of your essay. It should also be appropriate for your topic. A serious topic calls for a serious title, and a thoughtfully presented argument deserves a thoughtfully selected title.

GRAMMAR IN CONTEXT

Contractions versus Possessive Pronouns

Be especially careful not to confuse the contractions *it's, who's, they're,* and *you're* with the possessive forms *its, whose, their,* and *your.*

INCORRECT	<u>Its</u> not always clear <u>who's</u> responsibility it is to promote green initiatives on campus.
CORRECT	<u>It's</u> not always clear <u>whose</u> responsibility it is to promote green initiatives on campus.

A title does not need to surprise or shock readers. It also should not be long and wordy or something many readers will not understand. A simple statement of your topic ("Going Green") or of your position on the issue ("College Campuses Should Go Green") is usually all that is needed. If you like, you can use a quotation from one of your sources as a title ("Green Is Good").

⊙ EXERCISE 7.13 EVALUATING POSSIBLE ESSAY TITLES

Evaluate the suitability and effectiveness of the following titles for an argumentative essay on green campuses. Be prepared to explain the strengths and weaknesses of each title.

- Green Campuses
- It's Not Easy Being Green
- The Lean, Clean, Green Machine
- What Students Can Do to Make Their Campuses More Environmentally Responsible
- Why All Campuses Should Be Green Campuses
- Planting the Seeds of the Green Campus Movement
- The Green Campus: An Idea Whose Time Has Come

Checking Format

Finally, make sure that your essay follows your instructor's guidelines for documentation style and manuscript format. (The student paper on p. 278 follows MLA style and manuscript format. For additional sample essays illustrating MLA and APA documentation style and manuscript format, see Chapter 10 and Appendix B, respectively.)

⊙ The following student essay, "Going Green," argues that colleges should make every effort to create green campuses.

GOING GREEN

SHAWN HOLTON

Introduction

In recent years, the pressure to go green has led colleges and   1
universities to make big changes. The threats posed by climate change
are encouraging campus leaders to push beyond early efforts, such as
recycling, to become models of sustainability. Today, in the interest of
reducing their environmental impact, many campuses are seeking to
overhaul their entire infrastructure. Although many students, faculty,
staff, and administrators are excited by these new challenges, some
question this need to go green. Is it worth the money? Is it promoting "a moral and behavioral agenda rather than an educational one"
(Butcher)? In fact, greening will ultimately save institutions money
while providing their students with the educational opportunities necessary to help them solve the crisis of their generation. Despite the
expense, colleges should make every effort to create and sustain green

Thesis statement

campuses because by doing so they will not only improve their own
educational environment but also ensure their institutions' survival and
help solve the global climate crisis.

**Body paragraph:
Background of green
movement**

Although the green movement has been around for many years,   2
green has become a buzzword only relatively recently. Green political
parties and groups began forming in the 1960s to promote environmentalist goals ("Environmentalism"). These groups fought for "grassroots
democracy, social justice, and nonviolence" in addition to environmental protections and were "self-consciously activist and unconventional"
in their strategies ("Environmentalism"). Today, however, *green* denotes
much more than a political movement; it has become a catchall word
for anything eco-friendly. People use *green* to describe everything from
fuel-efficient cars to fume-free house paint. Green values have become
more mainstream in response to evidence that human activities, particularly those that result in greenhouse-gas emissions, may be causing
global warming at a dramatic rate ("Call for Climate Leadership" 4). To
fight this climate change, many individuals, businesses, and organizations have chosen to go green, making sustainability and preservation
of the environment a priority.

Greening a college campus means moving toward a sustainable campus that works to conserve the earth's natural resources. It means reducing
the university's carbon footprint by focusing on energy efficiency in every
aspect of campus life. This is no small task. Although replacing incandes-
cent lightbulbs with compact fluorescent ones and offering more locally
grown food in dining halls are valuable steps, meaningful sustainability
requires more comprehensive changes. For example, universities also
need to invest in alternative energy sources, construct new buildings and
remodel old ones, and work to reduce campus demand for nonrenewable
products. Although these changes will eventually save universities money,
in most cases, the institutions will need to spend money now to reduce
costs in the long term. To achieve this transformation, many colleges—
individually or in cooperation with other schools—have established formal
"climate commitments," set specific goals, and developed tools to track
their investments and evaluate their progress.

3 Body paragraph: Definition of *green* as it applies
to colleges

Despite these challenges, there are many compelling reasons to act
now. Saving money on operating costs, thus making the school more competitive in the long term, is an appealing incentive. In fact, many schools
have made solid and sometimes immediate gains by greening some aspect
of their campus. For example, by changing its parking and transit systems
to encourage more carpooling, biking, and walking, Cornell University
has saved 417,000 gallons of fuel and cut costs by $36 million over the last
twelve years ("Call for Climate Leadership" 10). By installing geothermal
wells and replacing its old power plant with a geothermal pump system, the
University of Central Missouri (UCM) is saving 31 percent in energy costs,
according to a case study in *Climate Neutral Campus Report* (Trane). These
changes were not merely a social, or even a political, response, but a necessary part of updating the campus. Betty Roberts, the UCM vice president for
administration, was faced with the problem of how to "make a change for
the benefit of the institution . . . with no money." After saving several million
dollars by choosing to go green, Roberts naturally reported that the school
was "very happy!" with its decision (qtd. in Trane). There is more to be
gained than just savings, however. Oberlin College not only saves money by
generating its own solar energy (as shown in Fig. 1) but also makes money
by selling its excess electricity back to the local power company (Petersen).
Many other schools have taken similar steps, with similarly positive results.

4 Body paragraph: First
argument in support of
thesis

Body paragraph:
Second argument
in support of
thesis

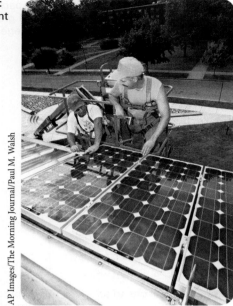

AP Images/The Morning Journal/Paul M. Walsh

Fig. 1. Solar panels on the roof of
the Adam Joseph Lewis Center for
Environmental Studies, Oberlin
College. 2008. Oberlin.edu.

Attracting the attention of the   5
media, donors, and—most significantly—
prospective students is another practical
reason for schools to go green. As one
researcher explains, "There is enough
evidence nationwide to detect an arms-
race of sorts among universities competing for green status" (Krizek et al. 27).
The *Princeton Review* now includes a
"green rating," and according to recent
studies, more than two thirds of college
applicants say that they consider green
ratings when choosing a school (Krizek
et al. 27). A school's commitment to the
environment can also bring in large private donations. For example, Carnegie
Mellon University attracted $1.7 million
from the National Science Foundation for
its new Center for Sustainable Engineering (Egan). The University of California,
Davis, will be receiving up to $25 million
from the Chevron Corporation to research biofuel technology ("Call for
Climate Leadership" 10). While greening certainly costs money, a green
commitment can also help a school remain financially viable.

Body paragraph: Third
argument in support of
thesis

In addition to these practical reasons for going green, universi-   6
ties also have another, perhaps more important, reason to promote
and model sustainability: doing so may help solve the climate crisis.
Although an individual school's reduction of emissions may not notice-
ably affect global warming, its graduates will be in a position to make
a huge impact. College is a critical time in most students' personal and
professional development. Students are making choices about what kind
of adults they will be, and they are also receiving the training, education,
and experience that they will need to succeed in the working world. If
universities can offer time, space, and incentives—both in and out of the
classroom—to help students develop creative ways to live sustainably,
these schools have the potential to change the thinking and habits of a
whole generation.

Many critics of greening claim that becoming environmentally friendly is too expensive and will result in higher tuition and fees. However, often a very small increase in fees, as little as a few dollars a semester, can be enough to help a school institute significant change. For example, at the University of Colorado–Boulder, a student-initiated $1 increase in fees allowed the school to purchase enough wind power to reduce its carbon emissions by 12 million pounds ("Call for Climate Leadership" 9). Significantly, the students were the ones who voted to increase their own fees to achieve a greener campus. Although university faculty and administrators' commitment to sustainability is critical for any program's success, few green initiatives will succeed without the enthusiastic support of the student body. Ultimately, students have the power. If they think their school is spending too much on green projects, then they can make a change or choose to go elsewhere.

7 Refutation of first opposing argument

Other critics of the trend toward greener campuses believe that schools with commitments to sustainability are dictating how students should live rather than encouraging free thought. As one early critic has claimed, "Once [sustainability literacy] is enshrined in a university's public pronouncements or private articles, then the institution has diminished its commitment to academic inquiry" (Butcher). This kind of criticism overlooks the fact that figuring out how to achieve sustainability requires and will continue to require rigorous critical thinking and creativity. Why not apply the academic skills of inquiry, analysis, and problem solving to the biggest problem of our day? Not doing so would be irresponsible and would confirm the perception that universities are ivory towers of irrelevant knowledge. In fact, the presence of sustainability as both a goal and a subject of study has the potential to reaffirm academia's place at the center of civil society.

8 Refutation of second opposing argument

Creating a green campus is a difficult task, but universities must rise to the challenge or face the consequences. If they do not commit to changing their ways, they will become less and less able to compete for students and for funding. If they refuse to make a comprehensive commitment to sustainability, they also risk irrelevance at best and institutional collapse at worst. Finally, by not rising to the challenge, they will be giving up the opportunity to establish themselves as leaders in addressing the climate crisis. As the coalition of American College and University Presidents states in its Climate Commitment, "No other institution has the influence,

9 Conclusion

Concluding statement

the critical mass and the diversity of skills needed to successfully reverse global warming" ("Call for Climate Leadership" 13). Now is the time for schools to make the choice and pledge to go green.

Works Cited

Butcher, Jim. "Keep the Green Moral Agenda off Campus." *Times Higher Education*, 19 Oct. 2007, www.timeshighereducation.com/news/keep -the-green-moral-agenda-off-campus/310853.article.

"A Call for Climate Leadership." *American College and University Presidents Climate Commitment*, Aug. 2009, www2.presidentsclimatecommitment .org/html/documents/ACUPCC_InfoPacketv2.pdf.

Egan, Timothy. "The Greening of America's Campuses." *New York Times*, 8 Jan. 2006, www.nytimes.com/2006/01/08/education/edlife/egan _environment.html?scp=1&amp%3Bsq=The&_r=0.

"Environmentalism." *Encyclopaedia Britannica Online*, 2015, www.britannica .com/topic/environmentalism.

Krizek, Kevin J., Dave Newport, James White, and Alan R. Townsend. "Higher Education's Sustainability Imperative: How to Practically Respond?" *International Journal of Sustainability in Higher Education*, vol. 13, no. 1, 2012, pp. 1–33. DOI: 10.1108/14676371211190281.

Petersen, John. "A Green Curriculum Involves Everyone on Campus." *Chronicle of Higher Education*, vol. 54, no. 41, 2008, p. A25. *ERIC Institute of Education Services*, eric.ed.gov/?id=EJ801316.

Trane. "University of Central Missouri." *Climate Neutral Campus Report*, Kyoto Publishing, 14 Aug. 2009, secondnature.org/wp-content /uploads/09-8-14_ClimateNeutralCampusReportReleased.pdf.

⊙ EXERCISE 7.14 PREPARING A FINAL DRAFT

Edit and proofread your essay, paying special attention to parenthetical documentation and to your works-cited page, and check to make sure your essay's format is consistent with your instructor's requirements. When you have finished, give your essay a title, and print out a final copy.

⊙ EXERCISE 7.15 EVALUATING VISUAL ARGUMENTS

Write a paragraph in which you evaluate the visual in the student essay on pages 278–82. Does it add valuable support to the essay, or should it be deleted or replaced? Can you suggest a visual that could serve as a more convincing argument in support of green campuses?

Using Sources to Support Your Argument

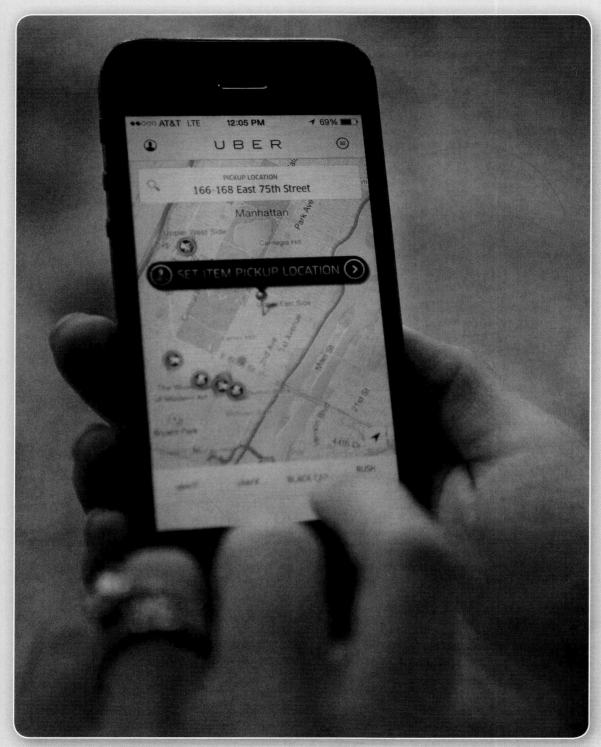

Victor J. Blue/Bloomberg/Getty Images

Finding and Evaluating Sources

AT ISSUE

Is Technology a Serious Threat to Our Privacy?

The internet and social media have become deeply woven into our lives, to the point where Facebook has over 2.23 billion users worldwide. Not surprisingly, social media sites have become a primary tool for people—from marketers to cybercriminals—who want to access personal information, for better and for worse. High profile data breaches have raised concerns too. Facebook faced a scandal in 2018 when it revealed that over 87 million of its users' data had been shared with Cambridge Analytica, a political consulting firm that sought data on American political behavior.

Most people agree that such breaches are bad and that protecting privacy is important. But they disagree over approaches to the problem. Some want stricter government regulation; others think free markets will address the issue; still, others argue that the only way to ensure privacy is for individuals to avoid sharing personal information online.

Later in this chapter, you will evaluate several sources to determine whether they are acceptable for an argumentative essay about technology and privacy. In Chapter 9, you will learn how to integrate sources into an essay on this topic. In Chapter 10, you will see an MLA paper on one aspect of the topic: whether it is ethical for employers to access information posted on job applicants' social-networking sites. Finally, in Chapter 11, you will learn how to use sources responsibly while considering the question, "Where should we draw the line with plagiarism?"

Finding Sources

In some argumentative essays, you can use your own ideas as evidence in support of your position. In many others, however, you have to do **research**—collect information (in both print and electronic form) from magazines, newspapers, books, journals, and other sources—to supplement your own ideas.

The obvious question is, "How does research help you to construct better arguments?" The answer is that research enables you to explore the ideas of others, consider multiple points of view, and expand your view of your subject. By doing so, you get a better understanding of the issues surrounding your topic, and as a result, you are able to develop a strong thesis and collect the facts, examples, statistics, quotations, and expert opinion that you will need to support your points. In addition, by taking the time to find reliable, up-to-date sources, you demonstrate to readers that your discussion is credible and that you are someone worth listening to. In short, doing research enables you to construct intelligent, authoritative, and convincing arguments.

As you do research, keep in mind that your argumentative essay should not be a collection of other people's ideas. It should present an original thesis that you develop with your own insights and opinions. You use the information you get from your research to provide additional support for your thesis and to expand your discussion. In other words, your voice, not the voices of your sources, should control the discussion.

Finding Information in the Library

When most students do research, they immediately go to the internet. Unfortunately, by doing this, they ignore the most reliable source of high-quality information available to them: their college library.

Your college library contains both print and electronic resources that you cannot find anywhere else. Although the internet gives you access to an almost unlimited amount of material, it does not offer the consistently high level of reliable information found in your college library. For this reason, you should always begin your research by surveying the resources of the library.

The best way to access your college library is to visit its website, which is the gateway to a great deal of information—for example, its online catalog, electronic databases, and reference works.

> **The Online Catalog:** The **online catalog** lists all the books, journals, newspapers, magazines, and other material housed in the library. Once you gain access to this catalog, you can type in keywords that will lead you to sources related to your topic.

> **NOTE**
>
> Many libraries have a **discovery service** that enables you to use a
> single search box to access a wide variety of content—for example,
> the physical items held by a library as well as content from e-books,
> journal articles, government documents, and electronic databases. Most
> discovery services return high-quality results quickly and (like Google)
> rank them according to relevancy.

Online Databases: All college libraries subscribe to **databases**—collections of digital information that you access through a keyword search. The library's online databases enable you to retrieve bibliographic citations as well as the full text of articles from hundreds of publications. Some of these databases—for example, *Expanded Academic ASAP* and *Proquest Research Library*—provide information on a wide variety of topics. Others—for example, *Business Source Premier* and *Sociological Abstracts*—provide information on a particular subject area. Before selecting a database, check with the reference librarian to determine which will be most useful for your topic.

Reference Works: All libraries contain **reference works**—sources of accurate and reliable information such as dictionaries, encyclopedias, and almanacs. These reference works are available both in print and in electronic form. **General encyclopedias**—such as the *New Encyclopaedia Britannica* and the *Columbia Encyclopedia*—provide general information on a wide variety of topics. **Specialized reference works**—such as *Facts on File* and the *World Almanac*—and **special encyclopedias**—such as the *Encyclopedia of Law and Economics*—offer detailed information on specific topics.

> **NOTE**
>
> Although a general encyclopedia (print or electronic) can provide
> an overview of your topic, encyclopedia articles do not usually treat
> topics in enough depth for college-level research. Be sure to check your
> instructor's guidelines before you use a general encyclopedia in your
> research.

Finding Information on the Internet

Although the internet gives you access to a vast amount of information, it has its limitations. For one thing, because anyone can publish on the web, you cannot be sure if the information found there is trustworthy, timely, or authoritative. Of course, there are reliable sources of information on the web. For example, the information on your college library's website is reliable. In addition, Google Scholar provides links to some scholarly sources that are as good as those found in a college library's databases. Even so, you have to approach this material with caution; some articles accessed through Google Scholar are pay-per-view, and others are not current or comprehensive.

USING GOOGLE SCHOLAR

Google Scholar is a valuable research resource. If you use it, however, you should be aware of its drawbacks:

- It includes some non-scholarly publications. Because it does not accurately define scholar, some material may not conform to academic standards of reliability.

- It does not index all scholarly journals. Many academic journals are available only through a library's databases and are not accessible on the internet.

- Google Scholar is uneven across scholarly disciplines—that is, it includes more information from some disciplines than others. In addition, Google Scholar does not perform well for publications before 1990.

- Google Scholar does not screen for quality. Because Google Scholar uses an algorithm, not a human being, to select sources, it does not always filter out junk journals.

- Some of the articles in Google Scholar are pay-per-view. Before you pay to download an article, check to see if your college library gives you free access.

A **search engine**—such as Google—helps you to locate and to view documents that you search for with keywords. Different types of search engines are suitable for different purposes:

- **General-Purpose Search Engines: General-purpose search engines** retrieve information on a great number of topics. They cast the widest possible net and bring in the widest variety of information. The disadvantage of general-purpose search engines is that you get a great deal of irrelevant material. Because each search engine has its own unique characteristics, you should try a few of them to see which you prefer. The most popular general-purpose search engines are Google, Bing, Yahoo!, and Ask.com.

- **Specialized Search Engines: Specialized search engines** focus on specific subject areas or on a specific type of content—for example, business, government, or health services. The advantage of specialized search engines is that they eliminate the need for you to wade through pages of irrelevant material. By focusing your search on a specific subject area, you are more likely to locate information on your particular topic. You can find a list of specialized search engines on the Search Engine List (thesearchenginelist.com).

- **Metasearch Engines:** Because each search engine works differently, results can (and do) vary. For this reason, if you limit yourself to a single search engine, you can miss a great deal of useful information. **Metasearch engines** solve this problem by taking the results of several search engines and presenting them in a simple, no-nonsense format. The most popular metasearch engines are Dogpile, ixquick, MetaGer, MetaCrawler, and Sputtr.

Evaluating Sources

When you **evaluate** a source, you assess the objectivity of the author, the credibility of the source, and its relevance to your argument. Whenever you locate a source—print or electronic—you should always take the time to evaluate it.

Although a librarian or an instructor has screened the print and electronic sources in your college library for general accuracy and trustworthiness, you cannot simply assume that these sources are suitable for your particular writing project. Material that you access online presents particular problems. Although some material on the internet (for example, journal articles that are published in both print and digital format) is reliable, other material (for example, personal websites and blogs) may be unreliable and unsuitable for your research. Remember, if you use an untrustworthy source, you undercut your credibility.

To evaluate sources, you use the same process that you use when you evaluate anything else. For example, if you are thinking about buying a

Sources must be evaluated carefully.

laptop computer, you use several criteria to help you make your decision—
for example, price, speed, memory, reliability, and availability of technical
support. The same is true for evaluating research sources. You can use the
following criteria to decide whether a source is appropriate for your research:

- Accuracy
- Credibility
- Objectivity
- Currency
- Comprehensiveness
- Authority

The illustrations on page 291 show where to find information that can
help you evaluate a source.

Accuracy   A source is **accurate** when it is factual and free of errors.
One way to judge the accuracy of a source is to compare the information
it contains to that same information in several other sources. If a source
has factual errors, then it probably includes other types of errors as well.
Needless to say, errors in spelling and grammar should also cause you to
question a source's general accuracy.

You can also judge the accuracy of a source by checking to see if the
author cites sources for the information that is discussed. Documentation
can help readers determine both the quality of information in a source and
the range of sources used. It can also show readers what sources a writer
has failed to consult. (Failure to cite an important book or article should
cause you to question the writer's familiarity with a subject.) If possible,
verify the legitimacy of some of the books and articles that a writer cites by
seeing what you can find out about them online. If a source has caused a
great deal of debate or if it is disreputable, you will probably be able to find
information about the source by researching it on Google.

Credibility   A source is **credible** when it is believable. You can begin
checking a source's credibility by determining where a book or article was
published. If a university press published the book, you can be reasonably
certain that it was **peer reviewed**—read by experts in the field to confirm
the accuracy of the information. If a commercial press published the book,
you will have to consider other criteria—the author's reputation and the
date of publication, for example—to determine quality. If your source is
an article, see if it appears in a **scholarly journal**—a periodical aimed at
experts in a particular field—or in a **popular magazine**—a periodical
aimed at general readers. Journal articles are almost always acceptable

TOMMIE SHELBY ——————— Author

We Who Are Dark

**The Philosophical Foundations
of Black Solidarity**

Publisher

The Belknap Press of
Harvard University Press
*Cambridge, Massachusetts
London, England 2005*

Date of publication

Sources cites

Library of Congress Cataloging-in-Publication Data

Shelby, Tommie, 1967–
We who are dark: the philosophical foundations of
Black solidarity/Tommie Shelby.
p. cm.

Includes bibliographical references and index.
Contents: Two conceptions of Black nationalism—Class, poverty, and
shame—Black power nationalism—Black solidarity after Black power—Race,
culture, and politics—Social identity and group solidarity.

ISBN 0-674-01936-9 (alk. paper)

1. African Americans—Politics and government. 2. African Americans—
Race identity. 3. African Americans—Social conditions—1975–
4. Black nationalism—United States. 5. Black power—United States.
6. Ethnicity—Political aspects—United States. 7. Racism—Political
aspects—United States. 8. United States—Race relations—Political aspects.
I. Title.

E185.615.S475   2005
305.896'073—dc22   2005045329

research sources because they are usually documented, peer reviewed, and written by experts. (They can, however, be difficult for general readers to understand.) Articles in high-level popular magazines, such as the *Atlantic* and the *Economist*, may also be suitable—provided experts wrote them. However, articles in lower-level popular magazines—such as *Sports Illustrated* and *Time*—may be easy to understand, but they are seldom acceptable sources for research.

You can determine how well respected a source is by reading reviews written by critics. You can find reviews of books by consulting *Book Review Digest*—either in print or online—which lists books that have been reviewed in at least three magazines or newspapers and includes excerpts of reviews. In addition, you can consult the *New York Times Book Review* website—www.nytimes.com/pages/books/index.html—to access reviews printed by the newspaper since 1981. (Both professional and reader reviews are also available at Amazon.com.)

Finally, you can determine the influence of a source by seeing how often other scholars in the field refer to it. **Citation indexes** indicate how often books and articles are mentioned by other sources in a given year. This information can give you an idea of how important a work is in a particular field. Citation indexes for the humanities, the social sciences, and the sciences are available both in print and electronically.

Objectivity   A source is **objective** when it is not unduly influenced by a writer's personal opinions or feelings. Ideally, you want to find sources that are objective, but to one degree or another, all sources are **biased**.

The covers of the liberal and conservative magazines shown here suggest different biases.

The New Yorker cover, June 19, 2017 by Barry Blitt, Conde Nast Publications, Inc.

The National Review

In short, all sources—especially those that take a stand on an issue—reflect the opinions of their authors, regardless of how hard they may try to be impartial. (Of course, an opinion is perfectly acceptable—as long as it is supported by evidence.)

As a researcher, you should recognize that bias exists and ask yourself whether a writer's assumptions are justified by the facts or are simply the result of emotion or preconceived ideas. You can make this determination by looking at a writer's choice of words and seeing if the language is slanted or by reviewing the writer's points and seeing if his or her argument is one-sided. Get in the habit of asking yourself whether you are being offered a legitimate point of view or simply being fed propaganda.

Currency A source is **current** when it is up to date. (For a book, you can find the date of publication on the copyright page, as shown on page 291. For an article, you can find the date on the front cover of the magazine or journal.) If you are dealing with a scientific subject, the date of publication can be very important. Older sources might contain outdated information, so you want to use the most up-to-date source that you can find. For other subjects—literary criticism, for example—the currency of the information may not be as important as it is in the sciences.

Comprehensiveness A source is **comprehensive** when it covers a subject in sufficient depth. The first thing to consider is whether the source deals specifically with your subject. (If it treats your subject only briefly, it will probably not be useful.) Does it treat your subject in enough detail? Does the source include the background information that you need to understand the discussion? Does the source mention other important sources that discuss your subject? Are facts and interpretations supported by the other sources you have read, or are there major points of disagreement? Finally, does the author include documentation?

How comprehensive a source needs to be depends on your purpose and audience as well as on your writing assignment. For a short essay for an introductory course, editorials from the *New York Times* or the *Wall Street Journal* might give you enough information to support your argument. If you are writing a longer essay, however, you might need to consult journal articles (and possibly books) about your subject.

Authority A source has **authority** when a writer has the expertise to write about a subject. Always try to determine if the author is a recognized authority or simply a person who has decided to write about a particular topic. For example, what other books or articles has the author written? Has your instructor ever mentioned the author's name? Is the author mentioned in your textbook? Has the author published other works on the same subject or on related subjects? (You can find this information on Amazon.com.)

You should also determine if the author has an academic affiliation. Is he or she a faculty member at a respected college or university? Do other established scholars have a high opinion of the author? You can often find this information by using a search engine such as Google or by consulting one of the following directories:

Contemporary Authors
Directory of American Scholars
International Who's Who
National Faculty Directory
Who's Who in America
Wilson Biographies Plus Illustrated

⊖ EXERCISE 8.1 EVALUATING SOURCES

Assume that you are preparing to write an argumentative essay on the topic of whether information posted on social-networking sites threatens privacy. Read the sources that follow, and evaluate each source for accuracy, credibility, objectivity, currency, comprehensiveness, and authority.

- Zeynep Tufekci, "The Privacy Debacle"

- David N. Cicilline and Terrell McSweeny, "Competition Is at the Heart of Facebook's Privacy Problem"

- Daniel Lyons, "Facebook: Privacy Problems and PR Nightmare"

This essay appeared in the January 30, 2018 issue of the *New York Times*.

THE PRIVACY DEBACLE

ZEYNEP TUFEKCI

Did you make a New Year's resolution to exercise more? Perhaps you down- 1
loaded a fitness app to help track your workouts, maybe one that allows you to share that data online with your exercise buddies?

If so, you probably checked a box to accept the app's privacy policy. For 2
most apps, the default setting is to share data with at least the company; for many apps the default is to share data with the public. But you probably didn't even notice or care. After all, what do you have to hide?

For users of the exercise app Strava, the answer turns out to be a lot more 3
than they realized. Since November, Strava has featured a global "heat map" showing where its users jogged or walked or otherwise traveled while the app was on. The map includes some three trillion GPS data points, covering more than 5 percent of the earth. Over the weekend, a number of security analysts

showed that because many American military service members are Strava users, the map inadvertently reveals the locations of military bases and the movements of their personnel.

Perhaps more alarming for the military, similar patterns of movement 4 appear to possibly identify stations or airstrips in locations where the United States is not known to have such operations, as well as their supply and logistics routes. Analysts noted that with Strava's interface, it is relatively easy to identify the movements of individual soldiers not just abroad but also when they are back at home, especially if combined with other public or social media data.

> "Data privacy is not like a consumer good."

Apart from chastening the cybersecurity experts in the Pentagon, 5 the Strava debacle underscores a crucial misconception at the heart of the system of privacy protection in the United States. The privacy of data cannot be managed person-by-person through a system of individualized informed consent.

Data privacy is not like a consumer good, where you click "I accept" and 6 all is well. Data privacy is more like air quality or safe drinking water, a public good that cannot be effectively regulated by trusting in the wisdom of millions of individual choices. A more collective response is needed.

Part of the problem with the ideal of individualized informed consent 7 is that it assumes companies have the ability to inform us about the risks we are consenting to. They don't. Strava surely did not intend to reveal the GPS coordinates of a possible Central Intelligence Agency annex in Mogadishu, Somalia—but it may have done just that. Even if all technology companies meant well and acted in good faith, they would not be in a position to let you know what exactly you were signing up for.

Another part of the problem is the increasingly powerful computational 8 methods called machine learning, which can take seemingly inconsequential data about you and, combining them with other data, can discover facts about you that you never intended to reveal. For example, research shows that data as minor as your Facebook "likes" can be used to infer your sexual orientation, whether you use addictive substances, your race and your views on many political issues. This kind of computational statistical inference is not 100 percent accurate, but it can be fairly close—certainly close enough to be used to profile you for a variety of purposes.

A challenging feature of machine learning is that exactly how a given sys- 9 tem works is opaque. Nobody—not even those who have access to the code and data—can tell what piece of data came together with what other piece of data to result in the finding the program made. This further undermines the notion of informed consent, as we do not know which data results in what privacy consequences. What we do know is that these algorithms work better the more data they have. This creates an incentive for companies to collect and store as much data as possible, and to bury the privacy ramifications, either in legalese or by playing dumb and being vague.

What can be done? There must be strict controls and regulations con- 10 cerning how all the data about us—not just the obviously sensitive bits—is collected, stored and sold. With the implications of our current data practices unknown, and with future uses of our data unknowable, data storage must move from being the default procedure to a step that is taken only when it is of demonstrable benefit to the user, with explicit consent and with clear warnings about what the company does and does not know. And there should also be significant penalties for data breaches, especially ones that result from under-investment in secure data practices, as many now do.

Companies often argue that privacy is what we sacrifice for the super- 11 computers in our pockets and their highly personalized services. This is not true. While a perfect system with no trade-offs may not exist, there are technological avenues that remain underexplored, or even actively resisted by big companies, that could allow many of the advantages of the digital world without this kind of senseless assault on our privacy.

With luck, stricter regulations and a true consumer backlash will force our 12 technological overlords to take this issue seriously and let us take back what should be ours: true and meaningful informed consent, and the right to be let alone.

This editorial was published in *WIRED* on April 24, 2018.

COMPETITION IS AT THE HEART OF FACEBOOK'S PRIVACY PROBLEM

DAVID N. CICILLINE AND TERRELL McSWEENY

Our data are being turned against us. Data powers disinformation campaigns 1 attacking democratic institutions. It is used to foment division and turn us against one another. Cambridge Analytica harvested the personal information of approximately 87 million Facebook users not just to target would-be vot-ers with campaign ads but, as former Cambridge Analytica staffer Christopher Wylie put it to the *New York Times*, to "fight a culture war in America."

Consumers are trusting companies with vast amounts of intimate data and 2 receiving very little assurance that it will be properly handled and secured. In turn, our data are used to power the connected services we use, and depending on the platform or app, are sold to advertisers. Sometimes, as in the case of Facebook, we receive services for free in exchange for our data.

But in this system individuals bear the risk that their data will be handled 3 properly—and have little recourse when it is not.

It is time for a better deal. Americans should have rights to and control over 4 their data. If we don't like a service, we should be free to move our data to another.

But Facebook's control of consumers' information and attention is 5 substantial and durable. There are more than 200 million monthly active Facebook users in the United States, and the company already owns two potential competitors—Instagram, a social photo-sharing company, and WhatsApp, a messaging service. Facebook also collects and mines consumers' data across the internet, even for consumers without Facebook accounts.

It is also difficult and time-consuming to move data between platforms.   6

The ability to control this data isn't just part of Facebook's business model; 7 it's also a vital component of creating choice, competition, and innovation online. The value of Facebook's network grows and depends on the number of people who are on it.

But unlike other networks—such as your phone company, which is required 8 to let you keep your existing phone number when switching service providers and make calls regardless of the carrier you use—Facebook and other technology companies also have the final say over whether you can take your key information to a competing service or communicate across different platforms.

The result of this asymmetry in control? The same network effect that 9 creates value for people on Facebook can also lock them into Facebook's walled garden by creating barriers to competition. People who may want to leave Facebook are less likely to do so if they aren't able to seamlessly rebuild their network of contacts, photos, and other social graph data on a competing service or communicate across services.

This friction effectively blocks new competitors—including platforms 10 that might be more protective of consumers' privacy and give consumers more control over their data—from entering the market. That's why we need pro-competitive policies that give power back to Americans through more rights and control over their data.

> "It is critical that we restore Americans' control over their data."   11

Privacy and competition are becoming increasingly interdependent conditions for protecting rights online. It is critical that we restore Americans' control over their data through data portability and interoperability requirements.

Data portability would reduce barriers to entry online by giving people 12 tools to export their network—rather than merely downloading their data—to competing platforms with the appropriate privacy safeguards in place.

Before it was acquired by Facebook, Instagram owed much of its immense 13 growth to the open APIs that allowed users of Twitter and Facebook to import their friend networks to a new, competing service.

And today, you can already use your Facebook account to import your 14 profile and contacts on Spotify and some other social apps.

Interoperability would facilitate competition by enabling communication 15 across networks in the way the Open Internet was designed to work.

The bottom line: Unless consumers gain meaningful control over their 16 personal information, there will continue to be persistent barriers to competition and choice online.

Of course, there need to be guardrails in place to protect the privacy and 17 security of users.

Legislators and regulators also need to more extensively reform data secu- 18 rity and privacy law to improve privacy, transparency, and accountability online—particularly among data brokers and credit reporting agencies like Equifax—and create more transparency in political advertisements and spending online.

But at a minimum, Americans should have real control over their data. 19 A procompetitive solution to reducing barriers to entry online will encourage platforms to compete on providing better privacy, control, and rights for consumers.

This essay was published by *Newsweek* on May 25, 2010.

FACEBOOK: PRIVACY PROBLEMS AND PR NIGHTMARE

DANIEL LYONS

Facebook's 26-year-old founder and CEO Mark Zuckerberg may be a brilliant 1 software geek, but he's lousy at public relations. In fact the most amazing thing about Facebook's current crisis over user privacy is how bad the company's PR machine is.

Instead of making things better, Facebook's spin doctors just keep making 2 things worse. Instead of restoring trust in Facebook, they just make the company seem more slippery and sneaky. Best example is an op-ed that Zuckerberg published earlier this week in the *Washington Post*, a classic piece of evasive corporate-speak that could only have been written by PR flacks.

In the op-ed, Zuckerberg pretends to believe that the biggest concern users 3 have is how complicated Facebook's privacy controls are. He vows to remedy that by making things simpler.

> "The problem is the privacy policy itself."

But the real problem isn't the com- 4 plexity of Facebook's privacy controls. The problem is the privacy policy itself. Of course Zuckerberg knows this. He's many things, but stupid isn't one of them. The real point of his essay, in fact, was that Facebook has no intention of rolling back the stuff that people are really upset about.

The company did revise its privacy policy this week, and some privacy 5 experts were appeased, while others said Facebook still has more work to do. For one thing, if you want to keep Facebook from sharing your info with Facebook apps and connected websites, you have to opt out—meaning, the default setting is you're sharing. From my perspective a better policy would just to have everything set to private, by default.

But at this point the details of the policy aren't even the real issue. The real 6 issue is one of perception, which is that sure, Facebook made some changes, but only because they had no choice. The perception is that Facebook got caught doing something wrong, and sheepishly backed down. That is the narrative that will be attached to this latest episode, and it's not a good one for Facebook.

As for that vapid op-ed earlier in the week, Facebook might also have 7 thought twice about publishing the piece in the *Washington Post*, since Donald E. Graham, chairman of the *Post*, also sits on Facebook's board of directors and has been an important mentor to Zuckerberg.

Everyone involved, including Graham himself, says nobody pulled any 8 strings, that Facebook just submitted the piece to the *Post* without Graham's knowledge, and the *Post* chose to run it because it was of interest to readers.

In other words we are asked to believe that though Graham and 9 Zuckerberg are close friends, and presumably Zuckerberg has been consulting with Graham (and other board members) over the privacy crisis, Zuckerberg and his team never mentioned to Graham the fact that Facebook was going to publish an op-ed in Graham's newspaper.

Okay. Maybe that's true. Nevertheless, of all the newspapers in the world, 10 why choose the one that's owned by one of your board members? Chalk up another clunker for the Facebook PR team.

Facebook's real problem now is that Zuckerberg and his PR reps have 11 made so many ludicrous statements that it's hard to believe anything they say. They've claimed that they're only changing privacy policies because that is what members want. They've said, when the current crisis began, that there was nothing wrong with the policy itself—the problem was simply that Facebook hadn't explained it well enough.

One gets the impression that Facebook doesn't take any of this stuff very 12 seriously. It just views the complaints as little fires that need to be put out. The statements Facebook issues aren't meant to convey any real information— they're just blasts from a verbal fire extinguisher, a cloud of words intended not to inform, but to smother.

Just keep talking, the idea seems to be, and it doesn't matter what you say. 13 In fact the more vapid and insincere you can be, the better. Eventually the world will get sick of the sound of your voice, and the whiners will give up and go away.

Of course Facebook wouldn't need to do any of this spinning if it would 14 just fix its privacy policy. It could, for example, go back to the policy it used in 2005, which said your info would only be shared with your friends.

No doubt Zuckerberg has performed a bunch of calculations, weighing 15 the cost of the bad publicity against the benefit of getting hold of all that user data. And he's decided to push on and endure the black eye.

Which tells you all you need to know about Mark Zuckerberg, and the 16 value of the information that Facebook is collecting.

⊘ EXERCISE 8.2 WRITING AN EVALUATION

Write a one- or two-paragraph evaluation of each of the three sources you read for Exercise 8.1. Be sure to support your evaluation with specific references to the sources.

Evaluating Websites

The internet is like a freewheeling frontier town in the old West. Occasionally, a federal marshal may pass through, but for the most part, there is no law and order, so you are on your own. On the internet, literally anything goes—exaggerations, misinformation, errors, and even complete fabrications. Some websites contain reliable content (for example, journal articles that are published in both print and digital format), but many do not. The main reason for this situation is that there is no authority—as there is in a college library—who evaluates sites for accuracy and trustworthiness. That job falls to you, the user.

Another problem is that websites often lack important information. For example, a site may lack a date, a sponsoring organization, or even the name of the author of the page. For this reason, it is not always easy to evaluate the material you find there.

ACCEPTABLE VERSUS UNACCEPTABLE INTERNET SOURCES

Before you use an internet source, you should consider if it is acceptable for college-level work:

Acceptable Sources

- Websites sponsored by reliable organizations, such as academic institutions, the government, and professional organizations
- Websites sponsored by academic journals and reputable magazines or newspapers
- Blogs by recognized experts in their fields
- Research forums

Unacceptable Sources

- Information on anonymous websites
- Information found in chat rooms or on discussion boards
- Personal blogs written by authors of questionable expertise
- Information on personal web pages
- Poorly written web pages

When you evaluate a website (especially when it is in the form of a blog or a series of posts), you need to begin by viewing it skeptically—unless you know for certain that it is reliable. In other words, assume that its information is questionable until you establish that it is not. Then apply the same criteria you use to evaluate any sources—*accuracy, credibility, objectivity, currency, comprehensiveness,* and *authority.*

The web page pictured on page 302 shows where to find information that can help you evaluate a website.

Accuracy Information on a website is **accurate** when it is factual and free of errors. Information in the form of facts, opinions, statistics, and interpretations is everywhere on the internet, and in the case of Wiki sites, this information is continually being rewritten and revised. Given the volume and variety of this material, it is a major challenge to determine its accuracy. You can assess the accuracy of information on a website by asking the following questions:

- **Does the site contain errors of fact?** Factual errors—inaccuracies that relate directly to the central point of the source—should immediately disqualify a site as a reliable source.

- **Does the site contain a list of references or any other type of documentation?** Reliable sources indicate where their information comes from. The authors know that people want to be sure that the information they are using is accurate and reliable. If a site provides no documentation, you should not trust the information it contains.

- **Does the site provide links to other sites?** Does the site have links to reliable websites that are created by respected authorities or sponsored by trustworthy institutions? If it does, then you can conclude that your source is at least trying to maintain a certain standard of quality.

- **Can you verify information?** A good test for accuracy is to try to verify key information on a site. You can do this by checking it in a reliable print source or on a good reference website such as Encyclopedia.com.

Credibility Information on a website is **credible** when it is believable. Just as you would not naively believe a stranger who approached you on the street, you should not automatically believe a site that you randomly encounter on the web. You can assess the credibility of a website by asking the following questions:

- **Does the site list authors, directors, or editors?** Anonymity—whether on a website or on a blog—should be a red flag for a researcher who is considering using a source.

- **Is the site refereed?** Does a panel of experts or an advisory board decide what material appears on the website? If not, what standards are used to determine the suitability of content?

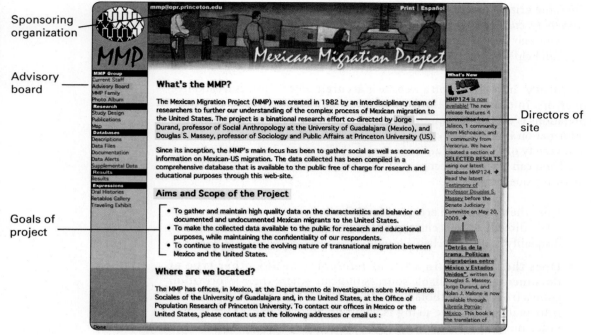

Courtesy from the Mexican Migration Project, mmp.opr.princeton.edu

- **Does the site contain errors in grammar, spelling, or punctuation?** If it does, you should be on the alert for other types of errors. If the people maintaining the site do not care enough to make sure that the site is free of small errors, you have to wonder if they will take the time to verify the accuracy of the information presented.

- **Does an organization sponsor the site?** If so, do you know (or can you find out) anything about the sponsoring organization? Use a search engine such as Google to determine the purpose and point of view of the organization.

Objectivity   Information on a website is **objective** when it limits the amount of **bias** that it displays. Some sites—such as those that support a particular political position or social cause—make no secret of their biases. They present them clearly in their policy statements on their home pages. Others, however, try to hide their biases—for example, by referring only to sources that support a particular point of view and not mentioning those that do not.

Keep in mind that bias does not automatically disqualify a source. It should, however, alert you to the fact that you are seeing only one side of an issue and that you will have to look further to get a complete picture. You can assess the objectivity of a website by asking the following questions:

- **Does advertising appear on the site?** If the site contains advertising, check to make sure that the commercial aspect of the site does not affect its objectivity. The site should keep advertising separate from content.

- **Does a commercial entity sponsor the site?** A for-profit company may sponsor a website, but it should not allow commercial interests to determine content. If it does, there is a conflict of interest. For example, if a site is sponsored by a company that sells organic products, it may include testimonials that emphasize the virtues of organic products and ignore information that is skeptical of their benefits.

- **Does a political organization or special-interest group sponsor the site?** Just as you would for a commercial site, you should make sure that the sponsoring organization is presenting accurate information. It is a good idea to check the information you get from a political site against information you get from an educational or a reference site—Ask.com or Encyclopedia.com, for example. Organizations have specific agendas, and you should make sure that they are not bending the truth to satisfy their own needs.

- **Does the site link to strongly biased sites?** Even if a site seems trustworthy, it is a good idea to check some of its links. Just as you can judge people by the company they keep, you can also judge websites by the sites they link to. Links to overly biased sites should cause you to reevaluate the information on the original site.

USING A SITE'S URL TO ASSESS ITS OBJECTIVITY

A website's **URL** (uniform resource locator) can give you information that can help you assess the site's objectivity.

Look at the domain name to identify sponsorship. Knowing a site's purpose can help you determine whether a site is trying to sell you something or just trying to provide information. The last part of a site's URL can tell you whether a site is a commercial site (.com and .net), an educational site (.edu), a nonprofit site (.org), or a governmental site (.gov, .mil, and so on).

See if the URL has a tilde (~) in it. A tilde in a site's URL indicates that information was published by an individual and is unaffiliated with the sponsoring organization. Individuals can have their own agendas, which may be different from the agenda of the site on which their information appears or to which it is linked.

AVOIDING CONFIRMATION BIAS

Confirmation bias is a tendency that people have to accept information that supports their beliefs and to ignore information that does not. For example, people see false or inaccurate information on websites, and because it reinforces their political or social beliefs, they forward it to others. Eventually, this information becomes so widely distributed that people assume that it is true. Numerous studies have demonstrated how prevalent confirmation bias is. Consider the following examples:

- A student doing research for a paper chooses sources that support her thesis and ignores those that take the opposite position.

- A prosecutor interviews witnesses who establish the guilt of a suspect and overlooks those who do not.

- A researcher includes statistics that confirm his hypothesis and excludes statistics that do not.

When you write an argumentative essay, do not accept information just because it supports your thesis. Realize that you have an obligation to consider all sides of an issue, not just the side that reinforces your beliefs.

Currency Information on a website is **current** when it is up-to-date. Some sources—such as fiction and poetry—are timeless and therefore are useful whatever their age. Other sources, however—such as those in the hard sciences—must be current because advances in some disciplines can quickly make information outdated. For this reason, you should be aware of the shelf life of information in the discipline you are researching and choose information accordingly. You can assess the currency of a website by asking the following questions:

- **Does the website include the date when it was last updated?** As you look at web pages, check the date on which they were created or updated. (Some websites automatically display the current date, so be careful not to confuse this date with the date the page was last updated.)

- **Are all links on the site live?** If a website is properly maintained, all the links it contains will be **live**—that is, a click on the link will take you to other websites. If a site contains a number of links that are not live, you should question its currency.

- **Is the information on the site up to date?** A site might have been updated, but this does not necessarily mean that it contains the most up-to-date information. In addition to checking when a website was last updated, look at the dates of the individual articles that appear on the site to make sure they are not outdated.

Comprehensiveness Information on a website is **comprehensive** when it covers a subject in depth. A site that presents itself as a comprehensive source should include (or link to) the most important sources of information that you need to understand a subject. (A site that leaves out a key source of information or that ignores opposing points of view cannot be called comprehensive.) You can assess the comprehensiveness of a website by asking the following questions:

- **Does the site provide in-depth coverage?** Articles in professional journals—which are available both in print and online—treat subjects in enough depth for college-level research. Other types of articles—especially those in popular magazines and in general encyclopedias, such as Wikipedia—are often too superficial (or untrustworthy) for college-level research.

- **Does the site provide information that is not available elsewhere?** The website should provide information that is not available from other sources. In other words, it should make a contribution to your knowledge and do more than simply repackage information from other sources.

- **Who is the intended audience for the site?** Knowing the target audience for a website can help you to assess a source's comprehensiveness. Is it aimed at general readers or at experts? Is it aimed at high school students or at college students? It stands to reason that a site that is aimed at experts or college students will include more detailed information than one that is aimed at general readers or high school students.

Authority Information on a website has **authority** when you can establish the legitimacy of both the author and the site. You can determine the authority of a source by asking the following questions:

- **Is the author an expert in the field that he or she is writing about?** What credentials does the author have? Does he or she have the expertise to write about the subject? Sometimes you can find this information on the website itself. For example, the site may contain an "About the Author" section or links to other publications by the author. If this information is not available, do a web search with the author's name as a keyword. If you cannot confirm the author's expertise (or if the site has no listed author), you should not use material from the site.

- **What do the links show?** What information is revealed by the links on the site? Do they lead to reputable sites, or do they take you to sites that suggest that the author has a clear bias or a hidden agenda? Do other reliable sites link back to the site you are evaluating?

■ **Is the site a serious publication?** Does it include information that enables you to judge its legitimacy? For example, does it include a statement of purpose? Does it provide information that enables you to determine the criteria for publication? Does the site have a board of advisers? Are these advisers experts? Does the site include a mailing address and a phone number? Can you determine if the site is the domain of a single individual or the effort of a group of individuals?

■ **Does the site have a sponsor?** If so, is the site affiliated with a reputable institutional sponsor, such as a governmental, educational, or scholarly organization?

⊙ EXERCISE 8.3 CONSIDERING TWO HOME PAGES

Consider the following two home pages—one from the website for the *Chronicle of Higher Education*, a publication aimed at college instructors and administrators, and the other from the website for *Glamour*, a publication aimed at general readers. Assume that on both websites, you have found articles about privacy and social-networking sites. Locate and label the information on each home page that would enable you to determine the suitability of using information from the site in your paper.

GLAMOUR

FASHION   BEAUTY   ENTERTAINMENT   WELLNESS   NEWS & CULTURE   VIDEO

CULTURE

Miss Universe Is Making History With the Pageant's First Openly Trans Contestant

HERE'S A TIP

This Is Exactly How Much You Should Tip When You Stay at a Hotel

UNLIKELY EXPERTS

The Best Beauty Gifts to Give, According to QVC Experts

⊖ EXERCISE 8.4 CONSIDERING TWO MISSION STATEMENTS

Here are the **mission statements**—statements of the organizations' purposes—from the websites for the *Chronicle of Higher Education* and *Glamour*, whose home pages you considered in Exercise 8.3. What

The Chronicle of Higher Education

The Chronicle of Higher Education has the nation's largest newsroom dedicated to covering colleges and universities. As the unrivaled leader in higher education journalism, we serve our readers with indispensable real-time news and deep insights, plus the essential tools, career opportunities, and knowledge to succeed in a rapidly changing world.

Our award-winning journalism is well-known at colleges and universities: More than 2 million people visit our website every month, and 1,650 organizations across the country make our journalism available to every one of their employees and students. Our newsroom is home to top experts in higher education who contribute to the ongoing conversation on the issues that matter.

The Chronicle, a privately owned, independent news and information organization, was founded in 1966 and originally owned by a nonprofit, Editorial Projects in Education. EPE sold The Chronicle in 1978 to Jack Crowl and Corbin Gwaltney, and The Chronicle of Higher Education Inc. was formed. Gwaltney bought the entire company in 1990, and he is co-chair of its board of directors, along with his wife, Pamela Gwaltney. The Chronicle of Higher Education Inc. publishes *The Chronicle of Higher Education*, *The Chronicle of Philanthropy*, *Arts & Letters Daily*, and *The Chronicle Review*.

Learn More About:

Account & Subscription FAQ

Community Guidelines

Copyright and Reprints

Submissions

Privacy Policy

How to Pitch Us

More Information

Advertise

Contact Us

Employment Opportunities

Internships

Newsletters

Subscribe

The Chronicle Store

The Chronicle of Philanthropy

The Chronicle of Philanthropy is an independent news organization that has been serving leaders, fundraisers, grant makers, and others involved in the philanthropic enterprise for almost 30 years. It offers a robust advice section to help nonprofit workers do their jobs as well as one of the biggest listings of career opportunities.

The Chronicle updates its website throughout the day and appears 12 times per year in print.

About Glamour

glamour.com   𝕩 f ▢ ℗ ⊙

Glamour is one of the biggest fashion and beauty media brands in the world, currently reaching an all-time high of one out of eight American women, with 9.7 million print readers, more than 11 million unique monthly users online, and over 14 million followers across social media platforms. Glamour believes in the power of women being themselves and stands with women as they do their own thing: honestly, authentically, and awesomely. Across every platform, Glamour is the ultimate authority for the next generation of changemakers.

Editor-in-Chief
Samantha Barry

Chief Business Officer
Susan Plagemann

additional information can you get from these mission statements? How do they help you to evaluate the sites as well as the information that might appear on the sites?

⊃ EXERCISE 8.5 EVALUATING MATERIAL FROM WEBSITES

Each of the following sources was found on a website: Bart Lazar, "Why We Need a Privacy Label on the Internet," page 308; Douglass Rushkoff, "You Are Not Facebook's Customer," page 309; and Igor Kuksov, "All Ears: The Dangers of Voice Assistants," page 309.

Assume that you are preparing to write an essay on the topic of whether information posted on social-networking sites threatens privacy. First, visit the websites on which the articles below appear, and evaluate each site for accuracy, credibility, objectivity, currency, comprehensiveness, and authority. Then, using the same criteria, evaluate each source.

This piece appeared on Politico on April 25, 2018.

WHY WE NEED A PRIVACY LABEL ON THE INTERNET

BART LAZAR

As Facebook and other internet companies deal with the fallout from security 1 lapses before and after the presidential election, lawmakers are increasingly concerned that lax oversight is resulting in major violations of Americans' privacy. When Facebook CEO Mark Zuckerberg testified before two committees earlier this month, even GOP lawmakers typically opposed to regulations said new rules to restrict the actions of Facebook and other internet companies may be necessary.

To finish reading this article and evaluate its source, Google search for Bart 2
Lazar's "Why We Need a Privacy Label on the Internet" or go to: https://www
.politico.com/agenda/story/2018/04/25/internet-privacy-label-000656.

This article was posted to Douglass Rushkoff's personal website.

YOU ARE NOT FACEBOOK'S CUSTOMER

DOUGLASS RUSHKOFF

The ire and angst accompanying Facebook's most recent tweaks to its interface 1
are truly astounding. The complaints rival the irritation of AOL's dial-up users
back in the mid-'90s, who were getting too many busy signals when they tried
to get online. The big difference, of course, is that AOL's users were paying
customers. In the case of Facebook, which we don't even pay to use, we aren't
the customers at all.

To continue reading this article and evaluate its source, Google search 2
for Douglass Rushkoff's "You Are Not Facebook's Customer" or go to:
www.rushkoff.com/you-are-not-facebooks-customer/.

This article originally appeared on Kaspersky Lab's website on February 28, 2017.

ALL EARS: THE DANGERS OF VOICE ASSISTANTS

IGOR KUKSOV

Nowadays the proverb "the walls have ears" is not as metaphoric as it used 1
to be.

"The telescreen received and transmitted simultaneously. Any sound that 2
Winston made, above the level of a very low whisper, would be picked up by
it. . . . There was of course no way of knowing whether you were being watched
at any given moment." That is George Orwell's description of Big Brother's
spying devices in the novel *1984*.

To continue reading this article and evaluate its source, Google search 3
for Igor Kuksov's "All Ears: The Dangers of Voice Assistants" or go to:
www.kaspersky.com/blog/voice-recognition-threats/14134/.

⊘ EXERCISE 8.6 EVALUATING A BLOG POST

Read the blog post below and then answer the questions on page 311.

This article first appeared on Mashable.com on February 6, 2012.

SHOULD ATHLETES HAVE SOCIAL MEDIA PRIVACY? ONE BILL SAYS YES

SAM LAIRD

Should universities be allowed to force student athletes to have their Facebook 1 and Twitter accounts monitored by coaches and administrators?

No, says a bill recently introduced into the Maryland state legislature.   2

The bill would prohibit institutions "from requiring a student or an appli- 3 cant for admission to provide access to a personal account or service through an electronic communications device"—by sharing usernames, passwords, or unblocking private accounts, for example.

Introduced on Thursday, Maryland's Senate Bill 434 would apply to all students but particularly impact college sports. Student-athletes' social media accounts are frequently monitored by authority fig-

> "Student-athletes' social 4
> media accounts are
> frequently monitored."

ures for instances of indecency or impropriety, especially in high-profile sports like football and men's basketball.

In one example, a top football recruit reportedly put his scholarship hopes 5 in jeopardy last month after a series of inappropriate tweets.

The bill's authors say that it is one of the first in the country to take on the 6 issue of student privacy in the social media age, according to the *New York Times*.

Bradley Shear is a Maryland lawyer whose work frequently involves sports 7 and social media. In a recent post to his blog, Shear explained his support for Senate Bill 434 and a similar piece of legislation that would further extend students' right to privacy on social media.

"Schools that require their students to turn over their social media user 8 names and/or content are acting as though they are based in China and not in the United States," Shear wrote.

But legally increasing student-athletes' option to social media privacy 9 could also help shield the schools themselves from potential lawsuits.

On his blog, Shear uses the example of Yardley Love, a former Univer- 10 sity of Virginia women's lacrosse player who was allegedly murdered by her ex-boyfriend, who played for the men's lacrosse team.

If the university was monitoring the lacrosse teams' social media accounts 11 and missed anything that could have indicated potential violence, it "may have had significant legal liability for negligent social media monitoring because it failed to protect Love," Shear wrote.

On the other hand, if the school was only monitoring the accounts of its 12 higher-profile football and basketball players, Shear wrote, then that could have been considered discrimination and the university "may have been sued for not monitoring the electronic content of all of its students."

Do you think universities should be allowed to force their athletes into 13 allowing coaches and administrators to monitor their Facebook and Twitter accounts?

Questions

1. What steps would you take to determine whether Laird's information is accurate?

2. How could you determine whether Laird is respected in his field?

3. Is Laird's blog written for an audience that is knowledgeable about his subject? How can you tell?

4. Do you think this blog post is a suitable research source? Why or why not?

5. This blog post was written in 2012. Do you think it is still relevant today? Why or why not?

This installation on Alcatraz Island from artist Ai Weiwei features a quotation from Edward Snowden, who became a notorious figure after leaking classified information about potentially privacy-invading surveillance programs to the public. AP Images/Eric Risberg

9 Summarizing, Paraphrasing, Quoting, and Synthesizing Sources

Is Technology a Serious Threat to Our Privacy? (continued)

In Chapter 8, you learned how to evaluate sources for an essay about the dangers of posting personal information online. In this chapter, you will learn how to take notes from sources that address this issue.

As you saw in Chapter 8, before you can decide what material to use to support your arguments, you need to evaluate a variety of potential sources. After you decide which sources you will use, you can begin thinking about where you might use each source. Then, you will need to consider how to integrate information from the sources you have chosen into your essay in the form of *summary*, *paraphrase*, and *quotation*. When you actually write your argument, you will *synthesize* source material into your essay, blending information from your sources with your own ideas and interpretations (as the student writer did when she wrote the MLA research paper in Chapter 10).

Summarizing Sources

A **summary** restates the main idea of a passage (or even of an entire book or article) in concise terms. Because a summary does not include the examples or explanations in the source, and because it omits the original source's rhetorical strategies and stylistic devices, it is always much shorter than the original. Usually, in fact, it consists of just a sentence or two.

WHEN TO SUMMARIZE

Summarize when you want to give readers a general sense of a passage's main idea or a source's position on an issue.

When you summarize information, you do not include your own opinions, but you do use your own words and phrasing, not those of your source. If you want to use a particularly distinctive word or phrase from your source, you may do so—but you must always place such words in quotation marks and **document** them. If you do not, you will be committing **plagiarism**. (See Chapter 10 for information on documenting sources; see Chapter 11 for information on avoiding plagiarism by using sources responsibly.)

The following paragraph appeared in a newspaper opinion essay.

ORIGINAL SOURCE

When everyone has a blog, a MySpace page, or Facebook entry, everyone is a publisher. When everyone has a cellphone with a camera in it, everyone is a paparazzo. When everyone can upload video on YouTube, everyone is a filmmaker. When everyone is a publisher, paparazzo, or filmmaker, everyone else is a public figure. We're all public figures now. The blogosphere has made the global discussion so much richer—and each of us so much more transparent. ("The Whole World Is Watching," Thomas L. Friedman, *New York Times*, June 27, 2007, p. 23)

The following effective summary conveys a general but accurate sense of the original paragraph without using the source's phrasing or including the writer's own opinions. (One distinctive and hard-to-reword phrase is placed in quotation marks.) Parenthetical documentation identifies the source of the material.

EFFECTIVE SUMMARY

The popularity of blogs, social-networking sites, cell phone cameras, and YouTube has enhanced the "global discussion" but made it very hard for people to remain anonymous (Friedman 23).

Notice that this one-sentence summary is much shorter than the original passage and that it does not include all the original's examples. Still, it accurately communicates a general sense of the original paragraph's main idea.

The following summary is not acceptable. Not only does it express the student writer's opinion, but it also uses the source's exact words without putting them in quotation marks or providing documentation. (This constitutes plagiarism.)

UNACCEPTABLE SUMMARY
It seems to me that nowadays blogs, social-networking sites, cell phone cameras, and YouTube are everywhere, and what this means is that we're all public figures now.

SUMMARIZING SOURCES

Do

- Convey the main idea of the original passage.
- Be concise.
- Use your own original words and phrasing.
- Place any distinctive words borrowed from your source in quotation marks.
- Include documentation.

Do not

- Include your own analysis or opinions.
- Include digressions.
- Argue with your source.
- Use your source's syntax or phrasing (unless you are quoting).

● EXERCISE 9.1 WRITING A SUMMARY

Write a two-sentence summary of the following passage. Then, edit your summary so that it is only one sentence long. Be sure your summary conveys the main idea of the original passage and includes proper documentation (see Chapter 10).

Make sure you represent your best self on any social network. On LinkedIn, that means crafting a professional persona. On Facebook, Snapchat, Instagram, and Twitter, even if you're mainly interacting with friends, don't forget that posts may still be public.

According to a CareerBuilder.com survey, 60 percent of employers research job candidates on social media, and over half are reluctant to hire candidates with no online presence. They're mainly looking for professionalism, whether you're a fit for the company and proof of qualifications.

If your social media profiles show you in that light, you're golden. (Alice Underwood, "9 Things to Avoid on Social Media While Looking for a New Job," *Glassdoor*, 3 Jan., 2018)

Paraphrasing Sources

A **paraphrase** is different from a summary. While a summary gives a general overview of the original, a paraphrase presents the source's ideas in detail, including its main idea, its key supporting points, and perhaps even its examples. For this reason, a paraphrase is longer than a summary. (In fact, it may be as long as the original.)

WHEN TO PARAPHRASE

Paraphrase when you want to communicate the key points discussed in a source—particularly a complex or complicated passage—in clear, accessible language.

Like a summary, a paraphrase uses your own words and phrasing, not the language and syntax of the original. Any distinctive words or phrases from your source must be placed in quotation marks. When you paraphrase, you may not always follow the order of the original source's ideas, but you should try to convey the writer's emphasis and most important points.

The following paragraph is from an editorial that appeared in a student newspaper.

ORIGINAL SOURCE

Additionally, as graduates retain their Facebook accounts, employers are increasingly able to use Facebook as an evaluation tool when making hiring decisions. Just as companies sometimes incorporate social functions into their interview process to see if potential hires can handle themselves responsibly, they may also check out a student's Facebook account to see how the student chooses to present him or herself. This may seem shady and underhanded, but one must understand that social networks are not anonymous; whatever one chooses to post will be available to all. Even if someone goes to great pains to keep an employer-friendly profile, his or her friends may still tag pictures of him or her which will be available to whoever wants to see them. Not only can unexpected Facebook members get information by viewing one's profile, but a user's personal information can also leak out by merely registering for the service. Both the user agreement and the privacy policy indicate that Facebook can give information to third parties and can supplement its data with information from newspapers, blogs, and instant messages. ("Beware What You Post on Facebook," *The Tiger*, Clemson University, August 4, 2006)

The following paraphrase reflects the original paragraph's emphasis and clearly communicates its key points.

EFFECTIVE PARAPHRASE

As an editorial in *The Tiger* observes, because students keep their accounts at social-networking sites after they graduate, potential employers can use the information they find there to help them evaluate candidates' qualifications. This process is comparable to the way a company might evaluate an applicant in person in a social situation. Some people may see the practice of employers checking applicants' Facebook pages as "shady and underhanded," but these sites are not intended to be anonymous or private. For example, a person may try to maintain a profile that will be appropriate for employers, but friends may post inappropriate pictures. Also, people can reveal personal information not only in profiles but also simply by registering with Facebook. Finally, as Facebook states in its membership information, it can supply information to others as well as provide data from other sources. ("Beware")

Notice that this paraphrase includes many of the details presented in the original passage and quotes a distinctive phrase, but its style and sentence structure are different from those of the original.

The following paraphrase is not acceptable because its phrasing and sentence structure are too close to the original. It also borrows words and phrases from the source without attribution and does not include documentation.

UNACCEPTABLE PARAPHRASE

As more and more college graduates keep their Facebook accounts, employers are increasingly able to use them as evaluation tools when they decide whom to hire. Companies sometimes set up social functions during the interview process to see how potential hires handle themselves; in the same way, they can consult a Facebook page to see how an applicant presents himself or herself. This may seem underhanded, but after all, Facebook is not anonymous; its information is available to all. Many people try to keep their profiles employer friendly, but their friends sometimes tag pictures of them that employers will be able to see. Besides, students' personal information is available not just on their profiles but also in the form they fill out when they register. Finally, according to their user agreement and their privacy policy, Facebook can give information to third parties and also add data from other sources.

PARAPHRASING SOURCES

Do

- Convey the source's ideas fully and accurately.
- Use your own words and phrasing.
- Convey the emphasis of the original.
- Simplify and clarify complex language and syntax.
- Put any distinctive words borrowed from the source in quotation marks.
- Include documentation.

Do not

- Use the exact words or phrasing of your source (unless you are quoting).
- Include your own analysis or opinions.
- Argue with or contradict your source.
- Wander from the topic of the source.

◑ EXERCISE 9.2 COMPARING SUMMARY AND PARAPHRASE

Write a paraphrase of the passage you summarized in Exercise 9.1. How is your paraphrase different from your summary?

◑ EXERCISE 9.3 WRITING A PARAPHRASE

The following paragraph is from the same Clemson University student newspaper article that was excerpted on pages 316–17. Read the paragraph, and then write a paraphrase that communicates its key ideas. Before you begin, circle any distinctive words and phrases that might be difficult to paraphrase, and consider whether you should quote them. Be sure to include documentation. (See Chapter 10.)

> All these factors make clear the importance of two principles: Responsibility and caveat emptor. First, people should be responsible about how they portray themselves and their friends, and employers, authorities, and the owners must approach this information responsibly and fairly. Second, "let the buyer beware" applies to all parties involved. Facebook users need to understand the potential consequences of the information they share, and outside viewers need to understand that the material on Facebook is often only a humorous, lighthearted presentation of one aspect of a person. Facebook is an incredibly valuable communications tool that will link the college generation more tightly than any before it, but users have to understand that, like anything good in life, they have to be aware of the downsides.

Quoting Sources

When you **quote** words from a source, you need to quote accurately—that is, every word and every punctuation mark in your quotation must match the source *exactly*. You also need to be sure that your quotation conveys the meaning its author intended and that you are not distorting the meaning by **quoting out of context** or by omitting an essential part of the passage you are quoting.

WHEN TO QUOTE

Quote a source's words only in the following situations:

- Quote when your source's words are distinctive or memorable.

- Quote when your source's words are so direct and concise that a paraphrase would be awkward or wordy.

- Quote when your source's words add authority or credibility to your argument (for example, when your source is a well-known expert on your topic).

- Quote a point when you will go on to refute it.

Remember, quoting from a source adds interest to your paper—but only when the writer's words are compelling. Too many quotations—especially long quotations—distract readers and make it difficult for them to follow your discussion. Quote only when you must. If you include too many quotations, your paper will be a patchwork of other people's words, not an original, unified whole.

QUOTING SOURCES

Do

- Enclose borrowed words in quotation marks.

- Quote accurately.

- Include documentation.

Do not

- Quote out of context.

- Distort the source's meaning.

- Include too many quotations.

➔ EXERCISE 9.4 IDENTIFYING MATERIAL TO QUOTE

Read the following paragraphs from a newspaper column. (The full text of this column appears in Exercise 9.5.) If you were going to use these paragraphs as source material for an argumentative essay, which particular words or phrases do you think you might want to quote? Why?

> How do users not know that a server somewhere is recording where you are, what you ate for lunch, how often you post photos of your puppy, what you bought at the supermarket for dinner, the route you drove home, and what movie you watched before you went to bed?
>
> So why do we act so surprised and shocked about the invasion of the privacy we so willingly relinquish, and the personal information we forfeit that allows its captors to sell us products, convict us in court, get us fired, or produce more of the same banality that keeps us logging on?
>
> We, all of us, are digital captives. (Shelley Fralic, "Don't Fall for the Myths about Online Privacy," *Calgary Herald*, October 17, 2015.)

➔ EXERCISE 9.5 SUMMARY AND PARAPHRASE: ADDITIONAL PRACTICE

Read the newspaper column that follows, and highlight it to identify its most important ideas. (For information on highlighting, see Chapter 2.) Then, write a summary of one paragraph and a paraphrase of another paragraph. Assume that this column is a source for an essay you are writing on the topic, "Is Technology a Serious Threat to Our Privacy?" Be sure to include documentation.

This column is from the *Calgary Herald*, where it appeared on page 1 on October 17, 2015.

DON'T FALL FOR THE MYTHS ABOUT ONLINE PRIVACY

SHELLEY FRALIC

If you are a Facebooker—and there are 1.5 billion of us on the planet, so 1 chances are about one in five that you are—you will have noticed yet another round of posts that suggest in quasi-legalese that you can somehow block the social network's invasion of your privacy.

This latest hoax cautions that Facebook will now charge $5.99 to keep 2 privacy settings private, and the copyright protection disclaimers making the rounds this week typically begin like this: "As of date-and-time here, I do not give Facebook or any entities associated with Facebook permission to use my pictures, information, or posts, both past and future. By this statement, I give notice to Facebook it is strictly forbidden to disclose, copy, distribute, or take any other action against me based on this profile and/or its contents. The content of this profile is private and confidential information."

Well, no, it's not.   3

This is a new-age version of an old story, oft-told. No one reads the fine   4 print. Not on contracts, not on insurance policies, and not on social media sites that are willingly and globally embraced by perpetually plugged-in gossipmongers, lonely hearts, news junkies, inveterate sharers, and selfie addicts.

Facebook's fine print, like that of many internet portals, is specific and   5 offers users a variety of self-selected "privacy" options.

But to think that any interaction with it, and its ilk, is truly private is   6 beyond absurd.

How can there still be people out there who still don't get that Netflix and   7 Facebook, Instagram and Twitter, Google and Tinder, and pretty much every keystroke or communication we register on a smartphone or laptop, not to mention a loyalty card and the GPS in your car, are constantly tracking and sifting and collating everything we do?

How do users not know that a server somewhere is recording where you   8 are, what you ate for lunch, how often you post photos of your puppy, what you bought at the supermarket for dinner, the route you drove home, and what movie you watched before you went to bed?

So why do we act so surprised and shocked about the invasion of the   9 privacy we so willingly relinquish, and the personal information we forfeit that allows its captors to sell us products, convict us in court, get us fired, or produce more of the same banality that keeps us logging on?

We, all of us, are digital captives.   10

But do we have to be so stupid about it?   11

And the bigger question is this: If we, the adults who should know better,   12 don't get it, what are we teaching our kids about the impact and repercussions of their online lives? What are they learn-ing about the voluntary and wholesale abandonment of their privacy? What are we teaching them about "sharing" with strangers?

> "We, all of us, are digital captives."

Worried about future generations not reading books or learning how to   13 spell properly or write in cursive? Worry more, folks, that internet ignorance is the new illiteracy.

Meantime, when another Facebook disclaimer pops up with a plea   14 to share, consider this clever post from a user who actually read the fine print:

"I hereby give my permission to the police, the NSA, the FBI and CIA,   15 the Swiss Guard, the Priory of Scion, the inhabitants of Middle Earth, Agents Mulder and Scully, the Goonies, ALL the Storm Troopers and Darth Vader, the Mad Hatter, Chuck Norris, S.H.I.E.L.D., The Avengers, The Illuminati . . . to view all the amazing and interesting things I publish on Facebook. I'm aware that my privacy ended the very day that I created a profile on Facebook."

Yes, it did.   16

Working Source Material into Your Argument

When you use source material in an argumentative essay, your goal is to integrate the material smoothly into your discussion, blending summary, paraphrase, and quotation with your own ideas.

To help readers follow your discussion, you need to indicate the source of each piece of information clearly and distinguish your own ideas from those of your sources. Never simply drop source material into your discussion. Whenever possible, introduce quotations, paraphrases, and summaries with an **identifying tag** (sometimes called a *signal phrase*), a phrase that identifies the source, and always follow them with documentation. This practice helps readers identify the boundaries between your own ideas and those of your sources.

It is also important that you include clues to help readers understand why you are using a particular source and what the exact relationship is between your source material and your own ideas. For example, you may be using a source to support a point you are making or to contradict another source.

Using Identifying Tags

Using identifying tags to introduce your summaries, paraphrases, or quotations will help you to accomplish the goals discussed above (and also help you to avoid accidental plagiarism).

> **SUMMARY WITH IDENTIFYING TAG**
> According to Thomas L. Friedman, the popularity of blogs, social-networking sites, cell phone cameras, and YouTube has enhanced the "global discussion" but made it hard for people to remain anonymous (23).

Note that you do not always have to place the identifying tag at the beginning of the summarized, paraphrased, or quoted material. You can also place it in the middle or at the end:

> **IDENTIFYING TAG AT THE BEGINNING**
> Thomas L. Friedman notes that the popularity of blogs, social-networking sites, cell phone cameras, and YouTube has enhanced the "global discussion" but made it hard for people to remain anonymous (23).

> **IDENTIFYING TAG IN THE MIDDLE**
> The popularity of blogs, social-networking sites, cell phone cameras, and YouTube, Thomas L. Friedman observes, has enhanced the "global discussion" but made it hard for people to remain anonymous (23).

IDENTIFYING TAG AT THE END
The popularity of blogs, social-networking sites, cell phone cameras, and YouTube has enhanced the "global discussion" but made it hard for people to remain anonymous, <u>Thomas L. Friedman points out (23).</u>

TEMPLATES FOR USING IDENTIFYING TAGS

To avoid repeating phrases like *he says* in identifying tags, try using some of the following verbs to introduce your source material. (You can also use "According to . . . ," to introduce a source.)

For Summaries or Paraphrases

[Name of writer]	notes	acknowledges	proposes	that [<u>summary or paraphrase</u>].
The writer	suggests	believes	observes	
The article	explains	comments	warns	
The essay	reports	points out	predicts	
	implies	concludes	states	

For Quotations

As [name of writer]	notes,	acknowledges,	proposes,	" _____ [quotation] _____ ."
As the writer	suggests,	believes,	observes,	
As the article	warns,	reports,	points out,	
As the essay	predicts,	implies,	concludes,	
	states,	explains,		

Working Quotations into Your Sentences

When you use quotations in your essays, you may need to edit them—for example, by adding, changing, or deleting words—to provide context or to make them fit smoothly into your sentences. If you do edit a quotation, be careful not to distort the source's meaning.

Adding or Changing Words When you add or change words in a quotation, use **brackets** to indicate your edits.

ORIGINAL QUOTATION
"Twitter, Facebook, Flickr, FourSquare, Fitbit, and the SenseCam give us a simple choice: participate or fade into a lonely obscurity" (Cashmore).

WORDS ADDED FOR CLARIFICATION

As Cashmore observes, "Twitter, Flickr, FourSquare, Fitbit, and the SenseCam [as well as similar social-networking sites] give us a simple choice: participate or fade into a lonely obscurity."

ORIGINAL QUOTATION

"The blogosphere has made the global discussion so much richer—and each of us so much more transparent" (Friedman 23).

WORDS CHANGED TO MAKE VERB TENSE LOGICAL

As Thomas L. Friedman explains, increased access to cell phone cameras, YouTube, and the like continues to "[make] the global discussion so much richer—and each of us so much more transparent" (23).

Deleting Words   When you delete words from a quotation, use **ellipses**— three spaced periods—to indicate your edits. However, never use ellipses to indicate a deletion at the beginning of a quotation.

ORIGINAL QUOTATION

"Just as companies sometimes incorporate social functions into their interview process to see if potential hires can handle themselves responsibly, they may also check out a student's Facebook account to see how the student chooses to present him or herself" ("Beware").

UNNECESSARY WORDS DELETED

"Just as companies sometimes incorporate social functions into their interview process, . . . they may also check out a student's Facebook account . . ." ("Beware").

DISTORTING QUOTATIONS

Be careful not to distort a source's meaning when you add, change, or delete words from a quotation. In the following example, the writer intentionally deletes material from the original quotation that would weaken his argument.

Original Quotation

"This incident is by no means an isolated one. Connecticut authorities are investigating reports that seven girls were sexually assaulted by older men they met online" ("Beware").

Distorted

"This incident is by no means an isolated one. [In fact,] seven girls were sexually assaulted by older men" they met online ("Beware").

➲ EXERCISE 9.6 INTEGRATING QUOTED MATERIAL

Look back at "Don't Fall for the Myths about Online Privacy" (p. 320). Select three quotations from this essay. Then, integrate each quotation into an original sentence, taking care to place the quoted material in quotation marks. Be sure to acknowledge your source in an identifying tag and to integrate the quoted material smoothly into each sentence.

➲ EXERCISE 9.7 INTEGRATING SUMMARIES AND PARAPHRASES

Reread the summary you wrote for Exercise 9.1 and the paraphrase you wrote for Exercise 9.3. Add three different identifying tags to each, varying the verbs you use and the position of the tags. Then, check to make sure you have used correct parenthetical documentation. (If the author's name is included in the identifying tag, it should not also appear in the parenthetical citation.)

Synthesizing Sources

When you write a **synthesis**, you combine summary, paraphrase, and quotation from several sources with your own ideas to support an original conclusion. You use a synthesis to identify similarities and differences among ideas, indicating where sources agree and disagree and how they support or challenge one another's ideas. In a synthesis, transitional words and phrases should identify points of similarity (*also*, *like*, *similarly*, and so on) or difference (*however*, *in contrast*, and so on). Identifying tags and parenthetical documentation should identify each piece of information from a source and distinguish your sources' ideas from one another and from your own ideas.

The following effective synthesis is excerpted from the student paper in Chapter 10. Note how the synthesis blends information from three sources with the student's own ideas to support her point about how the internet has affected people's concepts of "public" and "private."

EFFECTIVE SYNTHESIS

    Part of the problem is that the internet has fundamentally altered our notions of "private" and "public" in ways that we are only just beginning to understand. As Shelley Fralic observes in "Don't Fall for the Myths about Online Privacy," Facebook's privacy options do not really protect its users' privacy. On sites like Facebook, people often reveal intimate details of their lives to hundreds—perhaps even thousands—of strangers. This situation is unprecedented and, at least for the foreseeable future, irreversible. The French artist, film producer, and fashion designer Maripol has noted, "Andy Warhol said that everyone will be famous for fifteen minutes, but with social

    Student's original point

    Paraphrase

    Student's own ideas

    Quotation

media, everyone is famous all of the time" (qtd. in Hanra). In essence, we are all exhibitionists now, to some degree and our private lives are on display as never before. Given the changes in our understanding of privacy and the public nature of the internet, the suggestion that we should live our lives by the same rules we lived by thirty years ago simply does not make sense. As *New York Times* columnist Thomas Friedman noted prophetically in 2007, in the internet age, more and more of "what you say or do or write will end up as a digital fingerprint that never gets erased" (23).

Student's evaluation of source

Quotation

Compare the effective synthesis above with the following unacceptable synthesis.

UNACCEPTABLE SYNTHESIS

"The sheer volume of personal information that people are publishing online—and the fact that some of it could remain visible permanently—is changing the nature of personal privacy." On sites like Facebook, people can reveal the most intimate details of their lives to millions of total strangers. This development is unprecedented and, at least for the foreseeable future, irreversible. "When everyone has a blog . . . or Facebook entry, everyone is a publisher. . . . When everyone is a publisher, paparazzo, or filmmaker, everyone else is a public figure" (Friedman 23). Given the changes in our understanding of privacy and the essentially public nature of the internet, the analogy that David Hall makes in an essay about online behavior and workplace discrimination between an online post and a private conversation seems to be of limited use. In the internet age, more and more of "what you say or do or write will end up as a digital fingerprint that never gets erased."

Unlike the effective synthesis, the preceding unacceptable synthesis does not begin with a topic sentence that introduces the point the source material in the paragraph will support. Instead, it opens with an out-of-context quotation whose source (an essay by Alison George in *New Scientist*) is not identified. This quotation could have been paraphrased—its wording is not particularly memorable—and, more important, it should have been accompanied by documentation. (If source information is not provided, the writer is committing plagiarism even if the borrowed material is set in quotation marks.) The second quotation, although it includes parenthetical documentation (Friedman 23), is dropped into the paragraph without an identifying tag; the third quotation, also from the Friedman article, is not documented at all, making it appear to be from Hall. All in all, the paragraph is not a smoothly connected synthesis but a string of unconnected ideas. It does not use sources effectively and responsibly, and it does not cite them appropriately.

SYNTHESIZING SOURCES

Do

- Combine summary, paraphrase, and quotations from sources with your own ideas.

- Place borrowed words and phrases in quotation marks.

- Introduce source material with identifying tags.

- Document material from your sources.

Do not

- Drop source material into your synthesis without providing context.

- String random pieces of information together without supplying transitions to connect them.

- Cram too many pieces of information into a single paragraph; in most cases, two or three sources per paragraph (plus your own comments) will be sufficient.

⊘ EXERCISE 9.8 WRITING A SYNTHESIS

Write a synthesis that builds on the paraphrase you wrote for Exercise 9.2. Add your own original ideas—examples and opinions—to the paraphrase, and also blend in information from one or two of the other sources that appear in this chapter. Use identifying tags and parenthetical documentation to introduce your sources and to distinguish your own ideas from ideas expressed in your sources.

⊘ EXERCISE 9.9 INTEGRATING VISUAL ARGUMENTS

Suppose you were going to use this chapter's opening image of the Ai Weiwei art installation (p. 312) as a visual argument in an essay about whether technology poses a threat to our privacy, possibly taking into account the artist's personal history. Write a paragraph in which you introduce the image, briefly describe it, and explain its relevance to your essay's topic and how it supports your position.

Documenting Sources: MLA

When you are building an argument, you use sources for support. To acknowledge the material you borrow and to help readers evaluate your sources, you need to supply documentation. In other words, you need to tell readers where you found your information. If you use documentation responsibly, you will also avoid **plagiarism**, an ethical offense with serious consequences. (See Chapter 11 for more on plagiarism.)

WHY DOCUMENT SOURCES?

- To acknowledge the debt that you owe to your sources
- To demonstrate that you are familiar with the conventions of academic discourse
- To enable readers to judge the quality of your research
- To avoid plagiarism
- To make your argument more convincing

MLA documentation consists of two parts: **parenthetical references** in the text of your paper and a **works-cited list** at the end of the paper. (The references are keyed to the works-cited list.)

Using Parenthetical References

The basic parenthetical citation consists of the author's last name and a page number:

(Fielding 213)

If the author is referred to in the sentence, include only the page number in the parenthetical reference.

> According to environmental activist Brian Fielding, the number of species affected is much higher (213).

Here are some other situations you may encounter:

- When referring to a work by two authors, include both authors' names.

  > (Stange and Hogarth 53)

- When citing a work with no listed author, include a short version of the title.

  > ("Small Things" 21)

- When citing a source that is quoted in another source, indicate this by including the abbreviation *qtd. in.*

  > According to Kevin Kelly, this narrow approach is typical of the "hive mind" (qtd. in Doctorow 168).

- When citing two or more works by the same author, include a short title after the author's name.

  > (Anderson, *Long Tail* 47)

- If a source does not include page numbers, or if you are referring to the entire source rather than to a specific page, cite the author's name in the text of your paper rather than in a parenthetical reference.

You must document *all* information that is not **common knowledge**, whether you are summarizing, paraphrasing, or quoting. (See p. 357 for an explanation of common knowledge.) With direct quotations, include the parenthetical reference and a period *after* the closing quotation marks.

> According to Doctorow, this is "authorship without editorship. Or authorship fused with editorship" (166).

When quoting a passage of more than four lines, indent the entire passage half an inch from the left margin, and do not use quotation marks. Place the parenthetical reference *after* the final punctuation mark.

Doctorow points out that Wikipedia's history pages can be extremely informative:

> This is a neat solution to the problem of authority—if you want to know what the fully rounded view of opinions on any controversial subject looks like, you need only consult its entry's history page for a blistering eyeful of thorough debate on the subject. (170)

Preparing the Works-Cited List

Start your works-cited list on a new page following the last page of your paper. Center the heading Works Cited at the top of the page. List entries alphabetically by the author's last name—or by the first word (other than an article such as *a* or *the*) of the title if an author is not given. Double-space within and between entries. Each entry should begin at the left-hand margin, with subsequent lines indented one-half inch. (This format can be automatically generated if you use the "hanging indent" option in your word processing program.)

Citations need to identify elements of what MLA documentation refers to as a source's "container." If a source is part of a larger whole, that larger source is considered the container. When citing a chapter in a book, for example, the book itself would be considered the container. Not every work is held by a container, however. If you were citing a movie watched in a movie theater, the movie is the source and it has no container. But if the same movie is watched as part of a DVD boxed set, that set is the container. Other examples include songs, which are contained on an album; or individual blog posts, which are contained on a blog.

The following information should be included in the citation, in this order and when available: the *title of the container*; the *name of contributors* such as editors or translators; the *version or edition*; the *volume and issue numbers*; the *publisher*; the *date of publication*; and a *location* such as the page number, DOI, permalink, or URL. Which of these elements will be relevant or available for citation will depend on the container.

When you have completed your list, double-check your parenthetical references to make sure they match the items in your works-cited list.

The following models illustrate the most common kinds of references.

Periodicals

For periodical articles found online or through a full-text database, see page 339.

Guidelines for Citing a Periodical Article

To cite a print article in MLA style, include the following:

1. Author, last name first

2. Title of the article, in quotation marks

3. Title of the periodical, in italics

4. Volume and issue numbers

5. Date or year of publication

6. Page number(s) of the article

   (See images on page 333.)

Carton, Evan. "American Scholars: Ralph Waldo Emerson, Joseph Smith, John Brown, and the Springs of Intellectual Schism." *New England Quarterly,* vol. 85, no. 1, 2012, pp. 5–37.

Journals

Journals are periodicals published for experts in a field. Cite both volume number and issue number when available. In cases where only an issue number is available, cite just the issue.

> Minkler, Lanse. "Economic Rights and Political Decision-Making." *Human Rights Quarterly*, vol. 31, no. 2, 2009, pp. 369–93.
>
> Picciotto, Joanna. "The Public Person and the Play of Fact." *Representations*, no. 105, 2009, pp. 85–132.

Magazines

Magazines are periodicals published for a general audience. Do not include a magazine's volume and issue number, but do include the date (day, month, and year for weekly publications; month and year for those published less frequently). If pages are not consecutive, give the first page followed by a plus sign.

> Lansky, Sam. "Science fiction knows the future is female." *Time*, 26 Feb. 2018, pp. 95–97.
>
> Sancton, Tom. "Visionnaire." *Vanity Fair*, May 2018, pp. 92–99.

Title of periodical

THE JOURNAL OF ANGLO-SAXON STUDIES

Editors

Aarne Rolfsson   Ingrid Scholten
Eric Thorssen   Lynnette Wallis
Edmund Stitt   Nicole V. Brown

Volume and issue number — Volume LLXXIV   Number 3
August 2018

Date of publication

Copyright 2018 by The Journal of Anglo-Saxon Studies

Title of article

Author

☩☩☩☩☩☩☩☩☩☩☩☩☩☩☩☩☩☩☩☩☩☩☩☩☩☩☩☩

Þæs ofereode, þisses swa mæg: Applying
Political Lessons from *Deor* to
Contemporary American Politics

KARI GANNON

THE deeply bitter partisanship of contemporary American politics has been quietly growing for several decades. Each election cycle, the minority party—often recently disenfranchised, pledges to undermine and fight the administration. Yet today, in particular, the atmosphere is particularly virulent. I propose that, in examining how to move beyond the despair and anger, we draw not only from historical, philosophical, or moral precedent, but turn our attention to literature, in which can be found permutations and shades of the same struggles we face today. Often defying clear categorization (is it a traditional lament, an *ubi sunt*, a begging poem, an elegy?), the Anglo-Saxon poem *Deor's*[1] sorrowful retrospection and hopeful refrain provides a model for political reflection. Likewise, the interconnected episodes, revealing a medieval shared historical-folkloric tradition, reminds readers to look beyond closed borders and nationalistic values. The purpose of this paper may be best understood as twofold: to closely examine the context of the episodes detailed in *Deor* and their purpose in being related by the speaker, in order to argue that the poem, while tragic, is neither an elegy nor a *de casibus* tragedy, but ultimately contains an thin ray of stoic hope; and to apply the contextual messages within the poem to the contemporary political atmosphere, illustrating the universality and transience of political power shifts.

---

[1] *Deor* is widely available online, both in the original Anglo-Saxon and translations of varying quality. Anne Klinck's *The Old English Elegies* (1992) provides some useful commentary, and a thorough, though now somewhat dated, bibliography. Of course, placing *Deor* in a volume of elegies is, from the start, a debated critical choice.

Page number — 18

Newspapers

Include both the letter of the section and the page number. If an article continues on to a nonconsecutive page, give just the first page followed by a plus sign.

> Murphy, Sean P. "Eighty-seven, and left by the side of the road by Uber." *The Boston Globe*, 2 Nov. 2018, pp. A1+.

Editorial, Letter to the Editor, or Review

Include authors and titles where available as well as a descriptive label—for example Editorial, Letter, or Review. In the case of reviews, include the title and author of the work that is reviewed.

> Bernath, Dan. "Letter to the Editor." *The Washington Post*, 12 Apr. 2009, p. A16. Letter.
>
> Franklin, Nancy. "Whedon's World." Review of *Dollhouse*, directed by Joss Whedon. *The New Yorker*, 2 Mar. 2009, p. 45.
>
> "World Bank Responsibility." *The Wall Street Journal*, 28 Mar. 2009, p. A10. Editorial.

Political Cartoon or Comic Strip

Include the author and title (if available) of the cartoon or comic strip, followed by a descriptive label and publication information.

> Adams, Scott. "Dilbert." *The Chicago Tribune*, 10 Mar. 2012, p. C9. Comic strip.
>
> Pett, Joel. *Lexington Herald-Leader*, 30 Apr. 2012, p. A12. Cartoon.

Advertisement

Cite the name of the product or company that is advertised, followed by the descriptive label and the publication information.

> Subaru. *Wired*, Aug. 2017, p. 11. Advertisement.

Books

Guidelines for Citing a Book

To cite a book in MLA style, include the following:

1. Author, last name first

2. Title, in italics

3. Full publisher's name

4. Date of publication

┌────1────┐ ┌────2────┐ ┌──────3──────┐ ┌─4─┐
McKibben, Bill. *Oil and Honey.* St. Martin's Griffin, 2014.

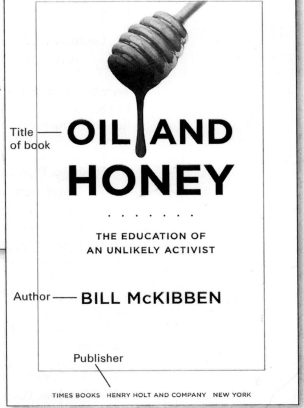

Text stock contains 20% post-consumer waste recycled fiber

OIL AND HONEY. Copyright © 2013, 2014 by Bill McKibben. All rights reserved. ——— Date of
Printed in the United States of America. For information, address   Publication
St. Martin's Press, 175 Fifth Avenue, New York, N. Y. 10010.

WWW.stmartins.com

Designed by Kelly S. Too

The Library of Congress has cataloged the Henry Holt edition as follows:

McKibben, Bill.
  Oil and honey : the education of an unlikely activist / Bill McKibben.
    p. cm.
  ISBN 978-0-8050-9284-4 (hardcover)
  ISBN 978-0-8050-9838-9 (e-book)
  1. McKibben, Bill.   2. Environmentalism—United States.   3. Climatic changes—
Environmental aspects.   4. Petroleum industry and trade—Environmental
aspects.   5. Petroleum industry and trade—Political aspects—United States.
6. Environmentalists—United States—Biography.   7. Beekeepers—United States—
Biography. 1. Title.
  GE197.M356 2013
  363.70092—dc23
  [B]   2013010995

ISBN 978-1-250-04871-4 (trade paperback)

St. Martin's Griffin books may be purchased for educational, business, or
promotional use. For information on bulk purchases, please contact Macmillan
Corporate and Premium Sales Department at 1-800-221-7745, extension 5442,
or write specialmarkets@macmillan.com

First published in hardcover by Times Books, an imprint of
Henry Holt and Company

First St. Martins's Griffin Edition: August 2014

10 9 8 7 6 5 4 3 2 1

Title —— OIL AND
of book

HONEY

• • • • • • •

THE EDUCATION OF
AN UNLIKELY ACTIVIST

Author —— **BILL McKIBBEN**

Publisher

TIMES BOOKS HENRY HOLT AND COMPANY NEW YORK

Jiri Hera/Shutterstock

Book by One Author

List the author, last name first, followed by the title (italicized). Include the full publisher's name, abbreviated when called for, and end with the date of publication.

> Goodwin, Doris Kearns. *Leadership*. Simon & Schuster, 2018.

Book by Two Authors

List authors in the order in which they are listed on the book's title page. List the first author with last name first, but list the second author with first name first.

> Singer, Peter, and Jim Mason. *The Way We Eat: Why Our Food Choices Matter*. Rodale, 2006.

Book by Three or More Authors

List only the first author, last name first, followed by the abbreviation et al. ("and others").

> Gould, Harvey, et al. *Advanced Computer Simulation Methods*. Pearson Education, 2009.

Two or More Books by the Same Author

List the entries alphabetically by title. In each entry after the first, substitute three unspaced hyphens, followed by a period, for the author's last name.

> Friedman, Thomas L. *Hot, Flat, and Crowded: Why We Need a Green Revolution—and How It Can Renew America*. Farrar, Strauss and Giroux, 2008.
>
> ---. *The World Is Flat: A Brief History of the Twenty-First Century*. Farrar, Strauss and Giroux, 2005.

Edited Book

If your focus is on the *author*, include the name of the editor (or editors) after the title, preceded by the abbreviation *Ed.* (for "edited by"). If the book is an edited collection of essays by different authors, treat it as an anthology.

> Whitman, Walt. *The Portable Walt Whitman*. Ed. by Michael Warner, Penguin Classics, 2004.

If your focus is on the *editor*, begin with the editor's name followed by editor or editors.

> Michael Warner, editor. *The Portable Walt Whitman*. Penguin
> Classics, 2004.

Translation

> Bolaño, Roberto. *The Savage Detectives*. Translated by Natasha
> Wimmer, Picador, 2008.

Revised Edition

> Smith, Steven S., et al., *The American Congress*. 4th ed., Cambridge
> UP, 2006.

Anthology

Include the name of the editor (or editors) of the anthology, followed by editor or editors.

> Browning, John Edgar, and Caroline Joan S. Picart, editors.
> *Speaking of Monsters*, Palgrave, 2012.

Work in an Anthology

> Malone, Dan. "Immigration, Terrorism, and Secret Prisons."
> *Keeping Out the Other: Immigration Enforcement Today*,
> edited by David C. Brotherton and Philip Kretsedemas,
> Columbia UP, 2008, pp. 44–62.

More Than One Work in the Same Anthology

To avoid repeating the entire anthology entry, you may provide a cross-reference from individual essays to the entire anthology.

> Adelson, Glenn et al., editors. *Environment: An Interdisciplinary*
> *Anthology*, Yale UP, 2008.
> Lesher, Molly. "Seeds of Change." Adelson, pp. 131–37.
> Marshall, Robert. "The Problem of the Wilderness." Adelson,
> pp. 288–92.

Section or Chapter of a Book

Tirado, Linda. "I'm Not Angry So Much as I'm Really Tired."
Hand to Mouth: Living in Bootstrap America, Berkeley,
2014, pp. 59–86.

Introduction, Preface, Foreword, or Afterword

Christiano, Thomas, and John Christman. Introduction.
Contemporary Debates in Political Philosophy. Edited by
Thomas Christiano and John Christman, Wiley, 2009,
pp. 1–20.

Multivolume Work

McNeil, Peter, editor. *Fashion: Critical and Primary Sources*. Berg
Publishers, 2009. 4 vols.

Article in a Reference Work

A **reference work** is a book (print or electronic)—such as an encyclopedia, a dictionary, a bibliography, an almanac, or a handbook—that contains factual information. If the entries in a reference work are arranged alphabetically, do not include page numbers or volumes. When citing a familiar encyclopedia that publishes new editions regularly, include only the edition (if given) and year. If the article's author is given, include that as well. For less well-known reference encyclopedias, include publication information.

"Human Rights." *Encyclopedia Americana*. 2003 ed.

"Seagrass Beds." *Ocean: A Visual Encyclopedia*. DK Publishing,
2015.

> **NOTE**
>
> Keep in mind that many instructors do not consider encyclopedia articles acceptable research sources. Before including a citation for an encyclopedia article in your works-cited list, check with your instructor.

Audiovisual Sources

TV Show

"Dance Dance Resolution." *The Good Place*, written by Megan
Amram, directed by Drew Goddard, NBC, 20 Sept. 2017.

Film

> *Get Out.* Directed by Jordan Peele, performances by Daniel
>   Kaluuya, Allison Williams, and Bradley Whitford, Universal
>   Pictures, 2017.

Internet Sources

Citing internet sources can be problematic because they sometimes lack basic information—for example, dates of publication or authors' names. When citing internet sources, include all the information you can find.

- For sites that are online editions of printed works, include as much of the original print information as is available, as well as the URL.

- For sites that exist only online, include (when available) the author, title, overall website title (if part of a larger project), the date it was last updated, and the URL.

- For works that are accessed through a library database, include the name of the database (in italics) and the URL or Digital Object Identifier (DOI). A DOI is a unique series of numbers assigned to electronic documents. The DOI remains the same regardless of where on the internet a document is located.

For particularly long URLs (three lines or greater), you may use the URL for the main website on which you found the content instead of the URL for the specific page which you are referencing. However, your instructor may not require a URL, so be sure to confirm their preference. It is always a good idea, however, to keep a record of the URLs for yourself in case you need to revisit your source.

If you type a URL into a works-cited entry that carries over to the next line, make sure that you break it at an appropriate place—for example, after a slash or a hyphen. If you paste a URL into a works-cited entry, Word will do this for you.

Guidelines for Citing a Website

To cite a website in MLA style, follow these guidelines:

1. Author (if any)
2. Title (if any)
3. Name of website or sponsor
4. Date the site was last updated
5. DOI or URL

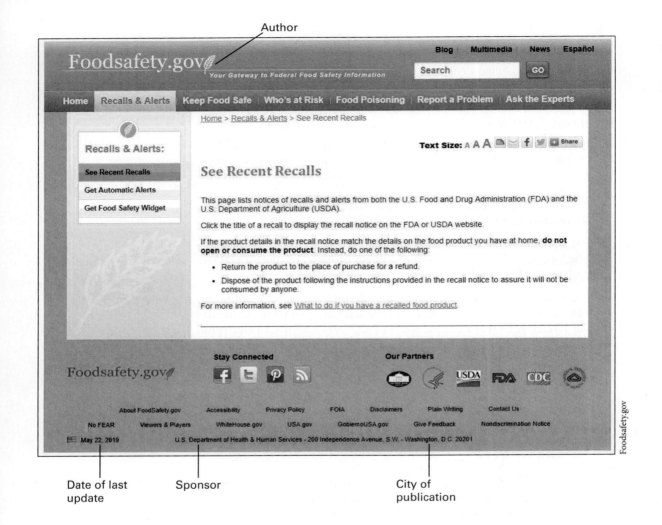

Author

Date of last update

Sponsor

City of publication

Foodsafety.gov

┌──── 1 ────┐ ┌──────── 2 ────────┐
Foodsafety.gov. "UBC Food Distributors Recalls Hot Curry Powder

┌─────────────┐ ┌──── 3 ────┐
and Curry Powder due to Lead." US Dept of Health and

┌──── 4 ────┐ ┌──── 5 ────┐
Human Services, 30 Oct. 2018. www.fda.gov/Safety/Recalls/

┌── 5 ──┐
ucm624397.htm

Entire Website

Include (if available) the author, title of the website, date of last update, and the URL.

Document within a Website

"Uniform Impunity: Mexico's Misuse of Military Justice to
    Prosecute Abuses in Counternarcotics and Public
    Security Operations." *Human Rights Watch*, Apr. 2009,
    www.hrw.org/report/2009/04/29/uniform-impunity
    /mexicos-misuse-military-justice-prosecute-abuses
    -counternarcotics.

Online Video

Baggs, Amanda. "In My Language." *YouTube*, 14 Jan. 2007,
    www.youtube.com/watch?v=JnylM1hl2jc.

Blog Posts and Blog Comments

Cimons, Marlene. "Why Cities Could Be the Key to Solving
    the Climate Crisis." *Thinkprogress.org*, Center for American
    Progress Action Fund, 10 Dec. 2015, thinkprogress.org
    /climate/2015/12/10/3730938/cities-key-to-climate-crisis/.

Parks, Tim. "Why Translation Deserves Scrutiny." *NYR Daily*,
    NYREV, 23 Oct. 2018, www.nybooks.com/daily/2018/10/23
    /why-translation-deserves-scrutiny/.

Tweet

Begin with the author's real name, followed by the user name in parentheses. Include only the user name if the real name is unknown. Next, include the entire text of the tweet in quotation marks, followed by the date, the time, and the medium (Tweet).

Barack Obama (@POTUS44). "Thank you for everything. My last
    ask is the same as my first. I'm asking you to believe—not in
    my ability to create change, but in yours." *Twitter*, 11 Jan. 2017,
    12:52 a.m., twitter.com/POTUS44/status/819044196371800065.
    Tweet.

Podcast

Koenig, Sarah. "A Bird in Jail Is Worth Two on the Street." *Serial,* Chicago Public Radio, 3 Oct. 2018, serialpodcast.org /season-one/1/the-alibi.

Ogg, Erica. "Google Tries to Rehab Its Antitrust Image." *CNET News Daily Podcast*, CBS Interactive, 8 May 2009, www.cnet.com /news/cnet-news-daily-podcast-google-tries-to-rehab-its -antitrust-image/.

Online Book

Doctorow, Cory. *Content: Selected Essays on Technology, Creativity, Copyright, and the Future of the Future,* Tachyon, 2008. *Craphound.com.*

Part of an Online Book

Zittrain, Jonathan L. "The Lessons of Wikipedia." *The Future of the Internet and How to Stop It,* Yale UP, 2008. *futureoftheinternet.org.*

Article in an Online Scholarly Journal

Johnston, Rebecca. "Salvation or Destruction: Metaphors of the Internet." *First Monday*, vol. 14, no. 4, 2009, firstmonday.org /article/view/2370/2158.

Magazine Article Accessed Online

Winter, Jessica. "Why Aren't Mothers Worth Anything to Venture Capitalists?." *The New Yorker*, 25 Sept. 2018, www.newyorker.com/business/currency/why-arent -mothers-worth-anything-to-venture-capitalists.

Newspaper Article Accessed Online

Twilley, Nicola. "With Bugs, You're Never Alone." *The New York Times*, 29 Oct. 2018, www.nytimes.com/2018/10/29/science /spider-insect-survey.html.

Article from a Library Database

Hartley, Richard D. "Sentencing Reform and the War on Drugs: An
Analysis of Sentence Outcomes for Narcotics Offenders
Adjudicated in the US District Courts on the Southwest Border."
Criminal Justice Policy Review, vol. 19, no. 4, 2008, pp. 414–37.
Sage Premier, doi: 10.1177/1043986208323264.

Legal Case

When citing a court opinion, provide the plaintiffs' names, the legal citation (volume, abbreviation of the source, page numbers), the name of the
court, the year of the decision, and any relevant information about where
you found it. In many cases, online versions of the opinions will include
only the first page; in those cases, supply that page number followed by a
plus sign.

Miranda v. Arizona, 384 US 436+. Supreme Court of the US. 1966.
FindLaw, Thompson Reuters, caselaw.findlaw.com
/us-supreme-court/384/436.html.

Government Document

Include the government agency or body issuing the document, followed by
publication information.

United States, Department of Homeland Security, *Estimates
of the Unauthorized Immigrant Population Residing in
the United States, Office of Immigration Policy,* Feb. 2009,
www.dhs.gov/sites/default/files/publications/ois_ill_pe_
2011_0.pdf.

MLA PAPER GUIDELINES

- An MLA paper should have a one-inch margin all around and be double-spaced.

- Indent the first line of every paragraph. Number all pages, including the first, consecutively. Type your name, followed by the page number, in the upper right-hand corner.

- An MLA paper does not typically have a title page. Type the following information at the top of the paper, one inch from the left-hand margin:

  Name

  Instructor

  Course

  Date submitted

- Center the title of the paper. Capitalize all important words of the title, except prepositions, articles, coordinating conjunctions, and the *to* in infinitives—unless the word is the first or last word of the title. Titles should never be italicized, underlined, or followed by a period.

- Begin the **works-cited list** on a new numbered page, after the body of the paper. (See page 331 for a discussion of the works-cited list.)

- Citations should follow MLA documentation style.

NOTE

In the student essay that follows, note that the blue annotations explain the student's choice of sources and the purple annotations highlight features of the student's use of documentation.

⊙ The following student research paper, "Should Data Posted on Social-Networking Sites Be 'Fair Game' for Employers?" by Erin Blaine, follows MLA documentation style as outlined in the preceding pages.

Blaine 1

Erin Blaine

Professor Adams

Humanities 101

4 March 2020

Should Data Posted on Social-Networking Sites

Be "Fair Game" for Employers?

The popularity of social-networking sites such as   1
Facebook, Instagram, LinkedIn, and Twitter has increased dramatically over the last several years, especially among college
students and young professionals. These sites provide valuable
opportunities for networking and for connecting socially. At the
same time, however, potential employers, human resources
professionals, and even college admissions officers routinely
use these sites to evaluate applicants. Because it is so easy
to access social-networking sites and because they provide
valuable information, this practice is certain to continue. Some
people concerned about this development argue that social-
networking sites should be off-limits because potential employers are seeing information out of context and are unable to
properly evaluate it. As long as applicants have freely posted
information in a public forum, however, there is no reason for
an employer not to consider it during the hiring process.

The number of employers and universities using   2
social-networking sites to evaluate candidates is growing
every year. A 2017 survey found that 35 percent of college
admissions officers acknowledged visiting sites like Facebook
to learn more about applicants, and 40 percent said that the
information they found "negatively impacted the applicant's
admissions chances" (Gurram). This practice also occurs in
the business world, where the numbers are even more
striking. One study found that 70 percent of employers use to
help them evaluate potential employees (Driscoll). The practice

This source and
the following
one supply
statistics that
support the
main point of
the paragraph.

Parentheti-
cal reference
identifies the
source, which is
included in the
works-cited list.

Blaine 2

Citations from
Driscoll and
Preston add
credibility.

of checking social media is so common that some employers
use outside companies, such as Social Intelligence Corp., to do
internet background checks on job candidates (Preston).

Not everyone is happy with this practice, though, and   3
some have strong objections. Becca Bush, a college student in
Chicago, argues that employers should not have the right to use
social media to evaluate potential employees. "It's a violation of
privacy," she says. "Twenty years ago, people still did the same
things as now," but the information "wasn't as widespread" (qtd.
in Cammenga). Marc S. Rotenberg, president of the Electronic
Privacy Information Center, agrees, saying, "Employers should
not be judging what people in their private lives do away from the
workplace." Rotenberg goes on to say that privacy settings on sites
like Facebook are often misunderstood. According to him, "People
are led to believe that there is more limited disclosure than there
actually is" (qtd. in Preston). Some people mistakenly think that
looking at an applicant's Facebook page is illegal (Cammenga).
Even though it is not, this practice can lead to discrimination,
which *is* illegal. An online search can reveal characteristics that an
applicant is not required to disclose to employers—for example,
race, age, religion, sex, national origin, marital status, or disability
(Preston).

Given the realities of the digital age, however, admissions   4
committees and job recruiters are acting reasonably when they
access social-networking sites. As a practical matter, it would be
almost impossible to prevent employers from reviewing online
sites as part of informal background and reference checks.
Moreover, those who believe that it is unethical for recruiters to
look at the online profiles of prospective job candidates seem
willing to accept the benefits of social-networking sites but
unwilling to acknowledge that these new technologies bring
new responsibilities and liabilities. Finally, the problems associated with employers' use of social-networking sites would not

Parenthetical
documentation
containing *qtd.
in* indicates a
source quoted
in another
source.

Quotes from
Rotenberg are
summarized
here to present
an opposing
viewpoint.

Blaine 3

be an issue in the first place if users of social-networking sites took full advantage of the available measures to protect themselves.

Part of the problem is that the internet has fundamentally altered our notions of "private" and "public" in ways that we are only just beginning to understand. As Shelley Fralic observes in "Don't Fall for the Myths about Online Privacy," Facebook's privacy options do not really protect its users' privacy, and thinking they do "is beyond absurd" (1). On sites like Facebook, people can reveal intimate details of their lives to millions of strangers. This situation is unprecedented and, at least for the foreseeable future, irreversible. The French artist, film producer, and fashion designer Maripol has noted, "Andy Warhol said that everyone will be famous for fifteen minutes, but with social media, everyone is famous all of the time" (qtd. in Hanra). In essence, we are all exhibitionists now, to some degree and our private lives are on display as never before. Given the changes in our understanding of privacy and the public nature of the internet, the suggestion that we should live our lives by the same rules we lived by thirty years ago simply does not make sense. As *New York Times* columnist Thomas Friedman noted prophetically in 2007, in the internet age, more and more of "what you say or do or write will end up as a digital fingerprint that never gets erased" (23).

Rather than relying on outdated notions of privacy, students and job seekers should accept these new conditions and take steps to protect themselves. Most college and career counseling services have easy-to-follow recommendations for how to maintain a positive online reputation. First on almost everyone's list is adjusting privacy settings. Understanding and employing these settings is a user's responsibility; misunderstanding such protections is no excuse. As Mariel Loveland suggests, those who want extra help can hire an online reputation-management company such as Reputation.com or Integrity Defenders or use services

5

6

Because the source and the author are named in an identifying tag, only the page numbers are needed parenthetically.

Distinctive key phrases are quoted directly.

Including a recognized authority, such as Friedman, adds credibility.

Internet source includes no page number in the parenthetical documentation.

such as those offered by Reppler. According to Sameer Somal, because many people judge a person solely on the basis of his or her online presence, it is important to make sure that your digital footprint is positive. Online reputation management companies identify questionable material across different social networks and take steps to protect your reputation.

The most important way for people to protect themselves against the possible misuse of personal information is for them to take responsibility for the information they post online. According to a recent article in *Education Week*, even middle school students should keep their future college and career plans in mind when they post information online ("Online Behavior"). In preparing students to apply for college, many high school counselors stress the "golden rule": "students should never post anything online they wouldn't want their parents to see" ("Online Behavior"). Students and job seekers must realize that a commonsense approach to the internet requires that they develop good "digital grooming" habits (Bond). For example, one self-described "cautious internet user" says that she "goes through the information on her [Facebook] account every few weeks and deletes statuses, messages, and other things" (Bond). She understands that a potential employer coming across an applicant's membership in a Facebook group such as "I Sold My Grandma for Crack-Cocaine!" or a picture of a student posing with an empty liquor bottle may not understand the tone, the context, or the joke. Students should also be careful about "friends" who have access to their online social networks, asking themselves whether these people really know them and would have good things to say about them if a prospective employer contacted them for a reference. According to one high school principal, 75 percent of the students at his school admitted to accepting a friend request from someone

7

Not every summary or paraphrase needs to include a quotation.

Brackets indicate that a quotation has been edited for clarity.

Paraphrasing provides readers with the key points of a source.

Blaine 5

they did not know ("Online Behavior"). Getting students to consider the repercussions of this kind of choice is central to many
social-media education programs.

Although social-networking sites have disadvantages, they [8]
also have advantages. These sites provide an excellent opportunity for job seekers to connect with potential employers and
to get their names and résumés in circulation. For example, a
job seeker can search the LinkedIn networks of a company's
executives or human resources staff for mutual connections. In
addition, a job seeker can post information calculated to appeal
to potential employers. Recruiters are just as likely to hire candidates based on social-media screening as they are to reject
them. A national survey conducted by Harris Poll on behalf of
CareerBuilder found that more than 57 percent of employers are
less likely to interview a candidate they can't find online. The
majority of companies will dig through social profiles, but find
it even more suspect if they see nothing at all (Driscoll). Another
article reports the following:

> However, one third (33 percent) of employers who
> research candidates on social networking sites say
> they've found content that made them more likely to
> hire a candidate. What's more, nearly a quarter (23 per-
> cent) found content that directly led to them hiring the
> candidate, up from 19 percent last year. ("Number of
> Employers")

In today's job market, people should think of their networks
as extensions of themselves. They need to take an active role
in shaping the image they want to project to future employers.
So even though students and job seekers should be careful [9]
when posting information online, they should not miss the
opportunity to take advantage of the many opportunities that
social-networking sites offer.

A quotation of more than four lines of text is double-spaced, indented one inch from the left margin, and typed as a block, without quotation marks. Parenthetical documentation comes after the final punctuation.

Blaine 6

Works Cited

Bond, Michaelle. "Facebook Timeline a New Privacy Test." *USA*
　　Today, 2 Nov. 2011, www.usatoday.com/tech/news
　　/internetprivacy/story/2011-11-02/facebook-timeline
　　-privacy/51047658/1.

Cammenga, Michelle. "Facebook Might Be the Reason You Don't
　　Get That Job." *Hub Bub*, Loyola University Chicago's School
　　of Communication, 23 Feb. 2012, blogs.luc.edu/hubbub
　　/reporting-and-writing/employers-screen-facebook/.

Driscoll, Kara. "Employers Less Likely to Hire Applicants with No
　　Social Media Presence." Dayton Daily News, 14 July 2017,
　　www.mydaytondailynews.com/business/employers
　　-less-likely-hire-applicants-with-social-media-presence
　　/MALOhAY4en0kok5WJfpVoK/.

Fralic, Shelley. "Don't Fall for the Myths about Online Privacy."
　　Calgary Herald, 17 Oct. 2015, p. 1.

Friedman, Thomas L. "The Whole World Is Watching." *The New York
　　Times,* 27 June 2007, p. A23.

Gurram, Mugdha. "Study Shows College Admissions Evaluate
　　Applicant's Social Media." *The Daily Free Press*, Boston
　　University, 20 Oct. 2017, dailyfreepress.com/blog/2017/10/20
　　/study-shows-college-admissions-evaluate-applicants
　　-social-media/.

Hanra, Hanna. "Maripol: 'Did I Discover Madonna? She Discovered
　　Me!'" *The Guardian*, Guardian News and Media, 20 Mar.
　　2015, www.theguardian.com/fashion/2015/mar/20
　　/maripol-madonna-photographer-stylist-polaroids-exhibition.

Loveland, Mariel. "Reppler Launches 'Reppler Image Score,'
　　Rates Social Network Profile Content for Potential
　　Employers." *Scribbal*, 27 Sept. 2011, www.scribbal.com
　　/reppler-launches-rates-social-network-profile-content-09-27-11/.

The works-cited list includes full information for all sources cited in the paper.

Blaine 7

"Number of Employers Passing on Applicants Due to
 Social Media Posts Continues to Rise." *CareerBuilder*,
 26 June 2014, www.careerbuilder.com/share/aboutus
 /pressreleasesdetail.aspx?sd=6%2F26%2F2014&id
 =pr829&ed=12%2F31%2F2014.

"Online Behavior Jeopardizing College Plans; Admissions Officers
 Checking Social-Networking Sites for Red Flags."
 Education Week, 14 Dec. 2011, p. 11. *Academic One File*,
 www.edweek.org/ew/articles/2011/12/08/14collegeadmit
 .h31.html.

Preston, Jennifer. "Social Media History Becomes a New Job
 Hurdle." *The New York Times*, 20 July 2011, www.nytimes.com
 /2011/07/21/technology/social-media-history-becomes
 -a-new-job-hurdle.html?_r=0.

Somal, Sameer. "Digital Reputation Management 101." *Medium*,
 12 Apr. 2018, medium.com/@SameerSomal
 /digital-reputation-management-101-5506eceb02cb.

Underwood, Alice. "9 Things to Avoid on Social Media While
 Looking for a New Job." *Glassdoor*, 3 Jan. 2018,
 www.glassdoor.com/blog/things-to-avoid-on-social
 -media-job-search/

Be sure that your data comes from recent sources.

11

Using Sources Responsibly

Where Should We Draw the Line with Plagiarism?

In recent years, a number of high-profile plagiarism cases have put a spotlight on how much "borrowing" from other sources is acceptable. Some critics—and many colleges and universities—draw little distinction between intentional and unintentional plagiarism, arguing that any unattributed borrowing is theft. Others are more forgiving, accepting the fact that busy historians or scientists (or students) might not realize that a particular sentence in their notes was not their original idea or might accidentally incorporate a source's exact words (or its unique syntax or phrasing) into their own work without attribution.

In the age of the internet, with its "cut-and-paste" culture, plagiarism has become easier to commit; however, with the development of plagiarism-detection software, it is also now much easier to detect. Still, some colleges and universities are uncomfortable with the idea of using such software, arguing that it establishes an atmosphere of distrust.

On college campuses, as in the professional world, many are questioning and reevaluating the concept of plagiarism. What exactly constitutes plagiarism? How serious a matter is it? Is there a difference between intentional and unintentional plagiarism? Why do people commit plagiarism? What should be done to prevent it? How should it be punished? What are its short- and long-term consequences?

These are some (although by no means all) of the questions to consider as you explore the sources at the end of this chapter. After reading these sources, you will be asked to write an argumentative essay that takes a position on the issue of what exactly constitutes plagiarism and how it should be dealt with.

Understanding Plagiarism

Plagiarism is the act of using the words or ideas of another person without attributing them to their rightful author—that is, presenting those borrowed words and ideas as if they are your own. When you plagiarize, you fail to use sources ethically or responsibly.

TWO DEFINITIONS OF PLAGIARISM

From *MLA Handbook*, Eighth Edition (2016)

Merriam-Webster's Collegiate Dictionary defines plagiarizing as committing "literary theft." Plagiarism is presenting another person's ideas, information, expressions, or entire work as one's own. It is thus a kind of fraud: deceiving others to gain something of value. While plagiarism only sometimes has legal repercussions (e.g., when it involves copyright infringement—violating an authors' exclusive legal right to publication), it is always a serious moral and ethical offense.

From *Publication Manual of the American Psychological Association*, Sixth Edition (2009)

Researchers do not claim the words and ideas of another as their own; they give credit where credit is due (APA Ethics Code Standard 8.11, Plagiarism). Quotation marks should be used to indicate the exact words of another. *Each time* you paraphrase another author (i.e., summarize a passage or rearrange the order of a sentence and change some of the words), you need to credit the source in the text.

The key element of this principle is that authors do not present the work of another as if it were their own work. This can extend to ideas as well as written words. If authors model a study after one done by someone else, the originating author should be given credit. If the rationale for a study was suggested in the Discussion section of someone else's article, that person should be given credit. Given the free exchange of ideas, which is very important to the health of intellectual discourse, authors may not know where an idea for a study originated. If authors do know, however, they should acknowledge the source; this includes personal communications.

For many people, defining plagiarism is simple: it is not "borrowing" but stealing, and it should be dealt with severely. For others, however, it is a more slippery term, seen as considerably more serious if it is intentional than if it is accidental (for example, the result of careless research methods). Most colleges and universities have guidelines that define plagiarism strictly and have penalties in place for those who commit it.

To avoid committing unintentional plagiarism, you need to understand exactly what it is and why it occurs. You also need to learn how to use sources responsibly and to understand what kind of information requires documentation and what kind does not.

Avoiding Unintentional Plagiarism

Even if you do not intentionally misuse the words or ideas of a source, you are still committing plagiarism if you present the work of others as your own. To avoid unintentional plagiarism, you need to maintain control over your sources, keeping track of all the material you use so that you remember where you found each piece of information.

As you take notes, be careful to distinguish your sources' ideas from your own. If you are copying a source's words into your notes, put them in quotation marks. (If you are taking notes by hand, circle the quotation marks; if you are typing your notes, put the quotation marks in boldface or in color.) If you photocopy material, write the full source information on the first page, and staple the pages together. When you download material from the internet, be sure the URL appears on every page. Finally, never cut and paste material from a source directly into your paper.

As you draft your paper, be sure to quote your sources' words accurately (even punctuation must be reproduced exactly as it appears in the source). Be careful not to quote out of context, and be sure that you are presenting your sources' ideas accurately when you summarize or paraphrase. (For information on quoting, paraphrasing, and summarizing source material, see Chapter 9.)

The most common errors that lead to unintentional plagiarism—and how to avoid them—are listed below.

COMMON ERROR	HOW TO AVOID IT
No source information is provided for borrowed material (including statistics).	Always include full parenthetical documentation and a works-cited list that make the source of your information clear to readers. (See Chapter 10.)
A source's ideas are presented as if they are your own original ideas.	Keep track of the sources you consult, and always keep full source information with your sources. Never cut and paste material from an electronic source directly into your paper.
The boundaries of borrowed material are unclear.	Be sure to use an identifying tag *before* and parenthetical documentation *after* borrowed material. (See Chapter 9.)

(Continued)

COMMON ERROR	**HOW TO AVOID IT**
The language of para-phrases or summaries is too close to that of the original source.	Be careful to use original phras-ing and syntax when you write summaries and paraphrases. (See Chapter 9.)
A friend's or tutor's words or ideas appear in your paper.	Be sure that any help you receive is in the form of suggestions, not additions.
Material you wrote for another course is used in your paper.	Always get permission from *both* instructors if you want to reuse work you did for another course, and be sure the material you use is substantially revised.

INTERNET SOURCES AND PLAGIARISM

The internet presents a particular challenge for students as they try to avoid plagiarism. Committing plagiarism (intentional or unintentional) with electronic sources is easy because it is simple to cut and paste material from online sources into a paper. However, inserting even a sentence or two from an internet source (including a blog, an email, or a website) into a paper without quotation marks and documentation constitutes plagiarism.

It is also not acceptable to use a visual found on the internet without acknowledging its source. This includes:

- Graphs
- Charts
- Tables
- Photographs

Finally, even if an internet source does not identify its author, the words or ideas you find there are not your own original material, so you must identify their source.

INTENTIONAL PLAGIARISM

Deliberately plagiarizing from a source, handing in another student's paper as your own, or buying a paper from an internet site is never acceptable. Such acts constitute serious violations of academic integrity. Creating your own original work is an important part of the educational experience, and misrepresenting someone else's work as your own undermines the goals of education.

Knowing What to Document

Documentation is the practice of identifying borrowed material and providing the proper bibliographic information for each source. Different academic disciplines require different formats for documentation—for example, English uses MLA, and psychology uses APA. For this reason, you should be sure to check with your instructor to find out what documentation style to use. (For information on MLA and APA documentation formats, see Chapter 10 and Appendix B, respectively.)

Regardless of the discipline, the following kinds of information should always be documented:

- Quotations from a source
- Summaries of a source's main points
- Paraphrases of a source's original ideas
- Opinions, judgments, and conclusions that are not your own
- Statistics from a source
- Visuals from a source
- Data from charts or graphs in a source

The following kinds of information, however, do not require documentation:

- **Common knowledge**—that is, factual information that can be found in several different sources. Examples of different sources include the following:
  - A writer's date of birth
  - A scientific fact
  - The location of a famous battle

- Familiar quotations—anything from proverbs to frequently quoted lines from Shakespeare's plays—that you expect readers will recognize

- Your own original opinions, judgments, and conclusions

⊘ EXERCISE 11.1 DECIDING WHAT TO DOCUMENT

Which of the following statements requires documentation, and why?

1. Doris Kearns Goodwin is a prize-winning historian.

2. Doris Kearns Goodwin's *The Fitzgeralds and the Kennedys* is a 900-page book with about 3,500 footnotes.

3. In 1994, Lynne McTaggart accused Goodwin of borrowing material from a book that McTaggart wrote.

4. My own review of the background suggests that Goodwin's plagiarism was unintentional.

5. Still, these accusations left Goodwin to face the "slings and arrows" of media criticism.

6. As Goodwin explains, "The more intensive and far-reaching a historian's research, the greater the difficulty of citation."

7. In her defense, Goodwin argued that the more research a historian does, the harder it is to keep track of sources.

8. Some people still remain convinced that Goodwin committed plagiarism.

9. Goodwin believes that her careful research methods, which she has described in exhaustive detail, should have prevented accidental plagiarism.

10. Some of Goodwin's critics have concluded that her reputation as a historian was hurt by the plagiarism charges.

⊘ EXERCISE 11.2 KNOWING WHEN TO DOCUMENT

Assume you are using the following editorial as a source. Identify two pieces of information you would need to document (for example, statistics). Then, identify two pieces of information you would *not* need to document (for example, common knowledge).

This editorial was first published on May 1, 2013.

WHEN BEYONCÉ'S INSPIRATION TURNS INTO IMITATION

ERIKA RAMIREZ

They say imitation is the sincerest form of flattery, but what if the person 1 imitating is a polarizing icon that should be doing otherwise—someone like Beyoncé?

On Monday (April 29), pop singer Kerli posted a side-by-side photo on her 2 Facebook page of her and Beyoncé donning the same Amato Haute Couture dress. The photo of Beyoncé comes from the pages of her 2013 *Mrs. Carter Show* tour book.

Except, it's not just the Furne One designed dress—which also Nicki Minaj 3 wore in her "Va Va Voom" video—that's similar in the photo. Both singers can be seen painted in white, from head to toe, and stylistically posed as sculptures.

No one owns a look, image, dance move (after all, how many artists have 4 pulled out signature Michael Jackson moves?), or in this case, an experimental costume. They're not copyrighted property, but filed as intellectual property.

Any artist, including Beyoncé, can wear whatever another artist wore, 5 but that multiplicity gets suspicious and easily pegged as stealing. And understandably so, when it's not only the look of the artist that is being traced, but his or her entire idea.

Beyoncé first caught flak for working up a dance similar to Josephine 6 Baker's iconic banana dance in her "Deja Vu" video, then was seen sporting a skirt with dangling bananas when performing the "B'Day" track. But let's be honest: that wasn't *that* serious, at least not at that point in her 20-year plus career. She later borrowed from Bob Fosse's routine, "Mexican Breakfast," in the video for her girls anthem, "Single Ladies (Put a Ring on It)." There are also references to "Rich Man's Frug" scene (of Bob Fosse's "Sweet Charity") in Bey's "Get Me Bodied" video.

> "There's a difference between inspiration and imitation."

There's a difference between inspiration and imitation. "Countdown" is 7 a good example of Beyoncé doing both in one piece of work. She references Audrey Hepburn's *Funny Face* dancing and both Hepburn and Peggy Moffitt's late 50's/early 60's fashion, then elaborates with color schemes and pairs the choreography perfectly with the pace of the soundscapes. She also samples Boyz II Men's countdown from their song, "Uhh Ahh."

As the video continues, we see Bey using the same choreography, cinema- 8 tography, and costumes that Belgian choreographer and dancer, Anne Teresa De Keersmaeker, used in "Rosas Danst Rosas." It's one thing to be inspired by someone else's work and revamp with one's personal style, but it's another to duplicate exact movements, which is ultimately violating the artist's intellectual property. Context matters.

Before the debut of "Countdown," Beyoncé was criticized for nearly repli- 9
cating Italian singer Lorella Cuccarini's live performance with her performance
of "Run the World (Girls)" at the 2011 Billboard Music Awards. She later stated
that she had hired the same choreographers that had worked on Cuccarini's
performance, but it's still puzzling as to why she didn't work with them to create a groundbreaking concept of her own.

The choreography, seen in the performance and the song's accompany- 10
ing music video, comes from Mozambique dance troupe Tofo Tofo. Instead of
thanking them for the inspiration after the fact, as she's done with Cuccarini
and Keersmaeker, Beyoncé brought them to the U.S. and hired them to dance
alongside her in the "Run the World (Girls)" video.

The 2011 song, off her fourth studio album *4* swipes the beat from Major 11
Lazer's 2009 "Pon De Floor." According to Diplo, one half of Major Lazer,
the making of "Run the World (Girls)" started out as a "joke" (whatever that
means).

Beyoncé's "1 + 1" video features scenes similar to the unfinished French 12
film, *Le'Enfer*, while her "Love On Top" video has dancing scenes much the
same as those in New Edition's "If It Isn't Love" video.

But more bothersome than Bey's inspiration-turned-imitation act—and 13
less subtle as her career progresses—is that she's playing off the risks that other
artists have been brave enough to take (and appropriately praised for) instead
of challenging herself and taken some herself.

Perhaps visual and dance concepts don't come as naturally to her as vocal 14
prowess, but I'm doubtful that she can recruit those for which it does. No
shots at Frank Gatson Jr. (but shots?) who is a director, visual artist developer,
creative director, and choreographer who's worked closely with greats like
Diana Ross, Mariah Carey, Tina Turner, and consecutively with Beyoncé.

Even as a vocal performer, Beyoncé is more of a canvas than a creator. 15
The majority of her discography was written (yes, some co-written) by other
singer-songwriters, from the likes of Ne-Yo to The-Dream. But the formula works
for her: she holds 19 top 10s on Hot R&B/Hip-Hop Songs chart with six No. 1s.

The bittersweet side of Beyoncé stealing imitable art is that when she does, 16
she does it well. Perhaps it's why we give the diva a pass, or two, and will in the
future. Let's also not forget that voice of hers and stage stamina that hypnotizes
many into disregarding such acts—after all, words and imagery can only strike
a chord or transcend to a degree if they're executed with astounding talent.

Revising to Eliminate Plagiarism

As you revise your papers, scrutinize your work carefully to be sure you
have not inadvertently committed plagiarism. To help you understand the
most common situations in which accidental plagiarism is likely to occur,
read this paragraph from page 1 of "Don't Fall for the Myths about Online
Privacy," by Shelley Fralic, which appears in Chapter 9 (p. 320).

Facebook's fine print, like that of many internet portals, is specific and offers a variety of self-selected "privacy" options.

But to think that any interaction with it, and its ilk, is truly private is beyond absurd.

How can there still be people out there who still don't get that Netflix and Facebook, Instagram and Twitter, Google and Tinder, and pretty much every keystroke or communication we register on a smartphone or laptop, not to mention a loyalty card and the GPS in your car, are constantly tracking and sifting and collating everything we do?

To avoid unintentional plagiarism when using material from this paragraph in an essay of your own, follow these four guidelines:

1. **Be sure you have identified your source and provided appropriate documentation.**

   PLAGIARISM

   Even though Facebook users can select from various privacy options, it makes no sense to assume that engaging with Facebook and similar sites guarantees privacy.

This student writer does not quote directly from Fralic's discussion, but his summary of her comments does not represent her original ideas and therefore needs to be documented.

The following correct use of source material includes both an **identifying tag** (a phrase that identifies Fralic as the source of the ideas) and a page number that directs readers to the exact location of the material the student is summarizing. (Full source information is provided in the works-cited list.)

   CORRECT

   According to Shelley Fralic, even though Facebook users can select from among various privacy options, it makes no sense to assume that engaging with Facebook and similar sites guarantees privacy (1).

2. **Be sure you have placed quotation marks around borrowed words.**

   PLAGIARISM

   According to Shelley Fralic, it is hard to imagine that people still don't understand that Facebook and similar sites are constantly tracking and sifting and collating everything we do (1).

Although the preceding sentence provides parenthetical documentation and includes an identifying tag indicating the source of its ideas, it uses Fralic's exact words without placing them in quotation marks.

To avoid committing plagiarism, the student needs to either place quotation marks around Fralic's words or paraphrase her comments.

> **CORRECT (BORROWED WORDS IN QUOTATION MARKS)**
>
> According to Shelley Fralic, it is hard to imagine that people still don't understand that Facebook and similar sites "are constantly tracking and sifting and collating everything we do" (1).

> **CORRECT (BORROWED WORDS PARAPHRASED)**
>
> According to Shelley Fralic, it is hard to imagine that people still don't understand that Facebook and similar sites are always following our posts (1).

3. **Be sure you have indicated the boundaries of the borrowed material.**

> **PLAGIARISM**
>
> Although Facebook users can select from among various privacy options, engaging with Facebook is not private. It is hard to imagine that anyone still believes that Facebook is not "constantly tracking and sifting and collating everything we do" (1).

In the preceding passage, the student correctly places Fralic's words in quotation marks and includes appropriate parenthetical documentation. However, she does not indicate that other ideas in the passage, although not quoted directly, are also Fralic's.

To avoid committing plagiarism, the student needs to use identifying tags to indicate the boundaries of the borrowed material, which goes beyond the quoted words.

> **CORRECT**
>
> According to Shelley Fralic, although Facebook users can select from among various privacy options, engaging with Facebook is not private. It is hard to imagine, Fralic observes, that anyone still believes that Facebook is not "constantly tracking and sifting and collating everything we do" (1).

4. **Be sure you have used your own phrasing and syntax.**

PLAGIARISM

As Shelley Fralic observes, Facebook's fine print offers various self-selected "privacy" options. However, she believes that it is beyond absurd to think that interacting with Facebook and its ilk is truly private. She questions how there can still be people who don't realize that sites like Netflix, Facebook, and Instagram—and pretty much every keystroke on our smartphones or laptops, and even our loyalty cards and GPS—are constantly tracking and sifting and collating everything we do (1).

The student who wrote the paragraph above does provide an identifying tag and parenthetical documentation to identify the source of his ideas. However, his paragraph's phrasing and syntax are almost identical to Fralic's.

In the following paragraph, the writer correctly paraphrases and summarizes Friedman's ideas, quoting a few distinctive passages. (See Chapter 9 for information on paraphrase and summary.)

CORRECT

According to Shelley Fralic, although Facebook does permit its users to choose among various privacy options, using the site is by no means a private activity. Fralic wonders how anyone can still not understand that the sites we visit—not just Facebook, but also Instagram, Twitter, and the rest—as well as "pretty much every keystroke or communication we register on a smartphone or laptop . . . are constantly tracking and sifting and collating everything we do" (1).

● EXERCISE 11.3 SYNTHESIZING SOURCES RESPONSIBLY

The following student paragraph synthesizes information from two different sources (which appear on pp. 364–65, following the student paragraph), but the student writer has not used sources responsibly. (For information on synthesis, see Chapter 9.) Read the sources and the paragraph, and then make the following changes:

- Insert quotation marks where the student has quoted a source's words.

- Edit paraphrased and summarized material if necessary so that its syntax and phrasing are not too close to those of a source.

■ Add parenthetical documentation where necessary to acknowledge the use of a source's words or original ideas.

■ Add identifying tags where necessary to clarify the scope of the borrowed material or to differentiate material from the two sources.

■ Check every quoted passage once more to see if the quotation adds something vital to the paragraph. If it does not, summarize or paraphrase the source's words instead.

STUDENT PARAGRAPH

In recent years, psychologists have focused on the idea that girls (unlike boys) face a crisis of self-esteem as they approach adolescence. Both Carol Gilligan and Mary Pipher did research to support this idea, showing how girls lose their self-confidence in adolescence because of sexist cultural expectations. Women's groups have expressed concern that the school system favors boys and is biased against girls. In fact, boys are often regarded not just as classroom favorites but also as bullies who represent obstacles on the path to gender justice for girls. Recently, however, this impression that boys are somehow privileged while girls are shortchanged is being challenged.

Source 1

That boys are in disrepute is not accidental. For many years women's groups have complained that boys benefit from a school system that favors them and is biased against girls. "Schools shortchange girls," declares the American Association of University Women. . . . A stream of books and pamphlets cite research showing not only that boys are classroom favorites but also that they are given to schoolyard violence and sexual harassment.

In the view that has prevailed in American education over the past decade, boys are resented, both as the unfairly privileged sex and as obstacles on the path to gender justice for girls. This perspective is promoted in schools of education, and many a teacher now feels that girls need and deserve special indemnifying consideration. "It is really clear that boys are Number One in this society and in most of the world," says Patricia O'Reilly, a professor of education and the director of the Gender Equity Center, at the University of Cincinnati.

The idea that schools and society grind girls down has given rise to an array of laws and policies intended to curtail the advantage boys have and to redress the harm done to girls. That girls are treated as the second sex in school and consequently suffer, that boys are accorded privileges and consequently benefit—these are things everyone is presumed to know. But they are not true.

—Christina Hoff Sommers, "The War against Boys"

Source 2

Girls face an inevitable crisis of self-esteem as they approach adolescence. They are in danger of losing their voices, drowning, and facing a devastating dip in self-regard that boys don't experience. This is the picture that Carol Gilligan presented on the basis of her research at the Emma Willard School, a private girls' school in Troy, N.Y. While Gilligan did not refer to genes in her analysis of girls' vulnerability, she did cite both the "wall of Western culture" and deep early childhood socialization as reasons.

Her theme was echoed in 1994 by the clinical psychologist Mary Pipher's surprise best seller, *Reviving Ophelia* (Putnam, 1994), which spent three years on the *New York Times* best-seller list. Drawing on case studies rather than systematic research, Pipher observed how naturally outgoing, confident girls get worn down by sexist cultural expectations. Gilligan's and Pipher's ideas have also been supported by a widely cited study in 1990 by the American Association of University Women. That report, published in 1991, claimed that teenage girls experience a "free-fall in self-esteem from which some will never recover."

The idea that girls have low self-esteem has by now become part of the academic canon as well as fodder for the popular media. But is it true? No.

—Rosalind C. Barnett and Caryl Rivers, "Men Are from Earth, and So Are Women. It's Faulty Research That Sets Them Apart"

Where Should We Draw the Line with Plagiarism?

dennizn/Alamy Stock Photo

Reread the At Issue box on page 353. Then, read the sources on the following pages. As you read these sources, you will be asked to answer questions and to complete some activities. This work will help you to understand the content and structure of the material you read. When you have read the sources, you will be ready to write an argumentative essay in which you take a position on the topic, "Where Should We Draw the Line with Plagiarism?"

SOURCES

 Trip Gabriel, "Plagiarism Lines Blur for Students in Digital Age," page 367

 Jennifer Mott-Smith, "Bad Idea about Writing: Plagiarism Deserves to Be Punished," page 371

 Richard A. Posner, "The Truth about Plagiarism," page 375

 Helen Rubinstein, "When Plagiarism Is a Plea for Help," page 378

 Dan Ariely, "Essay Mills: A Coarse Lesson in Cheating," page 382

 Visual Argument: Term Papers for Sale Advertisement (web page), page 385

This article is from the August 1, 2010, edition of the *New York Times.*

PLAGIARISM LINES BLUR FOR STUDENTS IN DIGITAL AGE

TRIP GABRIEL

At Rhode Island College, a freshman copied and pasted from a website's fre- 1
quently asked questions page about homelessness—and did not think he
needed to credit a source in his assignment because the page did not include
author information.

At DePaul University, the tip-off to one student's copying was the purple 2
shade of several paragraphs he had lifted from the web; when confronted by
a writing tutor his professor had sent him to, he was not defensive—he just
wanted to know how to change purple text to black.

And at the University of Maryland, a student reprimanded for copy- 3
ing from Wikipedia in a paper on the Great Depression said he thought its
entries—unsigned and collectively written—did not need to be credited since
they counted, essentially, as common knowledge.

Professors used to deal with plagiarism by admonishing students to give 4
credit to others and to follow the style guide for citations, and pretty much left
it at that.

But these cases—typical ones, according to writing tutors and officials 5
responsible for discipline at the three schools who described the plagiarism—
suggest that many students simply do not grasp that using words they did not
write is a serious misdeed.

It is a disconnect that is growing in the internet age as concepts of intel- 6
lectual property, copyright, and originality are under assault in the unbridled
exchange of online information, say educators who study plagiarism.

Digital technology makes copying and pasting easy, of course. But that is 7
the least of it. The internet may also be redefining how students—who came
of age with music file-sharing, Wikipedia, and web-linking—understand the
concept of authorship and the singularity of any text or image.

"Now we have a whole generation of students who've grown up with infor- 8
mation that just seems to be hanging out there in cyberspace and doesn't seem
to have an author," said Teresa Fishman, director of the Center for Academic
Integrity at Clemson University. "It's possible to believe this information is just
out there for anyone to take."

Professors who have studied plagiarism do not try to excuse it—many are 9
champions of academic honesty on their campuses—but rather try to understand why it is so widespread.

In surveys from 2006 to 2010 by Donald L. McCabe, a co-founder of the 10
Center for Academic Integrity and a business professor at Rutgers University, about 40 percent of 14,000 undergraduates admitted to copying a few
sentences in written assignments.

Perhaps more significant, the number who believed that copying from the 11 web constitutes "serious cheating" is declining—to 29 percent on average in recent surveys from 34 percent earlier in the decade.

Sarah Brookover, a senior at the Rutgers campus in Camden, N.J., said 12 many of her classmates blithely cut and paste without attribution.

"This generation has always existed in a world where media and intellec- 13 tual property don't have the same gravity," said Ms. Brookover, who at 31 is older than most undergraduates. "When you're sitting at your computer, it's the same machine you've downloaded music with, possibly illegally, the same machine you streamed videos for free that showed on HBO last night."

Ms. Brookover, who works at the 14 campus library, has pondered the differences between researching in the stacks and online. "Because you're not walking into a library, you're not physically hold-

> "Online, 'everything can belong to you really easily.'"

ing the article, which takes you closer to 'this doesn't belong to me,'" she said. Online, "everything can belong to you really easily."

A University of Notre Dame anthropologist, Susan D. Blum, disturbed by 15 the high rates of reported plagiarism, set out to understand how students view authorship and the written word, or "texts" in Ms. Blum's academic language.

She conducted her ethnographic research among 234 Notre Dame under- 16 graduates. "Today's students stand at the crossroads of a new way of conceiving texts and the people who create them and who quote them," she wrote last year in the book *My Word! Plagiarism and College Culture*, published by Cornell University Press.

Ms. Blum argued that student writing exhibits some of the same qualities 17 of pastiche that drive other creative endeavors today—TV shows that constantly reference other shows or rap music that samples from earlier songs.

In an interview, she said the idea of an author whose singular effort 18 creates an original work is rooted in Enlightenment ideas of the individual. It is buttressed by the Western concept of intellectual property rights as secured by copyright law. But both traditions are being challenged. "Our notion of authorship and originality was born, it flourished, and it may be waning," Ms. Blum said.

She contends that undergraduates are less interested in cultivating a unique 19 and authentic identity—as their 1960s counterparts were—than in trying on many different personas, which the web enables with social networking.

"If you are not so worried about presenting yourself as absolutely unique, 20 then it's O.K. if you say other people's words, it's O.K. if you say things you don't believe, it's O.K. if you write papers you couldn't care less about because they accomplish the task, which is turning something in and getting a grade," Ms. Blum said, voicing student attitudes. "And it's O.K. if you put words out there without getting any credit."

The notion that there might be a new model young person, who freely 21 borrows from the vortex of information to mash up a new creative work, fueled a brief brouhaha earlier this year with Helene Hegemann, a German teenager whose best-selling novel about Berlin club life turned out to include passages lifted from others.

Instead of offering an abject apology, Ms. Hegemann insisted, "There's no such thing as originality anyway, just authenticity." A few critics rose to her defense, and the book remained a finalist for a fiction prize (but did not win). 22

That theory does not wash with Sarah Wilensky, a senior at Indiana University, who said that relaxing plagiarism standards "does not foster creativity, it fosters laziness." 23

"You're not coming up with new ideas if you're grabbing and mixing and matching," said Ms. Wilensky, who took aim at Ms. Hegemann in a column in her student newspaper headlined "Generation Plagiarism." 24

"It may be increasingly accepted, but there are still plenty of creative people—authors and artists and scholars—who are doing original work," Ms. Wilensky said in an interview. "It's kind of an insult that that ideal is gone, and now we're left only to make collages of the work of previous generations." 25

In the view of Ms. Wilensky, whose writing skills earned her the role of informal editor of other students' papers in her freshman dorm, plagiarism has nothing to do with trendy academic theories. 26

The main reason it occurs, she said, is because students leave high school unprepared for the intellectual rigors of college writing. 27

"If you're taught how to closely read sources and synthesize them into your own original argument in middle and high school, you're not going to be tempted to plagiarize in college, and you certainly won't do so unknowingly," she said. 28

At the University of California, Davis, of the 196 plagiarism cases referred to the disciplinary office last year, a majority did not involve students ignorant of the need to credit the writing of others. 29

Many times, said Donald J. Dudley, who oversees the discipline office on the campus of 32,000, it was students who intentionally copied—knowing it was wrong—who were "unwilling to engage the writing process." 30

"Writing is difficult, and doing it well takes time and practice," he said. 31

And then there was a case that had nothing to do with a younger generation's evolving view of authorship. A student accused of plagiarism came to Mr. Dudley's office with her parents, and the father admitted that he was the one responsible for the plagiarism. The wife assured Mr. Dudley that it would not happen again. 32

⊙ AT ISSUE: SOURCES FOR UNDERSTANDING PLAGIARISM

1. Gabriel begins inductively, presenting three paragraphs of evidence before he states his thesis. Is this the best strategy, or should these examples appear later in his discussion? Explain.

2. In paragraph 5, Gabriel notes that "many students simply do not grasp that using words they did not write is a serious misdeed." Is this his thesis statement? Does he take a position, or is he just presenting information?

3. Why, according to Gabriel, is plagiarism so widespread? Do you think the reasons he cites in any way excuse plagiarism—at least accidental plagiarism? Does Gabriel seem to think they do?

4. What is *pastiche* (para. 17)? What is a collage (25)? How does the concept of pastiche or collage apply to plagiarism? Do you see the use of pastiche in TV shows or popular music (17) as different from its use in academic writing? Why or why not?

5. Summarize Sarah Wilensky's views (23–28) on the issue Gabriel discusses. Do you agree with her? Do you agree with Helene Hegemann's statement, "There's no such thing as originality anyway, just authenticity" (22)?

6. Do you think the anecdote in paragraph 32 is a strong ending for this article? Does the paragraph need a more forceful concluding statement? Explain.

This article appeared in *Insider Higher Education* on May 23, 2017.

BAD IDEA ABOUT WRITING: PLAGIARISM DESERVES TO BE PUNISHED

JENNIFER MOTT-SMITH

"College Plagiarism Reaches All-Time High"
"Studies Find More Students Cheating, With High Achievers No Exception"

Headlines like these from *the Huffington Post* and *the New York Times* scream at us about an increase in plagiarism. As a society, we feel embattled, surrounded by falling standards; we bemoan the increasing immorality of our youth. Plagiarism, we know, is an immoral act, a simple case of right and wrong, and as such, deserves to be punished. 1

However, nothing is simple about plagiarism. In fact, the more we examine plagiarism, the more inconsistencies we find, and the more confusion. 2

How we think about the issue of plagiarism is clouded by the fact that it is often spoken of as a crime. Plagiarism is not only seen as immoral; it is seen as stealing—the stealing of ideas or words. In his book *Free Culture*, Stanford law professor Lawrence Lessig questions what it can possibly mean to steal an idea. 3

> "I understand what I am taking when I take the picnic table you put in your backyard. I am taking a thing, the picnic table, and after I take it, you don't have it. But what am I taking when I take the good idea you had to put a picnic table in the backyard—by, for example, going to Sears, buying a table, and putting it in my backyard? What is the thing that I am taking then?"

Lessig gets at the idea that, when a person borrows an idea, no harm is done to the party from whom it was taken. But what about loss in revenues as a form of harm? Surely there is no loss of revenues when a student plagiarizes a paper. From Lessig's metaphor we can see that theft, and even copyright infringement, are not entirely apt ways to think about plagiarism. 4

But Lessig's metaphor does not help us understand that, in academic writing, acknowledgment of sources is highly valued. Neither does it reveal that taking ideas and using them in your own writing, with conventional attribution, is a sophisticated skill that requires a good deal of practice to master. 5

There are at least three important things to understand about the complexity of using sources. First, ideas are often a mixture of one's own ideas, those we read and those we discuss with friends—making it hard or even impossible to sort out who owns what. Second, writers who are learning a new field often "try out" ideas and phrases from other writers in order to master the field. That process, which allows them to learn, involves little or no deceit. And third, expectations for citing sources vary among contexts and readers, making it not only confusing to learn the rules but impossible to satisfy them all. 6

It is quite hard to separate one's ideas from those of others. When we read, 7 we always bring our own knowledge to what we're reading. Writers cannot say everything; they have to rely on readers to supply their own contribution to make meaning. One difficulty arises when you read an argument with unnamed steps. As a good reader, you fill them in so you can make sense of the argument. Now, if you were to write about those missing steps, would they be your ideas or those of your source?

Writers may reuse the ideas of others, but surely they know when they 8 reuse words, so should they attribute them? Perhaps not. Words are not discrete entities that can be recombined in countless ways, rather, they fall into patterns that serve certain ways of thinking, the very ways of thinking or habits of mind that we try to instill in students.

The fact is that language is formulaic, meaning that certain words com- 9 monly occur together. There are many idioms, such as "toe the line" or "cut corners" that need not be attributed. There are also many co-occurring words that don't quite count as idioms, such as "challenge the status quo," "it should also be noted that . . ." and "The purpose of this study is to . . ." that similarly do not require attribution. Those are called collocations. Student writers need to acquire and use a great number of them in academic writing. What this means is that not every verbatim reuse is plagiarism.

> "Much research has shown that patchwriting is not deceitful and therefore should not be punished."

Moreover, imposing strict rules 10 against word reuse may function to prevent student writers from learning to write in their fields. When student writers reuse patterns of words without attribution in an attempt to learn how to sound like a journalist, say, or a biologist, or a literary theorist, it is called *patchwriting*. In fact, not only student writers but all writers patch together pieces of text from sources, using their own language to sew the seams, in order to learn the language of a new field.

Because of the complex way in which patchwriting mixes text from var- 11 ious sources, it can be extremely difficult to cite one's sources. Despite this lack of attribution, much research has shown that patchwriting is not deceitful and therefore should not be punished. In fact, some scholars are interested in exploring how writing teachers could use the concept of patchwriting to help student writers develop their own writing skills.

The third reason that it is not always easy to acknowledge sources is that 12 expectations for referencing vary widely and what counts as plagiarism depends on context. If, for instance, you use a piece of historic information in a novel, you don't have to cite it, but if you use the same piece of information in a history paper, you do. Journalists typically do not supply citations, although they have fact checkers making sure their claims are accurate. In business, people often start their reports by cutting and pasting earlier reports without attribution. And in the academy, research has shown that the reuse of words in science articles is much more common and accepted than it is in the humanities.

In high school, student writers probably used textbooks that did not con- 13 tain citations, and once in college, they may observe their professors giving lectures that come straight from the textbook without citation, cribbing one another's syllabi and cutting and pasting the plagiarism policy into their syllabi. They may even notice that their university lifted the wording of its plagiarism policy from another institution!

In addition to those differing standards for different genres or fields of 14 study, research has also shown that individual "experts" such as experienced writers and teachers do not agree whether or not a given piece of writing counts as plagiarism. Given such wide disagreement over what constitutes plagiarism, it is quite difficult, perhaps impossible, for student writers to meet everyone's expectations for proper attribution. Rather than assuming that they are trying to pass off someone else's work as their own and therefore deserve punishment, we should recognize the complexity of separating one's ideas from those of others, mastering authoritative phrases and meeting diverse attribution standards.

While most people feel that plagiarism deserves punishment, some under- 15 stand that plagiarism is not necessarily deceitful or deserving censure. Today, many writers and writing teachers reject the image of the writer as working alone, using (God-given) talent to produce an original piece of work. In fact, writers often do two things that are proscribed by plagiarism policies: they recombine ideas in their writing and they collaborate with others.

Interestingly, the image of the lone, divinely inspired writer is only a few 16 hundred years old, a European construct from the Romantic era. Before the eighteenth century or so, writers who copied were respected as writers. Even today, rather than seeing copying as deceitful, we sometimes view it as a sign of respect or free publicity.

Today, millennial students often copy without deceitful intent. Reposting 17 content on their Facebook pages and sharing links with their friends, they may not cite because they are making an allusion; readers who recognize the source without a citation share the in-joke.

In school, millennials may not cite because they are not used to doing so 18 or they believe that having too many citations detracts from their authority. In either case, these are not students trying to get away with passing someone else's work off as their own, and, in fact, many studies have concluded that plagiarism, particularly that of second-language student writers, is not done with the intent to deceive.

Despite these complexities of textual reuse, most faculty members never- 19 theless expect student writers to do their "own work." In fact, student writers are held to a higher standard and punished more rigorously than established writers.

What is even more troublesome is that teachers' determinations of when 20 plagiarism has occurred is more complicated than simply noting whether a student has given credit to sources or not. Research has shown that teachers let inadequate attribution go if they feel the overall sophistication or authority of the paper is good, whereas they are stricter about citing rules when the sophistication or authority is weak. Furthermore, they tend to more readily recognize authority in papers written by students who are members of a powerful group (e.g., whites, native English speakers or students whose parents went to college). Thus, in some instances, plagiarism may be more about social inequity than individual deceit.

As we come to realize that writers combine their ideas with those of others 21 in ways that cannot always be separated out for the purposes of attribution, that writers often reuse phrases in acceptable ways, that citing standards themselves vary widely and are often in the eye of the beholder, and that enforcement of plagiarism rules is an equity issue, the studies and articles panicking over plagiarism make less and less sense. In looking at plagiarism from the different perspectives offered by collaborative writers and today's millennial student writers, we can see that much plagiarism is not about stealing ideas or deceiving readers.

Unless plagiarism is out-and-out cheating, like cutting and pasting an 22 entire paper from the internet or paying someone to write it, we should be cautious about reacting to plagiarism with the intent to punish. For much plagiarism, a better response is to relax and let writers continue to practice the difficult skill of using sources.

⊘ AT ISSUE: SOURCES FOR UNDERSTANDING PLAGIARISM

1. Many people, like law professor Lawrence Lessig (quoted in paragraph 3), see plagiarism as theft, but Mott-Smith disagrees. Why?

2. In paragraph 6, Mott-Smith introduces three key concepts to explain "the complexity of using sources." In your own words, summarize these three ideas.

3. What does Mott-Smith mean when she says that language is "formulaic" (para. 9)? Why does she believe this characterization explains—or even excuses—some plagiarism?

4. Mott-Smith points out that expectations for citing sources can vary from one situation to another. For example, different instructors and different kinds of writing tasks may have different citation standards. Do you believe that the fact that there is so little agreement about what constitutes plagiarism means that some kinds of plagiarism should not be punished? Is this what Mott-Smith believes?

5. How are Mott-Smith's ideas about student plagiarism like and unlike Richard Posner's ideas (p. 375) about plagiarism in professional settings?

6. According to Mott-Smith, what is the difference between "out-and-out cheating" (22) and the kind of casual, inadvertent plagiarism that occurs more widely? How does she believe each of these two kinds of plagiarism should be dealt with? What do you think?

This essay appeared in *Newsday* on May 18, 2003.

THE TRUTH ABOUT PLAGIARISM

RICHARD A. POSNER

Plagiarism is considered by most writers, teachers, journalists, scholars, and even 1
members of the general public to be the capital intellectual crime. Being caught
out in plagiarism can blast a politician's career, earn a college student expulsion,
and destroy a writer's, scholar's, or journalist's reputation. In recent days, for example, the *New York Times* has referred to "widespread fabrication and plagiarism"
by reporter Jayson Blair as "a low point in the 152-year history of the newspaper."

In James Hynes' splendid satiric novella of plagiarism, *Casting the Runes*, 2
the plagiarist, having by black magic murdered one of the historians whom he
plagiarized and tried to murder a second, is himself killed by the very same
black magic, deployed by the widow of his murder victim.

There is a danger of overkill. Plagiarism 3
can be a form of fraud, but it is no accident that,
unlike real theft, it is not a crime. If a thief steals
your car, you are out the market value of the car,

> "There is a
> danger of overkill."

but if a writer copies material from a book you wrote, you don't have to replace
the book. At worst, the undetected plagiarist obtains a reputation that he does
not deserve (that is the element of fraud in plagiarism). The real victim of his
fraud is not the person whose work he copies, but those of his competitors who
scruple to enhance their own reputations by such means.

The most serious plagiarisms are by students and professors, whose unde- 4
tected plagiarisms disrupt the system of student and scholarly evaluation.
The least serious are those that earned the late Stephen Ambrose and Doris
Kearns Goodwin such obloquy° last year. Popular historians, they jazzed
up their books with vivid passages copied from previous historians without
quotation marks, though with footnote attributions that made their "crime"
easy to detect. (One reason that plagiarism, like littering, is punished heavily,
even though an individual act of plagiarism usually does little or no harm, is
that it is normally very difficult to detect—but not in the case of Ambrose and
Goodwin.) Competing popular historians might have been injured, but I'm
not aware of anyone actually claiming this.

Abusive language

Confusion of plagiarism with theft is one reason plagiarism engenders 5
indignation; another is a confusion of it with copyright infringement. Wholesale copying of copyrighted material is an infringement of a property right, and
legal remedies are available to the copyright holder. But the copying of brief
passages, even from copyrighted materials, is permissible under the doctrine
of "fair use," while wholesale copying from material that is in the public
domain—material that never was copyrighted, or on which the copyright has
expired—presents no copyright issue at all.

Plagiarism of work in the public domain is more common than otherwise. 6 Consider a few examples: *West Side Story* is a thinly veiled copy (with music added) of *Romeo and Juliet*, which in turn plagiarized Arthur Brooke's *The Tragicall Historye of Romeo and Juliet*, published in 1562, which in turn copied from several earlier Romeo and Juliets, all of which were copies of Ovid's story of Pyramus and Thisbe.

Paradise Lost plagiarizes the book of Genesis in the Old Testament. 7 Classical musicians plagiarize folk melodies (think only of Dvorak, Bartok, and Copland) and often "quote" (as musicians say) from earlier classical works. Edouard Manet's most famous painting, *Déjeuner sur l'herbe*, copies earlier paintings by Raphael, Titian, and Courbet, and *My Fair Lady* plagiarized Shaw's play *Pygmalion*, while Woody Allen's movie *Play It Again, Sam* "quotes" a famous scene from *Casablanca*. Countless movies are based on books, such as *The Thirty-Nine Steps* on John Buchan's novel of that name or *For Whom the Bell Tolls* on Hemingway's novel.

Many of these "plagiarisms" were authorized, and perhaps none was 8 deceptive; they are what Christopher Ricks in his excellent book *Allusions to the Poets* helpfully terms *allusion* rather than *plagiarism*. But what they show is that copying with variations is an important form of creativity, and this should make us prudent and measured in our condemnations of plagiarism.

Especially when the term is extended from literal copying to the copy- 9 ing of ideas. Another phrase for copying an idea, as distinct from the form in which it is expressed, is dissemination of ideas. If one needs a license to repeat another person's idea, or if one risks ostracism by one's professional community for failing to credit an idea to its originator, who may be forgotten or unknown, the dissemination of ideas is impeded.

I have heard authors of history textbooks criticized for failing to doc- 10 ument their borrowing of ideas from previous historians. This is an absurd criticism. The author of a textbook makes no claim to originality; rather the contrary—the most reliable, if not necessarily the most exciting, textbook is one that confines itself to ideas already well accepted, not at all novel.

It would be better if the term *plagiarism* were confined to literal copying, 11 and moreover literal copying that is not merely unacknowledged but decep- tive. Failing to give credit where credit is due should be regarded as a lesser, indeed usually merely venial, offense.

The concept of plagiarism has expanded, and the sanctions for it, though 12 they remain informal rather than legal, have become more severe, in tandem with the rise of individualism. Journal articles are no longer published anon- ymously, and ghostwriters demand that their contributions be acknowledged.

Individualism and a cult of originality go hand in hand. Each of us 13 supposes that our contribution to society is unique rather than fungible° and so deserves public recognition, which plagiarism clouds.

This is a modern view. We should be aware that the high value placed on 14 originality is a specific cultural, and even field-specific, phenomenon, rather than an aspect of the universal moral law.

Replaceable

Judges, who try to conceal rather than to flaunt their originality, far from 15 crediting their predecessors with original thinking like to pretend that there is no original thinking in law, that judges are just a transmission belt for rules and principles laid down by the framers of statutes or the Constitution.

Resorting to plagiarism to obtain a good grade or a promotion is fraud and 16 should be punished, though it should not be confused with "theft." But I think the zeal to punish plagiarism reflects less a concern with the real injuries that it occasionally inflicts than with a desire on the part of leaders of professional communities, such as journalists and historians, to enhance their profession's reputation.

Journalists (like politicians) have a bad reputation for truthfulness, and 17 historians, in this "postmodernist"° era, are suspected of having embraced an extreme form of relativism and of having lost their regard for facts. Both groups hope by taking a very hard line against plagiarism and fabrication to reassure the public that they are serious diggers after truth whose efforts, a form of "sweat equity," deserve protection against copycats.

Postmodernism is a school of criticism that denies concepts such as scientific certainty and absolute truth.

Their anxieties are understandable; but the rest of us will do well to keep 18 the matter in perspective, realizing that the term *plagiarism* is used loosely and often too broadly; that much plagiarism is harmless and (when the term is defined broadly) that some has social value.

⊘ AT ISSUE: SOURCES FOR UNDERSTANDING PLAGIARISM

1. According to Posner, how do most people define *plagiarism*? How is the definition he proposes different from theirs? Do you think his definition is too broad? Too narrow?

2. Why does Posner believe that the plagiarisms committed by students and professors are the most serious? How would you argue against this position?

3. How do the examples Posner cites in paragraphs 6 and 7 strengthen his argument? Do you agree that the examples he gives here constitute plagiarism? Why or why not?

4. Explain the connection the author makes in paragraph 15 between judges and plagiarism. (Note that Posner himself is a federal judge.)

5. Why, according to Posner, do journalists and historians think plagiarism should be punished severely?

6. According to Posner, "the truth about plagiarism" is that "much plagiarism is harmless and (when the term is defined broadly) that some has social value" (para. 18). Does the evidence he presents in this essay support this conclusion? What connection do you see between this position and his comments about the rise of individualism and the "cult of originality" in paragraphs 12–14?

This article originally appeared in the *Chronicle of Higher Education* on March 30, 2016.

WHEN PLAGIARISM IS A PLEA FOR HELP

HELEN RUBINSTEIN

That summer night, at a dinner table surrounded by writing teachers, the plagiarism stories were hard to stop. There was the freshman who, given the writing prompt "Why Do I Procrastinate?," pasted in Yahoo Answers. I told about the senior who turned in an essay paraphrasing a scholarly article synonym by synonym, word by word. The winning story was the student who asked permission to study a novel written by his professor and then turned in an essay that copied text from the book jacket, including a line from the author bio: "She lives in Chicago with her two sons and their cat." 1

There was one I didn't tell. It's not a dinner-table story. It might not even be a story about plagiarism. For a while, every time I talked about it, I had to begin by saying, "I'm glad I'm not the kind of person who could feel responsible for something like this." What I meant was that people who believe the death of someone else could be their own fault are usually deluding themselves into a sense of omnipotence. "I'm glad I'm not the kind of person who could feel responsible," I repeated to myself. I needed that to be true. 2

My student—I'll call her "Susan"—dressed well. Big sweaters she'd tuck a knee into. Long hair, pale face, pretty. Twice that September, she had stayed after class to discuss the recommended reading—she'd actually *done* the recommended reading. When she was sick, she emailed: "Hello Professor! . . . My residence hall is currently experiencing 'the flu' epidemic and just my luck I believe I have it now." She was a freshman, keen to succeed: "Do you think I should soldier through the sickness and come to class anyway? . . . I've never been sick in college before and your class happens to be the only mandatory one I must attend." 3

It wasn't just the flu that was spreading that semester—so was the plagiarism. One weekend I plowed through 36 first drafts, and Susan's was not the first or the last to be of sketchy origin in that stack. "Why are there so many smokers on campus?," her paper began—innocently enough. Then she turned to the topic of e-cigarettes, citing numbers and statistics without quote marks or attribution. None of it was in answer to the actual assignment. And it didn't take long to find the sources she'd copied. 4

Susan had already missed several classes because of illness, and sent me countless emails—messages with subject lines that shouted "Hospital" and "Emergency Please Read." "Just focus on getting better," I would respond. "Don't worry about the class." In another email she mentioned she had been "diagnosed with anxiety" recently and was on a "low dose of anxiety medication." She was absent again on the day I handed back the drafts and gave a speech about plagiarism for the benefit of the six or eight students I had caught. *Caught*—the word betrays how I sat hunched over those essays, feeling hunted even as I hunted. 5

My stern warning surprised students. Some didn't realize the word 6
"plagiarism"—with its trill of alarm—might describe what they'd done.
Some didn't know plagiarism would "count" in a draft. I didn't report
any of those students to the administration, but I did deduct points—
proportionate to the level of plagiarism in each case—that would reduce the
students' final grade. All they had to do to avoid further trouble was not
plagiarize the final paper.

Shortly after, I got an inquiry from the dean's office about Susan, identi- 7
fying her by her student number. She'd apparently been having difficulties in
other classes as well: Had I noticed any problems? I mentioned the plagiarism
incident and noted that she was coming to class again yet performing erratically. The dean's office advised me to "follow protocol"—make sure that she
understood what she had done wrong and that she did not repeat it.

But Susan did repeat it. She had thanked me for being so "tolerant, consid- 8
erate, and kindhearted" after the first incident but when she turned in her final
paper, I was stunned to find that it, too, was plagiarized. I sent Susan a message
expressing my dismay and telling her that I would have to both fail the essay
and submit a report on her plagiarism to the administration.

It's too easy, as a teacher, to let plagiarism propel you toward protocol, 9
that means of moving forward without thinking. It's too easy to feel that you
must turn the tables, prevent the student from *pulling one over* or *getting away
with it*—all of those terrible clichés that hide the reality of how plagiarism, to a
teacher, is the rare instance in which the student seizes power.

After emailing Susan, I met with a col- 10
league to seek his advice. Once the door was
closed, he told me not to bother with protocol or with reporting the student. It won't be
worth the trouble, he said—not worth the
onerousness of photocopying, scanning, providing evidence, and navigating the bureaucratic near-legalese.

> "How can you
> tell if a student is
> just stressed or
> out-of-control?"

I was still deciding whether to follow his advice when Susan emailed a long, 11
dense reply: "I will not be dragged down because one single professor does not
like me. . . . How can I respect a teacher that has done nothing but bully me and
find any loophole to make me fail? . . . I DO NOT DESERVE THIS PUNISH-
MENT." And: "I will use every ounce of my power to set this straight."

I read it again and again. At dinner with friends that night, I described the 12
email and quoted its subject line: "This Has Gone Far Enough."

"She's crazy," someone said. I had no way of knowing if that was the 13
case. How can you tell if a student is just stressed or out-of-control? But the
truth was: I did feel like I'd been pressuring Susan—with my feverish photocopying, my petty collection of evidence, and now this ha-ha dinnertime
story. "Report the plagiarism," my friends insisted. "Follow protocol. Cover
your ass."

We all want to write about the times we succeed in the classroom. But 14
what about the times we teach poorly? What about the times we fail?

After she died, her essay—with the big green F in my handwriting circled 15 and my comments scrawled across its cover page—sat on a chair in my house for weeks. One day I flipped it over. Eventually I moved it under the chair, then under a table. I'm not supposed to keep student work. Nor am I supposed to throw it away. Nor am I supposed to show it to Susan's parents without her permission. Nor would I ever, ever return this essay to them, with its angry-scrawled F.

A week later, I received the news of her death in an email from the 16 university, with the words "deceased student," followed by her student ID number. (Protocol.) Then came another email from the colleague I had consulted for advice: "Thank God you didn't report her and don't have that now on your conscience."

Except, as far as Susan knew, I *had* reported her. The notice didn't tell 17 me how she died. It explained that she withdrew from college the day after she'd emailed me, and passed away six days after that. Her death seemed to confirm my worst suspicions of myself: that I am heartless, overly bound by some cockeyed ideal of fairness, not in touch enough with my students' human selves. I trembled when I had to tell a room of 18-year-olds that their classmate had died, but I wasn't sure whether that was because I feared I would cry, or because I feared I wouldn't.

Three weeks later, the semester ended. The internet had informed us that 18 Susan died from an overdose of an illegal recreational drug, though I had little idea what to do with that information, what it might mean. The class shared a moment of silence in her memory. And then, after everyone else had left, one student approached my desk. "I can't stop thinking about Susan," he confessed. "I feel so guilty. She asked me where to buy pot and I told her."

I saw then that, in her wake, Susan had left behind a whole universe of 19 people who felt responsible for her death. "It's not your fault," I said with as much conviction as I could muster—hoping to persuade both the young man and myself that it was egotistical to believe any of us have that much power.

But we long for such power. I see the longing in my tendency to experience 20 plagiarism as personal—about me or my class. I see it in my nervousness when faced with a student's power to deceive—even though plagiarism is, more than anything, an expression of a student's powerlessness.

Plagiarism is a gag on the voice, a paper bag over the face. So what if—the 21 next time our students plagiarize—we tried harder to actually see them? What if we could understand plagiarism as an expression of exhaustion, of distress, maybe even a plea for help?

The thing that haunts me, after all, is not Susan's rage in her last message 22 to me, but my own rage in my last message to her. The angrily scrawled F is a guilty conscience I don't want to forget. I didn't kill Susan—I don't have that kind of power. But I did have the power to fail her. And that F is a reminder that the next time a student hides her thinking behind someone else's, what I'd like to do is not fail her, but try to help her *not* fail.

⊃ AT ISSUE: SOURCES FOR UNDERSTANDING PLAGIARISM

1. This essay appeared in a publication for college instructors and administrators. Given that this is her audience, do you think Rubinstein's purpose here is to explain or justify her actions? To create awareness of a problem? Or, does she expect her readers to propose—or even to take-some kind of action?

2. What attitude toward plagiarism do the professors discussed in the opening paragraph seem to have? How might you explain that attitude?

3. Why does Rubinstein say that the incident she will discuss "might not even be a story about plagiarism" (para. 2)? If the story isn't about plagiarism, what *is* it about?

4. According to Rubinstein, what exactly did Susan do that constituted plagiarism? What other details does Rubinstein give readers about Susan, and why? For example, why does Rubinstein enumerate the many emails she received from Susan?

5. In paragraph 9, Rubinstein says, "It's too easy, as a teacher, to let plagiarism propel you toward protocol, . . . " What does she mean? Is she questioning her own actions here? Explain.

6. In paragraph 13, Rubinstein asks, "How can you tell if a student is just stressed or out-of-control?" Does she answer this question? How would you answer it?

7. What steps do you think colleges—or individual instructors—could take to avoid a situation like the one Rubinstein describes? How do you suppose Rubinstein might react to your suggestions? Why?

8. Whom (or what) do you blame for the incident's tragic outcome? Why?

9. If Rubinstein were going to write an argumentative essay for the same publication taking a position on how academic plagiarism should be addressed, what would her position be? Suggest a thesis statement for this essay.

This essay originally appeared in the *Los Angeles Times* on June 17, 2012.

ESSAY MILLS: A COARSE LESSON IN CHEATING

DAN ARIELY

Sometimes as I decide what kind of papers to assign to my students, I worry 1
about essay mills, companies whose sole purpose is to generate essays for high
school and college students (in exchange for a fee, of course).

The mills claim that the papers are meant to be used as reference mate- 2
rial to help students write their own, original papers. But with names such as
echeat.com, it's pretty clear what their real purpose is.

Professors in general are concerned about essay mills and their effect on 3
learning, but not knowing exactly what they provide, I wasn't sure how concerned to be. So together with my lab manager Aline Grüneisen, I decided
to check the services out. We ordered a typical college term paper from four
different essay mills. The topic of the paper? Cheating.

Here is the prompt we gave the four essay mills: 4

"When and why do people cheat? Consider the social circumstances 5
involved in dishonesty, and provide a thoughtful response to the topic of cheating. Address various forms of cheating (personal, at work, etc.) and how each
of these can be rationalized by a social culture of cheating."

We requested a term paper for a university-level social psychology class, 6
12 pages long, using 15 sources (cited and referenced in a bibliography). The
paper was to conform to American Psychological Assn. style guidelines and
needed to be completed in the next two weeks. All four of the essay mills
agreed to provide such a paper, charging us in advance, between $150 and
$216 for the paper.

Right on schedule, the essays came, and I
have to say that, to some degree, they allayed
my fears that students can rely on the services
to get good grades. What we got back from the
mills can best be described as gibberish. A few
of the papers attempted to mimic APA style, but
none achieved it without glaring errors. Cita- 7
tions were sloppy. Reference lists contained outdated and unknown sources,
including blog posts. Some of the links to reference material were broken.

> "What we got back
> from the mills can
> best be described
> as gibberish."

And the writing quality? Awful. The authors of all four papers seemed 8
to have a very tenuous grasp of the English language, not to mention how to
format an essay. Paragraphs jumped bluntly from one topic to another, often
simply listing various forms of cheating or providing a long stream of examples
that were never explained or connected to the "thesis" of the paper.

One paper contained this paragraph: "Cheating by healers. Healing is 9 different. There is harmless healing, when healers-cheaters and wizards offer omens, lapels, damage to withdraw, the husband-wife back and stuff. We read in the newspaper and just smile. But these days fewer people believe in wizards."

This comes from another: "If the large allowance of study undertook on 10 scholar betraying is any suggestion of academia and professors' powerful yearn to decrease scholar betraying, it appeared expected these mind-set would component into the creation of their school room guidelines."

And finally, these gems: 11

"By trusting blindfold only in stable love, loyalty, responsibility, and 12 honesty the partners assimilate with the credulous and naive persons of the past."

"Women have a much greater necessity to feel special."   13

"The future generation must learn for historical mistakes and develop the 14 sense of pride and responsibility for its actions."

It's hard to believe that students purchasing such papers would ever do so 15 again.

And the story does not end there. We submitted the four essays to 16 WriteCheck.com, a website that inspects papers for plagiarism, and found that two of the papers were 35 percent to 39 percent copied from existing works. We decided to take action on the two papers with substantial plagiarizing and contacted the essay mills requesting our money back. Despite the solid proof we provided to them, the companies insisted they did not plagiarize. One company even threatened to expose us by calling the dean and saying we had purchased the paper.

It's comforting in a way that the technological revolution has not yet solved 17 students' problems. They still have no other option but to actually work on their papers (or maybe cheat in the old-fashioned way and copy from friends). But I do worry about the existence of essay mills and the signal that they send to our students.

As for our refund, we are still waiting.   18

⊃ AT ISSUE: SOURCES FOR UNDERSTANDING PLAGIARISM

1. Consider the title of this essay. What does the word *coarse* mean? What does it suggest in this context?

2. What is an essay mill? Look up the word *mill*. Which of the definitions provided applies to the word as it is used in the phrase *essay mill*?

3. Why does Ariely decide to investigate the services provided by essay mills? What does he want to find out? Is he successful?

383

4. What does Ariely conclude about the four companies he surveys? Does he provide enough evidence to support his conclusion? If not, what kind of evidence should he add?

5. In paragraph 15, Ariely says, "It's hard to believe that students purchasing such papers would ever do so again." Given the evidence Ariely presents, how do you explain the continued popularity of essay mills?

6. What information does Ariely provide in his conclusion? Do you think he is departing from his essay's central focus here, or do you think the concluding paragraph is an appropriate and effective summary of his ideas? Explain.

VISUAL ARGUMENT: TERM PAPERS FOR SALE ADVERTISEMENT (WEB PAGE)

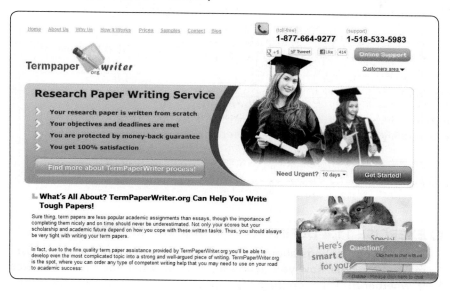

❷ AT ISSUE: SOURCES FOR UNDERSTANDING PLAGIARISM

1. The web page above is from a site that offers papers for sale to students. What argument does this web page make? What counter-argument could you present?

2. Identify appeals to *logos*, *pathos*, and *ethos* on the TermPaperWriter .org page. Which appeal dominates?

3. Study the images of students on the page. What message do these images convey?

4. Unlike the TermPaperWriter.org page, many other sites that offer papers for sale include errors in grammar, spelling, and punctuation. Search the web for some other sites that offer papers for sale. What errors can you find? Do such errors weaken the message of these ads, or are they irrelevant?

5. A different site offering similar services promises its papers are "100% plagiarism free." Does this promise make sense? Explain.

TEMPLATE FOR WRITING AN ARGUMENT ABOUT PLAGIARISM

Write a one-paragraph argument in which you take a position on where to draw the line with plagiarism. Follow the template below, filling in the blanks to create your argument.

To many people, plagiarism is theft; to others, however, it is not that simple. For example, some define *plagiarism* as _____

_____; others see it as _____

_____. Another thing to consider is

_____

_____. In addition, _____

_____. Despite these differences of opinion,

plagiarism is often dealt with harshly and can ruin careers and reputations. All things considered,

_____

_____.

⊙ EXERCISE 11.4 DEFINING PLAGIARISM: REVIEW

Discuss your feelings about plagiarism with two or three of your classmates. Consider how you define *plagiarism*, what you believe causes it, whether there are degrees of dishonesty, and so on, but focus on the *effects* of plagiarism—on those who commit it and on those who are its victims. Then, write a paragraph that summarizes the key points of your discussion.

⊙ EXERCISE 11.5 WRITING AN ESSAY

Write an argumentative essay on the topic, "Where Should We Draw the Line with Plagiarism?" Begin by defining what you mean by *plagiarism*, and then narrow your discussion down to a particular group—for example, high school or college students, historians, scientists, or journalists. Cite the sources on pages 366–85, and be sure to document the sources you use and to include a works-cited page. (See Chapter 10 for information on documenting sources.)

⊙ EXERCISE 11.6 REVIEWING THE ELEMENTS OF ARGUMENT

Review the four pillars of argument discussed in Chapter 1. Does your essay include all four elements of an effective argument? Add anything that is missing. Then, label the elements of your argument.

⊘ WRITING ASSIGNMENTS: USING SOURCES RESPONSIBLY

1. Write an argument in which you take a position on who (or what) is to blame for plagiarism among college students. Is plagiarism always the student's fault, or are other people (or other factors) at least partly to blame?

2. Write an essay in which you argue that an honor code will (or will not) eliminate (or at least reduce) plagiarism and other kinds of academic dishonesty at your school.

3. Reread the essays by Richard Posner and Jennifer Mott-Smith in this chapter. Then, write an argument in which you argue that only intentional plagiarism should be punished.

4. Do you consider student plagiarism a victimless crime that is best left unpunished? If so, why? If not, how does it affect its victims — for example, the student who plagiarizes, the instructor, the other students in the class, and the school?

Strategies
for Argument

Part 5: Strategies for Argument

Stasis Theory

Different writing purposes call for different argumentative strategies. One way to determine how to approach a topic is by using a rhetorical tool called **stasis theory.** The word *stasis* means "a slowing down" or "stopping." When you apply stasis theory, you ask questions that isolate a topic in order to determine the issue you will explore in your argument.

- What is the nature of the problem?

- What are its causes and its results?

- Is it a good thing or a bad thing?

- Is it right or wrong?

- What should be done?

Once you answer these questions, you can decide how best to approach your topic. For example, suppose you were going to develop an argument about animal testing. The topic "animal testing" is so broad that you couldn't effectively argue for or against it. Notice how the stasis questions enable you to focus your thinking to develop an effective argument.

- *What is the nature of the problem?* You could begin trying to determine exactly what animal testing is. What does it involve? What animals are used, and why? How are they treated? Is animal testing unnecessarily cruel? If these questions inspire interesting ideas, you could write an **argument by definition. (See Chapter 12.)**

- *What is the cause? What effects are associated with it?* At this point, you could move on to consider why animal testing is used and what results it has. Why do scientists use animals as testing subjects? Could computer models achieve the same result? Does animal testing make drugs and cosmetics safer? If questions such as these suggest a promising direction to explore, you could structure your essay as a **cause-and-effect argument. (See Chapter 13.)**

- *Is it a good thing or a bad thing?* Here you might examine the risks and/or benefits of animal testing. Is animal testing better than other kinds of testing? Is animal testing cheaper (or more expensive) than other kinds of testing? If these questions seem promising, you could write an **evaluation argument. (See Chapter 14.)**

- *Is it right or wrong?* Now, consider the moral and ethical issues associated with animal testing. Do animals have rights? Do the benefits of animal testing outweigh the harm it causes? If these questions seem useful, you could write an **ethical argument. (See Chapter 15.)**

- *What should be done?* Finally, you could consider how to solve the problems you have identified. What alternatives are there to animal testing? Which, if any, of these alternatives seem feasible? If these questions seem to be the most productive, you could write a **proposal argument. (See Chapter 16.)**

As you apply each of the questions above, you critically examine the topic you are considering. Thus, these questions help you to identify the kind of argument you are making and to understand the rhetorical choices you need to make in order to develop that argument.

Michael Brochstein/SOPA Images/LightRocket/Getty Images

Definition Arguments

Why Do We Need to Define Fake News?

We currently have access to more information now than at any time in human history. But this endless data stream—from Twitter notifications to Facebook posts—threatens to overwhelm us. Moreover, a good deal of this information is false. Certain misinformation can be relatively harmless, such as urban legends. But other types of information can be harmful, such as unsupported claims about the dangers of childhood vaccinations.

The 2016 election highlighted this problem when factually inaccurate stories and malicious rumors circulated endlessly on the internet. Sometimes these false stories appeared on social media sites or on fake news websites. Occasionally, they made their way into legitimate news outlets. A number of studies have found that many people cannot not tell the difference between what news is false and what news is real. Sites like Snopes.com and factcheck.org have tried to remedy this situation, but they can only verify a small portion of what appears in print and on the internet. Both Facebook and Instagram have tried to screen posts, but they too have found if virtually impossible to identify the overwhelming amount of false information that appears on their sites. Some critics point out that given our country's robust commitment to free speech, little can or should be done to address this issue. Others question if is appropriate for social media companies to monitor and possibly censor content—especially political content. Even so, the problem remains serious. Fake news can create confusion about what news is real and what news is false. At best, this problem can be frustrating; at worst it can undermine people's ability to understand important social and political issues.

Later in this chapter, you will be asked to think more about this issue. You will be given several sources to consider and write an argument by definition that takes a position on the issue of misinformation.

What Is a Definition Argument?

When your argument depends on the meaning of a key term or concept, it makes sense to structure your essay as a **definition argument**. In this type of essay, you will argue that something fits (or does not fit) the definition of a particular class of items. For example, to argue that Facebook's News Feed is a legitimate research source, you would have to define *legitimate research source* and show that Facebook's News Feed fits this definition.

Many arguments focus on definition. In fact, you encounter them so often that you probably do not recognize them for what they are. For example, consider the following questions:

- Is spanking child abuse?
- Should offensive speech be banned on campus?
- Should the rich pay more taxes than others?
- Are electric cars harmful to the environment?
- Is cheerleading a sport?
- Why do we need to define *fake news*?

You cannot answer these questions without providing definitions. In fact, if you were writing an argumentative essay in response to one of these questions, much of your essay would be devoted to defining and discussing a key term.

QUESTION	KEY TERM TO BE DEFINED
Is spanking child abuse?	*child abuse*
Should offensive speech be banned on campus?	*offensive speech*
Should the rich pay more taxes than others?	*rich*
Are electric cars harmful to the environment?	*harmful*
Is cheerleading a sport?	*sport*
Why do we need to define *fake news*?	*fake news*

Many contemporary social and legal disputes involve definition arguments. For example, did a coworker's actions constitute *sexual harassment*? Is an individual trying to enter the United States as an *undocumented worker* or an *illegal alien*? Is a person guilty of *murder* or of *manslaughter*? Did the CIA engage in *torture* or in *aggressive questioning*? Was the magazine cover *satirical* or *racist*? Is the punishment *just*, or is it *cruel and unusual*? The answers to these and many other questions hinge on definitions of key terms.

AP Images

The last public hanging in the United States took place in Owensboro, Kentucky, August 14, 1936. This spectacle would now be considered cruel and unusual punishment.

Keep in mind, however, that definitions can change as our thinking about certain issues changes. For example, fifty years ago the word *family* generally referred to one or more children living with two heterosexual married parents. Now, the term can refer to a wide variety of situations—children living with single parents, gay and lesbian couples, and unmarried heterosexual couples, for example. Our definition of what constitutes *cruel and unusual punishment* has also changed. Public hanging, a common method of execution for hundreds of years, is now considered barbaric.

Developing Definitions

Definitions explain terms that are unfamiliar to an audience. To make your definitions as clear as possible, avoid making them *too narrow*, *too broad*, or *circular*.

A definition that is **too narrow** leaves out information that is necessary for understanding a particular word or term. For example, if you define an *apple* as "a red fruit," your definition is too narrow since some apples are not red. To be accurate (and useful), your definition needs to be more inclusive and acknowledge the fact that apples can be red, green, or yellow: "An apple is the round edible fruit of a tree of the rose family, which typically has thin red, yellow, or green skin."

A definition that is **too broad** includes things that should not be part of the definition. If, for example, you define *chair* as "something that people sit on," your definition includes things that are not chairs—stools, park benches, and even tree stumps. To be accurate, your definition needs to be much more specific: "A chair is a piece of furniture that has a seat, legs, arms, and a back and is designed to accommodate one person."

A **circular definition** includes the word being defined as part of the definition. For example, if you define *patriotism* as "the quality of being patriotic," your definition is circular. For the definition to work, you have to provide new information that enables readers to understand the term: "*Patriotism* is a belief characterized by love and support for one's country, especially its values and beliefs."

> **NOTE**
>
> Sometimes you can clarify a definition by explaining how one term is different from another similar term. For example, consider the following definition:
>
> *Patriotism* is different from *nationalism* because *patriotism* focuses on love for a country while *nationalism* assumes the superiority of one country over another.

The success of a definition argument depends on your ability to define a term or concept so that readers (even those who do not agree with your position) will see its validity. For this reason, the rhetorical strategies you use to develop your definitions are important.

Dictionary Definitions (Formal Definitions)

When most people think of definitions, they think of the formal definitions they find in a dictionary. Typically, a formal **dictionary definition** has three parts: the term to be defined, the general class to which the term belongs, and the qualities that differentiate the term from other items in the same class.

TERM	CLASS	DIFFERENTIATION
dog	a domesticated mammal	that has a snout, a keen sense of smell, and a barking voice
naturalism	a literary movement	whose followers believed that writers should treat their characters' lives with scientific objectivity

⊙ EXERCISE 12.1 WRITING FORMAL DEFINITIONS

Write a one-sentence formal definition of each of the following words. Then, look each word up in a dictionary, and compare your definitions to the ones you found there.

Argument	Respect
App	Blog
Tablet	Fairness

Extended Definitions

Although a definition argument may include a short dictionary definition, a brief definition is usually not enough to define a complex or abstract term. For example, if you were arguing that *fake news* is a danger to society, you would have to include an **extended definition**, explaining to readers in some detail what you mean by *fake news* and perhaps giving some examples that fit your definition.

Examples are often used to develop an extended definition in an argumentative essay. For instance, you could give examples to make the case that a particular baseball player, despite his struggles with substance abuse, is a great athlete. You could define *great athlete* solely in terms of athletic prowess, presenting several examples of other talented athletes and then showing that the baseball player you are discussing possesses the same qualities.

For your examples to be effective, they have to be relevant to your argument. Your examples also have to represent (or at least suggest) the full range of opinion concerning your subject. Finally, you have to make sure that your readers will accept your examples as typical, not unusual.

Writing the Declaration of Independence, 1776 by Jean Leon Gerome Ferris (Virginia Historical Society)

Writing the Declaration of Independence in 1776 (oil on canvas)/
Ferris, Jean Leon Gerome (1863–1930)/VIRGINIA HISTORICAL
SOCIETY/Virginia Historical Society, Richmond, Virginia, USA/
Bridgeman Images

For example, in the Declaration of Independence, Thomas Jefferson presented twenty-five paragraphs of examples to support his extended definition of the king's tyranny. With these examples, he hoped to convince the world that the colonists were justified in breaking away from England. To accomplish his goal, Jefferson made sure that his examples supported his position, that they represented the full range of abuses, and that they were not unusual or atypical.

◐ EXERCISE 12.2 DEFINING A TERM

Choose one of the terms you defined in Exercise 12.1, and write a paragraph-length definition argument that takes a position related to that term. Make sure you include two or three examples in your definition.

Operational Definitions

Whereas a dictionary definition tells what a term means, an **operational definition** defines something by telling how it acts or how it works in a particular set of circumstances. Thus, an operational definition transforms an abstract concept into something concrete, observable, and possibly measurable. Children instinctively understand the concept of operational definitions. When a parent tells them to *behave*, they know what the components of this operational definition are: clean up your room, obey your parents, come home on time, and do your homework. Researchers in the natural and social sciences must constantly come up with operational definitions. For example, if they want to study the effects of childhood obesity, they have to construct an operational definition of *obese*. Without such a definition, they will not be able to measure the various factors that make a person obese. For example, at what point does a child become obese? Does he or she have to be 10 percent above normal weight? More? Before researchers can carry out their study, they must agree on an operational (or working) definition.

Structuring a Definition Argument

In general terms, a definition argument can be structured as follows:

- **Introduction:** Establishes a context for the argument by explaining the need for defining the term; presents the essay's thesis

- **Evidence (first point in support of thesis):** Provides a short definition of the term as well as an extended definition (if necessary)

- **Evidence (second point in support of thesis):** Shows how the term does or does not fit the definition

- **Refutation of opposing arguments:** Addresses questions about or objections to the definition; considers and rejects other possible meanings (if any)

- **Conclusion:** Reinforces the main point of the argument; includes a strong concluding statement

⬇ The following student essay includes all the elements of a definition argument. The student who wrote this essay is trying to convince his university that he is a nontraditional student and is therefore entitled to the benefits such students receive.

WHY I AM A NONTRADITIONAL STUDENT

ADAM KENNEDY

Ever since I started college, I have had difficulty getting the extra help I need to succeed. My final disappointment came last week when my adviser told me that I could not take advantage of the programs the school offers to nontraditional students. She told me that because I am not old enough, I simply do not qualify. This is confusing to me because I am anything but a "traditional" student. In fact, I am one of the most nontraditional students I know. In spite of my age—I am twenty-two—I have had experiences that separate me from most other students my age. The problem is that the school's definition of the term *nontraditional* is so narrow that it excludes people like me who should be able to qualify.

Thesis statement

According to researchers, the term *nontraditional student* is difficult to define. Studies show that a broad operational definition that acknowledges many factors is preferable to one that focuses on age alone. For example, the National Center for Educational Statistics bases its definition on whether or not a student has any of the following seven characteristics:

Evidence: Operational definition of *nontraditional student*

- Did not enter college right after high school
- Is a part-time student
- Does not depend on parents for money
- Has a full-time job
- Has children or a spouse

- Is a single parent
- Has a GED instead of a high school diploma (Kim et al. 405–6)

Evidence: Other schools' definitions of nontraditional student

Many colleges use similar, or even broader, criteria to define *nontraditional student.* For example, the University of Arkansas provides special services for older students as well as for students with other work- or family-related responsibilities. In fact, the school has a special department—Non-Traditional Student Services—to meet these students' needs. The university website says that a nontraditional student is someone who meets just one of the criteria listed above ("Non-Traditional Student Programs"). In addition, the university recognizes other factors, like whether the student is a veteran, an active member of the military, or the first in his or her family to go to college ("Non-Traditional Student Programs").

3

Evidence: Our school's definition of nontraditional student

According to the criteria from the National Center for Educational Statistics (listed above), I would have no problem qualifying as a nontraditional student at the University of Arkansas. Our school, however, has a much narrower definition of the term. When I went to Non-Traditional Student Services, I was told that my case did not fit the definition that the school had established. Here, a nontraditional student is someone who is twenty-five or older, period. The person I spoke to said that the school's intention is to give special help to older students. I was then told that I could appeal and try to convince the dean of Non-Traditional Student Services that I do not fit the definition of a traditional student.

4

Evidence: How writer fits the definition of nontraditional student

By any measure, I am not a "traditional student." After getting married at seventeen, I dropped out of high school and got a full-time job. Soon, my wife and I began to resent our situation. She was still a high school student and missed being able to go out with her friends whenever she wanted to. I hated my job and missed being a student. Before long, we decided it was best to end our marriage. Instead of going back to high school, however, I enlisted in the Army National Guard. After two years, I had completed a tour in Iraq and earned my GED. As soon as I was discharged from active duty, I enrolled in college—all this before I turned twenty-one.

5

Refutation of opposing argument

I can see how someone could say that I am too young to be considered a nontraditional student. However, I believe that my life experiences should qualify me for this program. My marriage and divorce, time in the army, and reentry issues make me very different from the typical first-year student. The special resources available to students who

6

qualify for this program—tutors, financial aid, special advising, support groups, and subsidized housing—would make my adjustment to college a lot easier. I am only four years older than the average first-year students, but I am nothing like them. The focus on age to define *nontraditional* ignores the fact that students younger than twenty-five may have followed unconventional paths to college. Life experience, not age, should be the main factor in determining whether a student is nontraditional.

The university should expand the definition of *nontraditional* to   7
include younger students who have followed unconventional career paths and have postponed college. Even though these students may be younger than twenty-five, they face challenges similar to those faced by older students. Students like me are returning to school in increasing numbers. Our situation is different from that of others our age, and that   Concluding statement
is exactly why we need all the help we can get.

Works Cited

Kim, Karen A., et al. "Redefining Nontraditional Students: Exploring the Self-Perceptions of Community College Students." *Community College Journal of Research and Practice,* vol. 34, 2009–10, pp. 402–22. Academic Search Complete, web.b.ebscohost.com.ezproxy.bpl.org/.

"Non-Traditional Student Programs." Office of Campus Life. *University of Arkansas at Little Rock*, 2018, ualr.edu/campuslife/ntsp/.

GRAMMAR IN CONTEXT

Avoiding *Is Where* and *Is When*

In a formal definition, you may find yourself using the phrase *is where* or *is when*. If so, your definition is incomplete because it omits the term's class. The use of *is where* or *is when* signals that you are giving an example of the term, not a definition. You can avoid this problem by making sure that the verb *be* in your definition is always followed by a noun.

INCORRECT	The university website says that a nontraditional student **is when** you live off campus, commute from home, have children, are a veteran, or are over the age of twenty-five.
CORRECT	The university website says that a nontraditional student is **someone** who lives off campus, commutes from home, has children, is a veteran, or is over the age of twenty-five.

⊖ EXERCISE 12.3 ANALYZING THE ELEMENTS OF A DEFINITION ARGUMENT

The following essay, "Athlete vs. Role Model" by Ej Garr, includes the basic elements of a definition argument. Read the essay, and then answer the questions that follow it, consulting the outline on pages 398–399 if necessary.

This blog post first appeared on August 31, 2014, in the Lifestyle section of newshub.com.

ATHLETE VS. ROLE MODEL

EJ GARR

Expectations of professional athletes have become such a touchy subject over 1 the years, and deciphering what defines a role model has become an even darker subject.

Kids who are into sports tend to look up to a favorite player or team and 2 find someone they say they want to be like when they grow up. Unfortunately, athletes today are not what they were decades ago when a paycheck was not the sole reason they wanted an athletic career.

Take Roger Staubach or Bart Starr for example. Both have multiple Super 3 Bowl titles. Both had tremendous NFL careers, and both conducted themselves in public with class and dignity. They deserved every accolade they received, both personally and professionally. Starr and his wife co-founded the Rawhide Boys Ranch, which helps kids who are in need of proper direction and might not have the family resources that can make a kid's life easier.

Roger Staubach was a class act, served in our Navy, and is a Vietnam vet. 4 These are just two examples of players who gained role model status because of how they acted and what they contributed, not simply because they played in the NFL, and earned a big paycheck. People rooted for them and looked up to them. Kids wanted to be like them. There were absolutely no discouraging words said about them from anyone who has ever met them. They had class, caring, and concern for other people, both on the field and off.

It is easy for kids, who hear about their favorite athlete who signed a mul- 5 timillion dollar contract, to say to themselves, "I wish I could do that." Do what? Become a pro or make lots of money? What about becoming a better person? What about giving back?

Many athletes do not think about how to be a better role model to those 6 kids that look up to them, how to make their community better, or what they can "give back" to the less fortunate.

Think back to Pete Rose, who was an amazing ballplayer when he was on 7 the field, but all he is known for today is gambling when he became a manager and being banned for life from baseball and the Hall of Fame. Pete Rose was a role model for every kid in his generation when he played baseball. Ran hard to first on a simple walk and gave every ounce of his being to the game. Then, that all went out the window and the role model moniker was gone faster than you could shake your head at what he did. He didn't think of those kids who looked up to him.

Then there's Ray Rice, who was on the cusp of being a role model with a 8 Super Bowl trophy in tow with the Baltimore Ravens. Kids looked up to him. Instead, he was caught on video dragging his unconscious wife out of an elevator after she "accidentally" put her face in front of his fist.

And who can ever forget Michael Vick, who went to prison on dog 9 fighting charges and arranging a death sentence for animals. It has been documented that he even placed a bet or two on those fights! Just recently, although not as criminally serious, USC's Josh Shaw lied about an injury that he claimed to receive when he rescued his nephew. He finally admitted he fabricated the story and all the facts are not out yet, but he went from a potential role model to a hero and then to a zero in record time. These guys sure aren't thinking about the kids who look up to them and want to be like them.

These days, sports newscasts are chock-filled with reports of pro ath- 10 letes using performance enhancing drugs. Over the years there's been Lance Armstrong, Alex Rodriguez, José Canseco, Shawne Merriman, Barry Bonds, and even gold medalist Marion Jones. It is well documented that Alex Rodriguez spent a lot of money buying performance enhancing drugs, rather than becoming a hardworking baseball player and using his money for good. Alex Rodriguez is only worried about Alex Rodriguez. That, unfortunately, is the ego that many athletes have today. I am me, you are you, and I can do what I want. And who cares if you're watching what I'm doing and looking up to me.

No sir! Athletes like this are arrogant and act like idiots, carrying guns, 11 hitting spouses, and taking drugs which are all, by the way . . . ILLEGAL in this country! Our world needs more role models like Staubach and Starr and less arrogant athletes who think society owes them something simply because they make big money and live in a big house and drive a nice car.

Professional athletes are not born role models. They are getting paid to 12 play a game. That far from constitutes the making of a role model. Perhaps this mentality of being better than anyone else starts at the college level. Even the NCAA [National Collegiate Athletic Association] has acknowledged that bringing in athletes to fill the stands is more important than

> "Will that make kids look up to you?"

making sure they get a quality education, because 75 percent of the athletes who play in college basketball or football are simply there to play their two years and move on to collect a big fat paycheck in the pros. Are they taught anything about giving back and setting a positive example?

A role model comes not from being an athlete and collecting that big pay- 13 check, but for what you do with and in your life. Throw a football and score three touchdowns today? Hey, good for you man. You will make the headlines, be highlighted on ESPN, and the press will come calling. Will that make kids look up to you? Sure it will, you won the game and had a great day, good for you. But you're not a role model.

Do you know why Derek Jeter, Drew Brees, and Tom Brady are true role 14 models? It's about how they carry themselves on and off the field. It's about how Jeter, during his rookie year in 1996, achieved his goal of establishing the Turn 2 Foundation, where he gives back and helps kids who are less fortunate. That is a role model! And Drew Brees is a great family man who gives of his time. Here, let me break it down for you. "Brittany and Drew Brees, and the Brees Dream Foundation, have collectively committed and/or contributed just over $20,000,000 to charitable causes and academic institutions in the New Orleans, San Diego, and West Lafayette/Purdue communities."[1]

He didn't buy his way into being a role model. He simply cares about the 15 people who he knows have supported him in his career.

Tom Brady has a beautiful supermodel wife and many guys are saying, "I 16 wish I was Tom Brady so I could be married to a supermodel and win Super Bowls." That doesn't make him a role model. It's because he is a class act who does a ton for the Boys and Girls Clubs of America and gives his time and money to help others.

I have the pleasure of hosting a radio show called *Sports Palooza Radio* 17 on Blogtalkradio. My wife and I interview professional athletes every Thursday on our two-hour show. Do you know what one of the biggest things is that we look for when we are booking guests? It's what the athlete does to make someone else's life a bit easier. Not everyone has it easy and gets spoon-fed money and material things in life. That's who kids should be looking up to.

There are former NFLers Dennis McKinnon and Lem Barney, who work 18 tirelessly with Gridiron Greats to help former football players. There's former New York Mets Ed Hearn, who is fighting his own health battle, but works with the NephCure Foundation and his own Bottom of the 9th Foundation. There's Roy Smalley, who is president of the Pitch in for Baseball foundation, an organization that collects baseball gear for children who don't have access to others. NFLer Calais Campbell has his own foundation and works hard to help others as well. There are so many other positive examples of athletes doing good things, but they aren't making the headlines. Those athletes are role models.

[1]See https://www.cuinsight.com/press-release/purdue-federal-brees-dream-foundation-give -50000-to-purdue-athletes-life-success-program-2.

And then there's Donald Driver. He didn't start out as role model material. 19
In his book, *Driven*, he tells the story of his rough childhood where he sold
drugs to make money and carried guns. But he cleaned up his act and became
a stellar NFL superstar, carrying himself with class and dignity. He is founder
of the Donald Driver Foundation and the recipient of the 2013 AMVETS
Humanitarian of the Year. If a kid looks up to him it's because he shows them
how to overcome and persevere. That's a role model.

Don't expect the athletes of today to be instant role models. Instantly 20
famous? Maybe that is a better description, but an athlete needs to earn the
role model status. That honor is not bestowed on you because you cashed a
nice paycheck for playing a game!

Identifying the Elements of a Definition Argument

1. This essay does not include a formal definition of *role model*. Why
   not? Following the template below, write your own one-sentence
   definition of *role model*.

   A *role model* is a _____ who _____

   _____

   _____

2. Throughout this essay, Garr gives examples of athletes who are
   and who are not role models. What does he accomplish with
   this strategy?

3. This essay was written in 2014. Do you think that Garr's thesis holds
   up? What contemporary athletes would you substitute for the ones
   Garr discusses?

4. In paragraph 16, Garr discusses why Tom Brady, quarterback for the
   NFL's New England Patriots, is a role model. Since this article was
   written, Brady was accused of deflating footballs during the 2015
   Super Bowl to give his team an unfair advantage. Although Brady
   denied the charges, the NFL gave him a four-game suspension. Does
   this scandal disqualify him from being a role model? Does Brady's
   scandal rise to the level of those involving Pete Rose, Ray Rice, and
   Michael Vick? Why or why not?

5. Where in the essay does Garr define the term *role model* by telling
   what it is not? What does Garr accomplish with this strategy?

6. Where does Garr introduce possible objections to his idea of a role model? Does he refute these objections convincingly? If not, how should he have addressed them?

7. In paragraph 17, Garr says that he and his wife host a radio show. Why does he mention this fact?

➲ EXERCISE 12.4 WRITING A DEFINITION ARGUMENT

According to former First Lady Eleanor Roosevelt, "We gain strength, and courage, and confidence by each experience in which we really stop to look fear in the face. . . . We must do that which we think we cannot." Each of the two pictures that follow presents a visual definition of *courage*. Study the pictures, and then write a paragraph in which you argue that they are (or are not) consistent with Roosevelt's concept of courage.

Firefighters at Ground Zero after the World Trade Center terrorist attacks on September 11, 2001, in New York City
Todd Maisel/New York Daily News Archive/Getty Images

The Tuskegee Airmen, a group of African-American men who overcame
tremendous odds to become U.S. Army pilots during World War II
Library of Congress, Prints & Photographs Division, [LC-DIG-ppmsca-13259]

Why Do We Need to Define Fake News?

Michael Brochstein/SOPA Images/
LightRocket/Getty Images

Go back to page 393 and reread the At Issue box, which gives some background on the question of why we need to define *fake news*. As the following sources illustrate, this question suggests a variety of possible responses.

As you read the sources that follow, you will be asked to answer some questions and to complete some simple activities. This work will help you understand both the content and the structure of the sources. When you are finished, you will be ready to write a **definition argument** on the topic, "Why Do We Need to Define Fake News?"

SOURCES

This piece first appeared in the November/December 2017 issue of Library Technology Reports as part of a longer feature on fake news.

HISTORY OF FAKE NEWS

JOANNA M. BURKHARDT

"Massive digital misinformation is becoming pervasive in online social media to the extent that it has been listed by the World Economic Forum (WEF) as one of the main threats to our society."[1]

Fake news is nothing new. While fake news was in the headlines frequently in the 2016 U.S. election cycle, the origins of fake news date back to before the printing press. Rumor and false stories have probably been around as long as humans have lived in groups where power matters. Until the printing press was invented, news was usually transferred from person to person via word of mouth. The ability to have an impact on what people know is an asset that has been prized for many centuries.

Pre–Printing Press Era

Forms of writing inscribed on materials like stone, clay, and papyrus appeared several thousand years ago. The information in these writings was usually limited to the leaders of the group (emperors, pharaohs, Incas, religious and military leaders, and so on). Controlling information gave some people power over others and has probably contributed to the creation of most of the hierarchical cultures we know today. Knowledge is power. Those controlling knowledge, information, and the means to disseminate information became group leaders, with privileges that others in the group did not have. In many early state societies, remnants of the perks of leadership remain—pyramids, castles, lavish household goods, and more.

Some of the information that has survived, carved in stone or baked on tablets or drawn in pictograms, extolled the wonder and power of the leaders. Often these messages were reminders to the common people that the leader controlled their lives. Others were created to ensure that an individual leader would be remembered for his great prowess, his success in battle, or his great leadership skills. Without means to verify the claims, it's hard to know whether the information was true or fake news.

In the sixth century AD, Procopius of Caesarea (500–ca. 554 AD), the principal historian of Byzantium, used fake news to smear the Emperor Justinian.[2] While Procopius supported Justinian during his lifetime, after the emperor's death Procopius released a treatise called *Secret History* that discredited the emperor and his wife. As the emperor was dead, there could be no retaliation, questioning, or investigations. Since the new emperor did not favor Justinian, it is possible the author had a motivation to distance himself from Justinian's court, using the stories (often wild and unverifiable) to do so.

Post–Printing Press Era

The invention of the printing press and the concurrent spread of literacy made 5 it possible to spread information more widely. Those who were literate could easily use that ability to manipulate information to those who were not literate. As more people became literate, it became more difficult to mislead by misrepresenting what was written.

As literacy rates increased, it eventually became economically feasible to 6 print and sell information. This made the ability to write convincingly and authoritatively on a topic a powerful skill. Leaders have always sought to have talented writers in their employ and to control what information was produced. Printed information became available in different formats and from different sources. Books, newspapers, broadsides, and cartoons were often created by writers who had a monetary incentive. Some were paid by a publisher to provide real news. Others, it seems, were paid to write information for the benefit of their employer.

In 1522, Italian author and satirist Pietro Aretino wrote wicked sonnets, 7 pamphlets, and plays. He self-published his correspondence with the nobility of Italy, using their letters to blackmail former friends and patrons. If those individuals failed to provide the money he required, their indiscretions became public. He took the Roman style of *pasquino*—anonymous lampooning— to a new level of satire and parody. While his writings were satirical (not unlike today's *Saturday Night Live* satire), they planted the seeds of doubt in the minds of their readers about the people in power in Italy and helped to shape the complex political reality of the time.[3]

Aretino's pasquinos were followed by a French variety of fake news known 8 as the canard. The French word *canard* can be used to mean an unfounded rumor or story. Canards were rife during the seventeenth century in France. One canard reported that a monster, captured in Chile, was being shipped to France. This report included an engraving of a dragon-like creature. During the French Revolution the face of Marie Antoinette was superimposed onto the dragon. The revised image was used to disparage the queen.[4] The resulting surge in unpopularity for the queen may have contributed to her harsh treatment during the revolution.

Jonathan Swift complained about political fake news in 1710 in his essay 9 "The Art of Political Lying." He spoke about the damage that lies can do, whether ascribed to a particular author or anonymous: "Falsehood flies, and truth comes limping after it, so that when men come to be undeceived, it is too late; the jest is over, and the tale hath had its effect."[5] Swift's descriptions of fake news in politics in 1710 are remarkably similar to those of writers of the twentyfirst century.

American writer Edgar Allan Poe in 1844 wrote a hoax newspaper article 10 claiming that a balloonist had crossed the Atlantic in a hot air balloon in only three days.[6] His attention to scientific details and the plausibility of the idea caused many people to believe the account until reporters failed to find the balloon or the balloonist. The story was retracted four days after publication. Poe is credited with writing at least six stories that turned out to be fake news.[7]

Mass Media Era

Father Ronald Arbuthnott Knox did a fake news broadcast in January 1926 called 11 "Broadcasting the Barricades" on BBC radio.[8] During this broadcast Knox implied that London was being attacked by Communists, Parliament was under siege, and the Savoy Hotel and Big Ben had been blown up. Those who tuned in late did not hear the disclaimer that the broadcast was a spoof and not an actual news broadcast. This dramatic presentation, coming only a few months after the General Strike in England, caused a minor panic until the story could be explained.

This fake news report was famously followed by Orson Welles's *War of the* 12 *Worlds* broadcast in 1938. *The War of the Worlds* was published as a book in 1898, but those who did not read science fiction were unfamiliar with the story. The presentation of the story as a radio broadcast again caused a minor panic, this time in the United States, as there

> "It is easy to see that fake news has existed for a long time."

were few clues to indicate that reports of a Martian invasion were fictional. While this broadcast was not meant to be fake news, those who missed the introduction didn't know that.[9]

On November 3, 1948, the *Chicago Daily Tribune* editors were so certain of the 13 outcome of the previous day's presidential election that they published the paper with a headline stating, "Dewey Defeats Truman." An iconic picture shows President Truman holding up the newspaper with the erroneous headline. The caption for the picture quotes Truman as saying, "That ain't the way I heard it."[10] The paper, of course, retracted the statement and reprinted the paper with the correct news later in the day. This incident is one reason that journalists at reputable news outlets are required to verify information a number of times before publication.

It is easy to see that fake news has existed for a long time. From the few examples described above, the effects of fake news have ranged widely, from amusement to death. Some authors of fake news probably had benign motivations for producing it. Others appear to have intended to harm individuals, families, or governments. The intended and unintended consequences of fake news of the pre-internet era were profound and far-reaching for the time. As the means of spreading fake news increased, the consequences became increasingly serious.

Internet Era

In the late twentieth century, the internet provided new means for disseminat- 15 ing fake news on a vastly increased scale. When the internet was made publicly available, it was possible for anyone who had a computer to access it. At the same time, innovations in computers made them affordable to the average person. Making information available on the internet became a new way to promote products as well as make information available to everyone almost instantly.

Some fake websites were created in the early years of generalized web 16 use. Some of these hoax websites were satire. Others were meant to mislead or deliberately spread biased or fake news. Early library instruction classes used these types of website as cautionary examples of what an internet user needed to look for. Using a checklist of criteria to identify fake news websites was relatively easy. A few hoax website favorites are

- *DHMO.org.* This website claims that the compound DHMO (Dihydrogen Monoxide), a component of just about everything, has been linked to terrible problems such as cancer, acid rain, and global warming. While everything suggested on the website is true, it is not until one's high school chemistry kicks in that the joke is revealed—DHMO and H_2O are the same thing.

- *Feline Reactions to Bearded Men.* Another popular piece of fake news is a "research study" regarding the reactions of cats to bearded men. This study is reported as if it had been published in a scientific journal. It includes a literature review, a description of the experiment, the raw data resulting from the experiment, and the conclusions reached by the researchers as a result. It is not until the reader gets to the bibliography of the article that the experiment is revealed to be a hoax. Included in the bibliography are articles supposedly written by Madonna Louise Ciccone (Madonna the singer), A. Schwartzenegger (Arnold, perhaps?), and Doctor Seuss and published in journals such as the *Western Musicology Journal, Tonsological Proceedings,* and the *Journal of Feline Forensic Studies.*

- *city-mankato.us.* One of the first websites to make use of website technology to mislead and misdirect was a fake site for the city of Mankato, Minnesota. This website describes the climate as temperate to tropical, claiming that a geological anomaly allows the Mankato Valley to enjoy a year-round temperature of no less than 70 degrees Fahrenheit, while providing snow year-round at nearby Mount Kroto. It reported that one could watch the summer migration of whales up the Minnesota River. An insert shows a picture of a beach, with a second insert showing the current temperature—both tropical. The website proudly announces that it is a Yahoo "Pick of the Week" site and has been featured by the *New York Times* and the *Minneapolis Star Tribune.* Needless to say, no geological anomaly of this type exists in Minnesota. Whales do not migrate up (or down) the Minnesota River at any time, and the pictures of the beaches and the thermometer are actually showing beaches and temperatures from places very far south of Mankato. It is true that Yahoo, the *New York Times,* and the *Minneapolis Star Tribune* featured this website, but not for the reasons you might think. When fake news could still be amusing, this website proved both clever and ironic.

- *MartinLutherKing.org.* This website was created by Stormfront, a white supremacist group, to try to mislead readers about the Civil Rights activist by discrediting his work, his writing, and his personal life.[11] The fact that the website used the .org domain extension convinced a number of people that it was unbiased because the domain extension was usually associated with nonprofit organizations working for good. The authors of the website did not reveal themselves nor did they state their affiliations. Using Martin Luther King's name for the website ensured that people looking for

information about King could easily arrive at this fake news website. This
website is no longer active.

Global Reach of Fake News

Initial forays into the world of fake news fall into the category of entertain- 17
ment, satire, and parody. They are meant to amuse or to instruct the unwary.
Canards and other news that fall into the category of misinformation and misdirection, like the Martin Luther King website, often have more sinister and
serious motives. In generations past, newspaper readers were warned that just
because something was printed in the newspaper did not mean that it was true.
In the twenty-first century, the same could be said about the internet. People
of today create fake news for many of the same reasons that people of the past
did. A number of new twists help to drive the creation and spread of fake news
that did not exist until recently.

Twenty-first-century economic incentives have increased the motivation to 18
supply the public with fake news. The internet is now funded by advertisers rather
than by the government. Advertisers are in business to get information about
their products to as many people as possible. Advertisers will pay a website owner
to allow their advertising to be shown, just as they might pay a newspaper publisher to print advertisements in the paper. How do advertisers decide in which
websites to place their ads? Using computing power to collect the data, it is possible to count the number of visits and visitors to individual sites. Popular websites
attract large numbers of people who visit those sites, making them attractive to
advertisers. The more people who are exposed to the products advertisers want to
sell, the more sales are possible. The fee paid to the website owners by the advertisers rewards website owners for publishing popular information and provides
an incentive to create more content that will attract more people to the site.

People are attracted to gossip, rumor, scandal, innuendo, and the unlikely. 19
Access Hollywood on TV and the *National Enquirer* at the newsstand have used
human nature to make their products popular. That popularity attracts advertisers.
In a *Los Angeles Times* op-ed, Matthew A. Baum and David Lazer report "Another
thing we know is that shocking claims stick in your memory. A long-standing
body of research shows that people are more likely to attend to and later recall a
sensational or negative headline, even if a fact checker flags it as suspect."[12]

In the past several years, people have created websites that capitalize on 20
those nonintellectual aspects of human nature. Advertisers are interested in how
many people will potentially be exposed to their products, rather than the truth
or falsity of the content of the page on which the advertising appears. Unfortunately, sites with sensational headlines or suggestive content tend to be very popular, generating large numbers of visits to those sites and creating an advertising
opportunity. Some advertisers will capitalize on this human propensity for sen-
sation by paying writers of popular content without regard for the actual content
at the site. The website can report anything it likes, as long as it attracts a large
number of people. This is how fake news is monetized, providing incentives for
writers to concentrate on the sensational rather than the truthful.

The problem with most sensational information is that it is not always based [21] on fact, or those facts are twisted in some way to make the story seem like something it is not. It is sometimes based on no information at all. For example:

> Creators of fake news found that they could capture so much interest that they could make money off fake news through automated advertising that rewards high traffic to their sites. A man running a string of fake news sites from the Los Angeles suburbs told NPR he made between $10,000 and $30,000 a month. A computer science student in the former Soviet republic of Georgia told the *New York Times* that creating a new website and filling it with both real stories and fake news that flattered Trump was a "gold mine."[13]

Technological advances have increased the spread of information and [22] democratized its consumption globally. There are obvious benefits associated with instantaneous access to information. The dissemination of information allows ideas to be shared and formerly inaccessible regions to be connected. It makes choices available and provides a platform for many points of view.

However, in a largely unregulated medium, supported and driven by adver- [23] tising, the incentive for good is often outweighed by the incentive to make money, and this has a major impact on how the medium develops over time. Proliferation of fake news is one outcome. While the existence of fake news is not new, the speed at which it travels and the global reach of the technology that can spread it are unprecedented. Fake news exists in the same context as real news on the internet. The problem seems to be distinguishing between what is fake and what is real.

Notes

1. Michela Del Vicario, Alessandro Bessi, Fabiana Zollo, Fabio Petroni, Antonio Scala, Guido Caldarelli, H. Eugene Stanley, and Walter Quattrociocchi, "The Spreading of Misinformation Online," *Proceedings of the National Academy of Sciences of the United States of America* 113, no. 3 (January 19, 2016): 534, https://doi.org/10.1073/pnas.1517441113.

2. Procopius, *Secret History,* trans. Richard Atwater (New York: Covici Friede; Chicago: P. Covici, 1927; repr. Ann Arbor: University of Michigan Press, 1961), https://sourcebooks.fordham.edu/basis/procop-anec.asp.

3. "Pietro Aretino," Wikipedia, last updated August 7, 2017, https://en.wikipedia.org/wiki/Pietro_Aretino.

4. Robert Darnton, "The True History of Fake News," *NYR Daily* (blog), New York Review of Books, February 13, 2017, http://www.nybooks.com/daily/2017/02/13/the-true-history-of-fake-news/.

5. Jonathan Swift, "The Art of Political Lying," *Examiner,* no. 14 (November 9, 1710), para. 9, repr. in Richard Nordquist, "The Art of Political Lying, by Jonathan Swift," ThoughtCo., last updated March 20, 2016, https://www.thoughtco.com/art-of-political-lying-by-swift-1690138.

6. Edgar Allan Poe, "The Balloon Hoax," published 1844, reprinted in PoeStories.com, accessed September 6, 2017, https://poestories.com/read/balloonhoax.

7. Gilbert Arevalo, "The Six Hoaxes of Edgar Allan Poe," HubPages, last updated March 30, 2017, https://hubpages.com/literature/The-Six -Hoaxes-of-Edgar-Allan-Poe.

8. A. Brad Schwartz, "Broadcasting the Barricades," A. Brad Schwartz website, January 16, 2015, https://abradschwartz.com/2015/01/16 /broadcasting-the-barricades/.

9. "The War of the Worlds (radio drama)," Wikipedia, last updated August 24, 2017, https://en.wikipedia.org/wiki/The_War_of_the_Worlds_(radio_drama).

10. Tim Jones, "Dewey Defeats Truman," *Chicago Tribune* website, accessed September 6, 2017, www.chicagotribune.com/news/nationworld/politics /chi-chicagodays-deweydefeats-story-story.html.

11. Keith Thomson, "White Supremacist Site Martin-LutherKing.org Marks 12th Anniversary," *The Blog,* HuffPost, last updated May 26, 2011, www .huffingtonpost.com/entry/white-supremacist-site-ma_b_809755.html.

12. Matthew A. Baum and David Lazer, "Google and Facebook Aren't Fight-ing Fake News with the Right Weapons," op-ed, *Los Angeles Times,* May 8, 2017, www.latimes.com/opinion/op-ed/la-oe-baum-lazer-how-to-fight -fake-news-20170508-story.html.

13. Angie Drobnic Holan, "2016 Lie of the Year: Fake News," PolitiFact, December 13, 2016, www.politifact.com/truth-o-meter/article/2016 /dec/13 /2016-lie-year-fake-news/.

⊘ AT ISSUE: SOURCES FOR DEVELOPING A DEFINITION ARGUMENT

1. Where does Burkhardt define fake news? Does she define this term in enough detail? If not, what could she have done to make her defini-tion more understandable?

2. In her essay, Burkhardt applies the term *fake news* to a treatise written in the sixth century AD and to two radio dramas broadcast in the twentieth century. Is the use of the term in these contexts accurate? Explain.

3. According to Burkhardt, the invention of both the printing press and the internet made it possible to spread information to a great number of people. In what sense are the printing press and the internet alike? How are they different?

4. How, according to Burkhardt, do the economic incentives of the internet increase "the motivation to supply the public with fake news" (para. 18)?

5. Burkhardt's purpose in writing this essay is mainly to convey infor-mation, to give the history of fake news. At what point in the essay does she indicate that she also might be trying to convince her read-ers of something? What is her thesis?

This piece originally appeared on the website Quora, in answer to a question about how to fight the spread of fake news.

WHAT WE CAN DO TO COMBAT FAKE NEWS

JIMMY WALES

There are (at least) two problems that give rise to the "fake news" phenome- 1 non. But let me pause for a minute first to define how I'm using the term for the purposes of this post.

I'm not talking about biased news, or errors made by major publications, 2 nor even irresponsible publication practices taken by what ought to be responsible publications. We'll get to that, as you'll see, but those aren't themselves "fake news" in the technical sense.

> "Various problems with traditional media have given rise to a real loss of trust, and this has given rise to plausibility and gullibility."

Fake news is "news" put forward 3 fraudulently by people just working the system at publications that aren't really news organizations. It can either be politically motivated and well-funded (in some cases perhaps by state-level actors) or it can just be spam. This news has catchy headlines and juicy stories but has absolutely zero concern for the truth, nor usually any concern for appearing truthful other than for just long enough to trick some poor sap into sharing it.

What gives rise to that?

First is the "distribution" problem—and this is something that Facebook 4 and Twitter and others are struggling to deal with. I think progress will be made here, just as progress has been made against spam email.

The second issue is the one I'm more interested in. And that's that various 5 problems with traditional media have given rise to a real loss of trust, and this has given rise to plausibility and gullibility. In short, when we get biased news, frequent errors, clickbait headlines, an extreme race to publish first (whether a story is confirmed or not), then the public doesn't know who to trust or what counts as real.

What's the solution to that? At WikiTribune what I'm really putting for- 6 ward is a strong ethos that we must *show our work*. If we have an interview, we should, to the maximum degree possible, post the audio and the transcript. If we have quotes from a source, we should to the maximum degree possible, name the person we are quoting. If we have documents, we should, to the maximum degree possible, publish the documents.

Not everyone will read all of that background material, of course. But it 7 will be there for a community of people who are interested in holding truth as a core value to read and to edit our work to improve it, in case someone has gone beyond what the source said, or written in a biased manner, etc.

Now I do want to add that in some cases, that kind of ultimate trans- 8 parency isn't possible. Sometimes you do need to protect a whistleblower. But even in those cases, there should be processes and procedures that are transparent and reasonable and verifiable and publicly signed off on to make sure that such things are being done in a responsible way.

If more media outlets take this approach, then the public understanding of 9 what "counts" as real news will shift. Just looking like a newspaper masthead won't be enough—people will expect to see the source documentation just a click away.

⊘ AT ISSUE: SOURCES FOR DEVELOPING A DEFINITION ARGUMENT

1. Wales defines fake news in paragraphs 2 and 3. How does his definition differ from the one Burkhardt includes in her essay? Which definition do you think is more accurate? Explain.

2. In paragraph 5, Wales refers to the "'distribution' problem." What do you think he means? What progress has been made against "spam email"?

3. What are the problems associated with traditional media? What is the result of these problems? According to Wales, how is WikiTribune, a Wikipedia-like news site, solving these problems?

4. What assumptions does Wales make about the readers of WikiTribune? Do you think his assumptions are justified? Explain.

5. In paragraph 9, Wales refers to "ultimate transparency." What does he mean? Why is ultimate transparency not possible in some cases?

6. In an article in the *Atlantic* about WikiTribune, Adrienne Lawrence says the following:

   So it's tempting to imagine a new kind of journalism site that tidily solves so many of the industry's problems—a site that's indifferent to the shrinking pool of available ad dollars, that gets people to carefully vet the information they encounter on a massive scale, a site that inspires people to spend their money on quality journalism, and a site that consistently produces it. This is ambitious stuff. Maybe too ambitious.

   What does Lawrence mean when she says, "This is ambitious stuff. Maybe too ambitious"?

This essay originally appeared in the *New Yorker* on September 4, 2017.

THE FAKE NEWS FALLACY

ADRIAN CHEN

On the evening of October 30, 1938, a seventy-six-year-old millworker in Grover's Mill, New Jersey, named Bill Dock heard something terrifying on the radio. Aliens had landed just down the road, a newscaster announced, and were rampaging through the countryside. Dock grabbed his double-barrelled shotgun and went out into the night, prepared to face down the invaders. But, after investigating, as a newspaper later reported, he "didn't see anybody he thought needed shooting." In fact, he'd been duped by Orson Welles's radio adaptation of *The War of the Worlds*. Structured as a breaking-news report that detailed the invasion in real time, the broadcast adhered faithfully to the conventions of news radio, complete with elaborate sound effects and impersonations of government officials, with only a few brief warnings through the program that it was fiction. 1

The next day, newspapers were full of stories like Dock's. "Thirty men and women rushed into the West 123rd Street police station," ready to evacuate, according to the *Times*. Two people suffered heart attacks from shock, the *Washington Post* reported. One caller from Pittsburgh claimed that he had barely prevented his wife from taking her own life by swallowing poison. The panic was the biggest story for weeks; a photograph of Bill Dock and his shotgun, taken the next day, by a *Daily News* reporter, went "the 1930s equivalent of viral," A. Brad Schwartz writes in his recent history, *Broadcast Hysteria: Orson Welles's* War of the Worlds *and the Art of Fake News*. 2

This early fake-news panic lives on in legend, but Schwartz is the latest of a number of researchers to argue that it wasn't all it was cracked up to be. As Schwartz tells it, there was no mass hysteria, only small pockets of concern that quickly burned out. He casts doubt on whether Dock had even heard the broadcast. Schwartz argues that newspapers exaggerated the panic to better control the upstart medium of radio, which was becoming the dominant source of breaking news in the thirties. Newspapers wanted to show that radio was irresponsible and needed guidance from its older, more respectable siblings in the print media, such "guidance" mostly taking the form of lucrative licensing deals and increased ownership of local radio stations. Columnists and editorialists weighed in. Soon, the Columbia education professor and broadcaster Lyman Bryson declared that unrestrained radio was "one of the most dangerous elements in modern culture." 3

The argument turned on the role of the Federal Communications Commission (F.C.C.), the regulators charged with ensuring that the radio system served the "public interest, convenience, and necessity." Unlike today's F.C.C., which is known mainly as a referee for media mergers, the F.C.C. of the 4 thirties was deeply concerned with the particulars of what broadcasters put in listeners' ears—it had recently issued a reprimand after a racy Mae West sketch that so alarmed NBC it banned West from its stations. To some, the lesson of the panic was that the F.C.C. needed to take an even more active role to protect people from malicious tricksters like Welles. "Programs of that kind are an excellent indication of the inadequacy of our present control over a marvellous facility," the Iowa senator Clyde Herring, a Democrat, declared. He announced a bill that would require broadcasters to submit shows to the F.C.C. for review before airing. Yet Schwartz says that the people calling for a government crackdown were far outnumbered by those who warned against one. "Far from blaming Mr. Orson Welles, he ought to be given a Congressional medal and a national prize," the renowned columnist Dorothy Thompson wrote.

Thompson was concerned with a threat far greater than rogue thespians. 5 Everywhere you looked in the thirties, authoritarian leaders were being swept to power with the help of radio. The Nazi Ministry for Public Enlightenment and Propaganda deployed a force called the Funkwarte, or Radio Guard, that went block by block to ensure that citizens tuned in to Hitler's major broadcast speeches, as Tim Wu details in his new book, *The Attention Merchants*. Meanwhile, homegrown radio demagogues like Father Charles Coughlin and the charismatic Huey Long made some people wonder about a radio-aided Fascist takeover in America. For Thompson, Welles had made an "admirable demonstration" about the power of radio. It showed the danger of handing control of the airwaves over to the state. "No political body must ever, under any circumstances, obtain a monopoly of radio," she wrote. "The greatest organizers of mass hysterias and the mass delusions today are states using the radio to excite terrors, incite hatreds, inflame masses."

Donald Trump's victory has been a demonstration, for many people, of 6 how the internet can be used to achieve those very ends. Trump used Twitter less as a communication device than as a weapon of information warfare, rallying his supporters and attacking opponents with hundred-and-forty-character barrages. "I wouldn't be here without Twitter," he declared on Fox News in March. Yet the internet didn't just give him a megaphone. It also helped him peddle his lies through a profusion of unreliable media sources that undermined the old providers of established fact. Throughout the campaign, fake-news stories, conspiracy theories, and other forms of propaganda were reported to be flooding social networks. The stories were overwhelmingly pro-Trump, and the spread of whoppers like "Pope Francis Shocks World, Endorses Donald Trump for President"—hardly more believable than a Martian invasion—seemed to suggest that huge numbers of Trump supporters were being duped by online lies. This was not the first campaign to be marred by misinformation, of course. But the sheer outlandishness of the claims being made, and believed, suggested to many that the internet had brought about a fundamental devaluing of the truth. Many pundits argued that the "hyper-democratizing" force of the internet had helped usher in a "post-truth" world, where people based their opinions not on facts or reason but on passion and prejudice.

Yet, even among this information anarchy, there remains an authority of 7 sorts. Facebook and Google now define the experience of the internet for most people, and in many ways they play the role of regulators. In the weeks after the election, they faced enormous criticism for their failure to halt the spread of fake news and misinformation on their services. The problem was not simply that people had been able to spread lies but that the digital platforms were set up in ways that made them especially potent. The "share" button sends lies flying around the web faster than fact checkers can debunk them. The supposedly neutral platforms use personalized algorithms to feed us information based on precise data models of our preferences, trapping us in "filter bubbles" that cripple critical thinking and increase polarization. The threat of fake news was compounded by this sense that the role of the press had been ceded to an arcane algorithmic system created by private companies that care only about the bottom line.

Not so very long ago, it was thought that the tension between commercial 8 pressure and the public interest would be one of the many things made obsolete by the internet. In the mid-aughts, during the height of the Web 2.0 boom, the pundit Henry Jenkins declared that the Internet was creating a "participatory culture" where the top-down hegemony of greedy media corporations would be replaced by a horizontal network of amateur "prosumers" engaged in a wonderfully democratic exchange of information in cyberspace—an epistemic agora that would allow the whole globe to come together on a level playing field. Google, Facebook, Twitter, and the rest attained their paradoxical gatekeeper status by positioning themselves as neutral platforms that unlocked the internet's democratic potential by empowering users. It was on a private platform, Twitter, where pro-democracy protesters organized, and on another private platform, Google, where the knowledge of a million public libraries could be accessed for free. These companies would develop into what the tech guru Jeff Jarvis termed "radically public companies," which operate more like public utilities than like businesses.

But there has been a growing sense among mostly liberal-minded observ- 9 ers that the platforms' championing of openness is at odds with the public interest. The image of Arab Spring activists using Twitter to challenge repressive dictators has been replaced, in the public imagination, by that of ISIS propagandists luring vulnerable Western teenagers to Syria via YouTube videos and Facebook chats. The openness that was said to bring about a democratic revolution instead seems to have torn a hole in the social fabric. Today, online misinformation, hate speech,

> "The openness that was said to bring about a democratic revolution instead seems to have torn a hole in the social fabric."

and propaganda are seen as the front line of a reactionary populist upsurge threatening liberal democracy. Once held back by democratic institutions, the bad stuff is now sluicing through a digital breach with the help of irresponsible tech companies. Stanching the torrent of fake news has become a trial by which the digital giants can prove their commitment to democracy. The effort has reignited a debate over the role of mass communication that goes back to the early days of radio.

The debate around radio at the time of *The War of the Worlds* was 10 informed by a similar fall from utopian hopes to dystopian fears. Although radio can seem like an unremarkable medium—audio wallpaper pasted over the most boring parts of your day—the historian David Goodman's book *Radio's Civic Ambition: American Broadcasting and Democracy in the 1930s* makes it clear that the birth of the technology brought about a communications revolution comparable to that of the internet. For the first time, radio allowed a mass audience to experience the same thing simultaneously from the comfort of their homes. Early radio pioneers imagined that this unprecedented blurring of public and private space might become a sort of ethereal forum that would uplift the nation, from the urban slum dweller to the remote Montana rancher. John Dewey called radio "the most powerful instrument of social education the world has ever seen." Populist reformers demanded that radio be treated as a common carrier and give airtime to anyone who paid a fee. Were this to have come about, it would have been very much like the early online-bulletin-board systems where strangers could come together and leave a message for any passing online wanderer. Instead, in the regulatory struggles of the twenties and thirties, the commercial networks won out.

Corporate networks were supported by advertising, and what many pro- 11 gressives had envisaged as the ideal democratic forum began to seem more like Times Square, cluttered with ads for soap and coffee. Rather than elevating public opinion, advertisers pioneered techniques of manipulating it. Who else might be able to exploit such techniques? Many saw a link between the domestic on-air advertising boom and the rise of Fascist dictators like Hitler abroad. Tim Wu cites the leftist critic Max Lerner, who lamented that "the most damning blow the dictatorships have struck at democracy has been the compliment they have paid us in taking over and perfecting our prized techniques of persuasion and our underlying contempt for the credulity of the masses."

Amid such concerns, broadcasters were under intense pressure to show 12 that they were not turning listeners into a zombified mass ripe for the Fascist picking. What they developed in response is, in Goodman's phrase, a "civic paradigm": radio would create active, rational, tolerant listeners—in other words, the ideal citizens of a democratic society. Classical- music-appreciation shows were developed with an eye toward uplift. Inspired by progressive educators, radio networks hosted "forum" programs, in which citizens from all walks of life were invited to discuss the matters of the day, with the aim of inspiring tolerance and political engagement. One such program, *America's*

Town Meeting of the Air, featured in its first episode a Communist, a Fascist, a Socialist, and a Democrat.

Listening to the radio, then, would be a "civic practice" that could cre- 13 ate a more democratic society by exposing people to diversity. But only if they listened correctly. There was great concern about distracted and gullible listeners being susceptible to propagandists. A group of progressive journalists and thinkers known as "propaganda critics" set about educating radio listeners. The Institute for Propaganda Analysis, co-founded by the social psychologist Clyde R. Miller, with funding from the department-store magnate Edward Filene, was at the forefront of the movement. In newsletters, books, and lectures, the institute's members urged listeners to attend to their own biases while analyzing broadcast voices for signs of manipulation. Listening to the radio critically became the duty of every responsible citizen. Goodman, who is generally sympathetic to the proponents of the civic paradigm, is alert to the off notes here of snobbery and disdain: much of the progressive concern about listeners' abilities stemmed from the belief that Americans were, basically, dim-witted—an idea that gained currency after intelligence tests on soldiers during the First World War supposedly revealed discouraging news about the capacities of the average American. In the wake of *The War of the Worlds* panic, commentators didn't hesitate to rail against "idiotic" and "stupid" listeners. Welles and his crew, Dorothy Thompson declared, "have shown up the incredible stupidity, lack of nerve, and ignorance of thousands."

Today, when we speak about people's relationship to the internet, we 14 tend to adopt the nonjudgmental language of computer science. Fake news was described as a "virus" spreading among users who have been "exposed" to online misinformation. The proposed solutions to the fake-news problem typically resemble antivirus programs: their aim is to identify and quarantine all the dangerous nonfacts throughout the web before they can infect their prospective hosts. One venture capitalist, writing on the tech blog Venture Beat, imagined deploying artificial intelligence as a "media cop," protecting users from malicious content. "Imagine a world where every article could be assessed based on its level of sound discourse," he wrote. The vision here was of the news consumers of the future turning the discourse setting on their browser up to eleven and soaking in pure fact. It's possible, though, that this approach comes with its own form of myopia. Neil Postman, writing a couple of decades ago, warned of a growing tendency to view people as computers, and a corresponding devaluation of the "singular human capacity to see things whole in all their psychic, emotional, and moral dimensions." A person does not process information the way a computer does, flipping a switch of "true" or "false." One rarely cited Pew statistic shows that only four percent of American internet users trust social media "a lot," which suggests a greater resilience against online misinformation than overheated editorials might lead us to expect. Most people seem to understand that their social-media streams represent a heady mixture of gossip, political activism, news, and entertainment. You might see this as a problem, but turning to Big Data–driven algorithms to

fix it will only further entrench our reliance on code to tell us what is important about the world—which is what led to the problem in the first place. Plus,
it doesn't sound very fun.

The various efforts to fact-check and label and blacklist and sort all the 15
world's information bring to mind a quote, which appears in David Goodman's
book, from John Grierson, a documentary filmmaker: "Men don't live by
bread alone, nor by fact alone." In the nineteen-forties, Grierson was on an
F.C.C. panel that had been convened to determine how best to encourage a
democratic radio, and he was frustrated by a draft report that reflected his
fellow-panelists' obsession with filling the airwaves with rationality and fact.
Grierson said, "Much of this entertainment is the folk stuff . . . of our technological time; the patterns of observation, of humor, of fancy, which make a
technological society a human society."

In recent times, Donald Trump supporters are the ones who have most 16
effectively applied Grierson's insight to the digital age. Young Trump enthusiasts turned internet trolling into a potent political tool, deploying the "folk
stuff" of the web—memes, slang, the nihilistic humor of a certain subculture
of web-native gamer—to give a subversive, cyberpunk sheen to a movement
that might otherwise look like a stale reactionary blend of white nationalism
and anti-feminism. As crusaders against fake news push technology companies to "defend the truth," they face a backlash from a conservative movement,
retooled for the digital age, which sees claims for objectivity as a smoke screen
for bias.

One sign of this development came last summer, in the scandal over Face- 17
book's "Trending" sidebar, in which curators chose stories to feature on the
user's home page. When the tech website Gizmodo reported the claim of an
anonymous employee that the curators were systematically suppressing conservative news stories, the right-wing blogosphere exploded. Breitbart, the
far-right torchbearer, uncovered the social-media accounts of some of the
employees—liberal recent college graduates—that seemed to confirm the suspicion of pervasive anti-right bias. Eventually, Facebook fired the team and
retooled the feature, calling in high-profile conservatives for a meeting with
Mark Zuckerberg. Although Facebook denied that there was any systematic
suppression of conservative views, the outcry was enough to reverse a tiny first
step it had taken toward introducing human judgment into the algorithmic
machine.

For conservatives, the rise of online gatekeepers may be a blessing in 18
disguise. Throwing the charge of "liberal media bias" against powerful institutions has always provided an energizing force for the conservative movement, as the historian Nicole Hemmer shows in her new book, *Messengers of
the Right*. Instead of focussing on ideas, Hemmer focusses on the galvanizing
struggle over the means of distributing those ideas. The first modern conservatives were members of the America First movement, who found their
isolationist views marginalized in the lead-up to the Second World War and
vowed to fight back by forming the first conservative media outlets. A "vague

claim of exclusion" sharpened into a "powerful and effective ideological arrow in the conservative quiver," Hemmer argues, through battles that conservative radio broadcasters had with the F.C.C. in the nineteen-fifties and sixties. Their main obstacle was the F.C.C.'s Fairness Doctrine, which sought to protect public discourse by requiring controversial opinions to be balanced by opposing viewpoints. Since attacks on the mid-century liberal consensus were inherently controversial, conservatives found themselves constantly in regulators' sights. In 1961, a watershed moment occurred with the leak of a memo from labor leaders to the Kennedy Administration which suggested using the Fairness Doctrine to suppress right-wing viewpoints. To many conservatives, the memo proved the existence of the vast conspiracy they had long suspected. A fund-raising letter for a prominent conservative radio show railed against the doctrine, calling it "the most dastardly collateral attack on freedom of speech in the history of the country." Thus was born the character of the persecuted truthteller standing up to a tyrannical government—a trope on which a billion-dollar conservative-media juggernaut has been built.

Today, Facebook and Google have taken the place of the F.C.C. in the conservative imagination. Conservative bloggers highlight the support that Jack Dorsey, the C.E.O. of Twitter, has expressed for Black Lives Matter, and the frequent visits that Google's Eric Schmidt made to the Obama White House. When Facebook announced that it was partnering with a group of fact checkers from the nonprofit Poynter Institute to flag false news stories, conservatives saw another effort to censor them under the guise of objectivity. Brent Bozell, who runs the conservative media-watchdog group Media Research Center, cited the fact that Poynter received funding from the liberal financier George Soros. "Just like George Soros and company underwrote the Fairness Doctrine several years ago," he said, "this is about going after conservative talk on the internet and banning it by somehow projecting it as being false." 19

One lesson you get from Hemmer's research is that the conservative skepticism of gatekeepers is not without a historical basis. The Fairness Doctrine really was used by liberal groups to silence conservatives, typically by flooding stations with complaints and requests for airtime to respond. This created a chilling effect, with stations often choosing to avoid controversial material. The technical fixes implemented by Google and Facebook in the rush to fight fake news seem equally open to abuse, dependent, as they are, on user-generated reports. 20

Yet today, with a powerful, well-funded propaganda machine dedicated to publicizing any hint of liberal bias, conservatives aren't the ones who have the most to fear. As Facebook has become an increasingly important venue for activists documenting police abuse, many of them have complained that overzealous censors routinely block their posts. A recent report by the investigative nonprofit ProPublica shows how anti-racist activism can often fall afoul of Facebook rules against offensive material, while a post by the Louisiana representative Clay Higgins calling for the slaughter of "radicalized" Muslims was deemed acceptable. In 2016, a group of civil-rights activists wrote Facebook to demand that 21 steps be taken to ensure that the platform could be used by marginalized people and social movements organizing for change. There was no high-profile meeting with Zuckerberg, only a form letter outlining Facebook's moderation practices. The wishful story about how the internet was creating a hyper-democratic "participatory culture" obscures the ways in which it is biased in favor of power.

The online tumult of the 2016 election fed into a growing suspicion of 22 Silicon Valley's dominance over the public sphere. Across the political spectrum, people have become less trusting of the Big Tech companies that govern most online political expression. Calls for civic responsibility on the part of Silicon Valley companies have replaced the hope that technological innovation alone might bring about a democratic revolution. Despite the focus on algorithms, A.I., filter bubbles, and Big Data, these questions are political as much as technical. Regulation has become an increasingly popular notion; the Democratic senator Cory Booker has called for greater antitrust scrutiny of Google and Facebook, while Stephen Bannon reportedly wants to regulate Google and Facebook like public utilities. In the nineteen-thirties, such threats encouraged commercial broadcasters to adopt the civic paradigm. In that prewar era, advocates of democratic radio were united by a progressive vision of pluralism and rationality; today, the question of how to fashion a democratic social media is one more front in our highly divisive culture wars.

Still, Silicon Valley isn't taking any chances. In the wake of the recent, 23 deadly white-supremacist rally in Charlottesville, Virginia, a slew of tech companies banned the neo-Nazi blog the Daily Stormer, essentially blacklisting it from the web. Responding so directly to appeals to decency and justice that followed the tragedy, these companies positioned themselves less as neutral platforms than as custodians of the public interest.

Zuckerberg recently posted a fifty-seven-hundred-word manifesto 24 announcing a new mission for Facebook that goes beyond the neutral-seeming mandate to "make the world more open and connected." Henceforth, Facebook would seek to "develop the social infrastructure to give people the power to build a global community that works for all of us." The manifesto was so heavy on themes of civic responsibility that many took it as a blueprint for a future political campaign. Speculation has only grown since Zuckerberg embarked on a fifty-state tour this summer to meet American Facebook users, posting photos of himself with livestock and unhealthy local delicacies. Those who think that Zuckerberg is preparing for a Presidential bid, however, should consider the emerging vectors of power in the digital era: for the man who runs Facebook, the White House might well look like a step down.

➲ AT ISSUE: SOURCES FOR DEVELOPING A DEFINITION ARGUMENT

1. What is the significance of Chen's title? Why, according to Chen, is fake news a "fallacy"?

2. Chen begins his essay by describing people's reaction to Orson Welles's 1938 radio adaption of *The War of the Worlds*. What point about early radio is Chen making? Why did columnist Dorothy Thompson think that far from being punished, Wells "ought to be given a Congressional medal and a national prize" (para. 4)?

3. What is Chen's opinion of President Donald Trump and those who voted for him? What language in his essay leads you to your conclusion? Do you think his assessments are fair, or do they seem unduly biased? Explain.

4. In paragraph 6, Chen says that many pundits argue "that the 'hyper-democratizing' force of the internet" helped usher in a "'post-truth' world, where people based their opinions not on facts or reason but on passion and prejudice." What is a "post-truth world"? How do Google and Facebook "play the role of regulators" of "this information anarchy" (7)?

5. In paragraph 10, Chen says that both the internet and "radio at the time of *The War of the Worlds*" were informed by a "fall from utopian hopes to dystopian fears." What does he mean? Do you agree?

6. How is Silicon Valley reacting to the possibility of government regulation of the internet? Does Chen support or oppose this regulation? Explain.

7. At what points in his essay does Chen address opposing arguments? Does he adequately refute them? Explain.

This article first appeared in *Science* magazine on March 8, 2018.

FAKE NEWS SPREADS FASTER THAN TRUE NEWS ON TWITTER

KATIE LANGIN

During the 2016 U.S. presidential election, the internet was abuzz with discussion 1 when reports surfaced that Floyd Mayweather wore a hijab to a Donald Trump rally, daring people to fight him. The concocted story started on a sports comedy website, but it quickly spread on social media—and people took it seriously.

From Russian "bots" to charges of fake news, headlines are awash in 2 stories about dubious information going viral. You might think that bots—automated systems that can share information online—are to blame. But a new study shows that people are the prime culprits when it comes to the propagation of misinformation through social networks. And they're good at it too: Tweets containing falsehoods reach 1,500 people on Twitter six times faster than truthful tweets, the research reveals.

Bots are so new that we don't have a clear sense of what they're doing and 3 how big of an impact they're making, says Shawn Dorius, a social scientist at Iowa State University in Ames who wasn't involved in the research. We generally think that bots distort the types of information that reaches the public, but—in this study at least—they don't seem to be skewing the headlines toward false news, he notes. They propagated true and false news roughly equally.

The main impetus for the new research was the 2013 Boston Marathon 4 bombing. The lead author—Soroush Vosoughi, a data scientist at the Massachusetts Institute of Technology in Cambridge—says after the attack a lot of the stuff he was reading on social media was false. There were rumors that a student from Brown University, who had gone missing, was suspected by the police. But later, people found out that he had nothing to do with the attack and had committed suicide (for reasons unrelated to the bombing).

That's when Vosoughi realized that "these rumors aren't just fun things on 5 Twitter, they really can have effects on people's lives and hurt them really badly." A PhD student at the time, he switched his research to focus on the problem of detecting and characterizing the spread of misinformation on social media.

He and his colleagues collected 12 years of data from Twitter, starting from 6 the social media platform's inception in 2006. Then they pulled out tweets related to news that had been investigated by six independent fact-checking organizations—websites like PolitiFact, Snopes, and FactCheck.org. They ended up with a data set of 126,000 news items that were shared 4.5 million times by 3 million people, which they then used to compare the spread of news that had been verified as true with the spread of stories shown to be false. They found that whereas the truth rarely reached more than 1000 Twitter users, the most pernicious false news

> "False news propagated faster and wider for all forms of news."

stories—like the Mayweather tale—routinely reached well over 10,000 people. False news propagated faster and wider for all forms of news—but the problem was particularly evident for political news, the team reports today in *Science*.

At first the researchers thought that bots might be responsible, so they 7 used sophisticated bot-detection technology to remove social media shares generated by bots. But the results didn't change: False news still spread at roughly the same rate and to the same number of people. By default, that meant that human beings were responsible for the virality of false news.

That got the scientists thinking about the people involved. It occurred to 8 them that Twitter users who spread false news might have more followers. But that turned out to be a dead end: Those people had fewer followers, not more.

Finally the team decided to look more closely at the tweets themselves. As it 9 turned out, tweets containing false information were more novel—they contained new information that a Twitter user hadn't seen before—than those containing true information. And they elicited different emotional reactions, with people expressing greater surprise and disgust. That novelty and emotional charge seem to be what's generating more retweets. "If something sounds crazy stupid you wouldn't think it would get that much traction," says Alex Kasprak, a fact-checking journalist at Snopes in Pasadena, California. "But those are the ones that go massively viral."

The research gives you a sense of how much of a problem fake news is, 10 both because of its scale and because of our own tendencies to share misinformation, says David Lazer, a computational social scientist at Northeastern University in Boston who co-wrote a policy perspective on the science of fake news that was also published today in *Science*. He thinks that, in the short term, the "Facebooks, Googles, and Twitters of the world" need to do more to implement safeguards to reduce the magnitude of the problem. But in the long term we also need more science, he says—because if we don't understand where fake news comes from and how it spreads, then how can we possibly combat it?

◯ AT ISSUE: SOURCES FOR DEVELOPING A DEFINITION ARGUMENT

1. What is a *bot*? How does it disseminate information on the internet?

2. What is the relationship between bots and false news. According to Langin, what is the relationship of people to false news?

3. Throughout her essay, Langin uses the terms *fake news*, *false news*, and *misinformation*. Do you think these terms have the same meaning? If not, how would you differentiate among them?

4. Why does Langin think that fake news spreads faster than true news? According to her, why is this a problem?

5. Langan ends her essay by referring to David Lazer, a social scientist who studies fake news. What does Lazer think should be done to combat fake news? Do you agree? What other steps could be taken?

6. Is this essay structured inductively or deductively? Why do you think Langin made the choice she did?

This article first appeared on the *Forbes* magazine website on December 11, 2016.

HOW DATA AND INFORMATION LITERACY COULD END FAKE NEWS

KALEV LEETARU

At its core, the rise of "fake news" is first and foremost a sign that we have failed 1 as a society to teach our citizens how to think critically about data and information. Take that email from a Nigerian prince offering to transfer you ten million dollars if you'll just send him $10,000 to cover the wire costs. Enough people get that email each day and wire those ten thousand dollars that this scam continues in 2016. The internet has globalized the art of the scam and the reach of misinformation, allowing a single tweet to go viral across the planet, sowing chaos in countries on the other side of the world from the person sending it.

At the heart of all such news is the inability to think critically about the 2 information that surrounds us and to perform the necessary due diligence and research to verify and validate. In April 2013 when the AP's Twitter account was hacked and tweeted that there had been an explosion at the White House that left President Obama injured, automated stock trading algorithms took the news as fact and immediately launched a cascade of trading activity that plunged the Dow Jones by more than 100 points in less than 120 seconds. Human reporters, on the other hand, simply picked up the phone and called colleagues stationed at the White House to inquire if they were aware of any such attack and were quick to refute the false information.

Such triangulation lies at the root of basic fact checking, yet few today 3 go to such lengths when reviewing information online. How many countless memes have spread on Facebook falsely attributing a particularly poignant quote to someone in the news? During the 2016 election cycle, such memes were standard practice on both sides, with unflattering or damaging statements falsely attributed to both candidates. A quick Google search for the quote in question typically turned up in short order corroborating information either showing that the quote was a modification of an existing quote, was attributed to the wrong person, or was fabricated entirely.

Yet, when I ask an audience at one of my presentations to raise their hand 4 if they fact check such quotes before sharing them online, I have yet to see a single hand. In fact, I frequently see journalists at top tier outlets misattributing famous quotes. This is an area where technology could in fact play a powerful role—imagine a browser plugin that automatically flagged quoted statements and factual statements in an article and conducted a quick online search to see if there was strong disagreement on who made the statement or the specifics of the factual statement. While this would not tell whether the statement/fact is false, it would at least flag contentious issues for readers to let them know there is disagreement.

Even the nation's most respected newspapers face challenges when fact 5 checking events in foreign countries as a result of a steeply declining foreign bureau footprint. Whereas in the past a top newspaper might have any number of staff permanently stationed in key countries around the world to report on events firsthand, today a protest march or terror attack is more likely to be covered by stringers or through remote reporting.

A top U.S. paper reported in a front-page story earlier this year that the 6 main refugee housing center in a European country had been burned to the ground in a xenophobic arsonist attack. Yet, a quick English language Google search turned up local coverage of the arson which stated that the fire had merely scorched a few siding shingles and was quickly put out, with everyone back inside the building shortly afterwards. Local coverage even included copious photographs showing just how minor the damage was. Yet, one of the most respected newspapers in the United States failed to perform even basic fact checking on its claims that the building was burned to the ground in a country where there is plenty of English coverage and thus no language barrier to impede verification. Again, this is an area where automated triangulation tools could play a great role in reducing such incidents.

Indeed, when I ask my audiences how many of them have turned to Google 7 News and Google Translate to access local Nepalese press coverage about the latest developments in the nation's recovery from the 2015 earthquake, I have yet to see a single hand raised. Today we have access to all the world's information, yet we take no advantage of that information to be more informed citizens of the world. Similarly, the majority of Americans' understanding of Syria come from heavily mediated Western reporting, often brokered or expanded through stringers or statements from the various involved parties. Few Americans have visited Syria recently as disinterested parties to learn for themselves what conditions on the ground are like and to catalog play-by-play narratives of the war. Local sources here will not provide an unbiased view, but at the least will provide reporting from closer to the nexus of activity, offering a greater range of perspectives and reports to allow a reader to make a more informed assessment of local activity and to see it through local eyes.

> "Today we have access to all the world's information, yet we take no advantage to be more informed citizens of the world."

While media and technology pundits have touted fully automated solu- 8 tions that would simply read an article and flag it as "true" or "false," the reality is much more difficult in that "fake news" is not black and white, it is a hundred shades of gray. In short, much of what we might label as "fake news" is actually a difference of opinion in how people of different backgrounds and experiences interpret a common set of information. Just as one person might find a statement hilariously humorous, another might find it deeply offensive— so too might two different people come to very different conclusions regarding whether a political candidate's statements make him unfit for office or whether they are his main appeal.

Attempting to classify entire websites as "fake" or "truthful" is also prob- 9
lematic, as one plugin discovered when it mistakenly flagged a story about
veterans heading to Standing Rock as false because of its use of a blanket
domain-based blacklist, even though the story was actually correct and had
been widely reported in other outlets. In a twist of irony, the well-regarded
outlet Tech Crunch initially reported this as a new Facebook technology gone
awry, before later correcting its story to note that this was a third party plugin
and unrelated to Facebook in any way. Facebook itself subsequently banned
the plugin before reenabling it.

Yet, a Stanford study published last month demonstrates the problem with 10
the status quo of simply leaving fact checking to readers themselves and hoping things will get better as the younger born-digital generation takes over.
Through a series of tests, the authors found that at every level of education,
from middle school to high school to college students, digital natives found
themselves unable to perform even the most basic of tasks of recognizing a
news article from a paid advertisement or recognizing an editorial from hard
news reporting. This is made even more difficult by the increasing fluidity and
blending of these formats in the evolving world of journalism.

The notion of a magical technology that could instantly label every article on 11
the web as "fake" or "true" is a false promise due to the hundred shades of gray that
underlie how we interpret the information around us. Yet, technology could certainly help us understand the information environment around a topic of interest,
seeing all of the different perspectives and statements being attributed to the event
and allowing us to make more informed decisions about that information.

As noted earlier, a browser or Facebook plugin that automatically iden- 12
tified quotes and factual assertions from an article and compiled a list of all
reporting on those quotes and statements would at the very least allow a reader
to understand how contested those details are. For example, a rapidly spreading viral meme attributing a certain statement to President Obama this afternoon could instantly be flagged as actually being a quote by Abraham Lincoln
from a century and a half ago. A climate change claim that temperatures have
actually dropped by 20 degrees over the past century could show that this
number comes from a single personal blog, while all remaining reporting and
scientific journals report very different results. Or, in the breaking aftermath
of a major terror attack, such a tool could draw together all of the conflicting
reports of the death and injury toll to offer a better understanding of the extent
of the attack as new information emerges.

Such an approach avoids the problematic approach of attempting to enforce 13
a single label of "fact" or "fiction" that ignores those hundred shades of gray, but
rather provides the tools to create more informed consumers of information.

Similarly, one could imagine a browser plugin that takes all of the news 14
outlets reporting on an issue and visualizes them in a 3D graph. The X axis
would position each outlet by how positive or negative its average coverage
of the topic is, while the Y axis positions each outlet by how much coverage
it affords the topic and the Z axis by how polarized/emotional its coverage is.
From such a graph one can immediately segment highly partisan outlets from

outlets adopting a more clinical reserved view. Of course, an outlet clinically covering a topic is not necessarily any less misleading in its coverage than a highly emotional partisan one, but at the very least, it suggests that the author is at least attempting to be more detached in his or her coverage and writing in more journalistic style rather than editorial style. Such a graph can easily be automated through the use of various sentiment mining tools.

Similarly, a common approach used in fact checking is to assess the level 15 of concrete detail in a report. An article that is filled with vague emotional language is more likely to be problematic than one filled with concrete details, such as quotes and precise numbers that can be verified and validated. An article reporting the results of a secret CIA report in which no details can be revealed is far more difficult to fact check than an article in which all of the facts are available for both verification and reputation assessment.

Putting this all together, we see that fake news exists because as a society 16 we have failed to teach our citizens data and information literacy. As I've noted here before, I've seen senior policymakers make statements that numbers equate to facts and that data is truth. Yet, as the Stanford study shows, even digital natives who have grown up in the information-saturated online world do no better at discerning the credibility of information or even understanding the most basic concepts of what is a paid advertisement versus journalistic reporting. Suggestions like requiring programming and data science courses in school would certainly create more technically literate citizens, but this is not the same as data literacy and the kind of critical and devil's advocate thinking it requires. Technology is also not a panacea here, as there is no simple magic algorithm that can eliminate false and misleading news. Instead, to truly solve the issue of "fake news" we must blend technological assistance with teaching our citizens to be data literate consumers of the world around them.

⊘ AT ISSUE: SOURCES FOR DEVELOPING A DEFINITION ARGUMENT

1. Leetaru begins his essay by stating the problem. Why does he begin this way? Is this an effective strategy? Why or why not?

2. Does Leetaru assume that his readers already understand what fake news is? How do you know? Is he correct?

3. According to Kalev Leetaru, how can technology help people become more data literate? What are the limitations of technology?

4. In paragraph 8, Leetaru says that "'fake news' is not black and white, it is a hundred shades of gray." What does he mean?

5. At what point in his essay does Leetaru acknowledge opposing arguments? How effectively does he refute them?

6. Why, according to Leetaru, can't the problem of fake news be solved simply by leaving the fact-checking to readers?

VISUAL ARGUMENT

Mikhail Leonov/Shutterstock

⊘ AT ISSUE: SOURCES FOR DEVELOPING A DEFINITION ARGUMENT

1. What message does this visual convey?

2. What do the words used here—CNN, turn left, truth, one way— suggest to you? How do these words work together to communicate the visual's message? What does the green light suggest?

3. Does the image appeal mainly to *ethos*, *pathos*, or *logos*?

4. Do you think the visual is effective? Why or why not?

TEMPLATE FOR WRITING A DEFINITION ARGUMENT

Write a one-paragraph definition argument in which you take a position on the topic, "Why Do We Need to Define Fake News?" Follow the template below, filling in the blanks to create your argument.

Most people seem to agree that fake news is a problem in our society, but not everyone agrees on the definition. Before we can decide what to do to solve this problem, we have to determine what fake news is and what it is not. Many people seem to think that anything they don't like or agree with must be fake news. For example, _____
_____.

Others, however, define fake news as _____
_____
_____.

For instance,_____.
To solve this problem, we should _____
_____
_____.

⊃ EXERCISE 12.5 EXPANDING YOUR DEFINITION

Ask two or three of your instructors what they consider to be fake news. Then, revise the draft of the paragraph you wrote in the template so that it includes your instructors' opinions.

⊃ EXERCISE 12.6 WRITING A DEFINITION ARGUMENT

Write a definition argument on the topic, "Why Do We Need to Define Fake News?" Make sure that you define the term *fake news* and that you give examples to develop your definition. (If you like, you may incorporate the material you developed in the template and Exercise 12.5.) You can refer to the At Issue readings on pages 409–433 to find sources to support your position. Be sure to document the sources you use and to include a works-cited page. (See Chapter 10 for information on documenting sources.)

⊘ EXERCISE 12.7 REVIEWING THE FOUR PILLARS OF ARGUMENT

Review the four pillars of argument discussed in Chapter 1. Does your essay include all four elements of an effective argument? Add anything that is missing. Then, label the key elements of your essay.

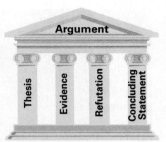

⊘ WRITING ASSIGNMENTS: DEFINITION ARGUMENTS

1. On most campuses, instructors have the right to pursue, teach, and discuss ideas without restriction. This principle is called *academic freedom*. Do you think that instructors should have academic freedom, or do you believe that this principle should be restricted? For example, are there any subjects or ideas an instructor should *not* be allowed to discuss? Write a definition argument in which you define *academic freedom* and take a position on this issue. For sources to incorporate into your argument, see Chapter 5.

2. Many colleges require students to perform community service before they graduate. Do you think that college students should have to do community service? Before you begin your argument, find a definition of the term *community service*. Be sure your argument focuses on the definition of this term.

3. Take detailed notes about the food and service in your campus cafeteria. Then, write an argumentative essay in which you rate the cafeteria as *excellent*, *good*, *bad*, or *poor*. Keep in mind that you are presenting *operational definitions* of these terms (see p. 398) and that you will have to explain the factors you examined to form your assessment.

Plume Creative/Getty Images

13

Cause-and-Effect Arguments

Does Our Reliance on Social Media Bring Us Together or Drive Us Apart?

In 2018, Facebook launched an advertising campaign with the slogan, "The Best Part of Facebook Isn't on Facebook." It seems odd for the world's biggest social-networking site to imply that offline connections are more important than the ones that we have online. However, it also shows a self-consciousness about what all that friending, liking, posting, and sharing is doing to us. The early years of the internet came with utopian visions of connectivity, bringing people around the world together to share their stories and help democratize the spreading of information. In some ways, this came true. For plenty of users, social networks are a genuine source of community, empowerment, and fun that could not have existed a generation earlier.

But social media also has a dark, dystopian side. Online trolls regularly engage in large-scale threats and harassment. Twitter, once a platform that brought different people around the world together to share information and conversation, now finds itself embroiled in controversies about the toxic content of its users. Cyberbullying has been labeled an "epidemic." Excessive screen time is linked to anxiety, depression, and suicide in teenagers—and these problems are not limited to young people. Social media allows users of all ages to isolate in the networks and opinions of like-minded people, reinforcing tribalism and polarization. So is all this connectivity making us more *disconnected*? Or is there still enough sense of community online to counteract the darker side? After reading a variety of perspectives on this complex issue, you will be writing a **cause-and-effect** argument that takes a position on social media.

What Is a Cause-and-Effect Argument?

Cause-and-effect arguments attempt to find causes (Why don't more Americans vote?) or identify possible effects (Does movie violence cause societal violence?). A cause-and-effect argument identifies the causes of an event or situation and takes a stand on what actually caused it. Alternatively, a cause-and-effect argument can focus on effects, taking a position on what a likely outcome is, has been, or will be.

Many of the arguments that you read and discuss examine causes and effects. In an essay on one of the following topics, for example, you would search for the causes of an event or a situation, examining a number of different possible causes before concluding that a particular cause was the most likely one. You could also consider the possible outcomes or results of a given event or situation and conclude that one possible effect would most likely occur:

- Are designated bicycle lanes really safer for cyclists?
- Is fast food making Americans fat?
- Is human activity responsible for climate change?
- Do mandatory minimum sentences discourage crime?
- Do charter schools improve students' academic performance?
- Does profiling decrease the likelihood of a terrorist attack?
- Does our reliance on social media bring us together or drive us apart?

⊜ EXERCISE 13.1 EXPLAINING CAUSE-AND-EFFECT ARGUMENTS

Bumper-sticker slogans frequently make cause-and-effect arguments that suggest the consequences of ignoring the message or the positive results of following the slogan's advice. Choose three of the bumper stickers from the following picture and explain the cause-and-effect argument each slogan makes.

Lucid Images/AGE Fotostock

Understanding Cause-and-Effect Relationships

Before you can write a cause-and-effect argument, you need to understand the nature of cause-and-effect relationships, some of which can be very complex. For one thing, a single event or situation can have many possible results, and not all of these will be equally significant. Identifying causes can be equally challenging because an event or situation can have more than one cause. For example, many factors might explain why more Americans do not vote. (The following diagram illustrates some possible causes.)

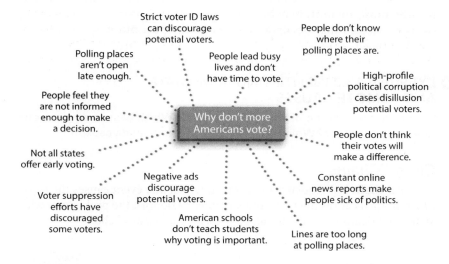

Main and Contributory Causes

In a cause-and-effect argument, your focus is on identifying the cause you believe is the most important and presenting arguments to convince readers *why* it is the most important (and why other causes are not as important).

The most important cause is the **main cause**; the less important causes are **contributory causes**. Typically, you will present the main cause as your key argument in support of your thesis, and you will identify the contributory causes elsewhere in your argument. (You may also identify factors that are *not* causes and explain why they are not.)

Identifying the main cause is not always easy; the most important cause may not always be the most obvious one. However, you need to figure out which cause is most important so you can structure and support your essay with this emphasis in mind.

❥ EXERCISE 13.2 UNDERSTANDING CAUSES

Look at the diagram on the previous page. Which causes do you see as the most and least important? Why? Do you think that any of the factors presented in the diagram are not really causes? Can you suggest any additional causes? If you were writing a cause-and-effect argument taking a position on the topic of why many Americans do not vote, which cause would you focus on? Why?

Immediate and Remote Causes

As mentioned earlier, identifying the main cause of a particular effect can be difficult because the most important cause is not necessarily the most obvious one. Usually, the most obvious cause is the **immediate cause**— the one that occurs right before an event. For example, a political scandal that erupts the day before an election might cause many disillusioned voters to stay home from the polls. However, this immediate cause, although it is the most obvious, may be less important than one or more **remote causes**—factors that occurred further in the past but may have had a greater impact.

❥ EXERCISE 13.3 IDENTIFYING IMMEDIATE AND REMOTE CAUSES

Look once more at the diagram on page 439. Which causes do you consider remote causes? Which one might be the immediate cause?

Causal Chains

A **causal chain** is a sequence of events in which one event causes the next, which in turn causes the next, and so on. For example, the problem of why many Americans do not vote can be presented as a causal chain.

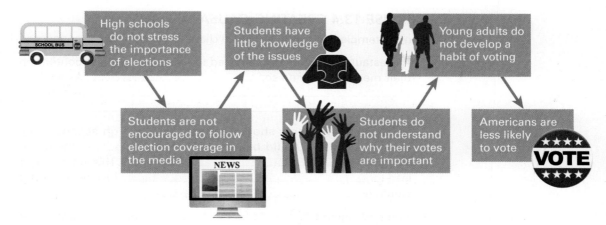

When you write a cause-and-effect argument, you can organize your essay as a causal chain, as the following outline illustrates.

Thesis statement: Because they do not encourage students to see voting as a civic duty, U.S. high schools are at least partly to blame for the low turnout in many elections.

- High schools do not stress the importance of elections.
- As a result, students do not follow election coverage in the media.
- Because they do not follow election coverage, students have little knowledge of the issues.
- With little knowledge of the issues, students do not understand that it is important to vote.
- Because they do not see voting as important, young adults do not develop a habit of regular voting.
- As a result, American adults are less likely to vote.

KEY WORDS FOR CAUSE-AND-EFFECT ARGUMENTS

When you write cause-and-effect arguments, choose verbs that indicate causal connections:

bring about	create	lead to	encourage
influence	contribute to	originate in	cause

Be sure to use transitional words and phrases such as *consequently* and *as a result* to help readers follow your argument. You should also try to repeat words like *cause*, *effect*, *outcome*, and *result* to help readers identify individual causes and effects.

⊝ EXERCISE 13.4 CREATING CAUSAL CHAINS

Fill in the templates to create a causal chain for each of these sequences:

1. All restaurants should be required to list fat and calorie content on their menus. If they do so, _____. As a result, _____. Eventually, _____.

2. Abstinence programs should be instituted in high schools. One immediate result would be _____. This could bring about _____. This in turn might lead to _____. Ideally, the result would be _____.

3. Taxes on cigarettes should be raised. If this step is taken, the first likely result would be _____. This might encourage _____. In a few years' time, the outcome might be _____.

Post Hoc *Reasoning*

Post hoc **reasoning** is the incorrect assumption that because an event precedes another event, it has caused that event. For example, you may notice that few of your friends voted in a recent election, and you may realize that many of your friends had previously decided to become science majors. This does not mean, of course, that their decision to choose careers in science has made them nonvoters. In fact, a scientist can be very interested in electoral politics. As you develop your cause-and-effect argument, be careful not to assume that every event that precedes another event has somehow caused it. (For information on avoiding *post hoc* **fallacies**, see Chapter 5.)

Structuring a Cause-and-Effect Argument

Generally speaking, a cause-and-effect argument can be structured in the following way:

- **Introduction:** Establishes a context for the argument by explaining the need to examine causes or to consider effects; states the essay's thesis

- **Evidence (first point in support of thesis):** Discusses less important causes or effects

- **Evidence (second point in support of thesis):** Discusses major causes or effects

- **Refutation of opposing arguments:** Considers and rejects other possible causes or effects

- **Conclusion:** Reinforces the argument's main point; includes a strong concluding statement

Other organizational patterns are also possible. For example, you might decide to refute opposing arguments *before* you have discussed arguments in support of your thesis. You might also include a background paragraph (as the student writer whose essay begins below does). Finally, you might decide to organize your essay as a **causal chain** (see pp. 440–442).

The following student essay illustrates one possible structure for a cause-and-effect argument. The student writer argues that, contrary to popular opinion, texting is not causing damage to the English language but is a creative force with the power to enrich and expand the language.

TEXTING: A BOON, NOT A THREAT, TO LANGUAGE
KRISTINA MIALKI

Certain technological developments of the last three decades have 1 a lot of people worrying about the state of the English language. Emailing, blogging, instant-messaging, tweeting, and texting have introduced new ways of writing and communicating, and the fear is that these technologies will encourage a sloppy, casual form of written English that will eventually replace "proper" English altogether. Texting, in particular, has people concerned because it encourages the use of a specialized, non-standard form of English. However, the effects of this new "textese" are misunderstood. Texting is not destroying the English language; in fact, it is keeping the language alive.

Thesis statement

Texting has become extremely popular because sending text 2 messages is instant, mobile, and silent. To make texting more efficient, texters have developed a shorthand—an abbreviated form of English that uses numbers and symbols in addition to letters. In textese, common phrases such as "see you later" or "talk to you later" become "cul8r" and "ttyl." Feelings and phrases are also expressed with emoji.

Background

Today, texting is the preferred method of communication for millions of people—especially young people, who are the most enthusiastic users of this technology. Not surprisingly, unwarranted fears that texting will destroy the language often focus on this group.

Refutation of opposing argument

Some people say texting will destroy the English language   3
because it encourages the use of an overly simplified form of written English that does not follow standard rules of spelling, grammar, and punctuation. The implication is that people who text, particularly children and teens, will not learn standard written English. However, there is no evidence that texting is having or will have this effect. In fact, as Margaret Rock observes, Australian researchers Nenagh Kemp and Catherine Bushnell at the University of Tasmania recently found just the opposite to be true. They demonstrated that students who were good at texting were also strong in reading, writing, and spelling (Rock). If, in fact, young people's language skills are weakening, researchers should look for the real causes for this decline rather than incorrectly blaming texting.

Evidence: First point in support of thesis

Despite what its critics charge, texting is a valuable way of com-   4
municating that actually encourages more writing and reading. Texters often spend hours each day engaged with language. This is time that would otherwise probably be spent talking on the phone, watching television, or playing video games, not reading or writing. Textese may not be standard written English, but it is a rich and inventive alternative form of communication, a creative modification of English for a particular purpose. For this reason, standard English is not in danger of being destroyed or replaced by textese. Just as most young people know not to talk to their teachers the way they talk to their friends, they know not to write essays the way they write text messages. Texting simply broadens young people's exposure to the written word. It also gets them reflecting on writing as a real-world process for a real-world audience. "As an act, texting provides opportunities to process experiences, as well as communicate and maintain relationships," write researchers Madhuri Kara and Missy Watson. "In addition, texting offers communicators regular practice with brainstorming, drafting, revising and editing" (Kara and Watson). Writing teachers and instructors, in particular, should take advantage of this.

Another reason texting is valuable is that it encourages creative use of language. Text messages are typically quick and brief, so the need for new and clever abbreviations is constant. Texters are continually playing with words and coming up with new ways of expressing themselves. Texting does not, as some fear, encourage sloppy, thoughtless, or careless writing. On the contrary, it rewards ingenuity and precision. One ongoing study by Canadian researchers aims to prove this point. They have already been able to demonstrate that texters are "creative and efficient at communicating" and use "novel forms of communications" (Shaw). Nenagh Kemp has also observed how texting encourages word play. Kemp maintains that texting shows "language is fluid and flourishing, rather than in a sad state of decline" (Rock). In other words, researchers recognize that texting is not damaging the English language but is actually enriching it and keeping it alive.

According to *Business Insider*, eighteen- to twenty-four-year-olds now send 2,022 texts per month and receive 1,831 texts (Cocotas). That averages out to around 67 texts per day. The exceptional popularity of texting and its fast growth over the last fifteen years explain why it is attracting attention. It is not, however, the threat that some believe it to be. It is neither destroying the language nor deadening people's thoughts and feelings. It is a lively, original, and creative way for people to play with words as they stay connected.

Margin notes:
5 Evidence: Second point in support of thesis

6

Concluding statement

Works Cited

Cocotas, Alex. "Chart of the Day: Kids Send a Mind Boggling Number of Texts Every Month." *Business Insider*, 22 Mar. 2013, www.businessinsider.com/chart-of-the-day-number-of-texts-sent-2013-3.

Karak, Madhuri, and Missy Watson. "Texting to New Perspectives." Inside Higher Ed, 21 July 2017, www.insidehighered.com/views/2017/07/31/intellectual-value-texting-essay.

Rock, Margaret. "Texting May Improve Literacy." *Mobiledia*, Mashable, 12 Sept. 2011, mashable.com/2011/09/12/texting-improves-literacy/#sCYnNT6VB8qL.

Shaw, Gillian. "Researchers Study Text Messages as Language Form." *Vancouver Sun*, 18 Jan. 2012, www.vancouversun.com/life/researchers+study+text+messages+language+form/6010501/story.html.

GRAMMAR IN CONTEXT

Avoiding "The Reason Is Because"

When you write a **cause-and-effect argument**, you connect causes to effects. In the process, you might be tempted to use the ungrammatical phrase *the reason is because*. However, the word *because* means "for the reason that"; therefore, it is redundant to say "the reason is because" (which actually means "the reason is for the reason that"). Instead, use the grammatical phrase "the reason is *that*."

INCORRECT	Another <u>reason</u> texting is so valuable <u>is because</u> it encourages creative use of language.
CORRECT	Another <u>reason</u> texting is so valuable <u>is that</u> it encourages creative use of language.

⊖ EXERCISE 13.5 IDENTIFYING THE ELEMENTS OF A CAUSE-AND-EFFECT ESSAY

The following essay, "Should the World of Toys Be Gender-Free?" by Peggy Orenstein, is a cause-and-effect argument. Read the essay carefully, and then answer the questions that follow it, consulting the outline on pages 442–443 if necessary.

This opinion column is from the December 29, 2011, *New York Times*.

SHOULD THE WORLD OF TOYS BE GENDER-FREE?

PEGGY ORENSTEIN

Now that the wrapping paper and the infernal clamshell packaging have 1
been relegated to the curb and the paying off of holiday bills has begun, the
toy industry is gearing up—for Christmas 2012. And its early offerings have
ignited a new debate over nature, nurture, toys, and sex.

Hamleys, which is London's 251-year-old version of F.A.O. Schwarz, 2
recently dismantled its pink "girls" and blue "boys" sections in favor of a
gender-neutral store with red-and-white signage. Rather than floors dedicated
to Barbie dolls and action figures, merchandise is now organized by types (Soft
Toys) and interests (Outdoor).

That free-to-be gesture was offset by Lego, whose Friends collection, 3
aimed at girls, will hit stores this month with the goal of becoming a holiday
must-have by the fall. Set in fictive Heartlake City (and supported by a $40
million marketing campaign), the line features new, pastel-colored blocks that

allow a budding Kardashian, among other things, to build herself a cafe or a beauty salon. Its tasty-sounding "ladyfig" characters are also taller and curvier than the typical Legoland denizen.

So who has it right? Should gender be systematically expunged from playthings? Or is Lego merely being realistic, earnestly meeting girls halfway in an attempt to stoke their interest in engineering?

> "Should gender be systematically expunged from playthings?" 4

Among the "10 characteristics for Lego" described in 1963 by a son of 5 the founder was that it was "for girls and for boys," as *Bloomberg Businessweek* reported. But the new Friends collection, Lego says, was based on months of anthropological research revealing that—gasp!—the sexes play differently.

While as toddlers they interact similarly with the company's Duplo blocks, 6 by preschool girls prefer playthings that are pretty, exude "harmony," and allow them to tell a story. They may enjoy building, but they favor role play. So it's bye-bye Bionicles, hello princesses. In order to be gender-fair, today's executives insist, they have to be gender-specific.

As any developmental psychologist will tell you, those observations are, 7 to a degree, correct. Toy choice among young children is the Big Kahuna of sex differences, one of the largest across the life span. It transcends not only culture but species: in two separate studies of primates, in 2002 and 2008, researchers found that males gravitated toward stereotypically masculine toys (like cars and balls) while females went ape for dolls. Both sexes, incidentally, appreciated stuffed animals and books.

Human boys and girls not only tend to play differently from one another— 8 with girls typically clustering in pairs or trios, chatting together more than boys, and playing more cooperatively—but, when given a choice, usually prefer hanging with their own kind.

Score one for Lego, right? Not so fast. Preschoolers may be the self- 9 appointed chiefs of the gender police, eager to enforce and embrace the most rigid views. Yet, according to Lise Eliot, a neuroscientist and the author of *Pink Brain, Blue Brain*, that's also the age when their brains are most malleable, most open to influence on the abilities and roles that traditionally go with their sex.

Every experience, every interaction, every activity—when they laugh, cry, 10 learn, play—strengthens some neural circuits at the expense of others, and the younger the child the greater the effect. Consider: boys from more egalitarian homes are more nurturing toward babies. Meanwhile, in a study of more than 5,000 3-year-olds, girls with older brothers had stronger spatial skills than both girls and boys with older sisters.

At issue, then, is not nature or nurture but how nurture becomes nature: 11 the environment in which children play and grow can encourage a range of aptitudes or foreclose them. So blithely indulging—let alone exploiting— stereotypically gendered play patterns may have a more negative long-term impact on kids' potential than parents imagine. And promoting, without forcing, cross-sex friendships as well as a breadth of play styles may be more beneficial.

There is even evidence that children who have opposite-sex friendships during their early years have healthier romantic relationships as teenagers.

Traditionally, toys were intended to communicate parental values and 12 expectations, to train children for their future adult roles. Today's boys and girls will eventually be one another's professional peers, employers, employees, romantic partners, co-parents. How can they develop skills for such collaborations from toys that increasingly emphasize, reinforce, or even create, gender differences? What do girls learn about who they should be from Lego kits with beauty parlors or the flood of "girl friendly" science kits that run the gamut from "beauty spa lab" to "perfume factory"?

The rebellion against such gender apartheid may have begun. Consider 13 the latest cute-kid video to go viral on YouTube: "Riley on Marketing" shows a little girl in front of a wall of pink packaging, asking, "Why do all the girls have to buy pink stuff and all the boys have to buy different-color stuff?" It has been viewed more than 2.4 million times.

Perhaps, then, Hamleys is on to something, though it will doubtless meet 14 with resistance—even rejection—from both its pint-size customers and multinational vendors. As for me, I'm trying to track down a poster of a 1981 ad for a Lego "universal" building set to give to my daughter. In it, a freckle-faced girl with copper-colored braids, baggy jeans, a T-shirt, and sneakers proudly holds out a jumbly, multi-hued Lego creation. Beneath it, a tag line reads, "What it is is beautiful."

Identifying the Elements of a Cause-and-Effect Argument

1. Where does Orenstein answer the question her title asks? How would you answer this question?

2. Orenstein's discussion of toys is based on the assumption that the world would be a better place if children were raised in a gender-neutral environment, but she does not offer any evidence to support this implied idea. Should she have? Is she **begging the question**?

3. In paragraph 7, Orenstein reports on two studies of primates. What conclusion does this evidence support? What conclusion does Lise Eliot's research (para. 9) support?

4. How do you react to Orenstein's use of the term *gender apartheid* (13)? What does this term mean? What connotations does it have? Given these connotations, do you think her use of this term is appropriate? Why or why not?

5. What effects does Orenstein claim stereotyped toys have on children? Does she support this claim?

6. Orenstein's thesis seems to leave no room for compromise. Given the possibility that some of her readers might disagree with her,

should she have softened her position? What compromise position might she have proposed?

7. This essay traces a causal chain. The first link in this chain is the "anthropological research revealing that . . . the sexes play differently" (5). Complete the causal chain by filling in the template below.

Anthropological research ⟶

⟶

⟶

⟶

Does Our Reliance on Social Media Bring Us Together or Drive Us Apart?

Reread the At Issue box on page 437. Then, read the sources on the pages that follow.

As you read each of these sources, you will be asked to respond to a series of questions and complete some simple activities. This work will help you to understand the content and structure of the material you read. When you are finished, you will be prepared to write a **cause-and-effect argument** in which you take a position on the topic, "Does Our Reliance on Social Media Bring Us Together or Drive Us Apart?"

Plume Creative/Getty Images

SOURCES

This essay was published in *The Week* on February 22, 2017.

I DON'T OWN A SMARTPHONE—AND I DON'T WANT ONE

LAURA BOGART

Whenever I'm making plans with a new acquaintance, there's often a moment when 1 our mutual enthusiasm turns to chagrin—and that moment is, inevitably, when we pull out our phones to swap contact information. My friend-to-be usually owns a smartphone, slim and sleek in a case that—whether leopard-patterned or festooned with images of some Saturday morning cartoon hero—manages to protect it while also subtly proclaiming the artful quirkiness of its owner's personality. I, however, own a "dumb phone" that can't connect me to Lyft or let me read restaurant reviews via a Yelp app, won't allow me to scroll through email or get into arguments on Facebook, let alone zone out to music on the metro, or even check the weather. My acquaintance's eyes widen as if I've just admitted to living in an underground bunker with a can of beans and a dented spoon. Unable to help herself, she'll outright ask if that is really my phone. And I'll mumble that yeah, really, it is.

Yes, I am among the narrow two-to-four percent of millennials who don't own 2 a smartphone. Never have, and likely never will. Most days, this causes me no pain at all. Thanks to the marvels of home computing, I can make reservations online and get directions to wherever I'm going, which I print out from MapQuest. I can charge an iPod and check the weather, and, of course, hold vicious political arguments on Facebook. I just can't do all of that at once, or on-the-go. And somehow, this has translated into a conception that beneath my favorite Oxford blouse beats the heart of a doomsday prepper. In her own essay about being a "dumb phone" user, Janet Burns wryly laments that dumb phones, particularly flip-phones, now only appear in media as "the personal tech go-to of onscreen drug dealers and serial killers." The last time I saw a young person using a phone just like mine was on a re-watch of *The Wire*. To be fair, I'm not entirely alone in eschewing the siren song of high-speed data and super-cool apps. Many of my fellow luddites cite familiar reasons for their wariness: the loss of everyday civility that knows how to ask a kind-faced stranger for directions; the freedom to not read the latest presidential tweet at the dinner table; the hyper-reliance on an eminently breakable, frequently replaceable, form of technology; and, of course, the cost. There are certain perks of a low-fi life, and a significant one is a kind of insularity—sometimes protective, sometimes productive—that comes from knowing that I can't be summoned back to work by an email, that I can navigate city blocks and curate new music playlists all on my lonesome, and that I have spared myself the temptation of constantly comparing my own grubby little life with the beach vacations and the new condos carefully staged to inflict maximum envy.

When the train cars and waiting rooms are filled with people squinting 3 into screens, I drift into daydream and conjure new essay ideas, or rearrange a chapter of my book-in-progress. Sometimes, I take out a small sketchpad and let rip with gesture drawings. Or I savor the tactile glide of book pages between my fingers. Imagination is a muscle, strengthened through repetition; sans smartphone, I've built those muscles up enough to sustain a career. I can understand why so many of my well-intentioned friends beg me to get myself to an Apple store, or "join the year 2017," or say "it will make your life so much better/easier/more complete"—and it may make *their* lives far better/easier/more complete, but I've done quite well as a scrappy contrarian. I've always had to.

Both of my parents grew up in a grit-under-the nails, dishpan hands kind of 4 working class. Their parents, dockworkers and waitresses, didn't benefit from the capitalist ebullience of the post-World War II years; they were abandoned by the same boon that gave well-heeled suburbanites their super-deluxe vacuums and color TVs, their video recorders and non-stick pans. So, in turn, my parents each developed a decidedly ambivalent approach to technology—the material possessions they valued had a very blunt, tangible usefulness: a house, food, good clothing, and a car to get you to and from work. By the time I was born, they were older, more entrenched in their fiscal conservatism. Whatever remained once the mortgage was paid went into savings, and that was that—even as PCs sprung up everywhere, even as teenaged me begged and begged for one, because I wanted to be like my friends, who were already lording my lack of an AOL username over me. The taunting made me feel terminally uncool; but this wasn't just a fleeting, teenage kind of feeling, it was a core-deep shame that my family hadn't kept up with the Joneses—we didn't have the same kind of house, the same kind of car, and, now, the same kind of computer. And we were dumber, duller, less "with it" for it.

My father finally caved and bought a white clunker of an IBM with dial-up inter- 5 net back when I was sophomore in high school, but only because, "I guess you need it for homework." Even then, many a Saturday night became a battle royale: I wanted to plunge down every long thread on the World Wide Web and my father wanted a manageable phone bill. Of course, the hours I spent staring at that boxy gray screen were some of the most transformative moments of my life—just as the hours I now spend in front of my laptop remain some of my most meaningful.

> "The hours I spent staring at that boxy gray screen were some of the most transformative moments of my life."

Still, as I get older, I better understand my parents' prioritizing thriftiness over modernity; though my only work-related aches and pains are eyestrain and stiff fingers, as a freelancer, I still live paycheck-to-paycheck, so I must make sharp, tactical decisions about priorities. And health insurance will come before an iPhone every day.

Sure, one could frame my entire reluctance toward getting on the treadmill 6 of constant fees from data plans and upgrades and ill-advised binges through the app store as a kind of hipster resistance against, like, documenting my life instead of living it, or being subsumed into the Borg of Instagram brunches. But much of my refusal to get a smartphone has more to do with cost and class. This pervasive clamor for adopting personal technology—and not just adopting it, but allowing it to become some ubiquitous, indispensable extension of the self—grates on me because it promotes consumerism-as-a lifestyle. And just as the suburban opulence of the 1950s left my grandparents behind, and the tech bubble of the '90s left my parents behind, I have been left behind by the 2010s' obsession with the smartphone and constant connectivity. There is a classist arrogance behind the assumption that everyone can, or should, or already does own a smartphone; and all of this "concern" would be far better spent working to alleviate the very real lack of access to computers and high-speed internet in underserved communities around the country.

I'm pretty much assured of being the only "grandma millennial" in any 7 room, and I'm pretty okay with that. My struggle is still with the people who make me feel dumber, duller, less "with it." However, at a recent confer-ence, I ran into an old acquaintance from school; a fellow writer I've always regarded as unimpeachably cool. As we went to swap digits, I braced myself for the familiar awkwardness of pulling out my "dumb phone" in the wild. And then, I saw it: the flip-phone in her hand. She looked down appreciatively at my app-less clunker. The same old lines—"Is that really your phone?" "Yeah, it is."—took on a rare, and powerful, pleasantness. Instead of mutual chagrin, we regarded each other with utter relief. For that moment, we were two old sol-diers who had, quite miraculously, found themselves back on the friendly side of the battle lines between those who are "with it" and the proud curmudgeons.

⊘ AT ISSUE: SOURCES FOR DEVELOPING A CAUSE-AND-EFFECT ARGUMENT

1. Despite acknowledging the many disadvantages of having a "dumb phone" (para. 1), Bogart insists she doesn't want a smartphone. Why not? Does her position make sense to you?

2. Fill in the following template to paraphrase Bogart's thesis:

   Even though _____, I do not own a smartphone because _____.

3. In paragraphs 3 and 4, Bogart cites the advantages of not owning a smartphone. Do you think these advantages outweigh the disadvan-tages? Why or why not?

4. In paragraph 3, Bogart identifies with her "fellow luddites." Who were the luddites? Do you think Bogart qualifies as a modern-day luddite?

5. Why does Bogart devote two paragraphs (5–6) to discussing her fam-ily and their experiences with technology? How do these paragraphs support her position? How did her parents' attitudes shape her own?

6. How would you characterize Bogart's tone in this essay? Would you say she is defensive? Defiant? Something else? Explain.

7. Throughout her essay, Bogart is critical of those who own smart-phones. What are some of her criticisms? Do you think they are valid?

8. Do you think a middle ground exists between Bogart's position and the position that those who own smartphones would take? Is Bogart committing the **either-or fallacy** in this essay? Explain.

This essay appeared on the author's blog on September 16, 2010.

SOCIAL MEDIA: BRINGING PEOPLE TOGETHER, VIRTUALLY AND PHYSICALLY

DMITRIY KOZLOV

I believe that the web and social media will, and have, brought us closer 1
together as a society by increasing our communication with each other and
understanding of each other with respect to greater society and culture. However, I don't believe that social is, or should be, a substitute for human contact
and personal interactions; rather, it enhances such connections.

Social media, by its very nature, relies on the growing connections 2
between its individual members. It has been a powerful tool in reconnect-
ing old friends and classmates to reunite, but it goes well beyond just recon-
necting. Social media breeds new connections between individuals that
otherwise could never have interacted because of social, geographical, and
other very real and practical barriers. These new connections breed social
interactions between like-minded individuals which often lead to very constructive collaborations.

In my own field (entrepreneurship), I see this very frequently. Many of 3
the business partners with whom I work, I met through social media . . . many
of them I have never actually met in person, yet trust them to be great friends
and business partners. In some cases, I
have seen people that met online build
entire successful companies from the
ideas that originated in Facebook
groups and online chat. Social Spin
and Buildingabrandonline are great examples. I know the co-founders personally (through social media, of course) and know that they all met each other
through social media and are now building and running thriving companies
together.

> "Social media is more than a technology."

Beyond the power of networking, social media, and the web (hi-tech) also 4
makes human connection (hi-touch) more possible and more easily attain-
able, hence the concept that social media is "hi-tech hi-touch." It does this by
building a bridge between people that otherwise may not connect, even if they
met directly in person and had no geographical boundaries. A great example
of this is the phenomenon experienced by many rising college freshmen, who
often find and connect with other students entering their freshman year at the
same college over the summer via Facebook. During orientation and the first
few weeks of classes, students recognize their peers from Facebook groups
and interactions, and find it much easier to approach each other and engage

in conversation; this is because despite their new environments and extremely varied backgrounds, they already have an acquaintance-like connection from Facebook. I have experienced this myself and know many others who have as well, and I can imagine that it has only increased since I was a first-year over 3 years ago. Bringing this same example back to the business world, one blogger discusses the impact that social media has had on face-to-face networking and communication: **http://www.lucorpmarketing.com/high-tech-requires -high-touch-article-about-victoria-trafton-and-referral-institute/**.

Yet another blogger and entrepreneur discusses the many tools within 5 social media that are available to further stimulate and increase authentic communication between its members:

On the platform side the tool allows you to effectively build a profile (here's mine), post articles, invite members to become a part of your network, join and create groups around community or themes, and create and promote local events.

On the harder to quantify side, the quality of engagement in this network far outstrips anything I've seen and been a part of in other networks. This comes through loud and clear in things like article comments and messages to new members.

The examples are endless from all corners of society, be it business, reli- 6 gion, music, sports, academics, whatever . . . the point is clear: social media is more than a technology, it is a cultural phenomenon that has allowed for greater connection (in quantity) and deeper communication (quality), not only within itself on the internet, but also in the offline societal community.

Just to perform a social (media) experiment, I decided to ask this question 7 on my Facebook status a few days ago, and got surprisingly similar responses to the thesis above . . . the two of the responses are reproduced for you below:

David H. Manning: "Social media gives us contact we would not normally have. However, taken to the extreme you have people in the same room tweeting and texting one another. Sending a hug online is no where near the real thing. I've connected with many people across the country in my business. This week at a convention in Dallas I was able to see them face to face, to shake their hands and to really hug them. Awesome. My philosophy: All things in moderation."

Donna Boccio Digilio: "I think it will do both depending upon what the person's situation is. I will use myself as an example. It brought me together with friends from high school that I had lost track off and we have gotten together many times and it is been great socially for me. But, if you do not physically connect like I just described you are depriving yourself from physical contact and the real time of reading someone's emotions on their face. Not actually seeing someone, reading their body language, facial expressions, etc., will retard if not debilitate your social instincts and social etiquette if you only do this by web and social media. If you have a social disability already it will only make matters worse. In order to feel confident socially and come together as people, it has to be face to face for me."

These responses indicate the power social media has to connect and 8 reconnect people, but still emphasize the importance of those connections leading to human contact.

⊘ AT ISSUE: SOURCES FOR DEVELOPING A CAUSE-AND-EFFECT ARGUMENT

1. What exactly is Kozlov's position on the issue of whether social media use unites or divides us? In one sentence, paraphrase his thesis.

2. In paragraph 4, Kozlov supports a point by saying, "I have experienced this myself." Where else does he use his own experience as support? Is this support convincing? What other kinds of support does he use?

3. Paragraph 2 traces a causal chain. List the elements of this sequence, using arrows to connect causes and effects.

4. What does Kozlov mean when he calls social media "hi-tech hi-touch" (para. 4)? Is this characterization consistent with his thesis? Explain.

5. In paragraph 6, Kozlov says, "The examples are endless from all corners of society." Do you think this statement is convincing? Do you think it would be more convincing if he toned it down or qualified it?

6. Kozlov is a student posting on his university's blog. How do you think other students would react to his ideas? How might members of the faculty or administration react?

7. What specific comments quoted in this post suggest that social media use is not a good substitute for human interaction? Do such comments support or undercut Kozlov's position?

8. This post was written in 2010. Are there any indications that it is not more current? Are the points it makes still valid? Explain your conclusion.

This piece was originally posted on the *Psychology Today* website on January 24, 2018.

DOES USING SOCIAL MEDIA MAKE YOU LONELY?

DAVID LUDDEN

Since the beginning of the internet, pundits have worried that computer-mediated 1
communication would have a pernicious effect on our social networks. Instead
of going out and interacting with others in traditional settings, the fearmongers fretted, people will stare at their computers all day typing messages to
people they've never even met. And if you'll look up from your smartphone a
moment, you'll see that everyone around you is engrossed in theirs. So maybe
the fearmongers were right.

There's even scientific evidence that suggests social media use is bad for 2
your psychological health. Some results show that people feel lonelier—and
experience drops in self-esteem—after using Facebook. These reports about
the dangers of social media use have even made it into the mainstream media.
You might have read some of these stories on Facebook.

A careful review of the literature, however, paints a more complicated 3
picture. It's certainly true that a number of studies have found a connection
between social media use and declines in well-being. But other studies have
found opposite results, with people feeling more socially connected as they
spend more time on social media.

And then there are the studies that find conflicting results. For exam- 4
ple, one study considered the relationship between the number of Facebook
friends and social adjustment in college freshmen and seniors. The more Facebook friends the freshmen had, the less socially adjusted they were to the college environment. But the result was the opposite for the seniors. The more
Facebook friends they had, the more socially adjusted they were.

Conflicting results such as these suggest the need to step back and look at 5
the larger context. The fundamental question that researchers have been asking is this: "Does using social media make you lonely?" But it now seems we've
been asking the wrong question. At least that's the conclusion Duke University
psychologist Jenna Clark and her colleagues came to in an article they recently
published in the journal, *Current Directions in Psychological Science.*

According to these researchers, 6
whether using social media makes you
lonely or not depends on what you
do with the social media. This point
is illustrated in the study of college
freshmen and seniors just mentioned.
As it turns out, the college freshmen

> "Whether using social
> media makes you lonely or
> not depends on what you
> do with the social media."

were using Facebook to keep in touch with their friends from high school. So
the more time they spent online, the less they had for building new friendships

457

on campus, leading to increased feelings of loneliness. In contrast, the college seniors were using Facebook mainly to communicate with friends on campus. So the more time they spent online, the more connected they felt.

Many people use social media as a substitute for in-person social 7 exchanges. Particularly for those who suffer from social anxiety—that is, the fear of interacting with other people, especially strangers—social media seems like a safe alternative. These people lack the necessary social skills to success-fully navigate interpersonal exchanges. As a result, their social networks are fragile and fail to support their need for connectedness. But when they go online, they carry with them this same set of inappropriate social behaviors.

Clark and colleagues warn of two pitfalls in social media use. The first 8 pitfall is what they call "social snacking." This involves activities such as brows-ing through other people's profiles or reading other people's comments without making any of your own. Social snacking may feel like social engagement, and while you're doing it you might temporarily forget your own feelings of lone-liness. But just as junk food makes you feel both bloated and empty afterward, social snacking only leaves you with much time wasted and more loneliness than before.

The second pitfall is self-comparison. On Facebook, other people's lives 9 seem so much more exciting and glamorous than your own. Of course, the socially savvy know when someone is just boasting, and they discount what that person says. But when you're all alone in the wee hours of the morning, the tall tales people tell on social media can make your own life seem insignif-icant by comparison.

As Clark and colleagues point out, these pitfalls aren't unique to social 10 media. Rather, they're the same traps that snare socially-isolated people in their attempts at interpersonal exchanges as well. Oftentimes, people with poor social skills will try to compensate by thrusting themselves into social situations, perhaps with the hope that if they just go where there are other peo-ple, someone will make friends with them. They join a church, hang out at the gym, or attend office parties. But they're too inhibited to initiate an exchange with anyone they don't already know, and when others do approach them, their awkwardness soon sends them away.

Some people engage in social snacking in real life too. Instead of interact- 11 ing with those around them, they stand back and watch as others chit-chat, laugh, and seem to have a grand old time. In the end, the spectacle only makes the socially awkward feel even lonelier. And they engage in maladaptive social comparisons as well. Because other people seem to have much happier and more fulfilling lives than they do, their self-esteem takes a heavy hit as well.

In the end, whether using social media makes you feel lonelier or not 12 depends on what you do when you're online. If you already have good social skills, you'll find Facebook a useful tool for keeping in touch with friends and family. In this way, social networking sites enrich our lives.

But if you find yourself passively browsing through social media to take 13 your mind off your loneliness, you'd be better off spending some time in self-help instead. There are plenty of sites on the internet—including here on *Psychology Today*—that give sound advice on how to improve your social skills. Take the advice to heart and practice it in public. As your social skills improve, so will the quality of the time you spend on Facebook.

Reference

Clark, J. L., Algoe, S. B., & Green, M. C. (2017). Social network sites and well-being: The role of social connection. *Current Directions in Psychological Science*. Advance online publication.

⊘ AT ISSUE: SOURCES FOR DEVELOPING A CAUSE-AND-EFFECT ARGUMENT

1. In his introductory paragraph, Ludden claims that "pundits" and "fearmongers" have been critical of the effects of social media. Does his essay refute their criticisms? Is he setting up a **straw man** here? Explain.

2. What negative effects of social media use does Ludden discuss? What positive results does he say studies have identified? On balance, do the effects of social media he identifies seem to be primarily positive or negative?

3. How does Ludden explain the "conflicting results" (para. 4) seen in a study correlating the number of Facebook friends students have with their level of social adjustment? Does his explanation seem logical to you in terms of your own observations and experiences? Why or why not?

4. Where does Ludden answer the question his title asks? Is this answer satisfactory to you, or do you think he is sidestepping the issue? Explain.

5. Explain the "two pitfalls" (8–9) of social media use that Ludden identifies. Do these pitfalls also occur in face-to-face interpersonal interaction?

6. In his conclusion, Ludden gives his readers some advice. What does this conclusion suggest about his motivation for writing this essay?

This essay was published in Toronto's *Globe and Mail* on April 5, 2018.

I QUIT FACEBOOK, AND I MISS IT

WENCY LEUNG

Last Sunday night, between putting away my laundry and brushing my teeth, I 1 deactivated my Facebook account. I'd like to say I did it with gusto, logging off for the last time with a triumphant "Ha!" But in reality, I felt torn.

I was now on the outside, with no way of even seeing what I was missing. No 2 more updates from my neighborhood groups about coming events and warnings of petty crimes. No more sweet—and okay, sometimes overabundant—photos of other people's children. No more ridiculous, but occasionally side-splitting, viral videos. (Did you see that one of the adorable dog who can't catch anything? Hilarious!) No more "Likes" to make me feel validated for my self-consciously crafted status updates.

I feared I would regret this decision. 3

Let me be straight with you. Quitting Facebook wasn't my idea. Of course, 4 I'd thought about doing it, long before the Cambridge Analytica scandal. In fact, for the past couple years, I thought about quitting almost daily. Facebook, for me, had become a bad habit, like biting my nails or slouching. I'd catch myself mindlessly checking it every few hours, between emails, before logging off at work, before going to bed. I didn't even enjoy being on Facebook most of the time. Scrolling through my feed was simply something I'd become accustomed to doing and I resented that I was hooked.

Still, I didn't seriously commit to deactivating my account until my edi- 5 tor asked me to give it a try, to see what it's like to heed the recent calls to #DeleteFacebook. In light of reports the British consulting firm Cambridge Analytica may have improperly gathered data of up to 87 million Facebook users, including 622,000 Canadians, an Angus Reid poll reportedly found 64 percent of Canadian respondents said they would change their privacy settings or use Facebook less in the future, while 10 percent said they would suspend or delete their accounts. At least I'd be in good company.

Back around 2006, joining Facebook wasn't entirely my idea either. Friends 6 and relatives overseas had coaxed me to sign on to the then-two-year-old network because it was a more convenient way of staying in touch and sharing photos than email. I was an easy convert. In those early days, it was thrilling to find long-lost friends and reconnect with old acquaintances through the site. (That thrill wore off when I received my first "friend request" from an ex. But by then, I was already a regular user.)

Gearing myself up to quit Facebook was hard. In fact, preparing to leave 7 the social network has, so far, proved to be harder than staying off it.

First, there were the practical preparatory steps. Facebook was my only 8 way of communicating with many friends, especially those in other parts of the world. Before leaving, I'd need to collect all their emails—or at least the emails of those whom I'd realistically write. (As far as user privacy is concerned, though, even that mode of communication is problematic; embarrassingly, I still have a Yahoo email account.) Friends' birthdays? That was a tough one. I jotted down a few birthdays into a notebook, but there's little chance I'll ever remember to wish people a happy birthday without Facebook's automatic reminders. There's even less chance anyone would remember mine. Worse, would anyone email me notices of marriages, births, and deaths?

Then, there was the psychological prep work. I needed to come to terms 9 with the fact that I'd likely lose contact with the vast majority of Facebook friends I'd accumulated over most of my adult life. Before Facebook, saying goodbye was a big deal whenever you left a job or school or city. There were inevitably people you'd likely never see or hear from again. But Facebook made it possible to do away with hard goodbyes in favor of a softer farewell: "Let's keep in touch!" Now, the process of deactivating my account felt like a definitive end to many relationships that had been artificially kept alive through occasional "Likes" and smiley face emoji. By disappearing from Facebook, I'd also cease to exist in other people's minds.

> "I needed to come to terms with the fact that I'd likely lose contact with the vast majority of Facebook friends I'd accumulated over most of my adult life."

I also needed to mentally say goodbye to all the groups I had joined. This 10 was probably one of the most anxiety-provoking parts of leaving Facebook. I was a member of a local parenting group, a couple of neighborhood groups, a group for former colleagues. By disconnecting from these groups, I feared I'd be totally in the dark.

How would I stay on top of what other parents are griping about or what 11 the social norms are around child-rearing these days? What if my child turns out to be a total misfit because I'm not on Facebook? How would I find out about the latest neighborhood news and gossip? Just days prior, a neighbor had alerted me via Facebook to a mugging incident that occurred nearby. Another neighbor posted that he needed to borrow a lemon to make a dish. How would I know the descriptions of potential muggers or respond to recipe emergencies if not for Facebook?

Leaving wouldn't be so hard if everyone else did the same. That way, we'd 12 probably be knocking on one another's doors a whole lot more or actually using our phones to make phone calls. As it is, it kind of felt like I was packing up and going home all by myself, when the party's still in full swing.

Finally, there was the process of quitting itself. After selecting to deacti- 13 vate my account, Facebook craftily showed me a lineup of my friends, whom, it claimed, would "miss" me. It then asked me to select my reason for leaving from a list including, "I have a privacy concern," "I don't find Facebook useful" and "I spend too much time on Facebook." No matter which one I clicked, it offered me tips on how I could address the problem—while, of course, remaining active on the site. As it turns out, this was the final push I needed. The more Facebook tried to convince me from leaving, the more I wanted to get out of there. "Deactivate Now." Click.

More than a week later, I'm still on the outside. I don't have any great rev-   14 elations about how much extra time I have or how productive I am, now that I'm no longer constantly checking my feed. It's not as though I've suddenly replaced Facebook with CrossFit or reading Dostoevsky. In spite of multiple studies that have linked Facebook use to depression, anxiety, and loneliness, I can't even say quitting the network has made me any happier or more social in real life. And I don't feel my online privacy is any more secure either. I still use Google. I still shop online. (And I still really need to get rid of that Yahoo account.)

Resisting the impulse to check Facebook is getting easier each day. I found   15 myself absentmindedly logging on less than 14 hours after I quit and immediately deactivated my account again before I could catch a glimpse of what I'd missed. This subconscious slip was an uncomfortable reminder of how ingrained Facebook had become in my life. It does make me feel better knowing I'm no longer bound to the network. Still, I can't promise myself I'll stay off for good.

I'm finally free of Facebook. And I'm really going to miss it.   16

⊙ AT ISSUE: SOURCES FOR DEVELOPING A CAUSE-AND-EFFECT ARGUMENT

1. What prompted Leung to give up Facebook? How did she prepare to separate from Facebook?

2. In what respects does Leung see Facebook as "a bad habit" (para. 4)?

3. In paragraph 12, Leung says, "Leaving wouldn't be so hard if everyone else did the same." What might be some short- and long-term results of "everyone else" leaving social media sites like Facebook and Instagram?

4. How did Facebook make it hard for Leung to deactivate her account? What effect did the obstacles it imposed have on her?

5. How has Leung's life changed in the brief time since she quit Facebook? How would you expect it to change in the future? Why?

6. On balance, does this essay highlight the positive or negative aspects of Facebook and similar sites?

This essay was published in the *New York Times* on April 21, 2012.

THE FLIGHT FROM CONVERSATION

SHERRY TURKLE

We live in a technological universe in which we are always communicating. 1
And yet we have sacrificed conversation for mere connection.

At home, families sit together, texting and reading email. At work exec- 2
utives text during board meetings. We text (and shop and go on Facebook)
during classes and when we're on dates. My students tell me about an important new skill: it involves maintaining eye contact with someone while you text
someone else; it's hard, but it can be done.

Over the past 15 years, I've studied technologies of mobile connection 3
and talked to hundreds of people of all ages and circumstances about their
plugged-in lives. I've learned that the little devices most of us carry around are
so powerful that they change not only what we do, but also who we are.

We've become accustomed to a new way of being "alone together." 4
Technology-enabled, we are able to be with one another, and also elsewhere,
connected to wherever we want to be. We want to customize our lives. We want
to move in and out of where we are because the thing we value most is control
over where we focus our attention. We have gotten used to the idea of being in a
tribe of one, loyal to our own party.

Our colleagues want to go to that board meeting but pay attention only to 5
what interests them. To some this seems like a good idea, but we can end up
hiding from one another, even as we are constantly connected to one another.

A businessman laments that he no longer has colleagues at work. He 6
doesn't stop by to talk; he doesn't call. He says that he doesn't want to interrupt them. He says they're "too busy on their email." But then he pauses and
corrects himself. "I'm not telling the truth. I'm the one who doesn't want to be
interrupted. I think I should. But I'd rather just do things on my BlackBerry."

A 16-year-old boy who relies on texting for almost everything says almost 7
wistfully, "Someday, someday, but certainly not now, I'd like to learn how to
have a conversation."

In today's workplace, young people who have grown up fearing conversa- 8
tion show up on the job wearing earphones. Walking through a college library
or the campus of a high-tech start-up, one sees the same thing: we are together,
but each of us is in our own bubble, furiously connected to keyboards and tiny
touch screens. A senior partner at a Boston law firm describes a scene in his
office. Young associates lay out their suite of technologies: laptops, iPods, and
multiple phones. And then they put their earphones on. "Big ones. Like pilots.
They turn their desks into cockpits." With the young lawyers in their cockpits,
the office is quiet, a quiet that does not ask to be broken.

In the silence of connection, people are comforted by being in touch with 9 a lot of people—carefully kept at bay. We can't get enough of one another if we can use technology to keep one another at distances we can control: not too close, not too far, just right. I think of it as a Goldilocks effect.

Texting and email and posting let us present the self we want to be. This 10 means we can edit. And if we wish to, we can delete. Or retouch: the voice, the flesh, the face, the body. Not too much, not too little—just right.

Human relationships are rich; they're messy and demanding. We have 11 learned the habit of cleaning them up with technology. And the move from connection is part of this. But it's a process in which we shortchange ourselves. Worse, it seems that over time we stop caring, we forget that there is a difference.

We are tempted to think that our little "sips" of online connection add 12 up to a big gulp of real conversation. But they don't. Email, Twitter, Facebook, all of these have their places—in politics, commerce, romance, and friendship. But no matter how valuable, they do not substitute for conversation.

Connecting in sips may work for gathering discrete bits of information 13 or for saying, "I am thinking about you." Or even for saying, "I love you." But connecting in sips doesn't work as well when it comes to understanding and knowing one another. In conversation we tend to one another. (The word itself is kinetic; it's derived from words that mean to move, together.) We can attend to tone and nuance. In conversation, we are called upon to see things from another's point of view.

Face-to-face conversation unfolds slowly. It teaches patience. When we com- 14 municate on our digital devices, we learn different habits. As we ramp up the volume and velocity of online connections, we start to expect faster answers. To get these, we ask one another simpler questions; we dumb down our communications, even on the most important matters. It is as though we have all put ourselves on cable news. Shakespeare might have said, "We are consum'd with that which we were nourish'd by."

> "We use conversation with others to learn to converse with ourselves."

And we use conversation with others 15 to learn to converse with ourselves. So our flight from conversation can mean diminished chances to learn skills of self-reflection. These days, social media continually asks us what's "on our mind," but we have little motivation to say something truly self-reflective. Self-reflection in conversation requires trust. It's hard to do anything with 3,000 Facebook friends except connect.

As we get used to being shortchanged on conversation and to getting by 16 with less, we seem almost willing to dispense with people altogether. Serious people muse about the future of computer programs as psychiatrists. A high school sophomore confides to me that he wishes he could talk to an artificial intelligence program instead of his dad about dating; he says the A.I. would have so much more in its database. Indeed, many people tell me they hope that as Siri, the digital assistant on Apple's iPhone, becomes more advanced, "she" will be more and more like a best friend—one who will listen when others won't.

During the years I have spent researching people and their relationships 17 with technology, I have often heard the sentiment "No one is listening to me." I believe this feeling helps explain why it is so appealing to have a Facebook page or a Twitter feed—each provides so many automatic listeners. And it helps explain why—against all reason—so many of us are willing to talk to machines that seem to care about us. Researchers around the world are busy inventing sociable robots, designed to be companions to the elderly, to children, to all of us.

One of the most haunting experiences during my research came when I 18 brought one of these robots, designed in the shape of a baby seal, to an elder-care facility, and an older woman began to talk to it about the loss of her child. The robot seemed to be looking into her eyes. It seemed to be following the conversation. The woman was comforted.

And so many people found this amazing. Like the sophomore who wants 19 advice about dating from artificial intelligence and those who look forward to computer psychiatry, this enthusiasm speaks to how much we have confused conversation with connection and collectively seem to have embraced a new kind of delusion that accepts the simulation of compassion as sufficient unto the day. And why would we want to talk about love and loss with a machine that has no experience of the arc of human life? Have we so lost confidence that we will be there for one another?

We expect more from technology and less from one another and seem increas- 20 ingly drawn to technologies that provide the illusion of companionship without the demands of relationship. Always-on/always-on-you devices provide three powerful fantasies: that we will always be heard; that we can put our attention wherever we want it to be; and that we never have to be alone. Indeed our new devices have turned being alone into a problem that can be solved.

When people are alone, even for a few moments, they fidget and reach for 21 a device. Here connection works like a symptom, not a cure, and our constant, reflexive impulse to connect shapes a new way of being.

Think of it as "I share, therefore I am." We use technology to define our- 22 selves by sharing our thoughts and feelings as we're having them. We used to think, "I have a feeling; I want to make a call." Now our impulse is, "I want to have a feeling; I need to send a text."

So, in order to feel more, and to feel more like ourselves, we connect. But 23 in our rush to connect, we flee from solitude, our ability to be separate and gather ourselves. Lacking the capacity for solitude, we turn to other people but don't experience them as they are. It is as though we use them, need them as spare parts to support our increasingly fragile selves.

We think constant connection will make us feel less lonely. The opposite is 24 true. If we are unable to be alone, we are far more likely to be lonely. If we don't teach our children to be alone, they will know only how to be lonely.

I am a partisan for conversation. To make room for it, I see some first, 25
deliberate steps. At home, we can create sacred spaces: the kitchen, the dining room. We can make our cars "device-free zones." We can demonstrate the
value of conversation to our children. And we can do the same thing at work.
There we are so busy communicating that we often don't have time to talk to
one another about what really matters. Employees asked for casual Fridays;
perhaps managers should introduce conversational Thursdays. Most of all,
we need to remember—in between texts and emails and Facebook posts—to
listen to one another, even to the boring bits, because it is often in unedited
moments, moments in which we hesitate and stutter and go silent, that we
reveal ourselves to one another.

I spend the summers at a cottage on Cape Cod, and for decades I walked 26
the same dunes that Thoreau once walked. Not too long ago, people walked
with their heads up, looking at the water, the sky, the sand, and at one another,
talking. Now they often walk with their heads down, typing. Even when they
are with friends, partners, children, everyone is on their own devices.

So I say, look up, look at one another, and let's start the conversation. 27

⋑ AT ISSUE: SOURCES FOR DEVELOPING A CAUSE-AND-EFFECT ARGUMENT

1. This essay was first published in 2012. Are Turkle's conclusions still valid—or perhaps even more valid—today? If you were updating this essay, what additional examples could you present to support (or challenge) her conclusions?

2. In paragraph 1, Turkle makes a distinction between *conversation* and *connection*. What is the difference? According to Turkle, how do we "shortchange ourselves" in the process of moving from conversation to connection (para. 11)?

3. In paragraph 3, Turkle presents information on her research methods. Why? Is she appealing here to *logos*, *ethos*, or *pathos*?

4. What does Turkle mean by "alone together" (4)? Do your own experiences and observations confirm or challenge the existence of this phenomenon?

5. In paragraph 20, Turkle claims, "We expect more from technology and less from one another and seem increasingly drawn to technologies that provide the illusion of companionship without the demands of relationship." Do you think this characterization of our plugged-in society is exaggerated? Overly pessimistic? Explain your views.

6. In paragraph 24, Turkle says, "We think constant connection will make us feel less lonely. The opposite is true." How does she explain this idea? Do you agree with her reasoning?

This essay first appeared in the *Huffington Post* on January 30, 2014.

CLOSER TOGETHER OR FURTHER APART? DIGITAL DEVICES AND THE NEW GENERATION GAP

ROBERT WEISS

Angry Birds: 1, Grandparents: 0

Last week Chuck and Janet Bloom gave their only daughter a night off by taking their grandchildren out for dinner at a local pizza parlor. Both were looking forward to a playful evening with the kids. But as soon as they sat at the table, even before the menus appeared, they noted with dismay that their beloved grandkids were more engaged with and attentive to their holiday-acquired digital devices than to their loving, pizza-partying grandparents. Miriam, their sweet 14-year-old granddaughter, had her eyes intently focused on the contents of her iPad Facebook page. Briana, the 11-year-old, was posting her whereabouts on Twitter, Facebook, and Foursquare. And at the far end of the table, 7-year-old Sam's lips pursed in silent focus as he furiously engaged in a PlayStation cowboy shootout. Feeling frustrated, hurt, and angry—like they might as well have dined alone—Chuck and Janet quietly launched into an oft-held discussion about how these devices are ruining not just their three grandkids, but young people in general.

At the very same moment and just one table over, half a dozen 20-something work friends were seated, also preparing to order pizza. And just one look over at that crowd affirmed Chuck and Janet's worries about a "lost generation." At that table, two of the diners amicably swapped office gossip, but the others were as engaged with their digital devices as the aforementioned grandkids. What the clucking Chuck and Janet failed to notice was that no one at this second table seemed even remotely concerned or bothered by the fact that technology held as much sway as actual people.

So, why were Chuck and Janet seething about the "digital snub" from their grandchildren, while everyone at the other table managed to enjoy themselves, completely unruffled by the ever-shifting sands of live conversation, texting, tweeting, and posting? In great part this difference stems from the fact that Chuck and Janet are digital immigrants, while their grandkids and the 20-somethings one table over are all digital natives—different generations divided by different definitions of personal respect, attentiveness, interpersonal communication, and what constitutes a meaningful relationship.

Digital Natives versus Digital Immigrants

Generally speaking, people born before 1980 are digital immigrants, and those born after are digital natives. This somewhat arbitrary dividing line attempts to separate those who grew up actively using the internet and those who did not. Another, and perhaps better, way of looking at things is to say that digital natives unquestioningly value and appreciate the role that digital technology plays in their lives, whereas digital immigrants hold mixed views on the subject. Not surprisingly, thanks to continual advances in digital technology (such as the introduction of internet-enabled smartphones a few years ago), the separation between digital natives and digital immigrants is widening almost by the day, resulting not so much in a generation gap as a generation chasm.

This new generation gap is evident in practically every facet of modern 5 life. For instance, there are extreme differences in the ways digital natives and digital immigrants conduct business, gather news and information, and spend their paychecks. They also differ significantly in the ways they define personal privacy, experience entertainment, and socially engage (as evidenced in the pizza restaurant scenario above). Simply put, in a mere 25 years our basic forms of interpersonal communication and interaction have been drastically reformatted, and those who prefer the old ways of mostly face-to-face contact often feel left out and unappreciated.

In some ways this new generation gap sounds a lot like every other generation gap in history. However, previous generation gaps have mostly centered on young people vocally, visually, and in-real-time challenging the beliefs and experiences of their elders. Today, the divide is more about the fact that young people neither see nor hear their elders because, from a communications standpoint, the two generations are not in the same room. For instance, in the pizza restaurant Chuck and Janet are "present" and interacting at the dinner table, while their grandkids are "present" and interacting in a completely different, entirely digital universe. In some ways, this means that Chuck and Janet are dinosaurs. Basically, because they're not texting, tweeting, or posting to social media, they're not effectively communicating with their grandkids. Thus it seems the 1960s mantra that Chuck and Janet used to utter, "Don't trust anyone over 30," has for their grandkids morphed into, "We don't care about anyone over 30 because we can't see or hear them."

Connection/Disconnection

Interestingly, many digital natives think that young people are isolated and 7 disconnected—more interested in machines than people. In reality, nothing could be further from the truth. In fact, no generation in history has been more interconnected than Generations Y and Z. Statistics readily back this up. One study found that in 2009 more than half of American teens logged on to a social media site at least once per day, and nearly a quarter logged on 10 or more times per day. In the same year, a study by the Pew Internet and American Life Project found that more than three-quarters of U.S. teens owned a cellphone, with 88 percent texting regularly. Boys were sending and receiving 30 texts per day, with girls averaging 80. A more recent Pew study, this one conducted in 2012, finds these numbers are rising rapidly among every Gen Y and Z demographic. In fact, the first sentence of the 2012 study's overview reads: "Teens are fervent communicators." Indeed!

This same survey also reveals (to the chagrin of many digital immigrants) 8 that texting is now the primary mode of communication between teens and their friends and family, far surpassing phone calls, emails, and face-to-face interactions. Depending on your age and point of view, of course, this may or may not be a bad thing.

Consider Brad, a tech-savvy digital immigrant who recently flew home 9 from the West Coast to visit his family in Chicago. One evening at dinner there were three generations—his parents, him and his sister, and his sister's kids. During dinner the oldest child, 17, asked him via text:

> "Are you going to marry that girl you brought home last year?"
> 10

He texted back: "Yes, but no one else knows yet. Is that OK?"

In response, she typed: "I'm so excited. I know you don't want your mom 11 and dad to know yet, but they are really hoping you will. They liked her. So just between us, can I be a bridesmaid?"

He texted: "I know my secret would be safe with you, and of course you 12 will be a bridesmaid!"

For Brad, this poignant conversation with his niece was one of the more 13 meaningful exchanges of his entire five-day visit. And it is possible that without the privacy shield provided by texting, his 17-year-old niece may not have had the courage to broach the subject, even if she'd been able to find a moment alone with him. For her, the digital buffer of texting made this sweet and intimate exchange possible. And the conversation was no less meaningful for either person just because it was conducted via text.

Talk versus Text: Does It Matter?

It is possible that human interactions are no less meaningful or productive 14 simply because they are digital rather than face-to-face. It is also possible the exact opposite is true. Frankly, it depends more on those doing the communicating than anything else. Most often, digital immigrants (Baby Boomer and Gen X types) tend to want/need/prefer in-person, live interactions, or at least telephone conversations where they can hear the other person's voice.

Digital natives, on the other hand, seem to feel that communication is 15 communication, no matter the venue. To them, it seems silly to wait until they run into someone when they can text that person right now and get an instant response. They ask: "Why would I be disconnected when I can post, tweet, and text to let my family and friends known what I'm doing and what I need, and they can do the same with me?" This, of course, is the crux of the current generation gap—shifting from a fully analog world to one that is increasingly digital.

In my recently released book *Closer Together, Further Apart,* my coauthor 16 Jennifer Schneider and I note that in today's world the best communicators are those who are willing and able to engage other people in whatever venue is most appropriate and useful at the time. They neither avoid nor insist on a particular mode of interaction. Instead, they work hard to make sure their message is fully understood by the intended audience no matter what. In other words, they embrace the idea that they need to live and communicate fluently in both the digital and analog worlds. As technology evolves, so do good communicators, and they do so without forgetting or discounting what has worked in the past, remaining constantly aware of the fact that some people may prefer the older methodology, while others prefer the new.

Unfortunately, as has always been the case when changes in technology 17 have swiftly and profoundly affected our day-to-day lives, many people, young and old alike, become entrenched in the belief that "the way we do it is the best way." The simple truth is that cultural/technological assimilation is rarely an easy task. Sometimes it can feel easier to judge and avoid, rather than to embrace and evolve. Thus we have the current communications-driven generation gap. That said, the effort of reaching out beyond our generational comfort zone is usually well worth the effort. Brad found that to be true with his niece, and Chuck and Janet might also find it to be the case if they were only willing to give it a shot.

⊘ AT ISSUE: SOURCES FOR DEVELOPING A CAUSE-AND-EFFECT ARGUMENT

1. Weiss opens his essay with a two-paragraph anecdote. What point does this anecdote illustrate? Is this an effective opening strategy? What other options might have been more effective?

2. The title of this essay introduces the two sides of the issue Weiss discusses. Does he take a side in this essay? If so, which side is he on?

3. What is the difference between a *digital native* and a *digital immigrant*? How is this distinction central to Weiss's thesis?

4. What is the "new generation gap" (para. 5)? According to Weiss, how is it different from previous generation gaps? Does he offer strategies for closing this gap? Can you suggest a strategy?

5. What does the text exchange reproduced in paragraphs 10–13 illustrate? How does it support Weiss's thesis? What other kinds of support does he include? Do you think he needs more (or different) supporting evidence? Why or why not?

6. In paragraph 15, Weiss says, "It is possible that human interactions are no less meaningful or productive simply because they are digital rather than face-to-face." How do you suppose Sherry Turkle (p. 463) would respond to this comment? Why?

VISUAL ARGUMENT: UNIVERSITY OF PITTSBURGH VIDEO

⊘ AT ISSUE: SOURCES FOR DEVELOPING A CAUSE-AND-EFFECT ARGUMENT

1. This visual is a still from a video reporting findings of scientists at the University of Pittsburgh School of Medicine. What message does it convey? Is it simply informative, or does it make an argument? Explain.

2. List the individual images depicted in this visual. Would its impact be greater if it used photographs of actual people and items instead of silhouettes? Why or why not?

3. The images in this visual are accompanied by a few lines of text. Is this text necessary, or could the same message be conveyed with just the images? Why are "2x the odds" and ">2" set in larger type than the other text?

TEMPLATE FOR WRITING A CAUSE-AND-EFFECT ARGUMENT

Write a one-paragraph cause-and-effect argument in which you take a position on whether our reliance on social media brings us closer together or drives us apart. Follow the template below, filling in the blanks to create your argument.

Although increased social media use is seen by many as a positive development, some people believe that it has had negative consequences as well. One positive result of the spread of social media has been _____

_____. Another positive result has been _____

_____

_____. Despite these developments, many people see social media as a negative influence. For example, they believe _____.

Others claim _____

_____.

These critics suggest _____

_____

_____.

Granted, _____

_____

_____.

Still, _____

_____.

All things considered, it seems clear that our use of social media [brings us together/drives us apart].

⊃ EXERCISE 13.6 RECONSIDERING YOUR CONCLUSIONS

Working with two or three of your classmates, discuss your feelings about your generation's use of social media. Write a paragraph that summarizes your group's conclusions.

⊙ EXERCISE 13.7 WRITING A CAUSE-AND-EFFECT ARGUMENT

Write a cause-and-effect argument on the topic, "Does Our Reliance on Social Media Bring Us Together or Drive Us Apart?" Begin by considering all possible problems associated in our increasing reliance on social media. Then, consider the advantages of social media use. After weighing both sides of this issue, write an essay that supports your position. (If you like you may incorporate material you developed for Exercise 13.7 and the paragraph you wrote following the template on page 472 into your essay.) Cite the readings on pages 451–471 where necessary, and be sure to document the sources you use and to include a works-cited page. (See Chapter 10 for information on documenting sources.)

⊙ EXERCISE 13.8 REVIEWING THE FOUR PILLARS OF ARGUMENT

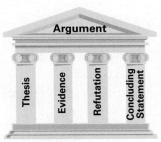

Review the four pillars of argument discussed in Chapter 1. Does your essay include all four elements of an effective argument? Add anything that is missing. Then, label the key elements of your essay.

⊙ WRITING ASSIGNMENTS: CAUSE-AND-EFFECT ARGUMENTS

1. What could your school do to encourage students to adopt healthier lifestyles? Write an editorial for your college newspaper in the form of a cause-and-effect argument. In your editorial, take one of these two positions:

   ■ If the university takes steps to encourage healthier lifestyles, students will benefit greatly.

   ■ If the university does not take steps to encourage students to adopt healthier lifestyles, the consequences could be serious.

2. Look at images of celebrities online, and consider the likely effects of these images on teenagers. Choose four or five of these images, and then write an essay arguing that such images help to encourage poor self-esteem, risky behavior, or eating disorders—or, that the celebrities pictured serve as positive role models for young people. Include some of the images in your essay, and analyze the impact of their visual elements as well as the effect of the words in the accompanying articles or captions.

3. In recent years, young children's lives have become more and more structured. Instead of the free play that their parents enjoyed, many of today's children are busy with scheduled sports, lessons, and play dates. Write an essay structured as a causal chain that traces the probable causes of this change as well as its likely effects on children and on their families. In your thesis statement, indicate whether you consider the effects positive or negative.

Evaluation Arguments

Do the Benefits of Fossil Fuels Outweigh the Environmental Risks?

We sometimes forget that fossil fuels like coal, oil, and natural gas come from plants and animals that died millions of years ago. Buried and pressurized, their organic remains formed substances rich in *hydrocarbons*. Hydrocarbons are highly combustible, which makes them a great fuel. While the use of these resources can be traced back to ancient Babylon, fossil fuels truly came of age during the Industrial Revolution. In the nineteenth and twentieth centuries, they not only provided fuel for factories and railroads but also for heating, lighting, driving, and countless other things that we take for granted. Today, the United States alone uses more than twenty million barrels of oil per day.

However, significant downsides do exist. Fossil fuels take millions of years to form: they are finite and nonrenewable. They give off carbon dioxide, which contributes to global warming. Even worse, coal releases toxins such as mercury into the air, soil, and water. Oil spills harm the environment, while the extraction of natural gas ("fracking") can poison drinking water and devastate landscapes. These problems have led people to explore alternative energy sources, such as wind, solar, and nuclear power, but these come with disadvantages, too, especially given the increasing scope and demands of the growing world economy. Later in this chapter, you will read essays that address the pros and cons of fossil fuels, and you will write an **evaluation argument** that takes a position on the issue of whether the benefits associated with fossil fuels outweigh the potential risks to the environment.

What Is an Evaluation Argument?

When you **evaluate**, you make a value judgment about something or someone—for example, a product, service, program, performance, work of literature or art, or candidate for public office.

Evaluation is part of your daily life: after all, before you make any decision, you need to evaluate your options. For example, you evaluate clothing and electronic equipment before you make a purchase, and you evaluate films, concerts, and TV shows before you decide how to spend your evening. Before you decide to go to a party, you evaluate its positive and negative qualities—who will be there, what music you are likely to hear, and what kind of food and drink will probably be on hand. You also evaluate your teachers, your classes, and even your friends.

When constructing an **evaluation argument**, you have several options: you can make a positive or negative judgment, you can assert that someone else's positive or negative judgment is not accurate or justified, or you can write a comparative evaluation, in which you demonstrate that one thing is (or is not) superior to another.

As a college student, you might read (or write) evaluation arguments based on topics such as the following:

- Is the college bookstore doing its best to serve students?
- Is a vegan diet really a practical option?
- Is *Moby-Dick* the great American novel?
- Is the SAT a valid testing instrument?
- Are portable e-book readers superior to print books?
- Are Crocs a marvel of comfort and design or just ugly shoes?
- Are hybrid cars worth the money?
- Is Beyoncé the most important musical artist of her generation?
- Do the benefits of fossil fuels outweigh the environmental risks?

⊖ EXERCISE 14.1 CHOOSING TOPICS FOR EVALUATION ARGUMENTS

List five additional topics that would be suitable for evaluation arguments.

MAKING EVALUATIONS

When you write an evaluation, you use terms such as the following to express judgments and indicate relative merits.

Superior/inferior	Important/trivial
Useful/useless	Original/trite
Efficient/inefficient	Innovative/predictable
Effective/ineffective	Interesting/dull
Successful/unsuccessful	Inspiring/depressing
Deserving/undeserving	Practical/impractical

◐ EXERCISE 14.2 MAKING EVALUATIVE STATEMENTS

Choose one word in each of the word pairs listed above, and use each word in a sentence that evaluates a service, program, or facility at your school.

IDENTIFYING BIAS

Everyone has biases, and these biases are likely to show up in evaluations, where strong opinions may overcome objectivity. As you read and write evaluation arguments, be on the lookout for evidence of bias:

- When you *read* evaluation arguments, carefully consider what the writer reveals (or actually states) about his or her values, beliefs, and opinions. Also be alert for evidence of bias in a writer's language and tone as well as in his or her choice of examples. (See "Detecting Bias in Your Sources" on pages 259–260 for more on this issue.)

- When you *write* evaluation arguments, focus on trying to make a fair assessment of your subject. Be particularly careful not to distort or slant evidence, quote out of context, or use unfair appeals or logical fallacies. (See "Being Fair" on pages 267–268 for more on how to avoid bias in your writing.)

Criteria for Evaluation

When you evaluate something, you cannot simply state that it is good or bad, useful or useless, valuable or worthless, or superior or inferior to something else; you need to explain *why* this is so. Before you can begin to develop a thesis and gather supporting evidence, you need to decide what **criteria for evaluation** you will use. To support a *positive* judgment, you need to show that something has value because it satisfies certain criteria;

to support a *negative* judgment, you need to show that something lacks value because it does not satisfy those criteria.

To make any judgment, then, you need to select the specific criteria you will use to assess your subject. For example, in an evaluation of a college bookstore, will you base your assessment on the friendliness of its service? Its prices? The number of books it stocks? Its return policy? The efficiency or knowledge of the staff? Your answers to these questions will help you begin to plan your evaluation.

The criteria that you establish will help you decide how to evaluate a given subject. If, for example, your criteria for evaluating musical artists focus on these artists' impact on the music industry, the number of downloads of their music, the number of corporate sponsors they attract, and their concert revenue, you may be able to support the thesis that Beyoncé is the most important musical artist of her generation. If, however, your main criterion for evaluation is the artist's influence on other contemporary performers, your case may be less compelling. Similarly, if you are judging health-care systems on the basis of how many individuals have medical coverage, you may be able to demonstrate that the Canadian system is superior to the U.S. system. However, if your criteria are referral time and government support for medical research, your evaluation argument might support a different position. Whatever criteria you decide on, a bookstore (or musical artist or health-care system) that satisfies them will be seen as superior to one that does not.

Beyoncé: The most important artist?

Kristina Kokhanova/Alamy Stock Photo

Consider another example. Suppose you want to evaluate the government's Head Start program, which was established in 1964 to provide preschool education to children from low-income families. The program also provides medical coverage and social services to the children enrolled, and in recent years it has expanded to cover children of migrant workers and children in homeless families. On what basis would you evaluate this program? Would you evaluate only the children's educational progress or also consider the program's success in providing health care? In considering educational progress, would you focus on test scores or on students' performance in school? Would you measure long-term effects—for example, Head Start students' likelihood of attending college and their annual earnings as adults? Or would you focus on short-term results—for example, students' performance in elementary school? Finally, would you evaluate only the children or also their families? Depending on the criteria you select for your evaluation, the Head Start program could be considered a success or a failure—or something in between.

⊛ EXERCISE 14.3 SELECTING CRITERIA FOR EVALUATION

Choose one of the topics you listed in Exercise 14.1, and list five possible criteria for an evaluation argument on that topic.

⊛ EXERCISE 14.4 EVALUATING YOUR TEXTBOOKS

By what criteria do you evaluate the textbooks for your college courses? Design? Content? Clarity? Comprehensiveness? Cost? Work with another student to decide on the most important criteria, and then write a paragraph in which you evaluate this textbook (or a textbook for another course).

Structuring an Evaluation Argument

In general terms, an evaluation argument can be structured like this:

- **Introduction:** Establishes the criteria by which you will evaluate your subject; states the essay's thesis

- **Evidence (first point in support of thesis):** Supplies facts, opinions, and so on to support your evaluation in terms of one of the criteria you have established

- **Evidence (second point in support of thesis):** Supplies facts, opinions, and so on to support your evaluation in terms of one of the criteria you have established

- **Evidence (third point in support of thesis):** Supplies facts, opinions, and so on to support your evaluation in terms of one of the criteria you have established

■ **Refutation of opposing arguments:** Presents others' evaluations and your arguments against them

■ **Conclusion:** Reinforces the main point of the argument; includes a strong concluding statement

⏺ The following student essay includes all the elements of an evaluation argument. The student who wrote the essay was evaluating a popular website, RateMyProfessors.com.

EVALUATION OF A WEBSITE: RATEMYPROFESSORS.COM

KEVIN MURPHY

Since 1999, both students and professors have been writing, reading, 1 defending, and criticizing the content on RateMyProfessors.com (RMP). With over 19 million ratings, 1.7 million professors rated, and millions of visitors per month, RMP continues to be the most popular site of its kind ("About RateMyProfessors.com"). However, the fact that a website is popular does not mean that it is reliable. Certainly RMP may be interesting and entertaining (and even, as *New York Times* writer Virginia Heffernan once wrote, "engrossing"), but is it useful? Will it help students to make informed decisions about the schools they choose to attend and the classes they choose to take? Are the ratings—as well as the site itself—trustworthy? Is the information about professors and schools comprehensive enough to be meaningful? No student wants to waste time in a course that is poorly taught by a teacher who lacks enthusiasm, **Thesis statement** knowledge, or objectivity. However, an evaluation of the reviews on RMP suggests that the site is not trustworthy or comprehensive enough to help college students make the right choices about the courses they take.

Evidence: First point in support of thesis The first question to ask about the reviews on RMP is, "Who is writing 2 them?" All reviews on the site are anonymous, and although anonymity protects the writers' privacy and may encourage them to offer honest feedback, it also raises a red flag. There is no guarantee that the reviews are written by students. In fact, anyone—even the professors themselves—can create RMP accounts and post reviews, and there is no way of knowing who is writing or what a writer's motivations and biases are. In addition, the percentage of students who actually write reviews is small. According to one recent survey, only 8 percent of students have ever written a review for an online professor-rating site; in other words, "a vocal minority" is running the show (Arden). Furthermore, the ratings for each individual professor vary greatly in number, quality, and currency. Even in the rare cases where a professor has hundreds of recent ratings, the score may represent the views of only a small percentage of that professor's students. This means that getting a representative sample is highly unlikely. Unless the website's managers institute rules and restrictions to ensure the legitimacy of the writer and the size of the sample, the RMP ratings will continue to be untrustworthy.

The second question to ask is, "Who controls RMP's content?" Although RMP posts "Site Guidelines" with a "Do" list and a "Do Not" list, these lists are merely suggestions. The RMP Site Moderation Team will remove obscene or unlawful posts, but it has no way to enforce other guidelines. For instance, one of the items on the "Do Not" list asks users not to "post a rating if you have not taken a class with the professor" ("Site Guidelines"). However, to sign up for an RMP account, a user does not have to identify his or her university or list the courses he or she has taken. The site asks only for a name, a birth date, and the right to share the user's personal information with its partner companies. This last question is a reminder that RMP is ultimately a commercial venture. The site is not owned by students or by their universities; it is owned by mtvU, a TV network that in turn is owned by media giant Viacom. The fact that each page of RMP content is surrounded on three sides by advertisements reminds users that the primary purpose of this site is to make money. When that fact is combined with the fact that the company has "the right to review, monitor, edit, and/or screen any content you post," it indicates that RMP does not warrant students' trust ("Terms of Use"). A for-profit corporation, not the student reviewers, controls all of the information on the site and may modify content to increase traffic and favorably impress advertisers.

3 Evidence: Second point in support of thesis

The last question to ask is, "Does RMP offer students the right kind of information—and enough in-depth information to give them a comprehensive understanding of a professor's effectiveness as a teacher?" In fact, the site offers ratings in only four categories: "Helpfulness," "Clarity," "Easiness," and "Hotness." As one highly rated professor points out, "None of the dimensions [of RMP's rating system] directly addresses how much students felt they learned" (qtd. in Arden). Moreover, no category addresses the professor's knowledge of the subject matter. The ratings tend

4 Evidence: Third point in support of thesis

to focus attention on superficial qualities rather than on substance, apparently assuming that most students are looking for "easy A" classes taught by attractive, pleasant instructors. To the site's credit, it recently phased out its infamous "chili pepper" rating for teacher attractiveness, which gave the site a reputation for gender bias and led to a backlash, as well as a potential boycott (Flaherty). Still, for students who are trying to make informed decisions about which classes to take, the site's limited criteria remain inadequate. As one frustrated student user explains, "One of my professors had a really negative rating and comments, but he came to be one of my favorites . . . his way of teaching matched me perfectly" (qtd. in Ross). The focus of RMP is not on giving substantial feedback about teaching effectiveness or information about the educational value of a class. Perhaps these kinds of feedback do not attract advertisers; feedback about a professor's "hotness"—the least important measure of effectiveness—apparently does.

Refutation of opposing arguments

Students who argue that RMP is a "useful resource" say that the site 5 helps them decide which professors to take and which to avoid (Davis). For example, one community college student says that checking professors' scores on RMP "helps me choose a professor who will suit my needs" (qtd. in Davis). Committed RMP users also say that they are able to sift through the superficial comments and find useful information about professors' teaching styles. As one junior at Baruch College in New York City says, "It's all about perspective, and you need to be aware of this when you use the site" (qtd. in Ross). Users claim that they can read reviews and understand that "the same course materials may work really well with one group of students and less well with another" (McGrath) and that "even though [a particular student] doesn't seem to like the professor, it sounds like I might" (qtd. in Davis). Students' ability to read between the lines, however, does not change the fact that the information on RMP is neither verifiable nor comprehensive. RMP's reviews are anonymous, and some of them are almost certainly not written by students who have taken the professors' classes. Professors' "Overall Quality" scores, which so many students rely on, are based on ratings by these untrustworthy reviewers. Furthermore, these "overall" ratings are based on only two factors: "Helpfulness" and "Clarity" ("Rating Categories"). A rating that is calculated on the basis of very limited information from questionable sources can hardly be a "useful resource." On balance, then, RMP does not give students the information they need to make informed decisions.

On RMP's home page, the site managers encourage visitors to [6] "join the fun!" ("About RateMyProfessors.com"). "Fun" is ultimately all users can hope to find at RMP. As Virginia Heffernan recommends, "Read it like a novel, watch it like MTV, study it like sociology. Just don't base any real decisions on it." Real students' honest and thorough reviews of professors are invaluable, but sites like RMP do not provide this kind of helpful feedback. When deciding between a commercial website and old-fashioned word of mouth, anyone who thinks that RMP offers more useful information should keep in mind who writes and controls the site's content. Because visitors to the site know almost nothing about the reviewers, they cannot know if their comments and ratings are trustworthy. Moreover, because they do know something about the site's owners, they should know enough to be wary of their motives. If students are looking for useful advice about which classes to take, they should look no further than the students on their own campuses.

Concluding statement

Works Cited

"About RateMyProfessors.com." *Rate My Professors*, MTV Networks, 2011, ratemyprofessors.com.

Arden, Patrick. "Rate My Professors Has Some Academics Up in Arms." *Village Voice*, 26 Oct. 2011, www.villagevoice.com/arts/rate-my -professors-has-some-academics-up-in-arms-7165156.

Davis, Mandi. "Rate My Professor Gains Popularity with MCCC Students." *Agora*, Monroe County Community College, 7 Dec. 2011, www .mcccagora.com/news/view.php/509769/Rate-My-Professor-gains -popularity-with-.

Flaherty, Colleen. "Bye, Bye, Chili Pepper." *Inside Higher Ed*, 2 July 2018, www.insidehighered.com/news/2018/07/02/rate-my-professors -ditches-its-chili-pepper-hotness-quotient.

Heffernan, Virginia. "The Prof Stuff." The *New York Times*, 11 Mar. 2010, www.nytimes.com/2010/03/14/magazine/14FOB-medium-t.html?_r=0.

McGrath, James F. "When My Son Discovered RateMyProfessors.com." *Inside Higher Ed*, 15 June 2015, www.insidehighered.com /views/2015/06/15/essay-about-professor-who-learns-his-son-has -discovered-ratemyprofessorscom.

"Rating Categories." *Rate My Professors*, MTV Networks, 2011, ratemyprofessors.com.

Ross, Terrance. "Professor Evaluation Website Receives Mixed Reviews." *Ticker*, Baruch College, City U of New York, 12 Sept. 2011, ticker .baruchconnect.com/article/professor-evaluation-website-receives -mixed-reviews/.

"Site Guidelines." *Rate My Professors*, MTV Networks, 20 June 2011, ratemyprofessors.com.

"Terms of Use." *Rate My Professors*, MTV Networks, 20 June 2011, ratemyprofessors.com.

GRAMMAR IN CONTEXT

Comparatives and Superlatives

When you write an **evaluation argument**, you make judgments, and these judgments often call for comparative analysis—for example, arguing that one thing is better than another or the best of its kind.

When you compare two items or qualities, you use a **comparative** form: *bigger, better, more interesting, less realistic*. When you compare three or more items or qualities, you use a **superlative** form: *the biggest, the best, the most interesting, the least realistic*. Be careful to use these forms appropriately.

■ **Do not use the comparative when you are comparing more than two things.**

INCORRECT Perhaps these kinds of feedback do not attract advertisers; comments about a professor's "Hotness"—<u>the less important measure</u> of effectiveness—apparently does.

CORRECT Perhaps these kinds of feedback do not attract advertisers; comments about a professor's "Hotness"—<u>the least important measure</u> of effectiveness—apparently does.

■ **Do not use the superlative when you are comparing only two things.**

INCORRECT When deciding between a commercial website and old-fashioned word of mouth, anyone who thinks that RMP offers <u>the most useful information</u> should keep in mind who writes and controls the site's content.

CORRECT When deciding between a commercial website and old-fashioned word of mouth, anyone who thinks that RMP offers <u>more useful information</u> should keep in mind who writes and controls the site's content.

⊙ EXERCISE 14.5 IDENTIFYING THE ELEMENTS OF AN EVALUATION ARGUMENT

The following commentary, "To Restore Civil Society, Start with the Library," includes the basic elements of an evaluation argument. Read the essay, and then answer the questions that follow it, consulting the outline on pages 476–480 if necessary.

This article was published in the *New York Times* on September 8, 2018.

TO RESTORE CIVIL SOCIETY, START WITH THE LIBRARY

ERIC KLINENBERG

Is the public library obsolete?   1

A lot of powerful forces in society seem to think so. In recent years, declines 2 in the circulation of bound books in some parts of the country have led prominent critics to argue that libraries are no longer serving their historical function. Countless elected officials insist that in the 21st century—when so many books are digitized, so much public culture exists online and so often people interact virtually—libraries no longer need the support they once commanded.

Libraries are already starved for resources. In some cities, even affluent ones 3 like Atlanta, entire branches are being shut down. In San Jose, Calif., just down the road from Facebook, Google, and Apple, the public library budget is so tight that users with overdue fees above $20 aren't allowed to borrow books or use computers.

But the problem that libraries face today isn't irrelevance. Indeed, in New 4 York and many other cities, library circulation, program attendance, and average hours spent visiting are up. The real problem that libraries face is that so many people are using them, and for such a wide variety of purposes, that library systems and their employees are overwhelmed. According to a 2016 survey conducted by the Pew Research Center, about half of all Americans ages 16 and over used a public library in the past year, and two-thirds say that closing their local branch would have a "major impact on their community."

Libraries are being disparaged and neglected at precisely the moment when they are most valued and necessary. Why the disconnect? In part it's because the founding principle of the public library—that all people deserve free, open access to our shared culture and heritage—is out of sync with the 5

> "Libraries are being disparaged and neglected at precisely the moment when they are most valued and necessary."

market logic that dominates our world. But it's also because so few influential people understand the expansive role that libraries play in modern communities.

Libraries are an example of what I call "social infrastructure": the physi- 6 cal spaces and organizations that shape the way people interact. Libraries don't just provide free access to books and other cultural materials, they also offer things like companionship for older adults, de facto child care for busy parents, language instruction for immigrants, and welcoming public spaces for the poor, the homeless, and young people.

I recently spent a year doing ethnographic research in libraries in New York City. 7 Again and again, I was reminded how essential libraries are, not only for a neighborhood's vitality but also for helping to address all manner of personal problems.

For older people, especially widows, widowers, and those who live alone, 8 libraries are places for culture and company, through book clubs, movie nights, sewing circles, and classes in art, current events, and computing. For many, the library is the main place they interact with people from other generations.

For children and teenagers, libraries help instill an ethic of responsibil- 9 ity, to themselves and to their neighbors, by teaching them what it means to borrow and take care of something public, and to return it so others can have it too. For new parents, grandparents, and caretakers who feel overwhelmed when watching an infant or a toddler by themselves, libraries are a godsend.

In many neighborhoods, particularly those where young people aren't 10 hyper-scheduled in formal after-school programs, libraries are highly popular among adolescents and teenagers who want to spend time with other people their age. One reason is that they're open, accessible, and free. Another is that the library staff members welcome them; in many branches, they even assign areas for teenagers to be with one another.

To appreciate why this matters, compare the social space of the library with 11 the social space of commercial establishments like Starbucks or McDonald's. These are valuable parts of the social infrastructure, but not everyone can afford to frequent them, and not all paying customers are welcome to stay for long.

Older and poor people will often avoid Starbucks altogether, because the 12 fare is too expensive and they feel that they don't belong. The elderly library patrons I got to know in New York told me that they feel even less welcome in the trendy new coffee shops, bars, and restaurants that are so common in the city's gentrifying neighborhoods. Poor and homeless library patrons don't even consider entering these places. They know from experience that simply standing outside a high-end eatery can prompt managers to call the police. But you rarely see a police officer in a library. This is not to say that libraries are always peaceful and serene. During the time I spent doing research, I witnessed a handful of heated disputes, physical altercations, and other uncomfortable situations, sometimes involving people who appeared to be mentally ill or under the influence of drugs. But such problems are inevitable in a public institution that's dedicated to open access, especially when drug clinics, homeless shelters, and food banks routinely turn away—and often refer to the library!—those who most need help. What's remarkable is how rarely these disruptions happen, how civilly they are managed, and how quickly a library regains its rhythm afterward.

The openness and diversity that flourish in neighborhood libraries were 13 once a hallmark of urban culture. But that has changed. Though American cities are growing more ethnically, racially, and culturally diverse, they too often remain divided and unequal, with some neighborhoods cutting themselves off from difference—sometimes intentionally, sometimes just by dint of rising costs—particularly when it comes to race and social class.

Libraries are the kinds of places where people with different backgrounds, 14 passions, and interests can take part in a living democratic culture. They are the kinds of places where the public, private, and philanthropic sectors can work together to reach for something higher than the bottom line.

This summer, Forbes magazine published an article arguing that libraries no 15 longer served a purpose and did not deserve public support. The author, an economist, suggested that Amazon replace libraries with its own retail outlets, and claimed that most Americans would prefer a free-market option. The public response—from librarians especially, but also public officials and ordinary citizens—was so overwhelmingly negative that Forbes deleted the article from its website.

We should take heed. Today, as cities and suburbs continue to reinvent 16 themselves, and as cynics claim that government has nothing good to contribute to that process, it's important that institutions like libraries get the recognition they deserve. It's worth noting that "liber," the Latin root of the word *library*, means both "book" and "free." Libraries stand for and exemplify something that needs defending: the public institutions that—even in an age of atomization, polarization, and inequality—serve as the bedrock of civil society.

If we have any chance of rebuilding a better society, social infrastructure 17 like the library is precisely what we need.

Identifying the Elements of an Evaluation Argument

1. Paraphrase Klinenberg's thesis by filling in the following template.

   Because _____,
   public libraries are not obsolete.

2. What criteria does Klinenberg use to evaluate public libraries? If he wanted to make the opposite case, what criteria might he use instead?

3. What benefits of public libraries does Klinenberg use to support his thesis? Can you think of additional benefits?

4. In his opening paragraphs, Klinenberg claims that "a lot of powerful forces in society" seem to see public libraries as obsolete. Why, according to Klinenberg, do they think so? How does he argue against this position?

5. In paragraph 7, Klinenberg says, "I recently spent a year doing ethnographic research in libraries in New York City." Why does he include this information?

6. How, according to Klinenberg, do the social spaces of Starbucks and McDonald's differ from those of public libraries? How does this contrast support the position he takes in this essay?

7. Where does Klinenberg identify the problems faced by public libraries? What explanations does he offer for these problems?

8. Evaluate Klinenberg's concluding statement. Do you think it is an appropriate conclusion for his essay, or do you think it overstates (or understates) his case? Explain.

Do the Benefits of Fossil Fuels Outweigh the Environmental Risks?

Citizens of the Planet/Education Images/UIG/Getty Images

Reread the At Issue box on page 475, which provides background on the question of whether the perceived advantages of fossil fuels outweigh concerns about possible environmental damage. Then, read the sources on the pages that follow.

As you read these sources, you will be asked to respond to some questions and complete some activities. This work is designed to help you understand the content and structure of the selections. When you are finished, you will be ready to decide on the criteria you will use to write an **evaluation argument** on the topic, "Do the Benefits of Fossil Fuels Outweigh the Environmental Risks?"

SOURCES

 Joseph L. Bast and Peter Ferrara, "The Social Benefits of Fossil Fuels Far Outweigh the Costs," page 489

 Juan Ramos, "Fossil Fuel Pros and Cons," page 492

 Bernard McNamee, "This Earth Day, Let's Accept the Critical Role That Fossil Fuel Plays in Energy Needs," page 496

 Sean Lennon, "Destroying Precious Land for Gas," page 499

 Bruno Comby, "The Benefits of Nuclear Energy," page 502

 Barbara Hurd, "Fracking: A Fable," page 508

 Visual Argument: "I Love Fossil Fuels," page 511

This article first appeared in the June 17, 2018, issue of the *Wall Street Journal*.

THE SOCIAL BENEFITS OF FOSSIL FUELS FAR OUTWEIGH THE COSTS

JOSEPH L. BAST AND PETER FERRARA

As several cities continue their suit against oil companies, *The People of the* 1 *State of California v. BP*, Judge William Alsup has boiled the case down to its pivotal question. In March he ordered the legal counsels of both parties to help him weigh "the large benefits that have flowed from the use of fossil fuels" against the possibility that such fuels may be causing global warming.

We sent the judge, and posted online, a 24-page document that answers 2 his question. The benefits of oil, coal, and gas are rarely acknowledged by environmental activists, who seek to regulate and tax these fuel sources out of existence. But an honest accounting shows that fossil fuels produce enormous social value that far outweighs their costs.

First, fossil fuels are lifting billions of people out of poverty, and in turn 3 improving health. "The most fundamental attribute of modern society is simply this," writes historian Vaclav Smil in his 2003 book on energy: "Ours is a high energy civilization based largely on combustion of fossil fuels."

Fossil fuels, and coal in particular, provided the energy that powered the 4 Industrial Revolution. Today, coal plants still produce most of the electricity that powers high-tech manufacturing equipment and charges mobile computing devices.

The alternative energy sources environmental activists favor are gener- 5 ally more expensive. Energy economists Thomas Stacey and George Taylor calculate that wind power costs nearly three times as much as existing coal generation and 2.3 times as much as combined-cycle gas. There is a negative correlation between energy prices and economic activity. A 2014 survey of economic literature by Roger Bezdek calculates that a 10 percent increase in U.S. electricity prices would eliminate approximately 1.3 percent of gross domestic product.

Cheap energy from fossil fuels also improves human well-being by powering labor-saving and life-protecting technologies, such as air-conditioning, modern medicine, and cars and trucks. Environmental activists often claim that prosperity speeds the depletion of resources and destruction of nature, but the opposite is true. As Ronald Bailey writes in *The End of Doom*: "It is in rich democratic capitalist countries that the air and water are becoming cleaner, forests

> "Cheap energy from fossil fuels improves human well-being by powering labor-saving and life-protecting technologies." 6

are expanding, food is abundant, education is universal, and women's rights respected."

Fossil fuels have increased the quantity of food humans produce and 7 improved the reliability of the food supply. The availability of cheap energy revolutionized agriculture throughout the world, making it possible for an ever-smaller proportion of the labor force to raise food sufficient to feed a growing global population without devastating nature or polluting air or water.

Fossil-fuel emissions create additional benefits, contributing to the green- 8 ing of the Earth. A 2017 study published in *Nature* magazine found that the global mass of land plants grew 31 percent during the 20th century. African deserts are blooming thanks to fossil fuels.

Finally, if fossil fuels are responsible for a significant part of the warm- 9 ing recorded during the second half of the 20th century, then they should also be credited with reducing deaths due to cold weather. Medical researchers William Richard Keatinge and Gavin Donaldson assessed this effect in a 2004 study. "Since heat-related deaths are generally much fewer than cold-related deaths, the overall effect of global warming on health can be expected to be a beneficial one."

They estimate the predicted temperature rise in Britain over the next 10 50 years will reduce cold-related deaths by 10 times the number of increased heat-related deaths. Other research shows climate change has exerted only a minimal influence on recent trends in vector-borne diseases such as malaria, dengue fever, and diseases spread by ticks.

Altogether, fossil fuels have produced huge benefits for mankind, many 11 of which continue today. But advocates of alternative energy sources usually manage to omit or diminish many of these benefits when calculating fossil fuels' "social cost."

Thankfully, President Trump and congressional Republicans understand 12 that the costs of fossil fuels must be weighed against their substantial benefits. They have decided wisely not to carry on the "war on fossil fuels" waged by the Obama administration, congressional Democrats, and their Golden State allies.

⊘ AT ISSUE: SOURCES FOR DEVELOPING AN EVALUATION ARGUMENT

1. How would you characterize the tone of this essay? Is this tone appropriate for the audience, readers of the *Wall Street Journal*, a national newspaper focusing on business and politics?

2. As the essay's title makes clear, this essay defends the use of fossil fuels. What criteria do the writers use for their evaluation?

3. List the specific advantages of fossil fuels that the writers identify to support their thesis. Do they include enough supporting evidence?

4. Throughout their essay, the writers summarize and refute arguments in support of other energy sources. Do you think they present these counterarguments fully enough? Do you think they refute them effectively? Explain.

5. Bast and Ferrara close paragraph 6 by quoting Ronald Bailey. Why do they include this statement? How does it support their position?

6. Consider the writers' use of past tense in the opening sentences of paragraphs 4 and 7. Does the use of past tense undercut their argument in any way? Explain.

7. How convincing do you find the argument presented in paragraphs 9–10? How might it be refuted?

8. Evaluate the concluding paragraph of this essay. What does it reveal about the writers' purpose?

This article was posted on September 23, 2018, on ScienceTrends.com.

FOSSIL FUEL PROS AND CONS

JUAN RAMOS

Fossil fuel pros and cons can be separated into inexpensive, globally available, 1 and compatibility with energy systems for fossil fuels pros compared to greenhouse gas emissions, finite resource, and environmentally damaging for fossil fuels cons.

There is an ongoing debate on the different kinds of fuel. Today, we want 2 to talk about the fossil fuels oil and gas. We will do so by exploring their pros and cons as we define the true advantage of oil and gas.

> "We are still a very long way from replacing the usage of fossil fuel by renewable energy sources."

When it comes to energy sources, fossil fuels are still indubitably the most 3 widely used energy sources globally. There are many different fossil fuels but the most largely used ones are natural gas, coal, and petroleum. When most people turn their lights on at home or at work, or when they ride cars or motorbikes, they would be using fossil fuels.

In recent years there have been great advances in the exploration of new 4 alternatives to fossil fuels. Unlike fossil fuels, which take millions of years to form, renewable sources of energy, like wind, solar, and hydropower are immediately available. But, we are still a very long way from replacing the usage of fossil fuel by renewable energy sources.

What Are Fossil Fuels?

There are essentially three fossil fuels: coal, petroleum (or oil), and natural gas. 5 It is worth looking at each one of them separately because, although they are often lumped together they are, in fact, quite different.

Coal is the result of millions of years of vegetation being accumulated 6 and altered. In order words, present-day coal is nothing but what remains of prehistoric vegetation. Coal is a great source of energy because of the solar energy that has been preserved in them. Solar energy is preserved by all living plants thanks to photosynthesis. When plants die any solar energy that they have stored is released. However, the vegetation that forms coal over millions of years after death do keep much of that solar energy.

Petroleum is a mixture of different hydrocarbons, usually found under the 7 surface of the earth. Petroleum is one of the most precious fossil fuels that are currently used. Petroleum includes the following different fractions:

- Gasoline
- Natural gas

- Naphtha
- Fuel oils
- Lubricating oils
- Kerosene
- Paraffin wax
- Asphalt

The one thing in common between the different fossil fuels is that they 8 are all the result of millions of years' worth of decomposition of plants and animals. This means, among other things, that these energy sources are finite. They all come with a "sell-by date" as it were. At some point, human beings will inevitably run out of fossil fuels. And this is one of the main reasons that the proponents of alternative energy sources deem essential that we find alternatives to fossil fuels as soon as possible.

But, the best to look at this issue is, to begin with by defining the pros and 9 cons of using fossil fuels.

What Are the Pros of Fossil Fuels?
There are, in fact, many pros of using fossil fuels.   10

Fossil Fuel Pros:

- Systems are set up to process and utilize oil and gas
- Widely available around the globe
- Low cost per unit energy
- Refineries, transportation, and plastics all rely heavily on oil and gas
- High energy output
- Employs millions of people globally
- The primary source of all plastics

Despite the undeniable fact that fossil fuels are finite, it is also true that 11 they are massively available still. Thanks to advances in technology among other reasons, we are able to access fossil fuels more than ever before. There are many places around the world that are rich in fossil fuels. Also fossil fuels such as oil and gas are relatively easy to find, particularly compared to some alternative energy sources. Most fossil fuels are close to the surface of the earth.

Their efficiency and ease of transport are also important pros that we 12 should take into account. In terms of efficiency, fossil fuels generate huge amounts of energy. Even the smallest piece of coal can generate phenomenal amounts of energy. But apart from this, they are also relatively easy to transport.

No matter the place of origin, fossil fuels can be transported to any part 13 of the planet with ease. You can see a contrast to alternative sources of energy such as wind or solar energy that can't really be deployed except in nearby areas to where they originate.

Finally, an important pro is that fossil fuel power plants are easy to set up. 14 So, anywhere fossil fuels are found, we are able to set up a plant to exploit it quickly enough.

What Are the Cons of Fossil Fuels?

But of course, there are also quite a few cons that should also be discussed.   15

Fossil Fuel Cons:

- Finite resource
- Large greenhouse gas emitter including CO_2
- Progressively harder to find oil and gas deposits
- Global movement toward limiting oil and gas and using renewable energy sources
- Environmentally damaging, with potential catastrophic damage from large oil spills
- Produces smog which harms human health

The main con is probably the environmental consequences of using 16 fossil fuels. The polluting effects of fossil fuels are widely known. Most scientists around the world argue that global warming is caused to a large extent by the burning of fossil fuels. These fuels are potentially very dangerous to our environment.

A related con is a direct impact this pollution has on human beings gen- 17 erally and, particularly, in children. Potentially mortal diseases such as asthma or lung cancer have been directly linked by scientists to the pollution caused by the burning of fossil fuels. This problem particularly affects people living in large cities and other areas exposed to a lot of traffic.

Another health-related issue is the danger that people who work in coal 18 mines have to deal with on a daily basis. The ingestion of coal dust has been proved to have seriously negative effects on people's health. Unfortunately, people who work in coal mines are bound to ingest this as they go about their work.

Another environmental problem is the potential of oil spills happening. 19 When this happens, oceans get polluted and birds and sea life suffer and often die. Although protections are always in place and oil spills are not all that common, they still happen from time to time. And every time, there is an oil spill, the environmental impact can result in the death of hundreds of animals, at the very least.

As we pointed out earlier, even though there are plenty of reserves still 20 available, fossil fuels are a finite source of energy. We will not be able to rely on these energy sources forever. At some point in the future, we will run out of them completely.

The final con is that as we rely more and more on these fuels and reserves 21 become more scarce, costs will go up. There are other factors that impact their costs and these are fairly unpredictable: war and other conflicts can also have an impact on prices and costs.

So, there are quite a few pros and cons to consider when discussing energy 22 sources. And this is no exception when it comes to oil and gas.

⊘ AT ISSUE: SOURCES FOR DEVELOPING AN EVALUATION ARGUMENT

1. As the title indicates, this essay presents both sides of the fossil fuel debate. Do you see the essay as an argument? Why or why not?

2. Why, according to Ramos, will fossil fuels eventually need to be replaced?

3. In paragraphs 5 through 8, Ramos explains what fossil fuels are. Why do you think he feels the need to include this explanation? What does this section of the essay tell you about how he views his audience?

4. In paragraphs 9 through 13, Ramos lists the advantages of fossil fuels. Which of the points on his bulleted list (para. 10) do you see as most and least important? Why?

5. In paragraphs 15 through 21, Ramos enumerates the disadvantages of fossil fuels. Which of these do you see as most and least important? Why?

6. Despite the controversial nature of its topic, this essay's conclusion is quite brief and understated. Rewrite it so it is more fully developed and more forceful. Do you think your new conclusion is more appropriate for this essay? Why or why not?

This essay was first posted on The Hill on April 17, 2018.

THIS EARTH DAY, LET'S ACCEPT THE CRITICAL ROLE THAT FOSSIL FUEL PLAYS IN ENERGY NEEDS

BERNARD MCNAMEE

Since its inception in 1970, Earth Day (April 22) has been a strange mix—a celebration of springtime and the great outdoors, combined with doom-and-gloom prophecies of destruction, centering on overpopulation, pollution, and capitalism.

But because Earth Day is an opportunity for reflection about our planet and the people who inhabit it, we should consider how man's use of natural resources has affected the environment and the human condition. In particular, we should honestly assess the data as to how fossil fuels impacted our planet, the environment, and quality of life. But like most things in life, the data does not always reflect the popular narrative.

> "Like most things in life, the data does not always reflect the popular narrative."

We have been told that fossil fuels are wrecking the environment and our health. The facts are that life expectancy, population, and economic growth all began to increase dramatically when fossil fuels were harnessed—and have continued to do so for the 200 years since the beginning of the Industrial Revolution.

When one thinks about it, it makes sense. Fossil fuels have allowed people to be more productive, to engage in less backbreaking manual labor, and to grow more food. Fossil fuel use for machines, transportation, electricity, and plastics allows us to build complex devices, travel longer distances, illuminate our homes, and build everyday products from toys to computers.

Consider this one example: gasoline in a car is used to transport an expectant mother to a hospital; coal and natural gas powers the electric lights and medical devices in a delivery room; that same electricity ensures that a prematurely born baby is kept warm in an incubator 24 hours a day, seven days a week; and petroleum-based plastics are used for tubing to supply that tiny baby with air and food.

Without oil, natural gas, and coal, none of this would be possible and available to so many people. In fact, many in developing countries can't save premature babies because they don't have access to the reliable electricity that fossil fuels provide Americans.

Fossil fuels have also allowed us to address hunger. In the United States, energy allows us to produce three times as much food as we did a century ago, in one-third fewer man-hours, on one-third fewer acres, and at one-third the cost. About 3 percent of the population now produces all the food that over 300 million Americans consume. From fertilizer produced with natural gas to tractors powered by diesel engines, and irrigation systems that pump water and refrigerators that prevent food from spoiling, natural gas, oil, and coal are the energy that feeds America.

Likewise, consider running water and sanitation. Natural gas, oil, and coal 8 help supply the electricity to pump clean, running water to our homes and allow us to operate wastewater and sewage plants so we don't pollute our rivers.

There is no doubt that the burning of fossil fuels has caused pollution. 9 But what is often not reported is how human ingenuity has reduced emissions. Since 1973, emissions have dropped 90 percent, even with a 123 percent increase in coal-fired electric generation. Since 1980, ozone is down 33 percent, nitrogen oxide down 57 percent, sulfur dioxide down 87 percent, carbon monoxide down 85 percent, and lead down 99 percent. Even U.S. carbon emissions from power generation have reached a 30-year low. In fact, these carbon emissions have been reduced primarily through the fracking revolution—in which hydraulic fracturing and directional drilling have made huge domestic quantities of natural gas available for electric power generation, offsetting dirtier coal.

Some suggest that we can replace fossil fuels with renewable resources 10 to meet our needs, but they never explain how. The challenges are clear: 80 percent of energy consumed (transportation, manufacturing, and electricity) in the U.S. comes from fossil fuels. About 63 percent of electricity generation comes from fossil fuels (coal, natural gas, petroleum, and other gases), with about 20 percent from nuclear energy. Renewable wind and solar, however, only provide about 7.6 percent of our electricity needs (6.3 percent wind and 1.3 percent solar)—and this is only when the sun is shining or wind is blowing.

This does not mean we should not use renewable energy. Of course we 11 should. But these facts do mean that we need to be honest about whether renewables can displace other energy resources in providing for our energy needs. Moreover, nearly 100 percent of the plastics we use every day are made from petroleum—and wind and the sun cannot be transformed into plastic.

America is blessed with an abundant supply of affordable natural gas, 12 oil, and coal. When we celebrate Earth Day, we should consider the facts, not the political narrative, and reflect about how the responsible use of America's abundant resources of natural gas, oil, and coal have dramatically improved the human condition—and continue to do so.

⊙ AT ISSUE: SOURCES FOR DEVELOPING AN EVALUATION ESSAY

1. McNamee begins and ends his essay with a discussion of Earth Day. Why? Is this an effective strategy? Explain.

2. In paragraph 2, McNamee says that when it comes to the fossil fuel debate, "the data does not always reflect the popular narrative." What "popular narrative" is he refuting here?

3. What specific advantages of fossil fuels (oil, natural gas, and coal) does McNamee enumerate? Does he identify any advantages that Ramos (p. 492) does not list?

4. In paragraph 9, McNamee concedes, "There is no doubt that the burning of fossil fuels has caused pollution." Is his refutation of this counterargument convincing? Why or why not?

5. In paragraph 10, McNamee refutes the claim that renewable energy sources can replace fossil fuels. How does he refute it? Is this refutation convincing? Why or why not?

6. What criteria does McNamee use to evaluate fossil fuel use? Are these the same criteria used by other writers whose essays appear in this chapter?

This op-ed ran in the *New York Times* on August 27, 2012.

DESTROYING PRECIOUS LAND FOR GAS

SEAN LENNON

On the northern tip of Delaware County, N.Y., where the Catskill Mountains 1 curl up into little kitten hills, and Ouleout Creek slithers north into the Susquehanna River, there is a farm my parents bought before I was born. My earliest memories there are of skipping stones with my father and drinking unpasteurized milk. There are bald eagles and majestic pines, honeybees and raspberries. My mother even planted a ring of white birch trees around the property for protection.

A few months ago I was asked by a neighbor near our farm to attend a 2 town meeting at the local high school. Some gas companies at the meeting were trying very hard to sell us on a plan to tear through our wilderness and make room for a new pipeline: infrastructure for hydraulic fracturing. Most of the residents at the meeting, many of them organic farmers, were openly defiant. The gas companies didn't seem to care. They gave us the feeling that whether we liked it or not, they were going to fracture our little town.

In the late '70s, when Manhattanites like Andy Warhol and Bianca Jagger 3 were turning Montauk and East Hampton into an epicurean Shangri-La for the Studio 54 crowd, my parents, John Lennon and Yoko Ono, were looking to become amateur dairy farmers. My first introduction to a cow was being taught how to milk it by hand. I'll never forget the realization that fresh milk could be so much sweeter than what we bought in grocery stores. Although I was rarely able to persuade my schoolmates to leave Long Island for what seemed to them an unreasonably rural escapade, I was lucky enough to experience trout fishing instead of tennis lessons, swimming holes instead of swimming pools, and campfires instead of cable television.

Though my father died when I was 5, I have always felt lucky to live 4 on land he loved dearly; land in an area that is now on the verge of being destroyed. When the gas companies showed up in our backyard, I felt I needed to do some research. I looked into Pennsylvania, where hundreds of families have been left with ruined drinking water, toxic fumes in the air, industrialized landscapes, thousands of trucks and new roads crosshatching the wilderness, and a devastating and irreversible decline in property value.

Natural gas has been sold as clean energy. But when the gas comes from 5 fracturing bedrock with about five million gallons of toxic water per well, the word "clean" takes on a disturbingly Orwellian tone. Don't be fooled. Fracking for shale gas is in truth dirty energy. It inevitably leaks toxic chemicals into the air and water. Industry studies show that 5 percent of wells can leak immediately, and 60 percent over 30 years. There is no such thing as pipes and concrete that won't eventually break down. It releases a cocktail of chemicals from a menu of more than 600 toxic substances, climate-changing methane, radium, and, of course, uranium.

> "Fracking for shale gas is in truth dirty energy."

New York is lucky enough to have some of the best drinking water in the 6 world. The well water on my family's farm comes from the same watersheds that supply all the reservoirs in New York State. That means if our tap water gets dirty, so does New York City's.

Gas produced this way is not climate-friendly. Within the first 20 years, 7 methane escaping from within and around the wells, pipelines, and compressor stations is 105 times more powerful a greenhouse gas than carbon dioxide. With more than a tiny amount of methane leakage, this gas is as bad as coal is for the climate; and since over half the wells leak eventually, it is not a small amount. Even more important, shale gas contains one of the earth's largest carbon reserves, many times more than our atmosphere can absorb. Burning more than a small fraction of it will render the climate unlivable, raise the price of food, and make coastlines unstable for generations.

Mayor Michael R. Bloomberg, when speaking for "the voices in the sen- 8 sible center," seems to think the New York State Association of County Health Officials, the American Academy of Pediatrics, the New York State Nurses Association, and the Medical Society of the State of New York, not to mention Dr. Anthony R. Ingraffea's studies at Cornell University, are "loud voices at the extremes." The mayor's plan to "make sure that the gas is extracted carefully and in the right places" is akin to a smoker telling you, "Smoking lighter cigarettes in the right place at the right time makes it safe to smoke."

Few people are aware that America's Natural Gas Alliance has spent 9 $80 million in a publicity campaign that includes the services of Hill and Knowlton—the public relations firm that through most of the '50s and '60s told America that tobacco had no verifiable links to cancer. Natural gas is clean, and cigarettes are healthy—talk about disinformation. To try to counteract this, my mother and I have started a group called Artists Against Fracking.

My father could have chosen to live anywhere. I suspect he chose to live 10 here because being a New Yorker is not about class, race, or even nationality; it's about loving New York. Even the United States Geological Survey has said New York's draft plan fails to protect drinking water supplies, and has also acknowledged the likely link between hydraulic fracturing and recent earthquakes in the Midwest. Surely the voice of the "sensible center" would ask to stop all hydraulic fracturing so that our water, our lives, and our planet could be protected and preserved for generations to come.

⊘ AT ISSUE: SOURCES FOR DEVELOPING AN EVALUATION ARGUMENT

1. Throughout this essay, Lennon is careful to establish himself as a resident of a rural area, a farmer, and someone who grew up swimming and fishing in an idyllic natural setting. Why does he do this? Does this information appeal to *logos*, *ethos*, or *pathos*? Explain.

2. Although Lennon mentions his parents in paragraphs 1 and 2, he doesn't identify them by name until paragraph 3. Why not? Is his readers' knowledge of who his parents were likely to add to, detract from, or not affect his credibility on the subject of fracking?

3. Why do you think Lennon tells readers in paragraph 4 that he "needed to do some research"? What did his research reveal?

4. Reread paragraph 8. Do you think Lennon is making an **ad hominem** attack on former New York City mayor Michael R. Bloomberg here? Why or why not?

5. What kind of evidence does Lennon present to support his position against fracking? Does he include enough evidence—as well as the right kind of evidence—to support his defense of the land he believes is threatened? Why or why not?

This essay appears on the website for the organization Environmentalists for Nuclear Energy at www.ecolo.org.

THE BENEFITS OF NUCLEAR ENERGY

BRUNO COMBY

Nuclear energy is a clean, safe, reliable, and competitive energy source. It is 1 the only source of energy that can replace a significant part of the fossil fuels (coal, oil, and gas) which massively pollute the atmosphere and contribute to the greenhouse effect.

If we want to be serious about climate change and the end of oil, we must 2 promote the more efficient use of energy, we must use renewable energies—wind and solar—wherever possible, and adopt a more sustainable lifestyle. But this will not be nearly enough to slow the accumulation of atmospheric CO_2, and satisfy the needs of our industrial civilization and the aspirations of the developing nations. Nuclear power should be deployed rapidly to replace coal, oil, and gas in the industrial countries, and eventually in developing countries.

An intelligent combination of energy conservation, and renewable 3 energies for local low-intensity applications, and nuclear energy for baseload electricity production, is the only viable way for the future.

Tomorrow's nuclear electric power plants will also provide power for elec- 4 tric vehicles for cleaner transportation. With the new high temperature reactors we will be able to recover fresh water from the sea and support hydrogen production.

We believe that the opposition of some environmental organizations 5 to civilian applications of nuclear energy will soon be revealed to have been among the greatest mistakes of our times.

Present Conditions

Resources: Our industrial civilization runs on energy and 85 percent of the 6 world's energy is provided by the fossil fuels, coal, oil, and gas.

Coal began to be used extensively in Britain when its forests were no lon- 7 ger able to satisfy the energy requirements of an embryo industrialization. Coal is found almost everywhere and reserves should last several centuries.

Petroleum began by replacing whale oil at the end of the 19th century, and 8 its use has grown ever since. Discoveries of new deposits are not keeping up with consumption and production of oil is about to peak. At the present rate of consumption, reserves are estimated to last a few decades, but consumption is growing rapidly. More than half the world's oil production today is located in the fragile and politically unstable area of the Persian Gulf, as is an even greater fraction of our future reserves.

Gas was at first a by-product of oil extraction and it was thrown away. It 9 has since been mastered to become a major source of energy. Reserves are similarly limited and estimated to last for a few decades.

These fossil fuels were laid down over geological times and it seems 10 likely they will have been totally exploited over the few centuries from about 1850 to 2100.

Environmental consequences: In burning fossil fuels, we inject 23 billion 11 tons of carbon dioxide every year into the atmosphere—730 tons per second. Half of it is absorbed in the seas and vegetation, but half remains in the atmosphere. This is significantly altering the composition of the atmosphere and seriously affecting the climate of our planet.

We have only this one fragile planet to live on. If we want it to remain 12 livable, to ensure the comfort of our modern lives and indeed the very continuation of our industrial civilization, then we must urgently adopt new lifestyles and find other energy sources.

What Is to Be Done?

Conservation and renewables: There are those who tell us we only need to 13 conserve energy and rely upon renewable energies. Solar and wind are the major renewables.

I agree, of course, that conservation is highly commendable, even essen- 14 tial. But in the light of the world's growing population, widespread economic development and enhanced life expectancy on the one hand (notably China and India which account for about 35 percent of the world's population) and finite fossil fuel resources on the other, conservation can only delay the crisis that will arise from the penury of oil and gas.

Energy efficiency and alternate sources of energy can and must be devel- 15 oped. Efficient light bulbs produce the same amount of light with 3 to 8 times less energy. Heat pumps can provide the same amount of heat with 2 to 5 times less energy. Solar heat and geothermal energy can and should be developed to a much greater extent than they are today.

Some environmentalists are enchanted by the simplicity of solar cells and 16 the pristine elegance of wind turbines, and they refuse to accept the fact that they are quantitatively incapable of supplying the energy required by an industrial civilization. I do not mean to say that these renewable energies should be excluded; they are useful and have important niche roles to play—in remote locations and under special circumstances. But they can make only a marginal contribution to the energy needs of a growing industrial civilization.

Let me give an example. To replace just one nuclear reactor, such as the 17 new EPR reactor which France is now building in Normandy, with the most modern wind turbines (twice as high as Notre Dame, the cathedral of Paris), they would have to be lined up all the way from Genoa in Italy to Barcelona in Spain (about 700 kilometers/400 miles). And, even so, they generate electricity only when the wind blows (their average yield is about 25 percent of their rated capacity).

There is much talk about biofuels, ethanol from sugar cane, for example. 18 The entire arable surface of the Earth could not produce enough biofuel to replace present oil consumption.

Mineral resources: By 2100, oil and natural gas reserves will likely be 19 exhausted. This leaves coal and nuclear energy.

As an environmentalist the idea of developing more coal, the most pollut- 20 ing energy source on the planet, and the greatest contributor to global warm- ing, is simply not acceptable. The process of sequestration or isolating millions and billions of tons of carbon dioxide is nothing but a pleasant dream at this point, still unproven and unlikely to be put into widespread practice.

Nuclear power: Nuclear power is clean, safe, reliable, compact, compet- 21 itive, and practically inexhaustible. Today over 400 nuclear reactors provide baseload electric power in 30 countries. Fifty years old, it is a relatively mature technology with the assurance of great improvement in the next generation. (Hundreds of nuclear reactors furnish reliable and flexible shipboard power: military ships of course. But the technology is adaptable to civilian maritime transport.)

Clean: Nuclear energy produces almost no carbon dioxide, and no sulfur 22 dioxide or nitrogen oxides whatsoever. These gases are produced in vast quan- tities when fossil fuels are burned.

Nuclear waste: One gram of uranium yields about as much energy as a 23 ton of coal or oil—it is the famous "factor of a million." Nuclear waste is corre- spondingly about a million times smaller than fossil fuel waste, and it is totally confined.

In the USA and Sweden, spent fuel is simply stored away. Elsewhere, spent 24 fuel is reprocessed to separate out the 3 percent of radioactive fission products and heavy elements to be vitrified (cast in glass) for safe and permanent stor- age. The remaining 97 percent—plutonium and uranium—is recovered and recycled into new fuel elements to produce more energy.

The volume of nuclear waste produced is very small. A typical French 25 family's use of nuclear energy over a whole lifetime produces vitrified waste the size of a golf ball.

Nuclear waste is to be deposited in deep geological storage sites; it does 26 not enter the biosphere. Its impact on the ecosystems is minimal. Nuclear waste spontaneously decays over time while stable chemical waste, such as arsenic or mercury, lasts forever.

Most fossil fuel waste is in the form of gas that goes up the smokestack. 27 We don't see it, but it is not without effect, causing global warming, acid rain, smog, and other atmospheric pollution.

Safe: Nuclear power is safe, as proven by the record of half a century of 28 commercial operation, with the accumulated experience of more than 12,000 reactor-years.

There have been only two serious accidents in the commercial exploita- 29 tion of nuclear power: Three Mile Island (TMI) in 1979 (in Pennsylvania, USA) and Chernobyl in 1986 (in the Soviet Union, now in Ukraine). TMI was the worst accident one can imagine in a Western power reactor. The core of the reactor melted down and much of it fell to the bottom of the reactor vessel. The radioactivity released was almost entirely confined within the reinforced concrete containment structure, the airtight silo-like building which houses the reactor—it was designed for that purpose. The small amount of radioactivity which escaped was quite innocuous. As a result, no one at TMI was seriously irradiated nor did anyone die. In fact, Three Mile Island was a real success story for nuclear safety. The worst possible accident occurred, a core meltdown, and yet no one died or was even injured.

Chernobyl was different. The reactors at Chernobyl had no contain- 30 ment structure. The reactor's faulty design made it unstable and Chernobyl was operated that night in a way known to be dangerous. In the execution of a test, all the security systems were deliberately bypassed. An uncontrollable surge in power occurred leading to a steam explosion. The 600-ton graphite moderator then caught fire and burned for several weeks. The smoke carried more than half the radioactive fission products directly into the atmosphere where they were swept far and wide by the winds. Fewer than 32 persons died within a few months, and about 200 more were severely irradiated but survived.

> "Far fewer fatalities have occurred in the civilian nuclear power industry in half a century than occurred in any year in the fossil fuel industries."

The inhabitants of the exclusion zone were also victims as they were hurriedly uprooted, evacuated, and resettled elsewhere. They lost their jobs and suffered psychological and social trauma in the dissolving Soviet Union. Their lives were disrupted and shortened. Since 1986, some 4,000 cases of thyroid cancer have been diagnosed in the surrounding regions, and successfully treated. Nine fatal cases have been reported. There has been some talk about long-term cancers. Some organizations and journalists speculate that there might be tens of thousands of victims still to come, but it should be noted that these are mostly the result of theoretical calculations based on an unsubstantiated hypothesis, the linear extrapolation of the effect of high doses and high-dose rates of radiation to the low-doses and low dose rates, applied in this case to populations in millions having received only low doses. It is scientifically well established that this linear extrapolation does not apply to doses below 100 mSv, and therefore these calculations are not relevant, except perhaps for those persons who were exposed to high doses above 100 mSv. Chernobyl was the perfect example of what not to do with a nuclear reactor: a faulty design, an unstable reactor, operated in an experiment with all security systems disconnected, followed by a panicked response by the civil authorities.

In sum, far fewer fatalities have occurred in the civilian nuclear power 31 industry in half a century (Chernobyl included) than occurred in any year in the fossil fuel industries. Coal mine accidents are common occurrences and often cause tens or hundreds of fatalities, reported one day and forgotten the next, adding up to about 15,000 per year worldwide, 6,000 of which are in China. The same may be said for oil field accidents. Oil tankers go aground or break up, accidents occur in refineries, oil and gas platforms have been lost with all hands. Accidents in high pressure gas pipelines are not infrequent. Just one example among many others is the gas pipeline accident at Ghislenghien, Belgium, on July 30, 2004, in which 21 persons died and 120 were injured.

Reliable: Nuclear reactors provide baseload power and are available over 32 90 percent of the time; intervals between refuelings have been extended and downtime for refueling has been reduced. In the USA, these improvements over the years have been the equivalent of adding one reactor a year to the existing fleet. Most reactors are designed for a life of 40 years; many are reaching that age in good condition and extensions of 20 years have usually been granted.

Competitive: The cost of nuclear power is competitive and stable. The cost 33 of nuclear fuel is a small part of the price of a nuclear kilowatt-hour, whereas fossil fueled power, especially oil and gas, is at the mercy of the market.

Inexhaustible: Uranium is found everywhere in the crust of the Earth—it 34 is more abundant than tin, for example. Major deposits are found in Canada and Australia. It is estimated that increasing the market price by a factor ten would result in 100 times more uranium coming to market. Eventually we will be able to recover uranium from seawater where 4 billion tons are dissolved.

Compact: A nuclear power station is very compact, occupying typically 35 the area of a football stadium and its surrounding parking lots. Solar cells, wind turbine farms, and growing biomass, all require large areas of land.

Radiation: Fear of the unknown is the merchandise of anti-nuclear "greens." 36 They preach fear of radiation in general, fear of radioactive waste in particular, fear of another major accident such as Three Mile Island or Chernobyl, and fear of nuclear weapons proliferation. Their campaign has been successful only because radiation is a mystery to most people, and very few are aware of the fact that radiation is present everywhere in the environment. The anti-nuclear organizations also exploit the widespread but mistaken interpretation of the studies of the health of the survivors of the Hiroshima and Nagasaki bombing: that even a small amount of radiation is deleterious to health (the linear no-threshold hypothesis), and the related concept of collective dose. In fact a moderate amount of radiation is natural and beneficial, if not essential, to life.

Radiation has been bathing our environment since the earliest history of 37 our planet, and it is present everywhere in nature. In fact, our sun and its planets including the Earth are the remnants of the giant explosion of a supernova. Everything is radioactive around us in nature and already was even before radioactivity was discovered. This radiation spontaneously decreases with time. When life first appeared on Earth, the natural radiation levels were about twice as high as today.

Most people are totally unaware of the fact that the human body itself is 38 naturally radioactive. Our bodies contain about 8,000 becquerels (8,000 atoms disintegrating every second), about half of which is potassium-40, a chemical element essential for health, as well as carbon-14.

Old fashioned attitudes: Ecological organizations such as Greenpeace 39 have consistently had an anti-nuclear bias which is more ideological than factual. An increasing number of environmentalists are now changing their minds about nuclear energy because there are very good, solid, scientific, and, above all, environmental reasons to be in favor of nuclear energy.

To conclude, it is our position that well-designed, well-constructed, 40 well-operated, and well-maintained nuclear energy is not only clean, but it is also safe, reliable, durable, and competitive.

⊘ AT ISSUE: SOURCES FOR DEVELOPING AN EVALUATION ARGUMENT

1. Comby's purpose here is to promote the clear advantage of nuclear energy over fossil fuels. What specific advantages does he cite to support the thesis that "Nuclear power should be deployed rapidly to replace coal, oil, and gas" (para. 2)?

2. What biases against nuclear energy does Comby think people have? How does he attempt to counter these preconceived ideas in this essay?

3. In a previous version of this essay, part of the text that now appears as paragraphs 1 through 5 was actually the conclusion. If you were editing this essay, which of these paragraphs (if any) would you relocate to the end? Why? Do you see any other paragraph in the essay that might work as a concluding statement?

4. Comby begins paragraph 2 with, "If we want to be serious about climate change and the end of oil." Is he begging the question here? Do you think he is correct to assume that his readers are "serious" about replacing fossil fuels? Explain.

5. Do you see this essay as appealing primarily to *logos, ethos,* or *pathos*? Explain.

6. What criteria does Comby use to evaluate nuclear energy? Does he apply the same criteria to his evaluation of fossil fuels (for examples, in paragraphs 11, 12, and 21)?

7. Comby devotes a good deal of space (29–32) to a discussion of the safety of nuclear power. Why? In what sense is this section of the essay a refutation?

This piece appeared in *Brevity*, a journal of literary nonfiction, on March 3, 2013.

FRACKING: A FABLE

BARBARA HURD

In the past, everything took forever. 1

Rain fell for centuries, and millions of years after that, the ancient Appa- 2 lachian Basin just west of what is now the East Coast spent even more millennia becoming a sprawling, shallow bowl. And then nothing much happened. Another million years passed. Mountain ranges slowly rose and receded, and continents wandered into each other and eventually the basin began to fill with seawater and for another million years, the surrounding mountains slid wetly down the slopes of themselves and settled into the bottom sludge of the basin.

More tens of thousands of centuries passed while the water sloshed and 3 the undersea mud thickened, and in all that time, no human ever stood on its shores, no blue crab ever scurried in the ooze. There were no witnesses. And even if there had been, who could have stood the boredom of watching that slow, barely breathing world? The only testimony ever made to that languid time was locked in the mud.

> "A few continents collided, some peaks rose, some valleys sank."

For yet another several million years, it piled up—thick, black, and putrid. Over the next millennia, miniscule creatures evolved: phytoplankton, 4 blue-green algae. They floated in the shallow seas until they died and drifted down to be entombed in the ooze that lay fifty, one hundred, two hundred feet deep.

Then came more mountains moving. A few continents collided, some 5 peaks rose, some valleys sank. Meanwhile, down in the black ooze, remnants of those tiny creatures that had been held in the mud were shoved more tightly together, packed side by side with sludged-in sediment, cemented together, cooked by the heat deep in the earth, and converted into hydrocarbons. Layer after layer of crammed-together particles and silt began to sink under the accumulating weight of the mountains that grew above. Wrung of its moisture, its pliability, its flow, the mud slowly, slowly, over millions of years, turned into gas-rich rock.

And there it lay, miles under the surface, as the old basin above it emp- 6 tied and rose and more continents meandered into each other and finally the sun dried the Appalachians, which eroded and softened, and three hundred million years after the first mud settled on the bottom of that basin, humans appeared. We developed with lightning speed—geologically speaking— our brains and vision and hands, our fast and furious tools, our drills and ingenuity, and all the while that ooze-become-rock lay locked and impenetrable, deep in the earth, farther than anything, including anyone's imagination, reached, until in the split second that is humankind's history on this planet we pushed a drill with a downhole mud-motor a mile deep and made it turn sideways and snaked it into that ancient rock speckled with evidence of another eon, and a few minutes later we detonated small explosives and blasted millions of gallons of slick water—sand and water and a bit of biocide in case anything was alive down there—into what hadn't seen water or light for four hundred million years.

The shale shattered, the black rock spider-webbed with skinny fissures as 7 the above world inserted its tendrils, and into those tiny rifts we rammed more sand to keep them wedged open wider.

And then—remember the blue-green algae?—the gas that had been 8 locked in that stony underworld for almost four hundred million years suddenly had an exit. It flowed through the intricate shudderings of brand new fissures and up the borehole through the limestone that had been laid down millions of years after the mud, and up through the bedrock just below someone's pasture and out into a world with air and fresh water where we humans, fur-less and in need of fuel to stay warm, exercised our resourceful minds.

And then in another split-second's time—geologically speaking—we 9 drilled another thousand wells, fracked another million tons of stony earth a mile beneath our feet.

And when the slick water was withdrawn from the fissures and small 10 slither-spaces and that prehistoric bedrock was lickety-split forever changed, no one could predict the impact, not even we inventive humans whose arrival on this planet is so recent, whose footprints, so conspicuous and large, often obliterate cautionary tales.

And soon the unpredictable, as always, occurred.   11

And now, in no time at all, not everything takes forever any longer.   12

⊖ AT ISSUE: SOURCES FOR DEVELOPING AN EVALUATION ESSAY

1. What is a fable? How is this essay similar to and different from fables with which you are familiar?

2. Is this "fable" also an argument? If so, what position does it take? Write a sentence that expresses this position.

3. What advantage might Hurd's labeling of this essay as a fable have given her? Can you see any disadvantages?

4. This essay makes an appeal to *pathos*. Do you think this kind of appeal is enough, or would Hurd have been more convincing if she had also appealed to *logos* and/or *ethos*? Explain.

5. What "cautionary tale" (para. 10) is the focus of this essay? How, according to Hurd, has it been "obliterated" by human beings?

6. Explain the essay's last sentence. How is the present imagined in this sentence different from the past referred to in the first sentence of the essay?

VISUAL ARGUMENT: "I LOVE FOSSIL FUELS"

⊘ AT ISSUE: DO THE BENEFITS OF FOSSIL FUELS OUTWEIGH THE ENVIRONMENTAL RISKS?

1. This website shows a T-shirt available for purchase in a variety of colors—including several shades of green. Why? Do you think this makes sense?

2. The website tell buyers that the purchase will "Show your support for the fossil fuel industry." Do you think the shirt's words and images would effectively convey the wearer's support for this industry? Do you think putting this message on a T-shirt trivializes the issue? Explain.

3. If you were going to design a T-shirt to discourage the use of fossil fuels, what words and images would you select? Why?

TEMPLATE FOR WRITING AN EVALUATION ARGUMENT

Write a one-paragraph evaluation argument in which you take a position on whether the benefits of fossil fuels are worth the environmental risks. Follow the template below, filling in the blanks to create your argument.

> Depending on the criteria used for evaluation, fossil fuels can be seen in a largely positive or negative light. If judged on the basis of _____, it seems clear that fossil fuels [are/are not] a valuable and necessary resource. Some people say that _____. They also point out that _____.
>
> Others disagree with this position, claiming that _____.
>
> However, _____.
>
> All things considered, _____.

⊘ EXERCISE 14.6 ASSESSING YOUR POSITION

In a group of three or four students, discuss your own opinions about the pros and cons of continuing to rely on fossil fuels rather than moving toward alternative energy sources, such as solar or wind power or nuclear energy. Write a paragraph that summarizes your group's conclusions.

⊘ EXERCISE 14.7 WRITING AN EVALUATION ESSAY

Write an evaluation argument on the topic, "Do the Benefits of Fossil Fuels Outweigh the Environmental Risks?" Begin by establishing the criteria by which you will evaluate both benefits and risks. Then, consider how well fossil fuels meet these criteria. (If you like, you may incorporate the material you developed in the template and Exercise 14.6 into your essay.) Cite the sources from Reading and Writing about the Issue earlier in this chapter, and be sure to document the sources you use and to include a works-cited page. (See Chapter 10 for information on documenting sources.)

⊘ EXERCISE 14.8 REVIEWING THE FOUR PILLARS OF ARGUMENT

Review the four pillars of argument discussed in Chapter 1. Does your essay include all four elements of an effective argument? Add anything that is missing. Then, label the key elements of your essay.

⊙ WRITING ASSIGNMENTS: EVALUATION ARGUMENTS

1. As a college student, you have probably had to fill out course-evaluation forms. Now, you are going to write an evaluation of one of your courses in the form of an argumentative essay that takes a strong stand on the quality of the course. Before you begin, decide on the criteria by which you will evaluate it—for example, what practical skills it provided to prepare you for your future courses or employment, whether you enjoyed the course, or what you learned. (You might begin by downloading an evaluation form and using it to help you brainstorm.)

2. Write an evaluation argument challenging a popular position on the quality of a product or service with which you are familiar. For example, you can defend a campus service that most students dislike, or you can write a negative review of a popular restaurant or film. Be sure you establish your criteria for evaluation before you begin. (You do not have to use the same criteria used by those who have taken the opposite position.)

3. Write a comparative evaluation—an essay in which you argue that one thing is superior to another. You can compare two websites, two streaming services, two part-time jobs, or any other two subjects you feel confident you can write about. In your thesis, take the position that one of your two subjects is superior to the other. As you would with any evaluation, begin by deciding on the criteria you will use.

AP Images/Mike Groll

CHAPTER

15

Ethical
Arguments

AT ISSUE

How Far Should Schools Go to Keep Students Safe?

Unfortunately, it is no longer unusual to read reports of shootings, robberies, muggings, and even murders in schools—both urban and rural. According to the Gun Violence Archive, from 2012 to 2018, there have been 239 school shootings nationwide, leaving 438 people wounded and 38 killed. But is this situation as bad as it seems? The Centers for Disease Control and Prevention (CDC) points out that, the vast majority of school-age children will never experience lethal violence at school. In addition, a number of studies suggest that college campuses experience less crime than society in general. Even so, the 2007 Virginia Tech massacre and the 2012 shooting at Sandy Hook Elementary have caused many people to worry that schools are no longer the safe environments they once were.

In response to pressure from parents, educators, students, and politicians, many public schools now require students to pass through metal detectors and teachers to lock classroom doors during school hours. Colleges have installed blue-light phones, card-access systems in dorms and labs, and surveillance cameras in parking garages and public areas. In addition, many colleges use text messages, automated phone calls, and emails to alert students and faculty to emergency situations.

Not everyone is happy about this emphasis on security, however. Some educators observe that public school buildings now look more like fortresses than places of learning. In addition, faculty members point out that colleges are supposed to promote free thought and that increased security undercuts this freedom by limiting access to campus and sanitizing the college experience. College students balk at having to wait in long lines to get into campus buildings as security guards examine and scan IDs.

Later in this chapter, you will be asked to think more about this issue. You will be given several research sources to consider and asked to write an **ethical argument** discussing how far schools should go to keep students safe.

What Is an Ethical Argument?

Ethics is the field of philosophy that studies the standards by which actions can be judged as right or wrong or good or bad. To make such judgments, we either measure actions against some standard (such as a moral rule like "Thou shall not kill") or consider them in terms of their consequences. Usually, making ethical judgments means examining abstract concepts such as *good*, *right*, *duty*, *obligation*, *virtue*, *honor*, and *choice*. **Applied ethics** is the field of philosophy that applies ethics to real-life issues, such as abortion, the death penalty, animal rights, and doctor-assisted suicide.

An **ethical argument** focuses on whether something should be done because it is good or right (or not done because it is bad or wrong). For example, consider the following questions:

- Does the United States have an obligation to help other countries?

- Is physician-assisted suicide ever justified?

- Is it wrong for Twitter to suspend people for posting inappropriate content?

- Is it right for the government to collect Americans' personal data?

- Is the death penalty ever justified?

- Do animals have rights?

Ethical arguments that try to answer questions like these usually begin with a clear statement that something is right or wrong and then go on to show how a religious, philosophical, or ethical principle supports this position. Consider how the last three questions on the list above can be examined in ethical arguments:

- **Is it right for the government to collect Americans' personal data?** You could begin your ethical argument by making the point that the government has a moral duty to protect its citizens. You could then go on to demonstrate that collecting personal data enables the United States government to accomplish this goal by addressing the threat of terrorism. You could end by saying that for this reason, the collection of personal data by the government is both moral and justified.

- **Is the death penalty ever justified?** You could begin your ethical argument by pointing out that because killing in any form is immoral, the death penalty is morally wrong. You could go on to demonstrate that despite its usefulness—it rids society of dangerous criminals— the death penalty hurts all of us. You could conclude by saying that because the death penalty is so immoral, it has no place in a civilized society.

- **Do animals have rights?** You could begin your ethical argument by pointing out that like all thinking beings, animals have certain basic rights. You could go on to discuss the basic rights that all thinking beings have—for example, the right to respect, a safe environment, and a dignified death. You could conclude by saying that the inhumane treatment of animals should not be tolerated, whether those animals are pets, live in the wild, or are raised for food.

Stating an Ethical Principle

The most important part of an ethical argument is the **ethical principle**—a general statement about what is good or bad, right or wrong. It is the set of values that guides you to an ethically correct conclusion.

- **You can show that something is good or right** by establishing that it conforms to a particular moral law or will result in something good for society. For example, you could argue in favor of a policy restricting access to campus by saying that such a policy will reduce crime on campus or will result in a better educational experience for students.

- **You can show that something is bad or wrong** by demonstrating that it violates a moral law or will result in something bad for society. For example, you could argue against the use of physician-assisted suicide by saying that respect for individual rights is one of the basic principles of American society and that by ignoring this principle we undermine our Constitution and our way of life.

Whenever possible, you should base your ethical argument on an ethical principle that is **self-evident**—one that needs no proof or explanation. (By doing so, you avoid having to establish the principle that is the basis for your essay.) Thomas Jefferson uses this strategy in the Declaration of Independence. When he says, "We hold these truths to be self-evident," he is saying that the ethical principle that supports the rest of his argument is so basic (and so widely accepted) that it requires no proof—in other words, that it is self-evident. If readers accept Jefferson's assertion, then the rest of his argument—that the thirteen original colonies owe no allegiance to England—will be much more convincing. (Remember, however, that the king of England, George III, would not have accepted Jefferson's assertion. For him, the ethical principle that is the foundation of the Declaration of Independence was not at all self-evident.)

Keep in mind that an ethical principle has to be self-evident to most of your readers—not just to those who agree with you or hold a particular set of religious or cultural beliefs. Using a religious doctrine as an ethical principle has its limitations, so doctrines that cut across religions and cultures are more suitable than those that do not. For example, every culture prohibits murder and theft. But some other doctrines—such as the Jehovah's Witness prohibition against blood transfusion or the Muslim dietary restrictions—are not universally accepted. In addition, an ethical principle must be stated so that it applies universally. For example, not all readers will find the statement, "As a Christian, I am against killing and therefore against the death penalty" convincing. A more effective statement would be, "Because it is morally wrong, the death penalty should be abolished" or "With few exceptions, taking the life of another person is never justified, and there should be no exception for the government."

Ethics versus Law

Generally speaking, an ethical argument deals with what is right and wrong, not necessarily with what is legal or illegal. In fact, there is a big difference between law and ethics. **Laws** are rules that govern a society and are enforced by its political and legal systems. **Ethics** are standards that determine how human conduct is judged.

Keep in mind that something that is legal is not necessarily ethical. As Socrates, St. Augustine, Henry David Thoreau, and Martin Luther King Jr. have all pointed out, there are just laws, and there are unjust laws. For example, when King wrote his famous "Letter from Birmingham Jail,"

Women march for the right to vote, New York, 1913.

Bettmann/Getty Images

For decades in America, African Americans were treated unfairly due to unjust laws.

Library of Congress

segregation was legal in many Southern states. According to King, unjust laws—such as those that institutionalized segregation—are out of harmony with both moral law and natural law. As King wrote, "We should never forget that everything Adolf Hitler did in Germany was 'legal.'" For King, the ultimate standard for deciding what is just or unjust is morality, not legality.

German Jews being sent to concentration camps.

Bettmann/Getty Images

There are many historical examples of laws that most people would now consider unjust:

- **Laws against woman suffrage:** In the late eighteenth century, various states passed laws prohibiting women from voting.

- **Jim Crow laws:** In the mid-nineteenth century, laws were passed in the American South that restricted the rights of African Americans.

- **Nuremberg laws:** In 1935, Nazi Germany passed a series of laws that deprived Jews of German citizenship. As a result, Jews could no longer vote, hold public office, or marry a German national.

- **Apartheid laws:** Beginning in 1948, South Africa enacted laws that defined and enforced racial segregation. These laws stayed in effect until 1994, when Nelson Mandela was elected South Africa's first black president.

Today, virtually everyone would agree that these laws were wrong and should never have been enacted. Still, many people obeyed these laws, with disastrous consequences. These consequences illustrate the importance of doing what is ethically right, not just what is legally right.

The difference between ethics and law can be seen in many everyday situations. Although we have no legal obligation to stop a drunk friend from driving, most people would agree that we should. In addition, although motorists (or even doctors) have no legal obligation to help at the scene of an accident, many people would say that it is the right thing to do.

An example of a person going beyond what is legally required occurred in Lawrence, Massachusetts, in 1995, when fire destroyed Malden Mills, the largest employer in town. Citing his religious principles, Aaron Feuerstein, the owner of the mill and inventor of Polartec fleece, decided to rebuild in Lawrence rather than move his business overseas as many of his competitors had done. In addition, he decided that for sixty days, all employees would receive their full salaries—even though the mill was closed. Feuerstein was not required by law to do what he did, but he decided to do what he believed was both ethical and responsible.

Understanding Ethical Dilemmas

Life decisions tend to be somewhat messy, and it is often not easy to decide what is right or wrong or what is good or bad. In many real-life situations, people are faced with **dilemmas**—choices between alternatives that seem equally unfavorable. An **ethical dilemma** occurs when there is a conflict between two or more possible actions—each of which will have a similar consequence or outcome.

The classic ethical dilemma is the so-called lifeboat dilemma. In this hypothetical situation, a ship hits an iceberg, and survivors are crowded

A scene from Alfred Hitchcock's *Lifeboat* (1944).

Ray Tamarra/The NY Times/Everett Collection

into a lifeboat. As a storm approaches, the captain realizes that he is faced with an ethical dilemma. If he does nothing, the overloaded boat will capsize, and all the people will drown. If he throws some of the passengers overboard, he will save those in the boat, but those he throws overboard will drown.

Another ethical dilemma occurs in William Styron's 1979 novel *Sophie's Choice*. The novel's narrator is fascinated by the story of Sophie, a woman who was arrested by the Nazis and sent along with her two children to the Auschwitz concentration camp. When she arrived, she was given a choice by a sadistic guard: one of her children would go to the gas chamber and one would be spared, but she had to choose which one. If she did not choose, both children would be murdered.

In the 1982 film *Sophie's Choice,* a mother (played by Meryl Streep) is forced to make a terrible decision.

Ethical dilemmas are not just the stuff of fiction; people confront them every day. For example, an owner of a business who realizes that costs must be cut faces an ethical dilemma. If the owner takes no action, the business will fail, and all the employees will lose their jobs. If the owner lays off some employees, they will be hurt, but the business might be saved and so might the jobs of the remaining workers. A surgeon who has to separate conjoined twins who share a heart also faces an ethical dilemma. If the surgeon does nothing, both twins will die, but if the surgeon operates, one of the twins might live although the other will be sacrificed.

Often, the only way to resolve an ethical dilemma is to choose the lesser of two evils. Simple "right or wrong" or "good versus bad" prescriptions will not work in such cases. For example, killing may be morally, legally, and ethically wrong, but what if it is done in self-defense? Stealing is also wrong, but what if a person steals food to feed a hungry child? Although it may be tempting to apply clear ethical principles, you should be careful not to oversimplify the situations you are writing about.

⊘ EXERCISE 15.1 CHOOSING AN ETHICAL PRINCIPLE

Consider the following topics for ethical arguments. Then, decide what ethical principle you could use for each argument. For example, if you were to argue against the legalization of marijuana, you could use the principle that getting high prevents people from making wise decisions as the basis for your argument. You could then demonstrate that society is harmed when large numbers of people smoke marijuana.

- The federal government should (or should not) legalize marijuana.

- A student's race should (or should not) be a consideration in college admissions.

- Homeless people should (or should not) be forcibly removed from city streets.

- Everyone should (or should not) be required to sign an organ-donor card.

- A witness to academic cheating should (or should not) report the cheater.

⊘ EXERCISE 15.2 IDENTIFYING UNJUST LAWS

Make a list of some rules or laws that you think are unjust. Then, next to each item on your list, write down the ethical principle on which you based your conclusion.

⊘ EXERCISE 15.3 ANALYZING VISUAL ARGUMENTS

Look at the following two images. In what sense do they make ethical arguments? What ethical principle underlies each image?

© Tread Lightly! Inc. (www.treadlightly.org)

Courtesy of People for the Ethical Treatment of Animals, www.peta.org

Structuring an Ethical Argument

In general, an ethical argument can be structured in the following way.

- **Introduction:** Establishes the ethical principle and states the essay's thesis

- **Background:** Gives an overview of the situation

- **Ethical analysis:** Explains the ethical principle and analyzes the particular situation on the basis of this principle

- **Evidence:** Presents points that support the thesis

- **Refutation of opposing arguments:** Addresses arguments against the thesis

- **Conclusion:** Restates the ethical principle as well as the thesis; includes a strong concluding statement

⏺ The following student essay contains all the elements of an ethical argument. The student takes the position that colleges should do more to help nontraditional students succeed.

ARE COLLEGES DOING ENOUGH FOR NONTRADITIONAL STUDENTS?

CHRIS MUÑOZ

Colleges and universities are experiencing an increase in the number of nontraditional students, and this number is projected to rise. Although these students enrich campus communities and provide new opportunities for learning, they also present challenges. Generally, nontraditional students are older, attend school part-time, and are self-supporting. With their years of life experience, they tend to have different educational goals from other students. Although many schools recognize that nontraditional students have unique needs, most schools ignore these needs and unfairly continue to focus on the "typical" student. As a result, nontraditional students frequently do not have the same access to educational opportunities as their younger counterparts. To solve this problem, universities need to do more to ensure equitable treatment of nontraditional students.

Most people's assumptions about who is enrolled in college are out of date. According to the educational policy scholar Frederick Hess, only 15 percent of all undergraduates attend a four-year college and live on campus. In other words, so-called typical college students are in the minority. In fact, 38 percent of today's undergraduates are over age twenty-five, 37 percent attend part-time, 32 percent work full-time, and many are responsible for dependents. In addition, real-world responsibilities cause many nontraditional students to delay starting school, to take a break in the middle, or to drop out entirely. According to Kris MacDonald, nearly 70 percent of all nontraditional students drop out of college. Although some argue that schools already provide extra help, such as advising and tutoring, others point out that asking nontraditional students to adapt to an educational model that focuses on the traditional student is a form of discrimination against them.

(margin notes)

Ethical principle established

Thesis statement

Background: Gives an overview of the situation

1

2

These people recommend that schools institute policies that reflect the growing number of nontraditional students on campus and address the challenges that these students face every day.

Most people would agree that diversity is highly valued on college campuses. In fact, most universities go to great lengths to admit a diverse group of students—including nontraditional students. However, as Jacqueline Muhammad points out, universities do not serve these students well after they are enrolled. By asking nontraditional students to assimilate into the traditional university environment, colleges marginalize them, and this is not ethical. Evidence of this marginalization is not difficult to find. As one college student acknowledges, "These students have a lot to offer, but often they don't feel included" (qtd. in Muhammad). This lack of inclusion is seen in many areas of campus life, including access to classes and services, availability of relevant programs and courses, and use of fair and appropriate classroom practices. To be fair, a university should ensure that all of its students have equal access to a meaningful and fulfilling education. By maintaining policies and approaches that are not inclusive, colleges marginalize nontraditional students.

3 Ethical analysis: Presents the ethical principle and analyzes the situation on the basis of this principle

To ensure the fair treatment of nontraditional students, colleges need to remove the barriers those students face. One of the first barriers that nontraditional students face is difficulty gaining access to classes and student services. Academic schedules, including the academic calendar and class times, frequently exclude working adults and parents. As Frederick Hess explains, "A semester system . . . works well for 19-year-olds used to the rhythms of high school, but that's hugely frustrating for workers." In addition, unless classes and services are available in the evening, on weekends, or online, they are inaccessible to many students. As one professional advocate for nontraditional students explains, "Most nontraditional students have obligations during the day that make it difficult to access on-campus resources that are only open during business hours" (qtd. in Muhammad). This situation makes it difficult (and sometimes impossible) for nontraditional students to schedule required courses or to get extra help, such as tutoring. As long as these barriers to equal access exist, nontraditional students will always be "second-class citizens" in the university.

4 Evidence: First point in support of the thesis

Evidence: Second point in support of the thesis

Schools also need to stop devaluing the kinds of programs in which   5
nontraditional students tend to enroll. Research shows that the reasons
older students want to continue their educations "indicate high motivation and commitment, but require accommodations to instruction"
(Newman, Deyoe, and Seelow 107). Many are taking courses in order to
return to work, change careers, or improve their chances for a promotion. According to Hess, although the greatest demand is for associate's
degrees, over 50 percent of nontraditional students are seeking "subbac-
calaureate" certification credentials. As Hess demonstrates, certification
programs are considered to be marginal, even in community colleges.
One reason for this situation is that most schools still judge their own
worth by factors—such as academic ranking or grant money—that have
little to do with teaching career skills. By devaluing practical training that
certification programs offer, schools are undermining the educational
experience that many nontraditional students want.

Evidence: Third point in support of thesis

Finally, universities need to do more to encourage inclusive   6
teaching approaches. According to Joshua L. Carreiro and Brian P.
Kapitulik, most educators assume their students are "traditional"—that
they are recent high school graduates from middle-class backgrounds
with little work experience (232). As a result, nontraditional students
"are frequently mis-served by direct instruction due to financial,
family, career, or learning style preferences" (Newman, Deyoe, and
Seelow 107). Carreiro and Kapitulik conclude that these assumptions
result in "an exclusive classroom environment" that excludes and
marginalizes nontraditional students (246). One way of addressing this
problem is for universities to expand online education offerings. Online
courses enable nontraditional students to gradually assimilate into
the college environment and to work at their own pace without fear of
ridicule. Universities can also encourage instructors to develop new
teaching approaches. If instructors want to be more inclusive, they can
acknowledge diversity by engaging students in diverse ways of thinking
and learning (Hermida). For example, they can ask students to relate
course material to their own experiences, and they can bring in guest
speakers from a variety of backgrounds. By acknowledging the needs of
nontraditional students, instructors can provide a better education for all
students.

Not everyone believes that colleges and universities need to change their basic assumptions about education. They concede that nontraditional students might need extra support, but they say that these students are adults and should be able to fend for themselves. Students' commitments outside of school—for instance, children or a full-time job—should not be a concern for colleges and universities. If these students need help, they can get support from one another, or they can turn to student-led organizations. Even those educators who are sympathetic to nontraditional students suggest that extra mentoring or advising is all that is necessary. However, the problems faced by these students need to be addressed, and according to Hermida, by ignoring institutional barriers and biases, colleges and universities are essentially burying their heads in the sand (22). To be more welcoming to nontraditional students, universities must fundamentally change some of the structures and practices that have traditionally defined them. Ultimately, everyone—the schools, the communities, and the students—will benefit from these adjustments.

7 Refutation of opposing arguments

According to Hermida, many of today's students are nontraditional (20). Most of the current research suggests that inclusion is their most pressing concern. As this population continues to grow, say Newman, Deyoe, and Seelow, educators should focus on offering "clear objectives, direct ties to life experience, and multiple opportunities" for nontraditional students to engage in the college community (122). Giving preferential treatment to some students while ignoring the needs of others is ethically wrong, so schools need to work harder to end discrimination against this increasingly large group of learners.

8

Concluding statement

Works Cited

Carreiro, Joshua L., and Brian P. Kapitulik. "Budgets, Board Games, and Make Believe: The Challenge of Teaching Social Class Inequality with Nontraditional Students." *American Sociologist,* vol. 41, no. 3, Oct. 2010, pp. 232–48. *Academic Search Complete*, www.ebscohost.com /academic.

Hermida, Julian. "Inclusive Teaching: An Approach for Encouraging Nontraditional Student Success." *International Journal of Research and Review,* vol. 5, no. 1, Oct. 2010, pp. 19–30. *Academic Search Complete*, www.ebscohost.com/academic.

Hess, Frederick. "Old School: College's Most Important Trend Is the Rise
of the Adult Student." *The Atlantic*, 28 Sept. 2011, www.theatlantic
.com/business/archive/2011/09/old-school-colleges-most-important
-trend-is-the-rise-of-the-adult-student/245823/.

MacDonald, Kris. "A Review of the Literature: The Needs of Non-
Traditional Students in Postsecondary Education." *Strategic
Management Quarterly*, 3 Jan. 2018, www.onlinelibrary.wiley.com
/doi/full/10.1002/sem3.20115.

Muhammad, Jacqueline. "New Coordinator to Address Nontraditional
Student Needs." *Daily Egyptian*, Southern Illinois University,
Carbondale, 8 Dec. 2011, archives.dailyegyptian.com/siu-2011
/2011/12/8/new-coordinator-to-address-non-traditional-student
-needs.html.

Newman, Dianna L., Meghan Morris Deyoe, and David Seelow. "Serving
Nontraditional Students: Meeting Needs through an Online Writing
Program." *Models for Improving and Optimizing Online and Blended
Learning in Higher Education*, edited by Jared Keengwe and
Joachim Jack Agamba, IGI Global, 2015, pp. 106–28.

GRAMMAR IN CONTEXT

Subordination and Coordination

When you write an argumentative essay, you need to show readers the
logical and sequential connections between your ideas. You do this by
using *coordinating conjunctions* and *subordinating conjunctions*—words
that join words, phrases, clauses, or entire sentences. Be sure to choose
conjunctions that accurately express the relationship between the ideas
they join.

Coordinating conjunctions—*and, but, for, nor, or, so,* and *yet*—
join ideas of equal importance. In compound sentences, they describe the
relationship between the ideas in the two independent clauses and show
how these ideas are related.

- "Colleges and universities are experiencing an increase in the number
  of nontraditional students, and this number is projected to rise." (*And*
  indicates addition.) (para. 1)

- "These students have a lot to offer, but often they don't feel included."
  (*But* indicates contrast or contradiction.) (3)

Subordinating conjunctions—*after, although, because, if, so that, where*, and so on—join ideas of unequal importance. In complex sentences, they describe the relationship between the ideas in the dependent clause and the independent clause and show how these ideas are related.

- "Although these students enrich campus communities and provide new opportunities for learning, they also present challenges." (*Although* indicates a contrast.) (1)

- "Although many schools recognize that nontraditional students have unique needs, most schools ignore these needs and unfairly continue to focus on the 'typical' student." (*Although* indicates a contrast.) (1)

- "As long as these barriers to equal access exist, nontraditional students will always be 'second-class citizens' in the university." (*As long as* indicates a causal relationship.) (4)

- "If instructors want to be more inclusive, they can acknowledge diversity by engaging students in diverse ways of thinking and learning." (*If* indicates condition.) (6)

⊘ EXERCISE 15.4 IDENTIFYING ELEMENTS OF AN ETHICAL ARGUMENT

The following essay includes the basic elements of an ethical argument. Read the essay, and then answer the questions that follow it, consulting the outline on page 523 if necessary.

This essay was published in the *Harvard Crimson* student newspaper on March 6, 2015.

THE ETHICAL CASE FOR EATING ANIMALS

SHUBHANKAR CHHOKRA

We were transplanting a row of eggplant as quickly as we could, trying to finish 1 before it got too hot. With one hand, Jake was placing seedlings a foot away from each other with uncanny precision and with the other he was stopping Maggie the dog from prancing all over them. I was right behind them covering the roots with soil, crawling on my stomach along the furrow like a soldier through a trench.

Jake usually got philosophical when we transplanted—it probably had 2 something to do with the wealth of intrigue offered by the task of putting plants into dirt. So I saw it coming when he asked me about halfway down the furrow about my thoughts on vegetarianism. Without looking up, I recited the religious and cultural implications of eating meat for certain people, talked about the potential health benefits, and said something about as vague and unsubstantiated as, "It's the ethical thing to do." He didn't say anything for a while. But Jake was a high school teacher first and a farmer second, and his instincts as the former must have kicked in.

"Ever hear of the Siberian fox experiment?" he asked. 3

He told me, once he saw my blank face, 4 about research that sounded like it came out of a science fiction novel. Against the backdrop of Soviet totalitarianism, scientist Dmitriy Belyaev attempted to recreate the evolution of wolves into dogs in a secret laboratory in some unexplored recess of Siberia. He and his team bred silver foxes, a cousin to the dog that had never been domesticated before, over multiple generations, selecting for traits like approachability and friendliness around humans.

> "Jake was a high school teacher first and a farmer second, and his instincts as the former must have kicked in."

After mere decades, Belyaev did what was previously thought took 5 millennia. Fourth generation foxes started showing the behavioral traits of tameness like wagging their tails and jumping into the laps of researchers. They also had what researchers call the "domestication phenotype"—physiological characteristics like floppier ears, curlier tails, and spottier coats. More strikingly, foxes born to aggressive mothers, but nurtured by tame ones, were nonetheless aggressive. Fifty years later, scientists continue his work, providing even more compelling evidence of the previously unthinkable—certain animals may be genetically predisposed to human contact, to domesticity.

Domesticity is a concept that's difficult to precisely define, but at its core, it 6 is the modification of animals over multiple generations for human benefit. The most prevalent use of domesticated animals is to produce meat, an exercise that many proponents of ethical vegetarianism take issue with on the grounds that since animals are sentient beings of similar moral value to humans, rearing and killing them cannot be justified. The doctrine of animal liberationism, defined by people like Peter Singer and organizations like PETA, distinguishes humans from the rest of the Animal Kingdom only in one regard: moral agency, which compels us to right our wrongs and to stop exploiting the farm animal.

But what Belyaev's research demonstrates—an idea that took a lot of time 7 for me to accept after Jake introduced it to me—is that historically, there have been more factors than just human intention in the process that has given us the beef steer and the broiler chicken. The ancestor of many of the animals we consider food species like pigs, cattle, and sheep derived much of their evolutionary competitiveness from mutations that caused them to be less afraid of humans, presenting an opportunity for humans to engage in symbiotic husbandry. Natural selection preceded artificial selection. At the risk of sounding reductive, farm animals were made to be farmed.

Animal liberationists conflate sentience with moral value, oversimplifying 8 the similarity between meat animals and humans and mischaracterizing human moral agency. Animals and humans are fundamentally and genetically different, and the moral responsibility of the human to animals exists only insofar as the need to care for them well. This human prerogative however cannot be overstated. Environmentalist Wendell Berry sets a good standard in his essay "The Pleasures of Eating" for responsible eating practices: "If I am going to eat meat," he wrote, "I want it to be from an animal that has lived a pleasant, uncrowded life outdoors, on bountiful pasture, with good water nearby and trees for shade."

Industrial or otherwise intensive farms, however, produce most of the 9 meat Americans eat by cruelly confining animals to inhabitable enclosures and slaughtering them in ways that yield inconceivable pain. Cows spend most of their lives walking knee-deep in their own waste. Chicken are fed and drugged until their breasts are so large that they spend the latter part of their lives keeled over. To that end, ethical vegetarians are only guilty of erring on the side of caution, refusing to be implicated in a process that is morally unacceptable regardless of the genetic origins of domesticity.

Man's control of the land is his crowning achievement. He revolutionized 10 the human diet by domesticating the plant and to the extent he was involved in domesticating the animal, he did so justifiably. Jake didn't change my eating practices in just one day. No, that would be a pedagogical nightmare. But he did accomplish what I think he wanted to. He challenged me to substantiate and eventually redefine my claims on ethical prudence. And more importantly, he made me thankful for gifts of nature and conversations like these.

Identifying the Elements of an Ethical Argument

1. What is the Siberian fox experiment? Why does Chhokra discuss it in his essay?

2. Look up the definition of *domesticity*? What does Chhokra mean when he says, "Domesticity is a concept that's difficult to precisely define" (para. 6)?

3. What ethical principle does Chhokra apply in his essay? At what point does he state this principle? Why do you think he states it where he does?

4. What does Chhokra mean when he says, "Animal liberationists conflate sentience with moral value, oversimplifying the similarity between meat animals and humans and mischaracterizing moral agency" (8)?

5. What is the problem with the way industrial farms raise animals? According to Chhokra, why is this method of producing meat "morally unacceptable" (9)?

6. In his essay, Chhokra uses all three appeals—*logos*, *pathos*, and *ethos*. Locate examples of each. How effective is each appeal? Explain.

7. What strategy does Chhokra use to conclude his essay? Do you think that his conclusion is effective? Explain.

How Far Should Schools Go to Keep Students Safe?

Go back and reread the At Issue box at the beginning of the chapter, which gives background on how far schools should go to keep their students safe. Then, read the sources on the pages that follow.

As you read this source material, you will be asked to answer some questions and to complete some simple activities. This work will help you understand both the content and the structure of the selections. When you are finished, you will be ready to write an **ethical argument** that takes a position on the topic, "How Far Should Schools Go to Keep Students Safe?"

AP Images/Mike Groll

SOURCES

Evie Blad, "Do Schools' 'Active-Shooter' Drills Prepare or Frighten?," page 533

Timothy Wheeler, "There's a Reason They Choose Schools," page 538

Sasha Abramsky, "The Fear Industry Goes Back to School," page 541

Michael W. Goldberg, "I'm a School Psychologist—And I Think Teachers Should Be Armed," page 548

Vann R. Newkirk II, "Arming Educators Violates the Spirit of the Second Amendment," page 551

Isothermal Community College, "Warning Signs: How You Can Help Prevent Campus Violence" (brochure), page 554

Visual Argument: Amy Dion, "Gone but Not Forgotten" (poster), page 558

This essay is from the September 19, 2017, issue of *Education Week*.

DO SCHOOLS' "ACTIVE-SHOOTER" DRILLS PREPARE OR FRIGHTEN?

EVIE BLAD

On "safety days," elementary students in Akron, OH, learn a new vocabulary word: barricade. 1

School-based police officers tell students as young as kindergartners how to stack chairs and desks against the classroom door to make it harder for "bad guys" to get in. "Make the classroom more like a fort," an officer says in a video of the exercise. 2

If a teacher asks you to climb out a window, listen to them, the officers instruct. And, in the unlikely event a "bad guy" gets into the classroom, scream and run around to distract him, officers tell students. 3

For some parents, the idea of such instruction is chilling. Others, though, say it's a sad, but necessary sign of the times. 4

Children around the country are increasingly receiving similar training as schools adopt more elaborate safety drills in response to concerns about school shootings. That leaves schools with a profound challenge: how to prepare young students for the worst, without provoking anxiety or fear. 5

"That's the fine balance," said Dan Rambler, the Akron school district's director of student services and safety. "We're not trying to panic people." A growing number of districts around the country have replaced or supplemented traditional lockdown drills—which teach students to quietly hide in their classrooms in the event of a school shooting—with multi-option response drills, which teach them a variety of ways to respond and escape. 6

Most controversially, the drills teach young students how to "counter" a shooter by running in zig-zag patterns, throwing objects, and screaming to make it difficult for a gunman to focus and aim. 7

Akron uses a protocol called ALICE (Alert, Lockdown, Inform, Counter, Evacuate). It was developed by former police officer Greg Crane and his wife, Lisa Crane, a former school principal, after the 1999 shootings at Colorado's Columbine High School. 8

It's grown more popular following the 2012 shootings at Sandy Hook Elementary School in Newtown, CT. About 4,000 school districts and 3,500 police departments have ALICE-trained personnel. 9

School safety consultant Kenneth Trump, who regularly writes about ALICE training, says it's not supported by evidence and "preys on the emotions of today's active shooter frenzy that is spreading across the nation." Trump and other critics say schools shouldn't train young children in the ALICE response when school shootings, typically the focus of such drills, are statistically rare. 10

But fires are also rare, Rambler said, and that doesn't stop schools from 11 conducting regular fire drills.

Greg Crane, ALICE's creator, says schools put children in danger if they 12 teach them to be "static targets."

Parents "don't have any problem discussing an abduction and giving chil- 13 dren quite aggressive tactics in response," Crane said. "What do we tell kids in stranger danger? Anything but go with the guy. Bite, kick, yell. Anything but go sit in the corner and be quiet."

Growing Use of Drills

Discussions over security are often sparked by media coverage of shootings. 14 Recently, a student at a Washington state high school shot and killed a class-mate and injured three others before he was subdued by a janitor.

Federal data show a growing use of school-shooter drills, though it 15 doesn't distinguish between lockdown drills and responses like ALICE. In the 2013–14 school year, 70 percent of public schools drilled students on how to respond to a school shooting, including 71 percent of elementary schools, according to the most recent data available. In 2003–4, 47 percent of schools involved students in shooter drills.

> "70 percent of pub-lic schools drilled students on how to respond to a school shooting."

A 2013 federal report, created in 16 response to Sandy Hook, outlined a safety response that called on school staff to "consider trying to disrupt or incapaci-tate the shooter by using aggressive force and items in their environment, such as fire extinguishers, and chairs. It didn't advocate involving students.

That report, released by the U.S. Department of Education on behalf of a 17 group of federal agencies, drew concern from some school safety consultants who said such a "run, hide, fight" approach is unproven by research and may even be dangerous in the event of an actual shooting.

But it also inspired states and districts to update safety plans, leading 18 many to adopt ALICE and similar training. A subsequent report by a task force convened by Ohio's attorney general, for example, recommended that schools train students and staff that, if a shooter enters a classroom, they try to inter-fere with his shooting accuracy by throwing books, computers, and phones. They may also need to subdue the intruder, the report said.

In Akron, parents can opt their children out of the training, though few 19 do. Elementary students are told briefly about countering techniques, but the focus of their discussions is on following teachers' directions in unpredictable situations. In middle school, training is "a little more complete," sometimes including foam props that students throw at school police officers as practice.

Countering an intruder "is literally the last resort," Rambler said. "That is, 20 'Do whatever you have to to stay alive.' It's not, 'Go find the gunman and throw something at them.'"

Planning a Response

Greg Crane said schools decide how detailed they want to be in their hypothet- 21 ical discussions of violence, but most involve students in some level of training.

The Cranes worked with a children's author to publish a book called *I'm* 22 *Not Scared . . . I'm Prepared!* that many schools use to train younger students. But some parents have been concerned about what some districts teach in ALICE drills, particularly when it comes to the counterstep.

In 2015, an Alabama middle school made headlines when its principal 23 asked students to keep canned goods in their desks to hurl at attackers. At the time, ALICE co-founder Lisa Crane said the use of canned goods is not something ALICE trainers would advocate, but it's also not something they would discourage.

In some districts, parents have started petitions or turned out to school 24 board meetings in opposition to active-shooter drills, saying they don't want to expose their young children to such discussions of violence.

"My daughter is 8 years old and she reads the newspaper and she gets ner- 25 vous about stories about murders and other things happening in the neighborhood, so I'm very concerned about what impact it will have on her to be told that there's a potential that someone might walk through the door and shoot her classroom," a father said at a public meeting after the Anchorage district announced ALICE training plans last year.

At the National Association of School Resource Officers (NASRO) con- 26 ference in Washington in July, Officer Ingrid Herriott told school-based police officers and safety directors how she customized ALICE training for elementary, middle, and high school students when she was a school resource officer at Southwest Allen County Schools in Fort Wayne, IN.

She showed a video she said schools could use to explain ALICE to 27 elementary school children. In it, a school officer explains "stranger danger" to a plush dog named Safety Pup. Police officers are in uniforms, teachers have lanyards and name tags, and strangers are other adults students don't recognize, the video says. The officer then explains ALICE, advising students to listen to their teacher for directions.

Middle school students quickly learn to barricade doors with desks, 28 Herriott said. She walked middle school students through drills by showing videos produced by the district's high school students using fake guns to act out school intruder scenarios. In one such video, a student in a library pretends to hit the gunman over the head with a chair.

At that age, the idea of a shooting "isn't something that's above and beyond 29 what they are seeing in the media and the video games they are playing," Herriot said. High school students were given internet surveys after training to learn about concerns, and had principals make follow-up videos to respond to those concerns.

NASRO worked with the National Association of School Psychologists 30 to address concerns about the psychological effects of safety drills. Recommendations call for plans that are as sensitive to local and regional concerns, like wildfires and earthquakes, as they are to statistically less probable events, like shootings.

Steve Brock, a professor of school psychology at California State Uni- 31 versity, Sacramento, helped draft that guidance. He said there's not enough research to support ALICE and similar training in schools.

Minimizing Student Anxiety

The most important thing a teacher can do in a shooting situation is lock the 32 classroom door, Brock said, and it's not necessary to "unnecessarily frighten" students by walking them through more elaborate hypothetical scenarios.

"When it comes to these kinds of activities, schools need to proceed cau- 33 tiously," he said.

Brock advocates for lockdown drills, which he calls "tried and true" for a variety of crises, ranging from intruders to an intoxicated parent. 34 Such drills have been shown to lessen student anxiety. Brock recommends schools train young students to pretend there's a strange dog in the hallway that they are trying to stay safe from, rather than talking about "bad guys" or shootings.

But some parents and teachers say responses like ALICE ease their fears 35 that children would be "sitting ducks" in a shooting situation.

After Matt Holland, a third-grade teacher in Alexandria, VA, learned 36 about ALICE in his own staff training this summer, he called his 7-year-old daughter's school in a neighboring district to ask leaders to transition away from a lockdown approach.

"While, yes, statistically speaking, the chances [of a shooting] are very 37 slim," Holland said, "I don't want, heaven forbid, something to happen to my students or my daughter and to say, 'There was a small chance it would happen, and it happened. And no one ever planned for it.'"

⊘ AT ISSUE: SOURCES FOR DEVELOPING AN ETHICAL ARGUMENT

1. Blad begins her essay by describing an active-shooter instruction session. Is this an effective opening strategy? Why or why not? What other strategy should Blad have used?

2. In paragraph 10, Blad refers to Kenneth Trump, who says that ALICE training is not supported by any evidence that it works. In paragraph 17, a group of school-safety consultants say that ALICE training was "unproven by research and may even be dangerous in the event of an actual shooting." Does Blad adequately address these criticisms? Explain.

3. What is the difference between a "lockdown drill" and ALICE training? Which do you think would be more effective when confronting an active shooter?

4. Why do some parents oppose active-shooter drills? Do you agree or disagree with them? In what sense do active shooter drills present these parents with an ethical dilemma?

5. In her conclusion, Blad quotes Matt Holland, a third-grade teacher, who acknowledges that "chances [of a shooting] are very slim" (para. 37). Does this weaken the argument in favor of active shooter drills? Explain.

6. Throughout her essay, Blad attempts to answer the question she asks in her title. Does she succeed? If not, why not?

This article is from the October 11, 2007, issue of *National Review*.

THERE'S A REASON THEY CHOOSE SCHOOLS

TIMOTHY WHEELER

Wednesday's shooting at yet another school has a better outcome than most in 1 recent memory. No one died at Cleveland's Success Tech Academy except the perpetrator. The two students and two teachers he shot are in stable condition at Cleveland hospitals.

What is depressingly similar to the mass murders at Virginia Tech and 2 Nickel Mines, Pennsylvania, and too many others was the killer's choice of venue—that steadfastly gun-free zone, the school campus. Although murderer Seung-Hui Cho at Virginia Tech and Asa Coon, the Cleveland shooter, were both students reported to have school-related grudges, other school killers have proved to be simply taking advantage of the lack of effective security at schools. The Bailey, Colorado, multiple rapes and murder of September 2006, the Nickel Mines massacre of October 2006, and Buford Furrow's murderous August 1999 invasion of a Los Angeles Jewish day-care center were all committed by adults. They had no connection to the schools other than being drawn to the soft target a school offers such psychopaths.

This latest shooting comes only a few weeks after the American Medical 3 Association released a theme issue of its journal *Disaster Medicine and Public Health Preparedness*. This issue is dedicated to analyzing the April 2007 Virginia Tech shootings, in which 32 people were murdered. The authors are university officials, trauma surgeons, and legal analysts who pore over the details of the incident, looking for "warning signs" and "risk factors" for violence. They rehash all the tired rhetoric of bureaucrats and public-health wonks, including the public-health mantra of the 1990s that guns are the root cause of violence.

Sheldon Greenberg, a dean at Johns Hopkins, offers this gem: "Reinforce 4 a 'no weapons' policy and, when violated, enforce it quickly, to include expulsion. Parents should be made aware of the policy. *Officials should dispel the politically driven notion that armed students could eliminate an active shooter*" (emphasis added). Greenberg apparently isn't aware that at the Appalachian School of Law in 2002 another homicidal Virginia student was stopped from shooting more of his classmates when another student held him at gunpoint. The Pearl High School murderer Luke Woodham was stopped cold when vice principal Joel Myrick got his Colt .45 handgun out of his truck and pointed it at the young killer.

Virginia Tech's 2005 no-guns-on-campus policy was an abject failure at 5 deterring Cho Seung-Hui. Greenberg's audacity in ignoring the obvious is typical of arrogant school officials. What the AMA journal authors studiously avoid are on one hand the repeated failures of such feel-good steps as no-gun policies, and on the other hand the demonstrated success of armed first responders. These responders would be the students themselves, such as the trained and licensed law student, or their similarly qualified teachers.

In Cleveland this week and at Virginia Tech the shooters took time to walk the halls, searching out victims in several rooms, and then shooting them. Virginia Chief Medical Examiner Marcella Fierro describes the locations of the dead in Virginia Tech's Norris Hall. Dead victims were found in groups ranging from 1 to 13, scattered throughout 4 rooms and a stairwell. If any one of the victims had, like the Appalachian School of Law student, used armed force to stop Cho, lives could have been saved.

> "Virginia Tech's . . . no-guns-on-campus policy was an abject failure."   6

The people of Virginia actually had a chance to implement such a plan 7 last year. House Bill 1572 was introduced in the legislature to extend the state's concealed-carry provisions to college campuses. But the bill died in committee, opposed by the usual naysayers, including the Virginia Association of Chiefs of Police and the university itself. Virginia Tech spokesman Larry Hincker was quoted in the *Roanoke Times* as saying, "I'm sure the university community is appreciative of the General Assembly's actions because this will help parents, students, faculty, and visitors feel safe on our campus."

It is encouraging that college students themselves have a much better grasp 8 on reality than their politically correct elders. During the week of October 22–26 Students for Concealed Carry on Campus will stage a nationwide "empty holster" demonstration (peaceful, of course) in support of their cause.

School officials typically base violence-prevention policies on irrational 9 fears more than real-world analysis of what works. But which is more horrible, the massacre that timid bureaucrats fear might happen when a few good guys (and gals) carry guns on campus, or the one that actually did happen despite Virginia Tech's progressive violence-prevention policy? Can there really be any more debate?

AMA journal editor James J. James, M.D., offers up this nostrum: 10

> We must meaningfully embrace all of the varied disciplines contributing to preparedness and response and be more willing to be guided and informed by the full spectrum of research methodologies, including not only the rigid application of the traditional scientific method and epidemiological and social science applications but also the incorporation of observational/empirical findings, as necessary, in the absence of more objective data.

Got that?

I prefer the remedy prescribed by self-defense guru Massad Ayoob. When 11 good people find themselves in what he calls "the dark place," confronted by the imminent terror of a gun-wielding homicidal maniac, the picture becomes clear. Policies won't help. Another federal gun law won't help. The only solution is a prepared and brave defender with the proper lifesaving tool—a gun.

⊘ AT ISSUE: SOURCES FOR DEVELOPING AN ETHICAL ARGUMENT

1. According to Wheeler, what is "depressingly similar" about the mass murders committed on campuses (para. 2)?

2. What is Wheeler's attitude toward those who said that "guns are the root cause of violence" (3)? How can you tell?

3. Why, according to Wheeler, do college administrators and bureaucrats continue to ignore the answer to the problem of violence on campus? How does he refute their objections?

4. Do you find Wheeler's argument in support of his thesis convincing? What, if anything, do you think he could have added to strengthen his argument?

5. How does Wheeler's language reveal his attitude toward his subject? (For example, consider his use of "gem" in paragraph 4 and "politically correct" in paragraph 8.) Can you give other examples of language that conveys his point of view?

6. How do you think Wheeler would respond to the ideas in "Warning Signs: How You Can Help Prevent Campus Violence" (p. 554)? Which suggestions do you think he would support? Which would he be likely to oppose? Explain.

This piece was published in *The Nation* on August 29, 2016.

THE FEAR INDUSTRY GOES BACK TO SCHOOL

SASHA ABRAMSKY

"Security was the number-one factor for me in choosing a school," explained 1 one of the mothers I met late last winter at a Montessori preschool in an affluent suburb of Salt Lake City. A quality-control expert at a dietary-supplement company, the woman said she vividly remembers the jolt of horror she felt when she first learned of the Columbine massacre in 1999. So when the time came to send her child to preschool, she selected one that markets itself not only as creative, caring, and nurturing, but also as particularly security-conscious.

To get the front door of the school to open, visitors had to be positively 2 ID'd by a fingerprint-recognition system. In the foyer, a bank of monitors showed a live feed of the activity in every classroom. After drop-off, many parents would spend 15 minutes to half an hour staring at the screens, making sure their children were being treated well by their teachers and classmates. Many of the moms and dads had requested internet access to the images, but the school had balked, fearing that online sexual predators would be able to hack into the video stream. All of the classroom doors had state-of-the-art lockdown features, and all of the teachers had access to long-distance bee spray—which, in the case of an emergency, they were instructed to fi re off at the eyes of intruders. The playground was surrounded by a high concrete wall, which crimped the kids' views of the majestic Wasatch Mountains. The imposing front walls, facing out onto a busy road, were similarly designed to stop predators from peering into the classrooms.

"I fear a gunman walking into my child's school and gunning up the place," 3 the mother continued. (I have withheld her name, and that of the school, upon request.) "And I fear someone walking onto the playground and swiping a kid. And I fear an employee of the school damaging my child. These things happen more commonly than people expect."

Actually, they don't. Despite the excruciating angst suffered by this woman 4 and so many other parents, school violence is a rarity in America. According to the National Center for Education Statistics (NCES), 34 children in the United States were murdered while in school during the 1992–93 school year. From 2008 to 2013, the most recent years for which the NCES provides data, the average annual figure was 19. In recent decades, the numbers have waxed and waned, hitting 34 again in 1997–98 and going as low as 11 in 2010–11. Generally, the trend has been downward.

If one adds the deaths of teachers and other staff, as well as suicides by 5 students during the school day, the numbers go up, of course. In the 20-year period covered by the NCES data, 2006–7 was the deadliest, with 63 violent deaths occurring in America's schools. That is unquestionably 63 too many violent deaths, and for the families directly affected by the killings, it represents unfathomable—and inextinguishable—anguish.

But it isn't quite the national epidemic that one might picture based on 6 the vast media coverage these killings receive. In fact, far more children and young adults are killed on the impoverished streets of America's large cities every year. By several orders of magnitude, far more kids die each year in car crashes or drowning accidents—or from asthma. And far more young lives are lost to a host of other diseases closely correlated with poverty.

There are approximately 55 million K–12 students in America and 7 roughly 3.5 million adults employed as teachers. There are, in addition, millions of support staff—janitors, nurses, cooks, after-school-program providers, and so on. Even in the deadliest years, the chance of a student or adult being killed at school is roughly one in a million. By contrast, roughly five out of every 100,000 American residents are murdered each year. Extrapolating from this, schools are somewhere in the region of 50 times safer than society overall.

And yet you'd never know that from the level of fear that exists around 8 schools—or from the vast amount of money we spend attempting to make them more secure. The research company IHS Technology recently estimated that schools and universities spent about $768 million on security measures in 2014—a sum that it predicted would rise to roughly $907 million for 2016. That's an awful lot of money to spend at a time when state and local budget cuts are limiting educational opportunities for students across the country.

The spike in spending on school security began in the mid-1990s, when the 9 Clinton administration, seeking to co-opt the prevailing tough-on-crime, zero-tolerance message, pushed an array of measures that led to the hiring of several thousand new "school resource officers." Thousands more police officers were funded by state and city grants, making the presence of armed police a daily reality in schools around the country. At the same time, one school after another, especially in inner cities, brought in airport-style metal detectors and introduced "clear bag" policies so that school officials could easily check everything students brought into the building.

As schools came to resemble prisons—which, perhaps not coincidentally, 10 were also expanding during these years—an increasing number of students ended up being arrested on school grounds. In cities like Stockton, California, where even nonpolice "resource officers" are granted arrest powers, thousands of kids have acquired criminal records for minor offenses. Students in these districts are arrested at rates far higher than those reported in places where resource officers aren't given such powers. The construction of this "school-to-prison pipeline" has disproportionately affected minority students—who, in turn, face harsher penalties once they come into contact with the criminal-justice system. Sometimes the confrontations with security officers can be horrendous. Last October, for example, students in a South Carolina school filmed an officer violently dumping a teenage girl out of her chair and dragging her across the floor before arresting her—all because she used her cell phone during math class.

In recent years, the school-security industry has expanded to include 11 high-tech surveillance among its offerings. The school district in Las Vegas has been installing surveillance cameras in schools since 2000, and they are now standard in new schools. All told, according to a 2014 article in the *Las Vegas Sun*, more than 12,000 surveillance cameras are recording in Sin City's schools, complementing the hundreds of cameras in school buses and on major thoroughfares, and the tens of thousands of cameras in the city's giant casinos. The *Sun* didn't report on how much this system cost, but a much smaller project at St. Mary's High School in St. Louis reportedly cost the school $500 a month to lease two cameras, or $15,000 to buy them outright.

Newark Memorial High School, in the San Francisco Bay Area, has 12 embedded ShotSpotter technology, an advanced sound-recognition sensor system deployed by police departments in many urban neighborhoods to identify when and where gunshots are occurring. Although the school hasn't had to pay ShotSpotter for the technology—the company views it as a testing ground for how such a system could be used in a school setting—police departments around the country pay anywhere from $65,000 to $90,000 per year for each square mile covered by the sensors.

And then there's the Indianapolis suburb of Shelbyville, where school 13 superintendent Paula Maurer recently became so worried about the possibility of a shooting that she installed a $400,000 security system in the town's high school. The entire campus, located in open countryside just outside of town, is now saturated with cameras linked into the nearest police station. Every teacher wears a panic button around his or her neck, and pressing it sends the entire campus into instant lockdown. For good measure, police officers watching from miles away can set off blinding smoke cannons and ear-splitting sirens at a moment's notice.

Much as anticrime advocates convinced government agencies in the 1990s 14 and 2000s to fund an increasing array of punitive programs, today school-security companies and trade associations are lobbying legislators in several states to change building codes so that schools will be mandated to spend more on their security systems. If they get their way, the Shelbyville experiment could well be a harbinger of things to come.

> "Lately, America's school-security fetish has reached a whole new level of bizarre."

Lately, America's school-security fetish has reached a whole new level of 15 bizarre. In the wake of the December 2012 Sandy Hook massacre in Newtown, Connecticut, one company after another has rushed to take advantage of the opportunities presented by the epidemic of fear that emerged in response to school violence, and to exploit the emotional vulnerabilities of terrified parents. As a result, a huge number of utterly inane products have entered the market.

School-security specialist Kenneth Trump, longtime president of 16 the Cleveland-based National School Safety and Security Services, likens the surge of "overnight experts, gadgets, and gurus who have popped up out of the blue" to a feeding frenzy. "Every time we have a high-profile shooting, we see another business or product, well intended but not well thought out," he says. After the Columbine massacre, Trump recalls, there was a "fairly reasonable conversation" about security. By contrast, in the years since the slaughter at Sandy Hook, "it's been the worst I've seen in 30-plus years, in terms of people responding emotionally and businesses preying on the emotions of people who are afraid."

Take, for example, Bullet Blockers, a company working out of Lowell, 17 Massachusetts, that manufactures bulletproof backpacks for elementary-school children. The ones for young girls come in raspberry pink or red plaid; the ones for boys come in red, black, navy blue, and more. The company also markets bulletproof jackets, bulletproof iPad cases, and bulletproof whiteboards for use in classrooms. It even sells a "survival pack and safety kit," complete with fire starters, first-aid guides, cold compresses, and other items that would allow a child to survive a prolonged school lockdown.

Bullet Blockers CEO Ed Burke won't divulge how many items his com- 18 pany has sold, but he does say that "since the Paris attacks [of November 13, 2015], our business has grown 80 percent and continues to grow." Have his products actually saved lives? "Thank God, none as yet," he answers— meaning that none of his products have thus far been used to foil an attacker in a school shooting. But "they've been tested randomly, to test ballistic capabilities."

None of Burke's clients would agree to talk for this article, but Burke 19 does aver that his company sold products to "a grandmother who lives in Sandy Hook, who got her grandchildren a couple of backpacks." He adds, "I got a phone call from a gentleman in California whose wife was involved in the massacre in San Bernardino. She was in the building. He wanted to get her a backpack." Burke also cited a family that ordered a man's farm coat, a woman's leather coat, a child's nylon jacket, and three backpacks, all bullet-proof as well.

In Hauppauge, New York, Derek Peterson runs a tech start-up called 20 Digital Fly, which enables school officials to monitor all social-media post-ings within a radius chosen by the school. The intent, which would be eerily familiar to government spy agencies the world over, is to drill down into communications used near schools as a way to identify potential shooters, bombers, bullies, or would-be suicides. The postings of everyone within that catchment area—whether they're students, local residents, or simply peo-ple passing through—are monitored. "My software will identify it," Peter-son enthuses, seemingly oblivious of (or indifferent to) the extraordinary privacy implications of his work. "The school administrator will get emails. At that point, every school has a different policy—they get the parents, the police involved. I provide you with a hammer: Here's the tools to build the house."

Peterson claims that his system is being used in more than 50 schools 21 around the country, as well as some in Ireland and South Africa. His ambitions are large. "It could go global," he says. "We're hoping it does. I'm a serial entrepreneur; this is right in my sweet spot. How do you put a price on protecting little ones? Unfortunately, we live in a crazy world where kids are targeted. So any way we can protect children, I'm all for it."

Much like Burke, Peterson acknowledges that he has no real way of know- 22 ing if Digital Fly is working—although he does claim that it helped prevent two suicides in New York City schools. But since he charges only $1.50 to $2.75 per student, Peterson hopes that schools will decide it's worth adding to their tool kit just on the off chance it works. He tells parents at PTA meetings that his service costs the equivalent of one can of soda per year for each kid, and then adds a spiel about how, if even one bloody nose is avoided, it will be money well spent. "Right now, there are 50 million K–12 matriculating students just in the U.S.," Peterson says as he ponders his company's future. "The sky is the limit."

Many experts worry that the new school-security measures can endanger the 23 people they're supposed to protect. Anti-intruder doors were installed in some schools in Ohio without overrides built in, making it hard for first responders to reach stranded kids in the event of a crisis. There is some anecdotal evidence that lockdown drills injure teachers; they have reputedly resulted in a flurry of workers'-compensation claims across the country. And at the Kaimuki Middle School in Honolulu, a lockdown drill in which a teacher ran through the school wielding a hammer and playing an attacker drew criticism after several young children were traumatized by the sight of their seemingly crazed teacher on a rampage.

The increasing cost of high-tech safety measures has become a concern 24 too. At a time when many schools can't rustle up enough money to keep art and music classes running, and when parents are often asked to purchase such necessities as notebooks, pencils, and even toilet paper, all of this militarization and surveillance represents a scandalous diversion of education funds.

Shelbyville's $400,000 security system, for example, could have been used 25 to pay the salaries and benefits of roughly eight full-time teachers for a year (the average salary for a teacher in the town is $43,000). That's not an insignificant fact in a city that shed five teachers in April 2010 as a way of saving $250,000 during the dog days of the recession. All told, according to the *Indiana Economic Digest*, Shelbyville schools lost access to over $1 million that year. Three years later, the school district cut the hours for scores of teaching aides, bus drivers, and other staff to avoid the cost of covering their health insurance under the terms of the Affordable Care Act.

Ronald Stephens, the executive director of the California-based National School Safety Center, who teaches a graduate course on school-safety issues at Pepperdine University, recalls talking with the superintendent of a school near his home in Oak Park, one of Los Angeles's many affluent suburbs. The superintendent explained that he was under tremendous public pressure to put security fences around the district's schools, at a cost of $1.6 million. He was resisting it because he believed the schools had bigger needs: The teachers hadn't received a pay raise in five years. 26

Back at the Montessori school in Utah, I met a father in his mid-40s who bemoaned the fact that kids could no longer roam freely, walking to and from school alone, playing unsupervised outdoors for hours with their friends, as he'd done growing up in the Bay Area. "Times are different now," he explained sadly. "There are more crazy people in the world." 27

The man, who worked for a large plumbing and air-conditioning company, had a bachelor's degree in criminal-justice studies. Intellectually, he knew the statistics. He knew that violent-crime rates were higher when he was growing up than they are today. So I asked him if he was sure that the environment was less safe for his 17-year-old daughter than it had been for him. "Probably not," he said after a long pause. "It's hard. She is way too sheltered. I'd love to let her spread her wings a little bit more. But we do keep our thumbs on her. There's always the fear of a kidnap, a traffic accident. Turn on the news at night—we watch the news while we eat dinner. The media loves to create a sense of panic. They love bad news." 28

On one level, he knew that the media were selling him a bill of goods. But he couldn't bring himself to turn away—and the more he watched, the more fearful he became. The man told me that he's had nightmares about mass shootings and kidnappings; his face got beet red with tension even while discussing it. 29

Unfortunately, this is the sort of circular reasoning that our society is increasingly trapped in when it comes to raising and educating our children. Television, newspapers, and social media focus on sensational but statistically anomalous horror stories about school violence. Parents and the broader community work themselves into a panic, prompting politicians to vow that they will do "whatever it takes" to make everyone safer. Security technologies emerge to fill the perceived need for stronger safety measures, and schools end up spending money they don't necessarily have to implement solutions they almost certainly will never need. The presence and the media coverage of these heightened security measures increase the public's sense of fear, and the spiral descends even further. 30

"We're preparing for the 1,000-year flood," says Ronald Stephens. "Children are safer at school than anywhere else." 31

⊘ AT ISSUE: SOURCES FOR DEVELOPING AN ETHICAL ARGUMENT

1. At what point in his essay does Abramsky state his thesis? Why do you think he states it where he does?

2. Does Abramsky structure his argument inductively or deductively? What is the advantage of his organization? Are there any disadvantages? Explain.

3. Abramsky begins his essay with several anecdotes. What point does he make with them? Why do you think he chose to begin his essay in this way?

4. According to Abramsky, what misconception about school shootings do many parents and school administrators have? How effectively does he address these misconceptions?

5. What kind of evidence does Abramsky provide to support his thesis? Does he provide enough evidence? Should he have provided other types of evidence? Explain.

6. Both Ed Burke (para. 18) and Derek Peterson (22) concede that they don't know for sure if their products actually work. How are they able to convince parents and school officials to purchase them? Do you find their explanations convincing?

7. In his conclusion, Abramsky quotes Ronald Stephens, the executive director of the National School Safety Center, who says about heightened security measures at school, "We're preparing for the 1,000-year flood" (31). What does he mean?

8. What ethical dilemma do parents and administrators face concerning spending on school security? If you were a parent at a school considering state-of-the-art surveillance, what would you advise school administrators to do?

The Nation published this article on August 29, 2016.

I'M A SCHOOL PSYCHOLOGIST—AND I THINK TEACHERS SHOULD BE ARMED

MICHAEL W. GOLDBERG

1 I've been a school psychologist for the past 20 years. In the wake of the school shootings in Florida, I am brought right back to December 7, 2017, the day of the deadly mass shooting at the high school I currently serve. In the aftermath, I helped to counsel students through the trauma caused by direct exposure to a murderous terrorist act—including nightmares, uncontrollable and unpredictable floods of tears, senseless "what if" questions, anxious obsessing, and survivors' guilt.

2 I also have a unique perspective on the school shooting problem, having been both a mental health professional and a licensed concealed firearm carrier for the past 24 years.

3 In addition to zero bullying tolerance, empathy building, and lockdown drills in our schools, we must bolster our self-defense. Specifically, law-abiding, psychologically stable, specially trained staff should carry concealed weapons.

4 This would reduce our students' trauma and has the potential to stop terror immediately—or deter it from occurring in the first place.

5 A Centers for Disease Control study commissioned by President Obama, "Priorities for Research to Reduce the Threat of Firearm-Related Violence," supports this idea. The report concludes that "self-defense can be an important crime deterrent":

> Studies that directly assessed the effect of actual defensive uses of guns (i.e., incidents in which a gun was "used" by the crime victim in the sense of attacking or threatening an offender) have found consistently lower injury rates among gun-using crime victims compared with victims who used other self-protective strategies.

6 A 1985 survey by the Justice Department, "Armed Criminal in America— A Survey of Incarcerated Felons," found that 54 percent of respondents agreed or strongly agreed with the statement, "A criminal is not going to mess around with a victim he knows is armed with a gun, and 74 percent also agreed that "One reason burglars avoid houses when people are at home is that they fear being shot." The study also reported that a third of the felons said they personally had been "scared off, shot at, wounded, or captured by an armed victim" and two-thirds said that they knew at least one other criminal who had been as well.

7 It follows that the majority of would-be school shooters would be deterred from attacking a school if they knew that they would likely be confronted by armed staff prior to accomplishing their evil deed.

Arming teachers is also likely to reduce trauma for our students.   8

In my experience counseling sessions after our school shooting, I found   9
that feeling totally defenseless increased the severity of the trauma for children
and staff. On the other hand, if both children and staff knew the school had
means to thwart the killer, this knowledge would serve to reduce their fear of a
potential traumatic assault. Many at my school needlessly experienced severe
emotional trauma because they were helpless to stop the violence. Helpless-
ness in the face of violence is an emotion that amplifies the effects of trauma,
and likely contributes to post-traumatic stress disorder. I'm convinced that if
highly trained school staff were armed, and the children were aware of it, the
emotional stress during any school shooting would be reduced significantly.
More importantly, school shootings may not even occur, and lost lives might
still be with us today.

Perhaps the greatest argument against
highly trained armed school staff is that
this would result in more deaths to students
through the accidental discharge of a firearm. This appears a reasonable concern, but
in reality is greatly exaggerated. For example,
In 2007, there were 220 unintentional firearm
deaths of children under age 13. Over 12 times
as many children died from drowning during
the same period. Because these accidental
gun death statistics include deaths caused
by drunks, drug users, children, criminals,
and novice gun users, in all likelihood, acci-

> "I'm convinced that   10
> if highly trained
> school staff were
> armed, and the chil-
> dren were aware of
> it, the emotional
> stress during any
> school shooting
> would be reduced
> significantly."

dents from guns occur a lot less frequently in the hands of highly trained and
responsible personnel. And we can never fully count the bodies saved from
deterrence and successful use of a gun for self-defense.

The topic of having guns on school grounds provokes strong visceral   11
reactions, but relying on reason and logic is the better way to save children's
lives. Guns, which have no intrinsic motivation of their own, stir phobic
responses and are assigned evil attributes. However, we need to stop our children from being slaughtered in a place they should feel safe and welcomed.
The next school shooting is imminent if we continue as is. I propose that
schools continue to fine-tune proactive measures like anti-bullying and empathy skill development, and defensive procedures that are proven effective (like
lockdown drills, but also consider a more active defense measure—carefully
screened and highly trained school staff willing to take on the enormous
responsibility of being competent and armed in a safe fashion on school
grounds. My own experience as a school psychologist and my understanding
of the research indicates that this would reduce emotional trauma as well as
reduce the amount of school shootings, saving and improving the lives of our
most valuable resource—our children.

⊃ AT ISSUE: SOURCES FOR DEVELOPING AN ETHICAL ARGUMENT

1. Goldberg begins his essay with an appeal to *ethos*. Is this appeal effective? Is he able to establish credibility? Explain.

2. In paragraph 1, Goldberg mentions that there was a deadly shooting at the school at which he works. Although his original publication included a link to a web page that gives additional information about the 2017 shooting, he doesn't provide much detail in his essay itself. Why do you think he chose to omit this information? Does this lack of detail strengthen or weaken his argument?

3. In paragraph 6, Goldberg cites a 1985 Justice Department study of armed criminals in America. In paragraph 7, he says that based on this study, "It follows that the majority of would-be school shooters would be deterred from attacking a school if they knew they would likely be confronted by armed staff." Do you think his conclusion is valid? If not, where is the flaw in his logic?

4. In paragraph 11, Goldberg concedes that "having guns on school grounds provokes strong visceral reactions." Does he do enough to address the concerns of those who have "strong visceral reactions" against his position?

5. In paragraph 10, Goldberg says that the greatest argument against having an armed school staff is the danger of a firearm accidentally discharging. Do you agree? What other dangers can you think of? Should Goldberg have addressed one or more of these?

6. In a response to Goldberg's essay, Aviva Miriam Patt, a teacher, said the following:

   > The people who want to arm teachers don't understand what makes us want to be teachers. The skill set that draws us to educate and nurture isn't the same skill set you need to shoot someone. Especially when the person with the gun is one of your students. We're trained to understand, empathize, and de-escalate—not to kill.

   What ethical principle is Patt stating? Is this principle self-evident, or does it apply just to those who believe as Patt does?

This piece ran on February 22, 2018, in the *Atlantic*.

ARMING EDUCATORS VIOLATES THE SPIRIT OF THE SECOND AMENDMENT

VANN R. NEWKIRK II

The Second Amendment is a remarkable piece of the Constitution. "A well 1 regulated Militia, being necessary to the security of a free State, the right of the people to keep and bear Arms, shall not be infringed," it reads.

Set aside for the moment questions about its practical interpretations today 2 and its usefulness as a legal tenet—the provision presents a starkly revolutionary moral and political theory. Written by the powerful men in charge of the nation, the amendment expressly preserves the right of individuals to protect themselves against the future tyranny of the powerful men in charge of the nation. In fact, it enshrines this as a moral obligation, mixing into the very core of American civics the expectation that uncivil disobedience might be a necessary patriotic duty should the government cease to serve the people.

That amendment is again front and center today, as the country continues 3 to grapple with serious questions about gun violence in the wake of the massacre at the Marjory Stoneman Douglas High School in Parkland, Florida. This particular incident seems to have shaken the public consciousness more than some previous shootings, and people on all sides of the political spectrum appear primed to at least consider solutions. Unfortunately for students, the solutions that appear to be gaining traction so far include further arming school police, arming students, and even giving schools drones. Not only is the efficacy of these measures dubious, they run counter to the ideals of the Second Amendment that are often invoked to justify them—extending the power of a militarized state at the expense of individual liberty.

President Trump has led the push for arming teachers for some time now. He 4 has repeatedly attacked gun-free zones in schools, arguing at an October 2015 presidential debate that such spaces provide "target practice for the sickos and for the mentally ill." He's kept up that critique as president in the wake of the Parkland shooting. While attempting to clarify or correct news reports suggesting that he wanted to arm teachers, he tweeted about his desire to arm teachers, endorsing giving "concealed guns to gun adept teachers with military or special training experience—only the best." He also tweeted that "a 'gun free' school is a magnet for bad people."

But Trump is merely the vanguard in a deepening movement to arm 5 educators in order to stop school shootings. Bills across the country have been proposed to allow concealed handguns in schools, some provisions already exist for postsecondary campuses, and there are initiatives to train teachers in the use of weapons. Education Secretary Betsy DeVos said in an interview last *week* that states "clearly have the opportunity and the option" to arm teachers. On Thursday at the Conservative Political Action Conference (CPAC), National Rifle Association Executive Vice President Wayne LaPierre echoed that sentiment, saying, "we must immediately harden our schools."

For many others, such "hardening" goes well beyond just arming teachers. In 6 the Florida county where the Parkland massacre took place, the sheriff announced yesterday that police officers will be allowed to carry rifles on school grounds.

Many other districts are already well beyond "hardened." Los Angeles 7 school police procured grenade launchers, rifles, and an armored personnel carrier through a federal surplus program. Police in Compton, California, are allowed to wear AR-15 rifles, and a Colorado district began distributing them *in 2016*. There are now plenty of school districts across America with armed school police officers, complete with metal detectors, body armor, and K-9 units. Even the patently outlandish suggestion of *Newsmax* host Wayne Root to provide schools with armed drones isn't so far from reality. Schools already have drones, though not (yet) armed.

As *Vox*'s Jane Coaston argued, these suggestions mostly amount to secu- 8 rity theater, and there is little data suggesting that armed school officials have a meaningful impact on student safety. Even metal detectors haven't really helped reduce violence, and that's against both the steady stream of more mundane events of gun violence that plague some schools and the annual massacres.

> "The 'good guy with a gun' theory has never had any real credibility beyond a few choice anecdotes." 9

Logically, even as Trump seemed to acknowledge in his backtracking, the idea of arming teachers is suspect. The "good guy with a gun" theory underpinning the movement has never had any real credibility beyond a few choice anecdotes, and the training required to make armed teachers anything more than a liability would be onerous. Teachers already work long hours for relatively little pay, and many school districts have dismissed the idea as simply impractical.

But the movement for hardening isn't just impractical or lacking in 10 evidentiary support; it's also a dystopian stroke of authoritarianism that runs deeply counter to the ideas embodied in the Constitution. Increasingly militarized school resource officers don't just passively wait for mass shootings; they have daily encounters with students that appear to be increasing in frequency. Brutality is endemic. *Mother Jones* chronicled 28 serious student injuries and one death from 2010 to 2015 in such encounters. The brunt of those brutal incidents and arrests falls on black students, and high-profile incidents of officers kicking students, choking them, handcuffing third-graders, and slamming students to the ground are all too common.

While most teachers are fiercely dedicated to their students, steady reports 11 of abuse from some teachers, as well as reports of racial slurs and racial bias, should be strong reasons to be skeptical of arming teachers. Especially in the often-fraught environments of under-resourced classrooms, it's probably not a good idea to have *anybody* with a gun present.

More broadly, hardening proposals posit that the only way to keep 12 kids safe is to raise them in police states, kept under guard by killer drones, assault rifles, and armed teachers. As Coaston writes, these setups will almost certainly tend towards gross violations of students' First Amendment rights to speech and Fourth Amendment rights to privacy, and will do so along already-established lines of race and class. As a person who attended a school where violence by resource officers was a fact of life for low-income black students, I can offer at least anecdotal support for this argument.

But hardening proposals also exhibit a circular logic that runs deeply 13 counter to the spirit of the Second Amendment. Again, that provision implies a duty to resist tyranny, in all the forms of military, surveillance, and governmental overreach that helped spark the revolution. Suggestions to create a police state in American schools, however, mirror other pro-authoritarian tendencies that run counter to this instinct. In the creation of the carceral state, in the expansion of drug laws, and in the extreme militarization of police in recent years, people have argued that placing more guns in the hands of authorities is the only way to keep people safe. But why would pro–Second Amendment enthusiasts be in favor of providing *more* firepower to the government?

One legal theory used to oppose the preferences of many defenders of the 14 Second Amendment is based on the fact that the militarized American police state has advanced far beyond the ability of any possible well-regulated militia to stop it. But lost in that observation is the fact that Americans—many of them staunch gun-rights advocates—have pushed repeatedly to bolster the military and the creep of militarism into other civic arenas. They've then trapped the country in an arms race between government and civilians, one in which civilians face severe losses from both state and private violence. And now students, protected in schools by the most basic tenets of the social contract, find themselves in the line of fire.

⊘ AT ISSUE: SOURCES FOR DEVELOPING AN ETHICAL ARGUMENT

1. Newkirk begins his essay with a three-paragraph discussion of the Second Amendment. What point does he make? How do these paragraphs prepare readers for the rest of the essay?

2. Does Newkirk treat those who don't agree with him fairly? How does he describe them? What language does he use when he deals with those with whom he disagrees?

3. In paragraph 8, Newkirk calls some efforts to "harden" schools "security theater." What does he mean? What evidence does he provide to support this contention? Do you agree with his assessment?

4. In paragraph 12, Newkirk says, "hardening proposals posit that the only way to keep kids safe is to raise them in police states." Is this a fair assessment, or is Newkirk engaging in hyperbole? Explain.

5. According to Newkirk, how do hardening proposals run "counter to the spirit of the Second Amendment" (para. 13)?

6. On the whole, does Newkirk support or oppose the Second Amendment's provision of the right to bear arms? How do you know?

7. A **paradox** is a contradictory statement that may indeed be true. In what sense does the last sentence of this essay express a paradox?

This brochure is available on the website for Isothermal Community College, isothermal.edu.

WARNING SIGNS: HOW YOU CAN HELP PREVENT CAMPUS VIOLENCE

ISOTHERMAL COMMUNITY COLLEGE

Isothermal Community College

2 ·····································

Things to

LOOK OUT FOR . . .

■ Any direct statement about the intention to harm him/her self or other members of the community

■ "Hints" that the individual intends to harm him/her self or other members of the community: For example, "I might not be around after this weekend;" "It would be a good idea for you to stay out of the cafeteria tomorrow;" "People might get hurt, if they're not careful"

■ Extreme difficulty adjusting to college life; for example, the student is isolated, depressed, and/or very angry with peers

■ Significant changes in behavior, appearance, habits, mood, or activities

■ Statements from individuals about access to firearms and suggestions that they may be bringing them to the campus or may already have them on campus

■ Behaviors that indicate that the individual is settling his/her affairs, which may include telling people goodbye, giving possessions away, and/or making statements about what they would like to have done should something happen to them

■ Fascination with violence, including some types of video games and music, and/or focusing on or admiring violent "role models"

■ Your own "gut feeling" that someone that you know intends to harm him/her self or others

Campus Security—289-1393. Isothermal Community College. Improve Life Through Learning. www.isothermal.edu.

At Isothermal Community College, we want all of our students, faculty, and staff to be safe and secure on campus.

In light of the tragic shootings at Virginia Tech and other recent events on college campuses and in schools around the country, it has become clear that friends, classmates, and acquaintances of troubled students may be the most likely individuals to be aware of potentially dangerous and/or self-destructive situations.

However, students often are not certain about what kinds of warning signs they should take seriously and/or whether reporting the signs to faculty or staff members is the right thing to do.

Isothermal Community College

. . . . 3

The tips in this brochure are aimed at helping you identify potential problems and behaviors that could lead to incidents of campus violence.

If you ever feel endangered or threatened at any time on campus, we ask that you immediately contact Isothermal security, an instructor, or an employee of the college for assistance.

Campus security can be reached at 289-1393. To contact the switchboard operator, dial **0** on any campus phone. You should also report any threatening activity to local law enforcement by dialing **911**. Don't forget to dial **9** for an outside line if using the campus phone system.

A lockdown procedure is in place for Isothermal Community College. Faculty and staff members periodically practice the procedure.

If you are informed of a lockdown situation, please cooperate with the proper authorities. Leaving the classroom or the building in such a situation may put you at greater risk.

POTENTIAL FOR VIOLENCE
Warning Signs in Others

Often people who act violently have trouble controlling their feelings. They may have been hurt by others and may think that making people fear them through violence or threats of violence will solve their problems or earn them respect. This isn't true. People who behave violently lose respect. They find themselves isolated or disliked, and they still feel angry and frustrated.

If you see these immediate warning signs, violence is a serious possibility:

- Loss of temper on a daily basis
- Frequent physical fighting
- Significant vandalism or property damage
- Increase in use of drugs or alcohol
- Increase in risk-taking behavior
- Detailed plans to commit acts of violence
- Announcing threats or plans for hurting others
- Enjoying hurting animals
- Carrying a weapon

Isothermal Community College

4 ·

If you notice the following signs over a period of time, the potential for violence exists:

- A history of violent or aggressive behavior
- Serious drug or alcohol use
- Gang membership or strong desire to be in a gang
- Access to or fascination with weapons, especially guns
- Threatening others regularly
- Trouble controlling feelings like anger
- Withdrawal from friends and usual activities
- Feeling rejected or alone
- Having been a victim of bullying
- Poor school performance
- History of discipline problems or frequent run-ins with authority
- Feeling constantly disrespected
- Failing to acknowledge the feelings or rights of others

Source: American Psychological Association

Isothermal Community College

⊘ AT ISSUE: SOURCES FOR DEVELOPING AN ETHICAL ARGUMENT

1. This brochure is designed to help students recognize people who have the potential to commit campus violence. What warning signs does the brochure emphasize?

2. What additional information, if any, do you think should have been included in this brochure? Why?

3. Are there any suggestions in this brochure that could possibly violate a person's right to privacy? Explain.

4. What additional steps do you think students should take to prevent campus violence?

This poster is from the UCDA Campus Violence Poster Project show at Northern Illinois University.

VISUAL ARGUMENT: GONE BUT NOT FORGOTTEN

AMY DION

Virginia Tech University
4·17·07 (32 dead)

Louisiana Technical College
2·8·08 (3 dead)

Northern Illinois University
2·14·08 (5 dead)

© Amy Dion, Art Director, SIU

⊘ AT ISSUE: SOURCES FOR DEVELOPING AN ETHICAL ARGUMENT

1. This poster shows a handprint on a background that repeats the phrase "Gone but not forgotten." What ethical argument does the poster make?

2. What other images does the poster include? How do these images reinforce its message?

3. Do you think posters like this one can really help to combat campus violence? Can they serve any other purpose? Explain.

TEMPLATE FOR WRITING AN ETHICAL ARGUMENT

Write a one-paragraph ethical argument in which you answer the question, "How far should schools go to keep students safe?" Follow the template below, filling in the blanks to create your argument.

> Recently, a number of schools have experienced violence on their campuses. For example,
>
> _____
>
> _____. Many schools have gone [too far/not far enough] in trying to prevent
>
> violence because _____
>
> _____
>
> _____
>
> _____. One reason _____
>
> _____.
>
> Another reason _____
>
> _____
>
> _____. Finally, _____
>
> _____
>
> _____. If schools really want to remain safe, _____
>
> _____
>
> _____
>
> _____.

> **EXERCISE 15.5 EXPANDING YOUR DEFINITION**
>
> Ask your friends and your teachers whether they think any of the steps your school has taken to prevent campus violence are excessive—or whether they think these measures don't go far enough. Then, revise the paragraph you wrote in the preceding template so that it includes their opinions.

> **EXERCISE 15.6 WRITING AN ETHICAL ARGUMENT**
>
> Write an ethical argument in which you consider the topic, "How Far Should Schools Go to Keep Students Safe?" Make sure you include a clear analysis of the ethical principle that you are going to apply. (If you like, you may incorporate the material you developed in the template and in Exercise 15.5 into your essay.) Cite the readings from this chapter, document the sources you use, and be sure to include a works-cited page. (See Chapter 10 for information on documenting sources.)

⊘ EXERCISE 15.7 REVIEWING THE FOUR PILLARS OF ARGUMENT

Review the four pillars of argument discussed in Chapter 1. Does your essay include all four elements of an effective argument? Add anything that is missing. Then, label the key elements of your essay.

⊘ WRITING ASSIGNMENTS: ETHICAL ARGUMENTS

1. Write an ethical argument in which you discuss whether hate groups have the right to distribute material on campus. Be sure to explain the ethical principle you are applying and to include several arguments in support of your position. (Don't forget to define and give examples of what you mean by *hate groups*. Remember to address arguments against your position.) You can refer to the readings on pages from earlier in this chapter to find sources to support your position.

2. Should English be made the official language of the United States? Write an ethical argument in which you take a position on this topic.

3. Many people think that celebrities have an ethical obligation to set positive examples for young people. Assume that you are a celebrity, and write an op-ed piece in which you support or challenge this idea. Be sure to identify the ethical principle on which you base your argument.

Protesters rallied in New York on April 25, 2012, the day that student loan debt reached $1 trillion. The protesters' proposals include debt forgiveness and no-interest student loans. Richard Levine/AGE Fotostock

16

Proposal Arguments

Should the Government Do More to Relieve the Student-Loan Burden?

In 2011, the protest movement Occupy Wall Street began in New York City's Zuccotti Park. Initially, the protestors focused on economic problems like inequality and unemployment. But other issues emerged, including a demand for student-loan forgiveness. Soon after, then-President Barack Obama announced a program of student-loan relief. For example, he reduced the maximum required payment on loans from 15 percent to 10 percent of a borrower's annual income. Since taking office in 2017, President Donald Trump has proposed his own reforms. But regardless of political party, policymakers agree that student debt—now over $1.5 trillion—is a problem.

According to some experts, the debt is a financial bubble that will eventually burst and cause more damage than the 2008 housing crisis. Many critics claim that reforms to the current student-loan program miss the root cause of the problem: the ever-increasing cost of tuition. In response, they propose restructuring federal aid in a way that rewards schools that reduce expenses and penalize schools that do not. Others argue that most students receive enough money from traditional grants and loans to offset tuition; in their view, the "crisis" is overblown. Still others say that students should simply realize that they must live up to their obligations and repay their loans.

Later in this chapter, you will be asked to think more about this issue. You will be given several sources to consider and asked to write a **proposal argument** that takes a position on whether the government should do more to relieve the student-loan burden.

Many college students apply for loans.

Andriy Popov/Alamy Stock Photo

What Is a Proposal Argument?

When you write a **proposal argument**, you suggest a solution to a problem. The purpose of a proposal argument is to convince people that a problem exists and that your solution is both feasible and worthwhile.

Proposal arguments are the most common form of argument. You see them every day on billboards and in advertisements, editorials, and letters to the editor. The problems proposal arguments address can be local:

- What steps should the community take to protect its historic buildings?
- How can the city promote the use of public transportation?
- What can the township do to help the homeless?
- What should be done to encourage recycling on campus?
- How can community health services be improved?

The problems addressed in proposal arguments can also be more global:

- Should the United States increase its military budget?
- What should be done to increase clean energy production?
- What can countries do to protect themselves against terrorism?
- What should be done to decrease gun violence?
- How can we encourage the ethical treatment of animals?

Many advertisements
try to influence
behavior.

The Advertising Archives

PROBLEM-SOLVING STRATEGIES

Because the purpose of a proposal argument is to solve a problem, you
should begin by considering both the problem and its significance. By
following a simple step-by-step process (alone or in a group), you can
analyze the problem and develop effective strategies for solving it.

Identify the problem.

⬇

Explore the possible causes of the problem.

⬇

Brainstorm possible solutions.

⬇

Examine the advantages and disadvantages of each solution.

⬇

Select the best option.

Remember, problem solving is a process. If you solve the problem, you
can begin to plan your proposal. If not, you should begin the problem-
solving process again, perhaps modifying the problem or its possible
solutions.

Stating the Problem

When you write a proposal argument, you should begin by demonstrating that a problem exists. In some cases, readers will be familiar with the problem, so you will not have to explain it in great detail. For example, it would not take much to convince students at your university that tuition is high or that some classrooms are overcrowded. Most people also know about the need to provide affordable health care to the uninsured or to reduce the rising level of student debt because these are problems that have received a good deal of media attention.

Other, less familiar issues need more explanation—sometimes a great deal of explanation. In these cases, you should not assume that readers will accept (or even understand) the importance of the problem you are discussing. For example, why should readers care about the high dropout rate at a local high school? You can answer this question by demonstrating that this problem affects not only the students who drop out but others as well:

- Students who do not have high school diplomas earn substantially less than those who do.

- Studies show that high school dropouts are much more likely to live in poverty than students who complete high school.

- Taxpayers pay for the social services that dropouts often require.

- Federal, state, and local governments lose the taxes that dropouts would pay if they had better jobs.

When you explain the situation in this way, you show that a problem that appears to be limited to just a few individuals actually affects society as a whole.

How much background information you need to provide about a problem depends on how much your readers already know about it. In many cases, a direct statement of a problem is not enough: you need to explain the context of the problem and then discuss it with this context in mind. For example, you cannot simply say that the number of databases to which your college library subscribes needs to be increased. Why does it need to be increased? How many new databases should be added? Which ones? What benefits would result from increasing the number of databases? What will happen if the number is not increased? Without answers to these questions, readers will not be able to understand the full extent of the problem. (Statistics, examples, personal anecdotes, and even visuals can also help you demonstrate the importance of finding a solution to the problem.) By presenting the problem in detail, you draw readers into your discussion and motivate them to want to solve it.

Proposing a Solution

After you have established that a problem exists, you have to propose a solution. Sometimes the solution is self-evident, so that you do not need to explain it in much detail. For example, if you want to get a new computer for the college newspaper, you do not have to give a detailed account of how you intend to purchase it. On the other hand, if your problem is more complicated—for example, proposing that your school should sponsor a new student organization—you will have to go into much more detail, possibly listing the steps that you will take to implement your plan as well as the costs associated with it.

Demonstrating That Your Solution Will Work

When you present a solution to a problem, you have to support it with **evidence**—facts, examples, and so on from your own experience and from research. You can also point to successful solutions that are similar to the one you are suggesting. For example, if you were proposing that the government should do more to relieve the student-loan burden, you could list the reasons why certain changes would be beneficial for many students. You might also point to student-friendly practices in other countries, such as Great Britain and Australia. Finally, you could use a visual, such as a chart or a graph, to help you support your position.

You also have to consider the consequences—both intended and unintended—of your proposal. Idealistic or otherwise unrealistic proposals almost always run into trouble when skeptical readers challenge them. If you think, for example, that the federal government should increase subsidies on electric cars to encourage clean energy, you should consider the effects of such subsidies. How much money would drivers actually save? How would the government make up the lost revenue? What programs would suffer because the government could no longer afford to fund them? In short, do the benefits of your proposal outweigh its negative effects?

Establishing Feasibility

Your solution not only has to make sense but also has to be **feasible**—that is, it has to be practical. Sometimes a problem can be solved, but the solution may be almost as bad as—or even worse than—the problem. For example, a city could drastically reduce crime by putting police on every street corner, installing video cameras at every intersection, and stopping and searching all cars that contain two or more people. These actions would certainly reduce crime, but most people would not want to live in a city that instituted such authoritarian policies.

Even if a solution is desirable, it still may not be feasible. For example, although expanded dining facilities might improve life on campus, the cost of a new student cafeteria would be high. If paying for it means that tuition would have to be increased, many students would find this proposal unacceptable. On the other hand, if you could demonstrate that the profits from the increase in food sales in the new cafeteria would offset its cost, then your proposal would be feasible.

Discussing Benefits

By presenting the benefits of your proposal, you can convince undecided readers that your plan has merit. How, for example, would students benefit from an expansion of campus parking facilities? Would student morale improve because students would get fewer parking citations? Would lateness to class decline because students would no longer have to spend time looking for a parking spot? Would the college earn more revenue from additional parking fees? Although not all proposals list benefits, many do. This information can help convince readers that your proposal has merit and is worth implementing.

Refuting Opposing Arguments

You should always assume that any proposal—no matter how strong—will be objectionable to some readers. Moreover, even sympathetic readers will have questions that they will want answered before they accept your ideas. That is why you should always anticipate and refute possible objections to your proposal. For example, if the federal government did more to relieve the student-loan burden, would some students try to take advantage of the program by borrowing more than they need? Would all students be eligible for help, even those from wealthy families? Would this proposal be fair to students who have already paid off their loans? Would students who worked while attending school be eligible? If any objections are particularly strong, concede them: admit that they have merit, but point out their shortcomings. For instance, you could concede that some students might try to abuse the program, but you could then point out that only a small minority of students would do this and recommend steps that could be taken to address possible abuses.

DALE SPARKS/AP Images

An image of an overcrowded campus parking lot can help convince your audience to see the merits of a proposal to make more parking available.

⊖ EXERCISE 16.1 SUPPORTING THESIS STATEMENTS

List the evidence you could present to support each of these thesis statements for proposal arguments.

1. Because many Americans are obese, the government should require warning labels on all sugared cereals.

2. The United States should ban all gasoline-burning cars in ten years.

3. Candidates for president should be required to use only public funding for their campaigns.

4. Teachers should carry handguns to protect themselves and their students from violence.

5. To reduce prison overcrowding, states should release all nonviolent offenders.

⊖ EXERCISE 16.2 IDENTIFYING PROBLEMS

Review the proposals in Exercise 16.1, and list two problems that each one could create if implemented.

⊖ EXERCISE 16.3 ANALYZING A PROPOSAL ARGUMENT

Read the following opinion column, "Why Medicare-for-All Is Good for Business" by Bernie Sanders. What problem does Sanders discuss? How does he propose to solve this problem? What benefits does he expect his solution to have? What evidence could he have added to strengthen his proposal?

This opinion column was published in *Fortune* on August 21, 2017.

WHY MEDICARE-FOR-ALL IS GOOD FOR BUSINESS

BERNIE SANDERS

Despite major improvements made by the Affordable Care Act (ACA), our health care system remains in crisis. Today, we have the most expensive, inefficient, and bureaucratic health care system in the world. We spend almost $10,000 per capita each year on health care, while the Canadians spend $4,644, the Germans $5,551, the French $4,600, and the British $4,192. Meanwhile, our life expectancy is lower than most other industrialized countries and our infant mortality rates are much higher.

Further, as of September 2016, 28 million Americans were uninsured and millions more underinsured with premiums, deductibles, and copayments that are too high. We also pay, by far, the highest prices in the world for prescription drugs.

The ongoing failure of our health care system is directly attributable to 3 the fact that it is largely designed not to provide quality care in a cost-effective way, but to make maximum profits for health insurance companies, the pharmaceutical industry, and medical equipment suppliers. That has got to change. We need to guarantee health care for all. We need to do it in a cost-effective way. We need a Medicare-for-all health care system in the U.S.

Let's be clear. Not only is our dysfunctional health care system causing 4 unnecessary suffering and financial stress for millions of low- and middle-income families, it is also having a very negative impact on our economy and the business community—especially small- and medium-sized companies. Private businesses spent $637 billion on private health insurance in 2015 and are projected to spend $1.059 trillion in 2025.

> "We need to guarantee health care for all. We need to do it in a cost-effective way."

But it's not just the heavy financial cost of health care that the business 5 community is forced to bear. It is time and energy. Instead of focusing on their core business goals, small- and medium-sized businesses are forced to spend an inordinate amount of time, energy, and resources trying to navigate an incredibly complex system in order to get the most cost-effective coverage possible for their employees. It is not uncommon for employers to spend weeks every year negotiating with private insurance companies, filling out reams of paperwork, and switching carriers to get the best deal they can.

And more and more business people are getting tired of it and are asking 6 the simple questions that need to be addressed.

Why as a nation are we spending more than 17 percent of our GDP on 7 health care, while nations that we compete with provide health care for all of their people at 9, 10, or 11 percent of their GDP? Is that sustainable? What impact does that have on our overall economy?

Why are employers who do the right thing and provide strong health 8 care benefits for their employees at a competitive disadvantage with those who don't? Why are some of the largest and most profitable corporations in America, like Walmart, receiving massive subsidies from the federal government because their inadequate benefits force many of their employees to go on Medicaid? Why are most labor disputes in this country centered on health care coverage? Is it good for a company to have employees on the payroll not because they enjoy the work, but because their families need the health insurance the company provides?

Richard Master is the owner and CEO of MCS Industries Inc., the nation's 9 leading supplier of wall and poster frames—a $200 million a year company based in Easton, Pa. "My company now pays $1.5 million a year to provide access to health care for our workers and their dependents," Master told Common Dreams. "When I investigated where all the money goes, I was shocked."

What he found was that fully 33 cents of every health care premium dollar 10 "has nothing to do with the delivery of health care." Thirty-three percent of his health care budget was being spent on administrative costs.

"I came to realize that insurers comprise a completely unnecessary mid- 11 dleman that not only adds little if any value to our health care system, it adds enormous costs to it," Master said.

It doesn't have to be this way. Every other major country on earth has a 12 national health care program that guarantees health care to all of their people at a much lower cost. In our country, Medicare, a government-run single-payer health care system for seniors, is a popular, cost-effective health insurance program. When the Senate gets back into session in September, I will be introducing legislation to expand Medicare to cover all Americans.

This is not a radical idea. I live in Burlington, Vt., 50 miles south of the 13 Canadian border. For decades, every man, woman, and child in Canada has been guaranteed health care through a single-payer, publicly funded health care program. Not only has this system improved the lives of the Canadian people, it has saved businesses many billions of dollars.

The American Sustainable Business Council, a business advocacy organization, 14 started a campaign in April in support of single-payer health care. To date, more than 170 business leaders have signed on to this initiative in more than 30 states.

Here is what these business leaders have written: 15

All supporters of the campaign believe that a single-payer health care system, which is what the vast majority of the industrialized world embraces, will deliver significant cost-savings, in large part by eliminating the wasteful practices of the insurance industry that are designed for financial advantage.

In my view, health care for all is a moral issue. No American should die 16 or suffer because they lack the funds to get adequate health care. But it is more than that. A Medicare-for-all single-payer system will be good for the economy and the business community.

⊖ EXERCISE 16.4 RESPONDING TO A PROPOSAL

Write a paragraph or two in which you argue for or against the recommendations Sanders proposes in "Why Medicare-for-All Is Good for Business." Be sure to present a clear statement of the problems he is addressing as well as the strengths or weaknesses of his proposal.

Structuring a Proposal Argument

In general, a proposal argument can be structured in the following way:

- **Introduction:** Establishes the context of the proposal and presents the essay's thesis
- **Explanation of the problem:** Identifies the problem and explains why it needs to be solved
- **Explanation of the solution:** Proposes a solution and explains how it will solve the problem

- **Evidence in support of the solution:** Presents support for the proposed solution (this section is usually more than one paragraph)

- **Benefits of the solution:** Explains the positive results of the proposed course of action

- **Refutation of opposing arguments:** Addresses objections to the proposal

- **Conclusion:** Reinforces the main point of the proposal; includes a strong concluding statement

The following student essay contains all the elements of a proposal argument. The student who wrote this essay is trying to convince the college president that the school should adopt an **honor code**—a system of rules that defines acceptable conduct and establishes procedures for handling misconduct.

COLLEGES NEED HONOR CODES

MELISSA BURRELL

Today's college students are under a lot of pressure to do well in   1
school, to win tuition grants, to please teachers and family, and to compete in the job market. As a result, the temptation to cheat is greater than ever. At the same time, technology, particularly the internet, has made cheating easier than ever. Colleges and universities have tried various strategies to combat this problem, from increasing punishments to using plagiarism-detection tools such as Turnitin.com. However, the most comprehensive and effective solution to the problem of academic dishonesty is an honor code, a campus-wide contract that spells out and enforces standards of honesty. To fight academic dishonesty, colleges should institute and actively maintain honor codes.

Thesis statement

Explanation of the problem: Cheating

Although the exact number of students who cheat is impossible to   2
determine, 68 percent of the students in one recent survey admitted to cheating (Musto). Some students cheat by plagiarizing entire papers or stealing answers to tests. Many other students commit so-called lesser offenses, such as collaborating with others when told to work alone, sharing test answers, cutting and pasting material from the internet, or misrepresenting data. All of these acts are dishonest; all amount to cheating. Part of the problem, however, is that students are often unsure whether

their decisions are or are not ethical (Dimon). Because they are unclear about expectations and overwhelmed by the pressure to succeed, students can easily justify dishonest acts.

An honor code solves these problems by clearly presenting the rules and by establishing honesty, trust, and academic honor as shared values. According to recent research, "setting clear expectations, and repeating them early and often, is crucial" (Grasgreen). Schools with honor codes require *every* student to sign a pledge to uphold the honor code. Ideally, students write and manage the honor code themselves, with the help of faculty and administrators. According to Timothy M. Dodd, however, to be successful, the honor code must be more than a document; it must be a way of thinking. To accomplish this, all first-year students should receive copies of the school's honor code at orientation. At the beginning of each academic year, students should be required to reread the honor code and renew their pledge to uphold its values and rules. In addition, students and instructors need to discuss the honor code in class. (Some colleges post the honor code in every classroom.) In other words, Dodd believes that the honor code must be part of the fabric of the school. It should be present in students' minds, guiding their actions and informing their learning and teaching.

3 Explanation of the solution: Institute honor code

Studies show that serious cheating is 25 to 50 percent lower at schools with honor codes (Dodd). With an honor code in place, students cannot say that they do not know what constitutes cheating or that they do not understand what will happen to them if they cheat. Studies also show that in schools with a strong honor code, instructors are more likely to take action against cheaters. One study shows that instructors frequently do not confront students who cheat because they are not sure the university will back them up (Vandehey, Diekhoff, and LaBeff 469) and another suggests that students are more likely to cheat when they feel their instructor will be lenient (Hosny and Fatima 753). When a school has an honor code, however, instructors can be certain that both the students and the school will support their actions.

4 Evidence in support of the solution

When a school institutes an honor code, a number of positive results occur. First, an honor code creates a set of basic rules that students can follow. Students know in advance what is expected of them and what will happen if they commit an infraction. In addition, an honor code promotes honesty, placing more responsibility and power in the

5 Benefits of the solution

hands of students and encouraging them to act according to a higher standard. As a result, schools with honor codes often permit unsupervised exams that require students to monitor one another. Finally, according to Dodd, honor codes encourage students to act responsibly. They assume that students will not take unfair advantage of each other or undercut the academic community. As Dodd concludes, in schools with honor codes, plagiarism (and cheating in general) becomes a concern for everyone—students as well as instructors.

Refutation of opposing arguments

Some people argue that plagiarism-detection tools such as Turnitin .com are more effective at preventing cheating than honor codes. However, these tools focus on catching individual acts of cheating, not on preventing a culture of cheating. When schools use these tools, they are telling students that their main concern is not to avoid cheating but to avoid getting caught. As a result, these tools do not deal with the real problem: the decision to be dishonest. Rather than trusting students, schools that use plagiarism-detection tools assume that all students are cheating. Unlike plagiarism-detection tools, honor codes fight dishonesty by promoting a culture of integrity, fairness, and accountability. By assuming that most students are trustworthy and punishing only those who are not, schools with honor codes set high standards for students and encourage them to rise to the challenge.

6

The only long-term, comprehensive solution to the problem of cheating is campus-wide honor codes. No solution will completely prevent dishonesty, but honor codes go a long way toward addressing the root causes of this problem. The goal of an honor code is to create a campus culture that values and rewards honesty and integrity. By encouraging students to do what is expected of them, honor codes help create a confident, empowered, and trustworthy student body.

7

Concluding statement

Works Cited

Dimon, Melissa. "Why Students Cheat—And What to Do About It." *Edutopia*, 17 Apr. 2018. https://www.edutopia.org/article /why-students-cheat-and-what-do-about-it.

Dodd, Timothy M. "Honor Code 101: An Introduction to the Elements of Traditional Honor Codes, Modified Honor Codes and Academic Integrity Policies." *Center for Academic Integrity, Clemson U*, 2010, www .clemson.edu/ces/departments/mse/academics/honor-code.html.

Grasgreen, Allie. "Who Cheats, and How." *Inside Higher Ed,*
    16 Mar. 2012, www.insidehighered.com/news/2012/03/16
    /arizona-survey-examines-student-cheating-faculty-responses.

Hosny, Manar and Shameem Fatima. "Attitude of Students towards Cheating
    and Plagiarism: University Case Study." *Journal of Applied Sciences,*
    vol. 14, no. 8, 2014, pp. 748–57.

Musto, Pete. "How Many College Students Admit to Cheating?" *VOA,* 1 Dec.
    2018. https://www.voanews.com/a/how-many-college-students-admit
    -to-cheating/4095674.html.

Vandehey, Michael, et al. "College Cheating: A Twenty Year Follow-Up and the
    Addition of an Honor Code." *Journal of College Student Development,*
    vol. 48, no. 4, July/August 2007, pp. 468–80. *Academic OneFile,* go
    .galegroup.com/.

GRAMMAR IN CONTEXT

Will versus *Would*

Many people use the helping verbs *will* and *would* interchangeably. When you write a proposal, however, keep in mind that these words express different shades of meaning.

Will expresses certainty. In a list of benefits, for example, *will* indicates the benefits that will definitely occur if the proposal is accepted.

> First, an honor code will create a set of basic rules that students can follow.

> In addition, an honor code will promote honesty.

Would expresses probability. In a refutation of an opposing argument, for example, *would* indicates that another solution could possibly be more effective than the one being proposed.

> Some people argue that a plagiarism-detection tool such as Turnitin.com would be simpler and a more effective way of preventing cheating than an honor code.

◉ EXERCISE 16.5 ANALYZING A PROPOSAL ARGUMENT

The following essay, "The Road to Fear-Free Biking in Boston" by Michelle Wu, includes the basic elements of a proposal argument. Read the essay, and answer the questions that follow it, consulting the outline on page 571 if necessary.

This opinion column appeared in the *Boston Globe* on July 12, 2016.

THE ROAD TO FEAR-FREE BIKING IN BOSTON

MICHELLE WU

I don't own a bicycle. But I recently reclaimed my inner cyclist as part of the   1
Boston Green Ribbon Commission's Climate Innovations study tour to Northern Europe. Our agenda included experiencing sustainable mobility with a bicycle tour of Copenhagen, voted world's best city for cyclists.

You might expect Cycling City to be a mecca of Lycra on wheels. But   2
among the hundreds of riders on the road, no one looked like a Boston bicyclist, suited up for commuter battle.

> "Stress-free city cycling? Never heard of it."

Our tour guide, Niels, was helmet-   3
less and dressed in a sharp blue suit. Spandex and gear, he explained, are for exercise cycling in the countryside. On the daily commute to work or school, the Danish take it easy, with relaxed, stress-free city cycling.

Stress-free city cycling? Never heard of it.   4

My head filled with flashbacks to the two previous bike tours I've joined in   5
Boston: sweaty hands gripping handlebars where Massachusetts Avenue meets Columbia Road in a six-way intersection; silent prayers as cars zoomed by too close for comfort on River Street in Mattapan.

Crash fear is all too often justified in Greater Boston. In the first four   6
months of 2016, 8 people were killed and 307 injured from crashes on Boston streets, up 20 percent compared to the same period in 2015. Last month, another fatal crash in Cambridge underscored the urgency of VisionZero and making our streets safe for all.

Many of these crashes are entirely preventable with street design that puts   7
a buffer between cars and bikes—called "protected bike lanes" or "cycle tracks." Separating cars from cyclists also makes pedestrians safer, with less sidewalk riding, slower vehicle speeds, shorter crossing distances, and safer intersections.

Pedaling through Copenhagen, I saw that safety is just the baseline benefit of   8
world-class cycling infrastructure. When every street has bike lanes shielded from cars by a curb or median, cyclists ride without fear, and more people become cyclists: women, seniors, even kids riding alongside their parents. Safe infrastructure means cycling becomes an affordable transportation option open to all.

In Copenhagen, cyclists make up 45 percent of all commuters, and city   9
planners have quantified the benefits. Adding up costs avoided by reducing traffic congestion, noise, crashes, wear and tear on infrastructure, and air pollution, they estimate 64 cents of net social gain from every mile traveled by bike instead of car. More residents getting regular exercise drives down health care costs by an estimated 61 cents per mile cycled.

But fitness and sustainability won't motivate commuters to abandon their   10
cars. To get nonprofessional riders on bicycles, cities must make bike com-

mutes safe and convenient. In Copenhagen, cycle tracks receive top priority for snow clearance, followed by pedestrian sidewalks, then car lanes. Every detail of street design accommodates cyclists, from separately timed bicycle signals to plentiful bike parking at train stations.

Boston's streets, on the other hand, are designed for conflict. Painted bike 11 lanes function as space for double-parked delivery trucks, pushing cyclists into traffic. Posted signs and "sharrows" unrealistically ask drivers and cyclists to get along. The result is that only 1.9 percent of Boston commuters are willing to risk a bicycle trip—the bravest and most aggressive cyclists, who often provoke anxiety and rage in drivers.

We can do better.   12

Mayor Walsh and the Boston Transportation Department are leading 13 a comprehensive effort to engage residents in planning our transportation future. We must reimagine our streets as spaces for all, not just cars.

For Boston, the urgency goes well beyond safety. Our continued economic 14 growth depends on solving our transportation crunch. With a struggling public transit system that won't be expanding service anytime soon, already gridlocked roadways will have to absorb many of the more than hundred thousand additional commuters projected by 2030. Carving out space for protected bike lanes is the most cost-effective way to increase our transit capacity and move more people on our streets.

To be clear, building a seamless and convenient network of protected cycling 15 infrastructure will require trade-offs. On many streets, adding a cycle track means narrowing or removing car lanes, or eliminating on-street parking—scenarios that bring panic to car and business owners. Although research suggests that retail sales actually increase after switching parking for protected bike lanes, the proposals rarely see support from abutters. Yet we must acknowledge that our current transportation situation isn't working for all residents, and it will worsen unless we take bold action to empower more affordable and sustainable options.

We can solve the car-bike conflict, and the solution unlocks a brighter, 16 more inclusive economic and environmental future for Boston.

Identifying the Elements of a Proposal Argument

1. What is the essay's thesis statement? How effective do you think it is?
2. Where in the essay does Wu identify the problem she wants to solve?
3. According to Wu, why is Copenhagen a model for Boston?
4. Where does Wu present her solutions to the problems she identifies?
5. Where does Wu discuss the benefits of her proposal? What other benefits could she have addressed?
6. Where does Wu address possible arguments against her proposal? What other arguments might she have addressed? How would you refute each of these arguments?
7. Evaluate the essay's concluding statement.

Should the Government Do More to Relieve the Student-Loan Burden?

Richard Levine/AGE Fotostock

Reread the At Issue box on page 563, which gives background on whether the government should do more to relieve the student-loan burden. Then, read the sources on the following pages.

As you read this material, you will be asked to answer questions and to complete some simple activities. This work will help you understand both the content and structure of the selections. When you are finished, you will be ready to write a **proposal argument** that makes a case for or against having the government do more to relieve the student-loan burden.

SOURCES

 Rana Foroohar, "The US College Debt Bubble Is Becoming Dangerous," page 579

 Richard Vedder, "Forgive Student Loans?," page 582

 Ben Miller, "Student Debt: It's Worse than We Imagined," page 585

 Astra Taylor, "A Strike against Student Debt," page 587

 Sam Adolphsen, "Don't Blame the Government," page 590

 Visual Argument: "Student Debt Crisis Solution," page 593

This op-ed appeared in *Financial Times* on April 9, 2017.

THE US COLLEGE DEBT BUBBLE IS BECOMING DANGEROUS

RANA FOROOHAR

Rapid run-ups in debt are the single biggest predictor of market trouble. So   1
it is worth noting that over the past 10 years the amount of student loan debt
in the US has grown by 170 percent, to a whopping $1.4tn—more than car
loans, or credit card debt. Indeed, as an expert at the Consumer Financial
Protection Bureau (CFPB) recently pointed out to me, since 2008 we have
basically swapped a housing debt bubble for a student loan bubble. No wonder
NY Federal Reserve president Bill Dudley fretted last week that high levels of
student debt and default are a "headwind to economic activity."

In America, 44 million people have student debt. Eight million of those   2
borrowers are in default. That's a default rate which is still higher than pre-
crisis levels—unlike the default rate for
mortgages, credit cards, or even car loans.

Rising college education costs will not
help shrink those numbers. While the headline consumer price index is 2.7 percent,
between 2016 and 2017 published tuition and
fee prices rose by 9 percent at four-year state
institutions, and 13 percent at posher private colleges.

> "I was told to expect a $72,000 a year sticker fee for Ivy League and liberal arts colleges."   3

A large chunk of the hike was due to schools hiring more administrators   4
(who "brand build" and recruit wealthy donors) and building expensive facilities designed to lure wealthier, full-fee-paying students. This not only leads
to excess borrowing on the part of universities—a number of them are caught
up in dicey bond deals like the sort that sunk the city of Detroit—but higher
tuition for students. The average debt load individual graduates carry is up
70 percent over the past decade, to about $34,000.

Having just attended the first college preparation meeting at my daugh-   5
ter's high school, where I was told to expect a $72,000 a year sticker fee for Ivy
League and liberal arts colleges, I would feel lucky to get away with just that.

This is clearly, as Mr Dudley observed, a headwind to stronger consumer   6
spending. Growing student debt has been linked to everything from decreased
rates of first time home ownership, to higher rental prices, to lower purchases
of white goods, and all the things that people buy to fill homes. Indeed, given
their debt loads, I wonder how much of the "rent not buy" spending habits of
Millennials are a matter of choice.

But there are even more worrisome links between high student debt   7
loads and health issues like depression, and marital failures. The whole
thing is compounded by the fact that a large chunk of those holding

massive debt do not end up with degrees, having had to drop out from the stress of trying to study, work, and pay back massive loans at the same time. That means they will never even get the income boost that a college degree still provides—creating a snowball cycle of downward mobility in the country's most vulnerable populations.

How did we get here? Extreme politics played a role. In the US, the Koch 8 Brothers/Grover Norquist tax revolt camp of the Republican party has been waging a state by state war on public university funding for years now: states today provide about $2,000 less in higher education funding per student than before 2008, the lowest rate in 30 years.

Meanwhile, the subprime crisis cut the ability of parents to use home 9 equity loans to pay for their children's education (previously a common practice). This left the bulk of the burden to students, at a time when the unemployment rates for young people of all skill levels were rising.

The trend is not limited to the US, of course. In the UK and beyond, 10 completely free post-secondary education is a thing of the past. Beleaguered governments are pushing more and more of the responsibility for the things that make a person middle class—education, healthcare, and pension—on to individuals.

What are the fixes? For starters, we should look closely at the for-profit 11 sector, where default rates are more than double those at average private colleges. These institutions receive federal subsidies but typically spend a minuscule part of their budgets on instruction; in the US, nearly 50 percent goes to marketing to new students. It looks all too much like an educational Ponzi scheme.

Transparency is also key—the student loan market as a whole is hopelessly 12 opaque. In one recent US study, only a quarter of first year college students could predict their own debt load to within 10 percent of the correct amount. Truth in lending documents would help, as would loan counseling paid for by colleges. Sadly, the agency that is leading the fight on both—the CFPB—is under attack from Trump himself.

But the administration will not be able to hide from the student debt 13 bubble. In an eerie echo of the housing crisis, debt is already flowing out of the private sector, and into the public. Before 2007, most student loans were underwritten by banks or other private sector financial institutions. Today, 90 percent of new loans originate with the Department of Education. Socialization of risk continues to be the way America deals with its debt bubbles.

Would that we considered making college free, as Bernie Sanders sug- 14 gested. Even Mr Dudley called this "a reasonable conversation." That way we could socialize the benefits of education too.

⊘ AT ISSUE: SOURCES FOR DEVELOPING A PROPOSAL ARGUMENT

1. What does Foroohar mean when she says, "we have basically swapped a housing debt bubble for a student loan bubble" (para. 1)?

2. In the first ten paragraphs of her essay, Foroohar examines the problems associated with the student loan situation. Why do you think she spent so much time discussing these problems?

3. In paragraphs 3 and 4, Foroohar discusses the increasing cost of college tuition, but she never says what colleges should do about this situation. Should she have? What suggestions could she have made?

4. In paragraph 5, Foroohar says that she has just attended a college preparation meeting at her daughter's high school. Why does she include this information?

5. According to Foroohar, how can the loan problem be fixed? How convincing are her suggestions?

6. How optimistic is Foroohar about the government's ability to solve the student-debt problem? How do you know?

7. In her conclusion, Foroohar raises the possibility of making college free. Is this an effective way for her to end her essay? Explain.

The blog entry was posted to *National Review Online* on October 11, 2011.

FORGIVE STUDENT LOANS?

RICHARD VEDDER

As the Wall Street protests grow and expand beyond New York, growing 1 scrutiny of the nascent movement is warranted. What do these folks want? Alongside their ranting about the inequality of incomes, the alleged inordinate power of Wall Street and large corporations, the high level of unemployment, and the like, one policy goal ranks high with most protesters: the forgiveness of student-loan debt. In an informal survey of over 50 protesters in New York last Tuesday, blogger and equity research analyst David Maris found 93 percent of them advocated student-loan forgiveness. An online petition drive advocating student-loan forgiveness has gathered an impressive number of signatures (over 442,000). This is an issue that resonates with many Americans.

Economist Justin Wolfers recently opined that "this is the worst idea ever." 2 I think it is actually the second-worst idea ever—the worst was the creation of federally subsidized student loans in the first place. Under current law, when the feds (who have basically taken over the student-loan industry) make a loan, the size of the U.S. budget deficit rises, and the government borrows additional funds, very often from foreign investors. We are borrowing from the Chinese to finance school attendance by a predominantly middle-class group of Americans.

But that is the tip of the iceberg: Though the ostensible objective of the 3 loan program is to increase the proportion of adult Americans with college degrees, over 40 percent of those pursuing a bachelor's degree fail to receive one within six years. And default is a growing problem with student loans.

Further, it's not clear that college imparts much of value to the average 4 student. The typical college student spends less than 30 hours a week, 32 weeks a year, on all academic matters—class attendance, writing papers, studying for exams, etc. They spend about half as much time on school as their parents spend working. If Richard Arum and Josipa Roksa (authors of *Academically Adrift*) are even roughly correct, today's students typically learn little in the way of critical learning or writing skills while in school.

Moreover, the student-loan program has proven an ineffective way to 5 achieve one of its initial aims, a goal also of the Wall Street protesters: increasing economic opportunity for the poor. In 1970, when federal student-loan and grant programs were in their infancy, about 12 percent of college graduates came from the bottom one-fourth of the income distribution. While people from all social classes are more likely to go to college today, the poor haven't gained nearly as much ground as the rich have: With the nation awash in nearly a trillion dollars in student-loan debt (more even than credit-card

obligations), the proportion of bachelor's-degree holders coming from the
bottom one-fourth of the income distribution has fallen to around 7 percent.

> "The sins of the loan
> program are many. Let's
> briefly mention just five."

6

The sins of the loan program are
many. Let's briefly mention just five.

First, artificially low interest rates are set by the federal government—
they are fixed by law rather than market forces. Low-interest-
rate mortgage loans resulting from loose Fed policies and the
government-sponsored enterprises Fannie Mae and Freddie Mac
spurred the housing bubble that caused the 2008 financial crisis.
Arguably, federal student financial assistance is creating a second
bubble in higher education.

Second, loan terms are invariant, with students with poor prospects of
graduating and getting good jobs often borrowing at the same interest rates as those with excellent prospects (e.g., electrical-engineering
majors at MIT).

Third, the availability of cheap loans has almost certainly contributed to
the tuition explosion—college prices are going up even more than
health-care prices.

Fourth, at present the loans are made by a monopoly provider, the same
one that gave us such similar inefficient and costly monopolistic
behemoths as the U.S. Postal Service.

Fifth, the student-loan and associated Pell Grant programs spawned the
notorious FAFSA° form that requires families to reveal all sorts of
financial information—information that colleges use to engage in
ruthless price discrimination via tuition discounting, charging
wildly different amounts to students depending on how much
their parents can afford to pay. It's a soak-the-rich scheme on
steroids.

*Free Application for Federal
Student Aid*

Still, for good or ill, we have this unfortunate program. Wouldn't loan 7
forgiveness provide some stimulus to a moribund economy? The Wall Street
protesters argue that if debt-burdened young persons were free of this alba-
tross, they would start spending more on goods and services, stimulating
employment. Yet we demonstrated with stimulus packages in 2008 and 2009
(not to mention the 1930s, Japan in the 1990s, etc.) that giving people more
money to spend will not bring recovery. But even if it did, why should we
give a break to this particular group of individuals, who disproportionately
come from prosperous families to begin with? Why give them assistance while
those who have dutifully repaid their loans get none? An arguably more equitable and efficient method of stimulus would be to drop dollars out of airplanes
over low-income areas.

Moreover, this idea has ominous implications for the macro economy. 8 Who would take the loss from the unanticipated non-repayment of a trillion dollars? If private financial institutions are liable for some of it, it could kill them, triggering another financial crisis. If the federal government shoulders the entire burden, we are adding a trillion or so more dollars in liabilities to a government already grievously overextended (upwards of $100 trillion in liabilities counting Medicare, Social Security, and the national debt), almost certainly leading to more debt downgrades, which could trigger investor panic. This idea is breathtaking in terms of its naïveté and stupidity.

The demonstrators say that selfish plutocrats are ruining our economy 9 and creating an unjust society. Rather, a group of predominantly rather spoiled and coddled young persons, long favored and subsidized by the American taxpayer, are complaining that society has not given them enough—they want the taxpayer to foot the bill for their years of limited learning and heavy partying while in college. Hopefully, this burst of dimwittery should not pass muster even in our often dysfunctional Congress.

⊘ AT ISSUE: SOURCES FOR DEVELOPING A PROPOSAL ARGUMENT

1. According to Vedder, forgiveness of student debt is "the second-worst idea ever" (para. 2). Why? What is the worst idea?

2. In paragraphs 3–6, Vedder examines the weaknesses of the federally subsidized student-loan program. List some of the weaknesses he identifies.

3. Why do you think Vedder waits until paragraph 7 to discuss debt forgiveness? Should he have discussed it sooner?

4. Summarize Vedder's primary objection to forgiving student debt. Do you agree with him? How would you refute his objection?

5. Throughout his essay, Vedder uses rather strong language to characterize those who disagree with him. For example, in paragraph 8, he calls the idea of forgiving student loans "breathtaking in terms of its naïveté and stupidity." In paragraph 9, he calls demonstrators "spoiled and coddled young persons" and labels Congress "dysfunctional." Does this language help or hurt Vedder's case? Would more neutral words and phrases have been more effective? Why or why not?

6. How would Vedder respond to Astra Taylor's solution to the student-loan crisis (p. 587)? Are there any points that Taylor makes with which Vedder might agree?

This commentary was published in the *New York Times* on August 26, 2018.

STUDENT DEBT: IT'S WORSE THAN WE IMAGINED

BEN MILLER

Millions of students will arrive on college campuses soon, and they will share a 1 similar burden: college debt. The typical student borrower will take out $6,600 in a single year, averaging $22,000 in debt by graduation, according to the National Center for Education Statistics.

There are two ways to measure whether borrowers can repay those loans: 2 There's what the federal government looks at to judge colleges, and then there's the real story. The latter is coming to light, and it's not pretty.

> "The new data makes clear that the federal government overlooks early warning signs." 3

Consider the official statistics: Of borrowers who started repaying in 2012, just over 10 percent had defaulted three years later. That's not too bad—but it's not the whole story. Federal data never before released shows that the default rate continued climbing to 16 percent over the next two years, after official tracking ended, meaning more than 841,000 borrowers were in default. Nearly as many were severely delinquent or not repaying their loans (for reasons besides going back to school or being in the military). The share of students facing serious struggles rose to 30 percent over all.

Collectively, these borrowers owed over $23 billion, including more than 4 $9 billion in default.

Nationally, those are crisis-level results, and they reveal how colleges are ben- 5 efiting from billions in financial aid while students are left with debt they cannot repay. The Department of Education recently provided this new data on over 5,000 schools across the country in response to my Freedom of Information Act request.

The new data makes clear that the federal government overlooks early 6 warning signs by focusing solely on default rates over the first three years of repayment. That's the time period Congress requires the Department of Education to use when calculating default rates.

At that time, about one-quarter of the cohort—or nearly 1.3 million 7 borrowers—were not in default, but were either severely delinquent or not paying their loans. Two years later, many of these borrowers were either still not paying or had defaulted. Nearly 280,000 borrowers defaulted between years three and five.

Federal laws attempting to keep schools accountable are not doing enough 8 to stop loan problems. The law requires that all colleges participating in the student loan program keep their share of borrowers who default below 30 percent for three consecutive years or 40 percent in any single year. We can consider anything above 30 percent to be a "high" default rate. That's a low bar.

Among the group who started repaying in 2012, just 93 of their colleges 9 had high default rates after three years and 15 were at immediate risk of losing access to aid. Two years later, after the Department of Education stopped tracking results, 636 schools had high default rates.

For-profit institutions have particularly awful results. Five years into 10 repayment, 44 percent of borrowers at these schools faced some type of loan distress, including 25 percent who defaulted. Most students who defaulted between three and five years in repayment attended a for-profit college.

The secret to avoiding accountability? Colleges are aggressively push- 11 ing borrowers to use repayment options known as deferments or forbearances that allow borrowers to stop their payments without going into delinquency or defaulting. Nearly 20 percent of borrowers at schools that had high default rates at year five but not at year three used one of these payment-pausing options.

The federal government cannot keep turning a blind eye while almost 12 one-third of student loan borrowers struggle. Fortunately, efforts to rewrite federal higher-education laws present an opportunity to address these short-comings. This should include losing federal aid if borrowers are not repaying their loans—even if they do not default. Loan performance should also be tracked for at least five years instead of three.

The federal government, states, and institutions also need to make sig- 13 nificant investments in college affordability to reduce the number of students who need a loan in the first place. Too many borrowers and defaulters are low-income students, the very people who would receive only grant aid under a rational system for college financing. Forcing these students to borrow has turned one of America's best investments in socioeconomic mobility—college—into a debt trap for far too many.

⊘ AT ISSUE: SOURCES FOR DEVELOPING A PROPOSAL ARGUMENT

1. In paragraph 2, Miller says, "There's what the federal government looks at to judge colleges, and then there's the real story." What does he mean by "the real story"?

2. Why, according to Miller, is the amount of student debt at "crisis level" (para. 5)?

3. What early warning signs concerning student debt does the federal government overlook? Why is this a problem?

4. How do colleges avoid accountability? Why do you think for-profit colleges have "particularly awful results" (10)?

5. Why, according to Miller, is the current student-loan program unfair to low-income students?

6. Has Miller defined the problem he is addressing in enough detail? Explain.

7. How does Miller propose to solve the burgeoning student-loan problem? Are his suggestions reasonable? Do they seem feasible?

Taylor's op-ed appeared on February 27, 2015, in the *New York Times*.

A STRIKE AGAINST STUDENT DEBT

ASTRA TAYLOR

This week a group of former students calling themselves the Corinthian 1
15 announced that they were committing a new kind of civil disobedience:
a debt strike. They are refusing to make any more payments on their federal
student loans.

Along with many others, they found themselves in significant debt after 2
attending programs at the Corinthian Colleges, a collapsed chain of for-profit
schools that the Consumer Financial Protection Bureau has accused of running a "predatory lending scheme." While the bureau has announced a plan
to reduce some of the students' private loan debts, the strikers are demanding
that the Department of Education use its authority to discharge their federal
loans as well.

These 15 students are members of the Debt Collective, an organization 3
that evolved out of a project I helped start in 2012 called the Rolling Jubilee.
Until now, we have worked in the secondary debt market, using crowdfunded
donations to buy portfolios of medical and educational debts for pennies on
the dollar, just as debt collectors do.

Only, instead of collecting on them, we abolish them, operating under the 4
belief that people shouldn't go into debt for getting sick or going to school.
This week, we erased $13 million of "unpaid tuition receivables" belonging to
9,438 people associated with Everest College, a Corinthian subsidiary.

But this approach has its limits. Federal loans, for example, are guaranteed 5
by the government, and debtors can be freed of them—via bankruptcy—only
under exceedingly rare circumstances. That means they aren't sold at steep
discounts and remain out of our reach. What's more, America's mountain of
student debt is too immense for the Jubilee to make a significant dent in it.

Real change will require more organized actions like those taken by the 6
Corinthian 15.

If anyone deserves debt relief— 7
morally and legally—it's these students. For-profit colleges are notorious
for targeting low-income minorities,
single mothers, and veterans with high-

> "If anyone deserves debt relief—morally and legally—it's these students."

pressure, misleading recruitment techniques. The schools slurp up about a
quarter of all federal student aid money, more than $30 billion a year, while their
students run up a lifetime of debt for a degree arguably worth no more than a
high school diploma.

But for-profit schools aren't the only problem. Degrees earned from tradi- 8 tional colleges can also leave students unfairly burdened.

Today, a majority of outstanding student loans are in deferral, delin- 9 quency, or default. As state funding for education has plummeted, public colleges have raised tuition. Private university costs are skyrocketing, too, rising roughly 25 percent over the last decade. That's why every class of graduates is more in the red than the last.

Modest fixes are not enough. Consider the interest rate tweaks or income- 10 based repayment plans offered by the Obama administration. They lighten the debt burden on some—but not everyone qualifies. They do nothing to address the $165 billion private loan market, where interest rates are often the most punishing, or how higher education is financed.

Americans now owe $1.2 trillion in student debt, a number predicted by 11 the think tank Demos to climb to $2 trillion by 2025. What if more people from all types of educational institutions and with all kinds of debts followed the example of the Corinthian 15, and strategically refused to pay back their loans? This would transform the debts into leverage to demand better terms, or even a better way of funding higher education altogether.

The quickest fix would be a full-scale student debt cancellation. For 12 students at predatory colleges like Corinthian, this could be done immediately by the Department of Education. For the broader population of students, it would most likely take an act of Congress.

Student debt cancellation would mean forgone revenue in the near term, 13 but in the long term it could be an economic stimulus worth much more than the immediate cost. Money not spent paying off loans would be spent elsewhere. In that situation, lenders, debt collectors, servicers, guaranty agencies, asset-backed security investors, and others who profit from student loans would suffer the most from debt forgiveness.

We also need to bring back the option of a public, tuition-free college 14 education once represented by institutions like the University of California, which charged only token fees. By the Rolling Jubilee's estimate, every public two- and four-year college and university in the United States could be made tuition-free by redirecting all current educational subsidies and tax exemptions straight to them and adding approximately $15 billion in annual spending.

This might sound like a lot, but it's a small price to pay to restore America's 15 place on the long list of countries that provide tuition-free education.

To get there, more groups like the Corinthian 15 will have to show 16 that they are willing to throw a wrench in the gears of the system by threatening to withhold payment on their debt. Everyone deserves a quality education. We need to come up with a better way to provide it than debt and default.

⊘ AT ISSUE: SOURCES FOR DEVELOPING A PROPOSAL ARGUMENT

1. Taylor begins her essay by discussing the Corinthian 15. How does this focus help her introduce the problem she wants to solve?

2. Paraphrase Taylor's thesis by filling in the following template.

   The Department of Education should solve the student debt crisis

   by _____

   _____.

3. What two problems does Taylor discuss? Does she describe them in enough detail? Explain.

4. What solutions does Taylor offer? How feasible are these solutions?

5. At what points in her essay does Taylor address objections to her proposal? Does she address the most important objections? If not, what other objections should she have addressed?

6. Taylor uses three terms that might be unfamiliar to some readers.

   - *secondary debt market* (para. 3)

   - *crowdfunded donations* (3)

   - *unpaid tuition receivables* (4)

   Look up these terms, and then reread the paragraphs in which they appear. Do these terms help Taylor develop her argument, or could she have made her points without them?

7. What assumptions does Taylor assume are self-evident and need no proof? Do you agree? If not, what evidence should Taylor have included to support these assumptions?

This opinion piece was published online on May 1, 2012, at TheMaineWire.com.

DON'T BLAME THE GOVERNMENT

SAM ADOLPHSEN

I still remember the day. 1

I was sitting at my kitchen table, pen in hand, and I signed the dotted line 2 to borrow a significant amount of money to pay for my first year of college.

The funny thing was, despite what you might hear in the media these 3 days, no one was standing over my shoulder forcing me to. No government official told me I had to borrow the money. It was my decision then and it's my debt today. I weighed the price of borrowing against the value of a secondary degree, and I chose education.

My decision, my responsibility. 4

That's not what you are hearing today from most of America's youth 5 though. There are rallies in the streets of Portland, and in cities across America, with "Occupy" inspired students and graduates whining about their debt and how they need a way out. Students that have borrowed too much, of their own free will, for degrees that haven't led to a job, are now demanding a handout.

My generation is looking for a bailout. It doesn't matter that many of them 6 are in tough positions, loaded with debt, because they made poor choices. It doesn't matter that borrowing money is a personal decision and requires personal responsibility. They want the easy way out.

> "They want the easy way out."

Take the example of Stephanie, featured in 7 a recent story from the *Philadelphia Inquirer* that re-ran in the *Portland Press Herald*. Stephanie, the story laments, owes over $100,000 in student loans. Poor Stephanie. Then we find out that, for one, Stephanie is in law school (really, becoming a lawyer costs money? Who knew . . .) and even worse, we find out that Stephanie, had a FREE RIDE to Rutgers, but instead chose to borrow money to go to a smaller private school because she "fell in love with it."

So Stephanie didn't have to take on student loan debt. She chose to. Why 8 should I feel sorry for her? Why should the government lower her interest rates so taxpayers can help her pay those loans back? It's her debt. Not the taxpayers of America.

Other decisions factor into this discussion as well. The *Press Herald* ran 9 another story a couple days ago, highlighting several students who carried student loan debt. One of the students was a Social Worker who owes $97,000 in student loan debt. A cursory search of the internet will tell you that social workers don't earn enough to warrant that kind of debt. The same goes for a Maine student who will owe more than $27,000 for his degree in Philosophy.

Seriously, I know Walt Disney told my generation we can "be whatever we 10 want to be" if we "believe in ourselves" but borrowing $27,000 for a career in philosophy . . . in Maine? That's a questionable decision at best, and it's not the government's fault.

The government already stepped in quietly and took over the student loan 11 industry as part of Obamacare, and they already used taxpayer money to lower interest rates on current government student loans to 3.4 percent. Now those taxpayer subsidized interest rates are set to expire, and more than double, and the "gimme gimme" nation doesn't like it.

Naturally, those who want government to take care of them are calling 12 for the interest rates to be held at 3.4 percent, with the taxpayers chipping in for the difference. But make no mistake, even if those rates are held, this won't be the end of the discussion. Now that the government holds all student loans, they have the opportunity to "bail out students" by forgiving loans. "Occupy" camps in a park near you are already chanting to the beat of the "forgive all student loans" drum, and you can expect that cry to get louder this summer. (It's warm so they can start "occupying" again.)

Now don't get me wrong. I agree that college costs are too high. And that 13 IS partly government's fault. Consider the University of Maine, piling on raises for their teachers, while simultaneously jacking up rates for students. In just a few years, university salaries were up 29 percent overall while at the same time tuition costs jumped 30 percent. That's unacceptable and it's a problem that needs to be addressed.

It's also the government's fault that anybody considers a bailout a legitimate 14 solution to our problems. The bank bailouts and Obama's absolute boondoggle "American Recovery Act" set the precedent and taught my generation that poor decisions and failure can be fixed with a government check. Shame on them for that, and shame on us for looking to government to bail out students now.

Ultimately, students and their parents make the decision to borrow money 15 for school. And it's their responsibility to pay it back. I'm tired of the whining, I'm tired of the blame game, and I'm tired of people relying on government to bail them out.

It's your debt. Pay it yourself.   16

◑ AT ISSUE: SOURCES FOR DEVELOPING A PROPOSAL ARGUMENT

1. Adolphsen states his thesis in paragraph 4: "My decision, my responsibility." In your own words, write an alternate one-sentence thesis statement for this essay on the lines below.

Thesis Statement: _____

_____

_____ .

Is your thesis more or less effective than Adolphsen's? Explain.

2. Adolphsen uses two examples to support his point that some people in his generation "want the easy way out" (para. 6). Are these examples enough to support his point? What other evidence could he have provided?

3. Could Adolphsen be accused of oversimplifying a complex issue? In other words, does he make **hasty or sweeping generalizations**? Does he **beg the question**? If so, where?

4. Where in his essay does Adolphsen concede a point to those who disagree with him? How effectively does he deal with this point?

5. How does Adolphsen characterize those who want student-debt relief? Are his characterizations fair? Accurate? Do these characterizations help or hurt his credibility? Explain.

6. In what sense is Adolphsen's essay a refutation of Astra Taylor's essay (p. 587)?

VISUAL ARGUMENT: STUDENT DEBT
CRISIS SOLUTION

Richard Levine/AGE Fotostock

⊖ AT ISSUE: SOURCES FOR DEVELOPING A
PROPOSAL ARGUMENT

1. This image, which appeared at the beginning of this chapter, shows
   protesters rallying on April 25, 2012, the day that student loan debt
   reached $1 trillion. The 1T Day movement proposed that government
   should cover higher education costs, with any necessary loans to be
   granted without interest, and for debt forgiveness of past loans. How
   do the images in their protests connect to this proposal?

2. Is it easy to understand the group's aims and solutions from their
   signs and props?

3. How do the images in the protest help support the argument and proposal being made by this group?

TEMPLATE FOR WRITING A PROPOSAL ARGUMENT

Write a one-paragraph proposal argument in which you consider the topic, "Should the Government Do More to Relieve the Student-Loan Burden?" Follow the template below, filling in the blanks to create your proposal.

The current federal student-loan program has some problems that must be addressed. For example, _____ _____. In order to address this situation, _____. First, _____ _____ _____. Second, _____ _____ _____. Finally, _____ _____ _____.

Not everyone agrees that this is the way to solve these problems, however. Some say _____ _____ _____. Others point out that _____ _____. These objections make sense, but _____ _____ _____. All in all, _____ _____ _____ _____.

◉ EXERCISE 16.6 EXPANDING YOUR PROPOSAL

Ask several of your instructors and your classmates whether they think the government should do more to relieve the student-loan burden. Then, add their responses to the paragraph you wrote using the template above.

◉ EXERCISE 16.7 WRITING A PROPOSAL

Write a proposal arguing that the government should do more to relieve the student-loan burden. Be sure to present examples from your own experience to support your arguments. (If you like, you may incorporate the material you developed for the template and for Exercise 16.7 into your essay.) Cite the readings on pages 578–592, and be sure to document your sources and include a works-cited page. (See Chapter 10 for information on documenting sources.)

◉ EXERCISE 16.8 REVIEWING THE FOUR PILLARS OF ARGUMENT

Review the four pillars of argument discussed in Chapter 1. Does your essay include all four elements of an effective argument? Add anything that is missing.

◉ WRITING ASSIGNMENTS: PROPOSAL ARGUMENTS

1. Each day, students at college cafeterias throw away hundreds of pounds of uneaten food. A number of colleges have found that by simply eliminating the use of trays, they can cut out much of this waste. At one college, for example, students who did not use trays wasted 14.4 percent less food for lunch and 47.1 percent less for dinner than those who did use trays. Write a proposal to your college or university in which you recommend eliminating trays from dining halls. Use your own experiences as well as information from your research and from interviews with other students to support your position. Be sure to address one or two arguments against your position.

2. Look around your campus, and find a service that you think should be improved. It could be the financial aid office, the student health services, or the writing center. Then, write an essay in which you identify the specific problem (or problems) and suggest a solution. If you wish, interview a few of your friends to get some information that you can use to support your proposal.

3. Assume that your college or university has just received a million-dollar donation from an anonymous benefactor. Your school has decided to solicit proposals from both students and faculty on ways to spend the money. Write a proposal to the president of your school in which you identify a good use for this windfall. Make sure you identify a problem, present a solution, and discuss the advantages of your proposal. If possible, address one or two arguments against your proposal—for example, that the money could be put to better use somewhere else.

Part 5 Review: Combining Argumentative Strategies

In Chapters 12–16, you have seen how argumentative essays can use different strategies to serve particular purposes. The discussions and examples in these chapters highlighted the use of a single strategy for a given essay. However, many (if not most) argumentative essays combine several different strategies.

For example, an argument recommending that the United States implement a national sales tax could be largely a **proposal argument**, but it could present a **cause-and-effect argument** to illustrate the likely benefits of the proposal, and it could also use an **evaluation argument** to demonstrate the relative advantages of this tax as compared to other kinds of taxes.

The following two essays—"RFK's Still a Leadership Role Model for Youth" and "Fulfill George Washington's Last Wish—a National University"— illustrate how various strategies can work together in a single argument. (The first essay includes marginal annotations that identify the different strategies the writer uses to advance his argument.)

This article first appeared in the *Atlanta Journal-Constitution* on June 8, 2018.

RFK'S STILL A LEADERSHIP ROLE MODEL FOR YOUTH

ROBERT M. FRANKLIN

At a moment when moral leadership is desperately needed in America and 1 across the globe, we need to remember Bobby Kennedy and his style of moral leadership. Another American hero who was killed by a gun in 1968 at the age of 42, U.S. Senator Kennedy demonstrated the art of bringing diverse people together for the purpose of improving the nation, and he repeatedly expressed his great faith that young people and students would lead us to achieve a better world.

Proposal argument

Fifty years later, today's students are mobilizing to make changes in 2 gun laws, police behavior, respecting women, the environment, and many other social concerns. They need to take a page from the playbook of Bobby Kennedy.

For years, I have anticipated and dreaded the arrival of 2018, a perfectly 3 ambivalent time zone of ecstasy and pain. We are here now, and far from being re-traumatized by painful memories, I am grateful for the lives of, and surprised by the abiding relevance of Bobby Kennedy and Martin King.

Ethical argument

In times of moral ambiguity and deep division, we need moral leaders 4 who can bring us together and offer guidance, correction, and hope. That's what Kennedy did on the night that Rev. King was murdered just two short months before his own assassination.

> "In times of moral ambiguity and deep division, we need moral leaders who can bring us together and offer guidance, correction, and hope."

I was a high school student in 5 Chicago and felt crushed by the news of King's death in Memphis. Searching for a way to make sense of the senseless theft of the life of another good man, on the radio I heard the soft and wavering but confident remarks of Robert F. Kennedy as he spoke impromptu to a crowd of people gathering in the streets of Indianapolis.

Kennedy did what moral leaders do. He started with empathy. He reminded 6 people, especially African Americans angered by King's murder that his own brother was also murdered, but this did not cause him to hate. His four-minute speech became King's first eulogy as he said, "What we need in the United States is not division; what we need in the United States is not hatred; what we need in the United States is not violence or lawlessness; but love and wisdom, and compassion toward one another, and a feeling of justice toward those who still suffer within our country, whether they be white or they be black."

In a haunting coincidence in 1966, almost two years to the day of his own 7 assassination, Bobby spoke to members of the National Union of South African Students at the University of Cape Town as they mobilized to dismantle apartheid.

In 2006, my wife and I were in South Africa for the 40th anniversary of 8 that speech and visited with the senator's daughter, Rory Kennedy, after she delivered a speech to remember the occasion. We all celebrated his empathy and his truthfulness as he spoke of America's freedom struggle and the courageous black and white students who were dismantling racism in America.

Bobby said, "Each nation has different obstacles and different goals, 9   Ethical argument shaped by the vagaries of history and of experience. Yet as I talk to young people around the world I am impressed not by the diversity but by the closeness of their goals, their desires and their concerns and their hope for the future." Then he cited the many examples of social evil in the world that "reflect the imperfections of human justice" and reminded them that the youth today represent "the only true international community" as he applauded their willingness to make sacrifices on behalf of a better society.

I teach classes at Emory University that attempt to understand the prin- 10 Definition argument ciples and practices of moral leaders. We delve into their personal qualities or virtues, their ways of thinking about justice, and the outcomes they have. We believe that they have integrity, courage, and imagination for serving the common good while inviting others to join them. They have a knack for standing in places of suffering and conflict to offer words of hope, justice, and the possibility of reconciliation.

In so many ways, Bobby Kennedy represented the best qualities of a moral 11 Evaluation argument leader. He had his faults and never pretended to be perfect, but he possessed integrity, courage, and imagination aimed at serving the common good.

Bobby and Martin were relatively privileged men. Both were well- 12 Evaluation argument educated, reared by loving parents in comfortable households, and could have enjoyed lives of personal prosperity, fame, and power. Instead, both responded to the call of conscience and crisis in their democracy. Their service, their sacrifice, and their service merit our attention today and compel us to dare greatness once again by repairing the faults of the promising nation that they loved.

❍ REVIEW EXERCISE 1

1. In "RFK's Still a Leadership Role Model for Youth," Robert M. Franklin uses various argumentative strategies, which are identified in the annotations. Why is each strategy used?

2. How does each strategy support the argument the writer makes?

3. Does one particular strategy seem to dominate the essay—that is, do you see it as largely a proposal argument, an ethical argument, or something else?

4. What effects did Robert Kennedy's speeches have on Franklin? Do paragraphs 5 through 9, which explain Franklin's reactions, develop a cause-and-effect argument? Explain.

This article first appeared on CNN.com on March 2, 2015.

FULFILL GEORGE WASHINGTON'S LAST WISH—A NATIONAL UNIVERSITY

KEVIN CAREY

In 1796, in his final annual address to Congress, President George Washington 1
called for the creation of:

". . . a National University; and also a Military Academy. The desirableness 2
of both these Institutions, has so constantly increased with every new view
I have taken of the subject, that I cannot omit the opportunity of once for all,
recalling your attention to them."

The Military Academy was soon built at West Point. But despite leaving 3
$22,222 for its establishment (a lot of money back then) in his last will and
testament, Washington's National University never came to pass.

Instead, lawmakers chose to rely on state governments and religious 4
denominations to build and finance new colleges and universities.

Today, the American higher education system is in crisis. The price of col- 5
lege has grown astronomically, forcing students and parents to take out loans that
now exceed $1.2 trillion in outstanding debt. Many of those loans are falling into
default as graduates struggle to find work. The latest research suggests that our
vaunted universities are producing graduates who haven't learned very much.

The time has come to revive George Washington's great idea, in 21st cen- 6
tury form. Advances in information technology that would have seemed like
pure magic in colonial times mean we can now create a 21st Century National
University that will help millions of students get a high-quality, low-cost
college education—without hiring any professors, building any buildings, or
costing the taxpayers a dime.

Washington's Role

To see how, it helps to understand the
three ways the federal government currently supports higher education.

Two of them are well known. First,
the Defense Department, National Institutes of Health, and other federal agencies spend hundreds of billions of dollars
financing university-based research,
contributing to countless scientific

"Second, the U.S. 7
Department of Education
provides $150 billion 8
annually in grants and
loans to help students pay
for college."

breakthroughs and commercial innovations. Second, the U.S. Department of
Education provides $150 billion annually in grants and loans to help students
pay for college.

As tuitions rise and states continue to slash funding for public universities 9 (Wisconsin Gov. Scott Walker recently proposed $300 million in new cuts), the federal government has become the college financier of last resort.

But there is a third essential federal role in higher education that is far less 10 well known. In many ways, it's the most important of them all, and the key to creating a 21st Century National University. In addition to funding colleges, the federal government approves colleges.

It does this through a little-understood process called accreditation. To be 11 eligible for those billions of research and financial aid dollars, colleges must be accredited. Technically, accreditors are nonprofit organizations run by consortia of existing colleges. But in order to make a college eligible for federal money, accreditors must first be approved by the federal government. Without that approval and the money that goes along with it, both colleges and accreditors would immediately close up shop. In other words, Uncle Sam ultimately decides who gets to be an American college and grant college degrees.

A University with No Buildings

So, here's the big idea: In order to build a 21st Century National University, all 12 the federal government has to do is something very simple: Approve itself.

In George Washington's days, this would have been only the first step 13 of a process subsequently involving the construction of an actual university. Doing this today would accomplish little in solving the higher education crisis, because physical universities cost billions of dollars to construct from scratch and can still only enroll a handful of the many students who can't afford a good education.

Fortunately, there's no need for new buildings—or, for that matter, admin- 14 istrators, libraries, faculty, and all the rest. Existing colleges and universities, flush with federal dollars, have already created all the essential building blocks for National U. Anyone with an internet connection can log on to Coursera, edX, saylor.org, and many other websites offering high-quality online courses, created by many of the world's greatest universities and taught by tenured professors, for free.

Tens of millions of students have already signed up for these courses over 15 the last four years. Yet enrollment in traditional colleges hasn't flagged, and prices have continued to rise. The reason is clear. The free college providers can't (or won't) give online students the one thing they need more than anything else: a college degree. Elite universities like Harvard and Stanford don't want to dilute their exclusive brands. Nonelite universities don't want to give away something they're currently selling for a lot of money.

That's where the federal government comes in. With some authoriz- 16 ing language from Congress and a small, one-time start-up budget, the U.S. Department of Education could create a nonprofit, bipartisan organization with only two missions: approving courses and granting degrees.

Don't worry, federal bureaucrats won't be in charge of academic mat- 17
ters. Instead, National U. would hire teams of leading scholars to evaluate and
approve courses. Some of the decisions shouldn't be difficult.

For example, this week, edX is launching a free, nine-week-long online 18
course called "Introduction to Computational Thinking and Data Science." It
will be taught by Dr. Eric Grimson, who is the chancellor of the renowned
Massachusetts Institute of Technology, and Dr. John Guttag, who leads the
MIT Computer Science and Artificial Intelligence Laboratory's Data Driven
Medical Research Group. The course materials mirror those taught to
some of the smartest students in the world on MIT's campus in Cambridge,
Massachusetts.

It seems likely that this is a good course.   19

A Degree from National U.

National U., moreover, wouldn't be limited to courses from existing colleges. 20
Any higher education provider, public or private sector, could submit a course
for approval. Those that aren't already accredited would pay a fee to cover the
cost of evaluation.

National U. would also map out which courses students need to take to 21
earn an associate or bachelor's degree. This won't be difficult, since existing
colleges have already established a standard set of requirements: a certain
number of approved lower- and upper-division courses, plus an approved
sequence in an academic major, adding up to 60 or 120 credits. Once students
complete the credits, National U. will grant them a degree.

While many of the courses will be free, students will bear small costs for 22
taking exams through secure online channels or in-person testing facilities.
(Textbooks will be free and open-source.) Students will also pay a modest fee
of a few hundred dollars for the degree itself, enough to defray the operating
costs of National U.

Lower-income students will be able to pay for those expenses using the 23
same federal grant and loan programs they currently use to pay tuition at
accredited colleges. Since National U. will likely be much cheaper, this will
actually save the taxpayers money in the long run.

If it all sounds too good to be true, keep in mind that free online courses 24
from the likes of MIT are a very recent phenomenon. Higher education policies just haven't adapted to them—yet.

The federal government's higher education approval powers are long- 25
established. Now it just needs to use them on behalf of students, instead of
traditional colleges and universities that are charging far too much. George
Washington was right all along.

⊘ REVIEW EXERCISE 2

1. What proposal argument does Carey make in this essay?

2. Label the argumentative strategies used in this essay, following the model of Robert M. Franklin's essay on page 598.

3. Where does Carey make a cause-and-effect argument? What causes and effects does he identify?

4. Where does Carey make an evaluation argument? What is he evaluating? On what criteria does he base his evaluation?

5. Does Carey include a definition argument in this essay? Does he include an ethical argument? If so, where? If not, where could he add these strategies?

6. How does each strategy contribute to the overall effectiveness of Carey's argument?

Debates, Casebooks, and Classic Arguments

David Paul Morris/Bloomberg/Getty Images

Should We Embrace Self-Driving Cars?

When writers and filmmakers imagine the future, they often include self-driving cars as part of their creations. The fictional worlds of Isaac Asimov, Philip K. Dick, Ray Bradbury, and many others contain detailed accounts of these vehicles. Such animate machines may be a convenience, as in the film *Total Recall* (1990), or they may be sinister, as in *Maximum Overdrive* (1986). But despite their futuristic connotations, driverless cars have a long pedigree in the history of technology and transportation. For example, in 1926, the electrical engineer Francis Houdina demonstrated a driverless automobile on the streets of New York: his radio-controlled car (The American Wonder) dazzled onlookers on Broadway and Fifth Avenue—before crashing into another car full of photographers. Since then, Japan's Tsukuba Mechanical Engineering Laboratory, Carnegie Mellon University, Mercedes-Benz, and other companies have developed and refined various prototypes. Now, however, these cars are on the verge of becoming a practical means of transportation, not just novelties. Google and Tesla have invested heavily into autonomous vehicles, and Uber has put these cars into service in a limited number of cities.

Supporters of self-driving cars tout their advantages: the elimination of human error from driving, fewer accidents, decreased traffic jams, and additional mobility for the elderly. Of course, there are potential disadvantages too. Uber's tests recently resulted in the first pedestrian death caused by a self-driving car; the accident occurred in 2018, when a forty-eight-year-old woman was killed in Arizona. In addition, autonomous vehicles raise numerous questions. Americans have long associated cars with individualism and freedom: are they willing to give up their autonomy to self-driving machines? How will government agencies and insurance underwriters treat these cars? What about the taxi drivers, truckers, and others whose jobs autonomous vehicles may eliminate?

The two essays that follow explore the ethical challenges presented by self-driving cars. For Karl Iagnemma, who supports these vehicles, abstract philosophical thought experiments are of little use when examining the practical effects of this evolving technology. In contrast, Olivia Goldhill says that driverless cars will allow philosophers to see their theories tested in a "very real way."

This piece was posted on the World Economic Forum on January 21, 2018.

WHY WE HAVE THE ETHICS OF SELF-DRIVING CARS ALL WRONG

KARL IAGNEMMA

A trolley barrels down a track at high speed. Suddenly, the driver sees five 1 people crossing the track up ahead. There's not enough time to brake. If the driver does nothing, all five will die. But there is enough time to switch onto a side track, killing one person instead. Should the driver pull the switch?

Philosophers have debated trolley problems like this for decades. It's a use- 2 ful thought experiment for testing our intuitions about the moral difference between doing and allowing harm. The artificial scenario allows us to ignore empirical questions that might cloud the ethical issue, such as could the trolley stop in time? Could the collision be avoided in another way?

Recently the trolley problem has been invoked within the real-world pol- 3 icy debate about regulating autonomous vehicles (AVs). The issue at hand is how AVs will choose between harms to one set of people or another.

In September 2016, the National Highway Traffic Safety Administration 4 (NHTSA) asked companies developing AVs to certify that they have taken ethical considerations into account in assessing the safety of their vehicles.

Engineers and lawyers actually working on AV technology, however, 5 largely agree that the trolley problem is at best a distraction and at worst a dangerously misleading model for public policy.

The trolley problem is the wrong guide for regulating AVs for three 6 reasons:

1. Trolley Problem Scenarios Are Extremely Rare

Even in a world of human-driven vehicles, for a driver to encounter a real- 7 world trolley problem, he or she must 1) perceive an imminent collision in time to consider alternative paths; 2) have only one viable alternative path, which just happens to involve another fatal collision; and yet 3) be able to react in time to steer the car into the alternative collision. The combination of these three circumstances is vanishingly unlikely. It's not surprising, then, that we never see trolley problem-like collisions in the news, let alone in judicial decisions.

But sadly, unlike trolley problems, fatal collisions are not rare. The National 8 Safety Council estimates that about 40,200 Americans died on the highway in 2016, a 6 percent increase over the previous year. By comparison, about 40,610 women in the US will die from breast cancer this year, as estimated by the American Cancer Society. A NHTSA study concluded that driver error is the critical reason for 94 percent of crashes. Policymakers need to keep the real causes of preventable highway deaths, like alcohol and texting, in mind to save lives.

> "A NHTSA study concluded that driver error is the critical reason for 94 percent of crashes."

2. Autonomous Vehicles Will Make Them Even Rarer

To the extent that trolley problem scenarios exist in the real word, AVs will 9 make them rarer, not more frequent. One might think that, since AVs will have superior perception and decision-making capacities and faster reaction times, an AV might be able to make trolley problem-like choices in situations where a human driver wouldn't. But those same advantages will also enable an AV to avoid a collision entirely—or reduce the speed and severity of impact—when a human driver wouldn't.

Unlike the track-bound trolley, an AV will almost never be restricted to two 10 discrete paths, both of which involve a collision. AVs are equipped with sensors that provide a continuously updated, three-dimensional, 360-degree representation of the world around the vehicle, enabling it to know, and be able to act on, many alternative paths. More importantly, since AVs are never drunk, drowsy, or distracted, they are less likely to be in near-collision situations in the first place.

3. There Is Not Much Regulators Can Do about Them

Even if trolley problems were a realistic concern for AVs, it is not clear what, if 11 anything, regulators or companies developing AVs should do about them. The trolley problem is an intensely debated thought experiment precisely because there isn't a consensus on what should be done.

Generally, if commentators applying the trolley problem to AVs give any 12 conclusions at all, they propose that AVs should not distinguish among different types of people, based on age, sex, or other characteristics. But it doesn't take a trolley problem to reach that common sense conclusion.

Focusing on the trolley problem could distract regulators from the 13 important task of ensuring a safe transition to the deployment of AVs, or mislead the public into thinking either that AVs are programmed to target certain types of people or simply that AVs are dangerous.

We are all vulnerable to the tendency to overestimate the likelihood of vivid, 14 cognitively available risks rather than statistically likelier, but less salient, risks. We often neglect the base rate of conventional traffic accidents, even though the statistical risk is high. Associating AVs with deadly trolley collisions could only exacerbate this problem.

Conflating thought experiments with reality could slow the deployment of 15 AVs that are reliably safer than human drivers. Let's not go down that wrong track when it comes to regulating self-driving cars.

❷ READING ARGUMENTS

1. Iagnemma opens his essay with a "thought experiment"? What is a *thought experiment*? What does this particular thought experiment allow us to do?

2. According to Iagnemma, the "trolley problem" is the wrong way to think about the safety benefits and risks of self-driving cars. Why?

3. Iagnemma argues that autonomous vehicles will make "trolley problem scenarios" (to the degree that it exists in the real world) rarer, not more frequent. What evidence does he use to support this claim? Do you find it convincing? Why or why not?

4. In paragraph 14, Iagnemma claims, "We are all vulnerable to the tendency to overestimate the likelihood of vivid, cognitively available risks rather than statistically likelier, but less salient, risks." Do you agree? Explain.

5. Iagnemma concludes by saying, "Conflating thought experiments with reality could slow the deployment of AVs that are reliably safe for human drivers" (para. 15). What does he mean? Is this an effective conclusion? Why or why not?

This piece was posted on the website Quartz on November 1, 2015.

SHOULD DRIVERLESS CARS KILL THEIR OWN PASSENGERS TO SAVE A PEDESTRIAN?

OLIVIA GOLDHILL

Imagine you're in a self-driving car, heading towards a collision with a group of pedestrians. The only other option is to drive off a cliff. What should the car do? 1

Philosophers have been debating a similar moral conundrum for years, but the discussion has a new practical application with the advent of self-driving cars, which are expected to be commonplace on the road in the coming years. 2

Specifically, self-driving cars from Google, Tesla, and others will need to address a much-debated thought experiment called The Trolley Problem. In the original set-up, a trolley is headed towards five people. You can pull a lever to switch to a different track, where just one person will be in the trolley's path. Should you kill the one to save five? 3

Many people believe they should, but this moral instinct is complicated by other scenarios. For example: You're standing on a footbridge above the track 4 and can see a trolley hurtling towards five people. There's a fat man standing next to you, and you know that his weight would be enough to stop the trolley. Is it moral to push him off the bridge to save five people?

Go Off the Cliff

When non-philosophers were asked how driverless cars should handle a sit- 5 uation where the death of either passenger or pedestrian is inevitable, most believed that cars should be programmed to avoid hurting bystanders, according to a paper uploaded to the scientific research site Arxiv this month.

The researchers, led by psychologist Jean-François Bonnefon from the 6 Toulouse School of Economics, presented a series of collision scenarios to around 900 participants in total. They found that 75 percent of people thought the car should always swerve and kill the passenger, even to save just one pedestrian.

Among the philosophers debating moral theory, this solution is compli- 7 cated by various arguments that appeal to our moral intuitions but point to different answers. The Trolley Problem is fiercely debated precisely because it is a clear example of the tension between our moral duty not to cause harm, and our moral duty not to do bad things.

The former school of thought argues that the moral action is that which 8 causes the maximum happiness to the maximum number of people, a theory known as utilitarianism. Based on this reasoning, a driverless car should take whatever action would save the most number of people, regardless of whether they are passenger or pedestrian. If five people inside the car would be killed in a collision with the wall, then the driverless car should continue on even if it means hitting an innocent pedestrian. The reasoning may sound simplistic, but the details of Utilitarian theory, as set out by John Stuart Mill, are difficult to dispute.

Who Is Responsible?

However, other philosophers who have weighed in on the Trolley Problem 9 argue that utilitarianism is a crude approach, and that the correct moral action doesn't just evaluate the consequences of the action, but also considers who is morally responsible.

Helen Frowe, a professor of practical philosophy at Stockholm University, 10 who has given a series of lectures on the Trolley Problem, says self-driving car manufacturers should program vehicles to protect innocent bystanders, as those in the car have more responsibility for any danger.

"We have pretty stringent obligations not to kill people," she tells Quartz. 11 "If you decided to get into a self-driving car, then that's imposing the risk."

The ethics are particularly complicated when Frowe's argument points to 12 a different moral action than utilitarian theory. For example, a self-driving car could contain four passengers, or perhaps two children in the backseat. How does the moral calculus change?

If the car's passengers are all adults, Frowe believes that they should die to 13 avoid hitting one pedestrian, because the adults have chosen to be in the car and so have more moral responsibility.

Although Frowe believes that children are not morally responsible, she 14 still argues that it's not morally permissible to kill one person in order to save the lives of two children.

> "But with enough driverless cars on the road, it's far from implausible that software will someday have to make a choice between causing harm to a pedestrian or passenger."

"As you increase the num- 15 ber of children, it will be easier to justify killing the one. But in cases where there are just adults in the car, you'd need to be able to save a lot of them—more than ten, maybe a busload—to make it moral to kill one."

It's Better to Do Nothing

Pity the poor software designers (and, undoubtedly, lawyers) who are trying 16 to figure this out, because it can get much more complicated. What if a pedestrian acted recklessly, or even stepped out in front of the car with the intention of making it swerve, thereby killing the passenger? (Hollywood screenwriters, start your engines.) Since driverless cars cannot judge pedestrians' intentions, this ethical wrinkle is practically very difficult to take into account.

Philosophers are far from a solution despite the scores of papers that 17 debate every tiny ethical detail. For example, is it more immoral to actively swerve the car into a lone pedestrian than to simply do nothing and allow the vehicle to hit someone? Former UCLA philosophy professor Warren Quinn explicitly rejected the utilitarian idea that morality should maximize happiness. Instead, he argued that humans have a duty to respect other persons, and so an action that directly and intentionally causes harm is ethically worse than an indirect action that happens to lead to harm.

Of course, cars will very rarely be in a situation where there are only two 18 courses of action, and the car can compute, with 100 percent certainty, that either decision will lead to death. But with enough driverless cars on the road, it's far from implausible that software will someday have to make such a choice between causing harm to a pedestrian or passenger. Any safe driverless car should be able to recognize and balance these risks.

Self-driving car manufacturers have yet to reveal their stance on the issue. 19 But, given the lack of philosophical unanimity, it seems unlikely they'll find a universally acceptable solution. As for philosophers, time will tell if they enjoy having their theories tested in a very real way.

⊖ READING ARGUMENTS

1. In her essay, Goldhill cites a 2015 study that asked nonphilosophers whether driverless cars should be programmed to protect passengers or to protect pedestrians. How did they respond? How would you respond?

2. What is the ethical utilitarianism? What results when you apply utilitarian theory to the trolley problem? Why do some philosophers "argue that utilitarianism is a crude approach" (para. 9)?

3. What is this essay's thesis? How would you state it in your own words?

4. According to Goldhill, car manufacturers are not likely to find a solution to the trolley problem. What real-world issues complicate this problem?

5. What is the purpose of paragraph 18 in this essay? How does it further the writer's argument?

⊘ AT ISSUE: SHOULD WE EMBRACE SELF-DRIVING CARS?

1. Both Iagnemma and Goldhill write about the ethical dilemmas associated with self-driving cars. Which writer's argument do you find more convincing? Do either (or both) of these articles change your view of autonomous vehicles? Why or why not?

2. Self-driving cars are already in use in some places. Do you think that car manufacturers, government regulators, insurance companies, and others need to work out most (or all) of the ethical implications of driverless cars *before* these vehicles become widespread? Do you think they will be able to resolve these issues? What regulations would you institute to make sure these cars are safe?

3. These two essays discuss the ethical implications of driverless cars with regard to safety. What *other* issues, problems, or difficult questions do autonomous vehicles raise for you—and for society, as a whole?

⊘ WRITING ARGUMENTS: SHOULD WE EMBRACE SELF-DRIVING CARS?

How do you view the future of self-driving cars? Do you think they are a good idea? Do their advantages outweigh their disadvantages? What do you see as their most serious problem? Write an essay in which you argue for or against the need for self-driving cars, making sure that you answer these questions.

CHAPTER 18

DEBATE

Should College Athletes Be Paid?

Before the middle of the nineteenth century, organized and school-sponsored sports played only a small role in college life. Modern collegiate athletics emerged, in part, from the disorganized and often violent intramural, rugby-like sports that students played on their own. To channel and manage these brutal contests, institutions decided to organize them in the interests of safety, physical fitness, and—as teams began representing colleges in competition against one another—school pride. College football led the way: the first intercollegiate game, between Rutgers University and Princeton University, took place on November 6, 1869. Baseball, basketball, and other sports followed suit. In the decades since, the rules and regulations of these games have changed greatly. The role of athletics in the contemporary university—and in American life—has changed greatly as well.

Today, college sports are a billion dollar industry. For example, in 2018, ESPN paid $7.3 billion to the National Collegiate Athletic Association (NCAA) for the rights to televise the college football playoffs. Likewise, CBS paid the NCAA $8.8 billion to broadcast the "March Madness" college basketball tournament. However, this business goes well beyond media contracts. In fact, a state's highest-paid public employee is likely to be a football or basketball coach at a public university. Throughout the country, the money flows in countless directions from what amounts to an enormous entertainment industry, yet the players—the athletes who provide the actual entertainment on the field or court—retain amateur status. Not only do many of them spend twenty to forty unpaid hours a week practicing or playing (often at great physical risk), but they are barred from earning any compensation from their names or images or from product endorsements. Some see this situation as unfair, exploitative, or even immoral, arguing that players should be compensated in some way (beyond scholarships). Others claim that amateurism protects the integrity of college sports, that players are already well compensated with scholarships, and that paying athletes will only lead colleges and universities to become more mercenary and avaricious than they already are.

The following essays provide two contrasting viewpoints on the issue. For the writers of "Point: Colleges and Universities Should

615

Provide Student-Athletes with Additional Compensation beyond Tuition, Room, and Board," college sports are unfairly "built on the backs of unpaid 20-year-olds who work full time." According to the writers of "Counterpoint: Colleges and Universities Have No Obligation to Provide Student-Athletes with Additional Compensation beyond Tuition, Room, and Board," however, students need to remain *students*, not employees.

This essay appeared as part of a point-counterpoint debate in *International Social Science Review* in early 2018.

POINT: COLLEGES AND UNIVERSITIES SHOULD PROVIDE STUDENT-ATHLETES WITH ADDITIONAL COMPENSATION BEYOND TUITION, ROOM, AND BOARD

RANDY BERTOLAS, JAYME KREJCI, AND ALIX STANLEY

There are few industries in which employees are required to work up to twenty 1 hours per week (in addition to the expected academic workload of a student), with only one day off—which sometimes is spent on a bus traveling to the next job site—all for no pay. Student-athletes raise money for their institutions, provide subsidized entertainment and inspiration for the student body, and supply colleges and universities with countless forms of promotional material, all without being paid. True, some athletes are fortunate enough to earn scholarships, but these awards are rarely the full-ride dream. If institutions are asking student-athletes to commit considerable time and effort to a sport from which the institution earns money and publicity, then the performers need to be compensated for their labor.

> "The NCAA has strict 'countability' hours limiting the amount of time student-athletes can spend in athletic-related endeavors."

The NCAA has strict "countability" hours limiting the amount of time student-athletes can spend in athletic-related endeavors.[1] Theoretically a student-athlete (with the exception of football players) cannot be engaged in athletic-related activities for more than twenty hours per week while in season. These twenty hours do not, however, include travel time, time spent in the training room, time spent training alone, "volunteer" activities in which players represent the team with or without a coach present, community service, or fund-raising activities. Interestingly, though athletes are limited to a maximum of four hours per day in athletic-related events, game day counts for only three hours no matter how much time is actually occupied by the athletic activity. For all of this time commitment, a student-athlete may or may not be compensated by a scholarship.

In a 2011 survey conducted by the NCAA, baseball players reported 3 spending an average of 42.1 hours per week involved in athletic-related events while in season.[2] That amount of time in almost any field of employment would be considered a full-time job. Few non-athlete college students work a full-time job on top of classes. University faculty members and administrators usually recommend that undergraduate students work no more than ten to fifteen hours per week if they are carrying a full course load so as to leave enough time for their studies.[3] Among athletes, not everyone on the team has a full-ride scholarship, hence they are taking on a recommended level of work but without monetary gain. On top of tuition, room, and board, student-athletes also need hygiene products, clothing, gas, and other incidentals—all things that require money and for which scholarships can rarely be used.

In addition to barring student-athletes from being paid a salary, NCAA 4 bylaws prohibit an athlete receiving compensation from any form of name recognition, or using their image or likeness.[4] By way of example, for student-athletes majoring in exercise science, college is the perfect time to acquire experience in their field while supporting themselves by working as a personal trainer. NCAA bylaws, however, deem it impermissible for student-athletes to endorse, or allow their name and/or image to be used for the purposes of promoting an event or endorsing a commercial product. This means student-athletes are unable to advertise their services or the services of their employers. The NCAA also closely regulates how student-athletes are paid by outside employers, requiring that they are paid at a rate comparable to their skills and experience in the field.[5]

Beyond the employment restrictions and time constraints, athletes who do 5 manage to find work—even part-time—often face difficulty finding jobs that fit with their schedules. Employers want employees with dependable schedules. The last thing an employer wants to hear is that an employee *might* be gone for two weeks of post-season competition, but they will not know until the Thursday before a Friday shift. Also, student-athletes are not able to work the same hours as their non-athlete counterparts due to the time commitments involved in playing sports. A student-athlete who might be able to work ten hours a week is not likely to obtain a job when a student with a regular schedule can work twenty-five.

Student-athletes should be paid for the time they spend in their sports. 6 They cannot use their own name to make money, are required to meet the terms of a contract which often includes much more than twenty hours of athletic-related activity per week, and are expected to balance class, homework, and athletics with no opportunity to earn necessary outside income. In any other industry, this practice would be illegal. However, when it comes to college football or March Madness—multimillion dollar industries—it is just deemed college athletics, built on the backs of unpaid twenty-year-olds who work full time and are expected to say thank-you for the privilege.

Endnotes

1. National Collegiate Athletic Association, "Countable Athletically Related Activities," ncaa.org/sites/default/files/2017DII_online-education -resources_CARA-DOC_20170807.pdf.

2. National Collegiate Athletic Association, "Division I Results from the NCAA GOALS Study on the Student-Athlete Experience," 8 Nov. 2011, https:// www.ncaa.org/sites/default/files/DI_GOALS_FARA_final_1.pdf.

3. Laura W. Perna, "Understanding the Working College Student," *American Association of University Professors*. July–August 2010, www.aaup.org.

4. National Collegiate Athletic Association, "Summary of NCAA Eligibility Regulations, 2017–18," www.ncaa.org/sites/.../2017-18DIREC_New _Legislation_Summary_20170531.pdf.

5. Jon Solomon, "10 ways college athletes can get paid and remain eligible for their sport," July 21, 2016, cbssport.com.

⊘ READING ARGUMENTS

1. According to the writers, what benefits do student-athletes provide to their colleges and universities?

2. Where is the thesis of this essay located? Restate it in your own words.

3. NCAA rules state that student-athletes (with the exception of football players) "cannot be engaged in athletic-related activities for more than twenty hours per week while in season" (para. 2). According to the writers, what are the problems with this policy?

4. If student-athletes seek paid employment, what restrictions do they face?

5. In what sense is this essay a **definition argument**? Could it be seen as a **proposal argument**?

This essay appeared as part of a point-counterpoint debate in *International Social Science Review* in early 2018.

COUNTERPOINT: COLLEGES AND UNIVERSITIES HAVE NO OBLIGATION TO PROVIDE STUDENT-ATHLETES WITH ADDITIONAL COMPENSATION BEYOND TUITION, ROOM, AND BOARD

RANDY BERTOLAS, JAYME KREJCI, AND ALIX STANLEY

Allowing college athletes to receive salaries for their participation on sports 1 teams would be the demise of college athletics as we know it. Salaries would essentially take the "student" out of "student-athlete" and shift college programs to a business model where athletes are employees first, demoting the importance of academics. Not allowing salaries for athletes upholds the integrity and student accountability of intercollegiate competition.

Allowing college athletes to receive a paycheck for their talents would be 2 fiscally unfeasible for a majority of higher education institutions. Nationwide, schools are already struggling to support their current athletic programs. In 2015, *The Chronicle of Higher Education* and *The Huffington Post* published an article revealing that, in order to continue financing their sports programs U.S. public universities had raised $10.3 billion over a five-year period, primarily by increasing student fees.[1]

In reality, the majority of college sports teams are not bringing in much 3 revenue. Division I men's football and basketball teams are the main sources of income for athletic programs, and not all D-I programs turn a profit. Since it is primarily these two sports that generate any revenue for sports programs, the argument could be made that it would only be feasible to pay football and basketball players. A system in which a college basketball player is earning a much higher paycheck than a less profitable athlete in another sport, however, would ultimately lead to a sense of income inequity and would create divisions between student-athletes. Such a system could potentially undermine equality advances achieved under Title IX as women's sports bring in substantially less revenue. Overall campus cohesion could also be undermined, as regular students graduating today with unprecedented high student loan debt might begin to question their schools spending so much on athletes while charging other students high tuition.

Student-athletes do provide benefits to their campuses, society, and the 4 sports entertainment industry, but most college athletes are far less valued within the economic market than what they self-estimate. NCAA survey researchers found that three-quarters of Division I basketball players, half of players in Division II, and one-quarter of those in Division III predict that they will be drafted into the NBA.[2] The reality is that only about 1 percent of all college athletes will ever play professionally. Student-athletes benefit much more by being eligible for scholarships and stipends rather than taxable, yearly salaries. Only professional athletes are the recipients of lucrative, high-paying contracts. By comparison, minor league baseball players are awarded a meager $13,000 per year base salary, with minor league basketball players not earning much more.

> "College scholarships are far more valuable for young athletes than either they or the public realize."

In the vast majority of cases, college scholarships are far more valuable 5 for young athletes than either they or the public realize. It is not unheard of for Division I athletes to be granted full-tuition scholarships, room and board, food and travel stipends, and countless extra opportunities. Student-athletes coming from low-income homes are still eligible for Pell Grants.[3] Student-athletes also benefit by having unlimited access to the best facilities, top strength and fitness programs, and the use of athletic trainers and sports medicine specialists. Moreover, while being NCAA athletes, they are also allowed to accept funding from the U.S. Olympic Committee,[4] which can be helpful to student-athletes in sports such as track and field and swimming, who may not be as likely to receive scholarships. Finally, a majority of student-athletes graduate college with little to no debt and a prestigious college degree in hand to aid in their career pursuits.

If colleges were mandated to pay student-athletes, these schools would be 6 much more likely to simply cut athletic programs leading to fewer collegiate teams, fewer scholarships, and fewer opportunities for student-athletes. To be sure, this logic held true when in 1972 Title IX called for equitable opportunities for women and men to participate in sports, leading to increased costs associated with ensuring equal access to equipment and practice time. Over 400 already-struggling athletic teams were eliminated due to a lack of equal funding.[5]

Clearly, college athletes already benefit immensely by being eligible 7 for non-taxable scholarships (the tuition portion of scholarships is tax free, however scholarships for room and board are taxable) worth far more than student-athletes' average market value. Additionally, student-athletes are rewarded with some of the best training and facilities, and are given opportunities for exposure to professional leagues. It must be remembered that college athletes are primarily students, not employees.

Endnotes

1. Brad Wolverton et al., Sports at Any Cost. *The Chronicle of Higher Education* and *The Huffington Post,* n. pag. 15 Nov. 2015.

2. National Collegiate Athletic Association, "NCAA Research: Estimated probability of competing in men's professional basketball," www.ncaa.org /about/.../research/estimatedprobability-competing-college-athletics.

3. Jon Solomon, "10 ways college athletes can get paid and remain eligible for their sport," July 21, 2016, cbssports.com.

4. Ibid.

5. Jonathon Yates and Andy Schwarz, "The Great Debate over Compensation for College Athletes." *CollegeAD*, n. pag. 8 Jan. 2018.

⊘ READING ARGUMENTS

1. According to the writers, paying athletes would be "fiscally unfeasible" (para. 2) for most colleges and universities. Why? How do they support this claim?

2. What percentage of college athletes will ever play professionally? Why is this number significant in the context of the writers' argument—and, more generally, in the context of this debate?

3. In the first paragraph, the writers claim that keeping student-athletes unpaid "upholds the integrity and student accountability of intercollegiate competition." What do you think they mean here by "integrity" and "student accountability"? Does their evidence and their argument support this opening claim convincingly? Explain.

4. In what respects is this essay a **cause-and-effect argument**? In what sense is it an **evaluation argument**?

⊙ AT ISSUE: SHOULD COLLEGE ATHLETES BE PAID?

1. In the second essay, the writers claim, "It is not unheard of for Division I athletes to be granted full-tuition scholarships, room and board, food and travel stipends, and countless extra opportunities" (para. 5). Do these benefits seem like compensation enough? How might the writers of the first essay respond to this information?

2. According to the writers of the counterpoint essay, paying student-athletes would undermine "campus cohesion" (3) not just among athletes, but among *all* students. Do you agree? Would you question the schools' compensating athletes while other students struggle with high tuition costs and student loans?

3. Neither of these essays incorporates the views or voices of actual student-athletes. Would including such sources strengthen either (or both) of the arguments? If so, how? If not, why not?

⊙ WRITING ARGUMENTS: SHOULD COLLEGE ATHLETES BE PAID?

Write an essay that takes a position on whether college athletes should receive a salary or other form of financial compensation for their work, time, and risks.

CHAPTER

19

Under What Circumstances Do Bystanders Have an Ethical Obligation to Intervene?

In 1964, twenty-eight-year-old Kitty Genovese was stabbed to death in her New York City neighborhood at 3:30 in the morning. The *New York Times* reported that thirty-eight of her neighbors heard her screams and did nothing to help, but recent research reveals that this account was overstated and that some of Genovese's neighbors actually did help—for example, one called out the window for her attacker to stop, two called the police, and another held her while she lay dying. Only two men who saw what happened failed to respond—one fled and the other was drunk. Still, the original, false story reinforced the public's fears that people could watch someone be murdered and do nothing to help. As a result, the story of Kitty Genovese entered the social consciousness, and we have been using it to ponder our ethical responsibility to help in a crisis ever since.

Some writers, such as Joe Nocera, the author of "It's Hard to Be a Hero," say that we have an unqualified obligation to help those in need. They praise individuals who respond in a crisis and condemn those who find reasons not to. Even if the Genovese case is overstated, scenarios like it—with more accurately documented group apathy—occur all the time. Nocera and others examine the "bystander effect," a psychological phenomenon popularized following Genovese's murder, which suggests that the larger the number of bystanders, the less likely any one of them is to help in an emergency.

On the other side of the debate, writers like Lenore Skenazy claim that we have taken our collective social guilt about Kitty Genovese too far, and as a result, we intervene when we should simply stand by and watch. This tendency leads to concerned neighbors' calling authorities whenever they see unaccompanied children walking down the street or playing in a park, whether they are in danger or not. The cost of this overabundant concern is substantial: it is expensive for law enforcement to respond to calls, and reacting to nonexistent problems pulls police away from situations in which they might actually be needed.

As you read the two essays that follow, try to think of ways to address this debate question. For example, how does the widespread ability to take pictures and videos with smartphones affect people's inclination to step in and help? Which group of bystanders are you most likely to fall into: those who act heroically, those who do nothing or those who panic and flee?

This essay appeared in *Time* on March 13, 2014.

HOW KITTY GENOVESE DESTROYED CHILDHOOD

LENORE SKENAZY

TIME

Kitty Genovese was stabbed to death 50 years ago today. She was 28. A tragedy. 1 The press reported 38 onlookers heard her screams and decided not to intervene. That account has since come under fire, but it nonetheless created a perception of ourselves (and certainly New Yorkers) as unconscionably reluctant to get involved.

We've been making up for it ever since—and that's too bad. 2

We may once have been too slow to call the cops (though that's still dis- 3 puted), but today we are definitely too fast. Oh, I don't mean we shouldn't dial 911 if we see someone being murdered, or threatened, or hurt. Of course we should! In fact, the simple 911 number to call for emergencies was developed partly in response to the Genovese murder: Now everyone could have a quick, easy way to summon the cops anytime, anyplace. A great leap forward.

The leap sideways, or perhaps downward, came as the general public grad- 4 ually became convinced that it not only had an obligation to help anyone in danger, it had the obligation to call the cops anytime it noticed people who could be in danger, especially kids, even if they were fine and dandy at the time.

This has given rise to a near mania for calling the cops when people spot 5 a child on his or her own anywhere in public. And so we have a Connecticut mom charged with "risk of injury to a minor" and failure to appear after police said she allowed her seven- and 11-year-old children to walk to buy pizza unsupervised.

That's right. Someone noticed kids off to get pizza and alerted the cops, as if stopping a potential tragedy. 6

> "Someone noticed kids off to get pizza and alerted the cops, as if stopping a potential tragedy."

Then there's the dad who was arrested for child endangerment after a woman 7
noticed "two children playing on the swings and slides alone without a guardian"
in a suburban Pittsburgh park for two hours. (The charges were later dropped.)

And let's not forget the mom in Jonesboro, Arkansas, who made her 8
10-year-old son walk 4.6 miles to school after he'd been suspended from the
school bus for bad behavior. A bank guard saw him walking alone—horrors!—
and called the cops. The mom was arrested for child endangerment. In the
end, she plead[ed] guilty and was fined $520.

None of these kids encountered any danger other than a concerned citi- 9
zen with 911 on speed dial. It has become so unusual to see children outside
on their own that a nervous public immediately picks up the phone at such a
sight, hyperventilating about danger.

"'If in doubt, call 911 to play it safe.' That's the lesson that was taken from 10
Kitty Genovese," says David Pimentel, a professor of law at Ohio Northern
University. "But it stems from a faulty assumption, which is that there's no
harm in calling." But unless the child is in true danger, "There is harm done.
The harm that comes from the overreaction of everybody to this." The courts
get involved, CPS gets involved. There are fines, arrests, the threat (and sometimes the reality) of jail time.

Most of the folks calling the cops—and most of the cops themselves— 11
remember walking to school and playing outside as kids. They are convinced
that times have changed and made these activities dicey, even though, nationally, the crime rate is down from what it was in the '70s, '80s, and '90s. (And
that's not because we don't let kids go outside anymore. The crime rate against
adults is down, too, and we don't helicopter them.)

So anyone who walked to the post office or the pizza shop as a kid was no 12
safer than a kid today. But back then, bystanders didn't dial 911 when they saw
kids on their own. They waved.

Maybe the lesson from the Kitty Genovese era should be this: Let's get 13
more people back outside, including children. That way we can be looking out
for each other, instead of freaking out.

◯ READING ARGUMENTS

1. Throughout this article, Skenazy uses the first-person plural (*we*).
   How does this usage affect the tone of her argument? How would
   her argument be different if she wrote entirely in the third-person
   plural (*they*)?

2. What cause-and-effect relationship does Skenazy try to establish in her
   three opening paragraphs? Do you find this introduction convincing?

3. Skenazy refers to a "near mania for calling the cops when people spot a child on his or her own anywhere in public" (para. 5). Does she provide enough evidence to support this assertion? Explain.

4. What specific problem does Skenazy address in this essay, and what is her suggestion for solving this problem? Would it be accurate to call this essay a proposal argument? Why or why not?

Nocera's opinion piece ran on December 7, 2012, in the *New York Times*.

IT'S HARD TO BE A HERO

JOE NOCERA

On a crisp January day in 2007, a 50-year-old construction worker named 1 Wesley Autrey became a New York hero when he rescued a man who had fallen onto the subway tracks.

A train had just left the station, so the platform was nearly empty except 2 for Autrey, his two daughters, and a young man who was having a seizure of some sort. The man fell onto the tracks, in a position, Autrey told me recently, "where he was going to lose his limbs." With another train fast approaching, Autrey instinctively jumped onto the tracks, positioned the man's body safely between the rails, and lay on top of him. Five cars passed over them before the train screeched to a halt.

What prompted me to telephone Autrey was the death on Monday of 3 Ki-Suck Han, a Queens man who was pushed onto the 49th Street subway tracks, allegedly by Naeem Davis, a drifter with whom police said he had been having an altercation. This time, there were plenty of people on the platform, most notably R. Umar Abbasi, a photographer who took some horrifying pictures as the subway train closed in on Han.

The 22 seconds or so between Han being pushed and the train reaching 4 him was about the same amount of time that Autrey had nearly six years earlier. Yet, on Monday, no one on the crowded platform made a move to help Han until it was too late. (A doctor tried to administer C.P.R., but he was already dead.)

"People were just standing in fear and shock, not really knowing what was 5 going on," one bystander told a crowd of reporters. "Some people started running out of the platform. Other people just stood there."

When one of Abbasi's gruesome photographs landed on the front page 6 of the *New York Post*, the reaction was fierce. "Someone's taking that picture," said Al Roker on NBC's *Today Show*. "Why aren't they helping this guy up?"

Abbasi defended himself in part by saying he used his flash to warn the   7
conductor, but he was also quick to point the finger at others: "Why didn't the
people who were close enough help him?" he asked. "If I had reached him in
time, I would have pulled him up," he insisted. We all harbor the hope that if
we found ourselves in the same position as Wesley Autrey—or Umar Abbasi—
we would act with courage instead of cowardice.

Yet behavioral science suggests otherwise. The most famous case of   8
bystanders failing to act took place in 1964, when Kitty Genovese, a young
woman living in a quiet Queens neighborhood, was brutally stabbed to death.
Despite her repeated screams for help, some 38 people who heard her from
their apartments did nothing—not even call the police.

A. M. Rosenthal, the renowned for-   9
mer executive editor of the *Times*, who was
then the metropolitan editor—and who
had gotten the tip that led to the story—

> "Why didn't anyone do anything?"

wrote a short book called *Thirty-Eight Witnesses*. In it, Rosenthal asked the question that haunted the country in the aftermath of the murder: *Why?*

Why didn't anyone do anything?   10

Rosenthal could only guess at the answer because there had been no   11
research on what is now known as "pro-social behavior." But after the story
gripped the country, two young social scientists—Bibb Latané, then at
Columbia University, and John Darley, who taught at New York University—
conducted a series of experiments on the behavior of bystanders.

Their startling conclusion, which is now known as the bystander effect, is   12
that the more people who witness a crime, the less likely any one of them will
come to the aid of the victim. Partly this is because when people see others not
doing anything, they become confused, not sure if it really is an emergency—"a
collective ignorance," says Latané. Another reason, though, is something called
the diffusion of responsibility. "You think to yourself, there are all these other
people here. This isn't entirely my problem," says Latané.

Go back to the beginning of this column. The crucial detail in 2007, when   13
viewed through the prism of behavioral science, is that the subway platform
was nearly empty. Autrey acted heroically—even leaving his two young children unattended to do so—because there was no one else who could help. On
Monday, the 49th Street subway platform was full of people, each possibly
thinking that someone else was closer, someone else was stronger, someone
else should be responsible for the heroic act. As a result, no one acted.

"I wouldn't do the wrong thing," one man waiting for a subway train told   14
the *Times* on Tuesday. That's what we all want to think. It's why we are so quick
to condemn those who do nothing at such moments.

But let's be honest: We don't really know how we'd act until the moment is   15
upon us. Sadly, the science says we're more likely to do nothing than respond
like Wesley Autrey.

⊘ READING ARGUMENTS

1. What prompted Nocera to write his essay? What question (or questions) did he want to answer?

2. According to Nocera, what is the "bystander effect"? What is the "diffusion of responsibility" (para. 12)?

3. What "crucial detail" (13) reveals the difference between Wesley Autrey's behavior and the behavior of those who failed to help Ki-Suck Han? How does this detail help explain Autrey's actions?

4. Nocera quotes a subway passenger who says, "I wouldn't do the wrong thing" (14). Is Nocera making an ethical argument here? If not, should he be doing so?

5. How would you describe Nocera's tone? Judgmental? Pedantic? Sarcastic? Neutral? Something else? Explain your answer.

⊘ AT ISSUE: UNDER WHAT CIRCUMSTANCES DO BYSTANDERS HAVE AN ETHICAL OBLIGATION TO INTERVENE?

1. Both Skenazy and Nocera mention the case of Kitty Genovese, but they use it to make different points. Explain how each writer interprets the story's significance and how each writer uses it to support his or her argument. Which writer uses the story more effectively? Why?

2. As Skenazy concedes, the commonly known version of the Kitty Genovese murder—in which no one helped Genovese—has "come under fire" (para. 1). According to contemporary accounts, several people did actually try to help Genovese. Does this factual discrepancy matter? Why do you think the original version of the event (regardless of its accuracy) continues to resonate?

3. Nocera writes that all of us would like to think we would act heroically to save another person in an emergency; as a result, he asserts, we are "quick to condemn those who do nothing at such moments" (para. 14). Do you agree with his conclusion? Why or why not?

⊘ WRITING ARGUMENTS: UNDER WHAT CIRCUMSTANCES DO BYSTANDERS HAVE AN ETHICAL OBLIGATION TO INTERVENE?

According to Skenazy, the public has passed a turning point, becoming "convinced that it not only had an obligation to help anyone in danger" but also had "the obligation to call the cops anytime it noticed people who could be in danger" (para. 4). In contrast, Nocera suggests that powerful social forces discourage people from helping those in danger. Using these two selections as sources, write an essay offering your own view of the ethical obligations of bystanders. (You might begin by considering fundamental differences between Skenazy's and Nocera's arguments.)

This giant poster was created by a Swiss nonprofit in support of a campaign to institute Universal Basic Income. Denis Balibouse/REUTERS.

DEBATE

Should the United States Establish a Universal Basic Income?

As George Zarkadakis points out in the essay that begins on page 636, the idea of a universal basic income (UBI) has a long history, proposed as early as 1516 in *Utopia*, a work of satirical fiction by the author, humanist, and Catholic saint Thomas More (1478–1535). In the nineteenth century, political economists and philosophers, such as John Stuart Mill, suggested that an equal sum of money be given to all members of the community to guarantee their basic subsistence. As the modern welfare state evolved in the twentieth century, various economists and policy makers refined and adapted the idea. In some cases, as in the United States, a form of guaranteed income was integrated into social insurance programs, such as Social Security, which pays benefits to the disabled, the elderly, and others. More direct and universal forms of UBI have also been proposed over the years. As the United Nations Educational, Scientific, and Cultural Organization (UNESCO) asserts: "The idea of an unconditional basic income is quite simple: every legal resident in a country receives a monthly stipend sufficient to live above the poverty line. Let's call this the 'no frills culturally respectable standard of living.'"

In the United States, discussion and advocacy of such programs waned in the 1980s and 1990s, but the twenty-first century is bringing new challenges that have led to a revival of interest in UBI. Many believe that automation will eliminate large sectors of the workforce in the future, as robotics already have in many fields. For these observers and policy makers, the UBI could ease some of the economic and social effects of high unemployment. For others, UBI is a practical solution to economic inequality and instability in the face of growing disparities between the wealthy and everyone else. Not surprisingly, proposals for a universal guaranteed income raise questions, problems, and criticisms: Who will pay for it? Would such a policy lead to wholesale welfare dependence—and create incentives for people *not* to work? How would it reshape our economy and our politics?

The following two essays provide views of this issue from two revealing angles. In "A Conservative Case for Universal Basic Income," Canadian writer Christian Bot argues that UBI, a policy generally associated with the economic and political left, may actually help maintain conservative social and cultural values, such as the preservation of the nuclear family. In contrast, science writer and artificial intelligence engineer George Zarkadakis makes a comprehensive case against UBI, arguing that it could lead to "an era of corporatist totalitarianism dressed up as representative democracy."

This essay was published in *Areo Magazine* on August 2, 2018.

A CONSERVATIVE CASE FOR UNIVERSAL BASIC INCOME

CHRISTIAN BOT

It hardly came as a surprise when the *National Review*, a leading American conservative publication, rushed to assail the idea of universal basic income (UBI for short) with its usual vigor, from almost its very first mention. The men and women manning the fort at the *Review*—most of whom are superlative, highly intelligent writers—have remained steadfast in their defense of quasi-libertarian free-market economics against the rising tide of Donald Trump's economic nationalism. It is of course within their rights to do so, and their principled persistence in an increasingly unpopular doctrine earns my commendation to some extent. But I feel they are mistaken.

But, first of all, what actually is UBI? There have been widely varying proposals, but the essential idea is to provide every citizen of a given jurisdiction with an unconditional sum of money at regular intervals. Its proponents typically insist that, if implemented, it will reduce poverty and income inequality, strengthen the economy by boosting consumer spending, and offer protection from the disruptive effects of workplace automation. The latter will become especially resonant in the coming years, as automation siphons off ever more jobs. But, as the *National Review* shows, it has been an uphill battle to convince many conservatives of the idea's viability or even its desirability. There is a critical element to this debate, however, that has thus far been almost entirely overlooked. UBI has the power to not only preserve the traditional nuclear family, but to raise its vitality and prestige to levels not seen in many years. As such, it ought to spur conservatives to see beyond their stubborn economic doctrines and acquaint themselves with the conservative case for UBI.

UBI is in essence a radical form of social welfare. But conservatives 3 take a gross misstep when they jump to the conclusion that UBI must therefore be an inherently left-wing idea. It is easy to see why this misconception has been allowed to spread. The very thought of showering individuals with unconditional money, regardless of their work situation, sets off alarm bells for fiscal conservatives, who find any initiative of this sort repellent. But the prime beneficiaries of UBI would be those permanently out of work thanks to automation. Conservatives have long professed sympathy with the "deserving" down-and-outs, and compassion, in any case, is not a monopoly of the left. Conservatives must reject being tethered to a callous and heartless individualism in a perverse race to the bottom to win the posthumous approval of Ayn Rand and her ilk. UBI is no more inherently left wing than salsa dancing is the domain of the right. Conservatives would be wise to step forward and discuss this very important and timely proposal. The image of the cold-hearted conservative need not reflect reality.

Nevertheless, conservative economic thought is stuck in neutral, owing 4 in large part to conservatives' unqualified support for *laissez-faire* capitalism. Little do they realize that capitalism has played a fundamental role in destabilizing the nuclear family—not only by leaving the poor, the struggling, and the destitute to fend for themselves without social assistance, but also by utterly alienating labor from the moral development of the worker. To better understand this, we must go far back in history and explore the changing nature of labor. I do not idealize the Middle Ages, but the undercurrent of religion that propped up so many areas of medieval life applied to labor too. The typical tradesman of, say, a Belgian town in around 1300 toiled under the understanding that his work was first and foremost a labor of love for God, and only secondarily a means, however necessary, of subsistence. This view was dealt a fatal blow by the Reformation, which shattered the socially cohesive power of the Catholic Church in precisely those areas of Northern Europe that soon began to embark on their mercantile ascendancy. When these regions industrialized in the nineteenth century, the uprooted workers, predictably, found no significant moral or political recourse to mitigate the horror of their plight.

The European nations in which the capitalist alienation of labor pro- 5 ceeded apace remained avowedly Christian. Paradoxically, it was the avowedly atheist Karl Marx who raised his voice more loudly than most against this outgrowth of unrestrained capitalism. Marx was quite explicitly an enemy of the traditional nuclear family. In *The Communist Manifesto*, he trumpeted wife-swapping and the abolition of the family, which he denigrated as a tool for the bourgeois domination of society. But he also observed that the ravages of mid-nineteenth-century capitalism were tearing families apart, through demoralizing overwork and abysmally low wages. In the Soviet Union under Lenin, abortion and divorce were legalized, with the predictable outcome of a declining birthrate. Lenin's successor Stalin, genocidal thug though he was, saw the writing on the wall and undid much of his forebear's radical work, notably by prohibiting abortion in most cases. There is more than a hint of the absurd at play when more can be said—at least nominally—for a mass-murdering communist dictator than for twenty-first century conservatives, who evince support for the nuclear family, but steadfastly refuse to take the necessary economic steps to protect it. The overwhelming hypocrisy of it all not only lets down struggling families but erodes their trust in the conservatives who are supposed to be helping them.

The precise channels by which economic strain lends itself to family 6 breakdown are varied and manifold, but the basic principle deserves some elucidation. Most people reading this can relate to the stress produced by the threat of economic hardship, perhaps even of insolvency and poverty. I emphasize *threat*, because the very fear of it often suffices to send whole families into free-fall, as surely as the mere whisper of financial catastrophe can throw Wall Street into an eight-hour terror. The modern mind prizes security above almost all else, but, paradoxically, capitalism in its current incarnation refuses most stubbornly to offer any meaningful measure of it to vast swaths of the population. The *zeitgeist* of the early twenty-first century demands that we ensure a certain level of material security, before we can even begin to discuss preserving the nuclear family. UBI will not, in itself, restore the idealistic medieval conception of labor, but—by alleviating millions of families' gnawing fears of poverty—it will make that conversation possible.

> "The precise channels by which economic strain lends itself to family breakdown are varied and manifold."

Conservatives, to their credit, have little problem detecting the deplorable social 7 outcomes of the family breakdown that they abhor. It is almost a truism among conservatives that children who emerge from broken and dysfunctional homes are at considerable risk of future delinquency, drug and alcohol abuse, and low educational achievement. They represent vast sums of sunk costs for the state, which most commonly takes the form of the inevitable welfare, disability, and unemployment payments that proportionately far too many of them will eventually draw upon. This is only one part of the story. The other includes medical costs stemming from substance abuse and its concomitant health problems—above all in countries that have socialized medicine, such as my native Canada—and the cost of law enforcement and detention, should they spend time in juvenile facilities or, later on in prison. All this money could have obviously been better spent elsewhere were it not so tragically necessary here. What, then, do we have to lose from an ambitious UBI scheme, laser focused on keeping families together and economically secure? We cannot know for sure at this early stage, but it seems likely that the cost of most mainstream UBI proposals will fall well short of the expense of mopping up the mess attributable to broken families.

Some have already hinted at the material basis needed to keep families happy 8 and secure. According to an apocryphal account, St. Thomas Aquinas believed that a pious soul suddenly plunged into the throes of spiritual sorrow ought to seek out a warm bath, a sleep, and a glass of wine. Authentic or otherwise, this attests to the necessity of possessing some degree of material security before you can even begin to think about the moral realm. One may take issue with scholasticism's habit of compounding virtually everything into a system of hierarchies, but the practice is eminently valid here. There exists a definite hierarchy of needs in asymmetrical relation to one another. At its base are man's material imperatives, and above these are his moral needs. One may be getting along quite well in the material sense while remaining morally dead, but the inverse is not equally true. This is much like saying that a tower without a foundation is doomed to collapse under its own weight, or that a pizza without toppings is still a pizza, but toppings without dough are not. To continue the culinary metaphor, conservatives never tire of insisting on the centrality of the masculine "breadwinner" figure. They ought to consider whether a family whose breadwinner is out of a job, and staring poverty in the face, can realistically tend to his and his family's moral growth. UBI, if implemented with commensurately pious intentions, can restore the foundation to the collapsing tower and become a force not only for newfound material abundance, but for moral excellence as well.

In a similar vein, there is more than a germ of truth to the old adage, "a 9 family that prays together stays together." Try as they might to deny the relevance of the moral realm, hardened atheists and agnostics would do well to take note of the objective benefits attached to personal spirituality, at both the individual and domestic levels. As the Institute for Family Studies observes, "Family prayer time is quality time together, time not spent in front of the television or a smartphone, but rather, time spent communicating on a deeply personal level." Individual prayer, too, is linked to "reduced stress, increased self-awareness, better communication, and a more empathetic and forgiving attitude towards others." It does not require a systematic and theological belief in God to appreciate the positive effects of prayer or of cultivating one's spiritual and moral development more broadly. This is scarcely possible in an atmosphere of squalor and perpetual economic insecurity. If conservatives wish to back up their appeals for more widespread religious commitment, there are few better ways to do so than by providing material peace of mind to those who desperately need it.

UBI is something that we are probably going to hear a lot more about in the 10 near future. The growing impact of automation will ensure that. But, just as economic libertarians are bound to put up a spirited fight against it, conservatives must be ready to vigorously defend it. There is a compelling conservative case to be made in its favor. I sense that a paradigm shift is coming in the age-old spat between liberals and conservatives, one in which conservatives will leave behind the doctrines of economic inaction inherited from a bygone age. The debate surrounding UBI offers an ideal stage on which to prove conservatives' commitment not only to the humanitarian values of social welfare and compassion, but also to the preservation, strengthening, and promotion of the traditional nuclear family. For far too long, conservatives have tolerated an appalling gap between their words and their deeds. If the conservative movement wishes to prove its enduring fealty to its rhetoric, that gap must now close.

⊘ READING ARGUMENTS

1. How does Bot characterize conservative opposition to universal basic income in his opening paragraph? What does this characterization suggest about his purpose and audience?

2. What does Bot accomplish with his use of **definition** in paragraph 3?

3. Bot identifies a number of **cause-and-effect** relationships. What point is he trying to make (or support) with this causal connection?

4. What "hypocrisy" does Bot identify in paragraph 5?

5. Bot believes that in the future, more people will be out of work. What key cause of future unemployment does he identify? How does he believe universal basic income would address this problem? Do you see this as a practical solution? Why or why not?

This essay was first published on the *Huffington Post* website on February 24, 2017.

THE CASE AGAINST UNIVERSAL BASIC INCOME

GEORGE ZARKADAKIS

Universal Basic Income (UBI) suggests that all adults should receive the same 1 minimum, guaranteed, income from the State irrespective of their other incomes. It is being put forward as the "solution" to the obliteration of jobs due to robots, artificial intelligence, and machine learning. In a future, when work will be intermittent or absent, UBI could provide safety net and replace the current, complex welfare systems—or so its advocates claim.

UBI is not a novel idea. Thomas Paine first proposed it in the late 19th 2 century, when he suggested that big landowners should be taxed and the dividends redistributed to every young man in America. Paine's economic argument rested on the idea of "rent": the owners of producing assets gain from the work of those who use these assets to produce goods and services. This gain is a rent because the owners do not participate in production. It is rather significant that the business models of the big high-tech companies in the modern digital economy are founded on rent. Think of digital platforms, or the cloud, or XaaS ("everything as a service") models. In a highly automated economy the owners of the automating technology will be akin to the Paine's big landowners. So why not tax them and redistribute the money to the rest of us?

There are several arguments against this, and I would like to separate 3 them in three categories: economic, political, and ethical. Let's start with economics. In a globalized economy capital is free to move to the lowest cost. In the absence of a world government that can enforce a tax regime on every country, the practicality of taxing the cash reserves of fully automated companies—as suggested by Thomas Piketty among others—is a moot point. Besides, such a tax would impact on those companies' ability to invest and innovate, which could result in losing their competitiveness. In such a scenario companies operating from low or zero tax regimes would win. By curbing innovation in their jurisdictions governments of today's advanced economies will also lose from the *productivity dividend* that automation is expected to deliver. Accordingly to a recent report by Accenture and Frontier Economics intelligent machines will raise the annual growth rate of gross value added (a close approximation of GDP) by 4.6 percent in US, 3.9 percent in UK, and 2.7 percent in Japan. Governments may like UBI because it is the sword that can cut through the messy Gordian knot of their welfare systems, which are generating generational poverty rather than helping anyone. But going for UBI may have adverse effects both on tax receipts as well as in losing the battle of the fourth industrial revolution to low tax competitors.

Politics comes into play as well. It is curious that big high-tech companies 4 in Silicon Valley are such fervent supporters of UBI. Perhaps they are fearful of replacing the bankers as the most-hated capitalist villains, or maybe they want to pass the bucket to governments and relieve themselves of the responsibility of destroying the livelihoods of many.

Nevertheless, many of those companies would be happy to contribute some of their vast wealth to fund UBI, for this will allow them to have much greater leverage on government decisions. There has been a tug of war between high-tech companies and energy companies for who will have the greatest influence over government—for 5

> "Quality of life requires a new way of thinking about work, not government handouts."

quite a while—and UBI seems to be fast becoming the new front line. While Bill Gates suggests a "robot tax" and Elon Musk advocates UBI, a conservative think tank led by notable republicans such as James Baker and Henry Paulson suggested a carbon tax for financing basic income. If you think that that the so-called "free-economy" is a euphemism for crony capitalism, wait till the automation era kicks in! But the deeper collusion of governments and capital can only lead to the further alienation of citizens. We are on the cusp of a citizen rebellion across the developed world. It would be foolhardy to suggest that, somehow, citizens will be quelled by UBI to the extent that they relinquished their rights, privacy, and well-being to decisions made behind closed doors between politicians and high tech, or energy, executives. Also, when we think of UBI we must ask ourselves: do we want to become financially dependent on the State? Especially on a State that is itself financially dependent on the owners of automation technologies?

Finally, there are many ethical problems with UBI. Quality of life is often 6
ignored in the current discussion. There are millions of people currently on
benefits whose life is miserable. Extending the idea of welfare to all under the
guise of UBI we are in danger of extending misery. There are certainly many
who would prefer to live poorly, as long as they do not have to get up in the
morning and do any work. To them UBI will be just some extra cash to spend
on life's little luxuries. But most people need to feel valued and productive, to
live meaningful lives, to support and nourish loving families, to be creative and
develop their full potential. For them a life of idleness on borderline poverty,
paid by taxing others who will be enjoying riches beyond imagination, does
not seem like a desirable future. Quality of life requires a new way of thinking
about work, not government handouts so we can stay home and play videog-
ames all day.

So if not UBI then what? How should we manage the transition to a post- 7
work future? There is too much hype about what AI can really do, and big
questions regarding how companies will adopt these new technologies in practice. But if for the sake of simplicity we assume that most jobs will become
obsolete by mid 21st century, then we ought to go back to the basics, rather
than patching up what has gone wrong with welfare. And the basics include
defining the role of citizens in a democratic society as the creators of wealth
and prosperity. Democracy is based on the assumption that citizens are the
producers of wealth and the owners of property. UBI is undermining the
foundations of democracy because it transforms citizen freedom to citizen
dependency. We must think beyond dependency, towards innovative systems
where machine intelligence leverages our creativity and self-development on
a bottom-up, rather than top-down, fashion. In short, we need to reinvent
democracy in a post-work future. The alternative would be to enter an era of
corporatist totalitarianism dressed up as representative democracy.

⊘ READING ARGUMENTS

1. Zarkadakis states that universal basic income is "not a novel idea"
   (para. 2). How does he support this claim?

2. According to Zarkadakis, arguments against universal basic income
   fall into three categories. What are they? How does he use these categories to structure his essay?

3. Zarkadakis notes that many high-tech companies support universal
   basic income. What does he suspect their motives are?

4. In Zarkadakis's view, what ethical problems are associated with universal basic income? Do you agree with his assumptions about how
   people might respond to the policy?

⊘ AT ISSUE: SHOULD THE UNITED STATES ESTABLISH A UNIVERSAL BASIC INCOME?

1. Bot focuses on making an ideologically "conservative" case for universal basic income. In contrast, Zarkadakis avoids explicit labeling but considers three different aspects of the issue. Which approach seems more effective and persuasive to you? Why?

2. Both writers address moral and ethical questions in their essays, but from different angles. How do you think that Bot would respond to Zarkadakis's ethical argument against universal basic income? Explain.

3. The two writers agree that automation, artificial intelligence, and robotics will lead to wider unemployment in the future. Do you agree with that assumption? Why or why not?

⊘ WRITING ARGUMENTS: SHOULD THE UNITED STATES ESTABLISH A UNIVERSAL BASIC INCOME?

After reading these two arguments, write an essay that argues either for or against establishing a universal basic income.

Should Every American Go to College?

Since Harvard College was founded in 1636, American higher education has reflected the history of the United States—economically, socially, and culturally. In the early days of the country, a college education was a privilege for the elite few. The nineteenth century—a period of economic expansion—saw the development of the state university system, which educated many engineers, teachers, agricultural experts, and other professionals who participated in the country's industrial boom. After World War I, the City College of New York provided a free, quality college education to many working-class students, including immigrants, at a time when they were effectively barred from other colleges. However, the most significant expansion in American higher education occurred after World War II, when the GI Bill gave returning veterans money for tuition and living expenses so they could attend college. Enrollment skyrocketed, and many people credit the GI Bill for helping to create postwar prosperity and a large middle class.

In the decades since the first GI Bill was passed, the number of colleges and universities in the United States has increased steadily: as of 2017, there were over 4,360 degree-granting institutions in the United States. Nearly 40 percent of Americans now have at least a two-year college degree, and roughly two thirds of high school graduates enroll in college after graduation. Statistics show that college graduates earn an average of about $17,500 more annually than those who have only a high school diploma. This financial reality, along with the need for a highly educated and competitive workforce in an increasingly global marketplace, has led some to argue that the federal government should do more than it already does to make sure that more—and perhaps even all—Americans attend college. Such proposals raise fundamental questions about higher education. How should colleges maintain academic standards even as they admit more students? How should such institutions control costs? Is higher education a right in the same way that a high school education is? Should everyone go to college? Wouldn't high-quality vocational training make more sense for many?

The following four essays address these and other questions, exploring the importance of a college degree and suggesting new ways of viewing postsecondary education. In "College's Value Goes Deeper than the Degree," Eric Hoover argues that a college education offers many tangible and intangible benefits. In "Stop Saying 'College Isn't for Everyone,'" Andre Perry argues that every student should be prepared to go to college, even if they ultimately do not attend. In "The College Trap," J. D. Vance argues that contrary to popular belief, subsidizing colleges is not an effective way to promote opportunity. Finally, in "What's Wrong with Vocational School?" Charles Murray argues that too many people are going to college and that some should consider vocational school as a viable alternative.

The *Chronicle of Higher Education* published this essay on April 22, 2015.

COLLEGE'S VALUE GOES DEEPER THAN THE DEGREE

ERIC HOOVER

Scholastic skepticism is contagious. Pundits and parents alike continue to second-guess the value of a college degree. After all, the recession has changed the way many Americans look at big-ticket purchases; plenty of families worry that today's expenses will not pay off tomorrow.

Not surprisingly, today's cost-conscious public views college price tags with a wary eye. According to the Pew Research Center survey of the American public, only 35 percent said colleges were doing a "good" job in terms of providing value to students and parents; 42 percent said "only fair," and 15 percent said "poor."

A curious thing happened when college graduates were asked about the value of their own degrees, however. In the Pew survey, 84 percent of those with degrees said college had been a good investment; only 7 percent said it had not.

Why? Perhaps it's because assessing the value of a college education is not a hard-and-fast calculation. Sure, diplomas help Americans land better jobs and earn higher salaries, and one can estimate the financial return on those investments. Yet the perceived benefits of attending college go well beyond dollars.

In the Pew survey, all respondents were asked about the "main purpose" of college. Forty-seven percent said "to teach knowledge and skills that can be used in the workplace," 39 percent said "to help an individual grow personally and intellectually," and 12 percent said "both equally."

These findings echo the words graduates often use to describe the benefits 6 of their college experiences. Typically, those benefits are intangible, immeasurable, and untethered to narrow questions about what a particular degree "got" them.

Evan Bloom's diploma will tell you only so much about him. As an 7 under-graduate at the University of California at Berkeley, Mr. Bloom considered several majors. He wanted to take hands-on courses that would require creative thinking. Finally, he settled on architecture.

After graduating, in 2007, Mr. Bloom worked in construction manage- 8 ment for a few years, but life inside a cubicle bored him. Recently, he decided to pursue a passion for which he has no credentials: cooking.

Mr. Bloom, 25, is the co-founder of Wise Sons Jewish Delicatessen, a 9 catering business in San Francisco. The venture, which serves the public out of rented space once a week, has yet to become a full-time, brick-and-mortar business. That's likely to change as soon as investors come aboard.

Mr. Bloom believes his out-of-classroom experiences prepared him to 10 become a restaurateur. At Berkeley he was active in the student government, honing his networking skills. As a member of the university's Hillel chapter, he and a friend, Leo Beckerman, cooked weekly meals for groups of 250. The experience inspired them to start Wise Sons together.

More than once, Mr. Bloom has thought about the power of connections 11 made in college. An alumnus of his fraternity helped him get an internship with the contractor for whom he later worked. And had he not met Mr. Beckerman at a bar one night years ago, he might still be doing something he enjoys less than making pastrami and rye bread.

"My classes were great, but it was really everything else I was doing that 12 mattered the most," Mr. Bloom said. "It was tapping into this whole sphere of influences."

"Basic, Fundamental Training"

The way her life unfolded, Vanessa Mera didn't end up needing her bach- 13 elor's degrees in psychology and economics. After graduating from the University of Miami in 2001, she and her sister took over their parents' import-export-distribution business, called VZ Solutions Inc., in Miami.

Still, Ms. Mera, 31, says her time in college was crucial. As a freshman, 14 she had expected to major in biology and go on to medical school. Over time, she realized that she didn't want to become a doctor. "In college, you come in thinking one thing about yourself," she said, "and you leave thinking in a completely different way."

Ms. Mera, who had attended a private all-girls high school, believes that 15 interacting with people of different backgrounds helped her overcome her shyness. So, too, did the time she spent studying in Spain.

Surrounded by many high-achieving students at Miami, Ms. Mera devel- 16 oped a competitive streak. If you want to land a good internship, she learned, you must put yourself out there.

"I realized that just because you had good grades didn't mean you were 17 going to get anywhere," Ms. Mera said. "Without those four years, I wouldn't be the businessperson I am today. I wouldn't have the confidence."

Jane Knecht can relate. She enrolled at the University of Virginia in the 18 late 1970s, unsure of what she wanted to study. She signed up for an introductory rhetoric course. "I didn't even know what the word meant," she said.

Soon, Ms. Knecht couldn't get enough. In a course on rhetoric and social 19 theory, she recalled, a professor gave students three unrelated pieces of writing and told them to synthesize an argument that tied them all together. At first, she froze up, worried that she couldn't do it. Then the writing flowed.

As Ms. Knecht practiced public speaking and wrote a mountain of papers, 20 her self-confidence soared: "It was basic, fundamental training."

Ms. Knecht graduated in 1982 with a degree in speech communications. 21 She had planned to go to law school, but instead spent seven years at home with her two children before entering the work force. At 52, she's now director of business development at the Water Environment Research Foundation, in Alexandria, Virginia.

Without a bachelor's degree, Ms. Knecht figures, she wouldn't have been 22 considered for the job. Many of her colleagues have master's degrees or Ph.D.'s. Moreover, she believes college prepared her for day-to-day challenges.

"Everything in my job is relationship-based," said Ms. Knecht, who on a 23 recent afternoon was preparing to run a conference call with business associates in Australia, followed by a board meeting. "My classes helped me recognize the importance of listening and effective negotiating, and how to go into new situations, which I do all the time."

Billy Ray, 59, described his degree as a door that led him to prosperity. 24 His parents were poor, as were most of his childhood friends. "We were on the bottom rung," he said. "I didn't like where I was, and I wanted to change that."

When Mr. Ray enrolled at Stephen F. Austin State University in 1970, he 25 found himself surrounded by people with fatter wallets and high aspirations. This inspired him. "I was associating with a different level of people," he said. He put himself through college by working for a construction company during the summers.

Mr. Ray says the contacts he made in college were just as crucial as the 26 courses he took. After graduating with a degree in business administration, Mr. Ray went to work for the construction company as a licensed plumber. Later, a good friend from Stephen F. Austin offered him a job selling trucks at a dealership. "I went from making good money to really good money," he said.

Mr. Ray, who lives in Lufkin, Texas, is now a regional manager for De 27 Lage Landen, a financial-services company. He and his wife, Alys, own a 3,000-square-foot house, and they recently purchased a second home, in Austin, where both of their sons graduated from the University of Texas.

Having written all those tuition checks, Mr. Ray understands why some 28 people question the value of college. "You're losing four years of work time and thousands of dollars," he said. "Do you ever get it back?"

Still, Mr. Ray, the only one of three brothers to finish college, said he would have a much lower-paying job without a bachelor's degree (his current position requires one). And the value of going to college, he believes, is only increasing. "If they don't get that degree," he said, "they're going nowhere."

> "And the value of going to college, he believes, is only increasing."   29

⊖ READING ARGUMENTS

1. In your own words, paraphrase Hoover's thesis.

2. Where does Hoover state his thesis? Why does he wait so long to do so? What information does he present before he states it? Why?

3. What is the relationship between paragraphs 6 and 7? What transition is Hoover making at this point in the essay?

4. Hoover supports his thesis with several anecdotal examples. What point do these examples make? What are the strengths and weaknesses of this kind of evidence? What other types of evidence could Hoover have included?

5. In what respects is this essay an evaluation argument?

This essay was published on The Hechinger Report, an education website, on September 1, 2015.

STOP SAYING "COLLEGE ISN'T FOR EVERYONE"

ANDRE PERRY

Let's admit that the "college isn't for everyone" cliché is really a euphemism for 1
those people aren't smart enough for college.

At historically black fraternity Kappa Alpha Psi's Grand Chapter Meeting, 2
or Conclave, in New Orleans last month, the phrase again reared its ugly head, when audience members repeatedly embedded it in questions to a panel in black male achievement hosted by the White House Initiative on Educational Excellence for African American Students.

The "college isn't for everyone" statement isn't false; it's just disingenu- 3
ous. According to the Lumina Foundation, a funder of The Hechinger Report, nearly 39 percent of Americans between 25 and 64 years old hold at least a two-year college degree. However, only 28 percent of blacks, 23 percent of Native Americans, and 20 percent of Latinos possess at least a two-year degree. Meanwhile, 44 percent of whites and 59 percent of Asians hold degrees.

Clearly, not everyone goes to college. But the "not for everyone" verbiage is most frequently used in conversations about improving education for low-income students. Soon thereafter comes the unimaginative bailout for underachieving kids—vocational training. 4

Let's be clear. We should prepare all students as if they are going to college. 5

There is a perception that trades require a completely different foundation than a college prep curriculum. The national push for career and technical education (vocational) focuses on "skills he or she can provide to a business" as opposed to those designed to prepare students for college. 6

This doesn't mean that all students shouldn't be prepared with rigorous courses. One study found that "students in career pathways outperformed their peers on the number of credits they earned in STEM and AP classes while also earning higher GPAs in their CTE classes." The study goes on to recommend rigorous curricula that don't hinder students' chances of going to college. 7

Intimating that we remove academic rigor because certain kids can't handle it actually downgrades professions as well as the academic sophistication needed to be successful for any career choice in the 21st century. There are high-paying jobs that only require a high school diploma. For instance, a college degree won't predict one's career performance as a coder. 8

Famous college dropouts like Steve Jobs, Mark Zuckerberg, and Bill Gates are often used as examples of how high-paying jobs are available for those with only high school or community college training. But Zuckerberg and Jobs aren't examples of why colleges don't work; they are examples of why colleges must change. These men shopped for courses they needed, gained networks, and acculturated (to a degree). 9

> "But Zuckerberg and Jobs aren't examples of why colleges don't work; they are examples of why colleges must change."

College and universities must change. Now acting as high-priced finishing schools where the middle-class networks, colleges need to become more affordable, flexible, relevant, and inclusive. In particular, they must create programs that are relevant and affordable to the populations they are supposed to serve. 10

What if the first two years of college were treated like the 13th and 14th grades? Obama's free community college plan addresses the reality that postsecondary education is requisite for personal and social vitality. The college debt argument within 'college isn't for everyone' debates is vital, but it's a red herring. If you think college is expensive, try living without a degree. 11

One may assume brothers of a black Greek letter organization, whose membership is predicated on the matriculation, initiation, and graduation of undergraduates, think that college is for everyone. Black Greek letter organizations, which represent one of higher education's most cherished traditions, must trumpet the college is for everyone horn. 12

I was happy to learn about Kappa Alpha Psi's Diamond in the Rough campaign at the "Klave." Diamonds in the rough exposes "young men across the nation to an intense college preparatory and scholarship access program." 13

The program provides resources for ACT/SAT test preparation and scholarships for each graduating class of "Kappa Leaguers" and increases access to scholarship opportunities for them nationally. Individual preparation is critical.

College isn't just for people whom we deem ready. We actually need to educate and transform people whom we're not ready for. Achievement as a result of selectivity isn't education—it's selectivity. 14

It's not a bourgie fantasy to expect plumbers and electricians to know the building blocks of language arts, math, and science. It's also not fantasy that fraternal organizations see people who are interested in the trades as future member/collegians. By growing membership and graduation rates, fraternities and sororities offer a bridge from low-income communities to college graduation stages. 15

College may not be for everyone, but it should be. 16

◯ READING ARGUMENTS

1. What is Perry's thesis? Where does he state it?

2. In paragraph 9, Perry refers to the examples of college dropouts like Mark Zuckerberg and Bill Gates. What point does he use them to make?

3. Perry writes, "It's not a bourgie fantasy to expect plumbers and electricians to know the building blocks of language arts, math, and science" (para. 15). What does *bourgie* mean? To what does the phrase *bourgie fantasy* refer?

4. What does Perry mean in paragraph 14 when he says, "We actually need to educate and transform people whom we're not ready for"?

5. In his opening sentence, Perry asserts, "Let's admit that the 'college isn't for everyone' cliché is really a euphemism for *those people aren't smart enough for college*." Why is "college isn't for everyone" a cliché? Do you agree with his assessment? Why or why not?

This essay appeared in the *National Review* in its January 9, 2014, issue.

THE COLLEGE TRAP
J. D. VANCE

A few years ago, a friend learned that a mutual acquaintance had accepted a job with an elite D.C. law firm, at a starting salary of $160,000. She turned pre-law almost overnight. Because I was thinking about law school myself, I knew that those high-paying jobs were vanishing for all but the luckiest graduates. My friend was undeterred: She took an extra year of classes to raise her GPA for the applications (incurring thousands in debt in the process) and crammed for the law-school admissions test. It was an admirable effort. But eventually the reality of the employment market set in, and she took a different job. She never did go to law school. 1

My friend displayed a classic middle- and working-class mindset. In his 2010 book *How Rich People Think*, Steve Siebold criticized the almost religious belief "that master's degrees and doctorates are the way to wealth." I had that belief too—it's why I wanted to go to law school in the first place—and so does virtually everyone I've ever known. When you grow up at the bottom or even in the middle, advanced education is the Holy Grail. Parents mortgage their homes and children donate their plasma (seriously) to pay for it.

Lately, writers have questioned whether many people spend too much on college and get too little in return. This fear has motivated recent proposals to encourage online education or make a $10,000 bachelor's degree available to everyone. But there is a deeper problem with the college cult than the diminishing value of certain degrees: In our zeal to give many a college education, we've made it an employment barrier for those who lack it.

You can imagine the reaction if, tomorrow, Congress passed a worker-identification law with the following provision: "Only those who carry their federal ID card may apply for jobs that pay more than $45,000; ID cards may be obtained from government vendors for $100,000." The country would erupt in protest. Yet this is what college does. When two people apply for a job, and they're alike in every way except schooling, the employer will almost always hire the more educated. That's true even of the many jobs that don't require a college degree. As economists Neeta Fogg and Paul Harrington recently found, a shocking 39 percent of new graduates are working such jobs.

Academics call this phenomenon "degree inflation." In an economy populated by college graduates, bachelor's degrees become necessary just to get your foot in the door. A host of professions—photographers, lab technicians, and equipment operators—have seen their ranks swell with college graduates, despite the absence of any obvious need for forklift drivers to have studied Michel Foucault. The *New York Times* recently reported that these new education requirements often have little to do with ensuring that employees possess a particular skill set. Instead, they're an easy way to winnow the applicant pool: There are so many degree holders these days that you can eliminate all non–degree holders and still have plenty of people to hire from.

Unfortunately for many working-class Americans, that winnowing process falls hardest on them. As it's currently played, the college-education game simply isn't fair.

Part of the problem is that bright low-income children don't apply to colleges that match their talents. The brutal irony is that, for the poor, the colleges with the highest sticker prices are free (or close to it) because of generous need-based aid. So there's much to be said for policies that make low-income students aware of the options they have.

Still, there are many subtle ways that colleges discriminate against working-class students. Take, for example, the admissions process. A common critique of modern affirmative action is that class is a far better metric of misfortune than race, and that colleges should adjust their admissions preferences accordingly. The underlying assumption is that a poor student gets no admissions boost relative to a "wealthy student. But this actually understates the problem: Poor students are actively disadvantaged in the process. In a recent study, Princeton sociologists Thomas Espenshade and Alexandria Radford discovered that at private colleges—whose graduates have, on average, significantly better employment prospects than graduates of public schools—a poor white student is three times less likely to receive an admissions offer than his wealthy counterpart with the exact same grades and SAT scores. Race doesn't explain this, and neither do grades or standardized tests.

What does explain it? One factor is that a lot of colleges are not "need-blind": They are simply less likely to accept students who will need more financial aid. Another answer is obvious to anyone who's applied to a prestigious college. To gain admission to these places, you don't just need scores and grades, you need a padded résumé—internships, sports, extracurriculars, and leadership positions. The Princeton Review, a test-coaching company, estimates that up to a third of the average college application is based on exactly these "soft factors." But for a working-class child, chess club, baseball, and student government usually give way to an after-school job. And admissions officers apparently care little about an applicant's experience bagging groceries.

When these students do get into college, they often encounter other barriers unique to their circumstances. Most parents complete their kid's financial-aid forms, for instance, but a lot of poor students must fight through the bureaucratic morass alone. That's harder than it sounds: For the 7.5 million impoverished kids living with single moms, filling out Dad's income figures on the annual financial-aid application requires serious detective work. One recent graduate I spoke with had to borrow money from a friend so that he could pay his first month's rent and security deposit. Even though he'd been awarded tens of thousands in financial aid, the money wasn't disbursed until a month after classes had started.

This is the minefield that progressives and many conservatives have labored to make the only path to the top in modern America. Of course, we married ourselves to college for all the right reasons: Policymakers wanted to help people, and statistics showed us that college graduates earned millions more than everyone else over a lifetime. The next step was obvious: Send more people to school. It was one of the truly bipartisan issues in our society. In the 2000 presidential campaign, Al Gore offered a $10,000 tuition deduction while George W. Bush promised more funding for scholarships and Pell Grants.

But to the extent that politicians viewed college education as a panacea for rising inequality and reduced upward mobility, they were wrong. The average college graduate may make more money, but anyone can tell you that a Harvard degree pays more than one from the online University of Phoenix—so statistics about the "average" graduate tell us little. The truth is that graduates of America's worst colleges have little to show for their time besides mountains of debt. And the graduates of those colleges are disproportionately poor.

Liberals justify the tens of billions we spend on college education on at least one other ground: that it ensures that our society is better prepared for the "new economy." President Obama has repeatedly committed the United States to leading the world in college-graduation rates by 2020, a goal that, if achieved, would allegedly cure many social ills. But if college is the key to the future, then it makes little sense that South Korea, Japan, and Canada—the best-educated societies on the planet—rank far behind the United States in per-person productivity. Meanwhile, Singapore and Switzerland, among the few countries that outrank us in terms of per capita GDP, lag behind the U.S. in college completion.

So, at the national level, the link between college education and productivity is virtually nonexistent. If we're not creating much value with the billions we spend on education, it's worth asking what those billions have bought. And the answer is: good jobs for university employees, and a social system that disadvantages the poor.   14

Economists have long understood that subsidies work best when producers are able to increase output. It's a very intuitive concept. If universities can't produce more employable graduates but are still taking in loads of cash, they'll spend it somewhere else. In practice, this meant that dorms grew plusher, professors earned more, administrative staffs swelled, and an industry of for-profit colleges sprouted from nowhere. A Goldwater Institute report found that since 1993, administrative outlays have increased by 61 percent per student. My own alma mater, Ohio State, employs six non-teachers for every full-time faculty member. This is where our education dollars go.   15

> "So, at the national level, the link between college education and productivity is virtually nonexistent."

Addressing this lack of practical skills, while helpful, is still only a partial solution. A big part of the problem is that by the time many of our poor kids reach college age, they're so far behind the curve that they'll never catch up. University of Chicago economist James Heckman, a winner of the Nobel Prize, has shown that far too many poor children lack the soft skills—such as the abilities to delay gratification and to cooperate—that help set the successful apart from everyone else. His research has found that high-quality early-childhood education is the most productive investment in the lower class. In fact, it's an investment that pays returns: We spend so much less in incarceration costs, welfare payments, and the like that we actually save tax dollars. The case for investing more in early-childhood education is based not just in fairness but in economics.   16

Not all early-childhood education is created equal. As progressives push for an expansion of the largely ineffective, federalized Head Start program, there is a better option: subsidizing early education in the same way we subsidize college education. Give people money and let them decide how to spend it.   17

Conservatives have supported vouchers for all the right reasons: Vouchers give kids the opportunity to escape a failing school, they give parents a choice, and they force educators to compete. Yet it needs to be said that vouchers grow less effective as children age. Skills beget skills, and knowledge begets knowledge: Heckman's research shows that a good preschool produces significantly better results for children than does a good high school. The most effective voucher programs will target our youngest kids, not those nearing adulthood.   18

This means that subsidizing college is a terrible way to promote opportunity. Of course, college still has value. There are millions of jobs that require advanced education. And many of our universities produce cutting-edge technologies that   19 create real growth and improve our nation's future. But we have reached a point of diminishing returns. Our society turns its nose up at 19-year-old plumbers while reinforcing the notion that every undergraduate is "going places." All the while, our government finances the creation of more undergraduates while doing little to help young kids close the skill gap.

The irony is that our economy needs more plumbers and fewer under- 20 graduates. And America's poor need more opportunity, not heavily subsidized pieces of paper.

⊙ READING ARGUMENTS

1. Vance begins his essay with an anecdote about a friend. What point does he make with this story? Is this an effective introduction? Explain.

2. In paragraph 3, Vance says that "there is a deeper problem with the college cult than the diminishing value of certain degrees." What does the "college cult" refer to? What is the "deeper problem"?

3. Where in his essay does Vance use an **argument by analogy**? Do you find it persuasive?

4. According to Vance, admission to a prestigious college or university is dependent on "soft factors" (para. 9). What are they? How does this situation disadvantage less affluent applicants?

5. Vance concedes that the "average college graduate may make more money" (12), but argues that this statistic tells us very little. Why?

6. In his conclusion, Vance says, "Our society turns its nose up at 19-year-old plumbers while reinforcing the notion that every undergraduate is 'going places'" (19). Do you think his generalization is true? Why or why not?

The *Wall Street Journal* published this opinion piece on January 17, 2007.

WHAT'S WRONG WITH VOCATIONAL SCHOOL?

CHARLES MURRAY

The topic yesterday was education and children in the lower half of the intelli- 1 gence distribution. Today I turn to the upper half, people with IQs of 100 or higher. Today's simple truth is that far too many of them are going to four-year colleges.

Begin with those barely into the top half, those with average intelligence. To 2 have an IQ of 100 means that a tough high-school course pushes you about as far as your academic talents will take you. If you are average in math ability, you may struggle with algebra and probably fail a calculus course. If you are average in verbal skills, you often misinterpret complex text and make errors in logic.

These are not devastating shortcomings. You are smart enough to engage 3 in any of hundreds of occupations. You can acquire more knowledge if it is presented in a format commensurate with your intellectual skills. But a genuine college education in the arts and sciences begins where your skills leave off.

In engineering and most of the natural sciences, the demarcation between 4 high-school material and college-level material is brutally obvious. If you cannot handle the math, you cannot pass the courses. In the humanities and social sciences, the demarcation is fuzzier. It is possible for someone with an IQ of 100 to sit in the lectures of Economics 1, read the textbook, and write answers in an examination book. But students who cannot follow complex arguments accurately are not really learning economics. They are taking away a mishmash of half-understood information and outright misunderstandings that probably leave them under the illusion that they know something they do not. (A depressing research literature documents one's inability to recognize one's own incompetence.) Traditionally and properly understood, a four-year college education teaches advanced analytic skills and information at a level that exceeds the intellectual capacity of most people.

There is no magic point at which a genuine-college-level education 5 becomes an option, but anything below an IQ of 110 is problematic. If you want to do well, you should have an IQ of 115 or higher. Put another way, it makes sense for only about 15 percent of the population, 25 percent if one stretches it, to get a college education. And yet more than 45 percent of recent high-school graduates enroll in four-year colleges. Adjust that percentage to account for high-school dropouts, and more than 40 percent of all persons in their late teens are trying to go to a four-year college—enough people to absorb everyone down through an IQ of 104.

No data that I have been able to find tell us what proportion of those stu- 6 dents really want four years of college-level courses, but it is safe to say that few people who are intellectually unqualified yearn for the experience, any more than someone who is athletically unqualified for a college varsity wants to have his shortcomings exposed at practice every day. They are in college to improve their chances of making a good living. What they really need is vocational training. But nobody will say so, because "vocational training" is second class. "College" is first class.

Large numbers of those who are intellectually qualified for college also 7 do not yearn for four years of college-level courses. They go to college because their parents are paying for it and college is what children of their social class are supposed to do after they finish high school. They may have the ability to understand the material in Economics 1 but they do not want to. They, too, need to learn to make a living—and would do better in vocational training.

Combine those who are unqualified with those who are qualified but not 8 interested, and some large proportion of students on today's college campuses—probably a majority of them—are looking for something that the four-year college was not designed to provide. Once there, they create a demand for practical courses, taught at an intellectual level that can be handled by someone with a mildly above-average IQ and/or mild motivation. The nation's colleges try to accommodate these new demands. But most of the practical specialties do not really require four years of training, and the best way to teach those specialties is not through a residential institution with the staff and infrastructure of a college. It amounts to a system that tries to turn out televisions on an assembly line that also makes pottery. It can be done, but it's ridiculously inefficient.

Government policy contributes to the problem by making college scholarships and loans too easy to get, but its role is ancillary. The demand for college is market-driven, because a college degree does, in fact, open up access to jobs that are closed to people without one. The fault lies in the false premium that our culture has put on a college degree. 9

For a few occupations, a college degree still certifies a qualification. For example, employers appropriately treat a bachelor's degree in engineering as a requirement for hiring engineers. But a bachelor's degree in a field such as sociology, psychology, economics, history, or literature certifies nothing. It is a screening device for employers. The college you got into says a lot about your ability, and that you stuck it out for four years says something about your perseverance. But the degree itself does not qualify the graduate for anything. There are better, faster, and more efficient ways for young people to acquire credentials to provide to employers. 10

> "A bachelor's degree in a field such as sociology, psychology, economics, history, or literature certifies nothing."

The good news is that market-driven systems eventually adapt to reality, and signs of change are visible. One glimpse of the future is offered by the nation's two-year colleges. They are more honest than the four-year institutions about what their students want and provide courses that meet their needs more explicitly. Their time frame gives them a big advantage—two years is about right for learning many technical specialties, while four years is unnecessarily long. 11

Advances in technology are making the brick-and-mortar facility increasingly irrelevant. Research resources on the internet will soon make the college library unnecessary. Lecture courses taught by first-rate professors are already available on CDs and DVDs for many subjects, and online methods to make courses interactive between professors and students are evolving. Advances in computer simulation are expanding the technical skills that can be taught without having to gather students together in a laboratory or shop. These and other developments are all still near the bottom of steep growth curves. The cost of effective training will fall for everyone who is willing to give up the trappings of a campus. As the cost of college continues to rise, the choice to give up those trappings will become easier. 12

A reality about the job market must eventually begin to affect the valuation of a college education: The spread of wealth at the top of American society 13 has created an explosive increase in the demand for craftsmen. Finding a good lawyer or physician is easy. Finding a good carpenter, painter, electrician, plumber, glazier, mason—the list goes on and on—is difficult, and it is a seller's market. Journeymen craftsmen routinely make incomes in the top half of the income distribution while master craftsmen can make six figures. They have work even in a soft economy. Their jobs cannot be outsourced to India. And the craftsman's job provides wonderful intrinsic rewards that come from mastery of a challenging skill that produces tangible results. How many white-collar jobs provide nearly as much satisfaction?

Even if forgoing college becomes economically attractive, the social 14 cachet of a college degree remains. That will erode only when large numbers of high-status, high-income people do not have a college degree and don't care. The information technology industry is in the process of creating that class, with Bill Gates and Steve Jobs as exemplars. It will expand for the most natural of reasons: A college education need be no more important for many high-tech occupations than it is for NBA basketball players or cabinetmakers. Walk into Microsoft or Google with evidence that you are a brilliant hacker, and the job interviewer is not going to fret if you lack a college transcript. The ability to present an employer with evidence that you are good at something, without benefit of a college degree, will continue to increase, and so will the number of skills to which that evidence can be attached. Every time that happens, the false premium attached to the college degree will diminish.

Most students find college life to be lots of fun (apart from the boring 15 classroom stuff), and that alone will keep the four-year institution overstocked for a long time. But, rightly understood, college is appropriate for a small minority of young adults—perhaps even a minority of the people who have IQs high enough that they could do college-level work if they wished. People who go to college are not better or worse people than anyone else; they are merely different in certain interests and abilities. That is the way college should be seen. There is reason to hope that eventually it will be.

⊖ READING ARGUMENTS

1. Construct a syllogism for the deductive argument Murray uses in his opening paragraphs. Do you find this argument persuasive? Why or why not?

2. Murray makes a distinction between engineering and the natural sciences (on the one hand) and the humanities and social sciences (on the other). What difference does he identify? Why is this difference important to his argument?

3. Murray claims that too many people are going to four-year colleges. What **cause-and-effect** arguments does he use to support this claim? How do these arguments support his position on the issue?

4. More than once in his essay, Murray notes that the "intellectually unqualified" probably do not want to attend a four-year college, and he implies that if given the chance, they would choose not to. Do you think this is true? Do you believe Murray's emphasis on personal choice strengthens his argument? Explain.

5. According to Murray, more people should go to vocational schools. What advantages does he see for those who choose careers in trades and crafts?

VISUAL ARGUMENT: WHY YOU SHOULD CONSIDER TRADE SCHOOL

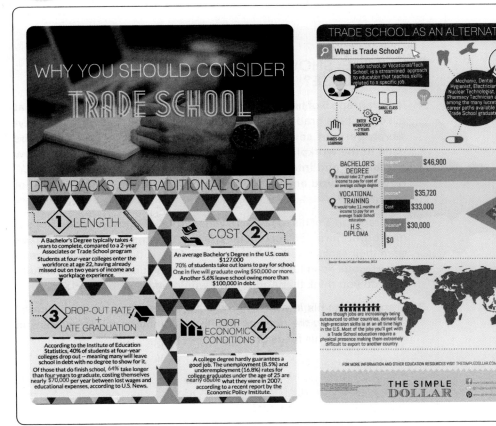

Bureau of Labor Statistics

�〜 READING ARGUMENTS

1. This visual is from a personal finance website and blog called The Simple Dollar. The site focuses on practical financial advice: eliminating debt, choosing a financial strategy, banking, and budgeting. How might the purpose of the site—and the nature of its audience—influence how the writers evaluate educational choices?

2. While this is a visual argument, it also requires a fair amount of reading. Are all these words necessary? Do you find the textual element of the graphic accessible and effective?

3. This visual has four different sections. Which is the strongest, or provides the best support for the main argument? Which element is the weakest? Explain.

�〜 AT ISSUE: SHOULD EVERY AMERICAN GO TO COLLEGE?

1. In paragraph 5 of his essay, Hoover cites a Pew Research Survey that asked college graduates about the main purpose of college: "Forty-seven percent said 'to teach knowledge and skills that can be used in the workplace,' 39 percent said 'to help an individual grow personally and intellectually,' and 12 percent said 'both equally.'" How would you answer this question about the main purpose of college?

2. In paragraph 5 of his essay, J. D. Vance writes: "A host of professions—photographers, lab technicians, and equipment operators—have seen their ranks swell with college graduates, despite the absence of any obvious need for forklift drivers to have studied Michel Foucault." How do you think that Andre Perry would respond to this claim?

3. Murray bases his argument on the IQ, or "intelligence distribution" (para. 1), among the general population. What are the strengths and weaknesses of his focus on IQ?

⊘ WRITING ARGUMENTS: SHOULD EVERY AMERICAN GO TO COLLEGE?

1. After reading and thinking about the four essays in this casebook, do you think more people should be encouraged to attend college, or do you think some people should be discouraged from doing so? Do you see higher education as a "right" (and a necessity) for most, or even all citizens? Write an argumentative essay in which you answer these questions.

2. Based on your own observations as well as the essays in this chapter, what is the biggest challenge—or challenges—that most students face as they make their way through a postsecondary education?

How Should We Solve the Opioid Problem?

In her essay "The Myth of What's Driving the Opioid Crisis" (p. 672), psychiatrist Sally Satel argues that our dominant narrative for explaining this epidemic is misleading. Regardless of the epidemic's various causes or storylines, however, few dispute that it is a serious problem. The crisis has its roots in the 1990s, when doctors began taking a greater interest in pain management. With some encouragement from the pharmaceutical industry, physicians began prescribing the newly developed oxycodone, a powerful, semisynthetic painkilling opiate. Some doctors began overprescribing opiates or writing long-term prescriptions for these highly addictive medications when perhaps only a few doses were needed to deal with a patient's short-term pain. In some cases, addicted patients moved from prescription drugs to illicit substances, such as heroin and fentanyl. The effects have been staggering. According to the Centers for Disease Control (CDC), 700,000 people died from drug overdoses between 1999 and 2017; on average, 130 Americans die daily from opioid overdoses. Such statistics, of course, do not reflect the economic and emotional toll the epidemic has taken on the many individual communities and families that have been devastated by opiates.

Health experts, politicians, and the general public all recognize the problem, and the president has designated it a national emergency. In fact, at a time of intense political polarization, this is one substantive issue that Americans of all political leanings agree needs to be addressed. But the question remains: How? Not surprisingly, government regulators, medical associations, and doctors have worked to restrict prescriptions for these drugs as well as to reduce their proliferation. The CDC has released more stringent guidelines on how and when to dispense opioids. Law-enforcement agencies have worked to make their responses to the crisis more effective and humane. In the private sector, churches and other organizations have also tried to help address the issue in their communities, and in the United States as a whole. So far, however, the crisis persists.

The four writers represented in this casebook all provide informed insight into the problem even as they approach its complexity from different points of view. For Ericka Andersen ("The Opioid Epidemic Is a Cultural Problem. It Requires Cultural Solutions"), top-down solutions, which rely on government intervention and regulation are not the answer. In "The Solution to the Opioid Crisis," Stanton Peele argues that our current conventional wisdom about the crisis—offered by public health officials like the U.S. Surgeon General—is useless, at best. He urges a radical rethinking of the problem—as well as a reframing of the model of addiction as a "disease." Peter Moore ("The Other Opioid Crisis") addresses an entirely different aspect of the opioid problem: the plight of chronic pain sufferers who cannot get the medications that they need to alleviate their pain. Finally, in "The Myth of What's Driving the Opioid Crisis," Sally Satel offers a comprehensive critique of our culture's current understanding of the problem and suggests some possible remedies.

This essay was published in the *Washington Examiner* on August 21, 2018.

THE OPIOID EPIDEMIC IS A CULTURAL PROBLEM. IT REQUIRES CULTURAL SOLUTIONS

ERICKA ANDERSEN

The Centers for Disease Control and Prevention announced last week that drug 1 overdose deaths rose to 72,000 in 2017, a 10 percent increase from 2016. This is more than the number of people who die each year from car crashes or suicides.

Overdose deaths are now close to the 7th leading cause of death in this 2 country, responsible for 1.5 percent of all deaths.

The national numbers mask even bigger spikes in some states. In Indiana, 3 overdose rates increased by 17 percent in 2017, one of the largest increases the nation has seen.

The spike in overdose deaths will result in renewed calls to regulate opi- 4 oids, which are responsible for two-thirds of overdose deaths. Already, nearly three-quarters of Americans believe the government should do more to address the problem, according to a CBS poll from earlier this year.

But the overdose crisis is a cultural problem that doesn't necessarily 5 respond to government solutions. As regulations surrounding prescription painkillers tighten, more dangerous black market opioids like fentanyl have taken their place. Deaths by such synthetic opioids increased by one-third last year, according to the CDC.

Rather than doubling down on top-down initiatives like pharmaceutical 6 restrictions and the drug war, policymakers and concerned citizens should focus on fostering bottom-up cultural change through local community support, church programs, awareness campaigns, and free access to recovery programs.

People don't stop using drugs because doctors and pharmacists curb 7 prescriptions or because police step up enforcement. They stop using drugs because they find a greater purpose, a supportive community, and a reason to live beyond the high.

Projects like Back on My Feet, where I was a volunteer leader for several 8 years, use running as a means to help recovering addicts overcome. I remain friends with at least one man from the program who has retained his sobriety for more than 7 years now.

Another example is The Phoenix, a gym whose only membership require- 9 ment is 48 straight hours of sobriety and offers a vital community aspect so many addicts are missing in their lives. Studies show that regular exercise may help in preventing drug addiction, due to the natural release of dopamine that is similar to that of a manufactured high.

You can also look to things like local YMCAs and community centers, which foster community engagement in a healthy way that promotes friendship, camaraderie, and purpose. Additionally, new churches in small communities attract individuals who had never attended church or hadn't attended in many years. It's clear there is a strong desire for this kind of life support, and yet it won't ever be the main focus for combating addiction in the media or on Capitol Hill.

> "Government efforts 10 to regulate opioid prescription may even exacerbate the epidemic."

Policymakers should prioritize funding these types of programs and pro- 11 mote more personalized kinds of help that has a lasting impact and addresses the root of the issue, rather than one of access and regulation. Empowerment of local communities to help their citizens where they are is a far better way than national regulations that consider all victims of addiction to require the same solutions.

Government efforts to regulate opioid prescription may even exacerbate the 12 epidemic by forcing those in pain onto the black market to use far more danger-ous and unregulated opioids. "The focus on prescription painkillers is especially misguided now that the vast majority of opioid-related deaths actually involve illegally produced drugs," said veteran journalist on the issue, Jacob Sullum.

I speak with the conviction of the converted. On a recent radio show, 13 where I discussed my support for government initiatives to regulate the phar-maceutical industry, a distressed caller educated me about her sister. She lives with chronic pain and is now unable to get the appropriate amount of painkill-ers she needs to control it. Her misery made me rethink my original support for tackling the crisis through regulations that put limits on drugs based on arbitrary quantities.

Adam Trosell of Pittsburgh, who has lived with chronic pain for 15 years 14 and has been unable to find a doctor to prescribe the opioids that had been providing him relief, noted that the depression that comes with chronic pain is horrific. He says government efforts to overregulate are "inhumane and cruel" to people like him. In the most extreme cases, some in chronic pain who are unable to access painkillers because of well-intended government regulations are considering or committing suicide.

As last week's overdose data demonstrates, government regulation is not 15 curbing the overdose epidemic. Cultural organizations like Back on My Feet, The Phoenix, and local community centers are more powerful, long-lasting solutions for addicts. Policymakers should give these a fresh look before doubling down on failed prohibition policies.

⊖ READING ARGUMENTS

1. Beyond introducing the topic, what do the first three paragraphs of this essay accomplish?

2. Where does Andersen introduce appeals to *ethos*? Do you find these appeals persuasive? Why or why not?

3. Where does Andersen use a **cause-and-effect** argument? In what sense is this essay a **proposal** argument?

4. According to Andersen, government efforts to regulate opioids may actually make the problem worse. Why?

5. Andersen makes several broad claims in paragraph 11. Does she support these claims with evidence? Explain.

This article first appeared in *Psychology Today* on March 6, 2017.

THE SOLUTION TO THE OPIOID CRISIS
STANTON PEELE

Here's What We Must Do to Improve Our Addictive Situation

In 2016, the American Surgeon General, Vivek Murthy, announced in a new 1 report on addiction, as though he had just discovered the structure of DNA, "Addressing the addiction crisis in America will require seeing addiction as a chronic illness, not as a moral failing. Addiction has been a challenge for a long time, but we finally have the opportunity and the tools to address it." At last, we're ready to solve addiction!

Murthy has lately been joined by such medical and social luminaries (both 2 of whom I admire) as Atul Gawande and J.D. Vance.

Instead of presenting solutions, however, Murthy simply rehashed our 3 tried-and-failed American bromides. In their place, I outline the actual strategies, almost the reverse of what he is proposing, to solve our addiction crisis.

Murthy's Bromides

1. Scare People (Even More!) about Opioid "Overdoses."
If people were to consume pure doses of heroin or other opioids, their likeli- 4
hood of accidental death is reduced to nearly naught. Yet the myth that people
typically develop an inordinate, insatiable desire for a single drug—when in
fact those most at risk are mixing a variety of substances in what can be considered either a chaotic pattern or an abandoned, intentionally self-destructive
one—still fatally misinforms our policies.

2. Convince People That Drugs Cause Addiction.
The headline news from the Surgeon General's report: "1 in 7 in USA will face 5
substance addiction." "We underestimated how exposure to addictive substances can lead to full blown addiction," Murthy told NPR. "Opioids are a good
example." Note to the Surgeon General: The definitive U.S. psychiatric guide,
DSM-5, no longer applies the term "addiction" to any substances, but only to
non-drug activity. How he rationalizes his perspective that drugs have an
insufficiently recognized special quality of addiction with the *DSM*-approved
possibility of becoming addicted to gambling, or the non-*DSM*-approved but
still-real possibility of becoming addicted to sex, love, the internet, or any other
compelling involvement, is anyone's guess.

Addiction is not in the thing. Addiction is in the life. And when addiction 6
is understood as being steeped in people's lives, we recognize that myriad drug
or non-drug experiences are liable to become compulsively destructive. The
thrust of Murthy's thinking—an impetus to further restrict access to certain
drugs—is as flawed conceptually as it is unachievable practically.

3. Emphasize "Prevention"—Meaning Avoiding Substance Use Altogether.
"The earlier people try alcohol or drugs," says the surgeon general's report, 7
"the more likely they are to develop a substance use disorder." Prevention,
to Murthy et al., means prevention of drug use, as opposed to what it should
mean: prevention of addiction or death.

These U.S. statistics are meaningless when considered outside of people's 8
life context in America, a context I provide in my book, *Addiction-Proof
Your Child*.

Consider that in Southern Europe, where people begin drinking legally at 9
much younger ages (typically 16), rates of problematic drinking are far lower than
in the U.S. and other temperance (Northern European and English-language)
countries. Consider that in the U.S., given restrictions on the use of alcohol and
other drugs, people's first experiences with them are likely to be binge episodes
with their peers, rather than moderate use with older, experienced family members. Consider that despite "Just Say No" being repeated to kids for decades,
40 percent have used marijuana by the time they leave high school, and 33 percent
have drunk alcohol in the last 30 days—the majority of whom, critically, have
engaged in binge-drinking. Both of the numbers rise rapidly following high
school and into people's early 20s.

Simply teaching people not to use drugs has gotten us where we are today. 10

4. Hype Supposed Biological Causes of Addiction and Minimize Social Causes.

"We now know from solid data that substance abuse disorders don't discrimi- 11
nate," Murthy told NPR. "They affect the rich and the poor, all socioeconomic
groups and ethnic groups. They affect people in urban areas and rural ones."

This is quite wrong. Addiction does affect people from all backgrounds, 12
but not at equal rates. It does discriminate. As discussed by Maia Szalavitz:

> "Addiction rates are higher in poor people—not because they are less
> moral or have greater access to drugs, but because they are more likely to
> experience childhood trauma, chronic stress, high school dropout, men-
> tal illness, and unemployment, all of which raise the odds of getting and
> staying hooked."

Murthy instead pursues a line of thinking, our neurochemical revolution, 13
that has yet to produce a single meaningful diagnostic or treatment tool: "Now
we understand that these disorders actually change the circuitry in your brain.
They affect your ability to make decisions, and change your reward system and
your stress response. That tells us that addiction is a chronic disease of the brain."

Murthy's misdirection supports our heavily funded medical efforts to 14
thwart addiction while we ignore the critical social levers for reversing our
addiction epidemic—an approach that would instead require major social
change to address the havoc in poor urban and rural communities that turns
them into addiction hubs.

5. Expand Our Drug Treatment Industry and Addiction Support Groups.

"We would never tolerate a situation where only one in 10 people with cancer or 15
diabetes gets treatment, and yet we do that with substance-abuse disorders," said
Murthy, speaking of an estimated 20.8 million Americans with these disorders.

Contrary to this perceived shortfall, no other country in the world provides 16
as much disease-oriented addiction treatment (i.e., 12-step and vaguely biomed-
ical treatment—"vaguely" since no treatments actually directly address supposed
brain centers of addiction) as does the US. Yet North America, as a global harm
reduction report notes, has the "highest drug-related mortality rate in the world."

Research repeatedly demonstrates that those addicted to drugs regularly 17
solve their addictions given supportive life conditions. In fact, the large majority of dependent drug users reverse addiction on their own—most who ever
qualify for a substance use disorder diagnosis move past it by their mid-30s.

How are we providing so much treatment with such bad outcomes? This 18
is because we are incapable of acknowledging that most addiction treatment is
no more effective than the ordinary course of the "disease." And, thus, we can't
focus on what about people's lives enables them to recover, and to encourage
these conditions, rather than thrusting more and more people into treatment.

I Would Remedy (Well, Improve) America's Drug and Addiction Problems

What, instead, are the messages that the U.S. surgeon general *should* be 19
spreading?

1. Loudly advertise the dangers of drug-mixing. Spread this message 20 widely, including in schools, along with other critical information about drugs, while teaching drug-use and life skills.

2. Call for legal regulation of heroin and other currently illegal drugs to 21 protect users from unwittingly consuming the haphazard, fraudulent, and dangerous combinations often sold on the street. Call for painkillers to be available to people who want them under medical supervision, along with heroin maintenance sites, while making medical or other trained supervision of use available.

It is worth noting here that just as the Surgeon General's addiction report came 22 out, the *British Medical Journal (BMJ)* issued a clarion call: "The war on drugs has failed: doctors should lead calls for drug policy reform." The *BMJ*'s report does not contain the words "brain," "disease," or "addiction." Instead, it asserts:

> ". . . a thorough review of the international evidence concluded that governments should decriminalize minor drug offenses, strengthen health and social sector approaches, move cautiously towards regulated drug markets where possible."

3. The SG's report does note the usefulness of medication-assisted 23 **treatment** including drugs like methadone and buprenorphine to assist in quitting heroin with greatly reduced risk, but fails to recognize that, time and again, medications like naltrexone and baclofen are insufficient in themselves, and hardly improve overall outcomes, in quitting a drug or alcohol addiction.

4. Demand the full-scale deployment of other harm reduction services 24 **and supplies,** from naloxone (Narcan) to syringe access to supervised drug consumption rooms—an expansion that will not only save many lives, but also do far more to reduce the stigmatization of people who use drugs than the empty words in the current report.

5. Make clear that addiction is not a disease and therefore, that it is 25 escapable and not a lifelong identity. Instead, point out, it is a phenomenon driven by psychological and social factors, and therefore inseparable from the realities of people's daily lives. Publicly tell politicians that if they really care about reducing addiction, taking meaningful steps to address inequality and absence of opportunity and to rebuild meaningful community would be the single best thing they could do.

> "We must normalize and rationalize the reality of our drug use."

6. Declare that we must abandon the futile goal of a drug-free society, 26 which decades of efforts and billions of dollars have been unable to accomplish. Instead, recognize that we are all drug users—from caffeine and alcohol to prescribed medications to commonplace Adderall use by students. Affirm that drugs are a normal part of human experience, that they provide benefits, and that they are even enjoyed—despite their potential dangers. This is how we approach experiences and involvements—from driving to love and sex—that can have dangerous or overwhelming effects. It's how alcohol is used throughout Southern Europe—indeed, this is how the large majority of Americans who drink think about alcohol.

Radical as this is to American ears, we must normalize and rationalize the 27 reality of our drug use—as opposed to encouraging uncontrolled and chaotic use of drugs while simultaneously vilifying and demonizing them.

As Murthy's report trumpets by way of perversely recommending more of 28 what has long failed us: An American dies every 19 minutes from narcotics-related drug use. Or, as Gawande points out, more Americans now die of overdoses (they're not overdoses, see above) than died of AIDS at the peak of that epidemic. He recommends better prescription practices—which is a lot like proposing tax (or health care) reform. After it passes (if it *does* pass) the new system is immediately assailed for a whole new host of problems.

Vance simply announces in his *New York Times* op-ed that he is "found- 29 ing an organization to combat Ohio's opioid epidemic," but doesn't offer a single opioid-related solution. Actually, Vance's book *Hillbilly Elegy: A Memoir of a Family and Culture in Crisis*, shows that purpose and community are the cure—just as their absence is the problem. Let's hope that Vance, a moral and brilliant man, is able to affect these critical factors in Ohio, setting a model for proceeding elsewhere.

But what we really need is a whole new way of thinking. 30

○ READING ARGUMENTS

1. In his third paragraph, Peele criticizes former Surgeon General Vivek Murthy for his response to the opioid crisis: "Instead of presenting solutions, . . . Murthy simply rehashed our tried-and-failed American bromides." What is a bromide? What connotation does the word have? According to Peele, what are some of the specific problems with Murthy's suggestions?

2. How does Peele use **definition** to criticize Murthy's proposals—and to further his own argument?

3. According to Peele, what is the relationship between socioeconomic class and addiction? Why is it important to recognize the relationship?

4. The "disease model" has long been used to explain addiction. Peele argues, however, that we must make clear that addiction *is not* a disease. Why? What problems does he identify with that view?

5. Peele argues, "Radical as this is to American ears, we must normalize and rationalize the reality of our drug use—as opposed to encouraging uncontrolled and chaotic use of drugs while simultaneously vilifying and demonizing them" (para. 27). Do you agree? Why or why not?

This article appeared in *Prevention* magazine on February 1, 2018.

THE OTHER OPIOID CRISIS

PETER MOORE

Lauren Deluca had never thought much about her pancreas until it attacked her. 1
One day in 2015, she felt searing abdominal pain that worsened when she ate. "It
was like the scene in *Alien*," she recalls—the one where an extraterrestrial creature erupts from a space traveler's abdomen. The flare-ups were worst after meals,
when they sometimes also included nausea and vomiting. Her doctors were initially stumped in their efforts to diagnose the otherwise healthy 35-year-old, even
as her pain worsened. She made repeated trips to the emergency room, where she
engaged a series of doctors in an attempt to understand what was wrong and to
secure prescription opioids to help her cope.

Unfortunately for Deluca, her quest bore the marks of *doctor shopping*, a term 2
for the way in which people addicted to opioids accumulate overlapping prescriptions to feed their cravings. Deluca says she was doing nothing of the sort but feels
she was blackballed in her pursuit of treatments—of any kind—that would help
her survive her workdays as a business insurance broker in Worcester, MA.

She was eventually diagnosed with chronic pancreatitis, in which the 3
organ repeatedly becomes inflamed and sustains irreversible damage during
acute attacks. As the disease ran its course, she lost 11 percent of her pancreatic
function, vital for digestion, and dropped 20 lb from an already lean frame.
She's 37 now but says she feels older: Pain wears the body down.

Curbing a Crisis

In the past few years, the United States has grappled with the widespread use 4
of opioids, a class of drugs that includes prescription oxycodone (Oxycontin)
and hydrocodone with acetaminophen (Vicodin), as well as illegal versions
like heroin.

In 2015 alone, nearly 92 million people in the US—both prescription 5
drug users and illegal users—took opioids for various ailments, for both
short and long periods. About 13 million of these people misused them—
by obtaining and taking them illegally or by taking prescribed drugs they
no longer needed—according to a report published in the *Annals of Internal
Medicine*.

As the opioid crisis has mushroomed, these users typically seek out the 6
drugs on the street or switch to illegal drugs like heroin and fentanyl when
their access to a prescription ends. This has led to fatal overdoses in numbers that keep ticking alarmingly upward: The Centers for Disease Control
and Prevention tallied more than 200,000 fatal overdoses between 1999 and
2016; there were another 42,000 in 2016 alone, and the numbers were still
rising in 2017. As a result, federal and state governments have cracked down

on the drugs' availability, often by restricting the quantities doctors can prescribe.

The new policies are choking off access to the medications for some of the 7 87.5 million chronic-pain patients who take them according to their prescriptions and don't misuse them. Like Deluca, these people rely on regular access to often-modest doses of the medications to live productive lives. The "solution" to the opioid crisis—making the drugs scarcer—has, in effect, created a new kind of medical emergency, leaving people cut off from necessary medicine and cast under a cloud of suspicion.

Terri Lewis is a clinical specialist in rehabilitation and mental health in 8 Tennessee, a hotbed of opioid overdoses, who advocates for chronic-pain patients trying to find treatment and medication support. Lewis is also a prominent expert on patient abandonment, in which chronic-pain patients lose access to doctors concerned about running afoul of government-mandated restrictions. "It is a catastrophic situation," she says. "People are being cut off cold turkey by their doctors. They have no health care, they have no physician, and they have nowhere to go."

That includes Deluca, whose home state imposed strict regulations on 9 opioid prescriptions the year before she suffered her first pancreatic attack. She wasn't about to try to buy them illegally. She finally received medication from a doctor last December, but the dosage is too low, and she's still struggling to recover from the damage sustained when she was denied care. Now she manages the best she can—and has become an advocate for change.

Pain and Prescriptions

Until the early 1990s, pain was barely recognized as a symptom and, hence, 10 largely ignored—at least by doctors. Patients didn't have that luxury. They enrolled in the "bite on a stick" school of pain remediation, says Mary Lynn McPherson, a professor of palliative care at the University of Maryland.

Then, in the 1990s, the pain-treatment pendulum swung in favor of drug 11 interventions with the advent of powerful synthetic medications such as Oxycontin. These new drugs gave patients levels of relief they had not experienced previously. Urged along by "education" programs sponsored by the pharmaceutical industry, primary care physicians began prescribing them in greater quantities.

What doctors didn't necessarily account for: Pain comes in many forms. 12 There is acute pain, the kind you feel when you break a bone. Strong drugs can blunt the effects of that sort of trauma. Then there's chronic pain, which can result from a wrenched back, a botched surgery, a degenerative condition— and which delivers such a payload of hurt that it can rewire the body's nervous system. The American Chronic Pain Association lists more than 120 maladies that can cause persistent pain, without counting the likes of sports injuries or dental abscesses. Chronic pain affects more than 100 million adults, according to the National Academy of Sciences.

Sometimes, even after the injury or disease heals, the agony continues. 13 And when the pain lasts, the drugs often have to, too—which is not ideal when the most-prescribed medicines also hold a grave risk of addiction. Patients in these situations can safely take carefully calibrated doses of opioids at levels that don't trigger addiction for decades, says Richard W. Rosenquist, chair of pain management at Cleveland Clinic. People's reactions to the drugs are unique to them. Those who have constant, chronic pain take medication more frequently just to get through their days, and these patients are more likely to develop a tolerance and need higher doses. Others take low-strength doses only when they expect flare-ups. The key is to match the dosage to the patient.

An Overreaching Crackdown

But when the new category of opioids came out, some doctors prescribed them 14 in large quantities to sufferers of all kinds of pain. Pharmaceutical companies marketed them aggressively and played down the risk of addiction, according to the *American Journal of Public Health*. For a broken bone, opioids are meant to provide short-term help, says Sameer Awsare, an internist at Kaiser Permanente Santa Clara Medical Center in California. "If it will hurt for only 2 or 3 days, you should get 10 pills, not 200 pills, which is what ended up happening," he says. "People got addicted and took more."

That's how a limited, but effective, medicine became a scourge. The 15 United States makes up 4.6 percent of the world's population; 80 percent of all opioids are consumed here, including 99 percent of the hydrocodone, says Awsare.

As the number of overdoses grew, all 50 states launched legislative 16 assaults on the problem, including seven that declared public health emergencies. (Massachusetts was the first, in 2014.) They mandated rollbacks in the number and duration of opioid prescriptions, established registries of users, began monitoring pharmacies, and closely watched and placed restrictions on doctors who were prescribing the drugs. In addition to *doctor shopping*, the term *pill mill* (a clinic that is loose with prescriptions) entered the lexicon. Last August, President Donald Trump declared the opioid crisis a national emergency, pledging funds and extra enforcement (with no tangible results to date beyond the measures already in place).

Predictably, opioids taken under any circumstance were swept up in 17 the panic around illegal use. According to the CDC, 40 million fewer opioid prescriptions were written in 2016 than 2 years earlier, the lowest rate in more than a decade. But opioid-related deaths continue to soar, largely because of an influx of street drugs that have effects that are similar to those of the medication. And the pressure on doctors to curb prescriptions remains intense. "When you're a prescriber and the Drug Enforcement Administration is breathing over your shoulder," says the University of Maryland's McPherson, "you think, *Uh-huh, this is what I have to do.*"

Caught in the Middle

As a result of the crackdown, fewer doctors will even take a pain patient's appoint- 18
ment. Steven Wright, a physician who is also vice president of the Colorado Pain
Society, quit seeing patients 3 years ago. "I was becoming an administrator of a
drug-reduction plan rather than a clinician making decisions about the best thing
for the patient," he says.

This confluence of events leaves people like Zoe Haigh in a significant 19
bind. Haigh, 44, of Danville, CA, suffered a congenital hip dislocation as
an infant that wasn't discovered until she was 3 years old. She experiences
"bone rubbing on bone" whenever she moves and has taken opioids for
everyday pain since she was a child. She also takes hydromorphone (Dilaudid)
and extended-release morphine (Kadian) when she's going to be active and
fentanyl lozenges when she's in agony.

The opioid crisis has turned her into a suspected addict, she says. Bow- 20
ing to new restrictions, her doctor cut off her prescription last November,
Haigh says. Making things worse, she felt a social stigma on top of her pain.
"I was made to feel ashamed and a pariah for following my doctor's orders,"
she says.

Pain sufferers who can't get medication face the prospect of leading 21
diminished lives. Barbara Obstgarten, 69, an avid crafter from Long Island,
NY, had a 2008 knee replacement surgery that she says "went horribly wrong."
Her doctor went on vacation after the operation, and her rehabilitation was
unsupervised. She never recovered full use of her knee, and the pain has per-
sisted ever since.

> "For many, the prospect of being cut off triggers despair."

She takes hydrocodone with acetamin- 22
ophen (Norco) and tramadol to get through
the Christmas craft fair season and to handle flare-ups. "The day is going to come
when some of my doctors will not give
them to me," she says. "I've already had one
internist, whom I had a good relationship with for 30 years, tell me he won't give
me a prescription."

For many, the prospect of being cut off triggers despair. Wright, of the 23
Colorado Pain Society, cites a survey of 3,400 pain patients, doctors, and other
health care providers by the International Pain Foundation. Since the CDC
guidelines for opioid dosing came out, 84 percent of US patients surveyed said
they were experiencing more pain, and 42 percent admitted they were considering suicide due to their predicament.

It's no idle threat. Cathy Kean is a California pain patient and advocate 24
who maintains a database of fellow sufferers who have taken their own lives.
Her list—with references and personal histories—has 17 names. "I am fighting
for my life," Kean says. "But more than that, I'm fighting for the veteran who
has a gun to his head because he's in so much pain and feels nobody cares or
will listen."

The Battle for Access

Advocates like McPherson, of the University of Maryland, believe that health 25 care providers, including physicians, need to be skilled in pain management so they can minimize the risks. As Kristen Silvia, a rehabilitative specialist at the Maine Medical Partners in Portland, points out, there is ample evidence that asking questions about childhood trauma and family history of drug and alcohol abuse can help identify potential misusers. That could leave most patients, who are at less risk, free to access drugs that help them. And more research is needed to identify the best method for weaning patients off opioids, which currently isn't well understood.

Kean and others are calling for federal and state governments to adopt 26 more-nuanced policies and studies on the effects of opioids. Lauren Deluca, the pancreatitis patient, has formed a national nonprofit—the Chronic Illness Advocacy and Awareness Group (ciaag.net)—and taken lobbying trips to Washington, DC, to advocate for people like her. Her organization is pushing for the creation of "intractable pain" cards, similar to ones now issued for medical marijuana, that document the need for opioids. Says Deluca: "We are looking to put our medical care back into the hands of qualified physicians and get the DEA and Department of Justice out of our doctors' offices."

Stefan Kertesz, an addiction scholar and general internist at the University 27 of Alabama at Birmingham, recently spearheaded a petition submitted to the National Committee for Quality Assurance (NCQA), the nation's top health care accreditation organization, signed by 80 practitioners concerned about harm the restrictions are causing their patients. The petition asks the NCQA to avoid taking action that would push doctors to prescribe lower doses to stable patients. Last June, Kertesz presented a talk urging the CDC to clarify guidelines that have been widely misapplied, resulting in reduced dosages for all patients. Some regulators have told him they're aware of these issues, Kertesz says.

For people who are in pain every day, a new way of handling the opioid 28 epidemic—one with greater nuance that accommodates people with genuine needs—can't come soon enough.

⊖ READING ARGUMENTS

1. According to Moore, how many Americans took opioids—both legally and illegally—in 2015?

2. Before the 1990s, how was pain viewed and dealt with by doctors and others in the medical profession? What changed in the 1990s?

3. Moore includes anecdotal evidence in the form of personal stories about people suffering from pain. Do you find this evidence credible and persuasive? Why or why not?

4. What do you think Moore's purpose in writing this essay was? To inform? To persuade? To inspire some kind of action? Explain.

This article was published by the online magazine *Politico* on February 21, 2018.

THE MYTH OF WHAT'S DRIVING THE OPIOID CRISIS

SALLY SATEL

As an addiction psychiatrist, I have watched with serious concern as the opioid crisis has escalated in the United States over the past several years, and overdose deaths have skyrocketed. The latest numbers from the Centers for Disease Control and Prevention show fatalities spiraling up to about 42,000 in 2016, almost double the casualties in 2010 and more than five times the 1999 figures. The White House Council of Economic Advisers recently estimated that the opioid crisis cost the nation half a trillion dollars in 2015, based on deaths, criminal justice expenses, and productivity losses. Meanwhile, foster care systems are overflowing with children whose parents can't care for them, coroners' offices are overwhelmed with bodies, and ambulance services are straining small-town budgets. American carnage, indeed.

I have also watched a false narrative about this crisis blossom into conventional wisdom: The myth that the epidemic is driven by patients becoming addicted to doctor-prescribed opioids, or painkillers like hydrocodone (e.g., Vicodin) and oxycodone (e.g., Percocet). One oft-quoted physician refers to opioid medication as "heroin pills." This myth is now a media staple and a plank in nationwide litigation against drugmakers. It has also prompted legislation, introduced last spring by Senators John McCain and Kirsten Gillibrand—the Opioid Addiction Prevention Act, which would impose prescriber limits because, as a news release stated, "Opioid addiction and abuse is commonly happening to those being treated for acute pain, such as a broken bone or wisdom tooth extraction."

But this narrative misconstrues the facts. The number of prescription opioids in circulation in the United States did increase markedly from the mid-1990s to 2011, and some people became addicted through those prescriptions. But I have studied multiple surveys and reviews of the data, which show that only a minority of people who are prescribed opioids for pain become addicted to them, and those who do become addicted and who die from painkiller overdoses tend to obtain these medications from sources other than their own physicians. Within the past several years, overdose deaths are overwhelmingly attributable not to prescription opioids but to illicit fentanyl and heroin. These "street opioids" have become the engine of the opioid crisis in its current, most lethal form.

If we are to devise sound solutions to this overdose epidemic, we must understand and acknowledge this truth about its nature.

For starters, among people who are prescribed opioids by doctors, the rate of addiction is low. According to a 2016 national survey conducted by the Substance Abuse and Mental Health Services Administration (SAMHSA), 87.1 million U.S. adults used a prescription opioid—whether prescribed directly by a physician or obtained illegally—sometime during the previous year. Only 1.6 million of them, or about 2 percent, developed a "pain reliever use disorder," which includes behaviors ranging from over-use to overt addiction. Among patients with intractable, noncancer pain—for example, neurological disorders or musculoskeletal or inflammatory conditions—a review of international medical research by the Cochrane Library, a highly regarded database of systemic clinical reviews, found that treatment with long-term, high-dose opioids produced addiction rates of less than 1 percent. Another team found that abuse and addiction rates within 18 months after the start of treatment ranged from 0.12 percent to 6.1 percent in a database of half a million patients. A 2016 report in the *New England Journal of Medicine* concluded that in multiple published studies, rates of "carefully diagnosed" addiction to opioid medication averaged less than 8 percent. In a study several years ago, a research team purposely excluded chronic-pain patients with prior drug abuse and addiction from their data, and found that only 0.19 percent of the patients developed abuse and addiction to opioids.

Indeed, when patients do become addicted during the course of pain 6 treatment with prescribed opioids, often they simultaneously face other medical problems such as depression, anxiety, other mental health conditions, or current or prior problems with drugs or alcohol. According to SAMHSA's 2014 National Survey on Drug Use and Health, more than three-fourths of those who misuse pain medication already had used other drugs, including benzodiazepines and inhalants, before they ever misused painkillers. And according to CDC data, at least half of all prescription opioid-related deaths are associated with other drugs, such

> "For starters, among people who are prescribed opioids by doctors, the rate of addiction is low."

as benzodiazepines, alcohol, and cocaine; combinations that are often deadlier than the component drugs on their own. The physical and mental health issues that drive people to become addicted to drugs in the first place are very much part of America's opioid crisis and should not be discounted, but it is important to acknowledge the influence of other medical problems and other drugs.

Just because opioids in the medical context don't produce high rates of 7 addiction doesn't mean doctors aren't overprescribing and doing serious harm. The amount of opioids prescribed per person in 2016, though a bit lower than the previous year, was still considered high by the CDC—more than three times the amount of opioids dispensed in 1999. Some doctors routinely give a month's supply of opioids for short-term discomfort when only a few days' worth or even none at all is needed. Research suggests that patients given post-operation opioids don't end up needing to use most of their prescribed dose.

In turn, millions of unused pills end up being scavenged from medicine 8 chests, sold or given away by patients themselves, accumulated by dealers, and then sold to new users for about $1 per milligram. As more prescribed pills are diverted, opportunities arise for nonpatients to obtain them, abuse them, get addicted to them, and die. According to SAMHSA, among people who misused prescription pain relievers in 2013 and 2014, about half said that they obtained those pain relievers from a friend or relative, while only 22 percent said they received the drugs from their doctor. The rest either stole or bought pills from someone they knew, bought from a dealer or "doctor-shopped" (i.e., obtained multiple prescriptions from multiple doctors). So diversion is a serious problem, and most people who abuse or become addicted to opioid pain relievers are not the unwitting pain patients to whom they were prescribed.

While reining in excessive opioid prescriptions should help limit diversion 9 and, in theory, suppress abuse and addiction among those who consume the diverted supply, it will not be enough to reduce opioid deaths today. In the first decade of the 2000s, the opioid crisis almost seemed to make sense: The volume of prescribed opioids rose in parallel with both prescription overdose deaths and treatment admissions for addiction to prescription opioids. Furthermore, 75 percent of heroin users applying to treatment programs initiated their opioid addiction with pills, so painkillers were seen as the "gateway" to cheap, abundant heroin after their doctors finally cut them off. ("Ask your doctor how prescription pills can lead to heroin abuse," blared massive billboards from the Partnership for a Drug-Free New Jersey.) If physicians were more restrained in their prescribing, the logic went, fewer of their patients would become addicted, and the pipeline to painkiller addiction and ultimately to heroin would run dry.

It's not turning out that way. While the volume of prescriptions has 10 trended down since 2011, total opioid-related deaths have risen. The drivers for the past few years are heroin and, mostly, fentanyl, a synthetic opioid that is 50 times as potent as heroin. Fentanyl has legitimate medical use, but there is also illicit fentanyl, trafficked mostly from China, often via the Dark Web. Fentanyl and heroin (which itself is usually tainted to some extent with the fentanyl) together were present in more than two-thirds of all opioid-related deaths in 2016, according to CDC data. Painkillers were present in a little more than one-third of opioid-related deaths, but a third of those painkiller deaths also included heroin or fentanyl. While deaths from prescription opioids have basically leveled off, when you look at deaths in which prescription opioids *plus* heroin and fentanyl were present, then the recorded deaths attributed to prescription opioids continue to climb, too. (An especially pernicious element in the mix is counterfeiters with pill presses who sell illicit fentanyl in pill form deceptively labeled as OxyContin and other opioid pain relievers or benzodiazepines.)

Notably, more current heroin users these days seem to be initiating their 11 opioid trajectory with heroin itself—an estimated 33 percent as of 2015— rather than with opioid painkillers. In the first decade of the 2000s, about 75 to 80 percent of heroin users started using opioids with pills (though not necessarily pain medication prescribed by a doctor for that particular person). It seems that, far more than prescribed opioids, the unpredictability of heroin and the turbocharged lethality of fentanyl have been a prescription for an overdose disaster.

Intense efforts to curb prescribing are underway. Pharmacy benefit manag- 12 ers, such as CVS, insurers, and health care systems have set limits or reduction goals. Statebased prescription drug monitoring programs help doctors and pharmacists identify patients who doctor-shop, ER hop, or commit insurance fraud. As of July, 23 states had enacted legislation with some type of limit, guidance, or requirement related to opioid prescribing. McCain and Gillibrand's federal initiative goes even further, to impose a blanket ban on refills of the seven-day allotment for acute pain. And watchdog entities such as the National Committee for Quality Assurance have endorsed a system that compares the number of patients receiving over a certain dose of opioids with the performance rating for a physician.

A climate of precaution is appropriate, but not if it becomes so chilly that 13 doctors fear prescribing. This summer, a 66-year-old retired orthopedic surgeon who practiced in Northern California—I'll call her Dr. R—contacted me. For more than 30 years, she had been on methadone, a legitimate opioid pain medication, for an excruciating inflammatory bladder condition called interstitial cystitis. With the methadone, she could function as a surgeon. "It gave me a life. I would not be here today without it," she told me. But one day in July, her doctor said the methadone had to stop. "She seemed to be worried that she was doing something illegal," Dr. R told me.

Dr. R was fortunate. She found another doctor to prescribe methadone. 14 But her experience of nonconsensual withdrawal of opioids is not isolated. Last year, the nonprofit Pain News Network conducted an online survey among 3,100 chronic pain patients who had found relief with opioids and had discussed this in online forums. While not necessarily a representative sample of all individuals with chronic pain who are on opioids, the survey was informative: 71 percent of respondents said they are no longer prescribed opioid medication by a doctor or are getting a lower dose; 8 out of 10 said their pain and quality of life are worse; and more than 40 percent said they considered suicide as a way to end their pain. The survey was purposely conducted a few months after the CDC released guidelines that many doctors, as well as insurance carriers and state legislatures, have erroneously interpreted as a government mandate to discontinue opioids. In other accounts, patients complain of being interrogated by pharmacists about their doses; sometimes they are even turned away.

The most tragic consequence is suicide. Thomas F. Kline, an internist 15 in Raleigh, North Carolina, has chronicled 23 of them. His count is surely a harbinger of further patient abandonment to come. Meanwhile, so-called pain refugees—chronic pain patients whose doctors have dropped them— search out physicians to treat them, sometimes traveling more than a hundred miles or relocating. And in a recent Medscape survey, half the doctors who were polled expressed fear of violent reactions if patients were refused the prescription.

Knowing all this, what should we do about the opioid crisis? First, we 16 must be realistic about who is getting in trouble with opioid pain medications. Contrary to popular belief, it is rarely the people for whom they are prescribed. Most lives do not come undone, let alone end in overdose, after analgesia for a broken leg or a trip to the dentist. There is a subset of patients who are vulnerable to abusing their medication—those with substance use histories or with mental health problems. Ideally, they should inform physicians of their history, and, in turn, their doctors should elicit such information from them.

Still, given that diverted pills, not prescribed medication taken by patients 17 for pain, are the greater culprit, we cannot rely on doctors or pill control policies alone to be able to fix the opioid crisis. What we need is a demand-side policy. Interventions that seek to reduce the *desire* to use drugs, be they painkillers or illicit opioids, deserve vastly more political will and federal funding than they have received. Two of the most necessary steps, in my view, are making better use of anti-addiction medications and building a better addiction treatment infrastructure.

Methadone and buprenorphine are opioid medications for treating 18 addiction that can be prescribed by doctors as a way to wean patients off opioids or to maintain them stably. These medications have been shown to reduce deaths from all causes, including overdose. A third medication, naltrexone, blocks opioids' effect on the brain, and prevents a patient who tries heroin again from experiencing any effects. In 2016, however, only 41.2 percent of the nation's treatment facilities offered at least one form of medication, and 2.7 percent offered all three medications, according to a recent review of a national directory published by SAMHSA. We must move beyond the outmoded thinking and inertia that keep clinics from offering these medications.

Motivated patients also benefit greatly from cognitive behavioral therapy and from the hard work of recovery—healing family rifts, reintegrating into the workforce, creating healthy social connections, finding new modes of fulfillment. This is why treatment centers that offer an array of services, including medical care, family counseling, and social services, have a better shot at promoting recovery. That treatment infrastructure must be fortified. The Excellence in Mental Health Act of 2014, a Medicaid-funded project, established more robust health centers in eight states. In 2017, House and Senate bills were introduced to expand the project to 11 more. It's a promising effort that could be a path to public or private insurance-based community services and an opportunity to set much-needed national practice standards.

These two priorities are among the 56 recommendations put forth last 20 October by President Donald Trump's Commission on Combating Drug Addiction and the Opioid Crisis. Indeed, there is no dearth of ideas. In Congress, more than 90 bills aimed at the opioid crisis have been introduced in the 115th session, dozens of hearings have been held, and later this month, the House Energy and Commerce Committee will begin holding a week of legislative hearings on measures to fight the opioid crisis. The White House's 2019 budget seeks $13 billion over two years for the opioid epidemic, and the president recently nominated a "drug czar" to helm the Office of Drug Control Policy, though the candidate has minimal experience in the area.

As we sort through and further pursue these policies, we need to make 21 good use of what we know about the role that prescription opioids plays in the larger crisis: that the dominant narrative about pain treatment being a major pathway to addiction is wrong, and that an agenda heavily weighted toward pill control is not enough.

⊘ READING ARGUMENTS

1. In her opening sentence, is Satel appealing to *logos*, *ethos*, or *pathos*? Is this appeal convincing? Why or why not?

2. In the second paragraph, Satel refers to a "false narrative" that has become "conventional wisdom." What is this false narrative?

3. What is the purpose of paragraph 5? How does it both establish and advance the writer's argument?

4. In what respects is this a **proposal** argument? What remedies does Satel recommend? Where in her essay does she make these recommendations?

This public-service poster was created by a Canadian campaign to raise awareness about one particular danger of drug use.

 VISUAL ARGUMENT

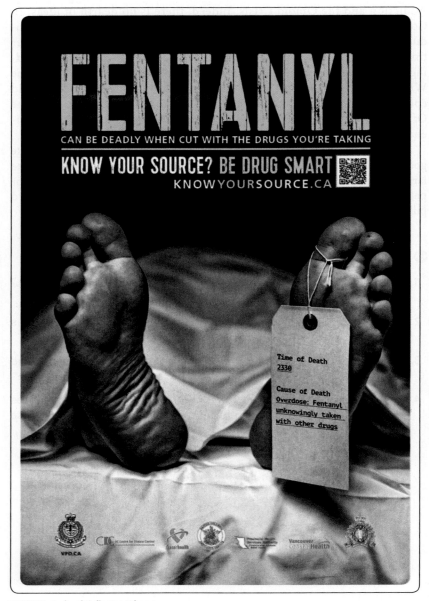

RMCP/Contraband Collection/Alamy

⊙ READING ARGUMENTS

1. Does this visual appeal primarily to *logos*, *pathos*, or *ethos*? Identify an element of each of these appeals in the image.

2. This visual uses both words and images to convey its message and emphasis. In one sentence, summarize this message. Which element (words or images) has the greater impact? Why?

3. This image was part of a campaign from the University of Calgary (Canada) Wellness Center. Who is the intended audience? What specific clues let you know?

⊙ AT ISSUE: HOW SHOULD WE SOLVE THE OPIOID PROBLEM?

1. In "The Myth of What's Driving the Opioid Crisis," Satel writes about a "false narrative" that has taken hold with regard to the opioid problem. To what degree are the three other writers in this casebook also addressing "false narratives"? What misleading or mistaken storylines is each trying to correct? Why is finding the "true" narrative so important in solving a problem like this one?

2. Think about how your own knowledge about alcohol, substance abuse, and addiction developed as you learned about them in school, from your friends and parents, from the media, and from medical professionals. What misunderstandings did you have about substance abuse or addiction? Did any of these essays surprise you, or change your mind about anything? Explain.

3. Stanton Peele writes that politicians need to be told that "if they really care about reducing addiction, taking meaningful steps to address inequality and absence of opportunity and to rebuild meaningful community would be the single best thing they could do." Do you think Ericka Andersen would agree with this statement? How might she respond to it?

⊙ WRITING ARGUMENTS: HOW SHOULD WE SOLVE THE OPIOID PROBLEM?

All the writers here not only address the opioid problem but also provide useful and substantive information about the crisis in their arguments. Write your own essay in which you take a position on this issue. How do you view the opioid problem? What do you see as the best solutions for addressing it?

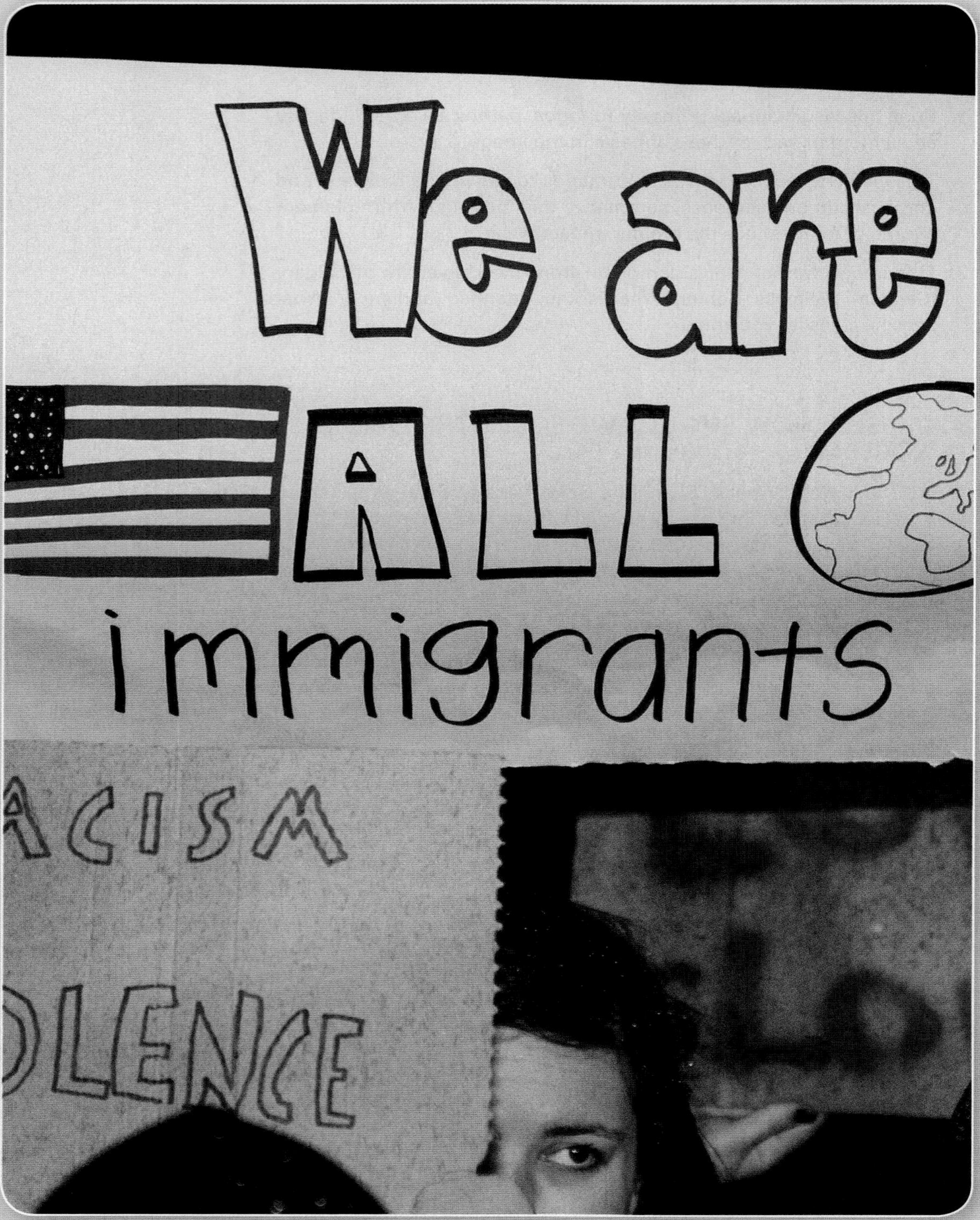

lynchpics/Alamy

Should the United States Have Open Borders?

For much of its history, the United States had—for all practical purposes—open borders. Before the United States was established, there was no national government to devise or implement policies on what were, in many ways, fluid and often-contested dividing lines between various nations, colonies, and territories. Moreover, the United States encouraged immigration during the late eighteenth century and much of the nineteenth century. In the era after the Civil War, however, the federal government took a more active role in regulating immigration and border control. The Immigration Act of 1882, for example, required immigrants to pay a fee for entry and blocked certain categories of people from immigrating, including criminals and any individual "unable to take care of him or herself without becoming a public charge." That same year, the Chinese Exclusion Act was passed, prohibiting the immigration of Chinese laborers. This was the first exclusionary U.S. immigration law based on nationality and ethnicity. During the first part of the twentieth century, waves of immigrants (over twenty-four million, in total) led to more regulation and legislation, including the Emergency Quota Act of 1921. This law placed limits on the number of people granted entry to the United States from any given country.

Throughout the rest of the twentieth century, and now in the twenty-first century, the question of who should be admitted to the United States, and how they should enter the country, has remained problematic, encompassing a variety of complex issues, such as nationalism, crime, sovereignty, national identity, labor, the environment, and the economy. President Donald Trump famously made border security the cornerstone of his campaign, and he has often framed the problem in apocalyptic terms. For example, he once tweeted, "Without Borders, we don't have a country. With Open Borders, which the Democrats want, we have nothing but crime! Finish the Wall!" In fact, illegal border-crossings have been at historic lows over the past few years. Moreover, illegal immigrants are *less likely* to commit crimes than native-born Americans. Still, many Americans agree with the president that our borders should be strictly controlled. Not surprisingly, then, border security and immigration continue to be highly polarized issues, even though most people on both sides of the partisan divide agree that new policies are needed. (And few, if any, elected Democrats or Republicans have publicly advocated for a literal "open borders" policy.)

Regardless of their specific viewpoints, all four of the writers whose essays appear in this casebook offer thoughtful, well-reasoned arguments on the topic. In "The Liberal Case for Reducing Immigration," Richard D. Lamm and Philip Cafaro argue for more restrictive immigration, basing their case on their concerns about preserving jobs for working-class Americans and ensuring environmental sustainability. In "The $100 Trillion Case for Open Borders," Nick Srnicek makes the case that opening borders (or loosening restrictions on immigration) would be "the single easiest way to improve the living standards of workers around the world—including those in wealthy countries." John Lee, in "Secure the U.S.-Mexico Border: Open It," believes that the United States needs a more rational, more discriminating immigration policy that allows the border patrol to focus on bad actors and criminals rather than on "good-faith" immigrants. Finally, Adam Ozimek ("Why I Don't Support Open Borders") sees less restrictive approaches as far too risky for the United States, which has too much to lose in the process.

This piece originally appeared in the *Denver Post* on February 16, 2018.

THE LIBERAL CASE FOR REDUCING IMMIGRATION

RICHARD D. LAMM AND PHILIP CAFARO

As Congress considers potential changes to immigration policy, the debate 1 seems to be breaking down along familiar lines. Conservatives argue for stricter enforcement of immigration laws and reduced immigration numbers, while liberals urge a new amnesty for undocumented immigrants and higher immigration levels.

Yet there are good liberal arguments for combating illegal immigration 2 and reducing historically high legal immigration. Many of these were articulated by the U.S. Commission on Immigration Reform, commonly known as the Jordan Commission, for its chairwoman, liberal icon Barbara Jordan. The Jordan Commission undertook the last comprehensive national study of immigration, publishing its final recommendations in 1997. It would serve the current immigration debate well to take another look at them.

The Jordan Commission began by stating the rationale for making immi- 3 gration policy in terms of the public good, broadly considered. "We decry hostility and discrimination towards immigrants as antithetical to the traditions and interests of the country," they wrote. "At the same time, we disagree with those who would label efforts to control immigration as being inherently anti-immigrant. Rather, it is both a right and a responsibility of a democratic society to manage immigration so that it serves the national interest."

A key aspect of this national interest for the commission was the well-being 4 of working-class people already in the country. Jordan observed that "immigrants with relatively low education and skills may compete for jobs and public services with the most vulnerable of Americans, particularly those who are unemployed or underemployed." She noted: "The Commission is particularly concerned about the impact of immigration on the most disadvantaged within our already resident society—inner city youth, racial and ethnic minorities, and recent immigrants who have not yet adjusted to life in the U.S." For these reasons, the Jordan Commission recommended sharp reductions in the numbers of less-educated, less-skilled immigrants coming into the country through chain migration. This, they reasoned, would help maintain employment opportunities for poorer Americans and decrease downward pressure on their wages.

When it came to numbers, the Jordan Commission recommended an 5 overall cut of 40 percent in total immigration. Given the increase in economic inequality since 1997, and forecasts that advances in artificial intelligence, robotics, and other automation technologies could cut millions of blue-collar jobs in coming decades, this recommendation seems more justified than ever—at least for those of us who believe that gross economic inequality is not compatible with a genuinely democratic society.

Like most Coloradans, we also believe in creating an ecologically sustain- 6 able society.

Climate change, water scarcity in the Western U.S., and other growing environmental challenges make this ever more imperative. While the Jordan Commission said little about the role of mass immigration in driving U.S. population growth, the reality is that current immigration levels are set to double our population to over 650 million by 2100. At reduced immigra-   7

> "Immigration policies are thus among our most crucial environmental policies—even though we don't usually think about them that way."

tion levels, our population instead could stabilize at under 400 million over the next three decades. Immigration policies are thus among our most crucial environmental policies—even though we don't usually think about them that way.

Ending U.S. population growth is the most important step we could take 8 as a nation to create a sustainable society. While that alone won't create such a society, without it ecological sustainability will be an ever-receding mirage. More people will, inevitably, undermine all the good work we do to use energy, water, and other resources more efficiently. More people will, inevitably, crowd other species off the landscape.

The goal of public policy is to confront new challenges boldly yet realistically. 9 Two great challenges we face in the 21st century are creating an ecologically sustainable society and sharing wealth more fairly among all our citizens. Reducing immigration, and thus reducing economic pressures on less wealthy Americans while stabilizing our population, will go a long way toward helping us meet these challenges successfully.

⊘ READING ARGUMENTS

1. In the second paragraph, the writers refer to the 1997 Jordan Commission, calling its chairwoman, Barbara Jordan, a "liberal icon." How is their use of this label consistent with their larger argument?

2. Whom do you think the writers see as their primary audience? How can you tell?

3. In its statements about protecting working-class Americans, what **causal argument** did the Jordan Commission recommendations rest upon? Do you see this as a valid argument? Why or why not?

4. What is the "most important step" Americans could take to create a "sustainable society" (para. 8)? What is the relationship between this "important step" and immigration policy?

5. In what sense is this a **definition** essay? What is being defined? What specific elements of definition can you identify?

This article appeared on The Conversation on February 8, 2017.

THE $100 TRILLION CASE FOR OPEN BORDERS

NICK SRNICEK

In an ideal world, we would all be able to freely move wherever we wanted. 1 The basic right of people to escape from war, persecution, and poverty would be accepted as a given, and no one would have their life determined by their place of birth.

But we don't live in this world, and national borders continue to block the 2 freedom of people to move. Around the world, protectionism is on the rise, as people are told to blame outsiders for threatening their way of life and, more importantly, stealing their jobs.

There is, however, an overwhelming case for open borders that can be 3 made even in the traditionally self-interested language of economics. In fact, our best estimates are that opening the world's borders could increase global GDP by $100 trillion.

That's $100,000,000,000,000

It sounds like a crazy idea, particularly when the media is dominated by sto- 4
ries about the need to control immigration and the right-wing tabloids trumpet "alternative facts" about how immigration hurts our economies. But every
piece of evidence we have says that ending borders would be the single easiest
way to improve the living standards of workers around the world—including
those in wealthy countries.

The argument is simple enough and has been made by more than one econ- 5
omist. Workers in poorer economies make less than they should. If they were to
have all of the benefits of rich countries—advanced education, the latest workplace technologies, and all the necessary infrastructure—these workers would
produce and earn as much as their rich country counterparts. What keeps them
in poverty is their surroundings. If they were able to pick up and move to more
productive areas, they would see their incomes increase many times over.

This means that opening borders is, by a massive amount, the easiest 6
and most effective way to tackle global poverty. Research shows that alternative approaches—for instance, microcredit, higher education standards, and
anti-sweatshop activism—all produce lifetime economic gains that would
be matched in weeks by open borders. Even small reductions in the barriers
posed by borders would bring massive benefits for workers.

Gains for All

Of course, the immediate fear of having open borders is that it will increase com- 7
petition for jobs and lower wages for those living in rich countries. This misses
the fact that globalization means competition already exists between workers
worldwide—under conditions that harm their pay and security. UK workers in
manufacturing or IT, for instance, are already competing with low-wage workers
in India and Vietnam. Workers in rich countries are already losing, as companies
eliminate good jobs and move their factories and offices elsewhere.

Under these circumstances, the function of borders is to keep workers 8
trapped in low-wage areas that companies can freely exploit. Every worker—
whether from a rich country or a poor country—suffers as a result. Ending
borders would mean an end to this type
of competition between workers. It would
make us all better off.

> "Under these circum-
> stances, the function of
> borders is to keep work- 9
> ers trapped in low-wage
> areas that companies can
> freely exploit."

The European Union has provided
a natural experiment in what happens
when borders between rich and poor
countries are opened up. And the evidence here is unambiguous: the long-
run effects of open borders improve the
conditions and wages of all workers. However, in the short-run, some groups
(particularly unskilled laborers) can be negatively affected.

The fixes for this are exceedingly simple though. A shortening of the work 10
week would reduce the amount of work supplied, spread the work out more
equally among everyone, and give more power to workers—not to mention,

more free time to everyone. And the strengthening and proper enforcement of labor laws would make it impossible for companies to hyper-exploit migrant workers. The overall impacts of more workers are exceedingly small in the short-run, and exceedingly positive in the long-run.

As it stands, borders leave workers stranded and competing against each 11 other. The way the global economy is set up is based entirely on competition. This makes us think that potential allies are irreconcilable enemies. The real culprits, however, are businesses that pick up and leave at the drop of a hat, that fire long-time workers in favor of cheaper newcomers, and that break labor laws outright, in order to boost their profits.

Borders leave us as strangers rather than allies. Yet this need not be the 12 case, and as a principle guiding political action, the abolition of borders would rank among the greatest of human achievements.

⊘ READING ARGUMENTS

1. What contrast does Srnicek use in his first two paragraphs? Why do you think he chose to begin his discussion in this way?

2. In the second paragraph, Srnicek refers to "protectionism." What does this term mean? What connotations does it have for him?

3. How would you define the reasoning in paragraph five of this essay? Does it seem to have an **inductive** or **deductive** structure? Explain.

4. How would you define the reasoning in paragraph six of this essay? Is it **inductive** or **deductive**? Explain.

5. Where do you see elements of a **proposal argument** in this essay?

This essay appeared on Open Borders, a blog and resource dedicated to making the case for open borders, on February 25, 2013.

SECURE THE U.S.-MEXICO BORDER: OPEN IT

JOHN LEE

The Associated Press has a great story out on what a "secure" U.S.-Mexico border 1 would look like. It covers perspectives from various stakeholders on border security, with opinions running the gamut from "The border is as secure as it can ever be" to "It's obviously incredibly unsafe." I am not sure if the AP is fairly representing opinions on the border issue, but the reporting of how life on the border has evolved over time is fascinating.

One thing that strikes me in this reporting is how casually drug smug- 2
glers/slave traffickers and good-faith immigrants are easily-conflated. Is a
secure border one where people who want to move contraband goods or
human slaves illegally cannot easily enter? Or is it one where well-meaning
people can be indefinitely kept at bay for an arbitrary accident of birth? This
passage juxtaposes the two quite different situations:

> And nearly all of more than 70 drug smuggling tunnels found along the
> border since October 2008 have been discovered in the clay-like soil of
> San Diego and Tijuana, some complete with hydraulic lifts and rail cars.
> They've produced some of the largest marijuana seizures in U.S. history.

> Still, few attempt to cross what was once the nation's busiest corridor
> for illegal immigration. As he waited for breakfast at a Tijuana migrant
> shelter, Jose de Jesus Scott nodded toward a roommate who did. He was
> caught within seconds and badly injured his legs jumping the fence.

> Scott, who crossed the border with relative ease until 2006, said he and a
> cousin tried a three-day mountain trek to San Diego in January and were
> caught twice. Scott, 31, was tempted to return to his wife and two young
> daughters near Guadalajara. But, with deep roots in suburban Los Angeles
> and cooking jobs that pay up to $1,200 a week, he will likely try the same
> route a third time.

The main thing that strikes me about the previously "unsecure" border 3
near San Diego is that border patrol agents were overwhelmed by a mass of
people until more staff and walls were brought to bear. But these masses
of people almost certainly were comprised in large part, if not near-entirely,
of good-faith immigrants. Smugglers and traffickers merely take advantage of the confusion to sneak in with the immigrants. If the immigrants
had a legal path to entry, if they did not have to cross the border unlawfully,
the traffickers would be naked without human crowds to hide in. If border
security advocates just want to reduce illegal trafficking, demanding "border security" before loosening immigration controls may well be putting the
cart before the horse.

Even so, as I've said before, the physical reality of a long border means 4
that human movement across it can never be fully controlled. Demanding
totalitarian control as "true border security" is about as unrealistic as, if not
even more so than an open borders advocate demanding the abolition of the
nation-state.

The AP covers some damning stories of peaceful Americans murdered 5
by drug traffickers in the same breath as it covers someone trying to get
to a job in suburban LA. Even if one insists that murdering smugglers and
restaurant cooks should be treated identically on account of being born
Mexican, it is difficult to see how one can demand that the U.S. border
patrol prioritize detaining them both equally. Yet as long as U.S. visa policy
makes it near-impossible for most good-faith Mexicans who can find work

in the U.S. to do so, the reality of the border means that thousands of Mexicans just looking to work will risk their lives crossing the border, alongside smugglers and murderers.

"The reality of the border means that thousands of Mexicans just looking to work will risk their lives crossing the border, alongside smugglers and murderers."

The more reasonable policy has to 6 be one that will allow U.S. border patrol to focus on catching the most egregious criminals. That means giving the good-faith immigrants a legal channel to enter the U.S. on a reasonable timeframe, reducing the flow of unlawful border crossings. This is not just my opinion, but that of even a former (Republican) U.S. Ambassador to Mexico:

Tony Garza remembers watching the flow of pedestrian traffic between Brownsville and Matamoros from his father's filling station just steps from the international bridge. He recalls migrant workers crossing the fairway on the 11th hole of a golf course—northbound in the morning, south-bound in the afternoon. And during an annual celebration between the sister cities, no one was asked for their papers at the bridge. People were just expected to go home.

Garza, a Republican who served as the U.S. ambassador to Mexico from 2002 to 2009, said it's easy to become nostalgic for those times, but he reminds himself that he grew up in a border town of fewer than 50,000 people that has grown into a city of more than 200,000.

The border here is more secure for the massive investment in recent years but feels less safe because the crime has changed, he said. Some of that has to do with transnational criminal organizations in Mexico and some of it is just the crime of a larger city.

Reform, he said, "would allow you to focus your resources on those activi-ties that truly make the border less safe today."

It's the view of those sheriffs who places themselves in harm's way to fight 7 those murderers and smugglers:

Hidalgo County Sheriff Lupe Trevino points out that drug, gun, and human smuggling is nothing new to the border. The difference is the attention that the drug-related violence in Mexico has drawn to the region in recent years.

He insists his county, which includes McAllen, is safe. The crime rate is falling, and illegal immigrants account for small numbers in his jail. But asked if the border is "secure," Trevino doesn't hesitate. "Absolutely not."

"When you're busting human trafficking stash houses with 60 to 100 peo-ple that are stashed in a two, three-bedroom home for weeks at a time, how can you say you've secured the border?" he said.

Trevino's view, however, is that those people might not be there if they had a legal path to work in the U.S.

"Immigration reform is the first thing we have to accomplish *before* we can say that we have secured the border," he said.

In Nogales, Sheriff Tony Estrada has a unique perspective on both border security and more comprehensive immigration reform. Born in Nogales, Mexico, Estrada grew up in Nogales, Ariz., after migrating to the U.S. with his parents. He has served as a lawman in the community since 1966.

He blames border security issues not only on the cartels but on the American demand for drugs. Until that wanes, he said, nothing will change. And securing the border, he added, must be a constant, ever-changing effort that blends security and political support—because the effort will never end.

"The drugs are going to keep coming. The people are going to keep coming. The only thing you can do is contain it as much as possible.

"I say the border is as safe and secure as it can be, but I think people are asking for us to seal the border, and that's unrealistic," he said.

Asked why, he said simply: "That's the nature of the border."

Simply put, if you want a secure U.S.-Mexico border, one where law enforce- 8
ment can focus on rooting out murderers and smugglers, you need open borders. You need a visa regime that lets those looking to feed their families and looking for a better life to enter legally, with a minimum of muss and fuss. When only those who cross the border unlawfully are those who have no good business being in the U.S., then you can have a secure border.

◒ READING ARGUMENTS

1. Lee begins by discussing an article on border security from the Associated Press. Why does he find the AP's coverage "fascinating"?

2. In paragraph 6, Lee identifies a "more reasonable policy" toward immigration. What is this policy? Why does he support it?

3. Where does Lee appeal to *ethos*? Point to a specific example and explain how the appeal works.

4. In Lee's view, what is the connection between immigration reform and a secure border policy? Do you see this connection as key to solving our immigration crisis, or do you think Lee is exaggerating its importance? Explain.

This piece was published by *Forbes* on February 26, 2017.

WHY I DON'T SUPPORT OPEN BORDERS

ADAM OZIMEK

I am a big fan of immigration, and I think we can easily absorb significantly 1
more immigrants than we do right now. But I am not a proponent of open borders, and I thought it would be useful to give a few fairly high level reasons why.

The big, fundamental meta question to me is: why is the U.S. richer than 2
the countries that most immigrants are coming from? It's a combination of
different levels of physical capital, human capital, technology, social capital,
and institutions. But the last two are extremely vague, and our knowledge of
how institutions and social capital emerge and evolve is not great. A decent
amount of immigration only changes these things slowly, but open borders
could change them very quickly.

Would these changes be positive or negative? We don't know, but given 3
that the U.S. is already very rich compared to the rest of the world the risks are
to the downside.

That said, if we could do better at directing immigration to parts of the 4
U.S. I think in some places the risks of massively increasing immigration flows
are outweighed by the benefits. Detroit, for example, is not doing nearly as well
as the U.S. overall. Ranked as a country by itself, one would not describe it as
doing so well that the risks are mostly to the downside.

It's true the U.S. overall has undergone successful massive changes in the 5
past, including due to large influxes of immigrants. According to a recent
National Academies report, the largest period of immigration influx as a share
of population since 1790 was from 1850 to 1860 when net international migration was 9.8 per 1,000 U.S. population. That's about triple today's rates, and
would translate to about 3 million immigrants a year. I'm fine with that rate,
it seems like a pretty aggressive expansion, and I'm not sure why we'd want
to start with something a lot higher than that. I think the risks outweigh the
rewards for pushing significantly above that.

The case against massive changes in the U.S. is also stronger today than 6
it was in the past. It was easier to support massive radical changes in previous centuries when we were constantly in the midst of huge fundamental
changes like the end of slavery, the rise of democracy, the industrial revolution, World Wars, and the emergence of the welfare state. In general, when
we questioned the status quo in the past we can say that the status quo was a
result of recent massive changes. In the past we also hadn't gone very far in
terms of well-being compared to previous centuries. But now, on the other

side of two industrial revolutions and 100 years of productivity growth, we have far much more to lose.

We're in an era of far fewer massive changes, and the U.S. is a big country 7 that is near the top of the list development-wise. If we're going to step outside of modern experience, I'd rather see it done somewhere else first.

Some, like the excellent Alex Nowrasteh, say we should wall off the welfare state from immigrants and natives rather than wall off the country. I think the welfare state is an important source of upward mobility and a driver of life-time well-being for natives and immigrants. I take his proposal as actually kind of telling about the sort of radicalism that might be required to potentially sustain open borders. Rather than spend a lot of energy arguing on behalf of things like public schools, food stamps, Medicaid, and the Earned Income Tax Credit, I'd rather simply point to this proposal and say "See? This kind of bad solution is what could potentially be required to sustain open borders!" 8

> "But now, on the other side of two industrial revolutions and 100 years of productivity growth, we have far much more to lose."

So that's my big vague case against open borders! We don't really know 9 enough about what generates the wealth of nations to make massive changes like this. It is very plausible that the people in a country play a big role in determining the wealth of that country, and the downside risks of massive changes in the U.S. tend to outweigh the upside risks.

⊙ READING ARGUMENTS

1. Why do you think Ozimek opens his essay by claiming to be a "big fan of immigration"? What does he gain by making this assertion?

2. In his second paragraph, Ozimek writes, "The big, fundamental meta question to me is: why is the U.S. richer than the countries that most immigrants are coming from?" What does he mean by "meta question"? Why is he asking this question?

3. Ozimek refers to "social capital" but claims that the term is "extremely vague" (para. 2). How would you define this term?

4. According to Ozimek, the "case against massive changes in the U.S. is also stronger today than it was in the past" (6). How does he explain this statement?

This image of families at the U.S.-Mexico border appeared in an ABC news story.

VISUAL ARGUMENT

John Moore/Getty Images

⊘ READING ARGUMENTS

1. This image is from an ABC News story about a Facebook campaign to raise money for immigrant families who have been separated at the U.S. border. What message does this image convey? What is your reaction to this message?

2. Describe the people who appear in this photograph. How does their presence affect your response to the image?

3. Which elements of this image are shown in sharp focus? Which are blurred? Do you think this difference in focus was intentional? If so, why did the photographer make this choice?

⊘ AT ISSUE: SHOULD THE UNITED STATES HAVE OPEN BORDERS?

1. Both Srnicek and Ozimek ground their arguments in the context of immigration and economic prosperity, but they reach different conclusions and support different approaches. Which writer do you find more persuasive, and why?

2. How do you think Lamm and Cafaro would respond to Srnicek's argument? Do you think they would agree on certain issues? Which ones?

3. The writers in this casebook address the question of borders and immigration in the context of different issues and problems, from crime and the environment to the job prospects of the American working class. After reading these four essays, what do you think is the most pressing issue related to border security and immigration?

⊘ WRITING ARGUMENTS: SHOULD THE UNITED STATES HAVE OPEN BORDERS?

After exploring this issue from a variety of angles, what is your view of the problem? Write an argument essay that takes a position on whether or not the United States should have open borders. (Alternatively, you may argue either for more restrictive immigration or less restrictive immigration—or for some other policy change outside the binary choice between open borders and no open borders.)

SCIENCE

CAN TELL YOU HOW TO CLONE A TYRANNOSAURUS REX

HUMANITIES

CAN TELL YOU WHY THIS MIGHT BE A BAD IDEA

The University of Utah, College of Humanities

24

Does It Pay to Study the Humanities?

At one time, students went to college to grow intellectually, to consider what they wanted to become, and to engage in the give-and-take of academic discourse. In the process, they could reexamine their ideas, develop new perspectives, and expand as thinkers and as human beings. Now, because students (and their parents) often have to take out loans to defray the high cost of tuition, they see a college education as an investment, not as a vehicle for intellectual growth. For this reason, they feel a great deal of pressure to ensure a return on their investment, and degrees in STEM subjects—an acronym that refers to courses in science, technology, engineering, and math—offer this return because STEM graduates earn more money than liberal arts majors. As a result, students flock to STEM majors in increasing numbers, and the humanities—art, literature, music, and history—become less and less important on college campuses. What good, students ask, is Michelangelo when it comes to developing a newer, better web app? How can an understanding of Tolstoy contribute to building a smarter smartphone?

Even though advocates for the humanities might concede that Tolstoy cannot help us to make a smartphone smarter, they would argue that all of us could benefit from reading Tolstoy. In addition, supporters of the humanities are concerned about what would be lost if we cut down on—or even eliminate—humanities courses. Although most people would agree that something is lost when we favor career skills over the humanities, they would have a difficult time pinpointing exactly what that "something" is. It is even harder to make the case for a liberal arts education when the average cost of a four-year degree is over $40,000 at a state school and over $135,000 at a private college.

In this chapter, you will read some essays that address the question of whether it pays to study the humanities. In "The Economic Case for Saving the Humanities," Christina H. Paxson, the president of Brown University, makes the point that society will benefit if it actively supports the humanities. In "Major Differences: Why Undergraduate Majors Matter," Anthony P. Carnevale and Michelle Melton argue that colleges have an obligation to give students the information they need to make intelligent decisions about their majors and their lives. In "Is It Time to Kill the Liberal Arts Degree?," Kim Brooks questions whether colleges are downplaying the obstacles that liberal arts graduates face when they try to find full-time employment. Finally, in "Course Corrections," Thomas Frank contends that in order to effectively defend the humanities, academics must first address the high cost of tuition.

Paxson's essay was published on August 20, 2013, in the *New Republic*.

THE ECONOMIC CASE FOR SAVING THE HUMANITIES

CHRISTINA H. PAXSON

What can we do to make the case for the humanities? Unlike the STEM disciplines (science, technology, engineering, and mathematics), they do not—on the surface—contribute to the national defense. It is difficult to measure, precisely, their effect on the GDP, or our employment rates, or the stock market.

And yet, we know in our bones that secular humanism is one of the greatest sources of strength we possess as a nation, and that we must protect the humanities if we are to retain that strength in the century ahead.

I do not exactly hail from the center of the humanities. I'm an economist, with a specialization in health and economic development. When you ask economists to weigh in on an issue, the chances are good that we will ultimately get around to a basic question: "Is it worth it?" Support for the humanities is more than worth it. It is essential.

We all know that there has been a fair amount of hostility to this idea recently in Congress and in State Houses around the country. Sometimes it almost feels as if there is a National Alliance against the Humanities. There are frequent potshots by radio commentators, and calls to reduce government spending in education and scholarship in the humanities.

It has become fashionable to attack government for being out of touch, bloated, and elitist; and humanities funding often strikes critics as an especially muddle-headed form of government spending. For that reason, the humanities are in danger of becoming even more of a punching bag than they already are.

In the current economic environment, these attacks have the potential to sway people. Any expenditure has to be clearly worth it. "Performance funding" links government support to disciplines that provide high numbers of jobs. Or, as in a Florida proposal that emerged last year, a "strategic" tuition structure would essentially charge more money to students who want to study the humanities and less money for those going into the STEM disciplines.

As a result, there is grave cause for concern. Federal support for the humanities is heading in the wrong direction. In fiscal year 2013, the National Endowment for the Humanities was funded at $139 million, down $28.5 million from FY 2010, at a time when science funding stayed mostly intact. This is part of a pattern of long-term decline since the Reagan years.

> "Federal support for the humanities is heading in the wrong direction." 7

I believe the question is fair. Are the humanities worth it? To push back against 8 the recent tide of criticism, I'd like to offer several strategies.

First, we need to argue that there are real, tangible benefits to the humanistic 9 disciplines—to the study of history, literature, art, theater, music, and languages. In the complex, globalized world we are moving toward, it will obviously benefit American undergraduates to know something of other civilizations, past and present. Any form of immersion in literary expression is helpful when we are learning to communicate and defend our thoughts. And it should not be that difficult to concur that a thorough and objective grounding in history is helpful and even inspiring when applying the lessons of our past to the future.

This point came home to me when, in my previous role as Dean of 10 Princeton's Woodrow Wilson School, I went to the university archives to read the reports and correspondence that concerned the formation of the School in 1929. The founding director of the School, DeWitt Clinton Poole, wrote that the need was not for "young men minutely trained in specific technicalities" but, instead, for a "broad culture that will enlarge the individual's mental scope to world dimensions." Accordingly, the curriculum was designed to ground students in both the social sciences and the humanities. At that time—on the eve of the Great Depression—there was concern that such an "impractical" education would be of little value. Indeed, one alumnus wrote that the curriculum "is not immediately useful to the boy who has to earn a living." Yet, if one looks back over the course of the school's rich history, it is evident that many of the men and women who were exposed to that curriculum went on to positions of genuine leadership in the public and private sectors.

We know that one of the best aspects of the undergraduate experience is the 11 fact that it is so multifaceted. Our scientists enjoy studying alongside our humanists and vice versa. They learn more that way, and they do better on each side of that not-very-precise divide. When I ask any of Brown's business-leader alumni what they valued most during their years at Brown, I am just as likely to hear about an inspirational professor of classics or religion as a course in economics, science, or mathematics.

Second, we need to better defend an important principle that centuries 12 of humanism have taught us—that we do not always know the future benefits of what we study and therefore should not rush to reject some forms of research as less deserving than others. In 1939, Abraham Flexner, the founding director of the Institute for Advanced Studies in Princeton, wrote an essay on this topic titled "The Usefulness of Useless Knowledge." It was published in *Harper's* in 1939, on the eve of World War II, a time when we can assume there was a high priority placed on military and scientific knowledge. In this essay, Flexner argued that most of our really significant discoveries have been made by "men and women who were driven not by the desire to be useful but merely the desire to satisfy their curiosity."

Flexner's essay underscores a very important idea—that random discover- 13 ies can be more important than the ones we think we are looking for, and that we should be wary of imposing standard criteria of costs and benefits on our scholars. Or perhaps I should put it more precisely: We should be prepared to accept that the value of certain studies may be difficult to measure and may not be clear for decades or even centuries.

After September 11, experts in Arabic and the history of Islam were sud- 14 denly in high demand—their years of research could not simply be invented overnight. Similarly, we know that regional leaders like Brazil, Indonesia, and South Africa will rise in relevance and connectivity to the United States over the next few decades, just as China and India already have. To be ready for those relationships, and to advance them, we need our humanists fully engaged.

And third, the pace of learning is moving so quickly that I would argue it 15 is all the more important that we maintain support for the humanities, precisely to make sure that we remain grounded in our core values. As many previous generations have learned, innovations in science and technology are tremendously important. But they inevitably result in unintended consequences. Some new inventions, if only available to small numbers, increase inequity or competition for scarce resources, with multiplying effects. We need humanists to help us understand and respond to the social and ethical dimensions of technological change. As more changes come, we will need humanists to help us filter them, calibrate them, and when necessary, correct them. And we need them to galvanize the changes that are yet to come. Our focus should not be only on training students about the skills needed immediately upon graduation. The value of those skills will depreciate quickly. Instead, our aim is to invest in the long-term intellectual, creative, and social capacity of human beings.

I started by saying that we should embrace the debate about the value of the 16 humanities. Let's hear the criticisms that are often leveled, and do what we can to address them. Let's make sure we give value to our students, and that we educate them for a variety of possible outcomes. Let's do more to encourage cross-pollination between the sciences and the humanities for the benefit of each. Let's educate all of our students in every discipline to use the best humanistic tools we have acquired over a millennium of university teaching—to engage in a civilized discourse about all of the great issues of our time. A grounding in the humanities will sharpen our answers to the toughest questions we are facing.

We don't want a nation of technical experts in one subject. We want a 17 scintillating civil society in which everyone can talk to everyone. That was a quality that Alexis de Tocqueville wrote of when he visited the United States at the beginning of the 1830s. Even in that era before mass communication, before the telegraph, before the internet, we were engaged in an American conversation that stretched from one end of the country to another. In a similar manner, Martin Luther King Jr. sketched a "web of mutuality" in his "Letter from Birmingham Jail," fifty years ago this year. We want politicians who have read Shakespeare—as Lincoln did. We want bankers and lawyers who have read Homer and Dante. We want factory owners who have read Dickens.

It is really important we get this right. A mountain of empirical evidence indi- 18 cates a growing inequality in our society. There is no better way to check this trend than to invest in education. And there is no better way to invest in education than to invest fairly, giving attention to all disciplines and short shrift to none.

Earlier generations have weighed these questions, and answered in the 19 affirmative. An early graduate of Brown, Horace Mann, trained in the humanities, was instrumental in creating the public school system of the United States. He knew that a broad, secular education, open to all, was one of the foundations of our democracy, and that it was impossible to expect meaningful citizenship without offering people the tools to inform themselves about all of the great questions of life. Horace Mann said, "Be ashamed to die until you have won some victory for humanity." In that spirit, let's continue this conversation, eager to engage the critics in a spirited conversation whose very richness depends on the humanistic values we cherish.

And in conclusion: yes, it's worth it. 20

⊖ READING ARGUMENTS

1. Paxson begins by acknowledging the difficulty of making "the case for the humanities" (para. 1). Why? Does this opening strategy undercut her argument in any way? Explain.

2. Does Paxson make a valid point in paragraph 2, or is she **begging the question**? Explain.

3. Where in the essay does Paxson appeal to *ethos*? Is this appeal effective in the context of her argument? Why or why not?

4. Paxson writes that "the humanities are in danger of becoming even more of a punching bag than they already are" (5). What evidence does she present to support this claim? Is this sufficient?

5. Paxson offers three strategies to stem the tide of criticism against the humanities. What are they? How effective have they been in stemming the "recent tide of criticism" (8)?

6. What point does Paxson make in her conclusion? Would a different concluding strategy have been more effective? Explain.

This essay was published in the Fall 2011 issue of *Presidency*, a publication of the American Council on Education.

MAJOR DIFFERENCES: WHY UNDERGRADUATE MAJORS MATTER

ANTHONY P. CARNEVALE AND MICHELLE MELTON

In the United States today, there is no more certain investment than a college education. In spite of the current gloomy economic forecast, college is still worth it. In fact, rising demand, coupled with the persistent undersupply of college-educated workers over the last 30 years, has driven up relative wages for these workers. On average, **college graduates make 84 percent more over a lifetime** than their high school–educated counterparts—up from 75 percent in 1999. While the current unemployment rate among recent college graduates is high (9 percent), it is still far lower than the average unemployment rate for recent high school graduates (35 percent). When it rains long enough and hard enough, everyone gets a little wet. Still, a college education is the best umbrella to shelter individuals from economic storms.

But that doesn't mean that all bachelor's degrees are created equal. While the focus recently has been on the value of higher education in general, we have failed to connect the dots between specific college majors and specific career trajectories. College offers many non-financial benefits, but there is new evidence of the oversize influence that certain majors have in preparing students for careers. Average salaries mask very real discrepancies between the economic advantages of different undergraduate majors. While everyone who attends college can expect a significant return on their investment, different undergraduate majors lead to markedly different careers—and significantly different earnings.

Disparity in Degrees

As we found in our recent study, *What's It Worth?: The Economic Value of College Majors,* because of the role it plays in occupational training, the choice of undergraduate major is as critical a choice as whether to get a college degree at all. In one of the most extreme examples, for instance, Counseling Psychology majors make an average of $29,000 per year, compared to $120,000 for Petroleum Engineering majors. That's a difference of 314 percent—or $4.1 million over a 45-year lifetime of work. A more typical example is the difference between two of the most popular majors, General Business and Elementary Education. A General Business major earns $60,000 annually, compared with $40,000 for an Education major. Over a lifetime, that's a difference in earnings of about $900,000.

Majors are so decisive for an individual's earnings because they are not just educational categories; majors are an essential component of career training. Critics constantly disparage higher education for not being more connected with the "real world," and for failing to more tightly align higher education and curricula with labor markets. Such criticism is off the mark; since the end of the Second World War, the growth in higher education has been in programs that connect learning with careers. Very few people today actually major in Ancient Greek, and you won't see any subway advertisements promoting class offerings in Classics. Fewer than 10 percent of bachelor's degrees in the U.S. economy are in Humanities and Liberal Arts. The growth areas of higher education have been, and will continue to be, in educational programs which stress career training. The for-profit sector has recognized this fact, and has profited handsomely from it. All of higher education would benefit from making the implicit relationships between education and careers more explicit.

The point is a simple one: while it is important to discuss the benefits of college in general, for too long we have treated all college degrees as though they had the same economic value. We have glossed over the differences between workers with a major in Mathematics and workers with a major in Drama and Theater Arts to the detriment of students. The plain truth is that the labor market does not treat these workers the same— and students deserve to know that. A love of Shakespeare should not deter students from becoming English majors. But we believe that students should know how their educational choices will affect the rest of their adult lives, in terms of the careers they will have, their expected earnings, and whether they are likely to need graduate education—which they may need to take out loans to get. 5

> "We have glossed over the differences between workers with a major in Mathematics and workers with a major in Drama and Theater Arts to the detriment of students."

We found that, for example, a Nursing major nearly always leads to a career in the Health Services industry, as do many other health preparatory majors (82 percent of Nursing majors end up in Health Professional occupations, and 6 percent are in management). Likewise, well over two-thirds of Education majors—especially Special Needs Education, Elementary Education, and Educational Administration and Supervision majors—end up in the Education Services industry. 6

Making the Arts Pay

That these particular majors lead to specific careers may be obvious—but what about Arts majors? Do most people who major in Arts actually become artists? In fact, only a quarter of Arts majors end up in Arts occupations, while about a third end up in either Office, Sales, or Education occupations. In other words, majoring in Arts only rarely leads to a career as an artist. Potential Arts majors should know this, and that they can expect median annual earnings of $44,000. 7

Of course, some Arts majors will end up going on to get a graduate degree (in fact, less than a quarter of Arts majors, 23 percent, do get a graduate degree). But Arts majors who get a graduate degree see a 23 percent boost in earnings. 8

Although it is slightly more remunerative than Arts, Humanities and 9
Liberal Arts majors are in the middle of the pack in terms of earnings ($47,000)
and graduate degree attainment (41 percent of Humanities and Liberal Arts
majors go to graduate school). Humanities and Liberal Arts majors that do
go on to graduate school see a 48 percent earnings boost for doing so, making
their median earnings $65,000 per year. This is a comfortable living, to be sure,
but even with a graduate degree, Humanities and Liberal Arts majors still make
significantly less than an Engineering major with a bachelor's degree. Moreover, in terms of all graduate earnings, Humanities and Liberal Arts majors
are still in the middle of the pack. They earn more than the Arts majors do,
but significantly less than many other major groups with a graduate degree,
including Engineering, Health, Social Sciences, and Agriculture and Natural
Resources.

In short, the Humanities and Liberal Arts may have unlimited intrinsic 10
value, but in terms of their more measurable market value, these graduates
simply do not fare as well as students whose majors equip them with more
technical and scientific skills.

The point is not for students to slavishly choose the majors with the high- 11
est earnings, instead of being driven by their interests. It is to provide the
information to students so that they are not solely driven by incomplete, anecdotal, or speculative evidence about their likely success, and to balance their
interests—both economic and humanistic—in making a decision about their
working lives.

Given information, students might make different decisions. We already 12
know that such decisions are complex and based on a combination of interests, values, knowledge, skills, and abilities. If a Social Work major is motivated by the desire to interact with and help others, he or she might decide
that, compared with $39,000 in Social Work, Nursing (at $60,000) might be
a better option that would also allow him or her to pursue interacting with
and helping others. The same might be true of a Biology major ($50,000), to
whom Nursing might be an appealing alternative path. Similarly, an English
major ($48,000) might decide that the small boost from majoring in Journal-
ism ($51,000) isn't worth the switch.

We have been embarrassingly slow to provide students with information 13
that will help them make these decisions. For the most part, this is because
higher education is balancing competing—and often contradictory—missions.
Many educators are wary about subjugating higher education's traditional role
to an economic one. Some are upset about the increasingly tight ties that bind
work and education. While training foot soldiers for capitalism is not the sole
mission of our education system, the inescapable reality is that ours is a society based on work. Those who are not equipped with the knowledge and skills
necessary to get—and keep—good jobs are denied full social inclusion and
tend to drop out of the mainstream culture, polity, and economy. In the worst
cases, they can be drawn into alternative cultures, political movements, and
economic activities that are a threat to mainstream American life. Therefore, if
postsecondary educators cannot fulfill their economic mission to help students

become successful workers and to better link postsecondary education with careers, they also will fail in their cultural and political missions to create good neighbors and good citizens.

⊘ READING ARGUMENTS

1. In paragraph 3, Carnevale and Melton say that "the choice of undergraduate major is as critical a choice as whether to get a college degree at all." What evidence do they provide to support this statement? Is this evidence convincing?

2. Carnevale and Melton write, "Critics constantly disparage higher education for not being more connected with the 'real world,' and for failing to more tightly align higher education and curricula with labor markets" (para. 4). Why do they believe that this criticism is "off the mark" (4)?

3. According to Carnevale and Melton, their purpose is to provide information about the "economic and humanistic" (11) trade-offs of different majors. Do you agree with the writers that many—or most—college students make decisions about their major based on "incomplete, anecdotal, or speculative evidence" (11)? Why or why not?

4. In what respects is this essay an evaluation argument? In what sense is it a proposal argument?

5. Where in this essay do the authors develop a **causal chain**? What point are they trying to make with this strategy? Are they successful? Explain.

This piece initially appeared in *Salon* on June 19, 2011.

IS IT TIME TO KILL THE LIBERAL ARTS DEGREE?

KIM BROOKS

Every year or two, my husband, an academic advisor at a prestigious Midwestern university, gets a call from a student's parent. Mr. or Mrs. So-and-so's son is a sophomore now and still insistent on majoring in film studies, anthropology, Southeast Asian comparative literature or, god forbid . . . English. These dalliances in the humanities were fine and good when little Johnny was a freshman, but isn't it time now that he wake up and start thinking seriously about what, one or two or three years down the line, he's actually going to do?

My husband, loyal first and foremost to his students' intellectual develop- 2
ment, and also an unwavering believer in the inherent value of a liberal arts
education, tells me about these conversations with an air of indignation. He
wonders, "Aren't these parents aware of what they signed their kid up for when
they decided to let him come get a liberal arts degree instead of going to weld-
ing school?" Also, he says, "The most aimless students are often the last ones
you want to force into a career path. I do sort of hate to enable this prolonged
adolescence, but I also don't want to aid and abet the miseries of years lost to a
misguided professional choice."

Now, I love my husband. Lately, however, I find myself wincing when he 3
recounts these stories.

"Well," I sometimes say, "what *are* they going to do?" 4

The answer, at least according to a recent article in the *New York Times*, is 5
rather bleak. Employment rates for college graduates have declined steeply in
the last two years, and perhaps even more disheartening, those who find jobs
are more likely to be steaming lattes or walking dogs than doing anything even
peripherally related to their college curriculum. While the scale and severity of
this post-graduation letdown may be an unavoidable consequence of an awful
recession, I do wonder if all those lofty institutions of higher learning, with
their noble-sounding mission statements and soft-focused brochure photos of
campus greens, may be glossing over the serious, at-times-crippling obstacles
a B.A. holder must overcome to achieve professional and financial stability. I'm
not asking if a college education has inherent value, if it makes students more
thoughtful, more informed, more enlightened and critical-minded human
beings. These are all interesting questions that don't pay the rent. What I'm
asking is far more banal and far more pressing. What I'm asking is: Why do
even the best colleges fail so often at preparing kids for the world?

When I earned my diploma from the University of Virginia in the spring 6
of 2000, it never occurred to me before my senior year to worry too seriously
about my post-graduation prospects. Indeed, most of my professors, advisors,
and mentors reinforced this complacency. I was smart, they told me. I'd spent
four years at a rigorous institution honing my writing, research, and critical-
thinking skills. I'd written an impressive senior thesis, gathered recommendations from professors, completed summer internships in various journalistic
endeavors. They had no doubt at all that I would land on my feet. And I did
(kind of), about a decade after graduating.

In the interim, I floundered. I worked as a restaurant hostess and tutored 7
English-as-a-second-language without a formal work visa. I mooched
off friends and boyfriends and slept on couches. One dreary night in San
Francisco, I went on an interview to tend bar at a strip club, but left demoral-
ized when I realized I'd have to walk around in stilettos. I went back to school
to complete the pre-medical requirements I'd shunned the first time through,
then, a week into physics, I applied to nursing school, then withdrew from
that program after a month when I realized nursing would be an environment where my habit of spacing out might actually kill someone. I landed a

$12-an-hour job as a paralegal at an asbestos-related litigation firm. I got an MFA in fiction.

Depending on how you look at it, I either spent a long time finding myself, or wasted seven years. And while all these efforts hardly add up to a tragedy (largely because I had the luxury of supportive parents willing to supplement my income for a time), I do have to admit feeling disillusioned as I moved from one gig to another, feeling as though my undergraduate education, far from preparing me for any kind of meaningful and remunerative work, had in some ways deprepared me, nurturing my natural strengths and predilections—writing, reading, analysis— and sweeping my weaknesses in organization, pragmatic problem-solving, decision-making under the proverbial rug. 8

Of course, there are certainly plenty of B.A. holders out there who, wielding the magic combination of competency, credentials, and luck, are able to land themselves a respectable, entry-level job that requires neither name tag nor apron. But for every person I know who parlayed a degree in English or anthropology into a career-track gig, I know two others who weren't so lucky, who, in that awful, post-college year or two or three or four, unemployed and uninsured and uncommitted to any particular field, racked up credit card debt or got married to the wrong person or went to law school for no particular reason or made one of a dozen other time- and money-wasting mistakes. 9

And the common thread in all these stories seems to be how surprised these graduates were by their utter unemployability, a feeling of having been misled into complacency, issued reassurances about how the pedigree or prestige of the institution they'd attended would save them. This narrative holds true whether their course of study was humanities or social sciences. My baby sitter, for example, who earned a degree in psychology from a Big Ten university, now makes $15 an hour watching my kids. 10

> "And the common thread in all these stories seems to be how surprised these graduates were by their utter unemployability."

"I was not the most serious student," she admits. "But I do wonder, why was I allowed to decide on a major without ever sitting down with my advisor and talking about what I might do with that major after graduating? I mean, I had to write out a plan for how I'd fit all my required courses into my schedule, but no one seemed to care if I had a plan once I left there. I graduated not knowing how to use Excel, write out a business plan, do basic accounting. With room and board and tuition, my time there cost $120,000." 11

I asked Sarah Isham, the director of career services of the College of Arts and Sciences at my alma mater about this discrepancy between curriculum and career planning, and she repeats the same reassurances I heard 10 years ago: "What we do is help students see how the patterns and themes of their interests, skills, and values, might relate to particular arenas. We do offer a few self-assessment tests, as well as many other resources to help them do this." 12

When I ask how well the current services are working—that is, how 13
many recent graduates are finding jobs, real jobs that require a degree—she
can only say that, "The College of Arts and Sciences does not collect statistics on post-graduation plans. I could not give you any idea of where these
students are going or what they are doing. Regrettably, it's not something in
place at this time."

I went on to ask her how the college's curriculum was adapting to meet the 14
demands of the recession and the realities of the job market, and she directed
me to a dean who asked not to be identified, and who expressed, in no uncertain terms, how tired he was of articles like mine that question the rationale,
rigor, or usefulness of a liberal arts education. He insisted that while he had no
suggestions regarding how a 22-year-old should weather a recession, the university was achieving its goal of creating citizens of the world.

When I asked him how a 22-year-old with no job, no income, no health 15
insurance, and, in some cases, six figures of college debt to pay off is supposed
to be a citizen of the world, he said he had no comment, that he was the wrong
person to talk to, and he directed me to another dean, who was also unable to
comment.

The chilliness of this response was a bit disheartening, but not terribly 16
surprising. When I was an undergrad, it seemed whenever I mentioned my
job-search anxieties, my professors and advisors would get a glassy look in
their eyes and mutter something about the career center. Their gazes would
drift toward their bookshelves or a folder of ungraded papers. And at the time,
I could hardly blame them. These were people who'd published dissertations
on Freud, written definitive volumes on Virginia Woolf. The language of real-
world career preparation was a language they simply didn't speak.

And if they did say anything at all, it was usually a reiteration of the typ- 17
ical liberal arts defense, that graduating with a humanities degree, I could do
anything: I could go on to earn a master's or a law degree or become an editor
or a teacher. I could go into journalism or nonprofit work, apply to medical
school or the foreign service. I could write books or learn to illustrate or bind
them. I could start my own business, work as a consultant, get a job editing
pamphlets for an alumni association, or raise money for public radio. The possibilities were literally limitless. It was a like being 6 years old again and trying
to decide if I'd become an astronaut or a ballerina. The advantage to a humanities degree, one professor insisted, was its versatility. In retrospect, though,
I wonder if perhaps this was part of the problem, as well; freedom can promote
growth, but it can also cause paralysis. Faced with limitless possibilities, a certain number of people will just stand still.

"So let me ask you something," my husband says, my wonderfully incisive 18
husband who will let me get away with only so much bitterness. "If your school
had forced you to declare a career plan or take an accounting class or study
web programming instead of contemporary lit, how would you have felt about
it at the time, without the benefit of hindsight?"

It's a good question, and the answer is, I probably would have transferred. 19

There were courses I took in college, courses in Renaissance literature and 20 the anthropology of social progress and international relations of the Middle East and, of course, writing, that will, in all likelihood, never earn me a steady paycheck or a 401K, but which I would not trade for anything; there were lectures on Shakespeare and Twain and Joyce that I still remember, that I've dreamt about and that define my sensibility as a writer and a reader and a human being. Even now, knowing the lost years that followed, I still wouldn't trade them in.

A new Harvard study suggests that it's not an abandonment of the college 21 curriculum that's needed, but a reenvisioning and better preparation. The study compares the U.S. system unfavorably to its European counterparts where students begin thinking about what sort of career they'll pursue and the sort of preparation they'll need for it in middle school. Could that be the answer?

At the end of my interview with Sarah Isham, she asks me if I might come 22 back to Charlottesville to participate in an alumni career panel. "We always have a lot of students interested in media and writing and the arts. It would be wonderful," she says "to have you come and talk to them." She asks me this, and I can't help but laugh.

"I don't think I'd be much of a role model," I say. "I don't have what you'd 23 call a high-powered career. I mostly do freelance work. Adjunct teaching. That sort of thing."

"Oh, that's fine," she insists. "Our students will love that. So many of them 24 are terrified of sitting in a cubicle all day."

They should be so lucky, I think. But I would never say that—not to them 25 and not to my own students. They'll have plenty of time later to find out just what a degree is and isn't good for. Right now, they're in those four extraordinary, exceptional years where ideas matter; and there's not a thing I'd do to change that.

⊙ READING ARGUMENTS

1. At two points in her essay, Brooks discusses her husband. Do you think these discussions help her advance her argument? If so, how?

2. Brooks's thesis occurs at the end of paragraph 5. Is this a logical place for it, or should it come earlier?

3. What evidence does Brooks use to support her points? Is this support convincing? What other kinds of evidence could she have used? What are the advantages and disadvantages of using such evidence?

4. What does Brooks mean when she says that the liberal arts graduates she interviewed have "a feeling of having been misled into complacency" (para. 10)?

5. How would you describe the tone of Brooks's essay? How does this tone affect your response to her argument?

6. What does Brooks think the purpose of college should be? Do you agree with her? Why or why not?

Harper's published this essay in its October 2013 issue.

COURSE CORRECTIONS

THOMAS FRANK

To the long list of American institutions that have withered since the dawn of the 1980s—journalism, organized labor, mainline Protestantism, small-town merchants—it may be time to add another: college-level humanities. Those ancient pillars of civilization are under assault these days, with bulldozers advancing from two different directions.

On the one hand, students are migrating away from traditional college subjects like history and philosophy. After hitting a postwar high in the mid-1960s, enrollments in the humanities dropped off sharply, and still show no signs of recovering. This is supposedly happening because recent college grads who chose to major in old-school subjects have experienced more difficulty finding jobs. Indeed, the folly of studying, say, English Lit has become something of an internet cliché—the stuff of sneering "Worst Majors" listicles that seem always to be sponsored by personal-finance websites.

On the other hand, an impressive array of public figures are eager to give the exodus from the humanities an additional push. Everyone from President Obama to Thomas Friedman knows where public support for education has to be concentrated in order to yield tangible returns both for individuals and for the nation: the STEM disciplines (science, technology, engineering, and math). *These* are the degrees American business is screaming for. These are the fields of study that will give us "broadly shared economic prosperity, international competitiveness, a strong national defense, a clean energy future, and longer, healthier, lives for all Americans," as a White House press release puts it.

> "Where does that leave the humanities, which don't contribute in any obvious way to national defense or economic prosperity?"

Where does that leave the humanities, which don't contribute in any obvious way to national defense or economic prosperity? The management theorist and financier Peter Cohan, addressing unemployment among recent college grads in the pages of *Forbes*, proposes a course of straightforward erasure: "To fix this problem, the answer is simple enough: cut out the departments offering majors that make students unemployable." Certain red-state governors seem eager to take up the task. Governor Pat McCrory of North Carolina, for example, dismisses gender studies as elitist woolgathering and announces, "I'm going to adjust my education curriculum to what business and commerce needs." Governor Rick Scott of Florida declares that "we don't need a lot more anthropologists in the state," while a panel he convened in 2012 has called for tuition prices to be subsidized for those willing to acquiesce to the needs of business and study practical things. Those who want to study silly stuff like divinity or Latin will have to pay ever more to indulge in their profligate pastimes.

And so the old battle is joined again: the liberal arts versus professional (i.e., 5 remunerative) studies. This time around, of course, it is flavored by all the cynical stratagems of contemporary politics. Take the baseline matter of STEM workers, the ones who supposedly hold our future in their hands. According to a recent study by the Economic Policy Institute, there is actually no shortage of STEM workers in the United States—and by extension, no need for all the incentives currently on the table to push more students into those fields. Oh, the demand of the business community for an ever greater supply of STEM grads is genuine enough. But their motive is the same as it was when they lobbied for looser restrictions on STEM workers from abroad: to keep wages down. Only this time the high-handed endeavor is being presented as a favor to students, who must be rescued from a lifetime of philology-induced uselessness.

A similar logic explains the larger attack on the humanities. The disci- 6 plines in the crosshairs have been the right's nemeses for many years. Maybe, in the past, conservatives stumped for some idealized core curriculum or the Great Books of Western Civ—but now that the option of demolishing these disciplines is on the table, today's amped-up right rather likes the idea. After all, universities are not only dens of liberal iniquity but also major donors to the Democratic Party.[1] Chucking a few sticks of dynamite into their comfy world is a no-brainer for any politician determined to "defund the left."

Fans of the banality of evil might appreciate the language with which this 7 colossal act of vandalism is being urged upon us. Florida's blue-ribbon commission, for example, sets about burying the humanities with a sandstorm of convoluted management talk:

> Four key policy questions must be addressed to accelerate Florida's progression toward world-class recognition as a system, particularly as its measurement framework transitions from simply reporting to collaborating toward clear goals. . . . Boards can advance effective cost management by helping to shape the conversation about aligning resources with goals and creating a culture of heightened sensitivity to resource management across the campus.

---

[1]According to statistics compiled by Neil Gross in *Why Are Professors Liberal and Why Do Conservatives Care?*, the most left-leaning divisions of the American university are the social sciences, closely followed by the humanities.

Let us assess the battle so far. In one corner, we have rhetoric like this: 8 empty, pseudoscientific jargon rubber-stamped by a Chamber of Commerce hack . . . who was appointed by the governor of Florida . . . who was himself elected by the Tea Party. It is not merely weak, it is preposterous; it is fatuity at a gallop.

In the other corner, we have the university-level humanities. Now, here 9 is an antagonist at the height of its vast mental powers. In polite and affluent circles, it is respected by all. Its distinctive, plummy tone seems daily to extend itself into more and more aspects of American life. The Opinion section of the Sunday *New York Times*, for example, is one long succession of professorial musings. So is much of NPR's programming. Former humanities students occupy many of the seats in President Obama's Cabinet.

That the exalted men and women of higher learning might take the field 10 against opponents like the authors of the Florida report and be defeated—it's almost impossible to believe. And yet that's precisely what is happening.

Stung by the attacks on their livelihood, the nation's leading humanists 11 have closed ranks, taken up their pencils, and tried to explain why they exist. The result is a train wreck of desperate rationalizations, clichés, and circular reasoning.

They insist that their work must not be judged by bogus metrics like the 12 employability of recent graduates. They scold journalists for getting the story wrong in certain of its details. They express contempt for the dunces in state legislatures. They tear into the elected philistines who badger them with what the academic superstar Homi Bhabha calls a "primitive and reductive view of what is essential."

And with touching earnestness, they argue that the humanities are 13 *plenty* remunerative. They tell of CEOs who demand well-rounded young employees rather than single-minded, vocationally focused drudges. They remind us that humanities grads get into law and medical schools, which in turn lead (as everyone knows, right?) to the big money. Besides, they point out, the humanist promise of explaining our mysterious country draws foreign students—and foreign currency—to college towns across the land. They even play the trump card of national security: wouldn't we have done better in the global "war on terror" if we had trained more Arabic linguists prior to the start of hostilities?

Their mission, after all, is not about money: it is about molding young 14 citizens for democracy! In making this traditional argument, no one today will venture quite as far as Bruce Cole, a former chairman of the National Endowment for the Humanities, who in 2004 claimed that the humanities were "part of our homeland defense." But we're getting pretty close. Consider the report issued a few months ago by the American Academy of Arts & Sciences, which asserts that our political system itself "depends on citizens who can think critically, understand their own history, and give voice to their beliefs while respecting the views of others." As proof, the authors of the report cite Thomas Jefferson's fondness for liberal education, and then proceed to trumpet the humanities as nothing less than "the keeper of the republic"—a phrase that is doubtless meant to out-patriot the various conservatives nipping at the academy's ankles.[2]

Others want nothing to do with such hackneyed arguments. Harvard University's effort to explain the high station of the humanities, a dense and confusing text issued in June, insists that these disciplines are designed in part to "unmask the operations of power," not to buttress them. The document then disavows Harvard's *previous* justification for the humanities, which had stressed the "civic responsibilities of American citizens living in and aspiring to preserve a free democratic society." No, that was last century's model—jingoistic junk. In 2013, the humanities are all about embracing ambiguity. And about determining exactly what the humanities are about. The humanists write:

> At the same time, therefore, that we aspire to ground our sense of ourselves on some stable understanding of the aim of life (e.g., the responsible citizen in a free society), we must constantly aspire to discover anew what the best way to characterize and cultivate such an aim might be. The humanities are the site where this tension is cultivated, nurtured, and sustained.[3]

The nurturing and sustaining of tensions—that's the stuff. Of course, some tensions are more desirable than others, and for all their excitement about the unmasking of power, the Harvard humanists have little interest in unmasking their own. Nor should their genuflection at the altar of ambiguity be taken as a call to knock down the disciplinary walls. No, according to Bhabha's navel-gazing appendix, even students interested in interdisciplinary studies will be D.O.A. unless they first encounter "disciplinary specificity *in its most robust expression.*" Ambiguity is a stern taskmaster, I guess.

Most touching, perhaps, is the argument advanced by Stanley Fish in a 2010 *New York Times* Opinionator column. After shooting down the many absurd defenses of the humanities that are floating around these days, Fish advises inhabitants of academia's more rarefied regions to forget even *trying* to

---

[2]The very same month that the Academy issued this report, its president was found not to have earned the Ph.D. ascribed to her on the organization's website.

[3]This deeply unpersuasive idea—that the humanities exist to teach us how to ponder the humanities—is so seductive to the authors that they repeat it, in slightly different form, a few pages later: "An understanding of the power of the humanistic enterprise, therefore, and an understanding of how responsibly to engage it and employ it, should be the central aims of any education in the humanities."

explain themselves to the public. Don't ask what "French theory" does for the man in the street, Fish writes. Instead, ask whether its

> insights and style of analysis can be applied to the history of science, to the puzzles of theoretical physics, to psychology's analysis of the human subject. In short, justify yourselves to your colleagues, not to the hundreds of millions of Americans who know nothing of what you do and couldn't care less and shouldn't be expected to care.

Once, academics like Fish dreamed of bringing young people to a full understanding of their humanity, and maybe even of changing the world. Now their chant is: We're experts because other experts say we're experts. We critique because we critique because we critique—but all critique stops at the door to the faculty lounge.

One thing the humanities warriors don't talk about very much is the cost of 17 it all. In the first chapter of Martha Nussbaum's otherwise excellent *Not for Profit*, the author declares that while the question of "access" to higher ed is an important one, "it is not, however, the topic of this book."

Maybe it should have been. To discuss the many benefits of studying the 18 humanities absent the economic context in which the humanities are studied is to miss the point entirely. When Americans express doubts about whether (in the words of Obama pollster Joel Benenson) "a college education was worth it," they aren't making a judgment about the study of history or literature that needs to be refuted. They are remarking on its price.

Tellingly, not a single one of the defenses of the humanities that I read 19 claimed that such a course of study was a good deal for the money. The Harvard report, amid its comforting riffs about ambiguity, suggests that bemoaning the price is a "philistine objection" not really worth addressing. (It also dismisses questions of social class with a footnote.) The document produced by the American Academy of Arts & Sciences contains numerous action points for sympathetic legislators, but devotes just two paragraphs to the subject of student debt and tuition inflation, declaring blandly that "colleges must do their part to control costs," then suggesting that the *real* way to deal with the problem is to do a better job selling the humanities.

But ignoring basic economics doesn't make them go away. It is supposed 20 to be a disaster when right-wingers in state legislatures threaten to destroy academic professions. However, one reason the world has so little sympathy for those professions is that everyone knows how they themselves cranked out Ph.D.'s for decades without considering whether there was a demand for said Ph.D.'s, thereby transforming their own dedicated disciples into the most piteous wretches on campus.

Still, the wretchedness they ought to be considering is of a different magni- 21 tude altogether. The central economic fact of American higher ed today is this: It costs a lot. It costs a huge amount. It costs so much, in fact—more than $60,000 a year for tuition plus expenses at a growing number of top private schools—that young people routinely start their postcollegiate lives with enormous debt loads. It's like forcing them to take out a mortgage when they turn twenty-two, only with no white picket fence to show for it.

This is the woolly mammoth in the room. I know the story of how it got there 22 is a complicated one. But regardless of how it happened, that staggering price tag has changed the way we make educational decisions. Quite naturally, parents and students alike have come to expect some kind of direct, career-prep transaction. They're out $240,000, for Christ's sake—you can't tell them it was all about embracing ambiguity. For that kind of investment, the gates to a middle-class life had better swing wide!

No quantity of philistine-damning potshots or remarks from liberal-minded 23 CEOs will banish this problem. Humanists couldn't stop the onslaught even if they went positively retro and claimed they were needed to ponder the mind of God and save people's souls. The turn to STEM is motivated by something else, something even more desperate and more essential than that.

What is required is not better salesmanship or reassuring platitudes. The 24 world doesn't need another self-hypnotizing report on why universities exist. What it needs is for universities to stop ruining the lives of their students. Don't propagandize for your institutions, professors: Change them. Grab the levers of power and pull.

⊖ READING ARGUMENTS

1. Frank observes that the debate about the value of a liberal arts education is nothing new: "And so the old battle is joined again: the liberal arts versus professional (i.e., remunerative) studies. This time around, of course, it is flavored by all the cynical stratagems of contemporary politics" (para. 5). What evidence does Frank provide to support this statement? Does he seem to favor one political party over another? Explain.

2. Frank quotes specific language from both detractors of a liberal arts education (such as the Florida commission [7]) and its defenders (such as the "Harvard humanists" [15]). Why does he focus on their language? How does his analysis support his main argument?

3. Frank repeatedly uses the word *philistine*—for example, when he refers to the "elected philistines who badger" liberal arts professors (12). What is a "philistine"? Why is the word significant in the context of this debate?

4. According to Frank, what is the "central economic fact of American higher ed today" (21)?

5. In his conclusion, Frank advises universities to "grab the levers of power and pull" (24). What does he mean? What other point (or points) could he have emphasized here?

This image was created by the College of the Humanities at the University of Utah to promote the value of humanities courses.

VISUAL ARGUMENT: MATH VS. HUMANITIES

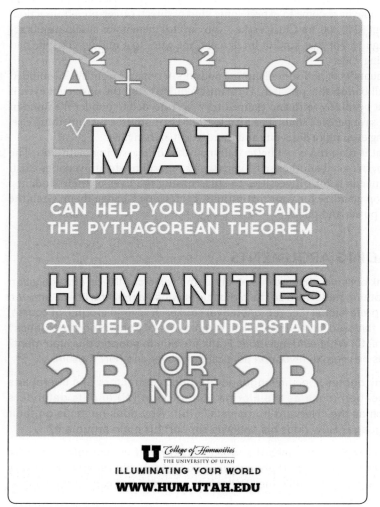

The University of Utah College of Humanities

⊘ READING ARGUMENTS

1. How would you summarize the argument of the visual in your own words?

2. What contemporary argument or issue is this visual addressing? Does it seem to be a refutation—that is, an argument against a specific position—or a clever restatement of conventional wisdom? Explain.

3. The image relies on a pun, or play on words, to make its point. How does this stylistic element support the overall argument of the visual? For example, what contrast is being highlighted?

⊘ AT ISSUE: DOES IT PAY TO STUDY THE HUMANITIES?

1. Carnevale and Melton write in paragraph 13 about the difficulties colleges and universities have trying to balance conflicting missions:

> Many educators are wary about subjugating higher education's traditional role to an economic one. Some are upset about the increasingly tight ties that bind work and education. While training foot soldiers for capitalism is not the sole mission of our education system, the inescapable reality is that ours is a society based on work.

Do you agree that there is a tension between these two "missions"? How should educators maintain a balance between their intellectual mission and the more practical demands of preparing graduates for work?

2. In her essay, Brooks asks, "Why do even the best colleges fail so often at preparing kids for the world?" (para. 5). How would you answer this question? When it comes to your college, do you agree or disagree with Brooks's contention?

3. According to Paxson, "We don't want a nation of technical experts in one subject. We want a scintillating civil society in which everyone can talk to everyone" (17). What does she mean? For example, what is a "civil society"? How are the values conveyed by the liberal arts related to civil society and public discourse? What problems might arise from having a nation composed almost entirely of highly specialized "technical experts in one subject"?

⊘ WRITING ARGUMENTS: DOES IT PAY TO STUDY THE HUMANITIES?

1. After reading the arguments in this casebook, develop your own ideas about whether it pays to study the humanities. Then, using these essays as sources, write an essay in which you argue for your position.

2. As Frank points out, educators, policymakers, politicians, and others have been strongly encouraging young Americans to major in a STEM discipline. Are you planning on studying one of these disciplines? If not, have you felt pressure from parents, teachers, or friends to pursue science, technology, engineering, or math? Write an essay that answers these questions and takes a position on the issue.

Plato

Jonathan Swift

James Baldwin

Betty Friedan

Rachel Carson

CHAPTER

25

THE ALLEGORY OF THE CAVE
PLATO

Plato (428 B.C.E.–347 B.C.E.) was an important Greek philosopher. In The Republic, *from which "The Allegory of the Cave" is drawn, Plato examines the nature of reality, how we know what we know, and how we should act. An* **allegory** *is a dramatic representation of abstract ideas by characters and events in a story or image. "The Allegory of the Cave" is an imagined dialogue between Plato's teacher (Socrates) and brother (Glaucon).*

And now, I said, let me show in a figure how far our nature is enlightened or 1 unenlightened:—Behold! human beings living in an underground den, which has a mouth open towards the light and reaching all along the den; here they have been from their childhood, and have their legs and necks chained so that they cannot move, and can only see before them, being prevented by the chains from turning round their heads. Above and behind them a fire is blazing at a distance, and between the fire and the prisoners there is a raised way; and you will see, if you look, a low wall built along the way, like the screen which marionette players have in front of them, over which they show the puppets.

I see. 2

And do you see, I said, men passing along the wall carrying all sorts of 3 vessels, and statues and figures of animals made of wood and stone and various materials, which appear over the wall? Some of them are talking, others silent.

You have shown me a strange image, and they are strange prisoners. 4

Like ourselves, I replied; and they see only their own shadows, or the 5 shadows of one another, which the fire throws on the opposite wall of the cave?

True, he said; how could they see anything but the shadows if they were 6 never allowed to move their heads?

And of the objects which are being carried in like manner they would only 7 see the shadows?

Yes, he said. 8

And if they were able to converse with one another, would they not 9 suppose that they were naming what was actually before them?

Very true. 10

And suppose further that the prison had an echo which came from the 11
other side, would they not be sure to fancy when one of the passers-by spoke
that the voice which they heard came from the passing shadow?

No question, he replied. 12

To them, I said, the truth would be literally nothing but the shadows of the 13
images.

That is certain. 14

And now look again, and see what will naturally follow if the prisoners are 15
released and disabused of their error. At first, when any of them is liberated
and compelled suddenly to stand up and turn his neck round and walk and
look towards the light, he will suffer sharp pains; the glare will distress him,
and he will be unable to see the realities of which in his former state he had
seen the shadows; and then conceive someone saying to him, that what he saw
before was an illusion, but that now, when he is approaching nearer to being
and his eye is turned towards more real existence, he has a clearer vision—what
will be his reply? And you may further imagine that his instructor is pointing
to the objects as they pass and requiring him to name them,—will he not be
perplexed? Will he not fancy that the shadows which he formerly saw are truer
than the objects which are now shown to him?

Far truer. 16

And if he is compelled to look straight at the light, will he not have a pain 17
in his eyes which will make him turn away to take refuge in the objects of
vision which he can see, and which he will conceive to be in reality clearer than
the things which are now being shown to him?

True, he said. 18

And suppose once more, that he is reluctantly dragged up a steep and rug- 19
ged ascent, and held fast until he is forced into the presence of the sun himself,
is he not likely to be pained and irritated? When he approaches the light his
eyes will be dazzled, and he will not be able to see anything at all of what are
now called realities.

Not all in a moment, he said. 20

He will require to grow accustomed to the sight of the upper world. And 21
first he will see the shadows best, next the reflections of men and other objects
in the water, and then the objects themselves; then he will gaze upon the light
of the moon and the stars and the spangled heaven; and he will see the sky and
the stars by night better than the sun or the light of the sun by day?

Certainly. 22

*Earth's star, often associated
in Plato's work with reason,
absolute good, intellectual
illumination, and God*

Last of all he will be able to see the sun,° and not mere reflections of him 23
in the water, but he will see him in his own proper place, and not in another;
and he will contemplate him as he is.

Certainly. 24

He will then proceed to argue that this is he who gives the season and the 25
years, and is the guardian of all that is in the visible world, and in a certain way
the cause of all things which he and his fellows have been accustomed to behold?

Clearly, he said, he would first see the sun and then reason about him. 26

And when he remembered his old habitation, and the wisdom of the den 27 and his fellow prisoners, do you not suppose that he would felicitate himself on the change, and pity them?

Certainly, he would. 28

And if they were in the habit of conferring honors among themselves on 29 those who were quickest to observe the passing shadows and to remark which of them went before, and which followed after, and which were together; and who were therefore best able to draw conclusions as to the future, do you think that he would care for such honors and glories, or envy the possessors of them? Would he not say with Homer,°

> Better to be the poor servant of a poor master,

and to endure anything, rather than think as they do and live after their manner?

A blind Greek poet from the eighth century B.C.E., author of the epics The Iliad *and* The Odyssey

Yes, he said, I think that he would rather suffer anything than entertain 30 these false notions and live in this miserable manner.

Imagine once more, I said, such a one coming suddenly out of the sun to 31 be replaced in his old situation; would he not be certain to have his eyes full of darkness?

To be sure, he said. 32

And if there were a contest, and he had to compete in measuring the shad- 33 ows with the prisoners who had never moved out of the den, while his sight was still weak, and before his eyes had become steady (and the time which would be needed to acquire this new habit of sight might be very consider- able), would he not be ridiculous? Men would say of him that up he went and down he came without his eyes; and that it was better not even to think of ascending; and if any one tried to loose another and lead him up to the light, let them only catch the offender, and they would put him to death.

No question, he said. 34

This entire allegory, I said, you may now append, dear Glaucon,° to the 35 previous argument; the prison house is the world of sight, the light of the fire is the sun, and you will not misapprehend me if you interpret the journey upwards to be the ascent of the soul into the intellectual world according to my poor belief, which, at your desire, I have expressed—whether rightly or wrongly God knows. But, whether true or false, my opinion is that in the world of knowledge the idea of good appears last of all, and is seen only with an effort; and, when seen, is also inferred to be the universal author of all things beautiful and right, parent of light and of the lord of light in this visible world, and the immediate source of reason and truth in the intellectual; and that this is the power upon which he who would act rationally either in public or pri- vate life must have his eye fixed.

Plato's brother, who responds to the questions, ideas, and arguments Socrates poses in The Republic

I agree, he said, as far as I am able to understand you. 36

Moreover, I said, you must not wonder that those who attain to this 37 beatific vision are unwilling to descend to human affairs; for their souls are ever hastening into the upper world where they desire to dwell; which desire of theirs is very natural, if our allegory may be trusted.

Yes, very natural. 38

And is there anything surprising in one who passes from divine contem- 39
plations to the evil state of man, misbehaving himself in a ridiculous manner;
if, while his eyes are blinking and before he has become accustomed to the surrounding darkness, he is compelled to fight in courts of law, or in other places,
about the images or the shadows of images of justice, and is endeavoring to
meet the conceptions of those who have never yet seen absolute justice?

Anything but surprising, he replied. 40

Anyone who has common sense will remember that the bewilderments of 41
the eyes are of two kinds, and arise from two causes, either from coming out
of the light or from going into the light, which is true of the mind's eye, quite
as much as of the bodily eye; and he who remembers this when he sees anyone
whose vision is perplexed and weak, will not be too ready to laugh; he will first
ask whether that soul of man has come out of the brighter life, and is unable to see
because unaccustomed to the dark, or having turned from darkness to the day is
dazzled by excess of light. And he will count the one happy in his condition and
state of being, and he will pity the other; or, if he have a mind to laugh at the soul
which comes from below into the light, there will be more reason in this than in
the laugh which greets him who returns from above out of the light into the den.

That, he said, is a very just distinction. 42

But then, if I am right, certain professors of education must be wrong 43
when they say that they can put a knowledge into the soul which was not there
before, like sight into blind eyes.

They undoubtedly say this, he replied. 44

Whereas, our argument shows that the power and capacity of learning 45
exists in the soul already; and that just as the eye was unable to turn from darkness to light without the whole body, so too the instrument of knowledge can
only by the movement of the whole soul be turned from the world of becoming
into that of being, and learn by degrees to endure the sight of being, and of the
brightest and best of being, or in other words, of the good.

Very true. 46

And must there not be some art which will effect conversion in the easiest 47
and quickest manner; not implanting the faculty of sight, for that exists already,
but has been turned in the wrong direction, and is looking away from the truth?

Yes, he said, such an art may be presumed. 48

And whereas the other so-called virtues of the soul seem to be akin to 49
bodily qualities, for even when they are not originally innate they can be
implanted later by habit and exercise, the virtue of wisdom more than anything
else contains a divine element which always remains, and by this conversion
is rendered useful and profitable; or, on the other hand, hurtful and useless.
Did you never observe the narrow intelligence flashing from the keen eye of a
clever rogue—how eager he is, how clearly his paltry soul sees the way to his
end; he is the reverse of blind, but his keen eyesight is forced into the service of
evil, and he is mischievous in proportion to his cleverness?

Very true, he said. 50

But what if there had been a circumcision of such natures in the days of 51
their youth; and they had been severed from those sensual pleasures, such as
eating and drinking, which, like leaden weights, were attached to them at their
birth, and which drag them down and turn the vision of their souls upon the
things that are below—if, I say, they had been released from these impediments
and turned in the opposite direction, the very same faculty in them would have
seen the truth as keenly as they see what their eyes are turned to now.

Very likely. 52

Yes, I said; and there is another thing which is likely, or rather a neces- 53
sary inference from what has preceded, that neither the uneducated and uninformed of the truth, nor yet those who never make an end of their education,
will be able ministers of State; not the former, because they have no single aim
of duty which is the rule of all their actions, private as well as public; nor the
latter, because they will not act at all except upon compulsion, fancying that
they are already dwelling apart in the islands of the blessed.

Very true, he replied. 54

Then, I said, the business of us who are the founders of the State will be to 55
compel the best minds to attain that knowledge which we have already shown
to be the greatest of all—they must continue to ascend until they arrive at the
good; but when they have ascended and seen enough we must not allow them
to do as they do now.

What do you mean? 56

I mean that they remain in the upper world: but this must not be allowed; 57
they must be made to descend again among the prisoners in the den, and par-
take of their labors and honors, whether they are worth having or not.

But is not this unjust? he said; ought we to give them a worse life, when 58
they might have a better?

You have again forgotten, my friend, I said, the intention of the legislator, 59
who did not aim at making any one class in the State happy above the rest; the
happiness was to be in the whole State, and he held the citizens together by
persuasion and necessity, making them benefactors of the State, and therefore
benefactors of one another; to this end he created them, not to please themselves, but to be his instruments in binding up the State.

True, he said, I had forgotten. 60

Observe, Glaucon, that there will be no injustice in compelling our philos- 61
ophers to have a care and providence of others; we shall explain to them that in
other States, men of their class are not obliged to share in the toils of politics:
and this is reasonable, for they grow up at their own sweet will, and the government would rather not have them. Being self-taught, they cannot be expected
to show any gratitude for a culture which they have never received. But we have
brought you into the world to be rulers of the hive, kings of yourselves and of
the other citizens, and have educated you far better and more perfectly than
they have been educated, and you are better able to share in the double duty.
Wherefore each of you, when his turn comes, must go down to the general
underground abode, and get the habit of seeing in the dark. When you have

acquired the habit, you will see ten thousand times better than the inhabitants of the den, and you will know what the several images are, and what they represent, because you have seen the beautiful and just and good in their truth. And thus our State, which is also yours, will be a reality, and not a dream only, and will be administered in a spirit unlike that of other States, in which men fight with one another about shadows only and are distracted in the struggle for power, which in their eyes is a great good. Whereas the truth is that the State in which the rulers are most reluctant to govern is always the best and most quietly governed, and the State in which they are most eager, the worst.

Quite true, he replied. 62

And will our pupils, when they hear this, refuse to take their turn at the 63
toils of State, when they are allowed to spend the greater part of their time with one another in the heavenly light?

Impossible, he answered; for they are just men, and the commands which 64
we impose upon them are just; there can be no doubt that every one of them will take office as a stern necessity, and not after the fashion of our present rulers of State.

Yes, my friend, I said; and there lies the point. You must contrive for your 65
future rulers another and a better life than that of a ruler, and then you may have a well-ordered State; for only in the State which offers this, will they rule who are truly rich, not in silver and gold, but in virtue and wisdom, which are the true blessings of life. Whereas if they go to the administration of public affairs, poor and hungering after their own private advantage, thinking that hence they are to snatch the chief good, order there can never be; for they will be fighting about office, and the civil and domestic broils which thus arise will be the ruin of the rulers themselves and of the whole State.

Most true, he replied. 66

And the only life which looks down upon the life of political ambition is 67
that of true philosophy. Do you know of any other?

Indeed, I do not, he said. 68

⊘ READING ARGUMENTS

1. Do you find Plato's allegory persuasive? What are its strengths and weaknesses?

2. According to Plato, what are the benefits of becoming educated about the true nature of reality? What are the drawbacks and costs of this process?

3. "The Allegory of the Cave" contains elements of a proposal argument. What does Plato propose? In what sense, if any, does his proposal apply to contemporary politics?

4. This argument is presented in the form of a dialogue, in which Glaucon responds to Socrates. How do Glaucon's responses move Plato's argument along?

⊘ WRITING ARGUMENTS

Both Plato and Thomas Jefferson (p. 732) discuss political leadership. How are their views similar? Where do their beliefs about the proper conduct and nature of political leaders differ? Which writer's argument seems more persuasive, and why? Develop your ideas in an argumentative essay.

TO HIS COY MISTRESS
ANDREW MARVELL

Andrew Marvell (1621–1678) was a member of the English Parliament for twenty years, starting in 1658. His poetry, which he wrote for his own enjoyment, was not published until after his death. "To His Coy Mistress" is his best-known poem.

Had we but world enough, and time,   1
This coyness, lady, were no crime.
We would sit down, and think which way
To walk, and pass our long love's day.
Thou by the Indian Ganges° side   5   *A river in India*
Should'st rubies find: I by the tide   *A river in England that flows past the city of Hull*
Of Humber° would complain.° I would   *To write poems or songs of unrequited love*
Love you ten years before the Flood,
And you should, if you please, refuse
Till the conversion of the Jews.°   10   *The belief that Jews would be converted to Christianity during the Last Judgment; the end of time*
My vegetable love° should grow
Vaster than empires, and more slow.
An hundred years should go to praise   *A slow-growing love*
Thine eyes, and on thy forehead gaze:
Two hundred to adore each breast: 15
But thirty thousand to the rest.
An age at least to every part,
And the last age should show your heart.
For, lady, you deserve this state,
Nor would I love at lower rate.   20
        But at my back I always hear
Time's wingèd chariot hurrying near;
And yonder all before us lie
Deserts of vast eternity.

Thy beauty shall no more be found,   25
Nor in thy marble vault shall sound
My echoing song; then worms shall try
That long preserved virginity,
And your quaint honor turn to dust,
And into ashes all my lust.   30
The grave's a fine and private place,
But none, I think, do there embrace.
      Now therefore, while the youthful hue
Sits on thy skin like morning dew,
And while thy willing soul transpires   35
At every pore with instant fires,
Now let us sport us while we may;
and now, like am'rous birds of prey,
Rather at once our time devour,

Slowly chewing jaws   Than languish in his slow-chapt° power,   40
Let us roll all our strength, and all
Our sweetness, up into one ball;
And tear our pleasures with rough strife

Through   Thorough° the iron gates of life.
Thus, though we cannot make our sun   45
Stand still, yet we will make him run.

➔ READING ARGUMENTS

1. "To His Coy Mistress" is divided into three sections. Paraphrase each section's main idea in a single sentence.

2. What does the phrase "coy mistress" suggest about the occasion and audience for the poem? How do you think the "coy mistress" would respond to the speaker's arguments?

3. How does the speaker's attitude toward time—and toward his relationship with the lady he addresses—change in line 21? How does this shift support his argument? What does he say will happen to the lady if she is not persuaded by his poem?

4. The concluding stanza of the poem begins with the phrase, "Now therefore." How does the speaker develop a deductive argument in the lines that follow?

➔ WRITING ARGUMENTS

1. Write a letter from the "coy mistress" to the poem's speaker refuting his arguments.

2. "To His Coy Mistress" is generally considered to be a poem on the theme of *carpe diem,* which means "seize the day." The full quotation comes from the Roman poet Horace: "Seize the day, and place no trust in tomorrow." Does this seem like a good philosophy of life? Write an argumentative essay that develops your position on this issue.

A MODEST PROPOSAL
JONATHAN SWIFT

Jonathan Swift (1667–1745) was a Protestant clergyman (dean of St. Patrick's Cathedral in Dublin) and a member of the Irish ruling class. His other works include A Tale of a Tub *(1704) and* Gulliver's Travels *(1726). "A Modest Proposal," written in 1729, addresses the wretched condition of the Irish people under English rule: drought had caused crop failures in Ireland, and English landowners ignored the widespread famine while thousands died of starvation.*

It is a melancholy object to those who walk through this great town or travel 1 in the country, when they see the streets, the roads, and cabin doors, crowded with beggars of the female sex, followed by three, four, or six children, all in rags and importuning every passenger for an alms. These mothers instead of being able to work for their honest livelihood, are forced to employ all their time in strolling to beg sustenance for their helpless infants: who as they grow up either turn thieves for want of work, or leave their dear native country to fight for the pretender in Spain,° or sell themselves to the Barbadoes.°

I think it is agreed by all parties that this prodigious number of children 2 in the arms, or on the backs, or at the heels of their mothers, and frequently of their fathers, is in the present deplorable state of the kingdom a very great additional grievance; and, therefore, whoever could find out a fair, cheap, and easy method of making these children sound, useful members of the commonwealth, would deserve so well of the public as to have his statue set up for a preserver of the nation.

But my intention is very far from being confined to provide only for the 3 children of professed beggars; it is of a much greater extent, and shall take in the whole number of infants at a certain age who are born of parents in effect as little able to support them as those who demand our charity in the streets.

As to my own part, having turned my thoughts for many years upon this 4 important subject, and maturely weighed the several schemes of our projectors, I have always found them grossly mistaken in their computation. It is true, a

James Francis Edward Stuart (1688–1766), descendant of the Stuart royal line. After the Stuarts were expelled from Protestant England in 1689, they took refuge in Catholic countries.

A New World colony in the Caribbean. The poor sometimes emigrated from Ireland to Barbados to find work.

Just born child just dropped from its dam° may be supported by her milk for a solar year, with little other nourishment; at most not above the value of 2s., which the mother may certainly get, or the value in scraps, by her lawful occupation of begging; and it is exactly at one year old that I propose to provide for them in such a manner as instead of being a charge upon their parents or the parish, or wanting food and raiment for the rest of their lives, they shall on the contrary contribute to the feeding, and partly to the clothing, of many thousands.

There is likewise another great advantage in my scheme, that it will pre- 5 vent those voluntary abortions, and that horrid practice of women murdering their bastard children, alas! too frequent among us! sacrificing the poor innocent babes I doubt more to avoid the expense than the shame, which would move tears and pity in the most savage and inhuman breast.

The number of souls in this kingdom being usually reckoned one million 6 and a half, of these I calculate there may be about 200,000 couple whose wives are breeders; from which number I subtract 30,000 couple who are able to maintain their own children (although I apprehend there cannot be so many, under the present distress of the kingdom); but this being granted, there will remain 170,000 breeders. I again subtract 50,000 for those women who miscarry, or whose children die by accident or disease within the year. There only remain 120,000 children of poor parents annually born. The question therefore is, how this number shall be reared and provided for? which, as I have already said, under the present situation of affairs, is utterly impossible by all the methods hitherto proposed. For we can neither employ them in handicraft nor agriculture; we neither build houses (I mean in the country) nor cultivate land; they can very seldom pick up a livelihood by stealing, till they arrive at six years old, except where they are of towardly parts, although I confess they learn the rudiments much earlier, during which time they can, however, be properly looked upon only as probationers; as I have been informed by a principal gentleman in the county of Cavan, who protested to me that he never knew above one or two instances under the age of six, even in a part of the kingdom so renowned for the quickest proficiency in that art.

I am assured by our merchants, that a boy or a girl before twelve years 7 old is no salable commodity; and even when they come to this age they will not yield above 3£. or 3£. 2s. 6d. at most on the exchange; which cannot turn to account either to the parents or kingdom, the charge of nutriment and rags having been at least four times that value.

I shall now therefore humbly propose my own thoughts, which I hope will 8 not be liable to the least objection.

I have been assured by a very knowing American of my acquaintance in 9 London, that a young healthy child well nursed is at a year old a most delicious, nourishing, and wholesome food, whether stewed, roasted, baked, or broiled; and I make no doubt that it will equally serve in a fricassee or a ragout.

I do therefore humbly offer it to public consideration that of the 120,000 10 children already computed, 20,000 may be reserved for breed, whereof only one-fourth part to be males; which is more than we allow to sheep, black cattle, or swine; and my reason is, that these children are seldom the fruits of marriage, a circumstance not much regarded by our savages; therefore one male will be sufficient to serve four females. That the remaining 100,000 may, at a year old, be offered in sale to the persons of quality and fortune through the kingdom; always advising the mother to let them suck plentifully in the last month, so as to render them plump and fat for a good table. A child will make two dishes at an entertainment for friends; and when the family dines alone, the fore and hind quarter will make a reasonable dish, and seasoned with a little pepper or salt will be very good boiled on the fourth day, especially in winter.

I have reckoned upon a medium that a child just born will weigh 11 pounds, and in a solar year, if tolerably nursed, will increase to 28 pounds.

I grant this food will be somewhat dear, and therefore very proper for 12 landlords, who, as they have already devoured most of the parents, seem to have the best title to the children.

Infants' flesh will be in season throughout the year, but more plentiful in 13 March, and a little before and after: for we are told by a grave author, an eminent French physician, that fish being a prolific diet, there are more children born in Roman Catholic countries about nine months after Lent than at any other season; therefore, reckoning a year after Lent, the markets will be more glutted than usual, because the number of popish infants is at least three to one in this kingdom: and therefore it will have one other collateral advantage, by lessening the number of papists° among us.

Catholics. The term papists suggests their allegiance to the Pope rather than to the Church of England.

I have already computed the charge of nursing a beggar's child (in which 14 list I reckon all cottagers, laborers, and four-fifths of the farmers) to be about 2s. per annum, rags included; and I believe no gentleman would repine to give 10s. for the carcass of a good fat child, which, as I have said, will make four dishes of excellent nutritive meat, when he has only some particular friend or his own family to dine with him. Thus the squire will learn to be a good landlord, and grow popular among the tenants; the mother will have 8s. net profit, and be fit for work till she produces another child.

Those who are more thrifty (as I must confess the times require) may flay 15 the carcass; the skin of which artificially dressed will make admirable gloves for ladies, and summer boots for fine gentlemen.

As to our city of Dublin, shambles° may be appointed for this purpose in 16 the most convenient parts of it, and butchers we may be assured will not be wanting: although I rather recommend buying the children alive, and dressing them hot from the knife as we do roasting pigs.

Butcher shops

A very worthy person, a true lover of his country, and whose virtues I 17 highly esteem, was lately pleased in discoursing on this matter to offer a refinement upon my scheme. He said that many gentlemen of this kingdom, having of late destroyed their deer, he conceived that the want of venison might be well supplied by the bodies of young lads and maidens, not exceeding fourteen years of age nor under twelve; so great a number of both sexes in every country being now ready to starve for want of work and service; and these to be disposed of by their parents, if alive, or otherwise by their nearest relations. But with due deference to so excellent a friend and so deserving a patriot, I cannot be altogether in his sentiments; for as to the males, my American acquaintance assured me from frequent experience that their flesh was generally tough and lean, like that of our schoolboys by continual exercise, and their taste disagreeable; and to fatten them would not answer the charge. Then as to the females, it would, I think, with humble submission be a loss to the public, because they soon would become breeders themselves: and besides, it is not improbable that some scrupulous people might be apt to censure such a practice (although indeed very unjustly), as a little bordering upon cruelty; which, I confess, has always been with me the strongest objection against any project, how well soever intended.

But in order to justify my friend, he confessed that this expedient was 18 put into his head by the famous Psalmanazar,° a native of the island Formosa, who came from thence to London about twenty years ago: and in conversation told my friend, that in his country when any young person happened to be put to death, the executioner sold the carcass to persons of quality as a prime dainty; and that in his time the body of a plump girl of fifteen, who was crucified for an attempt to poison the emperor, was sold to his imperial majesty's prime minister of state, and other great mandarins° of the court, in joints from the gibbet,° at 400 crowns. Neither indeed can I deny, that if the same use were made of several plump young girls in this town, who without one single groat° to their fortunes cannot stir abroad without a chair, and appear at the playhouse and assemblies in foreign fineries which they never will pay for, the kingdom would not be the worse.

George Psalmanazar (1679 [approx.]–1763), who falsely claimed to be the first person from Formosa (modern-day Taiwan) to visit Europe. He described Formosan native customs that included cannibalism.

Chinese nobles, court officials, or magistrates

A post for hanging; a gallows

A small coin

Some persons of a desponding spirit are in great concern about the vast num- 19 ber of poor people, who are aged, diseased, or maimed, and I have been desired to employ my thoughts what course may be taken to ease the nation of so grievous an encumbrance. But I am not in the least pain upon that matter, because it is very well known that they are every day dying and rotting by cold and famine, and filth and vermin, as fast as can be reasonably expected. And as to the young laborers, they are now in as hopeful condition: They cannot get work, and consequently pine away for want of nourishment, to a degree that if at any time they are accidentally hired to common labor, they have not strength to perform it; and thus the country and themselves are happily delivered from the evils to come.

I have too long digressed, and therefore shall return to my subject. I think 20 the advantages by the proposal which I have made are obvious and many, as well as of the highest importance.

For first, as I have already observed, it would greatly lessen the number of 21 papists, with whom we are yearly overrun, being the principal breeders of the nation as well as our most dangerous enemies; and who stay at home on purpose to deliver the kingdom to the Pretender, hoping to take their advantage by the absence of so many good Protestants, who have chosen rather to leave their country than stay at home and pay tithes against their conscience to an Episcopal curate.

Secondly, The poor tenants will have something valuable of their own, 22
which by law may be made liable to distress° and help to pay their landlord's
rent, their corn and cattle being already seized, and money a thing unknown.

Able to be seized to pay a debt

Thirdly, Whereas the maintenance of 100,000 children from two years 23
old and upward, cannot be computed at less that 10s. a-piece per annum, the
nation's stock will be thereby increased £50,000 per annum, beside the profit of
a new dish introduced to the tables of all gentlemen of fortune in the kingdom
who have any refinement in taste. And the money will circulate among ourselves, the goods being entirely of our own growth and manufacture.

Fourthly, The constant breeders beside the gain of 8s. sterling per annum 24
by the sale of their children, will be rid of the charge of maintaining them after
the first year.

Fifthly, This food would likewise bring great custom to taverns, where the 25
vintners will certainly be so prudent as to procure the best receipts for dressing
it to perfection, and consequently have their houses frequented by all the fine
gentlemen, who justly value themselves upon their knowledge in good eating;
and a skillful cook who understands how to oblige his guests, will contrive to
make it as expensive as they please.

Sixthly, This would be a great inducement to marriage, which all wise 26
nations have either encouraged by rewards or enforced by laws and penalties.
It would increase the care and tenderness of mothers toward their children,
when they were sure of a settlement for life to the poor babes, provided in
some sort by the public, to their annual profit instead of expense. We should
see an honest emulation among the married women, which of them would
bring the fattest child to the market. Men would become as fond of their wives
during the time of their pregnancy as they are now of their mares in foal, their
cows in calf, their sows when they are ready to farrow; nor offer to beat or kick
them (as is too frequent a practice) for fear of a miscarriage.

Many other advantages might be enumerated. For instance, the addition 27
of some thousand carcasses in our exportation of barreled beef, the propagation of swine's flesh, and improvement in the art of making good bacon, so
much wanted among us by the great destruction of pigs, too frequent at our
table; which are no way comparable in taste or magnificence to a well-grown,
fat, yearling child, which roasted whole will make a considerable figure at a
lord mayor's feast or any other public entertainment. But this and many others
I omit, being studious of brevity.

Supposing that 1,000 families in this city would be constant customers for 28
infants' flesh, besides others who might have it at merry-meetings, particularly
at weddings and christenings, I compute that Dublin would take off annually
about 20,000 carcasses; and the rest of the kingdom (where probably they will
be sold somewhat cheaper) the remaining 80,000.

I can think of no one objection that will possibly be raised against this 29
proposal unless it should be urged that the number of people will be thereby
much lessened in the kingdom. This I freely own, and it was indeed one principal design in offering it to the world. I desire the reader will observe, that

*The indigenous Sami people
of northern European
countries, including Sweden,
Norway, and Finland. The
term is now considered
pejorative.*

Brazil

*Jerusalem, which was
conquered by the Roman
commander Titus in 70 C.E.*

England

I calculate my remedy for this one individual kingdom of Ireland and for no other that ever was, is, or I think ever can be upon earth. Therefore let no man talk to me of other expedients: of taxing our absentees at 5s. a pound: of using neither clothes nor household furniture except what is of our own growth and manufacture: of utterly rejecting the materials and instruments that promote foreign luxury: of curing the expensiveness of pride, vanity, idleness, and gaming in our women: of introducing a vein of parsimony, prudence, and temperance: of learning to love our country, in the want of which we differ even from Laplanders,° and the inhabitants of Topinamboo:° of quitting our animosities and factions, nor acting any longer like the Jews, who were murdering one another at the very moment their city° was taken: of being a little cautious not to sell our country and conscience for nothing: of teaching landlords to have at least one degree of mercy toward their tenants: lastly, of putting a spirit of honesty, industry, and skill into our shopkeepers; who, if a resolution could now be taken to buy only our native goods, would immediately unite to cheat and exact upon us in the price, the measure, and the goodness, nor could ever yet be brought to make one fair proposal of just dealing, though often and earnestly invited to it.

Therefore I repeat, let no man talk to me of these and the like expedients, 30 till he has at least some glimpse of hope that there will be ever some hearty and sincere attempt to put them in practice.

But as to myself, having been wearied out for many years with offering vain, 31 idle, visionary thoughts, and at length utterly despairing of success, I fortunately fell upon this proposal; which, as it is wholly new, so it has something solid and real, of no expense and little trouble, full in our own power, and whereby we can incur no danger in disobliging England. For this kind of commodity will not bear exportation, the flesh being of too tender a consistence to admit a long continuance in salt, although perhaps I could name a country° which would be glad to eat up our whole nation without it.

After all, I am not so violently bent upon my own opinion as to reject 32 any offer proposed by wise men, which shall be found equally innocent, cheap, easy, and effectual. But before something of that kind shall be advanced in contradiction to my scheme, and offering a better, I desire the author or authors will be pleased maturely to consider two points. First, as things now stand, how they will be able to find food and raiment for 100,000 useless mouths and backs. And secondly, there being a round million of creatures in human figure throughout this kingdom, whose subsistence put into a common stock would leave them in debt 2,000,000£. sterling, adding those who are beggars by profession to the bulk of farmers, cottagers, and laborers, with the wives and children who are beggars in effect; I desire those politicians who dislike my overture, and may perhaps be so bold as to attempt an answer, that they will first ask the parents of these mortals, whether they would not at this day think it a great happiness to have been sold for food at a year old in the manner I prescribe, and thereby have avoided such a perpetual scene of misfortunes as they have since gone through by the oppression of landlords, the impossibility of paying rent without money or trade, the want of common sustenance, with neither house nor clothes to cover them from the inclemencies of the weather, and the most inevitable prospect of entailing the like or greater miseries upon their breed for ever.

I profess, in the sincerity of my heart, that I have not the least personal 33 interest in endeavoring to promote this necessary work, having no other motive than the public good of my country, by advancing our trade, providing for infants, relieving the poor, and giving some pleasure to the rich. I have no children by which I can propose to get a single penny; the youngest being nine years old, and my wife past childbearing.

⊙ READING ARGUMENTS

1. Swift's "A Modest Proposal" is **satire**: it takes a position that is so extreme that readers must necessarily disagree with it. By taking such a position, Swift ridicules the English political system that he considers corrupt and insensitive and implies another, more reasonable argument that the reader must infer. What is the real argument that Swift is making in "A Modest Proposal"? What social reforms does he propose?

2. Where does "A Modest Proposal" use inductive reasoning?

3. In what sense is "A Modest Proposal" an ethical argument?

4. Swift's use of **irony**—saying one thing but meaning another—is a useful technique for making an argument, yet it also has limitations. What are some of these limitations?

5. What elements of a proposal argument appear in this essay? Which elements, if any, are missing?

⊙ WRITING ARGUMENTS

1. Write your own "modest proposal." Choose a contemporary issue or controversy (political, cultural, or social). Then, write an argumentative essay that uses **irony**, **satire**, and **hyperbole** (intentional exaggeration) to make your point.

2. "A Modest Proposal" includes population data, economic projections, and other kinds of support. What point do you think Swift is making about actual proposals to solve social or political problems? Do you think his point is relevant today? Why or why not?

THE DECLARATION OF INDEPENDENCE

THOMAS JEFFERSON

Thomas Jefferson, born in 1743, was one of the founding fathers of the United States. He served in the Virginia House of Burgesses and the Continental Congress, as governor of Virginia, minister to France, secretary of state in President George Washington's cabinet, vice president, and president of the United States for two terms. He also founded the University of Virginia. In 1776, he was chosen to draft the Declaration of Independence, the founding document of American liberties. Jefferson died on July 4, 1826.

In Congress, July 4, 1776
The Unanimous Declaration of the
Thirteen United States of America

When in the Course of human events it becomes necessary for one people to   1
dissolve the political bands which have connected them with another, and to
assume among the powers of the earth, the separate and equal station to which
the Laws of Nature and of Nature's God entitle them, a decent respect to the
opinions of mankind requires that they should declare the causes which impel
them to the separation.

We hold these truths to be self-evident, that all men are created equal,   2
that they are endowed by their Creator with certain unalienable Rights,
that among these are Life, Liberty, and the pursuit of Happiness. That to
secure these rights, Governments are instituted among Men, deriving their
just powers from the consent of the governed. That whenever any Form
of Government becomes destructive of these ends, it is the Right of the
People to alter or to abolish it, and to institute new Government, laying
its foundation on such principles and organizing its powers in such form,
as to them shall seem most likely to effect their Safety and Happiness.
Prudence, indeed, will dictate that Governments long established should
not be changed for light and transient causes; and accordingly all experience hath shewn that mankind are more disposed to suffer, while evils are
sufferable, than right themselves by abolishing the forms to which they are
accustomed. But when a long train of abuses and usurpations, pursuing
invariably the same Object evinces a design to reduce them under absolute
Despotism, it is their right, it is their duty, to throw off such Government,
and to provide new Guards for their future security. Such has been the
patient sufferance of these Colonies; and such is now the necessity which
constrains them to alter their former Systems of Government. The history
of the present King of Great Britain is a history of repeated injuries and

usurpations, all having in direct object the establishment of an absolute Tyranny over these States. To prove this, let Facts be submitted to a candid° world.

Impartial, without prejudice

He has refused his Assent to Laws, the most wholesome and necessary for 3 the public good.

He has forbidden his Government to pass laws of immediate and press- 4 ing importance, unless suspended in their operation till his Assent should be obtained; and when so suspended, he has utterly neglected to attend to them.

He has refused to pass other Laws for the accommodation of large dis- 5 tricts of people, unless those people would relinquish the right of Representation in the Legislature, a right inestimable to them and formidable to tyrants only.

He has called together legislative bodies at places unusual, uncomfortable, 6 and distant from the depository of their Public Records, for the sole purpose of fatiguing them into compliance with his measures.

He has dissolved Representative Houses repeatedly, for opposing with 7 manly firmness his invasions on the rights of the people.

He has refused for a long time, after such dissolutions, to cause others to 8 be elected; whereby the Legislative Powers, incapable of Annihilation, have returned to the People at large for their exercise; the State remaining in the mean time exposed to all the dangers of invasion from without, and convulsions within.

He has endeavored to prevent the population of these States; for that pur- 9 pose obstructing the Laws for Naturalization of Foreigners; refusing to pass others to encourage their migration hither, and raising the conditions of new Appropriations of Lands.

He has obstructed the Administration of Justice, by refusing his Assent to 10 Laws for establishing Judiciary Powers.

He has made Judges dependent on his Will alone, for the tenure of their 11 offices, and the amount and payment of their salaries.

He has erected a multitude of New Offices, and sent hither swarms of 12 Officers to harass our people, and eat out their substance.

He has kept among us, in times of peace, Standing Armies without the 13 Consent of our legislatures.

He has affected to render the Military independent of and superior to the 14 Civil Power.

He has combined with others to subject us to a jurisdiction foreign to our 15 constitution, and unacknowledged by our laws; giving his Assent to their Acts of pretended Legislation: For quartering large bodies of armed troops among us: For protecting them, by a mock Trial, from punishment for any Murders which they should commit on the Inhabitants of these States: For cutting off our Trade with all parts of the world: For imposing Taxes on us without our Consent: For depriving us in many cases, of the benefits of Trial by Jury: For

Quebec, whose residents were deprived of political representation by the British government in 1774

transporting us beyond Seas to be tried for pretended offenses: For abolishing the free System of English Laws in a neighboring Province,° establishing therein an Arbitrary government, and enlarging its Boundaries so as to render it at once an example and fit instrument for introducing the same absolute rule into these Colonies: For taking away our Charters, abolishing our most valuable Laws and altering fundamentally the Forms of our Governments: For suspending our own Legislatures, and declaring themselves invested with power to legislate for us in all cases whatsoever.

He has abdicated Government here, by declaring us out of his Protection 16 and waging War against us.

He has plundered our seas, ravaged our Coasts, burnt our towns, and 17 destroyed the lives of our people.

He is at this time transporting large Armies of foreign Mercenaries to 18 complete the works of death, desolation and tyranny, already begun with circumstances of Cruelty & Perfidy scarcely paralleled in the most barbarous ages, and totally unworthy the Head of a civilized nation.

He has constrained our fellow Citizens taken Captive on the high Seas to 19 bear Arms against their Country, to become the executioners of their friends and Brethren, or to fall themselves by their Hands.

He has excited domestic insurrections amongst us, and has endeavored to 20 bring on the inhabitants of our frontiers, the merciless Indian Savages, whose known rule of warfare, is an undistinguished destruction of all ages, sexes, and conditions.

In every stage of these Oppressions We have Petitioned for Redress in 21 the most humble terms: Our repeated Petitions have been answered only by repeated injury. A Prince, whose character is thus marked by every act which may define a Tyrant, is unfit to be the ruler of a free people.

Nor have We been wanting in attention to our British brethren. We have 22 warned them from time to time of attempts by their legislature to extend an unwarrantable jurisdiction over us. We have reminded them of the circumstances of our emigration and settlement here. We have appealed to their native justice and magnanimity, and we have conjured them by the ties of our common kindred to disavow these usurpations, which would inevitably interrupt our connections and correspondence. They too have been deaf to the voice of justice and of consanguinity. We must, therefore, acquiesce in the necessity, which denounces our Separation, and hold them, as we hold the rest of mankind, Enemies in War, in Peace Friends.

We, THEREFORE the Representatives of the UNITED STATES OF 23 AMERICA, in General Congress, Assembled, appealing to the Supreme Judge of the world for the rectitude of our intentions, do, in the Name, and by Authority of the good People of these Colonies, solemnly publish and declare, That these United Colonies are, and of Right ought to be FREE AND INDEPENDENT STATES; that they are Absolved from all Allegiance to the British Crown, and that all political connection between them and the State of Great Britain, is and ought to be totally dissolved; and that as

Free and Independent States, they have full Power to levy War, conclude Peace, contract Alliances, establish Commerce, and to do all other Acts and Things which Independent States may of right do. And for the support of this Declaration, with a firm reliance on the protection of Divine Providence, we mutually pledge to each other our Lives, our Fortunes, and our sacred Honor.

⊙ READING ARGUMENTS

1. What are the purposes of the first and second paragraphs of the Declaration of Independence? Do these opening paragraphs present information deductively or inductively?

2. In paragraph 2, Jefferson writes, "Governments long established should not be changed for light and transient causes." Why is this qualification important to his argument? What objections does it anticipate?

3. According to the Declaration, what is the purpose of government? What makes a government legitimate?

4. In what sense is the Declaration of Independence a cause-and-effect argument?

5. What specific evidence does Jefferson supply to support his case? How effective is this evidence? What do you consider his most convincing piece of evidence?

⊙ WRITING ARGUMENTS

1. Write a one-page rhetorical analysis of the Declaration of Independence in terms of the Toulmin model. Begin by identifying the claim, the grounds, and the warrant. (See Chapter 6 for more on Toulmin argument; see Chapter 4 for information on writing a rhetorical analysis.)

2. Jefferson writes that revolutionary action should not be taken for "light and transient causes" (para. 2). After an armed uprising several years before the American Revolution, he also said, "God forbid we be 20 years without such a rebellion. . . . The tree of liberty must be refreshed from time to time with the blood of patriots and tyrants." In your view, what conditions or actions on the part of an established government justify its overthrow? Explain your answer in an argumentative essay.

THE GETTYSBURG ADDRESS

ABRAHAM LINCOLN

Abraham Lincoln (1809–1865) was the sixteenth president of the United States. Raised in frontier Kentucky and Indiana, he rose from rural poverty to become a lawyer, an Illinois state legislator, and a member of the U.S. House of Representatives. He also became one of America's mythic figures. Elected to the White House in 1861 and again in 1864, Lincoln led the United States through the cataclysm of the Civil War and was assassinated in 1865. His 1863 Gettysburg Address, delivered at the dedication of the Soldier's National Cemetery in Gettysburg, Pennsylvania, is arguably the most famous speech in American history.

Four score and seven years ago our fathers brought forth on this continent, a 1
new nation, conceived in Liberty, and dedicated to the proposition that all men
are created equal.

Now we are engaged in a great civil war, testing whether that nation, or 2
any nation so conceived and so dedicated, can long endure. We are met on a
great battle-field of that war. We have come to dedicate a portion of that field,
as a final resting place for those who here gave their lives that that nation might
live. It is altogether fitting and proper that we should do this.

But, in a larger sense, we can not dedicate—we can not consecrate—we can 3
not hallow—this ground. The brave men, living and dead, who struggled here,
have consecrated it, far above our poor power to add or detract. The world will
little note, nor long remember what we say here, but it can never forget what
they did here. It is for us the living, rather, to be dedicated here to the unfinished work which they who fought here have thus far so nobly advanced. It is
rather for us to be here dedicated to the great task remaining before us—that
from these honored dead we take increased devotion to that cause for which
they gave the last full measure of devotion—that we here highly resolve that
these dead shall not have died in vain—that this nation, under God, shall have
a new birth of freedom—and that government of the people, by the people, for
the people, shall not perish from the earth.

⊘ READING ARGUMENTS

1. According to Lincoln, what is the obligation of "the living" (para. 3)?
   Explain this obligation in your own words.

2. Does the Gettysburg Address make an argument? If so, is it a deductive argument or an inductive argument? Explain.

3. Lincoln gave this speech at the dedication of a cemetery, yet he concedes that "in a larger sense, we can not dedicate—we can not consecrate—we can not hallow—this ground" (3). Is he undercutting his own implicit purpose here? How does this concession support his larger point?

4. What strategies does Lincoln use to support his position? Does he make an ethical argument? A cause-and-effect argument? Is this speech in any sense a proposal argument?

◯ WRITING ARGUMENTS

1. Consider Lincoln's prose style—in particular, its rhythm and word choice. For example, is "Four score and seven years ago" (para. 1) the clearest, simplest phrasing he could have chosen? Rewrite this sentence—or any other sentence—in your own words. How does your version compare to Lincoln's? What do you learn about Lincoln's language—and his argument—when you try to paraphrase his speech?

2. In a well-known 1920 essay, the American critic H. L. Mencken lauded the Gettysburg Address as "eloquence brought to a pellucid and almost gem-like perfection—the highest emotion reduced to a few poetical phrases." However, Mencken qualified his praise of Lincoln's speech by saying, "But let us not forget that it is poetry, not logic; beauty, not sense." He said of Lincoln's main point: "It is difficult to imagine anything more untrue." How do you respond to Mencken's assessment? Do you find Lincoln's argument "true" or "untrue"? Do you think the speech's "eloquence," "poetry," and "beauty" undercut its "logic," "sense," and "truth"? Why or why not?

DECLARATION OF SENTIMENTS AND RESOLUTIONS

ELIZABETH CADY STANTON

Elizabeth Cady Stanton (1815–1902) was a prominent leader in the struggle for the rights of women, advocating for the right of women to vote, divorce, and be equal to men under law. In 1848, when Stanton's "Declaration of Sentiments and Resolutions" was written for a women's rights convention in Seneca Falls, New York, married women were not allowed to own property. Stanton's declaration is modeled on Thomas Jefferson's Declaration of Independence.

When, in the course of human events, it becomes necessary for one portion 1 of the family of man to assume among the people of the earth a position different from that which they have hitherto occupied, but one to which the laws of nature and of nature's God entitle them, a decent respect to the opinions of mankind requires that they should declare the causes that impel them to such a course.

We hold these truths to be self-evident: that all men and women are cre- 2 ated equal; that they are endowed by their Creator with certain inalienable rights; that among these are life, liberty, and the pursuit of happiness; that to secure these rights governments are instituted, deriving their just powers from the consent of the governed. Whenever any form of government becomes destructive of these ends, it is the right of those who suffer from it to refuse allegiance to it, and to insist upon the institution of a new government, laying its foundation on such principles, and organizing its powers in such form, as to them shall seem most likely to effect their safety and happiness. Prudence indeed, will dictate that governments long established should not be changed for light and transient causes; and accordingly all experience hath shown that mankind are more disposed to suffer, while evils are sufferable, than to right themselves by abolishing the forms to which they were accustomed. But when a long train of abuses and usurpations, pursuing invariably the same object evinces a design to reduce them under absolute despotism, it is their duty to throw off such government, and to provide new guards for their future security. Such has been the patient sufferance of the women under this government, and such is now the necessity which constrains them to demand the equal station to which they are entitled.

The history of mankind is a history of repeated injuries and usurpations 3 on the part of man toward woman, having in direct object the establishment of an absolute tyranny over her. To prove this, let facts be submitted to a candid world.

He has never permitted her to exercise her inalienable right to the elective 4 franchise.

He has compelled her to submit to laws, in the formation of which she had 5 no voice.

He has withheld from her rights which are given to the most ignorant and 6 degraded men—both natives and foreigners.

Having deprived her of this first right of a citizen, the elective franchise, 7 thereby leaving her without representation in the halls of legislation, he has oppressed her on all sides.

He has made her, if married, in the eye of the law, civilly dead.   8

He has taken from her all right in property, even to the wages she earns.   9

He has made her, morally, an irresponsible being, as she can commit many 10 crimes with impunity, provided they be done in the presence of her husband. In the covenant of marriage, she is compelled to promise obedience to her husband, he becoming, to all intents and purposes, her master—the law giving him power to deprive her of her liberty, and to administer chastisement.

He has so framed the laws of divorce, as to what shall be the proper causes, 11 and in case of separation, to whom the guardianship of the children shall be given, as to be wholly regardless of the happiness of women—the law, in all cases, going upon a false supposition of the supremacy of man, and giving all power into his hands.

After depriving her of all rights as a married woman, if single, and the 12 owner of property, he has taxed her to support a government which recognizes her only when her property can be made profitable to it.

He has monopolized nearly all the profitable employments, and from 13 those she is permitted to follow, she receives but a scanty remuneration. He closes against her all the avenues to wealth and distinction which he considers most honorable to himself. As a teacher of theology, medicine, or law, she is not known.

He has denied her the facilities for obtaining a thorough education, all 14 colleges being closed against her.

He allows her in Church, as well as State, but a subordinate position, 15 claiming Apostolic authority for her exclusion from the ministry, and, with some exceptions, from any public participation in the affairs of the Church.

He has created a false public sentiment by giving to the world a differ- 16 ent code of morals for men and women, by which moral delinquencies which exclude women from society, are not only tolerated, but deemed of little account in man.

He has usurped the prerogative of Jehovah himself, claiming it as his right 17 to assign for her a sphere of action, when that belongs to her conscience and to her God.

He has endeavored, in every way that he could, to destroy her confidence 18 in her own powers, to lessen her self-respect, and to make her willing to lead a dependent and abject life.

Now, in view of this entire disfranchisement of one-half the people of 19 this country, their social and religious degradation—in view of the unjust laws above mentioned, and because women do feel themselves aggrieved, oppressed, and fraudulently deprived of their most sacred rights, we insist that they have immediate admission to all the rights and privileges which belong to them as citizens of the United States.

In entering upon the great work before us, we anticipate no small amount 20 of misconception, misrepresentation, and ridicule; but we shall use every instrumentality within our power to effect our object. We shall employ agents, circulate tracts, petition the State and National legislatures, and endeavor to enlist the pulpit and the press in our behalf. We hope this Convention will be followed by a series of Conventions embracing every part of the country.

⊖READING ARGUMENTS

1. Why do you think Stanton chose to echo the style and structure of the Declaration of Independence? What point was she trying to make?

2. How do Stanton's general political aims contrast with Jefferson's goals in the Declaration of Independence (p. 732)?

3. According to Stanton, "The history of mankind is a history of repeated injuries and usurpations on the part of man toward woman, having in direct object the establishment of an absolute tyranny over her" (para. 3). How does she support this generalization? Do you find her evidence convincing? Why or why not?

4. Stanton writes that man has "usurped the prerogative of Jehovah himself, claiming it as his right to assign for [women] a sphere of action" (17). What do you think she means? Do you think her point is valid today?

5. In her conclusion, Stanton summarizes how women will fulfill the goals of her declaration. What specific steps does she expect women to take?

➲ WRITING ARGUMENTS

1. Stanton accuses male-dominated society not only of "monopoliz[ing] nearly all the profitable employments" (para. 13) but also of "giving to the world a different code of morals for men and women" (16). Do you think these gender restrictions and double standards still exist today? Write an argumentative essay that takes a stand on this issue.

2. In paragraph 2, Stanton quotes Thomas Jefferson's claim that "all experience hath shown that mankind are more disposed to suffer, while evils are sufferable, than to right themselves by abolishing the forms to which they were accustomed." What view of human nature is implied here? Do you agree with this view? Do you think it is still held by people today? Explain your views in an argumentative essay.

POLITICS AND THE ENGLISH LANGUAGE
GEORGE ORWELL

George Orwell was the pen name of journalist, critic, and novelist Eric Blair (1903–1950), best known for his allegorical satire Animal Farm *(1945) and his dystopian novel* 1984 *(1949). Orwell also wrote nonfiction about many different subjects, from his experiences in the Spanish Civil War to his affection for English cooking. He was especially preoccupied with language and political writing—for example, the ways in which political orthodoxy leads to a "lifeless, imitative style." Orwell himself rejected orthodoxy: he was a democratic socialist who criticized socialism, a lover of England who attacked British colonialism, and a literary highbrow who enjoyed popular culture. Although it was written in 1946, "Politics and the English Language" remains an excellent guide for avoiding the bad writing habits of "political conformity."*

Most people who bother with the matter at all would admit that the English 1 language is in a bad way, but it is generally assumed that we cannot by conscious action do anything about it. Our civilization is decadent and our language—so the argument runs—must inevitably share in the general collapse. It follows that any struggle against the abuse of language is a sentimental archaism, like preferring candles to electric light or hansom cabs to aeroplanes. Underneath this lies the half-conscious belief that language is a natural growth and not an instrument which we shape for our own purposes.

Now, it is clear that the decline of a language must ultimately have political 2 and economic causes: it is not due simply to the bad influence of this or that individual writer. But an effect can become a cause, reinforcing the original cause and producing the same effect in an intensified form, and so on indefinitely. A man may take to drink because he feels himself to be a failure, and then fail all the more completely because he drinks. It is rather the same thing that is happening to the English language. It becomes ugly and inaccurate because our thoughts are foolish, but the slovenliness of our language makes it easier for us to have foolish thoughts. The point is that the process is reversible. Modern English, especially written English, is full of bad habits which spread by imitation and which can be avoided if one is willing to take the necessary trouble. If one gets rid of these habits one can think more clearly, and to think clearly is a necessary first step towards political regeneration: so that the fight against bad English is not frivolous and is not the exclusive concern of professional writers. I will come back to this presently, and I hope that by that time the meaning of what I have said here will have become clearer. Meanwhile, here are five specimens of the English language as it is now habitually written.

These five passages have not been picked out because they are especially 3 bad—I could have quoted far worse if I had chosen—but because they illustrate various of the mental vices from which we now suffer. They are a little below the average, but are fairly representative samples. I number them so that I can refer back to them when necessary:

> (1) I am not, indeed, sure whether it is not true to say that the Milton who once seemed not unlike a seventeenth-century Shelley had not become, out of an experience ever more bitter in each year, more alien [*sic*] to the founder of that Jesuit sect which nothing could induce him to tolerate.
>
> Professor Harold Laski (Essay in *Freedom of Expression*)

(2) Above all, we cannot play ducks and drakes with a native battery of idioms which prescribes such egregious collocations of vocables as the basic *put up with* for *tolerate* or *put at a loss* for *bewilder*.

Professor Lancelot Hogben (*Interglossa*)

(3) On the one side we have the free personality: by definition it is not neurotic, for it has neither conflict nor dream. Its desires, such as they are, are transparent, for they are just what institutional approval keeps in the forefront of consciousness; another institutional pattern would alter their number and intensity; there is little in them that is natural, irreducible, or culturally dangerous. But *on the other* side, the social bond itself is nothing but the mutual reflection of these self-secure integrities. Recall the definition of love. Is not this the very picture of a small academic? Where is there a place in this hall of mirrors for either personality or fraternity?

Essay on psychology in *Politics* (New York)

(4) All the "best people" from the gentlemen's clubs, and all the frantic fascist captains, united in common hatred of Socialism and bestial horror of the rising tide of the mass revolutionary movement, have turned to acts of provocation, to foul incendiarism, to medieval legends of poisoned wells, to legalize their own destruction of proletarian organizations, and rouse the agitated petty-bourgeoisie to chauvinistic fervour on behalf of the fight against the revolutionary way out of the crisis.

Communist pamphlet

(5) If a new spirit *is* to be infused into this old country, there is one thorny and contentious reform which must be tackled, and that is the humanization and galvanization of the B.B.C. Timidity here will bespeak cancer and atrophy of the soul. The heart of Britain may be sound and of strong beat, for instance, but the British lion's roar at present is like that of Bottom in Shakespeare's *Midsummer Night's Dream*—as gentle as any sucking dove. A virile new Britain cannot continue indefinitely to be traduced in the eyes or rather ears, of the world by the effete languors of Langham Place, brazenly masquerading as "standard English." When the Voice of Britain is heard at nine o'clock, better far and infinitely less ludicrous to hear aitches honestly dropped than the present priggish, inflated, inhibited, school-ma'amish arch braying of blameless bashful mewing maidens!

Letter in *Tribune*

Each of these passages has faults of its own, but, quite apart from avoidable 4 ugliness, two qualities are common to all of them. The first is staleness of imagery: the other is lack of precision. The writer either has a meaning and cannot express it, or he inadvertently says something else, or he is almost indifferent as to whether his words mean anything or not. This mixture of vagueness and sheer incompetence is the most marked characteristic of modern English prose, and especially of any kind of political writing. As soon as certain topics are raised, the concrete melts into the abstract and no one seems able to think of turns of speech that are not hackneyed: prose consists less and less of *words* chosen for the sake of their meaning, and more and more of *phrases* tacked together like the sections of a prefabricated hen-house. I list below, with notes and examples, various of the tricks by means of which the work of prose-construction is habitually dodged:

Dying Metaphors

A newly invented metaphor assists thought by evoking a visual image, while on the other hand a metaphor which is technically "dead" (e.g., *iron resolution*) has in effect reverted to being an ordinary word and can generally be used without loss of vividness. But in between these two classes there is a huge dump of worn-out metaphors which have lost all evocative power and are merely used because they save people the trouble of inventing phrases for themselves. Examples are: *Ring the changes on, take up the cudgels for, toe the line, ride roughshod over, stand shoulder to shoulder with, play into the hands of, no axe to grind, grist to the mill, fishing in troubled waters, on the order of the day, Achilles' heel, swan song, hotbed.* Many of these are used without knowledge of their meaning (what is a "rift," for instance?), and incompatible metaphors are frequently mixed, a sure sign that the writer is not interested in what he is saying. Some metaphors now current have been twisted out of their original meaning without those who use them even being aware of the fact. For example, *toe the line* is sometimes written *tow the line*. Another example is *the hammer and the anvil*, now always used with the implication that the anvil gets the worst of it. In real life it is always the anvil that breaks the hammer, never the other way about: a writer who stopped to think what he was saying would be aware of this, and would avoid perverting the original phrase.

Operators or Verbal False Limbs

These save the trouble of picking out appropriate verbs and nouns, and at the same time pad each sentence with extra syllables which give it an appearance of symmetry. Characteristic phrases are: *render inoperative, militate against, make contact with, be subjected to, give rise to, give grounds for, have the effect of, play a leading part (role) in, make itself felt, take effect, exhibit a tendency to, serve the purpose of,* etc., etc. The keynote is the elimination of simple verbs. Instead of being a single word, such as *break, stop, spoil, mend, kill,* a verb becomes a *phrase,* made up of a noun or adjective tacked on to some general-purposes verb such as *prove, serve, form, play, render.* In addition, the passive voice is wherever possible used in preference to the active, and noun constructions are used instead of gerunds (*by examination of* instead of *by examining*). The range of verbs is further cut down by means of the *-ize* and *de-* formation, and the banal statements are given an appearance of profundity by means of the *not un-* formation. Simple conjunctions and prepositions are replaced by such phrases as *with respect to, having regard to, the fact that, by dint of, in view of, in the interests of, on the hypothesis that;* and the ends of sentences are saved from anticlimax by such resounding commonplaces as *greatly to be desired, cannot be left out of account, a development to be expected in the near future, deserving* *of serious consideration, brought to a satisfactory conclusion*, and so on and so forth.

Pretentious Diction

Words like *phenomenon, element, individual (as noun), objective, categorical,* 7 *effective, virtual, basic, primary, promote, constitute, exhibit, exploit, utilize, eliminate, liquidate,* are used to dress up simple statements and give an air of scientific impartiality to biased judgments. Adjectives like *epoch-making, epic, historic, unforgettable, triumphant, age-old, inevitable, inexorable, veritable,* are used to dignify the sordid processes of international politics, while writing that aims at glorifying war usually takes on an archaic color, its characteristic words being: *realm, throne, chariot, mailed fist, trident, sword, shield, buckler, banner, jackboot, clarion.* Foreign words and expressions such as *cul de sac, ancien régime, deus ex machina, mutatis mutandis, status quo, gleichschaltung, weltanschauung,* are used to give an air of culture and elegance. Except for the useful abbreviations *i.e., e.g.,* and *etc.,* there is no real need for any of the hundreds of foreign phrases now current in English. Bad writers, and especially scientific, political, and sociological writers, are nearly always haunted by the notion that Latin or Greek words are grander than Saxon ones, and unnecessary words like *expedite, ameliorate, predict, extraneous, deracinated, clandestine, subaqueous,* and hundreds of others constantly gain ground from their Anglo-Saxon opposite numbers.[1] The jargon peculiar to Marxist writing (*hyena, hangman, cannibal, petty bourgeois, these gentry, lackey, flunky, mad dog, White Guard,* etc.) consists largely of words and phrases translated from Russian, German, or French; but the normal way of coining a new word is to use a Latin or Greek root with the appropriate affix and, where necessary, the *-ize* formation. It is often easier to make up words of this kind (*deregionalize, impermissible, extramarital, nonfragmentatory,* and so forth) than to think up the English words that will cover one's meaning. The result, in general, is an increase in slovenliness and vagueness.

Meaningless Words

In certain kinds of writing, particularly in art criticism and literary criticism, 8 it is normal to come across long passages which are almost completely lacking in meaning.[2] Words like *romantic, plastic, values, human, dead, sentimental,*

---

[1]An interesting illustration of this is the way in which the English flower names which were in use till very recently are being ousted by Greek ones, *snapdragon* becoming *antirrhinum, forget-me-not* becoming *myosotis,* etc. It is hard to see any practical reason for this change of fashion: it is probably due to an instinctive turning-away from the more homely word and a vague feeling that the Greek word is scientific.

[2]Example: "Comfort's catholicity of perception and image, strangely Whitmanesque in range, almost the exact opposite in aesthetic compulsion, continues to evoke that trembling atmospheric accumulative hinting at a cruel, an inexorably serene timelessness . . . Wrey Gardiner scores by aiming at simple bull's-eyes with precision. Only they are not so simple, and through this contented sadness runs more than the surface bittersweet of resignation" (*Poetry Quarterly*).

natural, vitality, as used in art criticism, are strictly meaningless in the sense that they not only do not point to any discoverable object, but are hardly ever expected to do so by the reader. When one critic writes, "The outstanding feature of Mr. X's work is its living quality," while another writes, "The immediately striking thing about Mr. X's work is its peculiar deadness," the reader accepts this as a simple difference of opinion. If words like *black* and *white* were involved, instead of the jargon words *dead* and *living,* he would see at once that language was being used in an improper way. Many political words are similarly abused. The word *Fascism* has now no meaning except in so far as it signifies "something not desirable." The words *democracy, socialism, freedom, patriotic, realistic, justice,* have each of them several different meanings which cannot be reconciled with one another. In the case of a word like *democracy,* not only is there no agreed definition, but the attempt to make one is resisted from all sides. It is almost universally felt that when we call a country democratic we are praising it: consequently the defenders of every kind of régime claim that it is a democracy, and fear that they might have to stop using the word if it were tied down to any one meaning. Words of this kind are often used in a consciously dishonest way. That is, the person who uses them has his own private definition, but allows his hearer to think he means something quite different. Statements like *Marshal Pétain was a true patriot, The Soviet Press is the freest in the world, The Catholic Church is opposed to persecution,* are almost always made with intent to deceive. Other words used in variable meanings, in most cases more or less dishonestly, are: *class, totalitarian, science, progressive, reactionary, bourgeois, equality.*

Now that I have made this catalog of swindles and perversions, let me give 9 another example of the kind of writing that they lead to. This time it must of its nature be an imaginary one. I am going to translate a passage of good English into modern English of the worst sort. Here is a well-known verse from *Ecclesiastes:*

> I returned and saw under the sun, that the race is not to the swift, nor the battle to the strong, neither yet bread to the wise, nor yet riches to men of understanding, nor yet favor to men of skill; but time and chance happeneth to them all.

Here it is in modern English:

> Objective consideration of contemporary phenomena compels the conclusion that success or failure in competitive activities exhibits no tendency to be commensurate with innate capacity, but that a considerable element of the unpredictable must invariably be taken into account.

This is a parody, but not a very gross one. Exhibit (3), above, for instance, 10 contains several patches of the same kind of English. It will be seen that I have not made a full translation. The beginning and ending of the sentence follow the original meaning fairly closely, but in the middle the concrete illustrations— race, battle, bread—dissolve into the vague phrase "success or failure in competitive activities." This had to be so, because no modern writer of the kind I am discussing—no one capable of using phrases like "objective consideration of contemporary phenomena"—would ever tabulate his thoughts in that precise and detailed way. The whole tendency of modern prose is away from concreteness. Now analyze these two sentences a little more closely. The first contains forty-nine words but only sixty syllables, and all its words are those of everyday life. The second contains thirty-eight words of ninety syllables: eighteen of its words are from Latin roots, and one from Greek. The first sentence contains six vivid images, and only one phrase ("time and chance") that could be called vague. The second contains not a single fresh, arresting phrase, and in spite of its ninety syllables it gives only a shortened version of the meaning contained in the first. Yet without a doubt it is the second kind of sentence that is gaining ground in modern English. I do not want to exaggerate. This kind of writing is not yet universal, and outcrops of simplicity will occur here and there in the worst-written page. Still, if you or I were told to write a few lines on the uncertainty of human fortunes, we should probably come much nearer to my imaginary sentence than to the one from *Ecclesiastes*.

As I have tried to show, modern writing at its worst does not consist in 11 picking out words for the sake of their meaning and inventing images in order to make the meaning clearer. It consists in gumming together long strips of words which have already been set in order by someone else, and making the results presentable by sheer humbug. The attraction of this way of writing is that it is easy. It is easier—even quicker, once you have the habit—to say *In my opinion it is a not unjustifiable assumption that* than to say *I think*. If you use ready-made phrases, you not only don't have to hunt about for words; you also don't have to bother with the rhythms of your sentences, since these phrases are generally so arranged as to be more or less euphonious. When you are composing in a hurry—when you are dictating to a stenographer, for instance, or making a public speech—it is natural to fall into a pretentious, Latinized style. Tags like a *consideration which we should do well to bear in mind* or a *conclusion to which all of us would readily assent* will save many a sentence from coming down with a bump. By using stale metaphors, similes, and idioms, you save much mental effort, at the cost of leaving your meaning vague, not only for your reader but for yourself. This is the significance of mixed metaphors. The sole aim of a metaphor is to call up a visual image. When these images clash— as in *The Fascist octopus has sung its swan song, the jackboot is thrown into the melting pot*—it can be taken as certain that the writer is not seeing a mental image of the objects he is naming; in other words he is not really thinking. Look again at the examples I gave at the beginning of this essay. Professor Laski (1) uses five negatives in fifty-three words. One of these is superfluous, making nonsense of the whole passage, and in addition there is the slip *alien* for akin, making further nonsense, and several avoidable pieces of clumsiness which increase the general vagueness. Professor Hogben (2) plays ducks and drakes with a battery which is able to write prescriptions, and, while disapproving of the everyday phrase *put up with*, is unwilling to look *egregious* up in the dictionary and see what it means. (3), if one takes an uncharitable attitude towards it, is simply meaningless: probably one could work out its intended meaning by reading the whole of the article in which it occurs. In (4), the writer knows more or less what he wants to say, but an accumulation of stale phrases chokes him like tea leaves blocking a sink. In (5), words and meaning have almost parted company. People who write in this manner usually have a general emotional meaning—they dislike one thing and want to express solidarity with another—but they are not interested in the detail of what they are saying. A scrupulous writer, in every sentence that he writes, will ask himself at least four questions, thus: What am I trying to say? What words will express it? What image or idiom will make it clearer? Is this image fresh enough to have an effect? And he will probably ask himself two more: Could I put it more shortly? Have I said anything that is avoidably ugly? But you are not obliged to go to all this trouble. You can shirk it by simply throwing your mind open and letting the ready-made phrases come crowding in. They will construct your sentences for you—even think your thoughts for you, to a certain extent—and at need they will perform the important service of partially concealing your meaning even from yourself. It is at this point that the special connection between politics and the debasement of language becomes clear.

In our time it is broadly true that political writing is bad writing. Where 12 it is not true, it will generally be found that the writer is some kind of rebel, expressing his private opinions and not a "party line." Orthodoxy, of whatever color, seems to demand a lifeless, imitative style. The political dialects to be found in pamphlets, leading articles, manifestos, White Papers, and the speeches of under-secretaries do, of course, vary from party to party, but they are all alike in that one almost never finds in them a fresh, vivid, home-made turn of speech. When one watches some tired hack on the platform mechanically repeating the familiar phrases—*bestial atrocities, iron heel, bloodstained tyranny, free peoples of the world, stand shoulder to shoulder*—one often has a curious feeling that one is not watching a live human being but some kind of dummy: a feeling which suddenly becomes stronger at moments when the light catches the speaker's spectacles and turns them into blank discs which seem to have no eyes behind them. And this is not altogether fanciful. A speaker who uses that kind of phraseology has gone some distance towards turning himself into a machine. The appropriate noises are coming out of his larynx, but his brain is not involved as it would be if he were choosing his words for himself. If the speech he is making is one that he is accustomed to make over and over again, he may be almost unconscious of what he is saying, as one is when one utters the responses in church. And this reduced state of consciousness, if not indispensable, is at any rate favorable to political conformity.

In our time, political speech and writing are largely the defense of the 13 indefensible. Things like the continuance of British rule in India, the Russian purges and deportations, the dropping of the atom bombs on Japan, can indeed be defended, but only by arguments which are too brutal for most people to face, and which do not square with the professed aims of political parties. Thus political language has to consist largely of euphemism, question-begging, and sheer cloudy vagueness. Defenseless villages are bombarded from the air, the inhabitants driven out into the countryside, the cattle machine-gunned, the huts set on fire with incendiary bullets: this is called *pacification*. Millions of peasants are robbed of their farms and sent trudging along the roads with no more than they can carry: this is called transfer of *population* or *rectification of frontiers*. People are imprisoned for years without trial, or shot in the back of the neck, or sent to die of scurvy in Arctic lumber camps: this is called *elimination of unreliable elements*. Such phraseology is needed if one wants to name things without calling up mental pictures of them. Consider for instance some comfortable English professor defending Russian totalitarianism. He cannot say outright, "I believe in killing off your opponents when you can get good results by doing so." Probably, therefore, he will say something like this:

"While freely conceding that the Soviet régime exhibits certain features 14 which the humanitarian may be inclined to deplore, we must, I think, agree that a certain curtailment of the right to political opposition is an unavoidable concomitant of transitional periods, and that the rigors which the Russian people have been called upon to undergo have been amply justified in the sphere of concrete achievement."

The inflated style is itself a kind of euphemism. A mass of Latin words 15 falls upon the facts like soft snow, blurring the outlines and covering up all the details. The great enemy of clear language is insincerity. When there is a gap between one's real and one's declared aims, one turns as it were instinctively to long words and exhausted idioms, like a cuttlefish squirting out ink. In our age there is no such thing as "keeping out of politics." All issues are political issues, and politics itself is a mass of lies, evasions, folly, hatred, and schizophrenia. When the general atmosphere is bad, language must suffer. I should expect to find—this is a guess which I have not sufficient knowledge to verify—that the German, Russian, and Italian languages have all deteriorated in the last ten or fifteen years, as a result of dictatorship.

But if thought corrupts language, language can also corrupt thought. A 16 bad usage can spread by tradition and imitation, even among people who should and do know better. The debased language that I have been discussing is in some ways very convenient. Phrases like a *not unjustifiable assumption, leaves much to be desired, would serve no good purpose, a consideration which we should do well to bear in mind*, are a continuous temptation, a packet of aspirins always at one's elbow. Look back through this essay, and for certain you will find that I have again and again committed the very faults I am protesting against. By this morning's post I have received a pamphlet dealing with conditions in Germany. The author tells me that he "felt impelled" to write it. I open it at random, and here is almost the first sentence that I see: "(The Allies) have an opportunity not only of achieving a radical transformation of Germany's social and political structure in such a way as to avoid a nationalistic reaction in Germany itself, but at the same time of laying the foundations of a cooperative and unified Europe." You see, he "feels impelled" to write—feels, presumably, that he has something new to say—and yet his words, like cavalry horses answering the bugle, group themselves automatically into the familiar dreary pattern. This invasion of one's mind by ready-made phrases (*lay the foundations, achieve a radical transformation*) can only be prevented if one is constantly on guard against them, and every such phrase anaesthetizes a portion of one's brain.

I said earlier that the decadence of our language is probably curable. 17 Those who deny this would argue, if they produced an argument at all, that language merely reflects existing social conditions, and that we cannot influence its development by any direct tinkering with words and constructions. So far as the general tone or spirit of a language goes, this may be true, but it is not true in detail. Silly words and expressions have often disappeared, not through any evolutionary process but owing to the conscious action of a minority. Two recent examples were *explore every avenue* and *leave no stone unturned*, which were killed by the jeers of a few journalists. There is a long list of flyblown metaphors which could similarly be got rid of if enough people would interest themselves in the job; and it should also be possible to laugh the *not un-* formation out of existence,[3] to reduce the amount of Latin and Greek in the average sentence, to drive out foreign phrases and strayed scientific words, and, in general, to make pretentiousness unfashionable. But all these are minor points. The defense of the English language implies more than this, and perhaps it is best to start by saying what it does not imply.

To begin with it has nothing to do with archaism, with the salvaging 18 of obsolete words and turns of speech, or with the setting up of a "standard English" which must never be departed from. On the contrary, it is especially concerned with the scrapping of every word or idiom which has outworn its usefulness. It has nothing to do with correct grammar and syntax, which are of no importance so long as one makes one's meaning clear, or with the avoidance of Americanisms, or with having what is called a "good prose style." On the other hand it is not concerned with fake simplicity and the attempt to make written English colloquial. Nor does it even imply in every case preferring the Saxon word to the Latin one, though it does imply using the fewest and shortest words that will cover one's meaning. What is above all needed is to let the meaning choose the word, and not the other way about. In prose, the worst thing one can do with words is to surrender to them. When you think of a concrete object, you think wordlessly, and then, if you want to describe the thing you have been visualizing you probably hunt about till you find the exact words that seem to fit. When you think of something abstract you are more inclined to use words from the start, and unless you make a conscious effort to prevent it, the existing dialect will come rushing in and do the job for you, at

---

[3]One can cure oneself of the *not un-* formation by memorizing this sentence: *A not unblack dog was chasing a not unsmall rabbit across a not ungreen field.*

the expense of blurring or even changing your meaning. Probably it is better to put off using words as long as possible and get one's meaning as clear as one can through pictures or sensations. Afterwards one can choose—not simply *accept*—the phrases that will best cover the meaning, and then switch round and decide what impression one's words are likely to make on another person. This last effort of the mind cuts out all stale or mixed images, all prefabricated phrases, needless repetitions, and humbug and vagueness generally. But one can often be in doubt about the effect of a word or a phrase, and one needs rules that one can rely on when instinct fails. I think the following rules will cover most cases:

1. Never use a metaphor, simile, or other figure of speech which you are used to seeing in print.

2. Never use a long word where a short one will do.

3. If it is possible to cut a word out, always cut it out.

4. Never use the passive where you can use the active.

5. Never use a foreign phrase, a scientific word, or a jargon word if you can think of an everyday English equivalent.

6. Break any of these rules sooner than say anything outright barbarous.

These rules sound elementary, and so they are, but they demand a deep 19 change of attitude in anyone who has grown used to writing in the style now fashionable. One could keep all of them and still write bad English, but one could not write the kind of stuff that I quoted in those five specimens at the beginning of this article.

I have not here been considering the literary use of language, but merely 20 language as an instrument for expressing and not for concealing or preventing thought. Stuart Chase and others have come near to claiming that all abstract words are meaningless, and have used this as a pretext for advocating a kind of political quietism. Since you don't know what Fascism is, how can you struggle against Fascism? One need not swallow such absurdities as this, but one ought to recognize that the present political chaos is connected with the decay of language, and that one can probably bring about some improvement by starting at the verbal end. If you simplify your English, you are freed from the worst follies of orthodoxy. You cannot speak any of the necessary dialects, and when you make a stupid remark its stupidity will be obvious, even to yourself. Political language—and with variations this is true of all political parties, from Conservatives to Anarchists—is designed to make lies sound truthful and murder respectable, and to give an appearance of solidity to pure wind. One cannot change this all in a moment, but one can at least change one's own habits, and from time to time one can even, if one jeers loudly enough, send some worn-out and useless phrase—some *jackboot, Achilles' heel, hotbed, melting pot, acid test, veritable inferno,* or other lump of verbal refuse—into the dustbin where it belongs.

⊃ READING ARGUMENTS

1. What two qualities do Orwell's "five specimens" (para. 2) share? According to Orwell, what is the "most marked characteristic of modern English prose, and especially of any kind of political writing" (4)?

2. Where in this essay does Orwell use deductive reasoning?

3. How does Orwell use cause-and-effect argument in his essay? For instance, how does he use it to explain why political speech and writing are bad? What other examples of cause-and-effect argument can you identify?

4. Orwell argues that "political language" consists "largely of euphemism, question-begging, and sheer cloudy vagueness" (13). What is a euphemism? What does "question-begging" mean?

5. Where does Orwell make a proposal argument? What does he propose?

⊃ WRITING ARGUMENTS

1. In paragraph 16, Orwell concedes, "Look back through this essay, and for certain you will find that I have again and again committed the very faults I am protesting against." Find three examples of these "faults" in Orwell's prose. Then, write a paragraph for each "fault," explaining why it meets his standard for "bad" writing.

2. Surveying the state of the English language in 1946, Orwell asserts that "it is broadly true that political writing is bad writing" (para. 12). Is this still "broadly true"? Reread paragraphs 12 to 15 of Orwell's essay. Then, develop your own argument about the language of contemporary politics, updating Orwell's examples with contemporary examples.

THE OBLIGATION TO ENDURE

RACHEL CARSON

Rachel Carson (1907–1964) received a master's degree in zoology and worked as editor-in-chief of publications for the U.S. Bureau of Fisheries. Her books include Under the Sea-Wind *(1941);* The Sea around Us *(1951), a best seller and winner of the National Book Award;* The Edge of the Sea *(1955); and* The Sense of Wonder *(published in 1965 after her death). Her most famous work is*

Silent Spring (1962), from which "The Obligation to Endure" is drawn. In this book, Carson argues that agricultural pesticides are destructive to wildlife and to the environment, an idea that predates the modern environmental movement and to this day remains controversial. Silent Spring, an extremely influential work, led to bans of DDT as well as other chemicals.

The history of life on earth has been a history of interaction between living things 1 and their surroundings. To a large extent, the physical form and the habits of the earth's vegetation and its animal life have been molded by the environment. Considering the whole span of earthly time, the opposite effect, in which life actually modifies its surroundings, has been relatively slight. Only within the moment of time represented by the present century has one species—man—acquired significant power to alter the nature of his world.

During the past quarter century this power has not only increased 2 to one of disturbing magnitude but it has changed in character. The most alarming of all man's assaults upon the environment is the contamination of air, earth, rivers, and sea with dangerous and even lethal materials. This pollution is for the most part irrecoverable; the chain of evil it initiates not only in the world that must support life but in living tissues is for the most part irreversible. In this now universal contamination of the environment, chemicals are the sinister and little-recognized partners of radiation in changing the very nature of the world—the very nature of its life. Strontium 90, released through nuclear explosions into the air, comes to earth in rain or drifts down as fallout, lodges in soil, enters into the grass or corn or wheat grown there, and in time takes up its abode in the bones of a human being, there to remain until his death. Similarly, chemicals sprayed on croplands or forests or gardens lie long in soil, entering into living organisms, passing from one to another in a chain of poisoning and death. Or they pass mysteriously by underground streams until they emerge and, through the alchemy of air and sunlight, combine into new forms that kill vegetation, sicken cattle, and work unknown harm on those who drink from once pure wells. As Albert Schweitzer has said, "Man can hardly even recognize the devils of his own creation."

It took hundreds of millions of years to produce the life that now inhab- 3 its the earth—eons of time in which that developing and evolving and diversifying life reached a state of adjustment and balance with its surroundings. The environment, rigorously shaping and directing the life it supported, contained elements that were hostile as well as supporting. Certain rocks gave out dangerous radiation; even within the light of the sun, from which all life draws its energy, there were short-wave radiations with power to injure. Given time—time not in years but in millennia—life adjusts, and a balance has been reached. For time is the essential ingredient; but in the modern world there is no time.

The rapidity of change and the speed with which new situations are 4 created follow the impetuous and heedless pace of man rather than the deliberate pace of nature. Radiation is no longer merely the background radiation of rocks, the bombardment of cosmic rays, the ultraviolet of the sun that have existed before there was any life on earth; radiation is now the unnatural creation of man's tampering with the atom. The chemicals to which life is asked to make its adjustment are no longer merely the calcium and silica and copper and all the rest of the minerals washed out of the rocks and carried in rivers to the sea; they are the synthetic creations of man's inventive mind, brewed in his laboratories, and having no counterparts in nature.

To adjust to these chemicals would require time on the scale that is 5 nature's; it would require not merely the years of a man's life but the life of generations. And even this, were it by some miracle possible, would be futile, for the new chemicals come from our laboratories in an endless stream; almost five hundred annually find their way into actual use in the United States alone. The figure is staggering and its implications are not easily grasped—500 new chemicals to which the bodies of men and animals are required somehow to adapt each year, chemicals totally outside the limits of biologic experience.

Among them are many that are used in man's war against nature. Since the 6 mid-1940's over 200 basic chemicals have been created for use in killing insects, weeds, rodents, and other organisms described in the modern vernacular as "pests"; and they are sold under several thousand different brand names.

These sprays, dusts, and aerosols are now applied almost universally to 7 farms, gardens, forests, and homes—nonselective chemicals that have the power to kill every insect, the "good" and the "bad," to still the song of birds and the leaping of fish in the streams, to coat the leaves with a deadly film, and to linger on in soil—all this though the intended target may be only a few weeds or insects. Can anyone believe it is possible to lay down such a barrage of poisons on the surface of the earth without making it unfit for all life? They should not be called "insecticides," but "biocides."

The whole process of spraying seems caught up in an endless spiral. Since 8 DDT° was released for civilian use, a process of escalation has been going on in which ever more toxic materials must be found. This has happened because insects, in a triumphant vindication of Darwin's principle of the survival of the fittest, have evolved super races immune to the particular insecticide used, hence a deadlier one has always to be developed—and then a deadlier one than that. It has happened also because, for reasons to be described later, destructive insects often undergo a "flareback," or resurgence, after spraying, in numbers greater than before. Thus the chemical war is never won, and all life is caught in its violent crossfire.

Dichlorodiphenyltrichloroeth-ane, a synthetic pesticide that was widely used to control disease-spreading insect populations

Along with the possibility of the extinction of mankind by nuclear war, 9 the central problem of our age has therefore become the contamination of man's total environment with such substances of incredible potential for harm—substances that accumulate in the tissues of plants and animals and even penetrate the germ cells to shatter or alter the very material of heredity upon which the shape of the future depends.

Some would-be architects of our future look toward a time when it will be 10 possible to alter the human germ plasm by design. But we may easily be doing so now by inadvertence, for many chemicals, like radiation, bring about gene mutations. It is ironic to think that man might determine his own future by something so seemingly trivial as the choice of an insect spray.

All this has been risked—for what? Future historians may well be amazed 11 by our distorted sense of proportion. How could intelligent beings seek to control a few unwanted species by a method that contaminated the entire environment and brought the threat of disease and death even to their own kind? Yet this is precisely what we have done. We have done it, moreover, for reasons that collapse the moment we examine them. We are told that the enormous and expanding use of pesticides is necessary to maintain farm production. Yet is our real problem not one of *overproduction*? Our farms, despite measures to remove acreages from production and to pay farmers *not* to produce, have yielded such a staggering excess of crops that the American taxpayer in 1962 is paying out more than one billion dollars a year as the total carrying cost of the surplus-food storage program. And is the situation helped when one branch of the Agriculture Department tries to reduce production while another states, as it did in 1958, "It is believed generally that reduction of crop acreages under provisions of the Soil Bank will stimulate interest in use of chemicals to obtain maximum production on the land retained in crops."

All this is not to say there is no insect problem and no need of control. 12 I am saying, rather, that control must be geared to realities, not to mythical situations, and that the methods employed must be such that they do not destroy us along with the insects.

The problem whose attempted solution has brought such a train of disaster 13 in its wake is an accompaniment of our modern way of life. Long before the age of man, insects inhabited the earth—a group of extraordinarily varied and adaptable beings. Over the course of time since man's advent, a small percentage of the more than half a million species of insects have come into conflict with human welfare in two principal ways: as competitors for the food supply and as carriers of human disease.

Disease-carrying insects become important where human beings are crowded 14 together, especially under conditions where sanitation is poor, as in time of natural disaster or war or in situations of extreme poverty and deprivation. Then control of some sort becomes necessary. It is a sobering fact, however, as we shall presently see, that the method of massive chemical control has had only limited success, and also threatens to worsen the very conditions it is intended to curb.

Under primitive agricultural conditions the farmer had few insect prob- 15 lems. These arose with the intensification of agriculture—the devotion of immense acreages to a single crop. Such a system set the stage for explosive increases in specific insect populations. Single-crop farming does not take advantage of the principles by which nature works; it is agriculture as an engineer might conceive it to be. Nature has introduced great variety into the landscape, but man has displayed a passion for simplifying it. Thus he undoes the built-in checks and balances by which nature holds the species within bounds. One important natural check is a limit on the amount of suitable habitat for each species. Obviously then, an insect that lives on wheat can build up its population to much higher levels on a farm devoted to wheat than on one in which wheat is intermingled with other crops to which the insect is not adapted.

16   The same thing happens in other situations. A generation or more ago, the towns of large areas of the United States lined their streets with the noble elm tree. Now the beauty they hopefully created is threatened with complete destruction as disease sweeps through the elms, carried by a beetle that would have only limited chance to build up large populations and to spread from tree to tree if the elms were only occasional trees in a richly diversified planting.

17   Another factor in the modern insect problem is one that must be viewed against a background of geologic and human history: the spreading of thousands of different kinds of organisms from their native homes to invade new territories. This worldwide migration has been studied and graphically described by the British ecologist Charles Elton in his recent book *The Ecology of Invasions*. During the Cretaceous Period, some hundred million years ago, flooding seas cut many land bridges between continents and living things found themselves confined in what Elton calls "colossal separate nature reserves." There, isolated from others of their kind, they developed many new species. When some of the land masses were joined again, about 15 million years ago, these species began to move out into new territories—a movement that is not only still in progress but is now receiving considerable assistance from man.

18   The importation of plants is the primary agent in the modern spread of species, for animals have almost invariably gone along with the plants, quarantine being a comparatively recent and not completely effective innovation. The United States Office of Plant Introduction alone has introduced almost 200,000 species and varieties of plants from all over the world. Nearly half of the 180 or so major insect enemies of plants in the United States are accidental imports from abroad, and most of them have come as hitchhikers on plants.

19   In new territory, out of reach of the restraining hand of the natural enemies that kept down its numbers in its native land, an invading plant or animal is able to become enormously abundant. Thus it is no accident that our most troublesome insects are introduced species.

20   These invasions, both the naturally occurring and those dependent on human assistance, are likely to continue indefinitely. Quarantine and massive chemical campaigns are only extremely expensive ways of buying time. We are faced, according to Dr. Elton, "with a life-and-death need not just to find new technological means of suppressing this plant or that animal"; instead we need

the basic knowledge of animal populations and their relations to their surroundings that will "promote an even balance and damp down the explosive
power of outbreaks and new invasions."

Much of the necessary knowledge is now available but we do not use it. 21
We train ecologists in our universities and even employ them in our governmental agencies but we seldom take their advice. We allow the chemical death
rain to fall as though there were no alternative, whereas in fact there are many,
and our ingenuity could soon discover many more if given opportunity.

Have we fallen into a mesmerized state that makes us accept as inevita- 22
ble that which is inferior or detrimental, as though having lost the will or the
vision to demand that which is good? Such thinking, in the words of the ecologist Paul Shepard, "idealizes life with only its head out of water, inches above
the limits of toleration of the corruption of its own environment. . . . Why
should we tolerate a diet of weak poisons, a home in insipid surroundings,
a circle of acquaintances who are not quite our enemies, the noise of motors
with just enough relief to prevent insanity? Who would want to live in a world
which is just not quite fatal?"

Yet such a world is pressed upon us. The crusade to create a chemically 23
sterile, insect-free world seems to have engendered a fanatic zeal on the part
of many specialists and most of the so-called control agencies. On every hand
there is evidence that those engaged in spraying operations exercise a ruthless power. "The regulatory entomologists . . . function as prosecutor, judge
and jury, tax assessor and collector and sheriff to enforce their own orders,"
said Connecticut entomologist Neely Turner. The most flagrant abuses go
unchecked in both state and federal agencies.

It is not my contention that chemical insecticides must never be used. I do 24
contend that we have put poisonous and biologically potent chemicals indis-
criminately into the hands of persons largely or wholly ignorant of their poten-
tials for harm. We have subjected enormous numbers of people to contact
with these poisons, without their consent and often without their knowledge.
If the Bill of Rights contains no guarantee that a citizen shall be secure against
lethal poisons distributed either by private individuals or by public officials, it
is surely only because our forefathers, despite their considerable wisdom and
foresight, could conceive of no such problem.

I contend, furthermore, that we have allowed these chemicals to be used 25
with little or no advance investigation of their effect on soil, water, wildlife, and
man himself. Future generations are unlikely to condone our lack of prudent
concern for the integrity of the natural world that supports all life.

There is still very limited awareness of the nature of the threat. This is an 26
era of specialists, each of whom sees his own problem and is unaware of or
intolerant of the larger frame into which it fits. It is also an era dominated by
industry, in which the right to make a dollar at whatever cost is seldom challenged. When the public protests, confronted with some obvious evidence of
damaging results of pesticide applications, it is fed little tranquilizing pills of
half truth. We urgently need an end to these false assurances, to the sugar

coating of unpalatable facts. It is the public that is being asked to assume the risks that the insect controllers calculate. The public must decide whether it wishes to continue on the present road, and it can do so only when in full possession of the facts. In the words of Jean Rostand, "The obligation to endure gives us the right to know."

⊘READING ARGUMENTS

1. In her opening paragraphs, Carson makes broad and provocative claims about human beings and their place in the natural world. What evidence does she use to support these assertions? Do you find this evidence convincing?

2. According to Carson, what problem (in addition to the threat of nuclear war) was the greatest threat to human beings in the middle of the twentieth century?

3. In what sense is "The Obligation to Endure" an evaluation argument?

4. In paragraph 2, Carson refers to "man's assaults upon the environment." How does she characterize human beings throughout her essay? For example, how does she describe their interaction with the environment? How does her characterization of human beings support her essay's main point?

5. Where in her essay does Carson address opposing arguments? Do you think she refutes them effectively? Why or why not?

⊘WRITING ARGUMENTS

1. Carson contrasts the "heedless pace of man" with the "deliberate pace of nature" (para. 4). Is this distinction valid? Do you think her view of people and their relationship with the environment is accurate? For example, do you think human beings are engaged in a "war against nature" (6)? Do you generally share Carson's view of scientific progress and industrial society? Write an argumentative essay that takes a stand for or against her views.

2. As a result of Carson's book, DDT was banned worldwide. Since then, the World Health Organization has called for its limited use indoors in African countries to combat malaria, but it remains banned in the United States. Given the dramatic rise of insect-borne diseases (such as the West Nile virus, the Zika virus, Lyme disease, and Chagas disease), do you think the United States should reconsider its response to Carson's book and permit the use of DDT in some situations? Write an essay explaining your position.

THE IMPORTANCE OF WORK

BETTY FRIEDAN

An activist, an author, and the first president of the National Organization for Women, Betty Friedan (1921–2006) sparked the second wave of American feminism with her manifesto The Feminine Mystique. *This 1963 book examined the "problem that has no name"—the deep dissatisfaction of American women, who were trapped by domestic roles and feminine ideals that limited their individuality, freedom, and growth. In the following excerpt from this book, Friedan argues that women need "to break out of their comfortable concentration camps"—a metaphor that, like the book, remains shocking and controversial more than fifty years later.*

The question of how a person can most fully realize his own capacities and 1 thus achieve identity has become an important concern of the philosophers and the social and psychological thinkers of our time—and for good reason. Thinkers of other times put forth the idea that people were, to a great extent, defined by the work they did. The work that a man had to do to eat, to stay alive, to meet the physical necessities of his environment, dictated his identity. And in this sense, when work was seen merely as a means of survival, human identity was dictated by biology.

But today the problem of human identity has changed. For the work that 2 defined man's place in society and his sense of himself has also changed man's world. Work, and the advance of knowledge, has lessened man's dependence on his environment; his biology and the work he must do for biological survival are no longer sufficient to define his identity. This can be most clearly seen in our own abundant society; men no longer need to work all day to eat. They have an unprecedented freedom to choose the kind of work they will do; they also have an unprecedented amount of time apart from the hours and days that must actually be spent in making a living. And suddenly one realizes the significance of today's identity crisis—for women, and increasingly, for men. One sees the human significance of work—not merely as the means of biological survival, but as the giver of self and the transcender of self, as the creator of human identity and human evolution.

For "self-realization" or "self-fulfillment" or "identity" does not come 3 from looking into a mirror in rapt contemplation of one's own image. Those who have most fully realized themselves, in a sense that can be recognized by the human mind even though it cannot be clearly defined, have done so in the service of a human purpose larger than themselves. Men from varying disciplines have used different words for this mysterious process from which comes the sense of self. The religious mystics, the philosophers, Marx, Freud—all had different names for it: man finds himself by losing himself; man is defined by his relation to the means of production; the ego, the self, grows through understanding and mastering reality—through work and love.

The identity crisis, which has been noted by Erik Erikson° and others in 4 recent years in the American man, seems to occur for lack of, and be cured by finding, the work, or cause, or purpose that evokes his own creativity. Some never find it, for it does not come from busy-work or punching a time clock. It does not come from just making a living, working by formula, finding a secure spot as an organization man. The very argument, by Riesman and others, that man no longer finds identity in the work defined as a paycheck job, assumes that identity for man comes through creative work of his own that contributes to the human community: the core of the self becomes aware, becomes real, and grows through work that carries forward human society.

Erik Erikson (1902–1994): A German-born American psychologist who coined the phrase "identity crisis"

Work, the shopworn staple of the economists, has become the new fron- 5 tier of psychology. Psychiatrists have long used "occupational therapy" with patients in mental hospitals; they have recently discovered that to be of real psychological value, it must be not just "therapy," but real work, serving a real purpose in the community. And work can now be seen as the key to the problem that has no name. The identity crisis of American women began a century ago, as more and more of the work important to the world, more and more of the work that used their human abilities and through which they were able to find self-realization, was taken from them.

Until, and even into, the last century, strong, capable women were needed 6 to pioneer our new land; with their husbands, they ran the farms and plantations and Western homesteads. These women were respected and self-respecting members of a society whose pioneering purpose centered in the home. Strength and independence, responsibility and self-confidence, self-discipline and courage, freedom and equality were part of the American character for both men and women, in all the first generations. The women who came by steerage from Ireland, Italy, Russia, and Poland worked beside their husbands in the sweatshops and the laundries, learned the new language, and saved to send their sons and daughters to college. Women were never quite as "feminine," or held in as much contempt, in America as they were in Europe. American women seemed to European travelers, long before our time, less passive, childlike, and feminine than their own wives in France or Germany or England. By an accident of history, American women shared in the work of society longer, and grew with the men. Grade- and high-school education for boys and girls alike was almost always the rule; and in the West, where women shared the pioneering work the longest, even the universities were coeducational from the beginning.

The identity crisis for women did not begin in America until the fire and 7 strength and ability of the pioneer women were no longer needed, no longer used, in the middle-class homes of the Eastern and Midwestern cities, when the pioneering was done and men began to build the new society in industries and professions outside the home. But the daughters of the pioneer women had grown too used to freedom and work to be content with leisure and passive femininity.

It was not an American, but a South African woman, Mrs. Olive Schreiner, 8 who warned at the turn of the century that the quality and quantity of women's functions in the social universe was decreasing as fast as civilization was advancing; that if women did not win back their right to a full share of honored and useful work, woman's mind and muscle would weaken in a parasitic state; her offspring, male and female, would weaken progressively, and civilization itself would deteriorate.

The feminists saw clearly that education and the right to participate 9 in the more advanced work of society were women's greatest needs. They fought for and won the rights to new, fully human identity for women. But how very few of their daughters and granddaughters have chosen to use their education and their abilities for any large creative purpose, for responsible work in society? How many of them have been deceived, or have deceived themselves, into clinging to the outgrown, childlike femininity of "Occupation: housewife"?

It was not a minor matter, their mistaken choice. We now know that the 10 same range of potential ability exists for women as for men. Women, as well as men, can only find their identity in work that uses their full capacities. A woman cannot find her identity through others—her husband, her children. She cannot find it in the dull routine of housework. As thinkers of every age have said, it is only when a human being faces squarely the fact that he can forfeit his own life, that he becomes truly aware of himself, and begins to take his existence seriously. Sometimes this awareness comes only at the moment of death. Sometimes it comes from a more subtle facing of death: the death of self in passive conformity, in meaningless work. The feminine mystique prescribes just such a living death for women. Faced with the slow death of self, the American woman must begin to take her life seriously.

"We measure ourselves by many standards," said the great American psy- 11 chologist William James, nearly a century ago. "Our strength and our intelligence, our wealth and even our good luck, are things which warm our heart and make us feel ourselves a match for life. But deeper than all such things, and able to suffice unto itself without them, is the sense of the amount of effort which we can put forth."

If women do not put forth, finally, that effort to become all that they have 12 it in them to become, they will forfeit their own humanity. A woman today who has no goal, no purpose, no ambition patterning her days into the future, making her stretch and grow beyond that small score of years in which her body can fill its biological function, is committing a kind of suicide. For that future half a century after the child-bearing years are over is a fact that an American woman cannot deny. Nor can she deny that as a housewife, the world is indeed rushing past her door while she just sits and watches. The terror she feels is real, if she has no place in that world.

The feminine mystique has succeeded in burying millions of American 13 women alive. There is no way for these women to break out of their comfortable concentration camps except by finally putting forth an effort—that human effort which reaches beyond biology, beyond the narrow walls of home, to help shape the future. Only by such a personal commitment to the future can American women break out of the housewife trap and truly find fulfillment as wives and mothers—by fulfilling their own unique possibilities as separate human beings.

⊘READING ARGUMENTS

1. In what respects is this essay a definition argument? What key term is being defined? Why is the meaning of this term essential to Friedan's argument?

2. According to Friedan, how do modern people establish their identities? What gives these identities meaning?

3. In paragraph 6, Friedan writes about eighteenth- and nineteenth-century women who helped "to pioneer" the United States. How does she characterize these women? Why is their history important to her overall point?

4. In her next-to-last paragraph, Friedan refers to "a kind of suicide." What does she mean?

⊘WRITING ARGUMENTS

1. According to Friedan, men and women need work that satisfies their creativity and contributes to human society. Do you agree with her implication that doing paid work is the only way to create a meaningful life? Is it possible to find fulfillment by focusing on domestic tasks such as child-rearing? How do you view such questions in the context of your own life and career ambitions? Write an essay that responds to Friedan's argument about the importance of work—that is, of meaningful paid employment.

2. This essay is from Friedan's 1963 book *The Feminine Mystique*. Does the "identity crisis" that Friedan describes still exist? Many aspects of society have changed over the last five decades. Do her arguments seem relevant to men and women today? Why or why not? Write an essay that presents your point of view.

IF BLACK ENGLISH ISN'T A LANGUAGE, THEN TELL ME, WHAT IS?

JAMES BALDWIN

Although the Harlem-born novelist, playwright, poet, and critic James Baldwin spent much of his life abroad, he remained an American writer. That is evident in well-known works like Go Tell It on the Mountain *(1953),* Notes of a Native Son *(1955), and* The Fire Next Time *(1963), which explore the problem of race in the United States. He also wrote powerfully about class, culture, and sexual identity in both his fiction and his essays. Baldwin was especially perceptive about the complex relationship between "self" and "society," as is clear in the following essay. For Baldwin, language "reveals the private identity, and connects one with, or divorces one from, the larger, public, or communal identity."*

The argument concerning the use, or the status, or the reality, of black English 1
is rooted in American history and has absolutely nothing to do with the question the argument supposes itself to be posing. The argument has nothing to do with language itself but with the role of language. Language, incontestably, reveals the speaker. Language, also, far more dubiously, is meant to define the other—and, in this case, the other is refusing to be defined by a language that has never been able to recognize him.

People evolve a language in order to describe and thus control their cir- 2
cumstances or in order not to be submerged by a situation that they cannot articulate. (And if they cannot articulate it, they are submerged.) A French-man living in Paris speaks a subtly and crucially different language from that of the man living in Marseilles; neither sounds very much like a man living in Quebec; and they would all have great difficulty in apprehending what the man from Guadeloupe, or Martinique, is saying, to say nothing of the man from Senegal—although the "common" language of all these areas is French. But each has paid, and is paying, a different price for this "common" language, in which, as it turns out, they are not saying, and cannot be saying, the same things: They each have very different realities to articulate, or control.

What joins all languages, and all men, is the necessity to confront life, in 3
order, not inconceivably, to outwit death: The price for this is the acceptance, and achievement, of one's temporal identity. So that, for example, though it is not taught in the schools (and this has the potential of becoming a politi-cal issue) the south of France still clings to its ancient and musical Provençal, which resists being described as a "dialect." And much of the tension in the Basque countries, and in Wales, is due to the Basque and Welsh determination not to allow their languages to be destroyed. This determination also feeds the

flames in Ireland for among the many indignities the Irish have been forced to undergo at English hands is the English contempt for their language.

It goes without saying, then, that language is also a political instrument, 4 means, and proof of power. It is the most vivid and crucial key to identity: It reveals the private identity, and connects one with, or divorces one from, the larger, public, or communal identity. There have been, and are, times and places, when to speak a certain language could be dangerous, even fatal. Or, one may speak the same language, but in such a way that one's antecedents are revealed, or (one hopes) hidden. This is true in France, and is absolutely true in England: The range (and reign) of accents on that damp little island make England coherent for the English and totally incomprehensible for everyone else. To open your mouth in England is (if I may use black English) to "put your business in the street." You have confessed your parents, your youth, your school, your salary, your self-esteem, and, alas, your future.

Now, I do not know what white Americans would sound like if there 5 had never been any black people in the United States, but they would not sound the way they sound. *Jazz*, for example, is a very specific sexual term, as in *jazz me, baby*, but white people purified it into the Jazz Age. *Sock it to me*, which means, roughly, the same thing, has been adopted by Nathaniel Hawthorne's° descendants with no qualms or hesitations at all, along with *let it all hang out* and *right on! Beat to his socks*, which was once the black's most total and despairing image of poverty, was transformed into a thing called the Beat Generation,° which phenomenon was, largely, composed of *uptight*, middle-class white people, imitating poverty, trying to *get down*, to *get with it*, doing their *thing*, doing their despairing best to be *funky*, which we, the blacks, never dreamed of doing—we were funky, baby, like *funk* was going out of style.

Now, no one can eat his cake, and have it, too, and it is late in the day to 6 attempt to penalize black people for having created a language that permits the nation its only glimpse of reality, a language without which the nation would be even more *whipped* than it is.

I say that the present skirmish is rooted in American history, and it is. 7 Black English is the creation of the black diaspora. Blacks came to the United States chained to each other, but from different tribes. Neither could speak the other's language. If two black people, at that bitter hour of the world's history, had been able to speak to each other, the institution of chattel slavery could never have lasted as long as it did. Subsequently, the slave was given, under the eye, and the gun, of his master, Congo Square, and the Bible— or, in other words, and under those conditions, the slave began the formation of the black church, and it is within this unprecedented tabernacle that black English began to be formed. This was not, merely, as in the European example, the adoption of a foreign tongue, but an alchemy that transformed ancient elements into a new language: *A language comes into existence by means of brutal necessity, and the rules of the language are dictated by what the language must convey.*

Nathaniel Hawthorne (1804–1864), an American novelist and short story writer whose work often focused on Puritan New England

A group of post–World War II American writers that valued freedom, authenticity, spontaneous expression, antimaterialism, and nonconformity

There was a moment, in time, and in this place, when my brother, or my 8
mother, or my father, or my sister, had to convey to me, for example, the danger in which I was standing from the white man standing just behind me, and
to convey this with a speed and in a language, that the white man could not
possibly understand, and that, indeed, he cannot understand, until today. He
cannot afford to understand it. This understanding would reveal to him too
much about himself and smash that mirror before which he has been frozen
for so long.

Toni Morrison (1931–), an
African-American writer
who won the 1993 Nobel
Prize in Literature

Now, if this passion, this skill, this (to quote Toni Morrison°) "sheer intel- 9
ligence," this incredible music, the mighty achievement of having brought a
people utterly unknown to, or despised by "history"—to have brought this
people to their present, troubled, troubling, and unassailable and unanswer-
able place—if this absolutely unprecedented journey does not indicate that
black English is a language, I am curious to know what definition of languages
is to be trusted.

A people at the center of the western world, and in the midst of so hostile 10
a population, has not endured and transcended by means of what is patroniz-
ingly called a "dialect." We, the blacks, are in trouble, certainly, but we are not
inarticulate because we are not compelled to defend a morality that we know
to be a lie.

The brutal truth is that the bulk of the white people in America never had 11
any interest in educating black people, except as this could serve white purposes. It is not the black child's language that is despised. It is his experience. A
child cannot be taught by anyone who despises him, and a child cannot afford
to be fooled. A child cannot be taught by anyone whose demand, essentially, is
that the child repudiate his experience, and all that gives him sustenance, and
enter a limbo in which he will no longer be black, and in which he knows that
he can never become white. Black people have lost too many black children
that way.

And, after all, finally, in a country with standards so untrustworthy, a 12
country that makes heroes of so many criminal mediocrities, a country unable
to face why so many of the nonwhite are in prison, or on the needle, or standing, futureless, in the streets—it may very well be that both the child, and his
elder, have concluded that they have nothing whatever to learn from the people of a country that has managed to learn so little.

⊖ READING ARGUMENTS

1. How does Baldwin use deductive reasoning in the first three paragraphs of this essay? Construct a syllogism for this argument. Do you
   find the syllogism's conclusion persuasive? Why or why not?

2. Baldwin writes, "It goes without saying, then, that language is also a
   political instrument, means, and proof of power" (para. 4). What does

he mean? Does this really go "without saying"? In other words, is this point self-evident? How does he support his claim?

3. According to Baldwin, black people "created a language that permits the nation its only glimpse of reality" (6). What does he mean? Do you agree? Why or why not?

⊘ WRITING ARGUMENTS

1. For Baldwin, language is the "most vivid and crucial key to identity" (para. 4). He points out that when you speak, you reveal "your parents, your youth, your school, your salary, your self-esteem, and, alas, your future" (4). In your experience, have you found this to be true? Are these aspects of your life evident in the sounds of your own speech? Write an essay that presents your point of view on these questions.

2. Baldwin discusses black contributions to American English. He also points out how white Americans "purified" (5) certain black terms from jazz culture and transformed black poverty into the "Beat Generation." Why would people imitate the language of poverty? Is this process still at work today? If so, where do you see it? Address these questions in an argumentative essay, using examples to support your points.

Writing Literary Arguments

When you write an essay about literature, you have a number of options. For example, you can write a **response** (expressing your reactions to a poem, play, or story), or you can write an **explication** (focusing on a work's individual elements, such as a poem's imagery, meter, figurative language, and diction). You can also write an **analysis** of a work's theme, a character in a play or a story, or a work's historical or cultural context. Another option, which is discussed in the pages that follow, is to write a literary argument.

What Is a Literary Argument?

When you write a literary argument, you do more than just respond to, explicate, or analyze a work of literature. When you develop a **literary argument**, you take a position about a literary work (or works), support that position with evidence, and refute possible opposing arguments. You might, for example, take the position that a familiar interpretation of a well-known work is limited in some way, that a work's impact today is different from its impact when it was written, or that two apparently very different works have some significant similarities.

It is important to understand that not every essay about literature is a literary argument. For example, you might use a discussion of Tillie Olsen's short story "I Stand Here Ironing," with its sympathetic portrait of a young mother during the Great Depression, to support an argument in favor of President Franklin D. Roosevelt's expansion of social welfare programs. Alternatively, you might use Martín Espada's poem "Why I Went to College" to support your own decision to continue your education. However, writing a literary argument involves much more than discussing a literary work in order to support a particular position or referring to a character to explain a personal choice you made. A literary argument *takes a stand* about a work (or works) of literature.

Stating an Argumentative Thesis

When you develop an argumentative thesis about literature, your goal is to state a thesis that has an edge—one that takes a stand on your topic. Like any effective thesis, the thesis of a literary argument should be clearly worded and specific; it should also be more than a statement of fact.

INEFFECTIVE THESIS (TOO GENERAL)	In "A&P," Sammy faces a difficult decision.
EFFECTIVE THESIS (MORE SPECIFIC)	Sammy's decision to quit his job reveals more about the conformist society in which "A&P" is set than about Sammy himself.
INEFFECTIVE THESIS (STATES A FACT)	The theme of *Hamlet* is often seen as an Oedipal conflict.
EFFECTIVE THESIS (TAKES A STAND)	Although many critics have identified an Oedipal conflict in *Hamlet*, Shakespeare's play is also a story of a young man who is struggling with familiar problems—love, family, and his future.

Here are three possible thesis statements that you could support in a literary argument:

- Charlotte Perkins Gilman's short story "The Yellow Wallpaper," usually seen as a feminist story, is actually a ghost story.

- The two characters in August Strindberg's play *The Stronger* seem to be rivals for the affection of a man, but they are really engaged in a professional rivalry to see who gives the better performance.

- Although many readers might see Wilfred Owen's "Dulce et Decorum Est" as the more powerful poem because of its graphic imagery of war, Carl Sandburg's understated "Grass" is likely to have a greater impact on modern readers, who have been overexposed to violent images.

(For more on developing a thesis statement, see Chapter 7.)

Choosing Evidence

Like any argument, a literary argument relies on evidence. Some of this evidence can be found in the literary work itself. For example, to make a point about a character's antisocial behavior, you would cite specific examples of such behavior from the work. To make a point about a poet's use of biblical allusions, you would present examples of such allusions from the poem.

> **NOTE**
>
> Be careful not to substitute plot summary for evidence. For example, summarizing everything that happens to a character will not convince your readers that the character is motivated by envy. Choose only *relevant* examples—in this case, specific instances of a character's jealous behavior, including relevant quotations from the literary work.

Evidence can also come from **literary criticism**—scholarly articles by experts in the field that analyze and evaluate works of literature. For example, to argue that a particular critical theory is inaccurate, outdated, or oversimplified, you would first quote critics who support that theory and then explain why you disagree with their interpretation. (For more on evaluating potential sources for your essay, see Chapter 8.)

Writing a Literary Argument

The structure of a literary argument is similar to the structure of any other argument: it includes a **thesis statement** in the introduction, supporting **evidence**, **refutation** of opposing arguments, and a strong **concluding statement**. However, unlike other arguments, literary arguments follow specific conventions for writing about literature:

- In your essay's first paragraph, include the author's full name and the title of each work you are discussing.

- Use present tense when discussing events in works of literature. For example, if you are discussing "I Stand Here Ironing," you would say, "The mother *worries* [not *worried*] about her ability to provide for her child." There are two exceptions to this rule. Use past tense when referring to historical events: "The Great Depression *made* things difficult for mothers like the narrator." Also use past tense to refer to events that came before the action described in the work: "The mother is particularly vulnerable because her husband *left* her alone to support her children."

- Italicize titles of plays and novels. Put titles of poems and short stories in quotation marks.

- If you quote more than four lines of prose (or more than three lines of poetry), indent the entire quotation one inch from the left-hand margin. Do not include quotation marks, and add the parenthetical documentation after the end punctuation. Introduce the quotation with a colon, and do not add extra line spaces above or below it.

- When mentioning writers and literary critics in the body of your essay, use their full names ("Emily Dickinson") the first time you mention them and their last names only ("Dickinson," not "Miss Dickinson" or "Emily") after that.

- Use **MLA documentation style** in your essay, and include a works-cited list. (See Chapter 10 for information on MLA documentation.)

- In your in-text citations (set in parentheses), cite page numbers for stories, act and scene numbers for plays, and line numbers for poems. Use the word *line* or *lines* for the first in-text citation of lines from each poem. After the first citation, you may omit the word *line* or *lines*.

The following literary argument, "Confessions of a Misunderstood Poem: An Analysis of 'The Road Not Taken,'" proposes a new way of interpreting a poem that the student writer characterizes as "familiar but frequently misunderstood."

CONFESSIONS OF A MISUNDERSTOOD POEM: AN ANALYSIS OF "THE ROAD NOT TAKEN"

MEGAN MCGOVERN

Introduction (identifies titles and authors of works to be discussed)

    In his poem "Introduction to Poetry," Billy Collins suggests that rather than dissecting a poem to find its meaning, students should use their imaginations to experience poetry. According to Collins, they should "drop a mouse into a poem / and watch him probe his way out" (lines 5–6). However, Collins overstates his case when he implies that analyzing a poem to find out what it might mean is a brutal or

1

deadly process, comparable to tying the poem to a chair and "beating it with a hose" (15). Rather than killing a poem's spirit, a careful and methodical dissection can often help the reader better appreciate its subtler meanings. In fact, with patient coaxing, a poem often has much to "confess." One such poem is Robert Frost's familiar but frequently misunderstood "The Road Not Taken." An examination of Frost's "The Road Not Taken" reveals a complex and somewhat troubling message about the arbitrariness of our life choices and our need to idealize those choices.

The word *lines* is omitted from the in-text citation after the first reference to lines of a poem.

Thesis statement

On the surface, Frost's poem seems to have a fairly simple meaning. The poem's speaker talks about coming to a fork in the road and choosing the "less-traveled" path. Most readers see the fork in the road as a metaphor: the road represents life, and the fork represents an individual's choices in life. By following the less-traveled road, the speaker is choosing the less conventional — and supposedly more emotionally rewarding — route. At the end of the poem, the speaker indicates his satisfaction when he says his choice "made all the difference" (line 20). However, Frost himself, referring to "The Road Not Taken," advised readers "'to be careful of that one; it's a tricky poem — very tricky,'" encouraging readers not to accept the most appealing or obvious interpretation (qtd. in Savoie 7–8). Literary critic Bojana Vujin urges readers to look for "poetic booby traps such as irony or deceit" in this poem and to enjoy the pleasures and rewards of discovering instances of "deliberate deceit on the poet's part" (195). In fact, after the speaker's tone and word choice are carefully examined, the poem's message seems darker and more complicated than it did initially.

2 Refutation of opposing argument

The speaker's tone in the first three stanzas suggests indecision, regret, and, ultimately, lack of power. Rather than bravely facing the choice between one common path and one uncommon path, the speaker spends most of the poem considering two seemingly equal roads, "sorry" not to be able to "travel both" (2). Even after choosing "the other" road in line 6, the speaker continues for two more stanzas to weigh his options. The problem is that the two roads are, in fact, indistinguishable. As several critics have observed, "the difference between the two roads, at least when it comes to the amount of treading they

3 Evidence: Analysis and explication of Frost poem

Evidence: Literary criticism

have been exposed to, is but an illusion: "'they both that morning equally lay' and neither is particularly travelled by" (Vujin 197). The roads are worn "really about the same" (10). If there is virtually no difference between the two, then why does Frost draw our attention to this fork in the road—this seemingly critical moment of choice? If Frost had wanted to dramatize a meaningful decision, the roads would be different in some significant way.

Evidence: Literary criticism

One critic, Frank Lentricchia, argues that Frost is demonstrating   4 "'that our life-shaping choices are irrational, that we are fundamentally out of control'" (qtd. in Savoie 13). Similarly, another critic contends that Frost wants his readers "to feel his characters' inner conflicts and to feel as conflicted as his characters, who are all too often lost in them-

Evidence: Analysis and explication of Frost poem

selves" (Plunkett). These two critical views help to explain the speaker's indecision in the first three stanzas. The speaker impulsively chooses "the other" road but cannot accept the arbitrariness of his choice; therefore, he cannot stop considering the first road. He exclaims in the third stanza, "Oh, I kept the first for another day!" (13). In the next two lines, when he finally gives up the possibility of following that first road, he predicts, "Yet knowing how way leads on to way, / I doubted if I should ever come back" (14–15). Here, the speaker further demonstrates a lack of control over his own decisions. He describes a future guided not by his own active, meaningful choices but rather by some arbitrary force. In a world where "way leads on to way," he is a passive traveler, not a decisive individualist.

Evidence: Analysis and explication of Frost poem

Given the indecision that characterizes the previous stanzas, the   5 poem's last two lines are surprisingly decisive: "I took the one less traveled by / And that has made all the difference" (19–20). Is the speaker contradicting himself? How has he suddenly become clear about the rightness of his decision? In fact, the last stanza does not make sense unless the reader perceives the irony in the speaker's tone. The speaker is imagining himself in the future, "ages and ages hence," telling the story of his moment at the crossroads (17). He imagines how he will, in hindsight, give his choice meaning and clarity that it did not have at the time. As Vujin argues, the poem's speaker is already "mythologizing his self and his life" (198). The narrator, rather than anticipating the satisfaction that will come from having made the right and braver choice, is anticipating rewriting his own life story to make sense of an ultimately arbitrary chain of events. Vujin explains, "This is not a poem about individuality; this is a poem about self-deceit and the rewriting of one's own history" (198). Reading the last stanza ironically allows readers to make sense of the poem as a whole.

Evidence: Literary criticism

There are many possible interpretations of "The Road Not Taken," most of which can be supported with evidence from the poem itself. However, to understand these interpretations, readers need to take the poem apart, look at how its parts fit together, and reach a thoughtful and logical conclusion. To do so, readers must go against some of Billy Collins's well-meaning advice and be willing to tie the poem—and themselves—to a chair: to read it carefully, ask questions, and stay with it until it confesses.

6 *Conclusion*

Works Cited

Collins, Billy. "Introduction to Poetry." *Sailing Alone around the Room.* Random House, 1998, p. 16.

Frost, Robert. "The Road Not Taken." *Mountain Interval.* Henry Holt, 1920, *Bartleby.com*, www.bartleby.com/119/1.html.

Plunkett, Adam. "Robert Frost Was Neither Light Nor Dark." *New Republic*, 13 Jun. 2014, newrepublic.com/article/118046 /art-robert-frost-tim-kendall-reviewed-adam-plunkett.

Savoie, John. "A Poet's Quarrel: Jamesian Pragmatism and Frost's 'The Road Not Taken.'" *New England Quarterly*, vol. 77, no. 1, 2004, pp. 5–24. *Academic Search Premier*, www.ebscohost.com/academic /academic-search-premier.

Vujin, Bojana. "'I Took the Road Less Traveled By': Self-Deception in Frost's and Eliot's Early Poetry." *Annual Review of the Faculty of Philosophy*, vol. 36, no. 1, 2011, pp. 195–203.

🔽 The following literary argument, "Not Just a 'Girl,'" argues against the commonly held position that a key character in the 1925 Ernest Hemingway short story "Hills Like White Elephants" is a stereotype.

NOT JUST A "GIRL"
LOREN MARTINEZ

Introduction

In Ernest Hemingway's famous story "Hills Like White Elephants," 1
a couple, "the American and the girl with him," talk and drink while
waiting for a train to Madrid (Hemingway 69). Most readers agree that
the subject of their discussion is whether "the girl," called Jig, should
have an abortion. Most of the story is told through dialogue, and
although the word *abortion* is never mentioned, most readers agree
that the pregnancy is the source of the tension between them. However,
there are other aspects of the story about which readers do not agree.
For example, some critics believe that Hemingway's portrayal of "the
girl" is unfair or sexist. More specifically, some see in her the qualities
of "the typically submissive Hemingway woman" (Nolan 19). However,

Thesis statement

a close reading of the story reveals the opposite to be true: "the girl"
is not a one-dimensional stereotype but a complex, sympathetically
drawn character.

Refutation of
opposing arguments

Most critics who see Hemingway's portrayal of Jig as sexist base 2
their interpretation on Hemingway's reputation and not on the story
itself. For example, feminist critic Katherine M. Rogers points out that
because Hemingway himself "openly expressed fear of and hostility to
women" (263), it "seems fair" to see his male characters "as representative of Hemingway himself" (248). However, although "the American" in
this story may see Jig as just "a pleasant pastime," it would be an oversimplification to confuse the character's opinion of her with the writer's
as Rogers would encourage us to do (251). For example, one could
argue (as many critics have done) that because the name "Jig" has sexual connotations, it reveals the author's sexism (Renner 38). However,
as critic Howard Hannum points out, she is referred to by this name only
twice in the story, both times by the male character himself, not by the
narrator (qtd. in Renner 38). Critic Stanley Renner agrees with Hannum,
rejecting the idea that Hemingway's choice to refer to the character as
"the girl" is equally "belittling" (38). Renner argues that this use of the

word *girl* is necessary to show how the character changes and matures in this story. In fact, he sees "her achievement of mature self-knowledge and assertion [as] the main line of development in the story" (39). All in all, the evidence suggests that "the girl," not "the American," is actually the story's protagonist. Given this central focus on "the girl" and the complexity of her character, the accusations that Hemingway's sexism has led him to create a stereotype do not seem justified.

When students who are not familiar with Hemingway's reputation as a misogynist read "Hills Like White Elephants," they tend to sympathize more often with "the girl" than with "the American" (Bauer 126) and to see the female character's thoughtfulness and depth. Although "the American" refers to the abortion as "'really an awfully simple operation'" (Hemingway 72), downplaying its seriousness, "the girl" has a "more mature understanding" of what her decision might mean (Bauer 130). She recognizes that it is not so "simple," and she is not naive enough to think that having the baby will save the relationship. In fact, she responds to his own naive comments with sarcasm. He claims that they will be "'all right and happy'" if she goes through with the operation; he says he's "'known lots of people who have done it.' 'So have I,' said the girl. 'And afterward they were all so happy'" (Hemingway 73). Despite her sarcasm and her resistance to his suggestions, the man continues to insist that this problem will be easy to fix. Finally, the girl becomes irritated with him and, as readers can see by the dashes that end his lines midsentence, cuts him off, finishing his lines for him as he tries to tell her again how "perfectly simple" the operation is (Hemingway 76). Readers understand her pain and frustration when she finally says, "'Would you please please please please please please please stop talking?'" (Hemingway 76).

3 Evidence: First point in support of thesis

The argument that "the girl" is a flat, stereotypical character portrayed in sexist terms is hard to support. In fact, a stronger argument could be made that it is the man, "the American," who is the stereotype. As critic Charles J. Nolan Jr. points out, "Hemingway highlights Jig's maturity and superiority as he excoriates the selfishness and insensitivity of her companion" (19). Moreover, "the girl" is certainly the central character in this story—the one in conflict, the one who must make the final decision, and the one who grows over the course of the story. At times,

4 Evidence: Second point in support of thesis

she seems willing to listen to the man, even going so far as to say, "'Then I'll do it. Because I don't care about me'" (Hemingway 74). However, soon after, she responds defiantly to his comment, "'You mustn't feel that way'" with "'I don't feel any way'" (Hemingway 75). Thus, as Renner notes, Hemingway's dialogue reveals "the self-centered motives of his male character" while at the same time dramatizing the female character's complex inner struggle (38). By the end of the story, the shallow "American" still expects things to be all right between them. But when the man asks, "'Do you feel better?'" Hemingway shows the girl's quiet power—and her transformation—by giving her the final understated words of the story: "'I feel fine. . . . There's nothing wrong with me. I feel fine'" (Hemingway 77). Although we do not learn what her decision is, we can see that she is now in control: she has decided to shut down the conversation, and what the man has to say no longer matters.

Conclusion

In "Hills Like White Elephants," "the girl" proves herself to be neither "'weak *in* character'" nor "'weak *as* character'" as some have described Hemingway's female characters (Bauer 126). Far from being weak *in* character, she constantly questions and pushes against the male character's suggestions. And far from being weak *as* a character, she acts as the protagonist in this story, winning the reader's sympathies. A stereotypically drawn female character would not be able to carry off

Concluding statement

either of these feats. Although Hemingway may demonstrate sexism in his other stories—and demonstrate it in his own life—readers who evaluate *this* story will discover a complex, conflicted, sympathetic female character.

5

Works Cited

Bauer, Margaret D. "Forget the Legend and Read the Work: Teaching Two Stories by Ernest Hemingway." *College Literature*, vol. 30, no. 3, 2003, pp. 124–37. *Academic Search Premier*, www.ebscohost.com/academic/academic-search-premier.

Hemingway, Ernest. "Hills Like White Elephants." *Men without Women*. Charles Scribner's, 1927, pp. 69–77.

Nolan, Charles J., Jr. "Hemingway's Women's Movement." *Hemingway Review*, vol. 4, no. 1, 1984, pp. 14–22. *Academic Search Premier*, www.ebscohost.com/academic/academic-search-premier.

Renner, Stanley. "Moving to the Girl's Side of 'Hills Like White
  Elephants.'" *Hemingway Review*, vol. 15, no. 1, 1995, pp. 27–41.
  Academic Search Premier, www.ebscohost.com/academic
  /academic-search-premier.
Rogers, Katherine M. *The Troublesome Helpmate: A History of Misogyny
  in Literature*. U of Washington P, 1996.

Documenting Sources: APA

American Psychological Association (APA) documentation style is commonly used in the social sciences. In APA style, parenthetical references refer readers to sources in the list of references at the end of the paper.* Parenthetical citations must be provided for all sources that are not common knowledge, whether you are summarizing, paraphrasing, or quoting.

Using Parenthetical References

In APA style, parenthetical references refer readers to sources in the list of references at the end of the paper. A typical parenthetical reference includes the author's last name (followed by a comma) and the year of publication: (Vang, 2015). Here are some guidelines for specific situations.

- If the author's last name appears in the text, follow it with the year of publication, in parentheses: According to Vang (2015), recent studies suggest . . .

- When quoting from a source, include a page number, if available: (Vang, 2015, p. 33). Once you have cited a source, you can refer to the author a second time without the publication date so long as it is clear you are referring to the same source: Vang also found . . .

- If no author is identified, use a shortened version of the title: ("Mind," 2015).

- If you are citing multiple works by the same author or authors published in the same year, include a lowercase letter with the year: (Peters, 2014a), (Peters, 2014b), and so on.

---

*American Psychological Association, *Publication Manual of the American Psychological Association*, Sixth Edition (2010).

- When a work has two authors, cite both names, separated by an ampersand, and the year: (Tabor & Garza, 2006). For three to five authors, in the first reference, cite all authors, along with the year; for subsequent references, cite just the first author, followed by et al. When a work has six or more authors, cite just the first author, followed by et al. and the year: (McCarthy et al., 2010).

- Omit page numbers or dates if the source does not include them. (Try to find a .pdf version of an online source; it will usually include page numbers.)

- If you quote a source found in another source, cite the original author and the source in which you found it: Psychologist Gary Wells asserted . . . (as cited in Doyle, 2005, p. 122).

- Include in-text references to personal communications and interviews by providing the person's name, the phrase "personal communication," and the date: (J. Smith, personal communication, February 12, 2015). Do not include these sources in your reference list.

If a direct quotation is forty words or less, include it within quotation marks without separating it from the rest of the text. When quoting a passage of more than forty words, indent the entire block of quoted text one-half inch from the left margin, and do not enclose it in quotation marks. It should be double-spaced, like the rest of the paper. Place parenthetical documentation one space after the final punctuation.

Preparing a Reference List

Start your list of references on a separate page at the end of your paper. Center the title References at the top of the page, and follow these guidelines:

- Begin each reference flush with the left margin, and indent subsequent lines one-half inch. Double-space the reference list within and between entries.

- List your references alphabetically by the author's last name (or by the first major word of the title if no author is identified).

- If the list includes references for two sources by the same author, alphabetize them by title.

- Italicize titles of books and periodicals. Do not italicize article titles or enclose them in quotation marks.

- For titles of books and articles, capitalize the first word of the title and subtitle as well as any proper nouns. Capitalize words in a periodical title as they appear in the original.

When you have completed your reference list, go through your paper and make sure that every reference cited is included in the list in the correct order.

Examples of APA Citations

The following are examples of APA citations.

Periodicals

Article in a journal paginated by volume

Shah, N. A. (2006). Women's human rights in the Koran: An interpretive approach. *Human Rights Quarterly, 28,* 868–902.

Article in a journal paginated by issue

Lamb, B., & Keller, H. (2007). Understanding cultural models of parenting: The role of intracultural variation and response style. *Journal of Cross-Cultural Psychology, 38*(1), 50–57.

Magazine article

Von Drehle, D. (2015, April 20). Line of fire. *Time, 185*(14), 24–28.

Newspaper article

DeParle, J. (2009, April 19). Struggling to rise in suburbs where failing means fitting in. *The New York Times,* pp. A1, A20–A21.

Books

Books by one author

Jordan, Jennifer A. (2015). *Edible memory: The lure of heirloom tomatoes and other forgotten foods.* Chicago, IL: University of Chicago Press.

Books by two to seven authors

McFadden, J., & Al-Khalili, J. (2014). *Life on the edge: The coming of age of quantum biology.* New York, NY: Crown.

Books by eight or more authors

Barrett, J. M., Smith, V., Wilson, R. T., Haley, V. A., Clarke, P., Palmer, N. B., . . . Fraser, D. (2012). *How to cite references in APA style.* New York: Cambridge University Press.

Edited book

Brummett, B. (Ed.). (2008). *Uncovering hidden rhetorics: Social issues in disguise.* Los Angeles, CA: Sage.

Essay in an edited book

Alberts, H. C. (2006). The multiple transformations of Miami. In H. Smith & O. J. Furuseth (Eds.), *Latinos in the new south: Transformations of place* (pp. 135–151). Burlington, VT: Ashgate.

Translation

Piketty, T. (2015). *The Economics of inequality* (A. Goldhammer, Trans.). Cambridge, MA: Harvard University Press.

Revised edition

Johnson, B., & Christensen, L. B. (2008). *Educational research: Quantitative, qualitative, and mixed approaches* (3rd ed.). Los Angeles, CA: Sage.

Internet Sources
Entire website

Secretariat of the Convention on Biological Diversity. (2015). *Convention on biological diversity.* Retrieved from https://www.cbd.int/

Web page within a website

The great divide: How Westerners and Muslims view each other. (2006, July 6). In *Pew global attitudes project.* Retrieved from http://pewglobal.org/reports/display.php?ReportID=253

University program website

National security archive. (2009). Retrieved from George Washington University website: http://www.gwu.edu/~nsarchiv/

Journal article found on the web with a DOI

Because websites change and disappear without warning, many publishers have started adding a **Digital Object Identifier (DOI)** to their articles. A DOI is a unique number that can be retrieved no matter where the article ends up on the web.

To locate an article with a known DOI, go to the DOI system website at http://dx.doi.org/ and type in the DOI number. When citing an article that has a DOI (usually found on the first page of the article), you do not need to include a URL in your reference or the name of the database in which you may have found the article.

> Geers, A. L., Wellman, J. A., & Lassiter, G. D. (2009). Dispositional optimism and engagement: The moderating influence of goal prioritization. *Journal of Personality and Social Psychology, 94,* 913–932. doi:10.1037/a0014746

Journal article found on the web without a DOI

> Bendetto, M. M. (2008). Crisis on the immigration bench: An ethical perspective. *Brooklyn Law Review, 73,* 467–523. Retrieved from http://brooklaw.edu/students/journals/blr.php/

Journal article from an electronic database

The name and URL of the database are not required for citations if a DOI is available. If no DOI is available, provide the home page URL of the journal or of the book or report publisher.

> Staub, E., & Pearlman, L. A. (2009). Reducing intergroup prejudice and conflict: A commentary. *Journal of Personality and Social Psychology, 11,* 3–23. Retrieved from http://www.apa.org /journals/psp/

Electronic book

> Katz, R. N. (Ed.). (2008). *The tower and the cloud: Higher education in an era of cloud computing.* Retrieved from http://net .educause.edu/ir/library/pdf/PUB7202.pdf

Video blog post

> Green, J. (2015, July 7). Understanding the financial crisis in Greece [Video file]. Retrieved from https://www.youtube.com /watch?v=tigaryz-1y4

Presentation slides

> Hall, M. E. (2009) *Who moved my job!? A psychology of job-loss "trauma"* [Presentation slides]. Retrieved from http://www.cew .wisc.edu/docs/WMMJ%20PwrPt-Summry2.ppt

Student Essay

The following research paper, "The High Cost of Cheap Counterfeit Goods," follows APA format as outlined in the preceding pages.

APA PAPER GUIDELINES

- An APA paper should have a one-inch margin all around and be double-spaced throughout.

- The first line of every paragraph should be indented, and all pages of the paper, including the first, should be numbered consecutively.

- Every page should have a page header (an abbreviated title in all uppercase letters) typed one-half inch from the top of the page.

- An APA paper has four sections: the *title page*, the *abstract*, the *body of the paper*, and the *reference list*:

  1. The **title page** (page 1) should include a running head (in all uppercase letters) at the top:

     Running Head: COUNTERFEIT GOODS

  2. The title page should also include the title of the paper (upper- and lowercase letters), your name (first name, middle initial, last name), and your school.

  3. The **abstract** (page 2) should be a 150- to 250-word summary of the paper. Type the word **Abstract** (centered); skip one line; and do not indent. After the abstract, skip one line and type *Keywords* (italicized and indented), followed by keywords that will help researchers find your essay in a database.

  4. The **body of the paper** should begin on page 3. After the title page, each page of the paper should include the running head (in all uppercase letters), typed flush left, one-half inch from the top of the page:

     COUNTERFEIT GOODS

  5. The **reference list** should begin on a new page, after the body of the paper. (See pages A-14–A-15 for a discussion of how to format the reference list.)

- Citations should follow APA documentation style.

The High Cost of Cheap Counterfeit Goods

Deniz A. Bilgutay

Humanities 101, Section 1

Professor Fitzgerald

March 4, 2020

COUNTERFEIT GOODS   2

Abstract

The global trade in counterfeit products costs manufacturers of luxury goods millions of dollars each year. Although this illegal trade threatens the free market, employs underage labor, and may even fund terrorism, many people consider it a victimless crime. Studies show that some consumers even take pride in buying knock-off products. But a closer look at this illicit trade in counterfeit goods shows that consumers in the United States—and around the world—do not understand the ethical implications of the choices they make. Consumers should stop supporting this illegal business, and law enforcement officials should prosecute it more vigorously than they currently do. In the final analysis, this illegal practice hurts legitimate businesses and in some cases endangers the health and safety of consumers.

Keywords: counterfeiting, terrorism, ethics, crime

COUNTERFEIT GOODS   3

The High Cost of Cheap Counterfeit Goods

For those who do not want to pay for genuine designer   Introduction
products, a fake Louis Vuitton bag or knock-off Rolex watch
might seem too good to pass up. Such purchases may even
be a source of pride. According to one study, two-thirds of British
consumers said they would be "proud to tell family and
friends" that they bought inexpensive knock-offs (Thomas,
2007). The trade in counterfeit goods, however, is a crime—and
not a victimless crime. A growing body of evidence suggests
that the makers and distributers of counterfeit goods have
ties to child labor, organized crime, and even terrorism. In
addition, the global economic cost of counterfeiting is estimated at $600 billion a year, according to recent data from the
International Chamber of Commerce (Melik, 2011). For these   Thesis
                                                             statement
reasons, consumers should stop buying these products and
funding the illegal activities that this activity supports.

Much of the responsibility for the trade in counterfeit
goods can be placed on the manufacturers and the countries
that permit the production and export of such goods. For
example, China, which dominates the world counterfeit trade,
is doing very little to stop this activity. According to a recent
article in *USA Today* by Calum MacLeod (2011), "a major
obstacle is China's *shanzhai* culture, whereby some Chinese
delight in making cheap imitations, sometimes in parody, of
expensive, famous brands." Chinese counterfeiters have gone
so far as to create entire fake stores: fake Starbucks stores,
fake Abercrombie & Fitch stores, and even fake Apple stores.
Although some of these copycats have been prosecuted, there
is a high level of tolerance, even admiration, for counterfeiting in
China. This attitude toward *shanzhai* is reflected in the country's
lax intellectual property protection laws. As one Chinese
intellectual property lawyer observed, "The penalties don't

outweigh the benefits" (as cited in MacLeod, 2011). Given this situation, the production of counterfeit goods in China is not likely to slow down any time soon.

Despite such cultural justifications for counterfeiting, there is still an ethical problem associated with the purchase of knock-offs. As Dana Thomas (2007) has written in *The New York Times*, many of these counterfeit products are made by children who are "sold or sent off by their families to work in clandestine factories." To American consumers, the problem of children laboring in Chinese factories may be remote, but it is serious. If it is reasonable to place blame for this flourishing market on the countries that allow it, it is also reasonable to blame the people who buy most of the counterfeit goods—namely, consumers in the United States and Europe. According to a report by U.S. Customs and Border Patrol, 62% of fake goods seized in the United States in 2011 were produced in China (as cited in Coleman, 2012). In Europe, the numbers are even higher. According to *The Wall Street Journal*, 85% of goods seized in the European Union come from China (Nairn, 2011). Consequently, the simple act of buying a counterfeit Coach handbag implicates the consumer in the practice of forced child labor.

Immoral labor practices are not the only reason why the counterfeit market needs to be stopped. Organized crime is behind much of the counterfeit trade, so "every dollar spent on a knockoff Gap polo shirt or a fake Kate Spade handbag may be supporting drug trafficking, . . . and worse" ("Editorial: The True Cost," 2007). Consumer dollars may also be supporting narcotics, weapons, and child prostitution (Thomas, 2007).

This illicit international system also helps to finance groups even more sinister than crime syndicates. American consumers of counterfeit goods should understand that profits from

Evidence:
Point 1

Evidence:
Point 2

COUNTERFEIT GOODS   5

counterfeit goods support terrorist and extremist groups, including Hezbollah, paramilitary organizations in Northern Ireland, and
FARC, a revolutionary armed faction in Colombia (Thomas, 2007).
According to the International Anti-Counterfeiting Coalition, the   Evidence:
sale of knock-off T-shirts may even have funded the 1993 attack   Point 3
on the World Trade Center. Some observers speculate that terror-
ists annually receive about 2% of the roughly $500 billion trade in
counterfeit goods ("Editorial: The True Cost," 2007). According to
Ronald K. Noble, secretary-general of the international law
enforcement agency Interpol, crime involving counterfeit merchandise "is becoming the preferred method of funding for a
number of terrorist groups" (as cited in Langan, 2003).

Beyond the moral and ethical implications of its links to   Evidence:
child labor, crime, and terrorism, counterfeit merchandise also   Point 4
undermines the mainstay of Western business—respect for
intellectual property. In the context of a vast international market
of counterfeit luxury goods, the issue of intellectual property can
seem insignificant. But the creation of new products requires
time, energy, and money, and "unrestrained copying robs
creators of the means to profit from their works" (Sprigman,
2006). Copyright law exists to make sure that inventors and
producers will be motivated to create original work and be fairly
compensated for it. This principle applies to the designers of
luxury goods and fashion items as well. Christopher Sprigman   Opposing
(2006) disagrees, however, noting that although intellectual   argument
property law does little to protect fashion designs, this is as it
should be. "Trend-driven consumption," says Sprigman, is good
for the fashion industry because the industry's ability to create
trends "is based on designers' relative freedom to copy." But
even this argument—which addresses the influences of legitimate   Refutation
fashion designers and manufacturers—cannot be used to

justify allowing counterfeiters to copy Prada handbags or Hugo Boss suits and pass them off as genuine branded articles. Such illicit activity creates no trends—other than perhaps increasing the market for counterfeit products, which siphons off more profits from original designers.

Evidence: Point 5

The knock-off market is not limited to fashion and luxury goods. For example, fake products such as shoddy brake pads have directly injured many consumers. In addition, each year millions of people in the United States and abroad buy counterfeit drugs that do not work and in many cases are dangerous. Some sources estimate that the majority of drugs used to treat life-threatening diseases in Africa are counterfeit. Not coincidentally, many of the same people who are making and distributing counterfeit luxury goods are also manufacturing these drugs ("Editorial: The True Cost," 2007).

Conclusion

It is time for people to realize the harm that is done by counterfeit merchandise and stop buying it. One way to combat this problem is to educate consumers about the effects of their purchases. As James Melik (2011) of the BBC explains, "People try to save money without realizing that the purchase of counterfeit goods can actually harm themselves, the economy and ultimately, their own pockets." Melik urges consumers to "think twice" before buying "products which promote and fund crime." Another way to confront the problem is for law enforcement to address this issue aggressively. Not only should local authorities do more to stop this illegal trade, but national governments should also impose sanctions on countries that refuse to honor international treaties concerning intellectual property. Only by taking this issue seriously can we ensure that this "victimless" crime does not continue to spread and claim more victims.

COUNTERFEIT GOODS   7

References

Coleman, S. (2012, January 20). China still accounts for majority of US counterfeit goods. *Canadian Manufacturers and Exporters*. Retrieved from http://www.cme-mec.ca/?lid =JCKNC-E742G-1W6JA&comaction=show&cid=DVU6K -CVBRZ-C6TZQ

Editorial: The true cost: Illegal knockoffs of name-brand products do widespread harm [Editorial]. (2007, December 2). *The Columbus* [OH] *Dispatch*, p. 4G.

Langan, M. (2003, July 24). Counterfeit goods make real terrorism. *Pittsburgh Post-Gazette*, p. A17.

MacLeod, C. (2011, August 2). China takes knock-offs to a new level, copying entire stores. *USA Today*. Retrieved from http://www.usatoday.com/money/industries /technology/2011-07-31-China-counterfeiting-fake-Western -goods-stores_n.htm

Melik, J. (2011, December 18). Fake goods save money but at what cost? *BBC News*. Retrieved from http://www.bbc .co.uk/news/business-16087793

Nairn, G. (2011, October 18). Countering the counterfeiters. *The Wall Street Journal*. Retrieved from http://online.wsj.com /article/SB10001424052970204226204576600462442044764 .html

Sprigman, C. (2006, August 22). The fashion industry's piracy paradox [Online forum comment]. Retrieved from http:// www.publicknowledge.org/node/597

Thomas, D. (2007, August 30). Terror's purse strings. *The New York Times*, p. A23.

Accurate evidence: Evidence from reliable sources that is quoted carefully and in context.

***Ad hominem* fallacy:** The logical fallacy of undermining an argument by attacking the person who is making the argument instead of addressing the argument itself.

Allusion: A reference within a work to a person, literary or biblical text, or historical event. This shorthand device reminds the reader of something that enlarges the context of the situation being written about.

Analogy: An extended comparison that explains an unfamiliar item, concept, or situation by comparing it to a more familiar one.

Annotating: Making notes of your questions, reactions, and ideas on the document itself.

Antithesis: An opposing statement that tests whether an argumentative **thesis** is debatable.

Appeal to doubtful authority: The use of nonexperts to support an argument.

Applied ethics: The field of philosophy that applies **ethical principles** to real-life issues (such as abortion, the death penalty, animal rights, or doctor-assisted suicide).

Argument: A logical and persuasive presentation of **evidence** that attempts to convince people to accept (or at least to consider) the writer's position.

Argument by analogy: An argument that claims that its position is valid because it is similar in some ways to a position on another issue that readers are likely to accept.

Backing: In a **Toulmin argument**, the evidence that supports the warrant.

Bandwagon appeal: An attempt to convince people that something is true because it is widely held to be true.

Begging-the-question fallacy: An illogical assumption that a statement is self-evident (or true) when it actually requires proof.

Bias: Preconceived ideas or prejudices, which are often used in an argument instead of factual **evidence**.

Brainstorming: Making quick notes on a topic to generate ideas.

Causal chain: A sequence of events in which one event causes the next, which in turn causes the next, and so on.

Cause-and-effect argument: An argument that explains an event or a situation by considering its likely causes or outcomes.

Circular reasoning: An attempt to support a statement by simply repeating the statement in different terms.

Claim: In a **Toulmin argument**, the main point, usually stated as a **thesis**.

Clustering: Creating a diagram to map out your thoughts.

Common ground: Points of agreement that are shared by those on opposing sides of an argument.

Common knowledge: Factual information (such as a writer's date of birth, a scientific fact, or the location of a famous battle) that can be found in several credible sources. Common knowledge does not require documentation.

Conclusion: The last part of a **syllogism**.

Confirmation bias: The tendency that people have to accept information that supports their own beliefs and to ignore information that does not.

Confrontational argument: A kind of argument that is characterized by conflict and opposition.

Contributory causes: The less important causes in a **causal argument**.

Credibility: Trustworthiness. A credible source is believable.

Criteria for evaluation: Standards by which a subject (or source) is evaluated.

Critical response: A passage in which a writer examines the ideas that are presented in an argument and evaluates them.

Current source: A source containing up-to-date information. Current sources are especially important in discussions of scientific subjects and may be less important in other subjects.

Debatable thesis: A thesis statement that presents a position with which people might disagree.

Deductive reasoning: A form of reasoning that moves from general statements (or **premises**) to specific conclusions. See **inductive reasoning**.

Definition argument: An argument that is based on the idea that something fits or does not fit a particular definition of a key term.

Dictionary definition: A structure for definition that consists of the term to be defined, the general class to which the term belongs, and the qualities that differentiate the term from other items in the same class.

Dilemma: A choice between two or more unfavorable alternatives.

Distortion: An unfair tactic of argument in which the writer misrepresents evidence—for example, by presenting an opponent's view inaccurately or by exaggerating his or her position.

Documentation: Information that identifies the sources used in an argument.

Editing and proofreading: The final steps in the writing process, which check that an essay is well organized, convincing, and clearly written and has no distracting grammatical, spelling, and mechanical errors.

Either/or fallacy: Faulty reasoning that presents only two choices when there are actually three or more choices.

Enthymeme: A **syllogism** with one or two parts of its argument (usually the major premise) missing.

Equivocation: The use of two different meanings for the same key term in an argument.

Ethical argument: An argument that focuses on whether something should be done because it is good or right.

Ethical dilemma: A conflict between two or more possible actions, each of which will potentially have negative outcomes.

Ethical principles: A set of ideas or standards that guides someone to an ethically correct conclusion.

Ethics: The field of philosophy that studies the standards by which an act can be judged right or wrong or good or bad.

Ethos: An appeal to the trustworthiness or credibility of a speaker or writer.

Evaluate: To express an opinion about the quality of something.

Evaluation argument: An argument that presents a positive or negative judgment, asserts that someone else's positive or negative judgment is not accurate or justified, or demonstrates that one thing is or is not superior to another.

Evidence: The facts, observations, expert opinion, examples, and statistics that support a thesis statement. In a **Toulmin argument**, the evidence is called the **grounds**.

Fact: A statement that can be verified (proven to be true).

Fallacy: An error in reasoning that undermines the logic of an argument.

False dilemma: See **either/or fallacy**.

Formal argument: An argument developed according to set rhetorical principles in academic discussion and writing. See **informal argument**.

Formal outline: A presentation of an essay's main and subordinate points that uses a number/letter system to designate the order in which the points will be discussed.

Freewriting: Writing continuously for a set time to generate ideas without worrying about spelling or grammar.

Grounds: In a **Toulmin argument**, the evidence that is used to support the claim.

Hasty generalization: An error in reasoning that occurs when a conclusion is based on too little evidence or when the gap between the evidence and conclusion is too wide.

Highlighting: Using underlining and symbols to identify an essay's most important points.

Identifying tag: A phrase that identifies the source of a **quotation**, **paraphrase**, or **summary**.

Immediate cause: In a **causal argument**, the cause that occurs right before an event.

Inductive leap: In **inductive reasoning**, a stretch of the imagination that enables a writer to draw a reasonable conclusion from the existing information.

Inductive reasoning: A form of reasoning that begins with specific observations (or evidence) and moves to a general conclusion. See **deductive reasoning**.

Inference: A statement that uses what is known to draw a conclusion about what is unknown.

Informal argument: An **argument** that occurs in daily life about politics, sports, social issues, and personal relationships. See **formal argument**.

Informal outline: A list of the ideas that will be discussed in an essay. See **formal outline**.

Jumping to a conclusion: See **hasty generalization**.

Logic: The principles of correct reasoning that enable someone to tell whether a conclusion correctly follows from a set of statements or assumptions.

Logical fallacy: A flawed argument.

Logos: An appeal to logic.

Main cause: In a **causal argument**, the most important cause.

Major premise: See **syllogism**.

Means of persuasion: The appeals—*logos*, *pathos*, and *ethos*—that writers use to persuade their audience.

Metaphor: A comparison in which two dissimilar things are compared without the word *like* or *as*.

Middle term: The term in a **syllogism** that appears in both the major and minor premises but not in the conclusion.

Minor premise: See **syllogism**.

Misuse of statistics fallacy: When data are misrepresented.

Non sequitur **fallacy:** Illogical reasoning that occurs when a conclusion does not follow from the premises or is supported by weak or irrelevant evidence or by no evidence at all.

Objective source: A source that is not unduly influenced by personal opinions or feelings.

Operational definition: A definition of how something acts or works that transforms an abstract concept into something concrete, observable, and possibly measurable.

Opinion: A personal judgment; therefore, an idea that is open to debate.

Parallelism: The use of the same or a similar structure in the repetition of words, phrases, or clauses.

Paraphrase: A passage that presents a source's ideas in detail, including its main idea and key supporting points and perhaps key examples.

Parenthetical references: In MLA and APA **documentation**, citations that identify the source of a paraphrase, quotation, or summary.

Pathos: An appeal to the emotions.

Peer review: The process of having colleagues examine and critique written work. Informally, schoolwork is read by friends or classmates; formally, scholarly work is read by experts in the field to confirm its accuracy.

Persuasion: The act of influencing an audience to adopt a particular belief or to follow a specific course of action.

Plagiarism: The use of the words or ideas of another person without attributing them to their rightful author.

Popular magazine: A periodical that is aimed at general readers. It generally is not an acceptable source for research.

Post hoc **fallacy:** Faulty reasoning that asserts that because two events occur closely in time, one event must have caused the other.

Premises: Statements or assumptions on which an **argument** is based or from which a conclusion is drawn.

Previewing: During active reading, forming a general impression of a writer's position on an issue, the argument's key supporting points, and the context for the writer's remarks.

Propaganda: Biased or misleading information that is spread about a particular viewpoint, person, or cause.

Proposal argument: An argument that attempts to convince people that a problem exists and that a particular solution is both practical and desirable.

Qualifiers: In a **Toulmin argument**, statements that limit the **claim**.

Quotation: Words or sentences taken directly from a source.

Quoting out of context: Removing a quotation from its original setting for the purpose of distorting its meaning.

Reading critically: Questioning or challenging material instead of simply accepting it as true. This often involves assessing the accuracy of facts in sources and considering the evidence that supports them.

Reason: In a **Toulmin argument**, a statement that supports the **claim**.

Rebuttals: In a **Toulmin argument**, refutations of opposing arguments.

Red herring fallacy: An irrelevant side issue that diverts attention from the real issue.

Refutation: The section of an argumentative essay that identifies opposing arguments and presents arguments against them.

Refute: To disprove or call into question.

Relevant evidence: Evidence that applies specifically (not just tangentially) to the topic under discussion.

Remote causes: In a **causal argument**, incidents that occurred in the past but may have had a greater impact than more recent events.

Representative evidence: Evidence that is drawn from a fair range of sources, not just from sources that support a particular position.

Revision: The careful and critical review of a draft.

Rhetoric: The effect of various elements working together to form a convincing and persuasive **argument**.

Rhetorical analysis: A systematic examination of the strategies that a writer employs to achieve his or her purpose.

Rhetorical question: A question that encourages readers to reflect on an issue but does not call for a reply.

Rhetorical situation: The combination of the writer, the writer's purpose, the writer's audience, the topic, and the context.

Rhetorical strategies: The ways in which argument writers present ideas and opinions, including but not limited to thesis, organization, evidence, and stylistic techniques (**simile**, **metaphor**, **allusion**, **parallelism**, repetition, and **rhetorical questions**).

Rhetorical triangle: A graphic representation of the three kinds of appeals in an argument—*logos* (reason), *ethos* (credibility), and *pathos* (values and beliefs).

Rogerian argument: A model of argument that assumes that people of goodwill can avoid conflict by identifying **common ground** and points of agreement. It is based on the work of Carl Rogers, a twentieth-century psychologist who felt that traditional confrontational arguments could be counterproductive.

Scholarly journal: A periodical that is usually written by experts, documented, and peer reviewed.

Scientific method: A way of using induction to find answers to questions. It involves proposing a hypothesis, making a series of observations to test the hypothesis, and arriving at a conclusion that confirms, modifies, or disproves the hypothesis.

Self-evident: A proposition that requires no proof or explanation.

Simile: A figure of speech that compares two unlike things by using *like* or *as*.

Skeptical: Having an open mind but still needing to be convinced.

Slanting: An unfair tactic that makes an argument appear stronger by presenting only evidence that supports a particular position and ignoring evidence that challenges it.

Slippery-slope fallacy: An illogical argument that holds that one thing will cause a series of events that ends in an inevitable, unpleasant conclusion, usually with no evidence that such a sequence will actually occur.

Sound syllogism: A syllogism that is both true and valid.

Stasis theory: A rhetorical tool that determines the issue explored in a particular argument by slowing down and asking questions designed to isolate that topic.

Straw man fallacy: An intentional oversimplification of an opposing argument to make it easier to refute.

Sufficient evidence: Evidence that includes enough facts, statistics, and expert opinion to support the essay's thesis.

Summary: A concise restatement of the main idea of a passage (or article or book) without the examples, explanations, and stylistic devices of the source.

Sweeping generalization: See **hasty generalization**.

Syllogism: A model for **deductive reasoning** that includes a **major premise**, a **minor premise**, and a **conclusion**.

Synthesis: A combination of **summary**, **paraphrase**, **quotation**, and a writer's own ideas that supports an original conclusion.

Taking a stand: Expressing a position in the form of a **thesis statement**.

Thesis: The position that an argument supports.

Thesis statement: A single sentence in an argumentative essay that states a position on an issue.

Thinking critically: Questioning rather than accepting ideas at face value.

Toulmin argument: An argument that includes the **claim** (the main point), the grounds (the **evidence** a writer uses to support the claim), and the **warrant** (the inference—either stated or implied—that connects the claims to their grounds).

True syllogism: A syllogism in which the **premises** are consistent with the **facts**.

Unfair appeal: An appeal to an audience's fears or prejudices.

Valid syllogism: A system in which a conclusion follows logically from its premises.

Visual: An image—such as a chart, graph, table, photo, drawing, or diagram.

Visual argument: An advertisement, chart, graph, table, diagram, web page, photograph, painting, or other representation that communicates a position through images.

Warrant: In a **Toulmin argument**, the inference or assumption, either stated or implied, that connects a claim to its grounds.

Works-cited list: An alphabetical list of sources that appears at the end of an essay that follows MLA style.

Writing process: The process of planning, drafting, revising, and editing an argument.

You also fallacy (*tu quoque*): An illogical assertion that a statement is false because the speaker has said or done the opposite. It attacks a person for doing the thing that he or she is arguing against.

ACKNOWLEDGMENTS

Text Credits

Sasha Abramsky. "The Fear Industry Goes Back to Work." From *The Nation*, August 29/September 5, 2016. Copyright © 2016 The Nation Company. All rights reserved. Used under license.

Sam Adolphsen. "Student Loan Debt: It's Not the Government's Fault." From *The Maine Wire*, May 1, 2012. © 2012 Maine Heritage Policy Center. Reprinted by permission.

Erika Anderson. "The Opioid Epidemic is a Cultural Problem. It Requires Cultural Solutions." *The Washington Examiner*, August 21, 2018. Reprinted by permission.

Dan Ariely. "Essay mills: A coarse lesson in cheating," *The Los Angeles Times*, June 17, 2012. Reproduced with the permission of the author.

James Baldwin. "If Black English Isn't A Language, Then Tell Me, What Is?" From *The New York Times*, July 29, 1979. Collected in *James Baldwin: Essays*, published by Library of America. Copyright © 1979 James Baldwin. Reprinted by permission of The James Baldwin Estate.

Rosalind C. Barnett and Caryl Rivers. "Men Are from Earth, and So Are Women. It's Faulty Research That Sets Them Apart." *The Chronicle of Higher Education*, September 4, 2004. Reprinted by permission.

Rosalind C. Barnett and Caryl Rivers. "The Science Doesn't Support the Google Memo," *Recode*, August 11, 2017. Reprinted by permission of the authors.

Joseph L. Bast and Peter Ferrara. "The Social Benefits of Fossil Fuels Far Outweigh the Costs," *Wall Street Journal*, June 17, 2018. Copyright © 2018 Dow Jones & Company; permission conveyed through Copyright Clearance Center, Inc.

Bertolas et al. "Counterpoint: Colleges and Universities Have No Obligation to Provide Student-Athletes with Additional Compensation beyond Tuition, Room, and Board," *International Social Science Review*, Volume 94, Issue 1, Art. 21. Pgs. 5–8. Copyright © 2018 Pi Gamma Mu Honor Society. Reprinted by permission.

Bertolas et al. "Point: Colleges and Universities Should Provide Student-Athletes with Additional Compensation beyond Tuition, Room, and Board," *International Social Science Review*, Volume 94, Issue 1, Art. 21. Pgs. 3–5, 8. Copyright © 2018 Pi Gamma Mu Honor Society. Reprinted by permission.

Evie Blad. "Do School's 'Active Shooter' Drills Prepare or Frighten?" *Education Week*, September 19, 2017. Reprinted by permission.

Laura Bogart. "I Don't Own a Smartphone—and I Don't Want One," *The Week*, February 22, 2017. Reprinted by permission of The Week Publications, Inc.

Christian Bot. "A Conservative Case for Universal Basic Income," *Areo*, August 2, 2018. Reprinted by permission.

Kim Brooks. "Is it time to kill the liberal arts degree?" This article first appeared in Salon.com, at http://www.Salon.com. An online version remains in the Salon archives. Reprinted with permission.

Patrick Buchanan. "Immigration Time-Out." From http://buchanan.org/blog/immigration-time-out-163, October 31, 1994. Copyright © 1994 Patrick Buchanan. Reproduced with permission of Friedman, Inc. All rights reserved.

Joanna M. Burkhardt. "History of Fake News," *Library Technology Reports*, vol. 53, no. 8 (November/December 2017): 5–9. Reprinted with permission from The American Library Association.

Bryan Caplan. "What's College Good For?" *The Atlantic*, January/Februsry 2018. Reprinted by permission of the author.

Kevin Carey. "Fulfill George Washington's Last Wish—A National University." From CNN.com, March 2, 2015. Copyright © 2015 Turner Broadcast Systems. All rights reserved. Used under license.

Anthony P. Carnevale and Michelle Melton. "Major Differences: Why Undergraduate Majors Matter," Reprinted with permission from *The Presidency*, Fall 2011. © 2011 American Council on Education; permission conveyed through Copyright Clearance Center, Inc.

Rachel Carson. "The Obligation to Endure." From *Silent Spring*. Copyright © 1962 Rachel L. Carson, renewed 1990 by Roger Christie. Reprinted by permission of Houghton Mifflin Harcourt Publishing Company and Frances Collin Literary Agency.

Adrian Chen. "The Fake News Fallacy," *The New Yorker*, September 4, 2017. Copyright © Conde Nast. Reprinted by permission.

Shubhankar Chhokra. "The Ethical Case for Eating Animals," *The Harvard Crimson*, March 6, 2016. Copyright © 2016 The Harvard Crimson. All rights reserved. Reprinted with permission.

David N. Cicilline and Terrell McSweeny. "Competition is the Heart of Facebook's Privacy Problem," *Wired*, April 24, 2018. Copyright © 2018 Conde Nast. Reprinted by permission.

Bruno Comby. "The Benefits of Nuclear Energy," Environmentalists for Nuclear Energy. May 21, 2006. Reprinted by permission.

Mary C. Daly and Leila Bengali. "Is It Still Worth Going to College?" Reprinted from the Federal Reserve Bank of San Francisco's Economic Letter, May 5, 2014. The opinions expressed in this article do not necessarily reflect the views of the management of the Federal Reserve Bank of San Francisco or of the Board of Governors of the Federal Reserve System. https://www.frbsf.org/economic-research/publications/economic-letter/2014/may/is-college-worth-it-education-tuition-wages/.

Peter Moore. "The Other Opioid Crisis." From *Prevention* magazine, reprinted with permission of Hearst Magazines, Inc.

Charles Murray. "What's Wrong with Vocational School." Republished with permission from *The Wall Street Journal*, January 17, 2007. Copyright © 2007 Dow Jones Company; permission conveyed through Copyright Clearance Center, Inc.

Olivia Nicholas. "Op-Ed: What Are You Going to Do with That Major?" *Whitman Wire*, February 8, 2018. Reprinted by permission of the author.

Marty Nemko. "We Send Too Many Students to College" and "The Real Reason So Few Women Are In the Boardroom." From www.martynemko.com. Copyright © 2012 Marty Nemko. Reproduced with the permission of the author. All rights reserved.

Vann R. Newkirk. "Arming Educators Violates the Spirit of the Second Amendment," *The Atlantic*, February 22, 2018. Copyright © 2018 The Atlantic Media Company, as first published in the Atlantic Magazine. All rights reserved. Distributed by Tribune Content Agency LLC.

Joe Nocera. "It's Hard to Be a Hero." From *The New York Times*, December 8, 2012. Copyright © 2012 The New York Times. All rights reserved. Used under license.

Republished with permission of The Wall Street Journal, from Barbara Oakley. "Why Do Women Shun STEM? It's Complicated," July 13, 2018. Copyright © 2018 Dow Jones & Company; permission conveyed through Copyright Clearance Center Inc.

Peggy Orenstein. "Should the World of Toys Be Gender-Free?" From *The New York Times*, December 29, 2011. Copyright © 2011 The New York Times. All rights reserved. Used under license.

Adam Ozimek. "Why I Don't Support Open Borders," *Forbes*, February 26, 2017. Reprinted by permission of the author.

Christina H. Paxson. "The Economic Case for Saving the Humanities." From *The New Republic*, August 20, 2013. Copyright © 2013 New Republic. All rights reserved. Used under license.

Stanton Peele. "The Solution to the Opioid Crisis." *Psychology Today*, March 16, 2017. Reprinted by permission of the author.

Andre Perry. "Stop saying 'college isn't for everyone,'" *The Hechinger Report*, September 1, 2015. Reprinted by permission.

Richard A. Posner. "The Truth about Plagiarism." From *Newsday*, March 18, 2003. Copyright © 2003 by The Honorable Richard Posner. Reprinted by permission.

Erika Ramirez. "When Beyonce's Inspiration Turns Into Imitation," *Billboard*, May 1, 2013. Reprinted by permission.

Juan Ramos. "Fossil Fuel Pros and Cons," *Science Trends*, December 18, 2017. Reprinted by permission.

Rajeev Ravisankar. "Sweatshop Oppression," *The Lantern*, April 19, 2006. Copyright © 2006 Rajeev Ravisankar. Reproduced with permission of the author. All rights reserved.

Stuart Reges. "Why Women Don't Code," *Quilette*, June 19, 2018. Copyright © 2018 Quillette Pty Ltd. All rights reserved. Used under license.

Helen Rubinstein. "When Plagiarism Is a Plea for Help," *Chronicle of Higher Education*, March 30, 2016. Used with permission of The Chronicle of Higher Education. Copyright © 2016. All rights reserved.

Douglas Rushkoff. "You Are Not Facebook's Customer," https://rushkoff.com/you-are-not-facebooks-customer/. Reprinted by permission of the author.

Bernie Sanders. "Medicare for All Is Good for Business," *Fortune*, August 21, 2017. Reprinted by permission of Bernie Sanders.

Sally Satel, "The Myth of What's Driving the Opioid Crisis." Republished with permission from *Politico*, February 21, 2018. Copyright © 2018 Capitol News Company, LLC; permission conveyed through Copyright Clearance Center, Inc.

Ellen Ruppel Shell. "College May Not Be Worth It Anymore." From *The New York Times*, May 16, 2018. Copyright © 2018 The New York Times. All rights reserved. Used under license.

Jerome Sieger. "Sweatshops Are Good," *The Eagle*, February 15, 2017. Reprinted by permission.

Lenore Skenazy. "How Kitty Genovese Destroyed Childhood." From TIME.com, March 13, 2014. © 2014 TIME USA LLC. All rights reserved. Used under license. TIME.com and TIME USA LLC are not affiliated with, and do not endorse products or services of Macmillan Learning.

Nick Srnicek. "The $100 Trillion Case for Open Borders," *The Conversation*, February 8, 2018. Reprinted by permission.

Sol Stern. "The Unfree Speech Movement." From *The Wall Street Journal*, September 23, 2014. Reprinted by permission of the author.

Astra Taylor. "A Strike against Student Debt." From *The New York Times*, February 27, 2015. Copyright © 2015 The New York Times. All rights reserved. Used under license.

Dana Thomas. "Terror's Purse Strings." From The New York Times, August 30, 2007, Op Ed. Copyright © 2007 The New York Times. All rights reserved. Used under license.

John Tierney. "The Reign of Recycling." From *The New York Times*, October 3, 2015. Copyright © 2015 The New York Times. All rights reserved. Used under license.

The Times Editorial Board. "Grocery bags and takeout containers aren't enough. It's time to phase out all single-use plastic," *Los Angeles Times*, February 20, 2018. Reprinted by permission.

Zeynep Tufekci. "The Privacy Debacle." From *The New York Times*, January 30, 2018. Copyright © 2018 The New York Times. All rights reserved. Used under license.

Sherry Turkle. "The Flight From Conversation." From *The New York Times*, April 21, 2012. Copyright © 2012 The New York Times. All rights reserved. Used under license.

JD Vance. "The College Trap," *The National Review*, January 9, 2014. Copyright © 2014 National Review, Inc. Used with permission.

Richard Vedder. "Forgive Student Loans?" *The National Review*, October 11, 2011. Copyright © 2011 National Review, Inc. Used with permission.

Ayelet W. "Does College Still Matter in 2018?" University of the People, March 19, 2018. https://www.uopeople.edu/blog/does-college-still-matter-in-2018/. Reprinted with permission of University of the People.

Jimmy Wales. "What Can Be Done to Combat Fake News," *Quora*, May 3, 2017. https://www.quora.com/What-action-should-media-outlets-take-to-combat-fake-news. Reprinted by permission.

Robert Weiss. "Closer Together or Further Apart? Digital Devices and the New Generation Gap." *The Huffington Post*, January 30, 2014. Reprinted by permission of the author.

Timothy Wheeler. "There's A Reason They Choose Schools," *The National Review*, October 11, 2007. Copyright © 2007 National Review, Inc. Used with permission.

Michelle Wu. "The Road to Fear-Free Biking in Boston," *The Boston Globe*, July 12, 2016. Reprinted by permission of the author.

George Zarkadakis. "The Case Against Universal Basic Income," *The Huffington Post*, February 24, 2017. Reprinted by permission of the author.